Turkey and Ham
Casserole with Water
Chestnuts (page 127)

# COOK NOW

# SERVE LATER

The Reader's Digest Association, Inc.
Pleasantville, New York • Montreal

# COOK NOW
## SERVE LATER

PROJECT EDITOR: Gayla Visalli
PROJECT ART EDITORS: Marlene Rimsky
Henrietta Stern
ASSOCIATE EDITOR: Gerald Williams

### CONTRIBUTORS

EDITOR: Lee Fowler
EDITORIAL ASSISTANT: Carol T. Seabrooks
ART ASSISTANT: Eleanor Kostyk
COPY EDITOR: Mel Minter
INDEXER: Sydney Wolfe Cohen
ILLUSTRATORS: Ray Skibinski
Judy Skorpil

PHOTOGRAPHER: Rudy Muller
STYLIST: Hal Walter
FOOD STYLIST: Andrea B. Swenson
ASSISTANT FOOD STYLISTS: Cynthia W. Caldwell
Karen Hatt

### CONSULTANTS

CHIEF CONSULTANT: Jean Anderson
MICROWAVE CONSULTANT: Bea Cihak
NUTRITION CONSULTANT: Michele C. Fisher, Ph.D., R.D.
RECIPE DEVELOPERS: Jo Ann Brett-Billowitz
Georgia Downard
Sandra Rose Gluck
Paul E. Piccuito
Michele Scicolone

PHOTOGRAPH ON PAGE 109: Thom DeSanto

### READER'S DIGEST GENERAL BOOKS

EDITOR IN CHIEF: John A. Pope, Jr.
MANAGING EDITOR: Jane Polley
ART DIRECTOR: David Trooper
GROUP EDITORS: Norman B. Mack
Susan J. Wernert
Joel Musler (Art)
CHIEF OF RESEARCH: Monica Borrowman
COPY CHIEF: Edward W. Atkinson
PICTURE EDITOR: Robert J. Woodward
RIGHTS AND PERMISSIONS: Pat Colomban
HEAD LIBRARIAN: Jo Manning

The acknowledgments that appear on pages 310–311
are hereby made a part of this copyright page.

Library of Congress Cataloging in Publication Data

Cook now, serve later / Reader's Digest.
     p.   cm.
    Includes index.
    ISBN 0-89577-314-7
    1. Make-ahead cookery.   2. Quick and easy cookery.  I. Reader's
   Digest Association.
    TX652.C728 1989
    641.5′55 — dc 19              88-36564
                                     CIP

Printed in the United States of America
Second Printing, March 1990

# Contents

# Introduction

## ABOUT THIS BOOK

Cook Now, Serve Later, with its hundreds of prepare-in-advance recipes, is designed to help you serve yourself and your family nutritious, delicious meals each day of the year. Every dish is doable hours, days, or weeks in advance, and there are even tips on how to prepare such accompaniments as rice, cooked vegetables, tossed salads, and whipped cream ahead of time.

Of course, entertaining hasn't been neglected. An entire chapter is devoted to make-ahead dishes that are suitable for parties and holiday get-togethers, and many recipes throughout the book are excellent company fare. But the main beneficiaries will be you and your family; you're the ones who will enjoy the day-in, day-out convenience of ready-made, with the wholesomeness, fresh taste, and dollar-saving economy of homemade.

All recipes in Cook Now, Serve Later have been tested by professionals. Whenever practical, ingredients are listed in alternative units that make it easy to gauge how much you need to buy or have on hand as well as measure for preparation. The recipes have also been adjusted to avoid leaving small quantities of can or jar contents unused. In response to today's health concerns, nutritional information is listed under each recipe title, and fat and salt have been reduced.

Rest stops — points at which you can store the dish, indicated by triangular symbols — are included for many recipes, and storage times have been given for all of them. While some dishes might keep longer without spoiling, quality will begin to deteriorate. It is recommended that all cooked food be quickly cooled to room temperature before storing in the refrigerator or freezer. Its warmth would otherwise raise the temperature in these compartments and lessen their effectiveness.

Instructions for serving later tell you how to complete a dish or reheat it after it's been stored. Because the microwave oven speeds up defrosting and reheating of frozen dishes, recipes throughout the book include directions on using it for these purposes. The heating times are for a full-sized model with a wattage of 600 to 700. If your oven is less than 600 watts, you will have to increase the heating times.

Many Cook Now, Serve Later recipes utilize the food processor — another boon for the busy cook. If you don't own one already, you might consider adding it to your kitchen equipment. A blender can be substituted for some of the tasks, but puréeing of heavy foods takes longer and chopping capability is limited. (Note that when recipes in this book call for either a food processor or blender, the time indicated is for treatment in a food processor; add 20 to 30 seconds more for the blender.)

### Saving Time in the Kitchen

The main advantage to preparing meals ahead is that you can cook when it's convenient for you. But there are extra benefits, too. By grouping tasks, you save time overall and have fewer cleanup chores. For instance, if you double a casserole recipe, freezing half the food for a future meal, you'll spend nearly 50 percent less time than you would preparing it twice. And you clean up the kitchen only once!

Planned leftovers are another way to get more mileage from your cooking time. When preparing meat or poultry for Sunday supper, why not make an extra quantity for use in a salad, pasta dish, or soup later in the week? Do the same with rice and potatoes and other vegetables. At a weekend barbecue, you can grill a whole week's worth of food with very little effort and without ever heating up your kitchen!

The same method can be applied to other tasks. When chopping onions, sweet peppers, or garlic for one recipe, double or triple the quantity for later use. These will keep, covered, in the refrigerator for up to one week, in the freezer for up to six months; after freezing, though, they should be used only in cooked dishes. Combined with olive oil, minced garlic keeps for several months in the refrigerator.

If you wash greens and herbs as soon as you bring them home, they are ready whenever you need them, and you won't have to prepare them on several different occasions. Spin-dry them thoroughly, then store in plastic bags lined with paper toweling. Depending on type and freshness, greens will keep in the refrigerator for from three to six days; herbs, such as parsley and dill, for up to two weeks. Basil, which turns black in cold storage, can be kept for several months if stored in olive oil, like the minced garlic (above).

Whether you love to cook or consider the task tiresome, whether you cook for one or a family of ten, it is easy to appreciate the advantages of preparing food ahead: The approach permits flexibility, allows you to spend more time with the guests at company meals, and saves time and energy, leaving more of both for other pursuits.

The freezer can be a great help in do-ahead preparations. But while some foods freeze well and with minimal preparation, others require special handling, and some should not be frozen at all. To help you take full advantage of the freezer's capabilities, a few guidelines are set forth below.

## Do not freeze:

■ cooked egg whites and soft meringues

■ gelatin (it weeps), except in soufflés that will be eaten frozen

■ cake or pie with custard filling

■ cake icing that contains egg white

■ mayonnaise

■ cloves and imitation vanilla

■ sauces thickened with flour or cornstarch, except when used as a binder for other ingredients

■ milk, light cream, or sour cream

■ heavy cream, except when whipped

■ vegetables high in water content, such as celery, fennel, tomatoes, leafy salad greens, cucumbers, radishes, potatoes, zucchini, and eggplant, unless they have been cooked and finely chopped or puréed

■ raw vegetables (see *Blanching*, below)

## Blanching

Vegetables must be blanched before freezing to help set the color and to kill the enzymes that cause spoilage. The process takes but a few minutes.

Before blanching, wash vegetables thoroughly, taking extra care with the types that have compact heads, such as broccoli and cauliflower. While preparing them, bring a kettle of water to a boil over high heat — 1 gallon of water for each pound of vegetables.

Place the vegetables in a wire basket, insert the basket in the kettle, and cover. Begin timing (see chart) as soon as the water starts to boil again. When the time is up, immediately transfer the

basket to a large bowl of ice water, leave for a few minutes, then drain and pack. The blanching water can be re-used, with more added to maintain the proper level.

### How Long to Blanch
*(in minutes)*

| | |
|---|---|
| Asparagus | 3 |
| Bean sprouts | 4 to 6 |
| Black-eyed peas | 2 |
| Broccoli (split) | 3 to 4 |
| Brussels sprouts | 3 to 4 |
| Green beans | 2 |
| Lima beans | 1 |
| Carrots (sliced) | 3 |
| Cauliflower (florets) | 3 |
| Corn | 3 |
| Green peas | 2 |
| Mushrooms | 5 |
| Spinach | 2 |
| Summer squash (cut into ½-inch slices) | 3 |
| Winter squash | 5 to 6 |

## Freezing Tips

■ Because freezing has a tenderizing effect on meat, it is a good way to preserve this product. Freeze meats in small quantities to reduce thawing time and permit greater flexibility in use. Divide ground meat into patties; wrap steaks and chops individually; and cut boneless roasts in half.

■ Before freezing fish, dip it in lemon juice to help preserve its original taste and texture, then wrap it snugly in plastic wrap, followed by a layer of heavy-duty aluminum foil.

■ A convenient way to freeze egg whites is in an ice cube tray — 1 per cube. When solid, transfer the frozen egg-white cubes to freezer bags.

■ To prevent coagulation of egg yolks, stir ½ teaspoon salt or 2 teaspoons sugar into each ½ cup (6 to 7) yolks before freezing. When using, adjust recipes accordingly.

■ To freeze whole eggs, remove them from the shells and stir the whites and yolks together. Add ½ teaspoon salt or 2 teaspoons sugar per half-dozen eggs.

■ Cheddar, Swiss, Gouda, mozzarella, and Parmesan cheeses freeze well but should be frozen in portions of no more than 2 pounds. Wrap the cheese tightly, first in plastic wrap, then aluminum foil. Thaw in the refrigerator overnight to prevent crumbling.

■ Fruits that freeze well are berries, citrus fruits, figs, peaches, and cherries.

■ In the frozen state, fresh ginger is easier to peel and grate. It keeps for several months.

■ Freezing changes the character of some spices and herbs, often intensifying their flavor. You may prefer to salt and spice cooked foods after thawing and reheating them.

■ When you add items to your freezer, limit them to about 2 pounds a day for each cubic foot of freezer space. Always place these additions in the coldest part of the freezer — against the freezer wall or on the freezer floor — and keep some space between them so that the cold air can circulate.

■ Rotate foods in the freezer so that the older items don't become forgotten. Keep a list of freezer foods; when you remove a package, check it off.

■ When rotating frozen goods, handle them carefully so that the packaging doesn't get pierced or broken, exposing the contents to air.

■ A full freezer consumes less electricity than one that is half-full. Frozen food holds cold better than its equal volume in air space.

### Defrosting a Freezer

When there is 3/8 to 1/2 inch or more of frost buildup on your freezer walls, it's time to defrost. Set the dial at *defrost* or *off*, unload the freezing compartment, and tightly pack its contents into a cooler or cardboard carton (line a carton with thick layers of newspaper).

To reduce defrosting time, set pans of hot water on the freezer floor and work any loose ice free with a rubber spatula, which won't damage the surface. When completely clean, turn the freezer on and let it run for at least 15 minutes before reloading.

For periodic cleaning of a frostless freezer, unplug the appliance and store its contents as directed above. Plug in the freezer and let it cool to 0° F before reloading the food.

### Coping with Freezer Breakdowns

Food will remain frozen during a power outage or breakdown for up to 48 hours, provided the freezer is full and the door remains closed; if the freezer is half-full, the food will take up to 24 hours to thaw.

To help prevent frozen food from thawing, add dry ice (frozen carbon dioxide), usually available from ice

## Refrigerator and Freezer Storage Times

To maintain quality and prevent spoilage, food should be refrigerated at 34° F to 40° F and frozen at 0° F or lower. If the freezer temperature rises just 10 degrees above 0° F, the storage life of frozen goods is cut in half. Some foods may keep longer than the times listed, but they will gradually change in texture and flavor and will lose nutritional value. Dated dairy products, such as milk, cream, sour cream, and eggs, can be refrigerated until the expiration date stamped on the carton. Do not freeze them, except for raw eggs removed from their shells; cream cheese or yogurt mixed with other ingredients, as in a dip; and heavy cream that has been whipped. Blue-veined cheeses, such as Roquefort, can be frozen but will crumble when thawed.

| Food | Refrigerator (34° F–40° F) | Freezer (0° F or lower) |
|---|---|---|
| **Dairy Products** | | |
| Margarine | 4–6 weeks | 6–8 months |
| Butter | | |
| unsalted | 2–4 weeks | 4–6 months |
| salted | 2–4 weeks | 6–8 months |
| Cheese | | |
| soft (Brie, etc.) | 2 weeks | 4 months |
| semihard (Cheddar, Edam, etc.) | 2–3 months | 6 months |
| hard (Parmesan, Romano, etc.) | 4–6 weeks | 2 months |
| hard, grated | 2–4 weeks | 2 months |
| Eggs | | |
| hard-cooked | 1 week | Do not freeze |
| whites (raw) | 1 week | 12 months |
| yolks (raw) | 2 days | 6 months |
| Ice cream | — | 1–2 months |
| **Fish** | | |
| Lean fish, (cod, flounder, etc.) | 1 day | 6 months |
| Oily fish, (bluefish, mackerel, salmon) | 1 day | 3 months |

| Food | Refrigerator (34° F–40° F) | Freezer (0° F or lower) |
|---|---|---|
| **Poultry and Meats** | | |
| Chicken, turkey | 1–4 days | 6–7 months |
| Beef, lamb, veal | | |
| roasts, steaks | 2–4 days | 6–12 months |
| ground | 1–2 days | 3–4 months |
| cooked | 2–4 days | 2–3 months |
| Pork | | |
| roasts, chops | 2–4 days | 3–6 months |
| ground | 1 day | 1–3 months |
| sausage | 2–4 days | 2 months |
| cured ham, whole | 5 days | 2 months |
| cured ham, slices | 2–4 days | 2 months |
| bacon | 5–7 days | 1 month |
| Variety meats | 1–2 days | 2–3 months |
| **Bread** | | |
| Quick (baked) | 3–7 days | 3 months |
| Yeast (baked) | 7–14 days | 3 months |
| Yeast dough | 3–5 days | 1 month |
| **Desserts** | | |
| Cakes | | |
| frosted | 2–3 days | 2–4 months |
| unfrosted | 2–3 days | 6–8 months |
| Cookies | — | 3 months |
| Cookie dough | 2 weeks | 2 months |
| Pies (baked) | | |
| fruit | 3 days | 6–8 months |
| custard | 2 days | Do not freeze |

| Food | Refrigerator (34° F–40° F) | Freezer (0° F or lower) |
|---|---|---|
| **Fruit** | | |
| Apricots, berries, cherries | 2–3 days | 8–12 months |
| Melons, nectarines, peaches, pears, plums | 3–5 days | 8–12 months |
| Apples, citrus fruit, cranberries | 1–2 weeks | 8–12 months |
| **Vegetables** | | |
| Corn | 1 day | 8–12 months |
| Asparagus, green beans | 2–3 days | 8–12 months |
| Artichokes, broccoli, collards, eggplant,* lettuce,* lima beans, peas, spinach, turnip greens | 3–5 days | 8–12 months |
| Peppers, summer squash, radishes, ripe tomatoes | 1 week | Do not freeze |
| Beets, cabbage,* cauliflower, celery,* carrots, turnips,* winter squash | 2–3 weeks | 8–12 months |

*Do not freeze well unless finely chopped or puréed.

companies. Wear heavy gloves to handle it, ventilate the area, and don't let it touch the food. If dry ice is not available, tightly wrap your frozen goods in thick layers of newspaper and store in a cooler or other well-insulated container. Set the container in a cool place.

Discard thawed ice cream, also any frozen food that shows no ice crystals or has a strange odor or color. Eat immediately or discard defrosted cooked foods; cook and consume as soon as possible thawed uncooked products.

### Packaging

All wrapping material and containers used for storing food in the refrigerator or freezer should be moisture-proof. The best containers have tight-fitting lids and are square or rectangular (these use space more efficiently).

Take special care in covering food to be frozen. If any air penetrates the package through a thin wrapping or a hole, unpleasant freezer burn — dry, discolored areas — may result. Always use heavy-duty aluminum foil or freezer paper or heavy-duty plastic bags, preferably the type with a zip seal.

Wrap the food snugly, using one of the methods at right and pressing out as much air as possible. Then apply freezer or masking tape, if needed. When freezing food in a plastic bag, also eliminate as much air as possible. (An exception is made for liquids, which expand upon freezing. To allow for expansion, leave 1 to 2 inches above the top of the liquid, whether storing in a freezer bag or a jar.)

A label is essential. Use a self-sticking type or a piece of freezer tape, or write directly on the package with a freezer pen. Record *the recipe name, number of servings, cooking or reheating instructions, and date by which the food should be used.* Length of storage times is indicated for each recipe in this book. Additional times are given in the chart, opposite page.

## The Butcher Wrap

1 Place poultry or other irregularly shaped food diagonally on a square sheet of wrapping. Bring one corner over it, as shown.

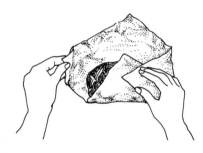

2 Fold the two adjoining corners toward the center.

3 Keeping the wrapping taut, pull the fourth corner snugly over the other three and seal with tape.

## The Drugstore Wrap

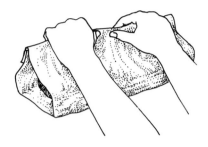

1 Place flat meat or a sandwich in the center of a rectangular sheet of wrapping; pull the long edges straight up; fold the edges over about 1 inch.

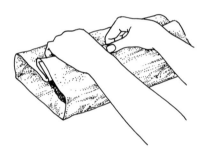

2 Continue folding the edges down until they are tight against the food, making an interlocking seam, as shown.

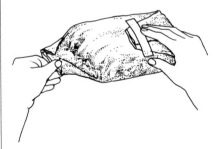

3 At each end, fold the two corners toward each other, forming triangles; bring the ends up and press them against the package. Seal with tape.

# COOKING TERMS AND TECHNIQUES

**baste** to ladle or brush drippings over food while it roasts or bakes to add flavor and prevent drying out

**batter** an uncooked mixture, usually of flour, eggs, liquid, and a leavening agent, that is thin enough to pour

**beat** to stir or mix rapidly in order to blend or make lighter

**blanch** to plunge vegetables, fruits, or nuts briefly into boiling water, then cold water to kill enzymes before freezing and/or set the color, or to loosen the skin for easy removal (nuts, peaches, or tomatoes)

**blend** to mix two or more ingredients together until smooth

**boil** to heat a liquid to the point at which large bubbles constantly break the surface (212° F for water)

**braise** to cook by browning in fat, then simmering, covered, in a small amount of liquid until tender

**combine** to form a uniform mixture by stirring two or more ingredients together until homogenous

**cream** to work shortening, butter, or margarine, sometimes with sugar, until soft and fluffy, usually with a wooden spoon or an electric mixer

**crimp** to pinch the edges of pastry together to form a fluted edge and/or to seal in a filling

**crisp-tender** cooked until tender enough to be pierced by a fork but still firm to the bite

**cube** to cut into cubes of ½ inch or larger

**dice** to cut into small cubes of less than ½ inch

**drizzle** to pour liquid such as melted butter over food in a thin stream

**dry pack** the method of freezing fruits without a syrup

**flake** to break a food into small pieces with a fork

**fold in** to blend a delicate substance, such as whipped egg whites, into a heavier one, such as custard, without losing volume

**flute** to make a decorative edge on the rim of a pie crust

**glaze** to give foods a shiny surface by coating them. A thin layer of jelly may be used on roasts or fruit tarts; an egg wash on baked goods

**grate** to rub food, such as citrus rind or ginger, against a fine grater

**grill** to cook on a rack over hot coals

**julienne** to cut into matchstick-like strips

**knead** to work bread dough by pulling and stretching it with the heels of the hands to blend the ingredients and develop the gluten

**marinate** to soak in a seasoned and/or acid liquid that imparts flavor and, as with meat or poultry, also tenderizes

**mince** to cut into very small pieces

**mold** to give food a specific form by pressing it into or letting it jell in a container of the desired shape

**parboil** to cook food briefly in boiling water, preparatory to further cooking (see also blanching)

**paste** a thick creamy mixture, made by mixing dry ingredients with a liquid or by pounding fresh herbs, meats, or nuts with a mortar and pestle

**pickle** to preserve food by immersing in a salt or vinegar solution

**poach** to cook food, usually eggs, fish, or poultry, by submerging in a simmering liquid

**purée** to reduce solids to a thick liquid or pulp by forcing them through a strainer or food mill or processing them in an electric blender or food processor

**reduce** to boil a liquid mixture, uncovered, until thicker and more intensely flavored

**sauté** to cook, uncovered, in a small amount of fat, turning frequently

**scald** to heat a liquid, usually milk, to the point just before boiling when tiny bubbles appear at the edge

**shred** to cut into thin, stringlike pieces, either with a knife or by rubbing against a coarse grater

**simmer** the point at which a heated liquid shows bubbles forming at the edges (185° F for water); also, to maintain a heated liquid at this point

**skim** to remove fat or scum from the surface of a liquid

**steam** to cook food, usually vegetables or rice, in a basket or colander set over boiling water in a covered saucepan

**stew** to cook foods slowly in liquid, usually in a heavy saucepan or flameproof casserole

**truss** to secure the legs and wings of a fowl with string so that it holds its shape during roasting

**whip** to introduce air into a substance, usually heavy cream or egg whites, by beating rapidly, thus increasing the volume

**whip to soft peaks** to beat just until the peaks that form curl over

**whip to stiff peaks** to beat until the peaks that form are firm enough to stand up straight

**whisk** to stir rapidly, using a whisk, to blend ingredients or introduce air

## Dicing

Hold the food firmly, fingertips tucked under; cut lengthwise into slices ¼ to ½ inch wide. Stack the slices on their sides and cut lengthwise again to the same width. Cut the sticks crosswise to the same width, forming cubes.

## Folding

Add the lighter mixture to the heavier one. Using a rubber spatula, cut down through the center and across the bottom of the bowl, scooping some of the heavier mixture on top. Rotate the bowl ¼ turn. Repeat until no streaks show.

## Trussing

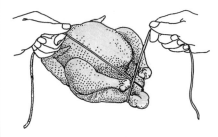

1 Place the bird on its back, leg tips facing you. Center a 3- to 4-foot length of white string under the tail; cross the string over the top of it.

## Fluting

1 **To form a pinch edge,** rest an index finger on the pastry rim; with thumb and index finger of the other hand, pinch the dough to form a V shape. Repeat around the entire rim.

## Kneading

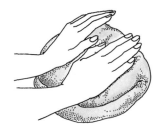

Fold the dough over toward you. Using the heels of your hands, push it down and, at the same time, away from you. Rotate ¼ turn. Repeat until the dough is elastic and satiny.

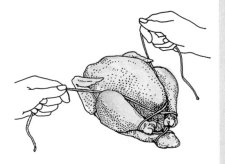

2 Bring the string around the legs, cross it over again, and pull the legs tightly together. Next, bring the string under the tip of the breastbone and back toward the wings.

## Making Cookie Baskets

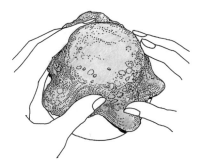

2 **To form a rope edge,** pinch the pastry with thumb and index finger at the angle shown. Repeat around the entire rim.

Let the cookies cool for 30 seconds (see recipe, page 270); mold each one over the bottom of a 2¼-inch tumbler.

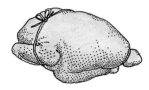

3 Turn the bird over onto its breast. Bring the string up and over the wings, pulling them snugly against the body. Tie a knot, leaving no slack, and trim the ends.

11

# GARNISHES

The presentation of any dish is enhanced by even a simple garnish, such as a sprig of watercress or parsley. With a little extra effort, it's possible to create a more elaborate embellishment, such as a twist, flower, or fan. Besides the garnishes described below, you can create vegetable or pastry cutouts with small cookie cutters, or decorative edgings and fillings with a pastry bag and plain or star tips. To accomplish any of these special effects takes just a little practice. It could become a habit.

### Green Onion Brushes

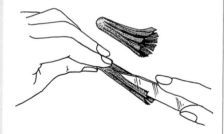

1 Cut off the root and most of the green and divide the remainder into 2-inch lengths. Using a paring knife, cut lengthwise for about 1 1/2 inches. Rotate 1/4 turn; make several more closely spaced, lengthwise cuts.

2 Drop into a bowl of ice water and leave for 20 minutes or until the tendrils curl outward.

### Cucumber Fans

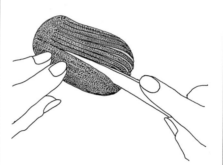

1 Cut the cucumber in half lengthwise, then crosswise, making 4 pieces. With the long, cut side down, use a sharp paring knife to make closely spaced lengthwise cuts, leaving 1/2 inch uncut at the sliced end.

2 Sprinkle with salt and let stand for 20 minutes to soften. Then wash off the salt and gently press with the flat side of a knife to fan out the slices.

### Cucumber Borders

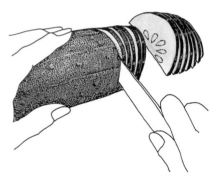

1 Slice the cucumber in half lengthwise and lay the cut side down on a board. Make seven thin cuts crosswise, leaving 1/4 inch uncut at one side. On the eighth cut, slice through, severing the segment. Repeat.

2 Fan out the slices; if desired, arrange the segments one next to the other around the edge of a serving dish, making a continuous border.

## Radish Flowers

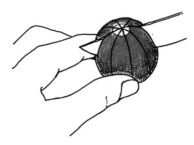

1 Wash and trim the radishes, leaving a little bit of stem, if desired. **To make flower #1**, hold the radish as shown and cut through the center almost to the base. Rotate ¼ turn and make a cut perpendicular to the first. Make two more cuts, each equidistant from the first two.

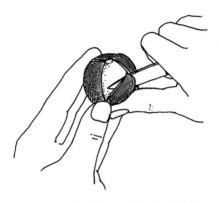

2 **To make flower #2**, hold the radish as shown; score, then cut a thin petal of skin almost to the base. Repeat, making 4 more petals.

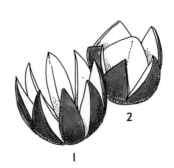

3 Drop the radish flowers into a bowl of ice water and leave for 20 minutes or until they open out.

## Tomato Rose

1 Using a thin paring knife, peel a firm-ripe tomato in one long continuous strip, beginning at the base and ending at the stem.

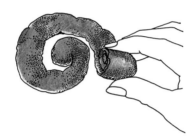

2 Place the strip flesh side down on a flat surface. Beginning with the stem end, coil it, skin side in.

3 When most of the skin has been rolled, turn it over and wrap the last bit of the strip around the bottom to form the base of the "rose."

## Tomato Sunflower

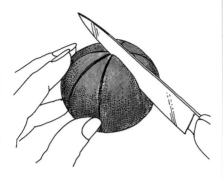

1 Set a cherry tomato, stem side down on a board. Cut through the top and down the sides of the center, penetrating just the skin and leaving ¼ inch uncut at the base. Make a second cut like the first but perpendicular to it.

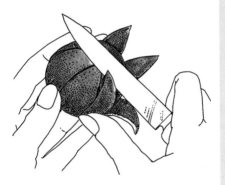

2 Make 2 more cuts, each equidistant from the first two, dividing the tomato skin into 8 equal segments.

3 Peel the skin back almost to the base, forming the "petals."

13

## Fluted Mushrooms

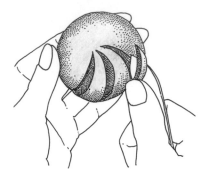

1 Holding a very fresh mushroom as shown and using a sharp paring knife, gently make a curved cut from the center of the cap out to the edge.

2 Make a second, flatter, cut next to the first, carving out a thin wedge of mushroom to form a groove. Continue around the mushroom. Trim the stem even with the cap. Dip in lemon juice and water to prevent darkening.

## Citrus Twists

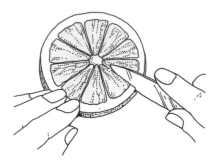

1 Cut the fruit into thin slices. Lay each slice on a board and make a cut from the center to the edge.

2 Twist the two sections in opposite directions.

## Chocolate Curls

Let a thick bar of chocolate (milk chocolate works best) stand in a warm place for 15 minutes to soften. With a swivel-bladed vegetable peeler or a thin knife, shave off long, thin slices. Lift the curls with a toothpick to avoid breakage.

## Chocolate Leaves

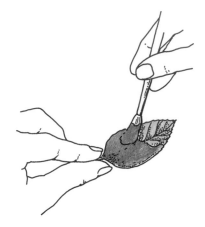

1 In a small saucepan, heat 1 to 2 ounces of milk chocolate or semi-sweet chocolate over very low heat or simmering water until just melted. Using a small paintbrush, spread a thin coating of chocolate on the top side of small, sturdy, preferably deep-veined leaves. Lay them on a cookie sheet and freeze until firm — about 15 minutes.

2 Remove from the freezer, let stand at room temperature for a minute or two; carefully peel each leaf from the chocolate. Store the chocolate leaves in the freezer until ready to use.

# Magic Mixes and TV Dinners

Two of today's most convenient food preparations are the packaged mix and the TV dinner. But if, like many people, you are tired of what's available on the shelves, would prefer your mixes without artificial additives, or won't trade convenience for homemade freshness, then this chapter is for you. The mixes include breads, sauces, stuffings, and salad dressings. The dinners were specially developed to appeal to many tastes.

If you like, use the TV dinner recipes for inspiration, adjusting them to suit your needs, or substituting some of your own favorites. Success stems from knowing what to select and how long to precook it. A meat, fish, or poultry recipe should have a sauce. Fresh vegetables should be cooked but still quite crisp; frozen vegetables must be added directly to the dinner container without thawing. If including rice, parboil it; if using potatoes, cook and mash them.

Several types of containers for TV dinners are available today. Among them are divided pans made of aluminum for a conventional oven, or plastic for a microwave oven. One divided aluminum model has a special coating that makes it suitable for either type of oven. Also, aluminum pie plates or any sort of microwave-safe dish will do nicely for this purpose.

# Griddle Quick-Mix

Per ½ cup: Calories 214; Protein 8 g; Carbohydrate 43 g; Fat 1 g; Sodium 458 mg; Cholesterol 7 mg.

*You'll be eating a lot more pancakes and waffles with this handy mix on the shelf. It's great for muffins, too. If desired, substitute nonfat dry milk powder for the buttermilk powder and omit the baking soda.*

| | |
|---|---|
| 4½ | cups all-purpose flour |
| 1 | cup dried buttermilk powder |
| ⅓ | cup sugar |
| 5 | teaspoons baking powder |
| 1¾ | teaspoons salt |
| ¼ | teaspoon baking soda |

1 In a large mixing bowl, stir together all of the ingredients until they are well mixed.

2 Transfer to a container with a tight-fitting lid, label, and store in a cool, dry place for up to 3 months. Makes about 6 cups.

Use this mix in the following recipes: Feather-Light Pancakes (page 230), Golden Waffles (page 230), Simple Muffins (page 230), Onion-Sage Bread (page 230).

# Shortcut Biscuit Mix

Per ½ cup: Calories 289; Protein 6 g; Carbohydrate 37 g; Fat 13 g; Sodium 467 mg; Cholesterol 12 mg.

*With this mix, you can make fresh-from-the-oven biscuits and shortcakes in a breeze.*

| | |
|---|---|
| 4 | cups all-purpose flour |
| ¼ | cup nonfat dry milk powder |
| 2 | tablespoons baking powder |
| 1 | tablespoon sugar |

| | |
|---|---|
| 1½ | teaspoons salt |
| 7 | tablespoons vegetable shortening |
| ¼ | cup (½ stick) unsalted butter or margarine |

1 In a large mixing bowl, stir the flour, dry milk powder, baking powder, sugar, and salt until well blended. With a pastry blender or 2 knives, cut in the shortening and butter until the mixture becomes crumbly and all the fat has been absorbed.

2 Refrigerate in a container with a tight-fitting lid for up to 6 weeks. Makes about 5¼ cups.

Use this mix in the following recipes: Shortcut Biscuits (page 231), Herb Biscuit Variation (page 231), Ham-and-Cheese Biscuit Variation (page 231), Shortcake Variation (page 231).

# Basic Cookie Mix

Per ½ cup: Calories 220; Protein 5 g; Carbohydrate 48 g; Fat tr; Sodium 315 mg; Cholesterol 1 mg.

| | |
|---|---|
| 4 | cups sifted all-purpose flour |
| 2½ | cups sugar |
| 1½ | cups nonfat dry milk powder |
| 5½ | teaspoons baking powder |
| 1½ | teaspoons salt |

1 In a large bowl, combine all the ingredients. Sift the mixture twice. Store in a tightly covered, labeled container for up to 3 months in a cool, dry place. Makes about 8 cups.

Use this mix in the following recipes: Sugar Cookies (page 268), Chocolate Chip Cookies (page 269), Brownies (page 269), Peanut Butter Cookies (page 269).

# Flaky Pie Crust Mix

Per ⅓ cup: Calories 278; Protein 3 g; Carbohydrate 21 g; Fat 20 g; Sodium 315 mg; Cholesterol 0 mg.

| | |
|---|---|
| 5 | cups sifted all-purpose flour |
| 2 | teaspoons salt |
| 2 | cups vegetable shortening |

1 In a large bowl, combine the flour and salt. With a pastry blender or 2 knives, cut in the shortening until the mixture resembles coarse meal.

2 Transfer to an airtight container and store in the refrigerator for up to 2 months. Or divide among four 1-pint freezer bags, label, and freeze for up to 6 months at 0° F. Makes about 7 cups or enough for 2 double-crust or 4 single-crust pies.

Use this mix in the following recipes: Walnut Pie (page 273), Blueberry Pie (page 274), Peach Pie Variation (page 274), Apple Pie Variation (page 274), Mince-Pumpkin Pie (page 298).

# Herbed Stuffing Mix

Per ½ cup: Calories 131; Protein 3 g; Carbohydrate 13 g; Fat 8 g; Sodium 303 mg; Cholesterol 0 mg.

| | |
|---|---|
| 1 | pound sliced whole-wheat or white bread, cut into ¾-inch cubes |
| ½ | cup vegetable oil |
| 1 | teaspoon salt |
| 2 | cloves garlic, minced |
| 2 | tablespoons each dried parsley and dried minced onion, crumbled |
| 1 | teaspoon rubbed sage, crumbled |
| ½ | teaspoon dried thyme, crumbled |
| ½ | teaspoon black pepper |

1 Preheat the oven to 350° F. In a large bowl, toss together the bread, oil, salt, and garlic. Spread on two

baking sheets and bake, stirring occasionally, for 25 minutes or until crisp.

2 Remove from the oven and toss together with the parsley, onion, sage, thyme, and pepper. Let cool to room temperature — about 20 minutes. Transfer to a container with a tight-fitting cover and refrigerate for up to 2 months. Makes 8 cups.

Use this mix in the following recipes: Herbed Stuffing (page 296), Sausage Stuffing (page 296).

# White Sauce Mix

Per ½-inch slice: Calories 129; Protein 1 g; Carbohydrate 6 g; Fat 12 g; Sodium 246 mg; Cholesterol 31 mg.

- 1 cup (2 sticks) unsalted butter or margarine, at room temperature
- 1 cup all-purpose flour
- 2 teaspoons salt
- ½ teaspoon white pepper

1 In a medium-size bowl, mix all the ingredients with your hands until well blended.

2 Transfer the mixture to a sheet of aluminum foil and roll it up, shaping it into a log about 8 inches long. Seal the ends tightly, label, and freeze for up to 2 months at 0° F. Makes enough for 8 cups of white sauce.

Use the mix in these recipes: Basic White Sauce (page 221), Cream of Spinach Soup (page 56), New England Clam Chowder (page 56), Captain's Seafood Casserole (page 126).

*Two for the shelf —*
*Sweet-Bite Salad Dressing*
*Mix and Herb Salad*
*Dressing Mix*

# Sweet-Bite Salad Dressing Mix

Per tablespoon: Calories 16; Protein tr; Carbohydrate 4 g; Fat tr; Sodium 110 mg; Cholesterol 0 mg.

- 1 jar (6 ounces) prepared horseradish
- ½ cup whole-grain or Dijon or spicy brown mustard
- ⅓ cup honey
- 2 tablespoons dried minced onion
- 1½ teaspoons dried dill weed

1 In a medium-size bowl, whisk together all the ingredients until they are well mixed.

2 Transfer to a container with a tight-fitting lid. Refrigerate, labeled, for up to 2 months. Makes about 2 cups.

Use this mix in the following recipes: Saucy Sour Cream Dip (page 35), Sweet-Bite Salad Dressing (page 214).

# Herb Salad Dressing Mix

Per tablespoon: Calories 5; Protein 0 g; Carbohydrate 1 g; Fat 0 g; Sodium 2933 mg; Cholesterol 0 mg.

*Use for a quick vinaigrette or as seasoning for fish, poultry, or meat. Sprinkle also on boiled potatoes, carrots, or green beans.*

- 6 tablespoons salt
- 1 tablespoon dry mustard
- 1 tablespoon black pepper
- 1 tablespoon paprika
- 1½ teaspoons each garlic powder and onion powder
- 1½ teaspoons each dried oregano, dried thyme, and dried basil, crumbled

1 Put all the ingredients into a small jar with a tight-fitting lid and shake well. Store in a cool, dry place for up to 6 months. Makes about ¾ cup.

Use this mix in the following recipe: Herb Vinaigrette Dressing (page 214).

## Beef Paupiettes in Hunter's Sauce, Cheese Polenta, and Minted Peas

# Beef Paupiettes in Hunter's Sauce

Per serving: Calories 454; Protein 57 g; Carbohydrate 12 g; Fat 19 g; Sodium 386 mg; Cholesterol 145 mg.

- 2 shallots or 4 green onions, minced
- 2 tablespoons minced parsley
- ½ teaspoon salt
- ⅛ teaspoon black pepper
- 4 boneless chuck steaks (6 ounces each), trimmed and pounded to ¼-inch thickness
- 2 tablespoons all-purpose flour
- 1 tablespoon olive oil
- 1 tablespoon unsalted butter or margarine
- 1 small yellow onion, finely chopped
- 8 ounces mushrooms, trimmed and quartered
- ¼ cup dry white wine
- 1 can (14 ounces) crushed tomatoes
- ⅓ cup low-sodium beef broth or Beef Stock (page 48)
- ¼ teaspoon each dried basil, thyme, and rosemary, crumbled
- 1 bay leaf
- 2 cloves garlic, minced
- 2 tablespoons minced parsley for garnish (optional)

1 Preheat the oven to 350° F. In a small bowl, combine the shallots, parsley, ¼ teaspoon of the salt, and the pepper. Spread the mixture on the steaks and roll them up jelly-roll fashion; secure with string.

2 Dredge the beef rolls in the flour and sprinkle with the remaining ¼ teaspoon of salt and more pepper, if desired. Heat the olive oil and butter in a medium-size flameproof casserole over moderate heat for 1 minute. Add the meat rolls, and cook, turning, until browned on all sides — 5 to 7 minutes. Transfer to a platter.

3 Add the onion to the casserole, and cook, stirring, over moderate heat for 2 minutes. Add the mushrooms, and cook, stirring, 5 minutes more. Add the wine, boil for 1 minute, and then stir in the tomatoes, beef broth, basil, thyme, rosemary, bay leaf, and garlic. Return the meat to the casserole, transfer to the oven, and bake, covered, for 1 ½ hours or until tender. (Turn the beef rolls halfway through the cooking time.) Let cool and then skim any fat from the sauce.

4 Remove the string from the beef rolls; place one roll and some sauce in each of 4 freezable containers that can be reheated in a conventional or microwave oven. If you don't want the sauce to flavor the polenta and vegetables, use divided containers. Serves 4.

# Cheese Polenta

Per serving: Calories 125; Protein 3 g; Carbohydrate 12 g; Fat 6 g; Sodium 210 mg; Cholesterol 16 mg.

- 2 cups water
- ¼ teaspoon salt
- ½ cup yellow cornmeal
- 1½ tablespoons unsalted butter or margarine
- 3 tablespoons grated Parmesan cheese
- ⅛ teaspoon black pepper, or to taste

1 In a medium-size saucepan, combine the water, salt, and cornmeal. Whisk as you bring it to a boil over moderate heat. Reduce the heat to moderately low and simmer, whisking the mixture occasionally, for 15 minutes or until thick. Whisk in the butter, 2 tablespoons of the cheese, and the black pepper.

2 Transfer the mixture to 4 divided containers, filling one small section of each, or pour it into a buttered 6-inch pie plate or baking dish. Sprinkle the polenta with the remaining tablespoon of cheese, cover loosely, and chill for 1 hour or until firm. If you have used a pie plate or baking dish, cut the polenta into 4 wedges and divide among the containers. Serves 4.

# Minted Peas

Per serving: Calories 99; Protein 4 g; Carbohydrate 12 g; Fat 4 g; Sodium 111 mg; Cholesterol 11 mg.

- 2 cups fresh peas (about 2 pounds unshelled) or 2 cups frozen peas
- 4 pats (each ½ inch thick) frozen Mint Butter (page 223)

1 Bring 2 quarts of water to a boil in a large saucepan over moderate heat. Add the peas and boil for 2 minutes; drain and refresh under cold water. Divide among the freezable containers. If using frozen peas, wait until the beef rolls and polenta have cooled before placing the peas in the containers. Do not let them thaw.

2 Top each serving with 1 pat of the frozen Mint Butter. (If you don't have Mint Butter on hand, substitute 4 teaspoons lightly salted butter or margarine, plus a sprinkling of freeze-dried mint and pepper.) Serves 4.

*A Beef Paupiettes dinner in its handy freezable container*

**Packaging and freezing:** Cover each container with heavy-duty aluminum foil, label, and freeze. Will keep for up to 3 months at 0° F.

### Serving Later

**To reheat in the oven:** Preheat oven to 400° F. Bake foil-wrapped dinners for 20 to 30 minutes or until the beef rolls are heated through. Remove the foil and garnish with the minced pars-ley, if desired. **To microwave:** Remove foil. Cover with plastic wrap vented at one side. Heat on *High* (100% power) for 5 minutes. Turn beef rolls and rotate the plate 90 degrees; heat on *High* (100% power) another 4 minutes. Let stand for 2 minutes before uncovering. Garnish with the minced parsley, if desired.

*Tip: When preparing fresh vegetables for the TV dinners, be careful to cook them until just slightly tender. They will finish cooking as they are reheated.*

## French Pot Roast with Garden Vegetables

# French Pot Roast

Per serving: Calories 483; Protein 72 g; Carbohydrate 9 g; Fat 24 g; Sodium 362 mg; Cholesterol 224 mg.

*For the marinade:*
- 1½ cups dry red wine
- 1½ cups low-sodium beef broth or Beef Stock (page 48)
- 1 medium-size yellow onion, sliced
- 2 small carrots, peeled and sliced
- 2 stalks celery, sliced
- 2 cloves garlic, crushed
- ½ teaspoon each dried thyme and rosemary, crumbled
- 1 bay leaf, crumbled
- 5 sprigs parsley
- 2 whole cloves
- ½ teaspoon salt
- ¼ teaspoon black pepper

*For the pot roast:*
- 3 pounds boneless beef rump, sirloin tip, or chuck roast
- 2 tablespoons olive oil
- 5 teaspoons tomato paste
- 1 tablespoon cornstarch dissolved in 2 tablespoons Madeira or Port

1 In a large, glass or ceramic bowl, mix the wine, broth, onion, carrots, celery, garlic, thyme, rosemary, bay leaf, parsley, cloves, salt, and pepper. Add the beef, cover, and marinate overnight in the refrigerator, turning once or twice for even marination.

2 Preheat the oven to 350° F. Remove the meat from the marinade and pat it dry, reserving the vegetables and the marinade. Heat the olive oil in a large flameproof casserole over moderately high heat. Add the beef and brown on all sides — 5 to 7 minutes. Transfer to a platter.

3 With a slotted spoon, transfer the vegetables and seasonings from the marinade to the casserole. Cook, stirring, over moderately high heat for 5 minutes. Then stir in the marinade liquid and the tomato paste. Add the beef, transfer to the oven, and bake, covered, for 2 to 2½ hours or until the meat is tender.

▽ Recipe may be prepared in advance to this point, covered, and refrigerated overnight.

4 Transfer the meat to a cutting board. Skim any fat from the surface of the sauce; then strain sauce into a medium-size saucepan. Bring to a boil over moderately high heat. Reduce heat to low, whisk in the cornstarch mixture, and simmer, whisking, until slightly thickened — about 3 minutes.

5 Cut the meat into 12 slices and divide among six 9-inch pie plates or casseroles that can be reheated in a conventional or microwave oven. Spoon sauce over them. Serves 6.

# Garden Vegetables

Per serving: Calories 51; Protein 2 g; Carbohydrate 12 g; Fat tr; Sodium 27 mg; Cholesterol 8 mg.

*If desired, 2 cups of frozen mixed vegetables can be substituted for the fresh carrots and green beans.*

- 6 medium-size carrots, peeled, and cut diagonally into ½-inch pieces
- ¾ pound green beans, trimmed and cut into 2-inch pieces

1 Bring 2 quarts unsalted water to a boil in a medium-size saucepan over moderate heat. Add the carrots, and when the water returns to a boil, cook, uncovered, for 5 minutes; add the green beans and boil, uncovered, 2 minutes more or until the vegetables are just slightly tender. Drain and refresh under cold water. Divide among the freezable containers, cover with sauce, and let cool.

2 If using frozen vegetables, place them directly in the freezable containers; don't allow them to thaw. Be sure the sauce is cool before you pour it over them. Serves 6.

**Packaging and freezing:** Cover each container with heavy-duty aluminum foil, label, and freeze. Freeze any leftover sauce to use on grilled meats or chicken. The dinners and the sauce will keep for up to 3 months at 0° F.

## *Serving Later*

**To reheat in the oven:** Preheat oven to 400° F. Bake foil-wrapped dinners for 25 to 35 minutes or until the meat is heated through. Remove foil and garnish with parsley, if desired. **To microwave:** Remove foil. Cover with plastic wrap vented at one side. Heat on *High* (100% power) for 4 minutes; turn beef slices over and heat on *High* (100% power) another 4 minutes. Let stand 1 minute before uncovering.

## Gingered Pepper Steak, Saffron Rice, and Vegetable Medley

# Gingered Pepper Steak

Per serving: Calories 470; Protein 51 g; Carbohydrate 8 g; Fat 25 g; Sodium 582 mg; Cholesterol 131 mg.

*For a richer, nuttier flavor, try adding the dark (also known as Oriental) sesame oil.*

- 1½ pounds lean boneless chuck steak, cut into 1-inch pieces
- 2 tablespoons all-purpose flour
- ⅛ teaspoon black pepper
- 2 tablespoons vegetable oil
- 4 green onions, sliced
- 2 cloves garlic, sliced
- 1½ teaspoons minced fresh ginger
- 1 cup low-sodium beef broth or Beef Stock (page 48)
- 5 teaspoons soy sauce
- 1 cinnamon stick, cracked
- 2 whole cloves
- 1½ teaspoons honey
- 1 medium-size sweet green pepper, cored and cut into 1½- by ½-inch strips
- 1½ teaspoons dark sesame oil (optional)

1 Dredge the steak in the flour and sprinkle with the black pepper. Heat the oil in a heavy 10-inch skillet over moderately high heat for 1 minute. Add the meat, and cook, turning, until browned on all sides — about 5 minutes. Add the green onions, garlic, and ginger; cook, stirring, for 2 minutes. Add the beef broth, soy sauce, cinnamon, cloves, and honey. Simmer, covered, over low heat for 1 hour or until the steak is tender. With a slotted spoon, transfer the meat to a platter.

2 Skim any fat from the broth, then strain through a sieve into a large saucepan; discard the strained solids. Add the steak and green pepper to the broth. Simmer, stirring, for 5 to 7 minutes or until the green pepper is just tender. Stir in the sesame oil, if desired. Divide mixture among 4 freezable containers that can be reheated in a conventional or microwave oven; let cool. If you don't want the sauce to flavor the rice and vegetables, use divided containers. Serves 4.

# Saffron Rice Pilaf

Per serving: Calories 212; Protein 6 g; Carbohydrate 38 g; Fat 4 g; Sodium 96 mg; Cholesterol 8 mg.

- 2 cups low-sodium chicken broth or Chicken Stock (page 48)
- 1 tablespoon unsalted butter or margarine
- ⅛ teaspoon saffron threads or ground turmeric
- 1 bay leaf
- ⅛ teaspoon each salt and black pepper
- 1 cup rice

1 In a large saucepan, bring the chicken broth, butter, saffron, bay leaf, salt, and pepper to a boil over moderately high heat. Stir in the rice; reduce the heat to low and simmer, covered, for 20 minutes or until all the liquid is absorbed. Discard the bay leaf and divide the saffron rice among the freezable containers. Serves 4.

# Vegetable Medley

Per serving: Calories 74; Protein 2 g; Carbohydrate 7 g; Fat 4 g; Sodium 93 mg; Cholesterol 12 mg.

*If desired, a 1-pound package of frozen mixed vegetables can be substituted for the fresh vegetables in this medley.*

- 2 medium-size carrots, peeled and sliced
- 1⅓ cups small cauliflower florets (about 4 ounces)
- 1⅓ cups small broccoli florets (about 4 ounces)
- 4 pats (each ½ inch thick) frozen Red Pepper Butter (page 222)

1 Bring 2 quarts unsalted water to a boil in a large saucepan over moderate heat. Add the carrots, and when the water returns to a boil, cook, uncovered, for 30 seconds. Add the broccoli and cauliflower and boil, uncovered, 2 minutes more. Drain and refresh the vegetables under cold water. Divide them among the freezable containers and let cool to room temperature. If you are using frozen vegetables, wait for the meat and rice to cool before dividing the vegetables among the containers. Do not let them thaw.

2 Top each serving with 1 pat frozen Red Pepper Butter. (If you don't have Red Pepper Butter on hand, sauté 2 tablespoons minced sweet red pepper in 2 tablespoons lightly salted butter or margarine. Spread over the vegetables and sprinkle with ⅛ teaspoon each black pepper and dried rosemary, crumbled.) Serves 4.

**Packaging and freezing:** Cover the containers with heavy-duty aluminum foil, label, and freeze. Will keep for up to 3 months at 0° F.

### Serving Later

**To reheat in the oven:** Preheat the oven to 400° F. Bake the foil-wrapped dinners for 25 to 35 minutes or until the steak is heated through. Remove the foil. **To microwave:** Remove foil. Cover with plastic wrap vented at one side. Heat on *High* (100% power) for 5 minutes. Turn the containers 90 degrees and heat on *High* (100% power) another 3 minutes. Let stand for 2 minutes before uncovering.

## Barbecued Pork Roast with Confetti Corn

# Barbecued Pork Roast

Per serving: Calories 365; Protein 37 g; Carbohydrate 2 g; Fat 22 g; Sodium 172 mg; Cholesterol 119 mg.

*For the pork:*
- 3 pounds boneless pork roast, such as shoulder or loin, trimmed of visible fat
- 3 cloves garlic, sliced thin
- ½ teaspoon each dried sage and thyme, crumbled
- ¼ teaspoon each salt and black pepper
- 2 tablespoons vegetable oil
- 1 medium-size yellow onion, sliced
- ½ cup low-sodium beef broth or Beef Stock (page 48)

*For the barbecue sauce:*
- 1 can (8 ounces) tomato sauce
- ¼ cup lemon juice
- ¼ cup chili sauce
- ¼ cup ketchup
- ¼ cup cider vinegar
- 3 tablespoons Worcestershire sauce
- 2 tablespoons brown sugar or honey
- 2 teaspoons Dijon or spicy brown mustard, or to taste
- ½ teaspoon paprika
- ⅛ teaspoon cayenne pepper, or to taste

1 Preheat the oven to 350° F. Make slits in the pork at regular intervals and insert the garlic slices. Rub the pork all over with the sage, thyme, salt, and pepper.

2 Heat the oil in a large flameproof casserole over moderately high heat for 1 minute. Add the pork, and cook, turning, until browned on all sides — 5 to 7 minutes. Add the onion; cook, stirring, until soft — about 5 minutes. Add the broth and bring the liquid to a simmer. Transfer to the oven and bake, covered, for 1 hour.

3 Meanwhile, prepare the sauce. In a medium-size mixing bowl combine the tomato sauce, lemon juice, chili sauce, ketchup, vinegar, Worcestershire sauce, brown sugar, mustard, paprika, and cayenne.

4 Remove the casserole from the oven and add the barbecue sauce. Return to the oven and bake, covered, 1 hour more; remove cover and bake an additional 15 minutes or until the pork is tender. Skim any fat from the sauce and let cool to room temperature.

▽ Recipe can be prepared in advance up to this point and refrigerated, covered, overnight.

5 Slice the meat into 12 slices and divide among 6 freezable containers that can be reheated in a conventional or microwave oven. If you do not want the sauce to flavor the corn, use divided containers. Cover each slice with 3 tablespoons sauce; let cool. Serves 6.

# Confetti Corn

Per serving: Calories 192; Protein 6 g; Carbohydrate 28 g; Fat 8 g; Sodium 77 mg; Cholesterol 20 mg.

- 8 medium-size ears fresh sweet corn or 2 cans (1 pound each) whole kernel corn
- 2 tablespoons unsalted butter or margarine
- 1 medium-size yellow onion, finely chopped
- ½ medium-size sweet green pepper, cored, seeded, and minced
- ½ medium-size sweet red pepper, cored, seeded and minced
- ⅛ teaspoon black pepper, or to taste
- ½ cup shredded Cheddar or Monterey Jack cheese

1 Remove the husks and silk from the ears of corn and cut off the kernels with a knife. Bring two quarts unsalted water to a boil in a medium-size saucepan. Add the corn and boil, uncovered, for 2 minutes; drain and refresh under cold water. If using canned corn, drain and set aside.

2 Melt the butter in a heavy, 10-inch skillet over moderate heat. Add the onion, and cook, stirring, for 4 minutes. Add the red pepper, green pepper, and black pepper, and cook, stirring, 1 minute more. Remove the skillet from the heat, add the corn, and mix well.

3 Divide the mixture among 6 freezable containers and sprinkle with the cheese. Serves 6.

**Packaging and freezing:** Cover each container with heavy-duty aluminum foil, label, and freeze. Will keep for up to 3 months at 0° F.

### Serving Later

**To reheat in the oven:** Preheat oven to 400° F. Bake foil-wrapped dinners for 20 to 30 minutes or until the meat is heated through. **To microwave:** Remove foil and cover with plastic wrap vented at the sides. Heat on *High* (100% power) for 4 minutes; turn pork slices over, then heat on *High* (100% power) 3 minutes more. Let stand for 1 minute before uncovering.

*The elements of a Barbecued Pork Roast dinner ready to be frozen for later use*

Chicken in Orange Sauce,
Rice with Almonds and
Raisins, Asparagus
with Dill Butter

# Chicken in Orange Sauce

Per serving: Calories 440; Protein 52 g;
Carbohydrate 18 g; Fat 15 g; Sodium 544 mg;
Cholesterol 148 mg.

*If you like dark meat as well as light,
substitute for the breasts a 3-pound
chicken, cut into serving-size pieces,
and increase the simmering time
to between 35 and 40 minutes.*

|   | |
|---|---|
| 2 | whole chicken breasts (about 14 ounces each), skinned and halved |
| 2 | tablespoons all-purpose flour |
| 3/4 | teaspoon salt |
| 1/4 | teaspoon black pepper |
| 2 | tablespoons unsalted butter or margarine |
| 1 | tablespoon olive oil |
| 1 | medium-size yellow onion, chopped |
| 1 | stalk celery, sliced |
| 1 | small carrot, peeled and sliced |
| 1/3 | cup dry white wine |
| 1 1/2 | cups low-sodium chicken broth or Chicken Stock (page 48) |
| 2 | teaspoons tomato paste |
| 2 | cloves garlic, minced |
| 3 | strips orange zest (colored part of the rind), 2 1/2 by 1 inch |
| 1/2 | teaspoon each dried sage and rosemary, crumbled |
| 3 | tablespoons red wine vinegar |
| 4 | teaspoons sugar |
| 1 | tablespoon cornstarch dissolved in 1 tablespoon orange-flavored liqueur or water |
| 1 | teaspoon grated orange rind Orange slices for garnish |

**1** Dredge the chicken in the flour and sprinkle with 1/2 teaspoon of the salt and 1/8 teaspoon of the pepper.

**2** Heat the butter and oil in a large flameproof casserole over moderately high heat for 1 minute. Add the chicken, and cook, uncovered, until no longer pink on the outside — about 5 minutes. Transfer to a platter.

**3** Add the onion, celery, and carrot to the casserole; cook, stirring, until the vegetables are golden — about 7 minutes. Add the wine and boil, uncovered, for 1 minute. Stir in the chicken broth, tomato paste, garlic, strips of orange zest, sage, and rosemary, and bring to a simmer. Return the chicken to the casserole and simmer, covered, for 15 to 20 minutes or until the juice runs clear when the chicken is pricked with a fork.

**4** Meanwhile, in a small heavy saucepan, combine the vinegar and sugar. Bring to a boil over moderate heat and cook 3 to 5 minutes, stirring often, until reduced to about 1 tablespoon.

**5** Remove the chicken from the casserole and strain the sauce into the vinegar mixture. Press liquid from the solids in the strainer and discard them. Cook the sauce over moderately high heat for 5 minutes, stirring often. Whisk in the cornstarch mixture and cook, stirring, until thickened. Add the grated orange rind, and remaining 1/4 teaspoon salt and 1/8 teaspoon pepper.

**6** Divide the chicken among 4 freezable containers that can be reheated in a conventional or microwave oven. If you don't want the orange sauce to spill into the rice and peas, use divided containers. Cover the chicken with sauce and let cool to room temperature. Serves 4.

# Rice with Almonds and Raisins

Per serving: Calories 237; Protein 5 g;
Carbohydrate 42 g; Fat 5 g; Sodium 291 mg;
Cholesterol 8 mg.

|   | |
|---|---|
| 1 | tablespoon unsalted butter or margarine |
| 1 | cup white rice |
| 1 | cup water |
| 1 | cup low-sodium chicken broth or Chicken Stock (page 48) |
| 2 | tablespoons toasted slivered almonds |
| 2 | tablespoons golden raisins |
| 1/2 | teaspoon salt |
| 1/8 | teaspoon black pepper |

**1** Melt the butter in a medium-size saucepan over moderate heat. Add the rice and stir to coat. Add the water and chicken broth; bring to a boil. Reduce the heat to low and simmer, covered, for 20 minutes or until all of the liquid is absorbed.

**2** Remove saucepan from the heat; stir in the almonds, raisins, salt, and pepper. Divide the rice among the freezable containers and, if desired, cover with some of the orange sauce. Let cool. Serves 4.

# Asparagus with Dill Butter

Per serving: Calories 64; Protein 3 g;
Carbohydrate 5 g; Fat 4 g; Sodium 46 mg;
Cholesterol 11 mg.

*If fresh asparagus is unavailable,
substitute another fresh or frozen
vegetable, such as broccoli or green
beans. Boil a fresh vegetable until
slightly tender — about 2 to 3
minutes — and refresh under cold
water. For a frozen vegetable, follow
directions below.*

*Chicken in Orange Sauce, with its accompaniments, served up elegantly on the spur of the moment.*

1 pound asparagus, trimmed, and cut to size of container to be used for the dinner, or 1 pound frozen asparagus or other frozen green vegetable
4 pats (each ½ inch thick) frozen Dill Butter (page 222)

1 Bring 2 quarts unsalted water to a boil in a medium-size saucepan over moderate heat. Add the fresh asparagus, and cook 2 minutes after water returns to a boil; drain and refresh under cold water. Divide among the containers; let cool. (If using frozen asparagus or another frozen vegetable, wait until the chicken and rice have cooled before dividing the frozen vegetables among the containers. Do not let the vegetables thaw.)

2 Top each serving with 1 pat frozen Dill Butter. (If you don't have Dill Butter on hand, substitute 4 teaspoons lightly salted butter or margarine, plus a sprinkling of dill weed and pepper.) Serves 4.

**Packaging and freezing:** Cover each container tightly with heavy-duty aluminum foil, label, and freeze. Will keep for up to 3 months at 0° F.

### Serving Later

**To reheat in the oven:** Preheat oven to 400° F. Bake foil-wrapped dinners for 25 to 35 minutes or until the chicken is heated through. Garnish with the orange slices. **To microwave:** Remove foil. Cover with plastic wrap vented at one side. Heat on *High* (100% power) for 5 minutes. Turn the containers 90 degrees; heat on *High* (100% power) another 4 minutes. Let stand for 1 minute before uncovering. Garnish with the orange slices.

25

Halibut Niçoise, Duchess Potatoes, and Green Beans with Garlic Butter

# Halibut Niçoise

Per serving: Calories 289; Protein 36 g; Carbohydrate 10 g; Fat 10 g; Sodium 455 mg; Cholesterol 86 mg.

*If you prefer, substitute fresh cod or haddock for the halibut in this recipe.*

| | |
|---|---|
| 1 | tablespoon olive oil |
| 1 | small yellow onion, thinly sliced |
| 1 | can (1 pound) tomatoes |
| 1 | clove garlic, minced |
| 2 | tablespoons minced fresh parsley |
| 1/4 | teaspoon each dried thyme and basil, crumbled |
| 1/4 | teaspoon grated lemon rind |
| 1/8 | teaspoon salt |
| | Black pepper to taste |
| 4 | halibut steaks (about 6 ounces each), 1 1/4 inches thick |
| 1 | bay leaf |
| 1/3 | cup dry white wine |
| 1 | tablespoon tomato paste |
| 2 | teaspoons cornstarch dissolved in 1 tablespoon water |
| 12 | pitted black or green olives |

1 Preheat the oven to 350° F. Heat the olive oil in a heavy 10-inch skillet over moderate heat for 1 minute. Add the onion, and sauté, stirring, until soft — about 5 minutes. Let cool.

2 Drain and chop the tomatoes, reserving 1/2 cup of the liquid. Add the tomatoes, garlic, parsley, thyme, basil, lemon rind, salt, and black pepper to the onions and mix well. Spoon half the mixture into a flameproof casserole large enough to hold the fish in one layer. Add the fish steaks, the remaining tomato mixture, and the bay leaf.

3 In a small bowl, whisk together the reserved tomato liquid, white wine, and tomato paste. Pour the liquid over the fish. Bake, covered, for 20 to 25 minutes or until the fish just flakes. Leaving the sauce in the casserole, transfer the fish to 4 freezable containers that can be reheated in a conventional or microwave oven.

4 In the casserole, bring the tomato sauce to a boil over moderate heat. Stir in the cornstarch mixture, and cook, stirring, over moderate heat until thickened. Spoon the sauce over the fish and garnish with the olives. Let cool. Serves 4.

# Duchess Potatoes

Per serving: Calories 154; Protein 3 g; Carbohydrate 23 g; Fat 6 g; Sodium 135 mg; Cholesterol 80 mg.

| | |
|---|---|
| 4 | medium-size red-skin potatoes (about 1 pound), peeled and quartered |
| 3 | tablespoons milk |
| 4 | teaspoons unsalted butter or margarine, at room temperature |
| 1 | egg yolk |
| 1/4 | teaspoon salt |
| 1/8 | teaspoon black pepper |
| | Grated nutmeg to taste |

1 Bring 2 quarts unsalted water to a boil in a large saucepan. Add the potatoes and boil for 20 minutes or until tender. Meanwhile, in a small saucepan, heat the milk until bubbles form at the edge. Stir in the butter.

2 Drain the potatoes and mash them. Beat in the egg yolk and milk. Add the salt, pepper, and nutmeg, and mix well. Divide the potatoes among the freezable containers. Let cool. Serves 4.

# Green Beans with Garlic Butter

Per serving: Calories 76; Protein 2 g; Carbohydrate 9 g; Fat 4 g; Sodium 45 mg; Cholesterol 11 mg.

| | |
|---|---|
| 1 | pound green beans, trimmed, or 1 1/2 cups frozen green beans |
| 4 | pats (each 1/2 inch thick) frozen Garlic Butter (page 223) |

1 Bring 2 quarts unsalted water to a boil in a medium-size saucepan. Add the fresh beans and boil for 3 minutes. Drain and refresh under cold water. Divide among the containers and let cool. (If using frozen beans, wait until the halibut and potatoes have cooled, then place the beans, still frozen, directly in the containers. Do not let them thaw.)

2 Top each serving with a pat of frozen Garlic Butter. (If you don't have garlic butter on hand, substitute 1 teaspoon of butter or margarine plus a sprinkling of garlic salt and black pepper.) Serves 4.

**Packaging and freezing:** Cover each container tightly with heavy-duty aluminum foil, label, and freeze. The dinners will keep for up to 3 months at 0° F. Serves 4.

### Serving Later

**To reheat in the oven:** Preheat oven to 400° F. Bake the foil-wrapped dinners for 20 to 30 minutes or until the fish is heated through. **To microwave:** Remove foil. Cover with plastic wrap vented at one side. Heat on *High* (100% power) for 6 minutes. Turn containers 90 degrees; heat on *High* (100% power) 6 minutes more. Let stand 2 minutes before uncovering.

*A wonderful prepare-ahead: Halibut Niçoise with Duchess Potatoes and Green Beans with Garlic Butter*

# Chicken Pot Pie

Per serving: Calories 875; Protein 40 g; Carbohydrate 65 g; Fat 48 g; Sodium 432 mg; Cholesterol 151 mg.

*Combining cold vegetable shortening with the butter makes a lighter, flakier crust. If, however, you don't have shortening on hand, you can use all butter or margarine.*

**For the pastry:**
- 2 cups sifted all-purpose flour
- 1/4 teaspoon salt
- 6 tablespoons (3/4 stick) cold unsalted butter or margarine
- 5 tablespoons cold vegetable shortening
- 4 to 5 tablespoons ice water
- 1 medium-size egg beaten with 2 teaspoons water (optional)

**For the filling:**
- 4 tablespoons (1/2 stick) unsalted butter or margarine
- 8 chicken thighs, skinned, boned, and cut into 1-inch pieces
- 1 medium-size yellow onion, chopped
- 1 stalk celery, sliced
- 8 ounces mushrooms, sliced
- 4 tablespoons all-purpose flour
- 1/2 cup dry white wine
- 2 1/2 cups low-sodium chicken broth or Chicken Stock (page 48)
- 1/2 teaspoon each dried tarragon and thyme, crumbled
- 1 bay leaf
- 1/4 teaspoon salt
- 1/8 teaspoon black pepper
- 4 medium-size carrots, peeled and sliced
- 1 cup shelled fresh peas (optional)
- 1/2 cup milk
- 2 tablespoons minced parsley Lemon juice to taste

1 To prepare the pastry: Combine the flour and salt in a large bowl. Cut in the butter and shortening until the mixture resembles coarse meal. Add the ice water 1 tablespoon at a time, mixing lightly with a fork, until the dough holds together. Seal in plastic wrap; chill for 30 minutes.

2 Meanwhile, prepare the filling: Melt the butter in a medium-size flame-proof casserole over moderate heat. Add the chicken, and cook, turning, until no longer pink on the outside — about 5 minutes. Add the onion, celery, and mushrooms, and cook, stirring, for 5 minutes. Sprinkle mixture with the flour; cook, stirring, 1 minute more. Add the wine and boil for 1 minute; then add the chicken broth, tarragon, thyme, bay leaf, salt, and black pepper. Simmer, covered, stirring occasionally, for 30 minutes or until the chicken is tender.

3 Meanwhile, bring 2 quarts unsalted water to a boil in a large saucepan. Add the carrots, and when the water returns to a boil, cook, uncovered, for 3 minutes. Add the peas, if desired, and boil 2 minutes more or until the vegetables are just tender. Drain and refresh under cold water.

4 Remove the chicken from the sauce and set aside. Strain the sauce into a large saucepan and skim off any fat. Cook over moderately high heat until thickened — 5 to 6 minutes. Stir in the milk, parsley, and lemon juice to taste. Remove from the heat and add the chicken and vegetables.

5 Preheat the oven to 400° F. Divide the mixture among four 1 1/2-cup ramekins that can be reheated in a conventional or microwave oven. Divide the pastry into 4 pieces; roll out. Cover each ramekin with pastry, crimping the edges decoratively.

▽ The pies can be prepared in advance to this point, covered with foil, and *refrigerated* overnight.

6 Cut 2 or 3 air slits in the top of each pie; then brush with the egg glaze, if desired. Bake pies, for 30 minutes or until the pastry is golden. Let cool to room temperature. Serves 4.

**Packaging and freezing:** Cover with heavy-duty aluminum foil, label, and freeze. Will keep for 3 months at 0° F.

## Serving Later

**To reheat in the oven:** Preheat oven to 400° F. Bake, uncovered, for 30 minutes. **To microwave:** Remove the foil and cover the ramekins with paper toweling. Microwave for 11 to 12 minutes on *High* (100% power). The crust will be soft. To crispen it, run the pie under a broiler for 2 to 3 minutes.

# Haddock and Shrimp Gratinée

Per serving: Calories 483; Protein 54 g; Carbohydrate 11 g; Fat 22 g; Sodium 683 mg; Cholesterol 289 mg.

*These individual casseroles are elegant enough to serve last-minute company for dinner. Since you will be freezing this dish, be sure to use fresh shrimp. Thawing frozen foods and then refreezing can breed bacteria.*

- 1 pound haddock, halibut, or monkfish fillet, skinned
- 6 ounces large shrimp, shelled and deveined
- 3 tablespoons unsalted butter or margarine
- 1 medium-size yellow onion, minced
- 3 tablespoons all-purpose flour
- 1 1/2 cups milk
- 2 tablespoons dry white wine
- 1 cup shredded Gruyère or Cheddar cheese (4 ounces)
- 1/8 teaspoon each salt and black pepper Minced parsley for garnish (optional)

1 Cut the haddock fillet into 8 equal strips crosswise and fold each strip in half. Place 2 strips in each of 4 greased 1 1/2-cup ramekins or gratin

dishes that can be reheated in a conventional or microwave oven. Divide the shrimp among the dishes, arranging it over and around the haddock.

2 Melt the butter in a medium-size saucepan over moderate heat. Add the onion; cook, stirring, until soft — about 5 minutes. Add the flour; cook, stirring, for 2 minutes. Add the milk and wine and simmer, stirring, for 4 to 5 minutes or until thickened. Remove sauce from heat, add ¾ cup of the cheese, and blend well. Season with the salt and pepper; let cool slightly.

3 Cover each serving of fish with the sauce and sprinkle with the remaining cheese. Serves 4.

**Packaging and freezing:** Wrap the ramekins tightly with heavy-duty aluminum foil, label, and freeze. Will keep for up to 3 months at 0° F.

### Serving Later

**To reheat in the oven:** Preheat oven to 400° F. Bake the foil-wrapped casseroles for 25 to 35 minutes or until heated through and bubbling. Then unwrap and run under the broiler, 4 inches from the heat, for 1 to 2 minutes to brown. Garnish with parsley, if desired. **To microwave:** Remove foil. Cover each ramekin with plastic wrap vented at one side. Heat on *High* (100% power) for 7 minutes. Let stand for 1 minute before uncovering. Serve with hot crusty bread and steamed spinach or broccoli.

*A hearty Chicken Pot Pie just hot from the oven*

# Macaroni, Spinach, and Cheese Casserole

Per serving: Calories 461; Protein 52 g; Carbohydrate 82 g; Fat 80 g; Sodium 696 mg; Cholesterol 90 mg.

- 12 ounces spinach, trimmed and washed well
- 4 tablespoons (½ stick) unsalted butter or margarine
- 1 large yellow onion, minced
- 6 ounces thinly sliced mushrooms (about 2 cups)
- 2 cloves garlic, minced
- ½ teaspoon each dried thyme, basil, and tarragon, crumbled
- 3 tablespoons all-purpose flour
- 2 cups milk
- ½ teaspoon salt
- ¼ teaspoon black pepper
- ½ cup grated Parmesan cheese
- 2 teaspoons Dijon or spicy brown mustard
- ½ cup elbow macaroni cooked according to package directions
- 1 cup ricotta cheese

1 Place spinach in a large saucepan, cover, and cook over moderate heat until wilted — 3 to 4 minutes. Drain, cool, and chop coarsely.

2 Melt 1 tablespoon of the butter in a heavy 10-inch skillet over moderately high heat. Add the onion and stir until slightly soft — about 2 minutes. Add the mushrooms, garlic, thyme, basil, and tarragon. Cook over moderate heat, stirring occasionally, until the liquid evaporates — about 5 minutes. Set aside to cool.

3 Melt the remaining 3 tablespoons of butter in a small saucepan over moderate heat. Blend in the flour and stir for 2 minutes. Add the milk and

bring to a simmer, stirring constantly. Reduce the heat to low and stir constantly for 5 minutes until thickened and smooth. Remove from the heat and stir in the salt, pepper, ¼ cup of the Parmesan cheese, and the mustard.

4 Mix 1 cup of sauce with the macaroni. Distribute the macaroni equally among 4 greased 1½-cup ramekins that can be reheated in a conventional or microwave oven. Stir ½ cup sauce into the mushroom mixture; then add the reserved spinach and the ricotta. Spoon the mixture over the macaroni and cover with the remaining sauce. Top casseroles with the remaining Parmesan cheese. Serves 4.

**Packaging and freezing:** Wrap each ramekin tightly with heavy-duty aluminum foil, label, and freeze. Will keep for up to 2 months at 0° F.

## Serving Later

**To reheat in the oven:** Preheat oven to 400° F. Bake the foil-covered casseroles for 30 minutes; uncover and cook until heated through and bubbling — about 15 minutes more. **To microwave:** Remove foil and cover with plastic wrap vented at the sides. Heat on *High* (100% power) for 7 minutes. Let stand 1 minute before uncovering.

*Macaroni, Spinach, and Cheese Casserole. A simple, but satisfying, meal-in-one*

# Appetizers

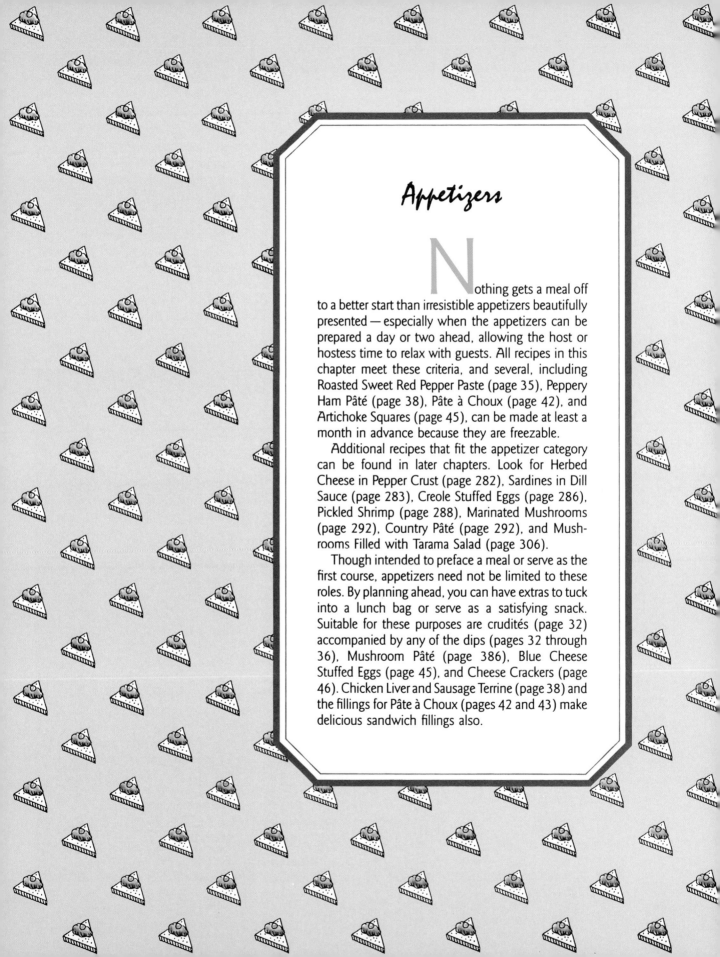

Nothing gets a meal off to a better start than irresistible appetizers beautifully presented — especially when the appetizers can be prepared a day or two ahead, allowing the host or hostess time to relax with guests. All recipes in this chapter meet these criteria, and several, including Roasted Sweet Red Pepper Paste (page 35), Peppery Ham Pâté (page 38), Pâte à Choux (page 42), and Artichoke Squares (page 45), can be made at least a month in advance because they are freezable.

Additional recipes that fit the appetizer category can be found in later chapters. Look for Herbed Cheese in Pepper Crust (page 282), Sardines in Dill Sauce (page 283), Creole Stuffed Eggs (page 286), Pickled Shrimp (page 288), Marinated Mushrooms (page 292), Country Pâté (page 292), and Mushrooms Filled with Tarama Salad (page 306).

Though intended to preface a meal or serve as the first course, appetizers need not be limited to these roles. By planning ahead, you can have extras to tuck into a lunch bag or serve as a satisfying snack. Suitable for these purposes are crudités (page 32) accompanied by any of the dips (pages 32 through 36), Mushroom Pâté (page 386), Blue Cheese Stuffed Eggs (page 45), and Cheese Crackers (page 46). Chicken Liver and Sausage Terrine (page 38) and the fillings for Pâte à Choux (pages 42 and 43) make delicious sandwich fillings also.

# Curried Chervil Dip

Per tablespoon: Calories 37; Protein 1 g;
Carbohydrate 1 g; Fat 3 g; Sodium 34 mg;
Cholesterol 9 mg.

*The tangy nip of this creamy dip is sure
to whet your guests' appetites.*

- 1 tablespoon unsalted butter
  or margarine
- 1½ teaspoons curry powder
- ½ cup plain low-fat yogurt
- ½ cup sour cream
- 3 ounces cream cheese, at
  room temperature
- 2 tablespoons snipped fresh
  chives or green onion tops
- 1 tablespoon minced parsley
- 1 tablespoon minced chervil or
  1 teaspoon dried chervil,
  crumbled
- 2 teaspoons lemon juice
- ½ teaspoon Dijon or spicy
  brown mustard
- ⅛ teaspoon salt
  Parsley for garnish (optional)

1 Melt the butter in a small heavy
skillet over moderately low heat.
Add the curry powder, stirring for 2
minutes; then set aside to cool.

2 In a medium-size bowl, cream together the yogurt, sour cream, and
cream cheese with an electric beater or
wooden spoon. Stir in the curry butter,
chives, parsley, chervil, lemon juice,
mustard, and salt.

3 Transfer the mixture to a small bowl
and cover tightly. Refrigerate for at
least 1 hour or overnight. Can be
refrigerated for up to 2 days. Garnish
with a parsley sprig, if desired. Serve
with such crudités as celery, cauliflower, or cucumbers. This goes well
also with chips or crackers. Makes
about 1¼ cups.

# Tarragon Lemon Dip

Per tablespoon: Calories 41; Protein 1 g;
Carbohydrate 1 g; Fat 4 g; Sodium 25 mg;
Cholesterol 11 mg.

*This zesty dip, rich in vitamin C, goes
well with unsalted chips, crisped
celery, or blanched green beans.*

- 8 ounces cream cheese, at
  room temperature
- 1 cup sour cream or plain low-
  fat yogurt
- 3 tablespoons lemon juice, or
  to taste
- ½ teaspoon fennel seeds,
  crushed
- ¼ cup minced tarragon or 2
  teaspooons dried tarragon,
  crumbled
- 1 slice lemon for garnish

1 In a medium-size mixing bowl,
cream together the cream cheese,
sour cream, and lemon juice with an
electric beater or wooden spoon. Blend
in the fennel seeds and tarragon.

2 Transfer the mixture to a serving
bowl and cover tightly. Refrigerate
for at least 1 hour or overnight. Can be
refrigerated for up to 2 days.

3 Serve, if desired, garnished with the
lemon slice, slit from the center
outward and twisted into an S. Serve
with chips, crackers, or crudités. Makes
about 2 cups.

---

*Tip: When it comes to
scooping up dips, crudités (raw
vegetables) are naturals. Much
lower in calories than chips,
crackers, or breads, these
healthful, colorful dippers make
for good munching.*

*In addition to old favorites —
carrot and celery sticks, green
and red pepper strips, broccoli
and cauliflower florets — try
cherry tomatoes, asparagus
spears, snow peas or sugar snap
peas, yellow squash, green
beans, and kohlrabi. For even
more exotic dippers, use enoki
mushrooms or jícama — a South
American, turniplike tuber.*

*When choosing crudités, keep
in mind the kind of dip they're
meant for. Bland or sweetish
vegetables — white mushrooms,
zucchini strips, or carrot
sticks — tend to go well with hot
or sharp-tasting dips. Vegetables
with a decided character —*
*radishes, fennel, green onions,
and Belgian endives —
complement milder-tasting dips.*

*Crisping. To crisp vegetables
for dipping, place them in a bowl
of water and ice cubes;
refrigerate for at least 1 hour.
(Do not crisp mushrooms this
way; they absorb too much of
the water.) Or, after cutting and
rinsing, put vegetables in plastic
bags and seal the bags tightly;
place in the refrigerator for at
least 2 hours or overnight.*

*Blanching. To blanch dip-size
vegetables, plunge them into a
pot of boiling water; remove
them when the water begins to
boil again. Rinse immediately
under cold water. Blanching
enhances the color of vegetables
and slightly softens their snap.
Vegetables that are improved
through blanching include
asparagus, green beans, and
snow peas.*

*An appealing array of crunchy crudités and creamy dips*

# Anchovy Parsley Dip

Per tablespoon: Calories 47; Protein 1 g;
Carbohydrate tr; Fat 4 g; Sodium 16 mg;
Cholesterol 0 mg.

*This dip can also be warmed and
served as a sauce over 1 pound of
pasta twists or linguine. For this
purpose, omit the bread.*

| | |
|---|---|
| 1 | large bunch parsley, stemmed |
| 1 | can (2 ounces) anchovy fillets, drained |
| 1 | tablespoon capers, drained and rinsed |
| 2 | cloves garlic |
| 1 | teaspoon coarsely ground black pepper |
| 2 | slices white bread, crusts removed and cubed |
| ½ | cup plus 2 tablespoons olive oil |
| 2 | tablespoons white wine vinegar |

1 Finely chop the parsley in an electric
blender or food processor by puls-
ing 6 to 8 times. Add and finely chop
the anchovies, capers, garlic, pepper,
and bread. With the motor running,
slowly add the oil and vinegar. Continue blending for about 30 seconds until
thick and smooth. Transfer to a medium-size serving bowl.

▽ At this point the dip can be
covered tightly with aluminum
foil or plastic wrap and stored. *Refrigerate* for up to 3 days.

2 Serve with such crudités as sweet
red pepper strips, cauliflower florets, and Jerusalem artichoke slices, or
serve with cooked, bite-size tortellini or
ravioli, speared with toothpicks. Makes
about 2 cups.

*A colorful spread of Anchovy Parsley
Dip, Roasted Sweet Red Pepper Paste,
and Pistachio Dip*

# Roasted Sweet Red Pepper Paste

Per tablespoon: Calories 17; Protein 0 g; Carbohydrate 1 g; Fat 1 g; Sodium 16 mg; Cholesterol 0 mg.

- 8 medium-size sweet red peppers (about 3 pounds)
- 1/3 cup plus 1 tablespoon olive oil
- 2 cloves garlic
- 1/2 teaspoon salt

1 Preheat the oven to 400° F. Place peppers in a shallow baking dish and rub them with 1 tablespoon of the olive oil. Roast the peppers, turning occasionally, until skin is blistered (about 30 minutes). Seal tightly in a plastic bag and let cool to room temperature. Peel, seed, and core the peppers, discarding any accumulated liquid. Blot dry with paper toweling.

2 In an electric blender or food processor, purée the peppers, garlic, and salt for 30 seconds, stopping to scrape down the container's sides when necessary. With the motor running, pour in the remaining 1/3 cup olive oil in a thin stream. Continue blending for 60 seconds.

▽ At this point the paste can be stored. Transfer it to a 1-quart container with a tight-fitting lid. *Refrigerate* for up to 3 days. Label and *freeze* for up to 1 month at 0° F.

3 Transfer to a serving bowl, and use as a spread for thinly sliced French bread or as a dip for such crudités as broccoli florets or zucchini sticks. Makes about 4 cups.

### Anchovy Variation

Per tablespoon: Calories 13; Protein tr; Carbohydrate 1 g; Fat 1 g; Sodium 8 mg; Cholesterol 0 mg.

To Roasted Sweet Red Pepper Paste, add 1 can (2 ounces) anchovy fillets, drained and finely chopped; 1 medium-size yellow onion, finely chopped; 1 tablespoon minced parsley; 1 teaspoon black pepper; and 2 teaspoons wine vinegar. Mix thoroughly, cover, and refrigerate for at least 3 hours or overnight. Can be refrigerated for up to 3 days. Makes about 2 cups.

# Saucy Sour Cream Dip

Per tablespoon: Calories 27; Protein tr; Carbohydrate 1 g; Fat 2 g; Sodium 47 mg; Cholesterol 5 mg.

- 3 tablespoons Sweet-Bite Salad Dressing Mix (page 17)
- 1 cup sour cream or plain low-fat yogurt
- 1/4 teaspoon each salt and black pepper

1 Combine all of the ingredients in a small bowl. Transfer to a serving bowl, cover tightly, and refrigerate for up to 2 days. Makes about 1 1/4 cups.

# Pistachio Dip

Per tablespoon: Calories 94; Protein 1 g; Carbohydrate 1 g; Fat 10 g; Sodium 39 mg; Cholesterol 10 mg.

- 1 large egg
- 2 tablespoons fresh lemon juice
- 1 tablespoon white wine vinegar
- 1/2 teaspoon dry mustard
- 1/2 teaspoon salt
- 2/3 cup vegetable oil
- 1/3 cup olive oil
- 1 clove garlic
- 1/3 cup parsley leaves
- 1/2 teaspoon dried tarragon, crumbled
- 2/3 cup pistachio nuts (about 8 ounces unshelled)
  Parsley for garnish (optional)

1 In an electric blender or food processor, blend the egg, lemon juice, vinegar, mustard, and salt until smooth. With the motor running, add the vegetable and olive oils a few drops at a time. Add the garlic, blending until finely chopped, then the parsley, tarragon, and pistachios, blending until they are chopped and the dip is flecked with green.

2 Transfer to a serving bowl. Cover tightly and refrigerate for up to 3 days. Garnish with parsley, if desired, and serve with crisp vegetable dippers such as celery, radishes, or broccoli florets. Makes about 1 2/3 cups.

# Artichoke Dip

Per tablespoon: Calories 41; Protein 1 g; Carbohydrate 3 g; Fat 3 g; Sodium 39 mg; Cholesterol 2 mg.

- 2 jars (6 ounces each) marinated artichoke hearts with their oil
- 2 cloves garlic
- 1/2 cup olive oil
- 1/4 cup lemon juice
- 1/4 teaspoon hot red pepper sauce, or to taste
- 1 cup shredded Cheddar cheese (about 4 ounces)
- 2 cups seasoned Italian-style bread crumbs

1 In an electric blender or food processor, purée the artichoke hearts, garlic, olive oil, lemon juice, and hot red pepper sauce — about 30 seconds. Pour the purée into a large bowl; stir in the cheese and bread crumbs. Transfer to a buttered 1-quart casserole.

▽ At this point the dip can be *refrigerated*, tightly covered, for up to 2 days.

2 Preheat the oven to 350° F. Cover the dip and bake for 15 to 25 minutes or until the cheese is melted. Serve warm with melba rounds or bread sticks. Makes about 4 cups.

# Tex-Mex Guacamole

Per tablespoon: Calories 25; Protein tr;
Carbohydrate 1 g; Fat 2 g; Sodium 33 mg;
Cholesterol 0 mg.

*For the tastiest guacamole, use the black-skinned Hass avocados from California. You can add more cilantro — as much as 1/4 cup, but remember that cilantro gets stronger as it sits. Substitute parsley if you prefer.*

- 2   medium-size avocados
- 2   teaspoons fresh lime or lemon juice
- 1/2   teaspoon salt
- 2   green onions, finely chopped
- 1   small tomato, seeded and finely chopped
- 1   clove garlic, minced
- 2   tablespoons seeded and finely chopped fresh or canned green chili pepper
- 1   tablespoon minced fresh cilantro or parsley, or to taste

1 Halve the avocados lengthwise and scoop the flesh into a medium-size bowl. Add the lime juice and salt and mash with a fork, mixing well.

2 Add the green onions, tomato, garlic, green chili pepper, and cilantro and blend. Serve immediately, or place a layer of plastic wrap directly on the surface to prevent browning, and refrigerate. Guacamole is best eaten the same day it is made, but it will keep, refrigerated, for 2 days. Serve with tortilla chips. Makes about 2 cups.

# Chili Nuts

Per tablespoon: Calories 64; Protein 3 g;
Carbohydrate 2 g; Fat 5 g; Sodium 7 mg;
Cholesterol 0 mg.

- 2   tablespoons chili powder
- 1   teaspoon onion powder
- 3/4   teaspoon garlic powder
- 1   teaspoon ground cumin (optional)

- 12   ounces oil-roasted, salted, skinless peanuts

1 Preheat the oven to 250° F. Combine the chili powder, onion powder, garlic powder, and cumin, if desired, in a medium-size bowl. Add the peanuts and toss until well coated with the spices.

2 Transfer the nuts to an ungreased 13" x 9" x 2" baking pan. Bake 10 minutes and then turn the nuts, using a metal serving spoon; bake 10 minutes more. Makes about 2 cups.

▽ At this point the nuts can be cooled to room temperature, then stored in a container with a tight-fitting lid. *Shelve* for up to 3 months. *Freeze* for up to 6 months at 0° F.

## Serving Later

**From freezer:** Preheat the oven to 250° F. Reheat the nuts in an ungreased 13" x 9" x 2" baking pan until warm — about 10 minutes.

# Best Bean Dip Bar None

Per tablespoon: Calories 31; Protein 2 g;
Carbohydrate 4 g; Fat 1 g; Sodium 27 mg;
Cholesterol 2 mg.

- 1   package (16 ounces) dried pinto beans
- 2   strips bacon
- 1   large yellow onion, finely chopped
- 1   clove garlic, minced
- 3   tablespoons chili powder
- 1   tablespoon ground cumin
- 1/2   teaspon salt, or to taste
- 2   tablespoons unsalted butter or margarine
- 1   cup shredded sharp Cheddar cheese (about 4 ounces)
- 1/2   teaspoon hot red pepper sauce

1 Pick over and rinse the pinto beans. Place in a large saucepan or flameproof casserole. Add enough unsalted water to cover and bring to a boil over high heat. Remove from the heat, cover, and let stand for 1 hour.

2 Meanwhile, in a 10-inch skillet, cook the bacon over moderate heat until crisp — about 5 minutes. Transfer to paper toweling and let cool. Crumble into bits, and reserve.

3 Add the bacon drippings, onion, garlic, chili powder, cumin, and salt to the beans. Bring to a boil over high heat; reduce the heat to low and simmer, covered, for 1 hour or until the beans are tender. Add 1 to 2 cups more water if necessary to prevent scorching.

4 When the beans are tender, drain them well in a colander. Add the butter, cheese, hot red pepper sauce, and reserved bacon. In an electric blender or food processor, purée the mixture in batches until smooth. Serve warm with tortilla chips, broken taco shells, or tostado rounds. Other dippers that go well with it include toasted French bread rounds, pita bread wedges, and crackers. Makes 5 cups.

## Canned Bean Dip Variation

Per tablespoon: Calories 23; Protein 1 g;
Carbohydrate 3 g; Fat 1 g; Sodium 59 mg;
Cholesterol 2 mg.

After cooking the bacon in Step 2 of Best Bean Dip Bar None, add the onion and garlic to the skillet. Cook over medium heat until the onion is soft — about 5 minutes. Add **2 cans (19 ounces each) drained and rinsed white kidney beans** and all remaining ingredients except the salt. Cook over low heat, stirring occasionally, until the butter and cheese are melted. Purée and serve as in Step 4.

*A trio of Southwestern favorites: Tex-Mex Guacamole, Chili Nuts, and Best Bean Dip Bar None*

# Chicken Liver and Sausage Terrine

Per serving: Calories 182; Protein 12 g; Carbohydrate 3 g; Fat 12 g; Sodium 435 mg; Cholesterol 251 mg.

- 4 tablespoons (½ stick) unsalted butter or margarine
- 12 ounces chicken livers, trimmed
- 2 eggs
- ⅓ cup Cognac
- 1 large yellow onion, coarsely chopped
- 2 cloves garlic, coarsely chopped
- 2 tablespoons all-purpose flour
- 1 teaspoon salt
- ½ teaspoon allspice
- ¼ teaspoon black pepper
- 8 ounces pork sausage, casings removed

*Optional garnishes:*
Chopped hard-cooked egg
Red onion slices

1 Preheat oven to 350° F. Melt the butter in a heavy 10-inch skillet over moderate heat. Add the chicken livers and cook, turning, until lightly browned — about 2 minutes.

2 In an electric blender or food processor, combine the chicken livers, eggs, Cognac, onion, garlic, flour, salt, allspice, and pepper, and purée — about 2 minutes. Add the sausage and pulse 4 or 5 times until just blended.

3 Grease a 6-cup terrine or a 9″ x 5″ x 3″ loaf pan. For easier removal from the pan cut a piece of aluminum foil to exactly fit the bottom. Pour mixture into the prepared pan and cover tightly with foil. Bake for 1 hour and 15 minutes or until juices run clear. Uncover, place pan upright on a wire rack, and let cool for 30 minutes.

4 Cover the pâté with foil, weight it with a loaf pan and a heavy can, and refrigerate overnight. Will keep, refrigerated, for 2 days.

5 To serve, let guests scoop pâté directly from the terrine. Or loosen the pâté around the edges of the pan with the tip of a knife, invert onto a serving platter, remove the foil, and cut into thin slices. Garnish with chopped hard-cooked egg and red onion slices, if desired. Accompany with French bread, crackers, or toasted pita bread wedges. Serves 12.

# Mushroom Pâté

Per tablespoon: Calories 38; Protein 1 g; Carbohydrate 1 g; Fat 4 g; Sodium 32 mg; Cholesterol 8 mg.

- 4 tablespoons (½ stick) unsalted butter or margarine, at room temperature
- 8 ounces mushrooms, finely chopped (about 2½ cups)
- 1 shallot or 2 green onions, minced
- 1 teaspoon lemon juice
- ¼ teaspoon hot red pepper sauce, or to taste
- ¼ teaspoon salt
- ¼ cup finely chopped walnuts
- 1 tablespoon minced parsley for garnish

1 Melt 2 tablespoons of the butter in a heavy 10-inch skillet over moderate heat. Add the mushrooms and shallot, and cook, stirring occasionally, until all of the liquid has evaporated — about 15 minutes. Transfer to a medium-size bowl.

2 Blend in the remaining 2 tablespoons of butter, the lemon juice, hot red pepper sauce, and salt. Stir in the walnuts. Spoon mixture into a small bowl or crock. Refrigerate, tightly covered, for up to 24 hours.

3 Before serving, let come to room temperature and sprinkle with the parsley. Serve with sliced pumpernickel bread, pita bread wedges, or crackers. Makes about 1 cup.

# Peppery Ham Pâté

Per tablespoon: Calories 31; Protein 2 g; Carbohydrate tr; Fat 2 g; Sodium 147 mg; Cholesterol 5 mg.

- 1½ teaspoons black peppercorns
- 3 tablespoons unsalted butter or margarine, at room temperature
- 2 cloves garlic
- ½ teaspoon ground cinnamon
- 1 pound baked ham, sliced thin
- ¼ cup mayonnaise
- 2 tablespoons Dijon or spicy brown mustard
- 1 tablespoon Cognac or brandy

1 Place peppercorns in a plastic bag. With a small heavy skillet or similar heavy object, gently pound peppercorns until coarsely crushed.

2 In an electric blender or food processor, blend the peppercorns, butter, garlic, and cinnamon until smooth — about 1 minute. With the motor running, add the ham slices, one at a time, and process until minced — about 15 seconds after each addition. Then blend in the mayonnaise, mustard, and Cognac.

▽ At this point the mixture can be transferred to a tightly covered container, labeled, and stored. *Refrigerate* for up to 5 days. *Freeze* for up to 3 months at 0° F.

3 Serve at room temperature with toasted French bread, hot biscuits, or crackers. Makes about 2½ cups.

*A substantial prelude: Chicken Liver and Sausage Terrine, Peppery Ham Pâté, and Cheese Potted with Black Walnuts*

# Cheese Potted with Black Walnuts

Per tablespoon: Calories 60; Protein 2 g; Carbohydrate tr; Fat 6 g; Sodium 42 mg; Cholesterol 10 mg.

*Black walnuts, with their unique flavor, are the first choice for this tasty spread. If they're not available, however, English walnuts or hazelnuts make an excellent substitute.*

4 ounces sharp Cheddar cheese, shredded
4 ounces Monterey Jack cheese, shredded
6 tablespoons (¾ stick) unsalted butter or margarine, at room temperature
2 tablespoons dry vermouth, sherry, or white wine
Pinch ground nutmeg or mace
½ cup finely chopped black walnuts, English walnuts, or toasted hazelnuts

In a large bowl, combine the cheeses, butter, vermouth, and nutmeg and beat until well blended. Stir in the nuts. Pack the mixture into a crock or bowl and press a piece of plastic wrap flat on the surface. Cover tightly with aluminum foil and store in the refrigerator. Can be kept in the refrigerator for up to 48 hours. Serve at room temperature with crackers or toast. Makes about 2 cups.

## Hot & Spicy Eggplant

Per tablespoon: Calories 9; Protein tr;
Carbohydrate 1 g; Fat tr; Sodium 39 mg;
Cholesterol 0 mg.

- 1 large eggplant (about 1 pound)
- 2 tablespoons olive oil
- 1 large yellow onion, finely chopped
- 1 medium-size sweet green pepper, cored and finely chopped
- 2 cloves garlic, minced
- 5 plum tomatoes, finely chopped (about 2 cups)
- 1/4 cup red wine vinegar
- 3 tablespoons chopped basil or 2 teaspoons dried basil, crumbled
- 4 teaspoons capers, drained
- 1 teaspoon salt
- 1/4 teaspoon cayenne pepper
- 1/8 teaspoon hot red pepper sauce, or to taste

1 Preheat oven to 350° F. Halve the eggplant lengthwise and place it, cut side down, on a lightly oiled baking sheet. Bake for 30 to 40 minutes or until it pierces easily with a fork. Cool.

2 Meanwhile, heat the oil in a heavy 12-inch skillet over moderate heat. Add the onion, green pepper, and garlic, and cook, stirring occasionally, until soft — about 5 minutes. Stir in the tomatoes, vinegar, basil, capers, salt, cayenne, and hot red pepper sauce.

3 Scoop the eggplant flesh into an electric blender or food processor and blend for 10 to 15 seconds, until nearly puréed. Stir the eggplant into the skillet mixture. Simmer, uncovered, for 15 minutes, stirring occasionally. Cool, cover, and refrigerate for several hours or until well chilled. Will keep, refrigerated, for up to 3 days. Serve with crackers, pita bread wedges, or French bread rounds. Makes about 4 cups.

## Prairie Caviar

Per tablespoon: Calories 13; Protein tr;
Carbohydrate 1 g; Fat 1 g; Sodium 36 mg;
Cholesterol 0 mg.

*This recipe makes enough for a good-size crowd, but it can easily be halved. For a hotter spread, add more jalapeño peppers.*

- 1 pound dried black-eyed peas
- 1/2 cup olive oil
- 1/4 cup red wine vinegar
- 3 cloves garlic, minced
- 1 medium-size sweet green pepper, cored and finely chopped
- 1 medium-size sweet red pepper, cored and finely chopped
- 3 medium-size yellow onions, finely chopped
- 6 green onions, chopped
- 2 jalapeño peppers, seeded and chopped, or 2 canned jalapeño peppers, rinsed, seeded, and chopped
- 1 teaspoon salt
  Lettuce leaves for garnish (optional)

1 Pick over and rinse the black-eyed peas and place in a large saucepan or flameproof casserole. Add enough unsalted water to cover, and bring to a boil over high heat. Remove from the heat, cover, and let stand for 1 hour.

2 Return peas to high heat and bring to a boil. Reduce the heat to low, cover, and simmer for 1 hour or until peas are tender, adding more water if necessary to prevent scorching. Drain.

3 Put 1 1/2 cups of the peas in an electric blender or food processor. Add the oil, vinegar, and garlic, and purée until smooth.

4 Transfer the purée to a large bowl. Add the remaining peas, the sweet green pepper, sweet red pepper, yellow onions, green onions, jalapeño peppers, and salt, and mix well. Cover and refrigerate overnight before serving. Will keep, refrigerated, for up to 48 hours. To serve, spoon onto a platter lined with lettuce, if desired, or into a serving bowl. Serve with tortilla chips, crackers, bread rounds, or pita bread wedges. Makes about 2 quarts.

## Tuna Log

Per tablespoon: Calories 41; Protein 3 g;
Carbohydrate tr; Fat 3 g; Sodium 64 mg;
Cholesterol 10 mg.

- 1 can (12 1/2 ounces) water-packed tuna, drained and flaked, or 2 cans (6 1/2 ounces each)
- 8 ounces cream cheese, at room temperature
- 1 tablespoon lemon juice
- 2 teaspoons grated yellow onion
- 1 teaspoon prepared horseradish
- 1/4 teaspoon salt
- 1/2 cup chopped pecans
- 3 tablespoons minced parsley

1 In a medium-size bowl, combine the tuna, cream cheese, lemon juice, onion, horseradish, and salt. Cover and chill for several hours or until firm enough to shape. Meanwhile, mix the pecans and parsley in a small bowl and set aside.

2 Spoon the cream cheese mixture onto a sheet of waxed paper, aluminum foil, or plastic wrap and shape into a 16- by 1 1/2-inch log. Sprinkle the pecan mixture over the log, rolling it until completely coated. Wrap tightly and chill. Will keep, refrigerated, for up to 48 hours. Serve with crackers, pita bread wedges, or bread rounds. Makes 2 1/2 cups.

# Roquefort Mousse Spread

Per tablespoon: Calories 30; Protein 1 g; Carbohydrate tr; Fat 3 g; Sodium 55 mg; Cholesterol 22 mg.

- 1 envelope unflavored gelatin
- ¼ cup cold water
- 4 eggs, separated
- 8 ounces Roquefort cheese, crumbled (about 1 ⅓ cups)
- ½ cup heavy cream, whipped to stiff peaks
- ½ cup finely chopped walnuts Walnut halves for garnish (optional)

1 In a small saucepan, combine the water and gelatin, and warm over low heat until the gelatin is completely dissolved; let cool for about 5 minutes.

2 Meanwhile, in a medium-size bowl, beat the egg yolks with an electric beater at high speed until creamy yellow and thick — 1 to 2 minutes. Gradually beat in the cooled gelatin until well blended; set aside.

3 In a medium-size bowl, beat the egg whites until soft peaks form. Gently fold them into the yolk mixture. Add the cheese, folding gently until well mixed; then fold in the whipped cream and nuts.

4 Spoon the mixture into a 4-cup mold, cover tightly with plastic wrap, and chill for 4 to 6 hours. Will keep, refrigerated, for 2 days.

5 To serve, dip mold quickly into warm (not hot) water. Loosen at the edges with the tip of a paring knife and invert onto a serving platter. Garnish with walnut halves, if desired. Serve with crackers or toasted French bread rounds. Makes about 4 cups.

*Fine party fare — Hot & Spicy Eggplant, Tuna Log, and Roquefort Mousse Spread*

# Pâte à Choux

Per bite-size unfilled puff: Calories 44; Protein 1 g; Carbohydrate 3 g; Fat 3 g; Sodium 22 mg; Cholesterol 37 mg.

*Try these with any of the savory fillings that follow, or fill them with your own favorite spread.*

- 1 cup water
- ½ cup ( 1 stick) unsalted butter or margarine
- ¼ teaspoon salt
- 1 cup all-purpose flour
- 4 eggs, at room temperature
- 1 egg yolk mixed with 1 tablespoon water (optional glaze)

1 Preheat the oven to 450° F. Combine the water, butter, and salt in a medium-size saucepan and bring to a boil over moderate heat. Add all the flour at once, and cook, stirring constantly, until the dough forms a mass in the pan. Remove the saucepan from the heat and let stand for 2 minutes.

2 Stir in the eggs, one at a time, beating vigorously after each addition. Make sure that one egg is well incorporated before adding the next. Dough should be smooth and glossy after all the eggs have been added.

3 Transfer dough to a pastry bag fitted with a plain large tip (number 6 or 8). Pipe out 1-inch mounds onto an ungreased baking sheet, leaving about 1 inch between mounds; or drop the mounds from a teaspoon. If desired, brush tops with the egg glaze, being careful not to let it drip down the sides (this could cause uneven rising).

4 Bake for 10 minutes at 450° F; then reduce the temperature to 350° F and bake 10 minutes more. Gently prick each puff with a fork, lower the temperature to 325° F, and bake an additional 5 to 7 minutes or until golden and crisp. Remove from the oven, transfer to wire racks, and cool to room temperature.

5 Slit the top of each puff and fill with a generous teaspoonful of filling; serve at room temperature. Or insert a 1" x 1" x ¼" piece of Brie into each puff and bake in a preheated 450° F oven for 6 to 8 minutes or until the Brie is soft. Makes 3 dozen bite-size puffs.

▽ If not serving the same day, *freeze* the puffs in a labeled freezer bag. Will keep for up to 2 months at 0° F.

## Serving Later

**From freezer:** Let the puffs stand at room temperature for ½ hour or reheat, in a 375° F oven, for about 10 minutes.

## Cheese and Onion Variation

Per bite-size puff: Calories 62; Protein 2 g; Carbohydrate 3 g; Fat 5 g; Sodium 34 mg; Cholesterol 42 mg.

After adding the eggs in Step 2 of Pâte à Choux, stir in **2 tablespoons grated onion, 1½ cups shredded Gruyère or Swiss cheese,** and **¼ teaspoon cayenne pepper.** Proceed as in Steps 3 and 4. Serve warm; no filling is needed. Makes 3 dozen bite-size puffs.

## Cheese and Green Chili Variation

Per bite-size puff: Calories 62; Protein 2 g; Carbohydrate 3 g; Fat 5 g; Sodium 34 mg; Cholesterol 42 mg.

After adding the eggs in Step 2 of Pâte à Choux, stir in **1½ cups (6 ounces) shredded Swiss cheese** and **2 tablespoons finely chopped, well-drained, canned green chilies.** Proceed as in Steps 3 and 4. Serve warm; no filling is needed. Makes 3 dozen bite-size puffs.

## Garlic Variation

Per bite-size puff: Calories 45; Protein 1 g; Carbohydrate 3 g; Fat 3 g; Sodium 22 mg; Cholesterol 37 mg.

After combining the butter, water, and salt in Step 1 of Pâte à Choux, add **12 garlic cloves, minced,** and **⅛ teaspoon black pepper.** Proceed as in Steps 2, 3, and 4. Serve warm; no filling is needed. Though these are flavorful puffs, they do not have the sharp "bite" of raw garlic. Makes 3 dozen bite-size puffs.

# Crabmeat Filling for Pâte à Choux

Per tablespoon: Calories 54; Protein 2 g; Carbohydrate 1 g; Fat 5 g; Sodium 84 mg; Cholesterol 11 mg.

- ¼ cup olive oil
- ¼ cup coarsely chopped blanched almonds (about 1 ounce)
- 6 ounces fresh, frozen, or canned crabmeat, cartilage and shells removed
- 1 tablespoon dry sherry or vermouth
- ¼ teaspoon salt
- 2 tablespoons minced parsley

1 Heat 2 tablespoons of the olive oil in a 7-inch skillet over moderate heat for 1 minute. Add the almonds; sauté until lightly browned — about 2 minutes. Drain on paper toweling.

2 Blend the almonds, half of the crabmeat, the sherry, and salt in an electric blender or food processor for 5 seconds. With the motor running, gradually add the remaining olive oil. Fold in the remaining crab and the parsley by hand. Makes 1 scant cup, enough to fill 3 dozen bite-size puffs. Can be refrigerated for up to 3 days.

*An elegant presentation of Pâte à Choux with Crabmeat Filling*

# Shrimp and Cheese Filling for Pâte à Choux

Per tablespoon: Calories 43; Protein 2 g;
Carbohydrate 1 g; Fat 3 g; Sodium 49 mg;
Cholesterol 20 mg.

*This quick and easy filling can also double as a dip for vegetables, or as a spread for sandwiches.*

- 4 ounces cream cheese, at room temperature
- 4 teaspoons curry powder
- 1 clove garlic, minced
- 1/4 cup sour cream
- 1/8 teaspoon salt
- 4 ounces cooked shrimp, cut into small pieces

In a small bowl, beat together the cream cheese, curry powder, and garlic with an electric beater or a wooden spoon until creamy. Stir in the sour cream, salt, and shrimp, being careful not to mash the shrimp. Can be refrigerated for up to 2 days. Makes 1 cup, enough to fill 3 dozen bite-size puffs.

# Tuna Filling for Pâte à Choux

Per tablespoon: Calories 42; Protein 3 g;
Carbohydrate tr; Fat 3 g; Sodium 83 mg;
Cholesterol 18 mg.

- 1 can (6 1/2 ounces) water-packed tuna, drained
- 1/3 cup finely chopped celery
- 1 hard-cooked egg, finely chopped
- 1 small yellow onion, grated
- 1/3 cup mayonnaise
- 2 teaspoons lemon juice
- 1 teaspoon Dijon or spicy brown mustard
- 1/4 teaspoon salt
- 1/8 teaspoon each black pepper and cayenne pepper

Combine the tuna, celery, egg, onion, mayonnaise, lemon juice, mustard, salt, black pepper, and cayenne pepper in a medium-size mixing bowl. Chill. Can be refrigerated for up to 3 days. Makes 1 1/3 cups or enough to fill 3 dozen bite-size puffs.

43

*Nice nibbles for a summer afternoon — Sardine Wheels, Artichoke Squares, and Watercress–Stuffed Eggs*

# Sardine Wheels

Per wheel: Calories 38; Protein 2 g; Carbohydrate 3 g; Fat 2 g; Sodium 82 mg; Cholesterol 5 mg.

*Once you've mastered the technique for making these attractive canapés, it's fun to develop your own variations.*

- 2 cans (3¾ ounces each) sardines, drained
- ¼ cup plus 2 tablespoons mayonnaise
- ¼ cup grated yellow onion
- 12 slices soft rye or pumpernickel bread
- ½ cup small dill sprigs or parsley leaves

1 In a small bowl, mash the sardines with a fork. Stir in the mayonnaise and grated onion.

2 Trim crusts from the bread, place slices on a flat surface, and flatten slightly with a rolling pin. Spread each slice with a heaping tablespoon of sardine mixture and roll up jelly-roll fashion. Pinch the seams to seal and trim off any ragged ends. Slice each roll into 4 wheels and then top each wheel with a pinch of dill.

3 Place wheels on a plate lined with a dampened kitchen towel and cover with plastic wrap. Refrigerate for up to 24 hours. Just before serving, transfer to a platter. Makes 4 dozen.

## Watercress and Cream Cheese Variation

Per wheel: Calories 33; Protein 1 g; Carbohydrate 3 g; Fat 2 g; Sodium 68 mg; Cholesterol 5 mg.

Mince **1 small bunch watercress leaves**. In a medium-size bowl, blend half of the watercress, **8 ounces cream cheese**, **1 tablespoon grated yellow onion**, and **⅛ teaspoon white pepper**. Proceed as in Steps 2 and 3 of Sardine Wheels. Top each wheel with a pinch of the remaining watercress.

# Artichoke Squares

Per 1-inch square: Calories 28; Protein 1 g; Carbohydrate 1 g; Fat 2 g; Sodium 33 mg; Cholesterol 21 mg.

- 2 jars (6 ounces each) artichoke hearts marinated in oil
- 1 small yellow onion, finely chopped
- 1 clove garlic, minced
- 4 eggs
- ¼ cup fine dry bread crumbs
- 2 tablespoons chopped parsley
- ⅛ teaspoon each black pepper and dried oregano, crumbled
- ⅛ teaspoon hot red pepper sauce
- 8 ounces Cheddar cheese, shredded (about 2 cups)

1 Preheat oven to 350° F. Drain the artichoke hearts, reserving 2 tablespoons of the oil, and chop fine. Heat the 2 tablespoons of reserved oil in a small heavy skillet over moderate heat. Add the onion and garlic, and cook, stirring frequently, until soft — about 5 minutes. Remove from the heat and cool for about 5 minutes.

2 In a medium-size bowl, beat the eggs until frothy. Stir in the bread crumbs, parsley, pepper, oregano, hot pepper sauce, cheese, artichokes, and cooled skillet mixture. Pour into a greased 8″ x 8″ x 2″ baking pan. Bake for 30 minutes or until lightly browned.

3 Cool for 10 minutes, then cut into 1-inch squares. Will keep, tightly covered and refrigerated, for 2 days. Can be wrapped in heavy-duty aluminum foil, labeled, and frozen for up to 1 month. Serve warm or at room temperature. Makes about 5 dozen 1-inch squares.

# Blue Cheese–Stuffed Eggs

Per half egg: Calories 75; Protein 4 g; Carbohydrate tr; Fat 6 g; Sodium 88 mg; Cholesterol 144 mg.

- 6 hard-cooked eggs, peeled
- ¼ cup crumbled blue cheese
- 2 tablespoons mayonnaise
- 2 tablespoons heavy cream
- 4 teaspoons tarragon vinegar
- 1 tablespoon chopped parsley
- ¼ teaspoon black pepper
  Minced parsley for garnish (optional)

1 Halve each egg lengthwise and transfer the yolks to a small bowl, reserving the whites. Mash the yolks; then add the blue cheese, mayonnaise, cream, vinegar, parsley, salt, and pepper and blend well.

2 Fill each half egg with the cheese mixture. Cover and chill for several hours. Will keep, refrigerated, for up to 24 hours. When ready to serve, garnish with minced parsley, if desired. Makes 12 egg halves.

## Watercress Variation

Per half egg: Calories 65; Protein 3 g; Carbohydrate 9; Fat 6 g; Sodium 79 mg; Cholesterol 139 mg.

Halve 6 hard-cooked eggs as in Step 1 of Blue Cheese–Stuffed Eggs. To the yolks, add ¾ cup minced watercress leaves (about 1 small bunch); 1 shallot or 2 green onions, minced; ½ teaspoon Dijon or spicy brown mustard; 3 tablespoons mayonnaise; ¼ teaspoon black pepper; ⅛ teaspoon salt; and lemon juice to taste. Proceed as in Step 2.

# Chinese Chicken Nuggets

Per nugget: Calories 29; Protein 5 g; Carbohydrate 1 g; Fat tr; Sodium 139 mg; Cholesterol 12 mg.

- ¼ cup soy sauce
- ¼ cup dry sherry or vermouth
- 1 tablespoon sugar
- 2 cloves garlic, minced
- 1 tablespoon grated fresh ginger or 1 teaspoon ground ginger
  Dash cayenne pepper
- 1 pound boneless, skinless chicken or turkey breast, cut into 1-inch-square pieces

1 In a shallow dish just large enough to hold the chicken in one layer, combine the soy sauce, sherry, sugar, garlic, ginger, and cayenne. Add the chicken, cover, and refrigerate for at least 4 hours or overnight.

2 Preheat broiler or grill. Thread chicken onto thin skewers. Broil or grill about 4 inches from the heat for 2 minutes. Turn and broil 2 minutes longer or until cooked through. Transfer to a serving platter. Serve hot or at room temperature, with toothpicks for spearing. Makes about 32 nuggets.

## Steak Wheels Variation

Per meat roll: Calories 43; Protein 4 g; Carbohydrate 1 g; Fat 2 g; Sodium 132 mg; Cholesterol 11 mg.

Substitute for the poultry in Chinese Chicken Nuggets 1 pound beef top round, about ½ inch thick. Cut the beef into strips ⅛ inch wide by 4 to 5 inches long (cut shorter lengths ¼ inch wide); roll each strip tightly. Thread onto thin skewers. Marinate, broil, and serve as directed. Makes about 32 wheels, 1 to 1½ inches in diameter.

# Cheese Crackers

Per cracker: Calories 64; Protein 2 g; Carbohydrate 3 g; Fat 5 g; Sodium 46 mg; Cholesterol 19 mg.

*You can bake these flavorful cheese snacks ahead of time or freeze the dough and have it on hand for unexpected company.*

- 1 cup (2 sticks) unsalted butter or margarine, at room temperature
- 8 ounces Cheddar cheese, shredded (2 cups)
- 2 cups sifted all-purpose flour
- ½ teaspoon salt
- ¼ teaspoon cayenne pepper
- 1 egg beaten with 1 tablespoon water (glaze)

1 In a large bowl, cream the butter and cheese with an electric beater until well blended — about 2 minutes. Blend in the flour, salt, and cayenne. Flatten dough into a patty, seal in plastic wrap, and chill for 2 hours.

▽ At this point, the dough can be *refrigerated* for 1 week or *frozen* for up to 6 months at 0° F.

2 Preheat the oven to 350° F. On a lightly floured surface, roll out the dough ¼ inch thick. Cut into any desired shape — a 2½-inch biscuit cutter works especially well. Place on ungreased baking sheets and brush with the egg glaze. Bake for 10 to 12 minutes or until crisp and golden. Let the crackers rest for 1 minute before transferring them to a rack. Will keep for 2 days in an airtight container. Makes 4½ dozen 2½-inch crackers.

## Caraway Cheese Sticks

Per stick: Calories: 51; Protein 1 g; Carbohydrate 3 g; Fat 4 g; Sodium 42 mg; Cholesterol 14 mg.

In Step 1 of Cheese Crackers add **2 tablespoons caraway seeds** and **1½ teaspoons dry mustard** to the butter and cheese. After rolling out the dough in Step 2, cut into 5- by ½-inch strips. Place ½ inch apart on ungreased baking sheets. Brush with the egg glaze, sprinkle with **3 tablespoons grated Parmesan cheese**, and bake as directed. Makes 6 dozen.

## Pecan Cheese Crackers

Per cracker: Calories: 70; Protein 2 g; Carbohydrate 4 g; Fat 5 g; Sodium 59 mg; Cholesterol 16 mg.

Reduce the butter in Cheese Crackers to ½ cup (1 stick) and the flour to 1⅓ cups. Add **½ teaspoon baking powder** and **¼ teaspoon baking soda** along with the flour. After the flour is blended in, stir in **1 cup finely chopped pecans**. Shape the mixture into 3 smooth cylinders 1½ inches in diameter and seal each one in plastic wrap. Chill until firm — at least 1 hour. Slice dough ¼ inch thick and place rounds on ungreased baking sheets. (Do *not* use the egg glaze.) Bake at 350° F until crisp and golden — about 15 minutes. Let cool before transferring to a rack. Makes 4 dozen.

### Serving Later

**From freezer:** For Pecan Cheese Crackers, slice off rounds ¼ inch thick; bake 10 to 14 minutes at 350° F. For Cheese Crackers and Caraway Cheese Sticks, place dough in refrigerator to thaw; roll out and bake as directed.

# Soups

One of the world's best make-aheads is soup. Not only does it keep well in the refrigerator or freezer, but it is also versatile, serving nicely as either a first course or an entrée. On the following pages are several soups that can make a satisfying meal when accompanied by bread and perhaps a salad. Among these are Tortilla Soup (page 52), Cheese Chowder (page 55), New England Clam Chowder (page 56), Tomato Soup with Veal Meatballs (page 64), Beef, Barley, and Yogurt Soup (page 66), and Chicken-Corn Soup (page 66).

If you think of soup primarily as winter fare, take a look at Lemon Soup, Summer Tomato Soup, and Gazpacho (all on page 50), Vichyssoise (page 54), Zucchini-Pepper Soup (page 59), Borscht (page 60), and Lentil Soup with Lime Juice (page 60).

Besides serving as the basis for many soups, the three stock recipes (pages 48 and 49) can also be used to flavor sauces and meat and vegetable dishes. Freeze the stock in ice cube trays for handy small quantities or in freezer bags — 1 or 2 portions per bag — for convenient reheating.

The more often you make soup, the sooner you will realize that it is one of the most adaptable of dishes. Use the recipes in this chapter as starting points and develop your own variations, adding whatever you have on hand that pleases you. Sunday's leftovers can flourish in Monday's soup.

# Beef Stock

Per 1-cup serving: Calories 16; Protein 3 g; Carbohydrate tr; Fat 0 g; Sodium 254 mg; Cholesterol 0 mg.

*The beef shanks used to flavor this recipe may be eaten later, topped by something flavorful, such as Spicy Tomato Sauce (page 216), Hot Cajun Sauce (page 218), or Firecracker Barbecue Sauce (page 219).*

| | |
|---|---|
| 2 | pounds beef or veal shanks, cut into 3-inch pieces |
| 2 | pounds beef or veal bones, cracked |
| 1 | large yellow onion, quartered |
| 1 | large carrot, peeled and cut in thick slices |
| 2½ | quarts water |
| 2 | stalks celery, cut in thick slices |
| 4 | whole cloves garlic |
| 12 | black peppercorns |
| ½ | teaspoon dried thyme, crumbled |
| 6 | sprigs parsley |
| 1 | teaspoon salt |
| 1 | bay leaf |
| 2 | whole cloves |

1 Preheat oven to 450° F. In a large, shallow baking pan, arrange the beef shanks, bones, onion, and carrot. Bake, uncovered, until the beef and vegetables are brown — about 1 hour. Transfer the beef and vegetables to a 6-quart stockpot. Pour off and discard the fat from the baking pan. To deglaze the pan, add 1 cup of the water, set it over moderately high heat, and with a wooden spatula scrape up any brown bits clinging to the bottom and sides.

2 Transfer the deglazing water to the stockpot. Add the celery, garlic, peppercorns, thyme, parsley, salt, bay leaf, cloves, and remaining water. Bring to a boil over moderately high heat, skimming occasionally. Simmer the stock, partially covered, for 4 hours.

3 Strain the stock through a large sieve or a colander lined with a double layer of cheesecloth or paper toweling into a large saucepan or heatproof bowl. When the stock cools to room temperature, refrigerate it, covered, overnight. Remove the fat from the surface. Makes about 2 quarts to use in any recipe that calls for beef stock.

▽ At this point the stock can be stored. *Refrigerate* in a tightly covered container for up to 3 days. *Freeze* in labeled, 1-quart freezer bags (2 cups per bag) for up to 6 months at 0° F. Or freeze the stock in ice cube trays and then seal the cubes in a freezer bag for convenient use in flavoring vegetable, meat, or chicken dishes.

## Serving Later

**From freezer:** Reheat stock in a covered stockpot over moderate heat until completely thawed — about 15 minutes. **To microwave:** Open a freezer bag 1 inch and stand it in a microwave-safe, deep, 1½-quart casserole. Microwave on *High* (100% power) for 4 minutes. Transfer the stock to the casserole, cover, and microwave on *High* (100% power) for 4 minutes. Turn the frozen block over. Cover and microwave 8 minutes longer.

# Chicken Stock

Per 1-cup serving: Calories 24; Protein 5 g; Carbohydrate 1 g; Fat 0 g; Sodium 254 mg; Cholesterol 0 mg.

*Easy to prepare, chicken stock is good to have on hand as the basis for many soups and stews. An old hen makes the most flavorful stock, but if a hen is not available, a capon or a roaster will do.*

| | |
|---|---|
| 1 | stewing or roasting chicken with giblets (5 to 6 pounds) |
| 1 | large yellow onion, quartered |
| 2 | stalks celery, quartered |
| 2 | medium-size carrots, peeled and quartered |
| 4 | sprigs parsley |
| 2 | bay leaves |
| 10 | black peppercorns |
| 1¼ | teaspoons salt |
| 1 | teaspoon dried rosemary, crumbled |
| 2 | quarts water |

1 In a 5-quart stockpot or heavy flameproof casserole, bring the hen with its giblets, the onion, celery, carrots, parsley, bay leaves, peppercorns, salt, rosemary, and water to a boil over high heat. Reduce the heat to low, cover, and simmer from 1½ to 2 hours or until the hen is tender.

2 Remove the hen from the broth and set it aside to cool. Strain the liquid into a large heatproof bowl through a large sieve or a cheesecloth-lined colander. Let it cool slightly; cover and refrigerate. When it has completely chilled, skim off and discard any solid fat. Makes about 2½ quarts. Use as a soup base or for gravy or sauce or any other recipes that call for chicken stock.

▽ At this point the stock can be stored. Follow the directions in Beef Stock (at left) for storing and serving later.

3 Discard the chicken skin. Remove meat from bones and save for recipes calling for cooked chicken meat.

# Vegetable Stock

Per 1-cup serving: Calories 33; Protein tr;
Carbohydrate tr; Fat 4 g; Sodium 196 mg;
Cholesterol 10 mg.

*For those who prefer a meatless stock,
this one can be used in any recipe for
vegetable soup.*

- 3  tablespoons unsalted butter
     or margarine
- 1  large yellow onion, chopped
- 3  leeks, well washed and
     sliced, including some green,
     or 2 bunches green onions
- 3  cloves garlic, crushed
- 3  bay leaves
- 4  sprigs thyme or ¼ teaspoon
     dried thyme, crumbled
- 1  teaspoon salt
- 5  medium-size carrots, peeled
     and thinly sliced
- 2  small parsnips, peeled and
     thinly sliced
- 2  stalks celery, thinly sliced
- 1  small celery root, pared and
     thinly sliced (optional)
- 8  sprigs parsley
- 2½ quarts cold water

1 Melt the butter in a 4-quart stock-pot over low heat. Add the onion, leeks, garlic, bay leaves, thyme, and salt, and cook, uncovered, stirring occasionally, until the vegetables are soft — about 10 minutes.

2 Add the carrots, parsnips, celery, and celery root, if desired, and stir to coat. Cover and cook, stirring occasionally, until the vegetables are softened — about 10 minutes longer. Add the parsley and water, bring to a boil over moderate heat, and then lower to a simmer and cook, partially covered, for 1 hour. Strain through a large sieve or cheesecloth-lined colander set over a large saucepan or heatproof bowl. Discard all solids. Makes about 2½ quarts.

▽ At this point the broth can be cooled to room temperature and stored. Follow directions in Beef Stock (page 48) for storing and serving later.

*Tip: Food that you might
otherwise throw away can be
used to make flavorful stocks.
Some possibilities are chicken
necks, backs, and wing tips
(freeze them until you have 4
to 5 pounds); scraps from meat
recipes; and wilting vegetables
or herbs.*

# Lemon Soup

Per serving: Calories 118; Protein 11 g; Carbohydrate 10 g; Fat 4 g; Sodium 445 mg; Cholesterol 174 mg.

*Traditionally, this delicious Greek soup, called Avgolemono, is served hot, but our cold version is equally appealing. It is most flavorful when prepared with a home-made chicken stock.*

- 6 cups Chicken Stock (page 48) or 3 cans (10¾ ounces each) condensed chicken broth diluted with 2 cups water
- ½ cup small pasta, such as egg pastina
- 3 eggs
- 2 tablespoons lemon juice, or to taste
- ¼ teaspoon each salt and white pepper

*Optional garnishes:*
Lemon slices
Minced parsley

1 In a large saucepan, bring the chicken stock to a boil over high heat; gradually stir in the pasta. Cook, uncovered, for 5 minutes. Remove from the heat. In a small mixing bowl, beat the eggs until frothy; then beat in the lemon juice.

2 Gradually whisk 2 cups of the warm stock into the egg mixture until well blended; then stir back into the saucepan. Add the salt and pepper. Cool to room temperature and refrigerate in a large, tightly covered container for at least 4 hours. Will keep for up to 24 hours.

3 To serve, stir the soup well and ladle into serving bowls. Garnish with lemon slices and minced parsley, if desired. Makes 7 cups, or enough for 5 or 6 servings.

*Tip: Canned chicken broth is available in full-strength and double-strength (condensed) forms; can sizes vary. Always check label descriptions to avoid confusion. For people on salt-restricted diets, low-sodium chicken broth (dehydrated) is available in packet form. One packet, rehydrated, makes about 1 cup broth.*

# Summer Tomato Soup

Per serving: Calories 194; Protein 5 g; Carbohydrate 22 g; Fat 10 g; Sodium 506 mg; Cholesterol 16 mg.

*Try this as a refreshing prelude to a summer lunch or dinner — or with crusty bread and a Bibb lettuce and watercress salad, as an impressive light meal in itself.*

- 2 tablespoons safflower or vegetable oil
- 2 large yellow onions, chopped
- 1 clove garlic, minced
- ¼ cup all-purpose flour
- 3 cups peeled and chopped fresh tomatoes (1¼ to 1½ pounds) or 1 can (28 ounces) crushed tomatoes
- 2 cups Chicken Stock (page 48) or canned chicken broth
- 1 teaspoon salt
- ¼ teaspoon each black pepper and ground allspice
- 1½ cups orange juice
- 1 tablespoon grated orange rind
- ¼ cup heavy cream

*Optional garnishes:*
Grated orange rind
Peeled, seeded, and finely chopped tomatoes

1 Heat the oil in a large saucepan over moderate heat. Add the onions and garlic, and sauté until the onion is soft — about 5 minutes. Blend in the flour a little at a time, and cook, stirring occasionally, for 3 to 5 minutes.

2 Stir in the tomatoes, chicken stock, salt, pepper, and allspice and bring to a boil, stirring constantly. Reduce the heat to low and simmer, covered, for 10 to 12 minutes. Cool slightly. Transfer to an electric blender or food processor and purée for 30 seconds.

3 Transfer to a large container with a tight-fitting lid. Stir in the orange juice, orange rind, and cream. Chill for at least 4 hours. Can be refrigerated for up to 3 days.

4 Ladle into soup bowls and garnish, if desired, with grated orange rind or chopped tomato. Makes about 6¼ cups, or enough for 4 or 5 servings.

*Tip: Cold soups are mistakenly thought of as appropriate or good only in summer weather. But they can be truly enjoyed in the other seasons as well. Chilling brings out flavor subtleties that hot servings sometimes obscure.*

# Gazpacho

Per serving: Calories 125; Protein 2 g; Carbohydrate 12 g; Fat 9 g; Sodium 382 mg; Cholesterol 0 mg.

*This thick, spicy soup has a high vitamin C content. Reduce preparation time by chilling the ingredients beforehand. A fresh green chili pepper substitutes nicely for the sweet pepper if you prefer a much spicier gazpacho.*

- 1 cup tomato juice
- 3 tablespoons olive oil
- 1 tablespoon wine vinegar

*Gazpacho — make it when the tomato season is at its peak.*

1   medium-size Spanish onion, quartered
1   clove garlic, crushed
½   teaspoon salt
4   large ripe tomatoes, peeled and coarsely chopped (about 2 pounds)
1   large cucumber, peeled, seeded, and chopped
1   small sweet green pepper, cored, seeded, and quartered
1   tablespoon minced cilantro (coriander leaves) or parsley
¼   teaspoon black pepper

In an electric blender or food processor, purée all of the ingredients for 30 seconds. Transfer to a large bowl and refrigerate, tightly covered, for at least 1 hour before serving. Will keep refrigerated for up to 3 days. Serve in chilled bowls or cups. Makes 6 cups, or enough for 5 or 6 servings.

## Chicken Gazpacho Variation

Per serving: Calories 183; Protein 13 g; Carbohydrate 12 g; Fat 10 g; Sodium 406 mg; Cholesterol 29 mg.

Before serving, stir in 1 boneless, skinless chicken breast (10 ounces), cooked, chilled, and cut into ½-inch cubes.

# Tortilla Soup

Per serving: Calories 348; Protein 13 g; Carbohydrate 17 g; Fat 27 g; Sodium 464 mg; Cholesterol 47 mg.

- 2 tablespoons unsalted butter or margarine
- 1 medium-size yellow onion, coarsely chopped
- 2 cloves garlic, minced
- 1 pound ripe tomatoes, cored, seeded, and coarsely chopped (about 2 cups), or 1 can (1 pound) crushed tomatoes
- 6 cups Chicken Stock (page 48) or canned chicken broth
- 1 teaspoon dried marjoram, crumbled
- 1/4 teaspoon hot red pepper sauce

*For the garnish:*
- 2 cups tortilla chips, broken into bite-size pieces
- 1 cup sour cream
- 1 ripe avocado, peeled and finely diced
- 1 cup shredded Cheddar cheese (about 4 ounces)

1 Melt the butter in a large saucepan over moderate heat. Reduce the heat to moderately low and sauté the onion and garlic until the onion is soft — about 5 minutes. Add the tomatoes, increase the heat to moderate, and cook, uncovered, 5 minutes longer. Stir in the chicken stock, marjoram, and hot red pepper sauce; bring the soup to boiling and cook, uncovered, for 1 minute.

▽ At this point the Tortilla Soup can be cooled to room temperature and stored. *Refrigerate* in a tightly covered container for up to 4 days. *Freeze* in labeled, 1-quart freezer bags (2 servings per bag) for up to 3 months at 0° F.

2 Ladle into soup bowls. Place serving bowls with tortilla chips, sour cream, avocado, and Cheddar cheese on the table for those desiring them. Makes about 9 cups, or enough for 6 to 8 servings.

## Serving Later

**From freezer:** Reheat in a covered saucepan over moderately low heat for 25 minutes. Serve as in Step 2. **To microwave:** Open a freezer bag 1 inch and stand it in a microwave-safe, deep, 1-quart casserole. Microwave on *High* (100% power) for 3 minutes. Transfer the soup to the casserole, cover, and microwave on *High* (100% power) for 4 minutes. Stir and gently break apart the frozen block. Cover and microwave 5 minutes longer; proceed as in Step 2.

# Soup of the Three Peppers

Per serving: Calories 129; Protein 5 g; Carbohydrate 11 g; Fat 8 g; Sodium 641 mg; Cholesterol 23 mg.

- 3 jars (4 ounces each) whole pimientos, drained
- 2 cups Chicken Stock (page 48) or canned chicken broth
- 2 tablespoons unsalted butter or margarine
- 2 tablespoons all-purpose flour
- 1 cup half-and-half or light cream
- 1 teaspoon salt
- 1 1/4 teaspoons lemon juice
- 1/2 teaspoon coarsely ground black pepper
  Hot red pepper sauce to taste
  Chopped parsley for garnish (optional)

1 Purée the pimientos and 1 cup of chicken stock in an electric blender or food processor for 20 seconds. Set aside. Melt the butter in a medium-size saucepan over moderately low heat. Blend in the flour, and cook, stirring constantly, until the mixture is bubbly — 1 to 2 minutes.

2 Gradually whisk in the remaining chicken stock and the puréed pimiento mixture. Cook, stirring constantly, over moderate heat for 5 to 8 minutes or until thickened and bubbly.

▽ At this point the soup can be cooled to room temperature and stored. *Refrigerate* in a tightly covered container for up to 3 days.

3 Add the half-and-half, salt, lemon juice, black pepper, and hot red pepper sauce to taste. Heat just to the simmering point; do *not* let it boil. Garnish with chopped fresh parsley, if desired. Makes about 6 cups, or enough for 4 servings.

## Serving Later

Reheat in a covered saucepan over moderate heat until the soup is warmed through — about 10 minutes. Proceed as in Step 3.

# Herbed Tomato Soup

Per serving: Calories 127; Protein 6 g; Carbohydrate 15 g; Fat 6 g; Sodium 823 mg; Cholesterol 15 mg.

- 2 tablespoons unsalted butter or margarine
- 1 stalk celery, diced
- 4 shallots or 8 green onions, minced
- 1 can (28 ounces) crushed tomatoes
- 2 tablespoons minced basil or 2 teaspoons dried basil, crumbled
- 1/2 teaspoon each dried oregano and thyme, crumbled, or to taste
- 3 tablespoons minced parsley
- 2 bay leaves
- 3 cups Chicken Stock (page 48) or canned chicken broth
- 1/4 teaspoon each salt and black pepper

1 Melt the butter in a large saucepan over moderate heat. Add the celery and shallots, and cook, uncovered, stirring occasionally, for 7 to 9 minutes or until the celery is tender.

2 Add the tomatoes, basil, oregano, thyme, parsley, bay leaves, chicken stock, salt, and pepper. Bring to a simmer, and cook, uncovered, over moderately low heat for 30 minutes, or until flavors are well blended. Remove and discard the bay leaves.

▽ At this point the Herbed Tomato Soup can be cooled to room temperature and stored. *Refrigerate* in a tightly covered container for up to 3 days. *Freeze* in labeled, 1-quart freezer bags (2 servings per bag) for up to 3 months at 0° F.

3 Transfer to soup bowls and serve with Italian or French bread. Makes about 5 cups, or enough for 4 servings.

### Serving Later

**From freezer:** Reheat the soup in a covered saucepan set over moderate heat. Stir occasionally until it is thawed — about 15 minutes. Bring the soup to a boil; then let it simmer until heated through — about 10 minutes.

**To microwave:** Open a freezer bag 1 inch and stand it in a microwave-safe, deep, 1-quart casserole. Microwave on *High* (100% power) for 4 minutes. Transfer the soup to the casserole, cover, and microwave on *High* (100% power) for 4 minutes. Stir and turn the frozen block of soup over. Cover and microwave until boiling — 4 to 5 minutes longer.

*Tortilla Soup with all the fixings — a light meal by itself and a festive treat for an informal gathering of friends*

# Potato Soup with Green Chilies

Per serving: Calories 217; Protein 12 g; Carbohydrate 15 g; Fat 13 g; Sodium 381 mg; Cholesterol 24 mg.

*This Southwestern soup is reminiscent of cocido, a green chili stew.*

- 2 tablespoons vegetable oil
- 1 small yellow onion, finely chopped
- 1 clove garlic, minced
- ½ teaspoon ground cumin
- ¼ teaspoon black pepper
  Pinch dried oregano, crumbled
- 2 medium-size all-purpose potatoes, peeled and cut into ½-inch chunks (about 11 ounces)
- 1 can (4 ounces) green chilies, drained and chopped (about ⅔ cup)
- 2 tablespoons drained and chopped canned jalapeño peppers (optional)
- 5 cups Chicken Stock (page 48) or canned chicken broth
- 1 cup shredded Monterey Jack cheese for garnish
- ¼ cup finely chopped cilantro (coriander leaves) for garnish (optional)

1 Heat the oil in a large saucepan over low heat. Add the onion and garlic, and cook, covered, until the onion is soft—about 5 minutes. Uncover and increase the heat to moderate. Stir in the cumin and black pepper; cook 2 or 3 minutes longer or until the onion begins to brown.

2 Add the oregano, potatoes, green chilies, the jalapeño peppers, if desired, and the chicken stock. Bring this to a simmer, cover, and cook over low heat for 45 minutes or until the potatoes are tender.

▽ At this point the soup can be cooled to room temperature and stored. *Refrigerate* in a tightly covered container for up to 3 days.

3 Ladle into soup bowls. Garnish with cheese and, if desired, the cilantro. Makes about 7 cups, or enough for 5 or 6 servings.

### Serving Later

Reheat in a saucepan over moderate heat until warmed through — about 15 minutes. Proceed as in Step 3.

# Leek and Potato Soup

Per serving: Calories 84; Protein 1 g; Carbohydrate 14 g; Fat 3 g; Sodium 493 mg; Cholesterol 8 mg.

- 3 medium-size all-purpose potatoes, peeled and sliced (about 1 pound)
- 3 leeks, trimmed and sliced (about 1 pound), or 3 small yellow onions, quartered
- 2 quarts water
- 2 teaspoons salt
  White pepper to taste
- 2 tablespoons unsalted butter or margarine at room temperature
- 2 tablespoons minced chives or parsley

1 In a large saucepan, bring the potatoes, leeks, water, and salt to a boil over moderate heat. Reduce the heat to moderately low, partially cover, and simmer for 40 to 50 minutes or until the vegetables are tender. Cool slightly.

2 Working in batches, purée the soup in an electric blender or food processor until smooth.

▽ At this point the soup can be cooled to room temperature and stored. *Refrigerate* in a tightly covered container for up to 3 days. *Freeze* in labeled, 1-quart freezer bags (2 servings per bag) for up to 1 month at 0° F.

3 Return the puréed soup to the saucepan and reheat. Stir in the pepper and butter. Ladle into bowls; sprinkle with the chives. Makes about 10 cups, or enough for 8 servings.

### Serving Later

**From freezer:** Reheat in a covered saucepan over low heat for about 25 minutes or until hot. Stir occasionally.

### Vichyssoise Variation

Per serving: Calories 99; Protein 2 g; Carbohydrate 15 g; Fat 4 g; Sodium 505 mg; Cholesterol 11 mg.

Proceed as in Leek and Potato Soup up to Step 3. Here, omit the butter and stir in **1 cup half-and-half.** Chill for at least 2 hours before serving. Garnish each serving with the minced chives. Serves 8.

### Green Vichyssoise Variation

Per serving: Calories 105; Protein 3 g; Carbohydrate 16 g; Fat 4 g; Sodium 517 mg; Cholesterol 11 mg.

In Step 1 of Leek and Potato Soup, cook the potatoes and the leeks for 40 minutes. Add **1 cup stemmed arugula, watercress,** or **turnip greens, 1 cup spinach leaves, 2 cups torn lettuce leaves,** and **1 cup fresh basil leaves.** Cook 10 minutes longer. Proceed as for Vichyssoise. Serves 8.

### Carrot Variation

Per serving: Calories 111; Protein 3 g; Carbohydrate 18 g; Fat 4 g; Sodium 514 mg; Cholesterol 11 mg.

In Step 1 of Leek and Potato Soup, add **3 medium-size carrots, peeled and sliced;** then proceed as for Vichyssoise. Makes enough for 8 servings.

## Cucumber Variation

Per serving: Calories 104; Protein 2 g; Carbohydrate 16 g; Fat 4 g; Sodium 506 mg; Cholesterol 11 mg.

Proceed as in Step 1 of Leek and Potato Soup. When puréeing the solids in Step 2, add **1 large cucumber, peeled, seeded, and cubed.** Pour the purée into a large mixing bowl; stir in **1 cup half-and-half** and a **pinch of ground nutmeg.** Omit the chives. Chill well before serving. Serves 8.

# Cheese Chowder

Per serving: Calories 502; Protein 23 g; Carbohydrate 31 g; Fat 30 g; Sodium 732 mg; Cholesterol 92 mg.

- 3 slices bacon
- 2 large yellow onions, chopped
- 1 clove garlic, minced
- ⅓ cup all-purpose flour
- 3 cups Chicken Stock (page 48) or canned chicken broth
- 3 medium-size all-purpose potatoes, peeled and cubed (about 1 pound)
- 1 bay leaf
- ¾ teaspoon white pepper
- ½ teaspoon salt
- 2 cups half-and-half
- 1 cup dry white wine
- 3 cups shredded sharp Cheddar cheese (12 ounces) Chopped fresh chives for garnish (optional)

1 In a large heavy saucepan or flameproof casserole, cook the bacon over moderately high heat until brown and crisp — about 5 minutes. Drain on paper toweling and set aside. Reserve the drippings in the saucepan.

2 Sauté the onions and garlic in the reserved drippings, stirring occasionally, until the onions are transparent — about 5 minutes.

*Leek and Potato Soup or its cold variation, Vichyssoise, is a simple yet impressive first course.*

3 Gradually blend in the flour. Cook, stirring constantly, until the vegetables are evenly coated and the mixture is bubbly — 1 to 2 minutes. Gradually blend in the chicken stock, and cook, stirring constantly, until thickened — about 3 minutes.

4 Add the potatoes, bay leaf, white pepper, and salt. Bring to a boil and reduce the heat to moderate; cover and cook for about 15 minutes or until the potatoes are tender.

▽ At this point the soup can be cooled to room temperature and stored. *Refrigerate* in a container with a tight-fitting lid. Keeps for up to 4 days.

5 Add the half-and-half and wine. Heat just to the simmering point. Do not let the soup boil or it may curdle. Reduce the heat to low and stir in the cheese. Continue stirring until the cheese is melted. Crumble the bacon into the soup. Garnish with chopped fresh chives, if desired. Makes about 8 cups, or enough for 6 servings.

### Serving Later

Reheat the soup in a covered saucepan over moderate heat until warmed through — about 15 minutes. Do not let it boil. Proceed as in Step 5.

# Cream of Spinach Soup

Per serving: Calories 399; Protein 10 g;
Carbohydrate 17 g; Fat 35 g; Sodium 663 mg;
Cholesterol 102 mg.

- 2 tablespoons unsalted butter or margarine
- 1 medium-size yellow onion, finely chopped
- 1 pound spinach, washed and trimmed
- 6 slices White Sauce Mix (page 17), each ½ inch thick
- 2 cups water
- 3 cups Chicken Stock (page 48) or canned chicken broth
  Pinch ground nutmeg
- ½ teaspoon salt
  Black pepper to taste
- ½ cup heavy cream

1 Melt the butter in a large saucepan over moderate heat. Add the onion, and cook, stirring frequently, until the onion is tender — about 5 minutes. Add the spinach, cover, and cook for 3 minutes or until the spinach is wilted. Cool slightly and then transfer to an electric blender or food processor. Purée until smooth — about 30 seconds.

2 In the same saucepan, melt the White Sauce slices over low heat — about 2 minutes. Remove from the heat and stir in the water. Return to the heat, and cook, stirring constantly, until the mixture comes to a boil. Cook 1 minute longer. Stir in the stock, spinach purée, nutmeg, salt, and pepper.

▽ At this point the soup can be cooled to room temperature and stored. *Refrigerate* in a tightly covered container for up to 3 days.

3 Bring the soup to a simmer. Just before serving, stir in the cream. Serve hot or, if you prefer, chill well and serve cold. Makes about 6 cups, or enough for 4 or 5 servings.

## Serving Later

Reheat in a covered saucepan over low heat for about 20 minutes. Proceed as in Step 3. Or, if you prefer, stir in the cream and serve cold.

# New England Clam Chowder

Per serving: Calories 373; Protein 13 g;
Carbohydrate 34 g; Fat 21 g; Sodium 699 mg;
Cholesterol 81 mg.

*You can make clam chowder with that good old-fashioned taste in a matter of minutes when using White Sauce Mix — a real time-saver. For a lighter soup, substitute an additional cup of milk for the cup of half-and-half.*

- 3 dozen small hard-shell clams or 2 cans (4 ounces each) chopped clams with their juice
- ½ cup cold water

*A bracing bowl of New England Clam Chowder will satisfy the winter appetite of the hungriest skier or skater.*

8 slices (1 stick) White Sauce Mix (page 17), each ½ inch thick

1 large yellow onion, finely chopped

4 large all-purpose potatoes, peeled and diced (about 2 pounds)

1 teaspoon salt

⅛ teaspoon white pepper

3 cups milk

1 cup half-and-half

1 Scrub clam shells with a stiff brush. Place in a 12-inch skillet or large saucepan with the cold water. Cover and cook over moderate heat until the clams open — 5 to 6 minutes. Discard any clams that haven't opened. Remove the clams from their shells and rinse away any sand. Chop up the clams and set aside. Pour the clam broth through a cheesecloth- or paper-toweling-lined strainer into a 1-quart measuring cup. If using canned clams, drain the clam broth into the measuring cup and set aside the clams. Add enough cold water to the broth to equal 3 cups.

2 In a large saucepan, cook the White Sauce Mix over low heat, stirring constantly, until melted and bubbly — about 2 minutes. Remove from the heat and add 2 cups of clam broth, stirring until smooth. Return to the heat, and cook, stirring constantly, until the mixture comes to a boil. Cook 1 minute more. Stir in the remaining clam liquid, the onion, and potatoes. Cook, covered, for 10 to 15 minutes or until the vegetables are tender. Stir in the reserved chopped clams.

▽ At this point the chowder can be cooled to room temperature and stored. *Refrigerate* it in a container with a tight-fitting lid for up to 2 days.

3 Add the salt, pepper, milk, and half-and-half to the chowder; bring to a simmer, stirring occasionally. Do not let it boil. Serve immediately with oyster crackers or Sage Corn Bread (page 236). Makes about 8 cups, or enough for 6 servings.

### Serving Later

Reheat in a large covered saucepan over moderate heat until warmed through — about 5 minutes. Proceed as in Step 3.

### Fish Variation

Per serving: Calories 308; Protein 27 g; Carbohydrate 28 g; Fat 9 g; Sodium 489 mg; Cholesterol 88 mg.

Omit the clams in New England Clam Chowder. In a large saucepan bring **3 cups water** to a simmer. Add **1½ pounds cod or haddock fillets** and **½ teaspoon salt**; cover and cook for 10 minutes or until the fish flakes. Strain the broth into a 1-quart measuring cup and add water, if necessary, to equal 3 cups. Proceed as in Steps 2 and 3,

# Creamy Carrot-Basil Soup

Per serving: Calories 221; Protein 8 g; Carbohydrate 21 g; Fat 12 g; Sodium 403 mg; Cholesterol 34 mg.

*This delicately flavored French soup makes a wonderful introduction to an elegant meal.*

- 3 tablespoons unsalted butter or margarine
- 2 large carrots, sliced
- 1 small yellow onion, finely chopped
- 4 cups Chicken Stock (page 48) or canned chicken broth
- 1 bay leaf
- 1 teaspoon dried basil, crumbled
- 1 teaspoon sugar
- ½ teaspoon ground nutmeg
- ⅓ cup long-grain white rice
- ½ cup half-and-half
  Pinch white pepper
  Croutons for garnish (optional)

1 Melt the butter in a medium-size saucepan over moderate heat. Add the carrots and onion, and cook, stirring, until the onion is soft — about 5 minutes. Add the chicken stock, bay leaf, basil, sugar, nutmeg, and rice. Bring to a boil and then reduce the heat to moderately low; simmer, covered, for 30 minutes or until the rice is tender. Discard the bay leaf.

2 Over a large saucepan or heatproof bowl, strain the liquid through a large sieve or a colander lined with cheesecloth or paper toweling. Transfer the solids to an electric blender or food processor. Add 1 cup liquid to the solids and purée for 30 seconds.

▽ At this point the soup can be cooled to room temperature and stored. *Refrigerate* in a tightly covered container for up to 3 days. *Freeze* in labeled 1-quart freezer bags (2 servings per bag) for up to 3 months at 0° F.

3 Return the purée to the saucepan and stir in the half-and-half and peppers. Warm over low heat until simmering. Ladle into soup bowls and garnish with the croutons, if desired. Makes about 5 cups, or 4 servings.

## Serving Later

**From freezer:** Reheat in a covered saucepan over moderate heat, stirring occasionally, until completely melted — about 15 minutes. Proceed as in Step 3. **To microwave:** Open a freezer bag 1 inch and stand it in a microwave-safe, deep, 1-quart casserole. Microwave on *High* (100% power) for 3 minutes. Transfer the soup to the casserole, cover, and microwave on *High* (100% power) for 4 minutes. Stir and turn the frozen block of soup over. Cover and microwave until boiling — 4 to 5 minutes longer. Stir in the half-and-half and pepper. Serve as in Step 3.

# Mushroom Soup

Per serving: Calories 156; Protein 7 g; Carbohydrate 16 g; Fat 6 g; Sodium 262 mg; Cholesterol 15 mg.

*To give this soup a subtler flavor, add ⅓ cup half-and-half after reheating.*

- 1 ounce dried mushrooms
- 1¼ cups boiling water
- 2 tablespoons unsalted butter or margarine
- 1 medium-size yellow onion, finely chopped
- 12 ounces fresh mushrooms, trimmed and sliced
- ⅛ teaspoon each salt and black pepper, or to taste
- ½ teaspoon dried thyme, crumbled
- ¼ cup all-purpose flour
- ½ cup dry white wine
- 3 cups Beef Stock (page 48) or canned beef broth
- 1 bay leaf

1 Place the dried mushrooms in a small bowl and cover with the boiling water; soak until soft — about 20 minutes. Drain the mushrooms in a cheesecloth-lined sieve set over a medium-size bowl. Squeeze excess moisture from the mushrooms with a spoon and then chop them. Reserve the mushroom liquid.

2 Melt the butter in a medium-size saucepan over moderate heat. Add the onion; cover and cook for 4 minutes, stirring occasionally. Add the fresh and dried mushrooms, salt, pepper, and thyme. Cook, covered, for 4 minutes, stirring occasionally. Uncover and continue to cook, stirring occasionally, until the liquid has evaporated and the fresh mushrooms are golden brown — 8 to 10 minutes.

3 Blend in the flour, and cook, stirring, for 2 minutes. Add the wine, beef stock, reserved mushroom liquid, and bay leaf. Bring to a simmer, stirring constantly, and then cook, covered, over moderately low heat for 15 minutes or until flavors are well blended. Remove the bay leaf, taste for salt and pepper, and adjust as needed. Ladle into soup bowls and serve with Italian or French bread. Makes about 5 cups, or enough for 4 servings.

▽ At this point the soup can be cooled to room temperature and stored. *Refrigerate* in a tightly covered container for up to 3 days. *Freeze* in labeled 1-quart freezer bags (2 servings per bag) for up to 3 months at 0° F.

## Serving Later

**From freezer:** Reheat in a covered saucepan over moderate heat, stirring occasionally, until thawed — about 15 minutes. Continue heating until the mixture simmers — about 10 minutes. **To microwave:** Open a freezer bag 1 inch and stand it in a microwave-safe, deep, 1-quart casserole. Microwave on

*High* (100% power) for 3 minutes. Transfer the soup to the casserole, cover, and microwave on *High* (100% power) for 3 minutes. Stir and break up the frozen block. Cover and microwave 3 minutes longer. Let stand 1 minute.

# Zucchini-Pepper Soup

Per serving: Calories 153; Protein 6 g; Carbohydrate 10 g; Fat 11 g; Sodium 454 mg; Cholesterol 22 mg.

- 4 small zucchini (about 1 pound), sliced ½ inch thick
- 2 medium-size sweet green peppers, cored, seeded, and chopped
- 3 medium-size yellow onions, chopped
- 4 cups Chicken Stock (page 48) or canned chicken broth
- 2 tablespoons chopped parsley
- 1 teaspoon salt
- ½ teaspoon black pepper
- 1½ cups sour cream or plain low-fat yogurt

*Optional garnishes:*
    Sour cream
    Thin slices of zucchini
    Parsley sprigs

1 In a large saucepan, bring the zucchini, green peppers, onions, and chicken stock to a boil over high heat. Reduce the heat to low and simmer, covered, for 15 minutes or until the vegetables are tender. Add the parsley, salt, and pepper; remove from the heat and cool slightly.

2 Over a saucepan or a heatproof bowl, strain the liquid through a large sieve or colander lined with cheesecloth or paper toweling, and transfer the solids to an electric blender or food processor. Add 1 cup of liquid from the saucepan and purée for about 30 seconds. Transfer the purée to the saucepan and stir until smooth.

▽ At this point the soup can be cooled to room temperature and stored. *Refrigerate* in a tightly covered container for up to 4 days.

3 To serve hot: Whisk in the sour cream. Heat through; do not boil. Ladle into soup bowls and, if desired, garnish with a dollop of sour cream, a zucchini slice, and a parsley sprig.

4 To serve cold: Whisk in the sour cream until well blended. Transfer the soup to a container with a tight-fitting lid. Refrigerate for at least 4 hours. With the sour cream added, the soup will keep for up to 2 days. Garnish as directed for hot soup. Makes about 8½ cups, or enough for 6 or 7 servings.

*Croutons floating on a sea of Creamy Carrot-Basil Soup: delightful for a summer lunch*

# Borscht

Per serving: Calories 52; Protein 4 g;
Carbohydrate 9 g; Fat tr; Sodium 337 mg;
Cholesterol 0 mg.

1 pound beef bones or ½
  pound boneless beef chuck,
  cut into 1-inch cubes
6 cups water
1 can (8 ounces) beets with
  their liquid, chopped
4 medium-size tomatoes,
  cored, peeled, and chopped
  (about 1 ½ pounds), or 1 can
  (28 ounces) crushed
  tomatoes
2 small carrots, peeled and
  chopped
½ small cabbage, cored and
  shredded
½ stalk celery, chopped
1 small yellow onion, chopped
1 teaspoon salt
¼ teaspoon black pepper
  Sour cream for garnish
  (optional)

1 In a large saucepan, bring the beef
  bones and water to a simmer over
moderate heat. Cook, covered, for 1
hour, skimming when necessary.

2 Add all remaining ingredients except the sour cream. Cover partially
and simmer 2 more hours. Remove and
discard the beef bones.

▽ At this point the borscht can be
  cooled to room temperature and
stored. *Refrigerate* in a tightly covered
container for up to 3 days.

3 Ladle into bowls and top each one
  with a dollop of sour cream, if
desired. Pumpernickel bread is a good
accompaniment. Makes about 10
cups, or enough for 8 servings.

## Serving Later

Reheat in a covered saucepan over
moderately low heat for about 15 minutes. Proceed as in Step 3.

## Cold Borscht Variation

Per serving: Calories 70; Protein 2 g;
Carbohydrate 9 g; Fat 3 g; Sodium 344 mg;
Cholesterol 6 mg.

Omit the beef bones or beef chuck.
Proceed as in Step 2, then chill the
soup for several hours or overnight. Just
before serving stir in ½ cup sour cream
or plain low-fat yogurt.

# Lentil Soup with Lime Juice

Per serving: Calories 335; Protein 19 g;
Carbohydrate 50 g; Fat 8 g; Sodium 354 mg;
Cholesterol 0 mg.

1 pound dried lentils, washed
  and picked over
8 cups cold water
1 teaspoon salt
½ teaspoon each black pepper
  and cumin seeds
1 teaspoon mint flakes or dried
  thyme or oregano, crumbled
3 bay leaves
1 can (4 ounces) mild green
  chilies, drained and chopped
1 medium-size sweet red
  pepper, cored, seeded, and
  finely chopped
1 medium-size carrot, peeled
  and finely chopped
⅓ cup fresh lime juice, or to
  taste
3 tablespoons olive oil

*Borscht — as pleasing to the eye as it is to the palate*

1 In a large saucepan, bring the lentils, water, salt, pepper, cumin, mint, and bay leaves to a boil over moderate heat, skimming occasionally. Lower the heat, cover, and simmer until lentils are very soft — about 45 minutes. (Uncover and skim from time to time.) Remove from the heat and discard the bay leaves.

2 In an electric blender or food processor, purée the chilies and 1 cup of the soup for about 30 seconds and then return to the saucepan. Bring to a simmer and stir in the sweet red pepper and the carrot.

▽ At this point the soup can be cooled to room temperature and stored. *Refrigerate* in a tightly covered container for up to 3 days. *Freeze* in labeled 1-quart freezer bags (2 servings per bag) for up to 3 months at 0° F.

3 Stir in the lime juice and olive oil; adjust the seasoning, if necessary. Serve hot or at room temperature. Makes about 9 cups, or enough for 6 to 8 servings.

### Serving Later

**From freezer:** Reheat in a covered saucepan over moderate heat for about 20 minutes. Add a little water if needed. Proceed as in Step 3. **To microwave:** Open freezer bag 1 inch and stand it in a microwave-safe, deep, 1-quart casserole. Microwave, uncovered, on *High* (100% power) for 3 minutes. Transfer the soup to the casserole, cover, and microwave on *High* (100% power) for 4 minutes. Stir and gently break apart the frozen block. Cover and microwave on *High* (100% power) 5 minutes longer. Let stand 1 minute. Proceed as in Step 3.

# Yellow Split Pea Soup with Spiced Yogurt

Per serving: Calories 186; Protein 10 g; Carbohydrate 29 g; Fat 4 g; Sodium 108 mg; Cholesterol 10 mg.

- 2 tablespoons unsalted butter or margarine
- 1 large yellow onion, diced
- 2 cloves garlic, minced
- 2 tablespoons minced fresh ginger, or to taste
- 1 bay leaf
- 1 teaspoon ground cumin, or to taste
- 1/8 teaspoon ground cloves
- 1 2/3 cups yellow split peas, soaked for 2 hours or overnight
- 2 stalks celery, diced
- 2 medium-size carrots, peeled and diced
- 7 cups water
- 1/4 teaspoon each salt and black pepper
- 1 tablespoon lemon juice, or to taste
- 2 teaspoons grated lemon rind

*For the spiced yogurt:*
- 1/2 cup plain low-fat yogurt
- 1/2 teaspoon each ground turmeric and paprika
- 1/4 teaspoon each cayenne pepper and ground cumin
  Pinch salt
  Minced fresh cilantro (coriander leaves) for garnish (optional)

1 Melt the butter in a large saucepan over moderate heat. Add the onion, garlic, ginger, bay leaf, cumin, and cloves, and cook, stirring, for 4 minutes. Add the peas, celery, carrots, and water. Bring to a boil and then reduce the heat to moderately low; simmer, uncovered, skimming occasionally, for 45 to 60 minutes or until the peas are soft. Cool slightly. Working in batches, purée in an electric blender or food processor — about 30 seconds for each batch.

▽ At this point the purée can be cooled to room temperature and stored. *Refrigerate* in a tightly covered container for up to 3 days. *Freeze* in labeled 1-quart freezer bags (2 servings per bag) for up to 3 months at 0° F.

2 Reheat the purée in a large saucepan and season with the salt, pepper, lemon juice, and lemon rind. Meanwhile, prepare the spiced yogurt by whisking the yogurt and spices in a small mixing bowl until well blended.

3 Serve in soup bowls, topped with the spiced yogurt and minced coriander, if desired. Makes 7 1/2 cups, or enough for 6 servings.

### Serving Later

**From freezer:** Reheat in a covered saucepan over moderate heat, stirring occasionally, until melted — about 15 minutes. Bring to a boil, reduce the heat to low, and simmer, uncovered, until heated through — about 10 minutes. Proceed as in Steps 2 and 3. **To microwave:** Open a freezer bag 1 inch and stand it in a microwave-safe, deep, 1-quart casserole. Microwave on *High* (100% power) for 3 minutes. Transfer the soup to the casserole, cover, and microwave on *High* (100% power) for 4 minutes. Stir and gently break up the frozen block. Cover and microwave 4 minutes longer. Let stand 1 minute. Proceed as in Steps 2 and 3.

*Tip: To dice an onion, cut it in half from stem to root. Place the flat side of one half on the cutting board and steady it with your fingers at the root end. Make thin slices lengthwise, perpendicular to the cutting board. Cut crosswise to desired thickness. Repeat with the other half.*

# Fresh Pea Soup

Per serving: Calories 209; Protein 9 g; Carbohydrate 18 g; Fat 12 g; Sodium 470 mg; Cholesterol 37 mg.

- 3 pounds shelled fresh green peas (9 pounds unshelled) or 3 bags (16 ounces each) frozen peas
- 3 cups Chicken Stock (page 48) or canned chicken broth
- ½ teaspoon black pepper
- 1 teaspoon salt
- 2 tablespoons unsalted butter or margarine
- ½ cup heavy cream

*Optional garnishes:*
  Fresh cooked peas
  Fresh mint sprigs or chopped mint
  Grated orange rind

1 In a large saucepan, bring 1 inch of water to a boil over high heat. Add the peas, let the water return to a boil, and reduce the heat to moderate. Cover and cook for 5 minutes; drain and cool slightly.

2 Working in batches, purée the peas in an electric blender or food processor, adding a little of the chicken stock to each batch and processing about 20 seconds. Return the puréed peas to the saucepan and stir in the remaining stock.

▽ At this point the soup can be cooled to room temperature and stored. *Refrigerate* in a tightly covered container for up to 5 days.

3 Reheat the soup over low heat. Add the salt, butter, and cream, and stir until heated through — about 5 minutes. Do *not* allow it to boil.

4 Ladle the fresh pea soup into bowls and garnish, if desired, with a sprinkling of cooked fresh peas, fresh mint sprigs, or grated orange rind. Makes 7 cups, or enough for 6 servings.

## Serving Later

Reheat in a covered saucepan over moderate heat until the soup is warmed through — about 15 minutes. Reduce the heat to low and proceed as in Steps 3 and 4.

# White Bean and Fresh Tomato Soup with Parsley Pesto

Per serving: Calories 219; Protein 7 g; Carbohydrate 22 g; Fat 12 g; Sodium 433 mg; Cholesterol 2 mg.

- ¾ cup (5 ounces) dried navy beans or white pinto beans
- 2½ quarts cold water
- 10 sage leaves or 1 teaspoon dried sage, crumbled
- 3 cloves garlic, peeled
- 3 bay leaves
- 6 sprigs thyme or ¼ teaspoon dried thyme, crumbled
- 3 tablespoons olive oil
- 2 cloves garlic, minced
- 1 medium-size yellow onion, finely chopped
- 1 pound ripe tomatoes, peeled, seeded, and chopped (about 2 cups)
- 1 teaspoon salt
- ¼ teaspoon black pepper
- ½ cup Parsley Pesto (page 222)

1 Pick over and rinse the beans. Put them in a large saucepan, add water to cover, and bring to a boil over high heat. Remove from the heat, cover, and let stand for 1 hour.

2 Pour off the liquid and discard it. Return the beans to the saucepan. Add 2½ quarts cold water, 5 of the sage leaves or ½ teaspoon of the dried sage, the 3 cloves of garlic, 2 of the bay leaves, the thyme, and 1 tablespoon of the olive oil. Bring to a boil over moder-

ate heat. Reduce the heat to moderately low and simmer, covered, until beans are soft (not mushy) — about 1 hour — skimming as necessary.

3 In a heavy 10-inch skillet, heat the remaining 2 tablespoons of olive oil over low heat. Add the remaining sage and bay leaf, the garlic, and the onion. Cook, uncovered, until the onion is soft — about 5 minutes. Stir in the tomatoes, salt, and pepper. Cover and cook for 10 minutes, stirring occasionally. Add the tomato mixture to the beans, and cook, covered, 10 minutes longer. Discard all bay leaves.

▽ At this point the soup can be cooled to room temperature and stored. *Refrigerate* in a tightly covered container for up to 4 days. *Freeze* in labeled 1-quart freezer bags (2 servings per bag) for up to 4 months at 0° F.

4 Ladle the soup into bowls; garnish each serving with a generous spoonful of the pesto. Makes about 8 cups, or enough for 6 or 7 servings.

## Serving Later

**From freezer:** Reheat in a large covered saucepan over low heat for about 25 minutes. Proceed as in Step 4. **To microwave:** Open a freezer bag 1 inch and stand it in a microwave-safe, deep, 1-quart casserole. Microwave on *High* (100% power) for 3 minutes. Transfer the soup to the casserole, cover, and microwave on *High* (100% power) for 4 minutes. Stir and gently break apart the frozen block. Cover and microwave 4 minutes longer. Let stand for 1 minute and proceed as in Step 4.

*Fresh Pea Soup, with a spring green color and an intense flavor that lingers long after the last spoonful*

# Tomato Soup with Veal Meatballs

Per serving: Calories 435; Protein 26 g; Carbohydrate 46 g; Fat 17 g; Sodium 712 mg; Cholesterol 137 mg.

- 2 tablespoons olive oil
- 1 medium-size carrot, peeled and finely chopped
- 1 medium-size yellow onion, finely chopped
- 1 stalk celery, finely chopped
- 1 tablespoon minced parsley
- 2 pounds ripe plum tomatoes, peeled, cored, seeded, and chopped (about 4 ½ cups), or 1 can (28 ounces) crushed tomatoes
- 2 quarts Chicken Stock (page 48) or canned chicken broth
- 2 slices white bread without crusts
- ½ cup milk
- ½ pound ground veal shoulder
- 1 tablespoon unsalted butter or margarine
- 2 shallots or 4 green onions, minced
- 2 egg yolks, lightly beaten
- ¾ teaspoon salt, or to taste
- ⅛ teaspoon black pepper
  Pinch ground nutmeg
- ¼ cup all-purpose flour
- 5 ounces vermicelli, broken into 1 ½-inch pieces (about 2 cups)

1 Heat the olive oil in a large stockpot over moderate heat for 1 minute. Add the carrot, onion, celery, and parsley; reduce the heat to low and cook, uncovered, until the vegetables are soft — about 10 minutes. Add the tomatoes and chicken stock; bring to a boil. Lower the heat, cover, and simmer for 1 hour.

2 While the soup simmers, make the meatballs. Soften the bread in the milk; then press out and discard the liquid. Mix the bread with the veal.

3 Heat the butter in a small skillet. Sauté the shallots over low heat until tender — about 4 minutes. Blend the shallots into the veal mixture along with the egg yolks, salt, pepper, and nutmeg. Form into 30 marble-size meatballs, roll the meatballs in the flour, and carefully drop them into the simmering stock. Cook for 10 minutes.

▽ At this point the soup can be cooled to room temperature and stored. *Refrigerate* in a tightly covered container for up to 4 days. *Freeze* in labeled 1-quart freezer bags (2 servings per bag) for up to 4 months at 0° F.

4 Stir in the vermicelli and cook, uncovered, for 5 to 7 minutes or until al dente. Serve as a main course with salad and bread. Makes about 8 cups, or enough for 6 servings.

## Serving Later

**From freezer:** Reheat in a covered stockpot over moderate heat until simmering — about 25 minutes. Proceed as in Step 4. **To microwave:** Open a freezer bag 1 inch and stand it in a microwave-safe, deep, 1-quart casserole. Microwave on *High* (100% power) for 3 minutes. Transfer the soup to the casserole, cover, and microwave on *High* (100% power) for 4 minutes. Stir and gently break apart the frozen soup. Cover and microwave 6 minutes longer. Add the vermicelli and cook 6 minutes more. Let stand for 2 minutes.

# Curried Winter Squash Soup

Per serving: Calories 192; Protein 15 g;
Carbohydrate 22 g; Fat 6 g; Sodium 871 mg;
Cholesterol 31 mg.

- 2 tablespoons unsalted butter or margarine
- 6 green onions, finely chopped
- 1 clove garlic, minced
- 1 small sweet green pepper, cored, seeded, and finely chopped
- 1/4 cup minced parsley
- 2 teaspoons minced basil or 1 teaspoon dried basil, crumbled
- 2 pounds butternut squash, peeled, seeded, and cubed
- 1 can (14 1/2 ounces) plum tomatoes with their juice
- 4 cups Chicken Stock (page 48) or canned chicken broth
- 1/2 teaspoon ground allspice
- 1/4 teaspoon ground mace

Pinch ground nutmeg
- 1 ham bone or 1/2 pound smoked ham
- 2 teaspoons curry powder
- 1/4 teaspoon each salt and black pepper
  Minced parsley for garnish (optional)

1 Melt the butter in a large saucepan over moderate heat. Add the green onions, garlic, green pepper, parsley, and basil. Cook, uncovered, for 5 minutes, stirring occasionally.

2 Stir in the squash, tomatoes, chicken stock, allspice, mace, and nutmeg and then add the ham bone. Bring to a boil over moderately high heat. Reduce the heat to moderately low and simmer, covered, for 50 to 60 minutes or until squash is very tender.

3 Remove and discard the ham bone; if using ham, reserve for another use. Over a large saucepan, strain the liquid through a large sieve or a colander lined with cheesecloth or paper toweling, and transfer the solids to an electric blender or food processor. Add 1 cup of the liquid to the solids and purée for 30 seconds or until smooth. Pour the purée back into the soup pan and stir in the curry powder. Bring to a boil over moderately high heat. Reduce the heat to moderately low and simmer for 10 minutes, uncovered, stirring often. Add the salt and pepper.

▽ At this point the soup can be cooled to room temperature and stored. *Refrigerate* in a tightly covered container for up to 3 days. *Freeze* in labeled 1-quart freezer bags (2 servings per bag) for up to 3 months at 0° F.

4 Ladle into bowls and garnish with parsley, if desired. Serve with bread, cheese, and a salad. Makes about 7 1/2 cups, or enough for 6 servings.

### Serving Later

**From freezer:** Reheat in a covered saucepan over moderate heat, stirring occasionally, until the soup is thawed — about 15 minutes. Bring the soup to a boil and then simmer until heated through — about 10 minutes. Proceed as in Step 4. **To microwave:** Open a freezer bag 1 inch and stand it in a microwave-safe, deep, 1 1/2-quart casserole. Microwave on *High* (100% power) for 3 minutes. Transfer the soup to the casserole, cover, and microwave on *High* (100% power) for 5 minutes. Stir and turn the frozen block over. Cover and microwave on *High* (100% power) 6 to 7 minutes longer. Proceed as in Step 4.

*Tomato Soup with Veal Meatballs — hearty, wholesome, and welcome on a wintry day*

# Beef, Barley, and Yogurt Soup

Per serving: Calories 342; Protein 24 mg; Carbohydrate 31 g; Fat 14 g; Sodium 297 mg; Cholesterol 148 mg.

- 3 tablespoons unsalted butter or margarine
- 1 medium-size yellow onion, finely chopped
- 1 clove garlic, minced
- ½ pound lean ground beef round
- 1½ teaspoons ground cumin
- ½ teaspoon ground allspice
- ¼ teaspoon black pepper
- 4 green onions, thinly sliced
- 2 tablespoons chopped mint or 1 tablespoon mint flakes, crumbled
- 1½ cups cooked barley
- 4 cups Chicken Stock (page 48) or canned chicken broth
- 2 large eggs, lightly beaten
- 3 cups plain low-fat yogurt Chopped mint leaves for garnish (optional)

1 Melt the butter in a medium-size saucepan over moderate heat. Add the onion and garlic, and cook, stirring, for 3 to 5 minutes. Add the beef, cumin, allspice, and pepper; cook until the meat is brown — 3 to 5 minutes. Stir in the green onions, mint, barley, and chicken stock.

▽ At this point the soup can be cooled to room temperature and stored. *Refrigerate* in a tightly covered container for up to 3 days. *Freeze* in labeled 1-quart freezer bags (2 servings per bag) for up to 3 months at 0° F.

2 In a medium-size mixing bowl, whisk together the eggs and yogurt. Blend a little of the hot soup into this mixture, then stir it back into the saucepan. Cook over moderately low heat, stirring, for 5 minutes or until slightly thickened. Do not let the soup boil. Ladle into soup bowls and garnish with chopped mint, if desired. Makes about 9 cups, or enough for 6 to 8 servings.

## Serving Later

**From freezer:** Reheat in a covered saucepan over moderate heat, stirring occasionally, until the soup is completely thawed — about 15 minutes. Bring to a simmer and then proceed as in Step 2. **To microwave:** Open a freezer bag 1 inch and stand it in a microwave-safe, deep, 1½-quart casserole. Microwave on *High* (100% power) for 3 minutes. Transfer the soup to the casserole, cover, and microwave on *High* (100% power) for 4 minutes. Stir and break up the frozen block. Cover and microwave 5 minutes longer. Meanwhile, whisk together the eggs and yogurt; then blend a little of the hot soup into this mixture. Whisk the mixture into the hot soup, cover, and microwave on *High* (100% power) for 2 minutes.

# Chicken-Corn Soup

Per serving: Calories 270; Protein 28 g; Carbohydrate 15 g; Fat 11 g; Sodium 552 mg; Cholesterol 133 mg.

*This traditional Pennsylvania Dutch recipe is a meal in itself.*

- 1 stewing fowl with giblets (about 5 pounds)
- 4 quarts water
- 2 large yellow onions, chopped
- 1 clove garlic, crushed
- 2 stalks celery, diced
- 1 tablespoon salt
- ¼ teaspoon black pepper
- 1 cup minced parsley
- 4 cups fresh whole-kernel corn (6 large ears) or 2 packages (10 ounces each) frozen whole-kernel corn
- 4 ounces wide egg noodles
- 2 hard-cooked eggs, chopped

1 Remove the giblets from the fowl. Put the liver and heart in a small mixing bowl, cover, and refrigerate.

2 Place the fowl and its neck and gizzard in a large stockpot. Add the 4 quarts water and bring to a simmer over moderate heat. Cover and cook until tender — about 2½ hours.

3 Remove stockpot from the heat. Lift the fowl and gizzard from the broth and set aside; discard neck. Strain the broth into a large heatproof mixing bowl through a large sieve or a cheese-cloth- or paper-toweling-lined colander. After the broth has cooled, skim off as much fat as possible; or chill for 1 hour and then remove solidified fat.

4 Return the broth to the stockpot and add the onions, garlic, and celery. Cover and simmer for 45 minutes. Add the salt and pepper; cover and simmer 45 minutes longer.

5 Skin and bone the fowl and cut it into bite-size pieces. Discard the skin and bones. Chop the gizzard, also the reserved liver and heart; add them along with the chicken to the stockpot. Stir in the parsley and simmer, uncovered, for 20 minutes.

▽ At this point the soup can be cooled to room temperature and stored. *Refrigerate* in a tightly covered container for up to 3 days. *Freeze* in labeled 1-quart freezer bags (2 servings per bag) for up to 3 months at 0° F.

6 Add the corn and noodles, cover, and simmer, stirring occasionally, until noodles are tender — 8 to 10 minutes. Stir in the chopped eggs and ladle into soup bowls. Serves 12.

## Serving Later

**From freezer:** Reheat in a covered stockpot over moderate heat, stirring occasionally, until thawed — about 15 minutes. Bring the soup to a boil, reduce the heat to low, and simmer, uncovered, stirring occasionally, until heated through — about 10 minutes. Proceed as in Step 6.

# Fish

Good cooks know that fish or other seafood is at its best when cooked and eaten as soon as possible after being caught. How then can it be prepared satisfactorily ahead of time?

One approach is to slowly cook or preserve seafood in lemon juice or vinegar. Poisson Mariné (page 70), Sea Scallops Creole (page 76), and Seviche (page 76) are all examples of this method.

Another technique is to flake cooked fish and incorporate it into a gelatin base, as in Curried Tuna Mousse and Layered Salmon Mousse (page 72), or an egg preparation, such as Flounder Soufflé (page 70).

Still another way, one that offers the greatest number of variations, is to prepare a sauce, then cook the fish and add it at the last minute. Typical of such recipes are Halibut in Wine Sauce (page 68) and Fiery Shrimp (page 74). Elsewhere in this book are several other do-ahead sauces suitable for fish. Among them are Spicy Salsa (page 218), Garlic Mayonnaise, and Piquant Sauce for Fish and Poultry (page 220). Also fine with grilled or poached fish are Dill Butter (page 222), Lemon Butter, and Parsley Butter (page 223).

Seafood dishes that retain their palatability and texture when reheated are also good make-aheads. Creamy Shrimp Curry (page 74), Scalloped Oysters (page 78), and Crab in Mustard-Madeira Sauce (page 299) are typical representatives.

# Halibut in Wine Sauce

Per serving: Calories 386; Protein 37 g; Carbohydrate 12 g; Fat 19 g; Sodium 389 mg; Cholesterol 85 mg.

- ¼ cup olive oil
- 1 large yellow onion, chopped
- 1 medium-size carrot, peeled and coarsely shredded
- 2 stalks celery, chopped
- 1 clove garlic, crushed
- 1 large tomato, peeled and chopped
- ¼ cup water
- ¾ cup dry white wine
- 4 halibut steaks (about 6 ounces each)
- 2 tablespoons all-purpose flour
- 1 tablespoon minced parsley
- ½ teaspoon salt
- ¼ teaspoon black pepper
  Parsley sprigs for garnish (optional)

1 Heat 2 tablespoons of the olive oil in a heavy 10-inch skillet over moderate heat. Add the onion, carrot, celery, and garlic, and cook, stirring occasionally, until softened — about 5 minutes. Add the tomato and water and bring to a boil. Reduce the heat to low, cover, and simmer for 10 minutes.

2 Transfer the vegetable mixture to an electric blender or food processor and purée for 15 to 20 seconds. Blend in the white wine; set aside.

▽ At this point, the sauce can be transferred to a small bowl, covered tightly, and *refrigerated* for up to 24 hours.

3 Rinse and dry each steak thoroughly with paper toweling. On a sheet of wax paper, combine the flour, minced parsley, salt, and pepper. Dredge the fish in the flour mixture, shaking off any excess.

4 Wipe out the skillet with paper toweling. Heat the remaining 2 tablespoons of oil in the skillet over moderate heat. Add the halibut steaks and sauté until golden brown — about 5 minutes per side. Transfer the fish to a platter lined with paper toweling.

5 Return the sauce to the skillet and add the halibut steaks. Bring to a simmer over moderate heat; then reduce the heat to low, cover, and simmer for 5 minutes or until the fish flakes easily when tested with a fork. Transfer the halibut steaks to a serving platter, cover with the sauce, and garnish with parsley sprigs, if desired. Serve accompanied by new potatoes with Dill Butter and steamed asparagus. Serves 4.

### Serving Later

Let the wine sauce come to room temperature. Proceed as in Steps 3, 4, and 5.

# Salmon in Three-Citrus Sauce

Per serving: Calories 434; Protein 34 g; Carbohydrate 6 g; Fat 29 g; Sodium 144 mg; Cholesterol 74 mg.

- 6 salmon steaks (about 6 ounces each)
- ½ teaspoon each grated orange rind, grated lemon rind, and grated lime rind
- ⅓ cup orange juice
- 2 tablespoons each lemon juice and lime juice
- ¼ cup grated yellow onion
- 1 tablespoon honey
- ½ teaspoon minced hot red chili pepper or ¼ teaspoon red pepper flakes
- 3 tablespoons lightly salted butter or margarine

1 In a shallow, glass or ceramic dish, arrange the salmon steaks in a single layer. In a small bowl, combine the orange, lemon, and lime rinds, the orange, lemon, and lime juices, the onion, honey, and hot red pepper. Mix well, pour over the salmon, cover, and refrigerate. Marinate the fish, turning occasionally, for at least 3 hours.

2 Preheat the broiler. In a small saucepan, melt 1 tablespoon of the butter. Using a slotted spoon, transfer the salmon to the broiler rack, reserving the marinade. Brush the steaks with the melted butter and broil 4 inches from the heat for 4 to 6 minutes on each side or until the steaks flake easily when tested with a fork. Transfer to a heated serving platter.

3 Meanwhile, strain the marinade into the saucepan and bring to a boil over moderate heat. Boil, uncovered, until slightly thickened — about 2 minutes. Blend in the remaining 2 tablespoons of butter and pour the sauce over the fish. Serve with scalloped potatoes and baby carrots rolled in butter and dill. Serves 6.

# Oriental Spiced Fish

Per serving: Calories 223; Protein 31 g; Carbohydrate 3 g; Fat 10 g; Sodium 524 mg; Cholesterol 75 mg.

- ½ cup soy sauce
- 2 tablespoons brown sugar
- 2 cloves garlic, minced
- ½ teaspoon cayenne pepper, or to taste
- 1 whole flounder (about 2 pounds), cleaned and dressed, or 1½ pounds mackerel or bluefish fillets, or 4 tuna steaks (6 ounces each)
- 4 tablespoons (½ stick) unsalted butter or margarine
- 4 tablespoons lemon juice

*Optional garnishes:*
  Julienned strips of carrot and sweet green pepper
  Radish flowers

*Oriental Spiced Fish — a popular dish from the Indonesian archipelago*

1 In a shallow baking dish, combine the soy sauce, brown sugar, garlic, and cayenne pepper. Add the fish, turning in the marinade to coat. Cover and refrigerate for at least 1 hour, and up to 12 hours, basting occasionally.

2 Preheat the broiler or grill and lightly brush the rack with oil. With a slotted spatula, gently transfer the fish to the broiler pan; set the marinade aside. Broil the fish 4 to 5 inches from the heat until it flakes easily when tested with a fork — 8 to 10 minutes per inch of thickness. Brush occasionally with the marinade. Fillets do not have to be turned; a whole fish or steaks should be turned once.

3 Meanwhile, melt the butter in a small saucepan over low heat. Stir in the lemon juice and pour the sauce into a sauceboat. Transfer the fish to a serving platter and garnish with the vegetable strips and radishes, if desired. Pass the lemon butter separately. Serve hot with steamed rice and stir-fried shredded zucchini; or at room temperature with Cold Sesame Noodles Oriental Style (page 154). Serves 4.

69

# Herbed Bluefish Fillets

Per serving: Calories 342; Protein 32 g; Carbohydrate tr; Fat 21 g; Sodium 192 mg; Cholesterol 119 mg.

- ½ small yellow onion, finely chopped
- 1 clove garlic, minced
- 1 tablespoon minced parsley
- 1 tablespoon Dijon or spicy brown mustard
- 1 teaspoon fennel seeds, crushed
- ½ teaspoon salt
- ¼ teaspoon black pepper
- 3 tablespoons vegetable oil
- 1 tablespoon lime or lemon juice
  Dash hot red pepper sauce, or to taste
  Dash Worcestershire sauce, or to taste
- 1½ pounds bluefish or mackerel fillets, cut into 4 serving-size pieces, or 4 tuna steaks (6 ounces each)

1 In a shallow baking dish just large enough to hold the fish in a single layer, stir together all ingredients except the fish. Add the fish, rubbing the marinade lightly into the flesh. Cover and refrigerate for at least 1 hour. Will keep, refrigerated, for up to 5 hours.

2 Preheat the broiler. With a slotted spatula, transfer the fillets to a lightly oiled broiler pan; set the marinade aside. Broil the bluefish or mackerel fillets, skin side down, 4 inches from the heat for 5 to 6 minutes or until the fish flakes easily when tested with a fork. Baste once with the marinade but do not turn. Broil the tuna steaks 4 inches from the heat for 4 to 6 minutes; turn, brush with the marinade, and broil 4 to 6 minutes more or until the fish flakes easily when tested with a fork. Serve with rice and Zucchini Slaw (page 196) or an arugula and tomato salad. Serves 4.

# Poisson Mariné

Per serving: Calories 299; Protein 49 g; Carbohydrate 1 g; Fat 10 g; Sodium 289 mg; Cholesterol 120 mg.

*In this traditional Provençal recipe, broiled fish is marinated for an especially rich flavor.*

- 3 pounds sea bass, striped bass, red snapper, or whiting fillets
- 1 tablespoon salt
- 2 cups white wine vinegar
- 1 large carrot, peeled and chopped
- 1 large yellow onion, chopped
- 2 shallots or 4 green onions, chopped
- 1 stalk celery, chopped
- 3 tablespoons minced parsley
- 3 bay leaves
- 1 teaspoon dried thyme, crumbled
- ¼ teaspoon black pepper
- 1 whole clove
- 4 tablespoons olive oil

*Optional garnishes:*
- 2 tablespoons minced parsley
- 2 lemons, sliced

1 In a large, shallow, glass or ceramic dish, lay the fillets in a single layer and sprinkle with the salt. Cover with plastic wrap and refrigerate for 3 hours.

2 Meanwhile, in a medium-size saucepan, bring the vinegar, carrot, onion, shallots, celery, parsley, bay leaves, thyme, pepper, and clove to a boil over high heat. Reduce the heat to low, cover, and simmer for 30 minutes. Set the marinade aside to cool.

3 Preheat the broiler. Using paper toweling, wipe excess salt from the fish fillets. Arrange on a lightly oiled broiler pan and broil 6 inches from the heat for 5 minutes or until the fish flakes easily when tested with a fork.

4 Meanwhile, wash and dry the dish used for salting the fish. Arrange the broiled fillets in it. Add the marinade, wrap tightly with plastic wrap, and refrigerate for 8 hours.

5 Using 2 spatulas, gently transfer the fillets to a platter and discard the marinade. Return the fillets to the marinating dish, brush well with the olive oil, and cover tightly with plastic wrap. Refrigerate 8 hours more.

6 Using 2 spatulas, gently transfer the fillets to a serving platter and, if you like, garnish with the parsley and lemon slices. Serve with a cold rice salad and sliced tomatoes sprinkled with coarsely chopped basil, black pepper, and olive oil. Serves 6.

# Flounder Soufflé

Per serving: Calories 258; Protein 16 g; Carbohydrate 7 g; Fat 18 g; Sodium 245 mg; Cholesterol 335 mg.

- 1 cup water
- 8 ounces fresh flounder, hake, haddock, or other white fish fillets
- 4 tablespoons (½ stick) unsalted butter or margarine
- 4 tablespoons all-purpose flour
- 2 tablespoons lemon juice
- ¼ teaspoon each salt and dill weed
- 1 teaspoon grated lemon rind
- 4 eggs, separated

1 In a 10-inch skillet, bring the water to a boil over moderately high heat. Add the flounder fillets. Reduce the heat to low, cover, and simmer until the fish flakes easily when tested with a fork — about 5 minutes. Drain, reserving the stock; set the fish aside to cool.

2 In a medium-size heavy saucepan, melt the butter over moderate heat. Blend in the flour, and cook, stirring constantly, until a smooth paste is formed — 1 to 2 minutes. Slowly add

the reserved fish stock and lemon juice, and cook, stirring, until thickened and smooth — about 5 minutes. Remove from the heat and stir in the salt, dill weed, and grated lemon rind.

3 In a small bowl, beat the egg yolks lightly. Stir in a small amount of the hot sauce. Add the egg mixture to the saucepan, and cook, stirring, over moderate heat until thickened and smooth — 2 to 3 minutes. Remove from the heat. Flake the fish with a fork and stir it into the sauce; set aside.

▽ At this point the fish sauce can be cooled to room temperature and stored. Cover tightly and *refrigerate* for up to 24 hours.

4 Preheat the oven to 375° F. In a medium-size bowl, beat the egg whites until stiff peaks form. Stir 2 spoonfuls of the egg whites into the fish mixture; then gently fold in the remaining whites.

5 Pour into a greased 6-cup casserole. Bake 35 to 40 minutes or until puffy and lightly browned. Serve immediately, accompanied by steamed broccoli with buttered bread crumbs or Baked Tomatoes Stuffed with Orzo (page 184) and a watercress and mushroom salad. Serves 4.

*Fish flakes dispersed in an edible cloud — Flounder Soufflé — a celestial experience*

# Curried Tuna Mousse

Per serving: Calories 193; Protein 20 g; Carbohydrate 5 g; Fat 11 g; Sodium 405 mg; Cholesterol 53 mg.

*This light flavorful mousse is very pretty to look at — an ideal dish for a special luncheon.*

- 1 envelope unflavored gelatin
- ½ cup water
- ½ cup tomato juice
- ½ cup low-calorie mayonnaise
- 2 tablespoons grated yellow onion
- 1 tablespoon cider vinegar
- 1 tablespoon Worcestershire sauce
- 2 teaspoons curry powder
- ½ cup heavy cream
- 2 cans (6½ ounces each) water-packed tuna, drained and flaked
- 1 tablespoon capers, drained and minced (optional)
  Lettuce leaves for garnish (optional)

**1** In a small saucepan, combine the gelatin with the water. Warm over low heat, stirring constantly, until the gelatin is dissolved — about 5 minutes.

**2** In a large bowl, combine the tomato juice, mayonnaise, onion, vinegar, Worcestershire sauce, and curry powder. Add the gelatin, and whisk together. Cover and chill until the mixture mounds slightly when dropped from a spoon — about 30 minutes.

**3** Meanwhile, in a medium-size bowl, whip the cream until stiff peaks form. Beat the thickened gelatin mixture lightly; then fold in the whipped cream, tuna, and capers, if desired. Pour into a lightly oiled 1-quart mold or bowl, cover tightly, and chill until firm — at least 4 hours. Can be kept, refrigerated, for up to 2 days.

**4** To unmold, loosen the tuna mousse with a thin-bladed spatula. Dip the mold in hot water for 30 seconds, invert the mousse onto a serving platter, and garnish, if you like, with lettuce leaves. Accompany with Summer Corn Salad (page 196) or Spring Vegetable Casserole (page 187) and a crusty rye bread. Serves 6.

# Layered Salmon and Cucumber Mousse

Per serving: Calories 227; Protein 18 g; Carbohydrate 9 g; Fat 14 g; Sodium 683 mg; Cholesterol 45 mg.

*Here is a refreshing combination that has special appeal on a hot summer night. One pound of boneless, skinless, poached or steamed salmon can be substituted for the canned.*

- 6 green onions, white parts only
- ¾ cup low-fat ricotta or low-fat cottage cheese
- 1 can (15½ ounces) salmon, drained
- ¾ cup low-calorie mayonnaise
- ¾ teaspoon salt
- 2 teaspoons Dijon or spicy brown mustard
- 2 tablespoons lemon juice
- ½ teaspoon hot red pepper sauce
  Dash Worcestershire sauce
- 1½ cups cold water
- 3 envelopes plus 1 teaspoon unflavored gelatin
- ½ cup fish stock or bottled clam juice
- 8 to 10 sprigs dill or watercress, large stems removed
- 1 large cucumber, peeled, seeded, and shredded
- 1 medium-size zucchini, shredded
- 1 medium-size sweet green pepper, cored, seeded, and minced
- 1 cup sour cream
- 2 tablespoons white wine vinegar

*Optional garnishes:*
  Lemon twists
  Dill sprigs

**1** In an electric blender or food processor, process 4 of the green onions, the ricotta, salmon, ¼ cup of the mayonnaise, ¼ teaspoon of the salt, the mustard, lemon juice, hot red pepper sauce, and Worcestershire sauce until smooth — 15 to 20 seconds.

**2** In a small saucepan, combine ½ cup of the water with 1 envelope of the gelatin and warm over low heat, stirring constantly, until dissolved — about 5 minutes. Add the gelatin to the salmon mixture, setting the saucepan aside to use later, and pulse 4 to 5 times. Pour the mixture into a lightly oiled, 6-cup fish or ring mold. Cover with plastic wrap and chill for 15 minutes or until slightly set.

**3** Meanwhile, in the small saucepan, combine the fish stock with the 1 teaspoon of gelatin and warm over low heat, stirring constantly, until dissolved — about 5 minutes. Arrange the dill sprigs on top of the salmon mousse, letting them push up the sides of the mold so they will be visible when unmolded. Spoon the gelatin mixture over the dill, and chill for at least 30 minutes or until tacky.

**4** Meanwhile, pat dry the cucumber, zucchini, and green pepper on paper toweling and put them in a large bowl. Mince the remaining 2 green onions and add them to the vegetables along with the sour cream, vinegar, and the remaining ½ teaspoon salt and ½ cup mayonnaise; mix well.

5 Rinse out the small saucepan; in it, combine the remaining 2 envelopes of gelatin with the remaining 1 cup water. Warm over low heat, stirring constantly, until dissolved — about 5 minutes. Add the gelatin to the vegetables and stir well. Spoon the mixture into the mold on top of the fish stock layer, cover with aluminum foil or plastic wrap, and chill for at least 5 hours or overnight. Can be referigerated for up to 2 days.

6 To unmold, loosen the gelatin mixture with a thin-bladed spatula and then dip the mold in a pan of hot water for 30 seconds. Invert onto a serving platter and garnish with the lemon twists and dill sprigs, if desired. Serve with cold asparagus, Herbed Rice Salad (page 209) and crusty rolls. Serves 6.

*Pleasing to the eye and the palate, Layered Salmon and Cucumber Mousse is a fine choice for a special occasion.*

# Fiery Shrimp

Per serving: Calories 212; Protein 25 g;
Carbohydrate 17 g; Fat 5 g; Sodium 605 mg;
Cholesterol 164 mg.

*Cayenne pepper gives this sauce much
of its fire. Begin with the ½ teaspoon
indicated and increase according to
your own preference.*

- 2 tablespoons unsalted butter
  or margarine
- 2 medium-size yellow onions,
  chopped
- 1½ medium-size sweet green
  peppers, cored, seeded, and
  chopped
- 2 stalks celery, chopped
- 1½ pounds tomatoes, peeled,
  seeded, and chopped, or 1
  can (28 ounces) crushed
  tomatoes
- 1 can (8 ounces) tomato sauce
- 1½ tablespoons minced jalapeño
  peppers
- 2 bay leaves
- ½ teaspoon each black pepper,
  cayenne pepper, and white
  pepper
- 2 cloves garlic, minced
- 2 bottles (8 ounces each) clam
  juice
- ¼ cup water
- 3 tablespoons brown sugar
- ½ teaspoon salt, or to taste
- 2 pounds large shrimp, shelled
  and deveined

1 Melt the butter in a large heavy
saucepan over moderate heat. Add
the onions, green peppers, and celery,
and cook, stirring, for 5 minutes or until
the onions are softened. Add the tomatoes, tomato sauce, jalapeño peppers,
bay leaves, cayenne pepper, white pepper, black pepper, and garlic, and mix
well. Cook, stirring, 3 minutes more.

2 Add the clam juice, water, sugar,
and salt and bring the mixture to a
boil. Reduce the heat to low; simmer,
uncovered, stirring occasionally, 20
minutes more or until the flavors are
well combined.

▽ At this point the sauce can be
cooled and stored. *Refrigerate* in
a tightly covered medium-size bowl for
up to 3 days. *Freeze*, in 2 labeled, 1-
quart freezer bags (4 servings per bag),
for up to 3 months at 0° F.

3 Add the shrimp to the sauce. Cover
the pan, raise the heat to high, and
bring the sauce to a boil. Cook for 1
minute. Remove the pan from the heat
and let stand, covered, for 7 to 10
minutes to let the shrimp finish cooking. Serve over a mound of hot rice,
accompanied by cucumbers with Yogurt Dressing (page 214). Serves 8.

## Serving Later

**From refrigerator:** Transfer the sauce
to a large heavy saucepan and warm,
uncovered, over medium heat, stirring
occasionally, until heated through —
about 10 minutes. Proceed as in Step
3. **From freezer:** Transfer the sauce to
a large heavy saucepan. Cover and
cook over low heat, stirring occasionally and breaking up the chunks, until
heated through — about 25 minutes.
Proceed as in Step 3. **To microwave 4
servings:** Open a freezer bag 1-inch
and place it in a microwave-safe, deep,
1-quart casserole. Cover and microwave on *High* (100% power) for 3
minutes. Transfer the sauce to the
casserole. Cover with plastic wrap and
microwave on *High* (100% power) for
4 minutes. Stir to break up the frozen
sauce block, re-cover, and microwave
on *High* (100% power) 5 minutes
more. Add 1 pound cooked shrimp. If
the shrimp are hot, serve immediately.
If cold, re-cover and microwave on
*High* (100% power) 1 minute more.

# Creamy Shrimp Curry

Per serving: Calories 254; Protein 24 g;
Carbohydrate 5 g; Fat 15 g; Sodium 356 mg;
Cholesterol 184 mg.

- 1½ pounds medium-size
  shrimp, in the shell
- 2 tablespoons unsalted butter
  or margarine
- 1 small yellow onion, finely
  chopped
- ½ small sweet green pepper,
  cored, seeded, and chopped
- 1 clove garlic, minced
- 8 ounces mushrooms, thinly
  sliced
- 1 teaspoon curry powder
- ½ teaspoon Worcestershire
  sauce
- ½ teaspoon salt
- ¼ teaspoon dry mustard
- ⅛ teaspoon white pepper
- 1 cup sour cream, at room
  temperature
- 2 tablespoons toasted slivered
  almonds

1 In a medium-size saucepan set over
high heat, bring 2 quarts water to a
boil. Add the shrimp, reduce the heat
to moderately low, and simmer, uncovered, just until they turn pink — 2 to 3
minutes. Drain and cool slightly; then
shell and devein.

2 Melt the butter in a heavy 10-inch
skillet over moderate heat. Add the
onion, green pepper, and garlic, and
sauté, stirring occasionally, until soft —
about 5 minutes. Add the mushrooms
and cook 5 minutes more. Stir in the
curry, Worcestershire sauce, salt, mustard, and white pepper, cook 1 minute
longer. Stir in the shrimp.

▽ At this point the mixture can be
cooled to room temperature and
*refrigerated* in a covered container for
up to 24 hours.

3 Stir in the sour cream and heat
through. Do not let the sauce boil
or it will curdle. To serve, pour over hot

rice and sprinkle with the toasted almonds. Accompany with Four-Fruit Chutney (page 226) and a green salad. Or serve at room temperature on lettuce leaves accompanied by Poppy Seed Bowknots (page 241). Serves 6.

(page 226)
(page 241)

### Serving Later

In a heavy 10-inch skillet, gently warm the shrimp mixture over low heat, being careful not to cook the shrimp any further. Proceed as in Step 3.

# Shrimp Bundles

Per serving: Calories 278; Protein 30 g; Carbohydrate 11 g; Fat 11 g; Sodium 534 mg; Cholesterol 208 mg.

- 2½ tablespoons olive or vegetable oil
-   1 medium-size yellow onion, sliced thin
-   2 small sweet red peppers, cored, seeded, and cut into ½-inch strips
- ¼ teaspoon each salt and black pepper
-   2 cloves garlic, minced
- ⅓ cup dry white wine
-   1 can (14½ ounces) tomatoes, drained and chopped
-   2 teaspoons tomato paste
- ½ teaspoon each dried thyme and basil, crumbled
- ½ teaspoon fennel seeds, crushed
-   1 teaspoon grated orange rind
- 1⅓ pounds large shrimp, shelled and deveined
-   2 tablespoons minced chives, basil, or parsley

1 Cut 4 pieces of aluminum foil, each measuring 12 inches wide by 14 inches long. Fold each piece in half crosswise to form a rectangle measuring 7 inches wide by 12 inches long. Beginning at the folded edge, and 2 inches from the top, cut the foil to form a heart when opened. Unfold and lay the pieces shiny side down. Brush the dull sides with ½ tablespoon of the olive oil.

2 In a heavy 10-inch skillet, warm the remaining 2 tablespoons of olive oil over moderately high heat for 1 minute. Add the onion, red peppers, salt, and black pepper, and cook, stirring, until the onion is golden — about 7 minutes. Add the garlic, wine, tomatoes, tomato paste, thyme, basil, fennel, and grated orange rind. Bring to a boil and simmer, covered, for 5 minutes. Let cool to room temperature.

3 For each serving, spoon a little of the sauce along one side of each heart and place one-quarter of the shrimp on top. Cover with more sauce, fold the other side of each heart over, and seal the edges securely.

▽ At this point the packages can be *refrigerated*, tightly sealed, for up to 8 hours.

4 Preheat the oven to 425° F. Place the packages on a baking sheet and bake for 15 to 20 minutes. Transfer each package to a plate and cut an "x" in the top. Fold back the foil to reveal the seafood and sprinkle with the fresh chives. Serve with orzo baked with feta cheese and a green salad. Serves 4.

### Serving Later

Preheat the oven to 425° F. Transfer the packages to a baking sheet and bake for 20 minutes. Serve as in Step 4.

*A Shrimp Bundle, with its mouth-watering morsels revealed*

# Sea Scallops Creole

Per serving: Calories 199; Protein 18 g; Carbohydrate 6 g; Fat 11 g; Sodium 445 mg; Cholesterol 213 mg.

- 1 cup dry white wine
- 1 cup water
- 6 sprigs parsley
- 2 stalks celery
- 1 medium-size yellow onion, stuck with a clove
- 6 black peppercorns
- 2 pounds sea scallops

*For the marinade:*
- 6 tablespoons olive oil
- 1/4 cup lemon juice
- 1 tablespoon white wine vinegar
- 1 teaspoon Dijon or spicy brown mustard
- 1 teaspoon dry mustard
- 1 small red onion, thinly sliced
- 1/2 cup sliced, pitted black olives
- 1 lemon, thinly sliced
- 3 tablespoons chopped pimiento
- 2 tablespoons chopped parsley
- 1 clove garlic, minced
- 1 bay leaf
- 1/2 teaspoon salt
- 1/4 teaspoon black pepper
- 1/8 teaspoon cayenne pepper

1 In a medium-size saucepan, bring the wine, water, parsley, celery, onion, and black peppercorns to a boil over high heat. Reduce the heat to low and simmer, partially covered, for about 30 minutes.

2 Add the scallops and bring to a boil over moderately high heat; reduce the heat to low and cook, uncovered, just until cooked through — about 5 minutes. Using a slotted spoon, transfer the scallops to a platter.

3 Meanwhile, in a large, glass or ceramic bowl, whisk together the olive oil, lemon juice, vinegar, Dijon mustard, and dry mustard. Add the onion, olives, lemon, pimiento, parsley, garlic, bay leaf, salt, black pepper, cayenne pepper, and scallops, and mix

well. Cover and refrigerate, stirring occasionally, for at least 2 and up to 8 hours. Serve on a bed of red leaf lettuce, accompanied by a mélange of cold steamed vegetables, French bread, and a mixed green salad. Serves 8.

# Broiled Scallops and Mushrooms in Lemon Sauce

Per serving: Calories 147; Protein 24 g; Carbohydrate 7 g; Fat 2 g; Sodium 391 mg; Cholesterol 268 mg.

*To make this recipe serve four people, increase the scallops to 1 1/3 pounds, the mushrooms to 10 ounces.*

- 1/4 cup fresh lemon juice
- 1/4 cup dry Vermouth or dry white wine
- 1/4 cup vegetable oil
- 2 tablespoons chopped parsley
- 1 clove garlic, crushed
- 1/2 teaspoon salt
- 1/4 teaspoon black pepper
- 1 pound sea scallops
- 8 ounces mushrooms, trimmed
  Lemon wedges for garnish

1 In a large bowl, combine the lemon juice, Vermouth, oil, parsley, garlic, salt, and pepper. Add the scallops and mushrooms and coat well. Cover and marinate in the refrigerator for at least 1 hour, but not more than 3 hours, turning occasionally.

2 Preheat the broiler. Using a slotted spoon, transfer the scallops and mushrooms to a lightly oiled broiler pan. Broil 5 inches from the heat for 4 minutes. Turn, brush with the marinade, and broil 4 minutes more or until cooked through. Garnish with lemon wedges. Serve with rice and sautéed cucumbers or broiled tomatoes and a green salad. Serves 3.

# Seviche

Per serving: Calories 153; Protein 18 g; Carbohydrate 9 g; Fat 5 g; Sodium 475 mg; Cholesterol 213 mg.

*When you marinate fish in fresh lemon or lime juice, the acid "cooks" the fish and gives it a delicious piquant flavor.*

- 6 tablespoons each fresh lemon juice and fresh lime juice
- 1 medium-size sweet green pepper, cored, seeded, and diced
- 1 medium-size sweet red pepper, cored, seeded, and diced
- 2 stalks celery, diced
- 3 tablespoons minced parsley
- 2 tablespoons chopped cilantro or 1/2 teaspoon dried cilantro or dried tarragon, crumbled
- 1 clove garlic, minced
- 2 teaspoons minced fresh ginger or 1/4 teaspoon ground ginger
- 2 teaspoons chili powder
- 1/2 teaspoon salt
- 1/4 teaspoon red pepper flakes
- 1 1/2 pounds bay scallops or other firm-fleshed fish, such as tuna, cut into bite-size pieces
- 2 tablespoons olive oil
  Lettuce leaves for garnish

1 In a medium-size, glass or ceramic bowl, mix the lemon juice, lime juice, green pepper, red pepper, celery, parsley, cilantro, garlic, ginger, chili powder, salt, and red pepper flakes. Add the scallops and toss well. Cover and refrigerate for at least 6 hours. Will keep, refrigerated, for up to 12 hours.

2 Before serving, add the olive oil and toss well. Arrange on a bed of lettuce. Accompany with Herbed Rice Salad (page 209). Serves 6.

*Colorful Seviche and Herbed Rice Salad (page 209) easily attract attention — and compliments.*

# Scalloped Oysters

Per serving: Calories 354; Protein 11 g; Carbohydrate 27 g; Fat 22 g; Sodium 528 mg; Cholesterol 99 mg.

- 1 pint shucked oysters
- 1½ cups whole kernel corn (about 4 ears) or 1 can (12 ounces) whole kernel corn, drained
- 1 small yellow onion, finely chopped
- 1 small sweet red pepper, cored, seeded, and finely chopped
- ½ cup light cream
- 2 tablespoons minced parsley
- ½ teaspoon salt
- ¼ teaspoon black pepper
- ⅛ teaspoon hot red pepper sauce
- ½ cup (1 stick) unsalted butter or margarine
- 2 cups saltine cracker crumbs

1 Drain the oysters, reserving ¼ cup of the liquor, and chop coarsely; set aside. In a medium-size bowl, mix the corn, onion, red pepper, cream, parsley, salt, black pepper, and the hot red pepper sauce; set aside.

2 In a small saucepan, melt the butter over low heat. Remove from heat, add the cracker crumbs, and mix well.

3 In 6 greased scallop shells or 4 greased 1¾-cup casseroles, alternate 3 layers of crumbs with 2 layers of oysters and 2 of corn mixture, beginning and ending with the crumbs. Pour a little oyster liquor over each.

▽ At this point the oysters can be stored. Cover with plastic wrap and *refrigerate* for up to 8 hours. Or cover with heavy-duty aluminum foil, label, and *freeze* for 1 month at 0° F.

4 Preheat the oven to 375° F. Bake the scallop shells, uncovered, for 15 to 20 minutes (the casseroles, uncovered, for 20 to 25 minutes) or until brown and bubbling. Serves 6 as a first course, 4 as an entrée.

**From refrigerator:** Remove the plastic wrap and proceed as in Step 4. **From freezer:** Remove foil. Bake the scallop shells, uncovered, at 375° F for 30 to 35 minutes (the casseroles at 425° F for 40 minutes) or until golden and bubbling. **To microwave 1 casserole:** Remove foil and cover with plastic wrap vented at one side. Microwave on *Low* (30% power) for 5 minutes. Microwave on *High* (100% power) for 2 minutes. Rotate casserole 90 degrees and microwave on *High* (100% power) 1½ minutes more. Let stand 1 minute, then run under the broiler to brown.

# Deviled Crab

Per serving: Calories 189; Protein 15 g; Carbohydrate 8 g; Fat 11 g; Sodium 431 mg; Cholesterol 139 mg.

- 3 tablespoons unsalted butter or margarine
- 1 cup soft white bread crumbs
- 1 small yellow onion, minced
- ½ small sweet green pepper, cored, seeded, and finely chopped
- 1 pound crabmeat, flaked, shell and cartilage removed
- 1 egg, lightly beaten
- ½ cup low-calorie mayonnaise
- ½ teaspoon salt
- ¼ teaspoon cayenne pepper

1 Melt the butter in a heavy 10-inch skillet over moderate heat. In a small bowl, blend 1 tablespoon of the butter with ⅔ cup of the bread crumbs; set aside to use for topping. Add the onion and green pepper to the skillet; cook over moderate heat, stirring frequently, until soft — about 5 minutes.

2 In a medium-size bowl, mix the crabmeat, the remaining ⅓ cup bread crumbs, the egg, mayonnaise, salt, and cayenne pepper. Add the onion mixture and stir well. Spoon into 6 greased scallop shells or a greased, 1-quart au gratin dish; sprinkle with the buttered bread crumbs.

▽ At this point the Deviled Crab can be cooled, tightly covered, and *refrigerated* for up to 6 hours.

3 Preheat oven to 350° F. Bake 25 to 30 minutes or until brown and bubbling. Serves 6 as a first course.

*Scalloped Oysters*

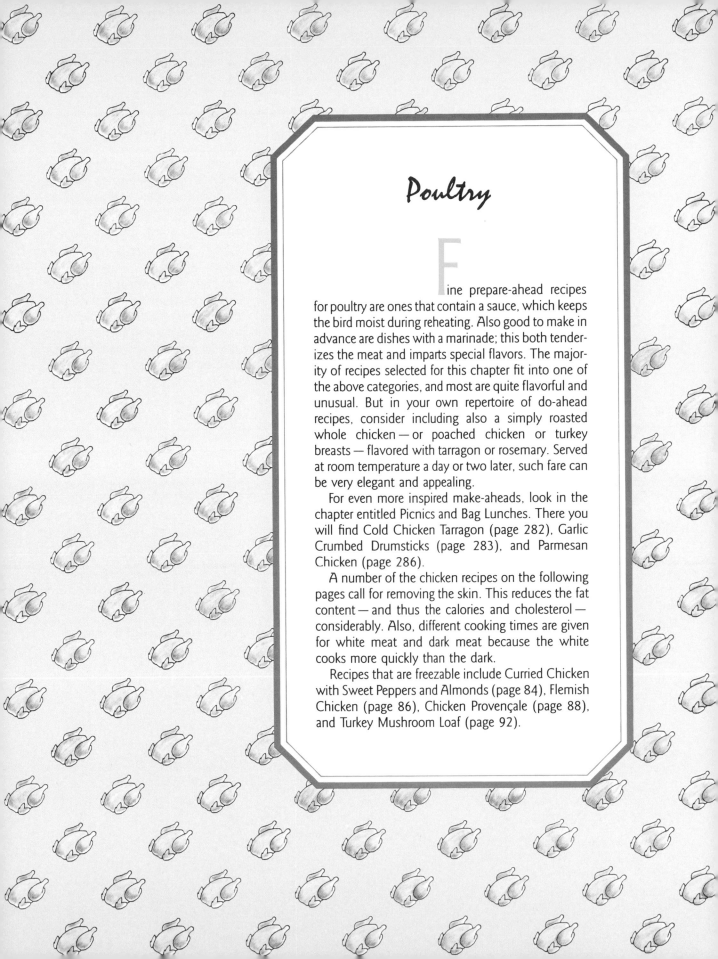

# Poultry

Fine prepare-ahead recipes for poultry are ones that contain a sauce, which keeps the bird moist during reheating. Also good to make in advance are dishes with a marinade; this both tenderizes the meat and imparts special flavors. The majority of recipes selected for this chapter fit into one of the above categories, and most are quite flavorful and unusual. But in your own repertoire of do-ahead recipes, consider including also a simply roasted whole chicken — or poached chicken or turkey breasts — flavored with tarragon or rosemary. Served at room temperature a day or two later, such fare can be very elegant and appealing.

For even more inspired make-aheads, look in the chapter entitled Picnics and Bag Lunches. There you will find Cold Chicken Tarragon (page 282), Garlic Crumbed Drumsticks (page 283), and Parmesan Chicken (page 286).

A number of the chicken recipes on the following pages call for removing the skin. This reduces the fat content — and thus the calories and cholesterol — considerably. Also, different cooking times are given for white meat and dark meat because the white cooks more quickly than the dark.

Recipes that are freezable include Curried Chicken with Sweet Peppers and Almonds (page 84), Flemish Chicken (page 86), Chicken Provençale (page 88), and Turkey Mushroom Loaf (page 92).

# Lime Chicken Stuffed with Goat Cheese

Per serving: Calories 596; Protein 45 g; Carbohydrate 1 g; Fat 66 g; Sodium 268 mg; Cholesterol 317 mg.

*This is a perfect dish for Sunday dinner or other special occasions. It's impressive looking, delicious, and surprisingly easy to make.*

- 4 ounces fresh mild goat cheese, such as Bucheron or Montrachet, or ricotta cheese that has been drained for 30 minutes in a sieve lined with cheesecloth
- 2 tablespoons unsalted butter or margarine, at room temperature
- 2 tablespoons minced parsley or cilantro (coriander leaves)
- ¼ teaspoon each salt and black pepper
- 1 whole roasting chicken (about 5 pounds)
- 2 tablespoons lime juice

1 In a small bowl, combine the cheese, butter, parsley, salt, and pepper. Carefully loosen the skin over the chicken breast with your fingertips and stuff the cheese mixture between the skin and the breast meat, arranging it in an even layer. Pull the skin back into place and truss the chicken.

▽ At this point the chicken can be stored. Transfer it to a platter, cover with plastic wrap, and *refrigerate* for up to 6 hours.

2 Preheat the oven to 475° F. Rub the chicken with the lime juice and set it breast side up on a rack in a roasting pan. Roast, uncovered, basting with the pan juices every 15 minutes, until golden — about 30 minutes.

3 Reduce the heat to 375° F and roast, uncovered, basting every 15 minutes, until the juices run clear when the chicken is pricked with a fork — 1 to 1¼ hours longer. Transfer the chicken to a serving platter and let rest for 15 minutes, covered loosely with aluminum foil, before carving. Accompany with Baked Carrot Ring filled with peas (page 173) or rice and wild rice cooked in chicken broth, and a salad of watercress and endive with a vinaigrette dressing. Serves 6.

# Piquant Chicken with Sausage and Raisins

Per serving: Calories 431; Protein 55 g; Carbohydrate 23 g; Fat 31 g; Sodium 672 mg; Cholesterol 133 mg.

- ⅓ cup dry sherry
- 3 tablespoons golden raisins
- 8 ounces chorizo or hot Italian sausage
- 6 chicken quarters (4½ to 5 pounds), skinned
- ½ teaspoon salt
- ¼ teaspoon black pepper
- ¼ cup vegetable oil
- 1 medium-size yellow onion, thinly sliced
- 2 serrano chilies, cored, seeded, and finely chopped, or ¼ cup finely chopped sweet red pepper plus ½ teaspoon red pepper flakes
- ¾ cup Chicken Stock (page 48) or canned chicken broth
- 1 can (1 pound) tomato purée
- 2 cloves garlic, minced
- ¼ cup fresh lime juice
- 4 medium-size carrots, peeled and cut into 2″ x ¼″ x ¼″ sticks
- 2 medium-size zucchini, cut into 2″ x ¼″ x ¼″ sticks
- 2 tablespoons toasted slivered almonds

1 In a small saucepan, bring the sherry to a simmer. Remove from the heat. Add the raisins, cover, and soak for 2 to 4 hours.

2 In a heavy 12-inch skillet, fry the chorizo over moderate heat until cooked through and slightly crisp — about 20 minutes. Transfer to a plate lined with paper toweling and let cool. Cut into ½-inch-thick slices.

3 Sprinkle the chicken quarters with the salt and black pepper. Heat the oil in a large, heavy, flameproof casserole over moderate heat for 1 minute. Add the chicken, 3 quarters at a time, and cook, turning, until no longer pink on the outside — about 10 minutes. Transfer to a platter lined with paper toweling and set aside.

4 Add the onion and chilies to the skillet, and sauté until tender — about 5 minutes. With a slotted spoon, remove the onion and chili mixture and set aside. Drain the fat from the skillet, leaving the crusty brown bits, and add the chicken stock. Bring the stock to a simmer over moderate heat, and cook, stirring and scraping up the brown bits, until the stock is reduced to ½ cup — 5 to 10 minutes.

5 Add the tomato purée and garlic to the stock. Cook, uncovered, over moderate heat for 5 minutes, stirring occasionally. Add the chorizo, lime juice, and chicken. Reduce heat to low, cover, and simmer for 15 minutes.

6 Strain the sherry into the chicken, setting the raisins aside. Then add the onion and chili mixture, carrots, and zucchini, and simmer, covered, 15 minutes longer or until the chicken is tender. Stir in the raisins.

*Lime Chicken Stuffed with Goat Cheese, and a Baked Carrot Ring (page 173), for those memorable get-togethers*

▽ At this point the chicken mixture can be cooled to room temperature and *refrigerated* in a tightly covered container for up to 2 days.

7 To serve, transfer the chicken and sauce to a serving bowl and sprinkle with the toasted almonds. Accompany with hot rice and a salad of lettuce, avocados, and oranges dressed with a tart vinaigrette. Makes 6 servings.

### Serving Later

Skim any fat from the the sauce. Transfer the chicken and sauce to a heavy 12-inch skillet. Cover and warm over moderately low heat, stirring occasionally, until the chicken is heated through and the sauce simmering — 20 to 25 minutes. Proceed as in Step 7.

# Andalusian Chicken

Per serving: Calories 418; Protein 39 g; Carbohydrate 23 g; Fat 15 g; Sodium 311 mg; Cholesterol 129 mg.

½ cup all-purpose flour
¼ teaspoon salt
⅛ teaspoon black pepper
1 chicken (3 to 3½ pounds), quartered and skinned
1 tablespoon olive or vegetable oil
1 tablespoon unsalted butter or margarine
5 shallots, minced, or 8 green onions, finely chopped
¼ cup Cognac
5 small tomatoes, peeled, seeded, and chopped, or 1 can (14½ ounces) crushed tomatoes
1 tablespoon minced tarragon or 1 teaspoon dried tarragon, crumbled
½ cup dry white wine or vermouth
½ cup Chicken Stock (page 48) or canned chicken broth
½ cup half-and-half
3 tablespoons minced parsley

1 In a shallow bowl or on a sheet of wax paper, combine the flour, salt, and pepper. Coat the chicken, shaking off any excess. Heat the oil and butter in a heavy 12-inch skillet over moderately high heat for 1 minute. Add the chicken and brown — about 10 minutes. Transfer to a platter lined with paper toweling.

2 Add the shallots to the skillet and cook, uncovered, over low heat, stirring occasionally, until soft — about 5 minutes. Add the Cognac, and cook

*Andalusian Chicken — the piquant flavors of sun-drenched Spain gently enhanced by tarragon*

2 minutes longer, stirring and scraping up the brown bits with a wooden spoon. Add the tomatoes and tarragon, increase heat to moderately high, and cook, uncovered, 5 minutes more.

3 Add the wine and chicken stock, increase the heat to high, and cook, uncovered, 5 minutes longer. Add the half-and-half and bring the sauce to a simmer. Reduce the heat to low, add the chicken thigh quarters, and cook, uncovered, 10 minutes more. Add the breast quarters, and cook, uncovered, 10 more minutes or until all of the chicken is tender and no longer pink at the bone.

▽ At this point the chicken and sauce can be cooled to room temperature and stored. Transfer to a tightly covered container and *refrigerate* for up to 3 days.

4 With a slotted spoon, transfer the chicken to a heated serving dish. Stir the parsley into the sauce and pour it over the chicken. Accompany with hot buttered rice mixed with green peas, and a salad of red leaf lettuce and sliced pears, topped with a dressing of sour cream and mayonnaise. Serves 4.

### Serving Later

Transfer the chicken and sauce to a heavy 12-inch skillet. Cover and warm over low heat, stirring occasionally, until the chicken is heated through and the sauce simmering — 15 to 20 minutes. Proceed as in Step 4.

# Chicken Marrakesh with Almonds and Chick Peas

Per serving: Calories 618; Protein 58 g; Carbohydrate 27 g; Fat 32 g; Sodium 909 mg; Cholesterol 155 mg.

- 1 cup blanched whole almonds (about 8 ounces)
- 3 tablespoons unsalted butter or margarine
- 1 chicken (3 to 3 1/2 pounds), quartered and skinned, or 4 chicken leg and thigh quarters, skinned
- 1 teaspoon each salt and white pepper
- 1/2 teaspoon ground ginger
- 1 cinnamon stick
- 1/4 teaspoon saffron threads, crumbled, or ground turmeric
- 2 medium-size Spanish onions, 1 finely chopped and 1 sliced thin
- 4 cups Chicken Stock (page 48), canned chicken broth, or water
- 1/4 cup minced parsley
- 1 cup canned chick peas, drained
- 2 tablespoons lemon juice, or to taste

1 In a small heavy saucepan, cover the almonds with cold water. Bring to a boil over moderate heat. Reduce the heat to its lowest point, cover, and simmer until soft — about 2 hours. Add more water, if necessary, to prevent scorching. Drain and set aside.

2 Melt the butter in a large, heavy, flameproof casserole over moderate heat. Add the chicken, salt, pepper, ginger, cinnamon stick, 1/8 teaspoon of the saffron, the finely chopped onion, and the chicken stock and bring to a simmer. Reduce the heat to low, cover, and cook for 30 minutes.

3 Add the sliced onion and the parsley, and cook, covered, 15 minutes longer. Uncover and cook for 15 minutes more or until the chicken is very tender and the flesh almost falling off the bones.

▽ At this point the chicken and sauce can be cooled to room temperature and *refrigerated* in the casserole for up to 24 hours.

4 With a slotted spoon, transfer the chicken to a heated serving platter and keep warm. Add the chick peas and bring to a boil over moderately high heat. Boil rapidly, uncovered, stirring occasionally, until the sauce is thickened — about 15 minutes.

5 Add the almonds and the remaining 1/8 teaspoon of saffron to the sauce and simmer, uncovered, for 2 minutes. Spoon the sauce over the chicken and sprinkle with the lemon juice. Accompany with hot rice or couscous and steamed carrots and zucchini. Serves 4.

### Serving Later

Skim any fat from the sauce. Cover and warm over low heat, stirring occasionally, until the chicken is heated through and the sauce simmering — about 20 minutes. Proceed as in Steps 4 and 5.

*Tip: Couscous, the ground golden heart of semolina wheat, is served in North Africa in place of rice or potatoes. When properly cooked it is very light and fluffy and an especially delicious foil for spicy foods. Look for it in health and specialty food stores, also in the better supermarkets.*

# Curried Chicken with Sweet Peppers and Almonds

Per serving: Calories 425; Protein 28 g; Carbohydrate 45 g; Fat 16 g; Sodium 489 mg; Cholesterol 66 mg.

- ¼ cup all-purpose flour
- 1 teaspoon salt
- ½ teaspoon black pepper
- 1 chicken (3 to 3½ pounds), skinned and cut into 8 serving-size pieces
- 3 tablespoons olive or vegetable oil
- 2 medium-size sweet green peppers, cored, seeded, and chopped
- 1 medium-size yellow onion, chopped
- 1 clove garlic, minced
- ⅓ cup minced parsley
- 1 tablespoon curry powder
- 1 can (28 ounces) tomatoes, with their liquid, chopped
- ½ cup currants or raisins
- ½ teaspoon each ground mace and dried thyme, crumbled
- 4 cups steamed white rice
- ½ cup toasted slivered almonds (about 2 ounces)

1 In a medium-size bowl, combine the flour, ½ teaspoon of the salt, and the black pepper. Dredge the chicken, shaking off any excess flour.

2 Heat the oil in a large flameproof casserole over moderately high heat for 1 minute. Add the chicken, and cook, uncovered, until no longer pink on the outside — about 5 minutes. With a slotted spoon, transfer to a platter lined with paper toweling.

3 To the casserole, add the green peppers, onion, garlic, parsley, and curry powder. Reduce the heat to moderate and cook, uncovered, stirring often, until the vegetables are soft — 7 to 10 minutes. Add the tomatoes, the remaining ½ teaspoon of salt, the currants, mace, and thyme. Increase

the heat to moderately high and bring the sauce to a simmer. Reduce the heat to low; simmer, covered, for 5 minutes.

4 Return the chicken to the casserole and simmer, covered, for 25 minutes. Check to see which pieces are done — fork tender and no longer pink on the inside. Transfer any cooked pieces to a platter and keep warm. Simmer 15 minutes more or until all of the chicken is done.

▽ At this point the curried chicken can be cooled to room temperature and stored. *Refrigerate* in the covered casserole for up to 2 days. Or *freeze* in a tightly sealed, labeled, 1-gallon freezer bag or freezable container for up to 1 month at 0° F.

5 Serve over the hot rice, garnished with the toasted almonds. Accompany with cucumbers topped by Yogurt Dressing (page 214). Serves 8.

## Serving Later

**From refrigerator:** Skim any fat from the sauce. Reheat, covered, over moderate heat, stirring occasionally, until the chicken is warmed through and the sauce simmering — 15 to 20 minutes. Serve as in Step 5. **From freezer:** Defrost the chicken overnight in the refrigerator. Transfer to a large flameproof casserole and reheat as above.

# Chicken in Yogurt with Indian Spices

Per serving: Calories 341; Protein 44 g; Carbohydrate 10 g; Fat 13 g; Sodium 506 mg; Cholesterol 135 mg.

- 2 tablespoons minced fresh ginger or 1½ teaspoons ground ginger
- ½ teaspoon salt
- ¼ teaspoon each ground coriander, ground cumin, and red pepper flakes
- ⅛ teaspoon each black pepper and ground cardamom
Pinch each ground cloves and ground cinnamon
- ¾ cup plain low-fat yogurt
- ¼ cup water
- 1 tablespoon lemon or lime juice
- 2 tablespoons peanut or vegetable oil
- 2 tablespoons ketchup
- 1 tablespoon honey
- 1 clove garlic, crushed
- 1 chicken (3 to 3½ pounds), skinned and cut into 8 serving-size pieces

1 In an electric blender or food processor, blend all the ingredients except the chicken until well combined — about 1 minute.

2 Arrange the chicken pieces in a single layer in a shallow, glass or ceramic bowl and pour the marinade over them. Cover and refrigerate for at least 12 hours but preferably 24, turning the pieces at least once.

3 Preheat the oven to 425° F. With a slotted spoon, transfer the chicken to a 13″ x 9″ x 2″ baking dish, arranging the pieces in a single layer; set the marinade aside. Bake, uncovered, for 15 minutes.

4 Lower the oven temperature to 375° F. Spoon the marinade over the chicken, cover the dish with foil, and bake 10 minutes longer. By this time the breast pieces should be done — no longer pink on the inside. Transfer any cooked pieces to a heated serving platter and keep warm.

5 Brush the remaining pieces with the marinade, re-cover with the foil, and cook until done — 15 to 20 minutes longer. Transfer the remaining chicken and the sauce to a heated platter. Accompany with hot rice cooked with raisins and diced dried apricots (see Tip, page 85), also with zucchini sticks sautéed in Dill Butter (page 222). Serves 4.

Tip: An easy way to dress
up rice is to add ¼ cup of diced
dried fruit with each cup of rice
when the cooking water
comes to a boil. Cook as directed
and serve with butter. Raisins,
currants, and diced dates, figs,
and apricots are all good.

# Himalayan Chicken

Per serving: Calories 243; Protein 42 g;
Carbohydrate 1 g; Fat 7 g; Sodium 170 mg;
Cholesterol 133 mg.

*Start this spicy dish the day before
you'd like to serve it because it must
marinate for at least 12 hours.*

⅓ cup vegetable oil
¼ cup white wine vinegar
⅓ cup lime or lemon juice
2 teaspoons soy sauce
1½ teaspoons paprika
2 cloves garlic, minced
1 tablespoon grated fresh
ginger or 1 teaspoon
ground ginger

¾ teaspoon ground cumin
½ teaspoon dry mustard
1 chicken (3 pounds), skinned
and cut into 8 serving-size
pieces

1 In a shallow dish just large enough
to contain the chicken in a single
layer, combine the oil, vinegar, lime
juice, soy sauce, paprika, garlic, ginger,
cumin, and mustard.

2 With a sharp knife, score the chick-
en at ¼-inch intervals. Place the
pieces in the dish in a single layer,
spoon the marinade over them, and
cover with plastic wrap. Refrigerate for
at least 12 hours and up to 24 hours,
turning the pieces frequently.

3 Preheat the oven to 350° F. With a
slotted spoon, transfer the chicken
pieces to a 13" x 9" x 2" baking
dish, arranging them in a single
layer. Set the marinade aside.

4 Bake the chicken, uncovered, for 10
minutes, then turn and baste with
the marinade. Bake, uncovered, 10
minutes longer. By this time the breasts
should be done — no longer pink on
the inside. Transfer any cooked pieces
to a heated serving platter; keep warm.

5 Turn the remaining chicken pieces,
baste again with the marinade, and
bake, uncovered, until all of the pieces
are done — 15 to 20 minutes more.
Transfer to the heated platter. Accompany with hot rice, and Sautéed Cucumbers (page 176). Serves 4.

*Chicken in Yogurt with
Indian Spices and fruited rice
(see Tip, above), a meal fit for a mogul
or anyone else special*

# Flemish Chicken Stew with Barley

Per serving: Calories 477; Protein 45 g; Carbohydrate 38 g; Fat 16 g; Sodium 923 mg; Cholesterol 272 mg.

- 1 chicken (2½ to 3 pounds), cut into 8 pieces
- 1 teaspoon salt
- ½ teaspoon white pepper
- 2 tablespoons unsalted butter or margarine
- 2 leeks, sliced ½ inch thick
- 2 medium-size carrots, peeled and sliced ½ inch thick
- 2 stalks celery, with leaves, sliced ½ inch thick
- 1 medium-size yellow onion, thinly sliced
- 6 sprigs parsley
- 2 sprigs fresh thyme or ½ teaspoon dried thyme, crumbled
- 5 whole cloves
- ¼ teaspoon ground nutmeg
- 4 cups Chicken Stock (page 48) or canned chicken broth
- 1 quart water
- ½ cup medium-pearl barley
- 2 egg yolks
- 2 tablespoons heavy cream
- 2 tablespoons lemon juice

*Optional garnishes:*
- 2 tablespoons minced parsley
- 4 thin slices lemon

1 Sprinkle the chicken pieces with ½ teaspoon of the salt and the pepper. Set aside. Melt the butter in a large, heavy, flameproof casserole over low heat. Remove from the heat and add the leeks, carrots, celery, and onion, arranging them in a bed. Place the parsley and thyme sprigs on top; then add the chicken, arranging the pieces in a single layer. Sprinkle the cloves and nutmeg over all. Cover and cook over moderately low heat for 10 minutes.

2 Add the chicken stock and simmer, covered, 30 to 35 minutes longer or until the chicken is tender. Remove from the heat and, with a slotted spoon, transfer the chicken to a platter. Let cool.

3 Strain the stock into a large saucepan or flameproof casserole, reserving the vegetables and discarding the parsley sprigs, thyme sprigs, and cloves. Skim any fat from the stock.

4 When the chicken is cool enough to handle, remove and discard the skin and bones. Cut the chicken into bite-size pieces. Add the chicken and vegetables to the stock.

▽ At this point the chicken stew can be cooled to room temperature and stored. *Refrigerate* in the covered casserole for up to 3 days. Or *freeze* in a labeled, 1-gallon freezer bag or freezable container for up to 1 month at 0° F.

5 In a medium-size saucepan, bring the water to a boil. Add the barley and the remaining ½ teaspoon salt. Cover and cook for 40 to 45 minutes or until the barley is tender. Drain, recover, and keep warm.

6 Bring the stock to a simmer over low heat. Meanwhile, in a small bowl, beat together the egg yolks, cream, and lemon juice with a fork. Gradually beat a ladleful of the simmering stock into the egg mixture. Then stir the mixture back into the casserole. Cook, uncovered, over low heat, stirring frequently, until slightly thickened — about 5 minutes.

7 To serve, transfer the barley to a large soup tureen or casserole and spoon the chicken stew over it. Garnish with the minced parsley and the lemon slices, if desired. Serve in soup plates and accompany with pumpernickel bread. Serves 4 to 6.

### Serving Later

**From refrigerator:** Reheat the stew over moderate heat until warmed through — 15 to 20 minutes. Proceed as in Steps 5, 6 and 7. **From freezer:** Thaw the stew overnight in the refrigerator. Transfer to a large flameproof casserole and reheat as directed above.

*Tip: Leeks, like spinach, have a tendency to be very gritty and should be carefully washed. First cut off the roots and the tops, leaving about 7 inches of leek. Soak for about 10 minutes. Then rinse several times under running water, fanning out the layers to remove any grit near the base. Or slice the leeks first according to recipe directions, put them in a colander, and wash thoroughly under running water.*

# Colombian Chicken and Potato Stew

Per serving: Calories 324; Protein 31 g; Carbohydrate 38 g; Fat 6 g; Sodium 520 mg; Cholesterol 81 mg.

*An authentic Ajiaco, as this dish is called in Colombia, is made from 6 to 12 varieties of potatoes. This modified version calls for 3.*

- 1 chicken (2½ to 3 pounds), skinned and cut into serving-size pieces
- 4 cups Chicken Stock (page 48) or canned chicken broth
- 1 cup water
- 1 large yellow onion, chopped
- 4 green onions, white part sliced; green part sliced and set aside
- 1 bay leaf
- ¼ teaspoon dried thyme, crumbled

*A dish that sticks to your ribs on cold windy days — Flemish Chicken Stew with Barley*

¼ cup minced cilantro (coriander leaves) or ¼ cup minced parsley plus ¼ teaspoon dried cilantro

2 medium-size baking potatoes, peeled and cubed

2 medium-size all-purpose potatoes, peeled and cubed

3 small new or red-skinned potatoes, peeled and quartered

2 small ears corn, cut into 1 ½-inch lengths

¾ teaspoon salt

½ cup half-and-half

2 tablespoons capers (optional)

1 small avocado, peeled, cubed, and sprinkled with lemon juice, for garnish (optional)

1 In a large flameproof casserole, bring the chicken, chicken stock, water, onion, white part of the green onions, bay leaf, thyme, 2 tablespoons of the cilantro, and the baking potatoes to a boil over moderately high heat. Reduce the heat to low, cover, and simmer for 45 minutes or until the dark meat is no longer pink on the inside.

2 With a slotted spoon, transfer the chicken to a platter. When cool enough to handle, remove and discard the bones, then cut the meat into bite-size chunks and set aside.

3 Meanwhile, add the all-purpose potatoes and new potatoes to the stock and return to a boil over moderately high heat. Cover, reduce the heat to moderately low, and simmer for 15 minutes. Add the corn and the chicken, re-cover, and simmer 15 minutes longer or until the corn is tender.

▽ At this point the stew can be cooled to room temperature and stored. *Refrigerate* in the casserole for up to 2 days.

4 Stir in the salt, half-and-half, the remaining 2 tablespoons of cilantro, the green onion tops, and the capers, if desired. Cover and bring to a simmer over moderately low heat. Serve garnished with the avocado, if desired. Accompany with garlic bread and a salad of romaine lettuce and sliced tomatoes. Serves 6.

### Serving Later

Bring to a simmer over moderately low heat. Proceed as in Step 4.

# Chicken Provençale

Per serving: Calories 285; Protein 41 g; Carbohydrate 9 g; Fat 8 g; Sodium 378 mg; Cholesterol 99 mg.

- 3 whole boneless, skinless, chicken breasts (about 12 ounces each), split
- 3 tablespoons all-purpose flour
- 1/4 teaspoon each salt and black pepper
- 4 teaspoons vegetable oil
- 1 medium-size yellow onion, chopped
- 1 medium-size sweet green pepper, cored, seeded, and chopped
- 1 clove garlic, minced
- 1 can (14 1/2 ounces) tomatoes, drained
- 1/2 cup white wine or Chicken Stock (page 48)
- 1/4 teaspoon dried thyme, crumbled
- 1/2 cup sliced pitted black olives
- 2 tablespoons minced parsley for garnish (optional)

1 Place each chicken breast between two sheets of waxed paper and flatten slightly with a meat mallet, a small heavy skillet, or a rolling pin.

2 In a shallow bowl, combine the flour, salt, and pepper and dredge the chicken, shaking off any excess. Heat the oil in a heavy 12-inch skillet over moderate heat for 1 minute. Add the chicken and brown on one side only for 5 minutes. Transfer to a platter lined with paper toweling.

3 To the skillet, add the onion, green pepper, and garlic, and cook, uncovered, until slightly softened — about 3 minutes. Add the tomatoes, wine, and thyme and bring to a boil. Add the chicken breasts, uncooked side down. Reduce the heat to low, and simmer, uncovered, for 8 minutes. Stir in the olives.

▽ At this point the Chicken Provençale can be cooled to room temperature and stored. *Refrigerate* in a tightly covered container for up to 2 days. Or *freeze* in a tightly sealed, labeled, 1-gallon freezer bag or 2-quart microwave-safe casserole for up to 1 month at 0° F.

4 Garnish with the minced parsley, if desired, and serve with buttered noodles, steamed broccoli, and a salad of chick peas, grated carrots, and sliced fennel with a creamy vinaigrette dressing. Serves 6.

## Serving Later

**From refrigerator:** Transfer to a heavy 12-inch skillet, cover, and heat over moderately low heat until warmed through — about 15 minutes. Serve as in Step 4. **From freezer:** Transfer to a heavy 12-inch skillet, cover, and heat over moderately low heat for 20 minutes. Turn the chicken breasts. Increase the heat to moderate, re-cover, and cook 10 minutes more or until warmed through. Serve as in Step 4. **To microwave:** Cover the casserole with plastic wrap vented at one side. Microwave on *Low* (30% power) for 20 minutes. Rotate the casserole 90 degrees, stir, re-cover, and microwave on *Low* (30% power) 10 minutes more. Microwave on *High* (100% power) for 2 minutes. Rotate the casserole 90 degrees and microwave on *High* (100% power) 2 minutes more. Serve as in Step 4.

# South-of-the-Border Chicken Rolls

Per serving: Calories 540; Protein 52 g; Carbohydrate 23 g; Fat 27 g; Sodium 1106 mg; Cholesterol 102 mg.

*A Mexican-style version of the classic Russian dish — Chicken Kiev — this recipe makes great party fare.*

- 4 whole boneless, skinless, chicken breasts (about 12 ounces each), split
- 1 can (7 ounces) green chilies, drained and minced
- 8 slices (1 ounce each) Monterey Jack cheese
- 3/4 cup fine dry bread crumbs
- 1/3 cup grated Parmesan cheese
- 1 1/2 tablespoons chili powder
- 1/4 teaspoon ground cumin, or to taste
- 1/4 teaspoon each salt and black pepper
- 6 tablespoons unsalted butter or margarine, melted
- 4 cups Spicy Tomato Sauce (page 216)
- 2 tablespoons minced cilantro (coriander leaves) or parsley for garnish (optional)

1 Place each piece of chicken between two sheets of wax paper and gently pound to a 1/4-inch thickness with a meat mallet, a small heavy skillet, or a rolling pin. Put 2 tablespoons (approximately) minced chilies and 1 slice of Monterey Jack cheese on each breast, leaving a narrow border all around. Roll up the breasts tightly, tucking in the ends, and secure with toothpicks or wire skewers.

2 In a medium-size bowl, combine the bread crumbs, Parmesan cheese, chili powder, cumin, salt, and black pepper. Coat each chicken roll with the butter, then the bread crumb mixture, gently patting crumbs onto the breasts until covered. Cover the chicken rolls with plastic wrap and chill for at least 4 hours or overnight.

3 Preheat the oven to 400° F. Arrange the chicken rolls seam side down in a greased 13″ x 9″ x 2″ baking dish and bake, uncovered, for 20 minutes or until golden. Meanwhile, in a covered medium-size saucepan, bring the Spicy Tomato Sauce to a simmer over moderate heat, stirring occasionally.

4 Transfer the chicken rolls to a heated serving platter and remove the toothpicks. Spoon some of the Spicy Tomato Sauce over each roll and garnish with the cilantro, if desired. Accompany with hot rice and a mixed green salad. Serves 8.

## Cheese-Stuffed Chicken Rolls

Per serving: Calories 298; Protein 48 g; Carbohydrate 8 g; Fat 7 g; Sodium 651 mg; Cholesterol 179 mg.

| | |
|---|---|
| 2 | medium-size tomatoes, peeled and coarsely chopped |
| ½ | cup tomato juice |
| 1 | small sweet green pepper, cored, seeded, and finely chopped |
| 1 | small yellow onion, finely chopped |
| 1 | clove garlic, minced |
| ½ | teaspoon salt |
| ⅛ | teaspoon black pepper |
| ¼ | teaspoon dried oregano, crumbled |
| 2 | whole skinless, boneless chicken breasts (about 12 ounces each), split |
| ½ | cup low-fat cottage or ricotta cheese |
| 1 | egg yolk |
| 1 | teaspoon minced parsley |
| 1 | teaspoon grated Parmesan cheese |
| ½ | cup shredded mozzarella cheese |

1 Preheat the oven to 350° F. In a medium-size saucepan, bring the tomatoes, tomato juice, green pepper, onion, garlic, salt, black pepper, and oregano to a boil over medium heat. Reduce the heat to low, cover, and simmer, stirring occasionally, until thickened — about 25 minutes.

2 Meanwhile, place each chicken breast between two sheets of wax paper and gently pound to a ¼-inch thickness with a meat mallet, a small heavy skillet, or a rolling pin.

3 In a small bowl, combine the cottage cheese, egg yolk, parsley, and Parmesan cheese. Spread 1 tablespoon (approximately) of the mixture in the center of each chicken piece, leaving a ½-inch border all around. Roll up and set aside.

4 Spoon half the tomato sauce into an 8-inch pie plate or baking dish. Arrange the chicken rolls on top, seam sides down. Pour the remaining tomato sauce over them and sprinkle with the shredded mozzarella.

▽ At this point the chicken rolls can be stored. Cover with plastic wrap and *refrigerate* for up to 6 hours.

5 Bake, uncovered, for 40 to 45 minutes or until the chicken is cooked through. Set one roll on each dinner plate and spoon some of the sauce over it. Accompany with buttered spinach noodles and a salad of arugula with a garlic vinaigrette dressing. Serves 4.

*Cheese-Stuffed Chicken Rolls, a culinary delight that beggars description*

*Sweet and Sour Chicken Chunks, a restaurant favorite that you can make in your own kitchen*

# Chicken Escabeche

Per serving: Calories 494; Protein 41 g; Carbohydrate 15 g; Fat 30 g; Sodium 383 mg; Cholesterol 99 mg.

*This colorful and piquant chicken dish from Chile is best served at room temperature. It's great for a picnic.*

- 4 medium-size carrots, peeled and sliced ½ inch thick
- 2 medium-size yellow onions, quartered
- 1 large sweet red pepper, cored, seeded, and cut into strips 1 inch wide
- ½ cup olive or vegetable oil
- ¼ cup tarragon or white wine vinegar
- ¼ cup dry white wine
- ½ teaspoon salt
- 8 black peppercorns
- 2 whole boneless, skinless, chicken breasts (about 12 ounces each), split

1 In a large flameproof casserole or a heavy 10-inch skillet, bring the carrots, onions, red pepper, olive oil, vinegar, white wine, salt, and peppercorns to a boil over moderate heat. Cover, reduce the heat to moderately low, and simmer for 30 minutes.

2 Add the chicken, increase the heat to moderately high, and bring the liquid, uncovered, to a boil. Cover, reduce the heat to moderately low, and simmer for 10 to 12 minutes or until the chicken is no longer pink at the center. Cool to room temperature, cover tightly, and refrigerate for at least 4 hours. Will keep for up to 2 days.

3 Let the chicken come to room temperature. Transfer it with some of the liquid to a serving platter. Accompany with Potatoes Roasted with Garlic and Rosemary (page 180) and a salad of avocados and tomatoes. Serves 4.

# Sweet and Sour Chicken Chunks

Per serving: Calories 591; Protein 43 g; Carbohydrate 46 g; Fat 23 g; Sodium 770 mg; Cholesterol 99 mg.

*The sauce for this favorite Chinese dish can be prepared a couple of days in advance; the chicken, up to 4 hours ahead and refrigerated. Last-minute preparation is minimal.*

- 6 tablespoons peanut or vegetable oil
- 1 medium-size yellow onion, cut into thin wedges
- 1 large sweet red or sweet green pepper, cored, seeded, and cut into thin strips
- 2 medium-size carrots, peeled and thinly sliced
- ¼ cup firmly packed brown sugar or 3 tablespoons honey
- ¼ cup rice wine vinegar, white wine vinegar, or cider vinegar
- 4 teaspoons ketchup
- 1 can (8 ounces) pineapple chunks, with juice drained and reserved
- 2 tablespoons soy sauce
- ⅛ teaspoon each cayenne pepper and ground ginger
- 2 whole boneless, skinless chicken breasts (about 12 ounces each), cut into pieces 1½ inches square
- 2 egg whites lightly beaten with 2 teaspoons water and a pinch of salt
- ⅔ cup cornstarch
- 2 teaspoons cornstarch, blended with ¼ cup cold water to form a paste

1 Heat 2 tablespoons of the peanut oil in a heavy 12-inch skillet over moderately high heat for 1 minute. Add the onion, red pepper, and carrots, and cook, stirring constantly, until lightly browned — about 5 minutes. Stir in the sugar, vinegar, ketchup, reserved pineapple juice, soy sauce, cayenne, and ginger. Reduce the heat to low and simmer, uncovered, stirring occasionally, until the flavors have blended — about 8 minutes.

▽ At this point the sauce can be cooled to room temperature and *refrigerated* in a tightly covered container for up to 3 days.

2 Dip each chicken piece first in the egg white mixture and then roll in the cornstarch to coat, shaking off any excess. Set aside.

3 Heat the remaining 4 tablespoons of the peanut oil in a heavy 10-inch skillet over moderately high heat for 1 minute. Add the chicken, and cook, uncovered, stirring occasionally, until crisp and browned — 4 to 5 minutes. With a slotted spoon, transfer to a platter lined with paper toweling.

4 In the heavy 12-inch skillet, bring the sauce to a simmer over moderate heat. Add the cornstarch paste, reduce the heat to low, and cook, stirring constantly, until thickened and clear — about 3 minutes. Add the chicken and pineapple chunks and simmer, uncovered, until heated through — about 3 minutes longer. Transfer to a heated serving platter and accompany with hot rice garnished with sliced green onions. Serves 4.

## Serving Later

Prepare the chicken as in Steps 2 and 3. In a heavy 12-inch-skillet, bring the sauce to a simmer over moderate heat and proceed as in Step 4.

*Tip: The vegetables for many Oriental dishes, or other recipes that call for them to be cut up, can be prepared up to a day in advance, sealed in airtight containers or plastic bags, and refrigerated until needed.*

# Herbed Turkey Roll

Per serving: Calories 285; Protein 30 g; Carbohydrate tr; Fat 18 g; Sodium 244 mg; Cholesterol 110 mg.

- 4 tablespoons (½ stick) unsalted butter or margarine, at room temperature
- 1 tablespoon each minced rosemary, sage, and parsley or 1 teaspoon each dried rosemary, sage, and parsley, crumbled
- ½ teaspoon each salt and black pepper
- 1 turkey breast (about 3 pounds), skinned, boned, and butterflied

1 In a small bowl, combine the butter, rosemary, sage, parsley, and ¼ teaspoon each of the salt and pepper.

2 Lay the turkey breast flat, smooth-side down, and sprinkle with the remaining ¼ teaspoon each salt and pepper. Spread all but 1 tablespoon of the herb butter over the turkey, roll it up tightly into a sausage shape, and tie securely with string. Rub the outside of the turkey roll with the remaining 1 tablespoon herb butter and wrap tightly with aluminum foil.

▽ At this point the turkey roll can be *refrigerated* for up to 8 hours before cooking.

3 Preheat the oven to 400° F. Place the foil-wrapped turkey roll in a baking pan and bake for 50 minutes.

▽ At this point, if the turkey roll is to be served cold, it can be cooled to room temperature and *refrigerated* for up to 2 days.

4 Remove the foil and slice ½ inch thick. Serve hot, accompanied by warm rolls, and Baked Carrot Ring (page 173) filled with peas or Baked Acorn Squash with Cranberries (page 183).

5 Or cool to room temperature, garnish with black olives, and tomato and cucumber slices, if desired, and accompany with potato or macaroni salad. Serves 6 to 8.

## Serving Later

Serve at room temperature, garnished as in Step 5. Do not reheat.

# Turkey Mushroom Loaf

Per serving: Calories 321; Protein 36 g; Carbohydrate 15 g; Fat 13 g; Sodium 465 mg; Cholesterol 178 mg.

*If you prefer to serve this versatile loaf cold, increase the thyme to ¾ teaspoon and the parsley to ½ cup.*

- 2 tablespoons unsalted butter or margarine
- 1 small yellow onion, minced
- 1 small sweet red pepper, cored, seeded, and minced
- 6 ounces mushrooms, trimmed and sliced
- ½ teaspoon each salt and black pepper
- 1¼ pounds ground turkey
- 1 clove garlic, minced
- ¼ teaspoon dried thyme, crumbled
- ½ cup fine dry bread crumbs
- 1 egg, beaten lightly
- ¼ cup milk
- 3 tablespoons minced parsley
- ½ cup shelled and blanched pistachio nuts (about 6 ounces unshelled) (optional)

1 Melt the butter in a heavy 10-inch skillet. Add the the onion and red pepper, and cook, stirring, over moderate heat for 3 minutes. Add the mushrooms and ¼ teaspoon each of the salt and black pepper, and cook, uncovered, stirring frequently, until the mushrooms have released almost all

their liquid — about 5 minutes. Transfer the mixture to a large bowl and let cool to room temperature.

2 Combine the turkey, garlic, thyme, bread crumbs, egg, milk, parsley, the remaining salt and pepper, and the pistachios, if desired, with the mushroom mixture. Shape the mixture into a round loaf about 8 inches in diameter.

▽ At this point the loaf can be stored. Transfer to a buttered, 9-inch pie plate, cover with plastic wrap, and *refrigerate* overnight. Or *freeze*, wrapped in heavy-duty aluminum foil and labeled, for up to 2 months at 0° F.

3 Preheat the oven to 350° F. Bake, uncovered, in a buttered 9-inch pie plate for 45 to 60 minutes or until the juices run clear. Serve hot, accompanied by Basic Brown Sauce with Madeira (page 221) and mashed, buttered sweet potatoes, or at room temperature accompanied by Gazpacho Aspic with Avocado Dressing (page 212) and Herbed Rice Salad (page 209). Serves 4.

## Serving Later

**From refrigerator:** Proceed as in Step 3. **From freezer:** Preheat the oven to 325° F. Place the foil-wrapped loaf on a buttered, 9-inch pie plate and bake 40 minutes. Remove the foil and bake 20 to 30 minutes more or until the juices run clear. Serve as in Step 3. **To microwave:** Remove the aluminum foil and place the loaf on a 9-inch, microwave-safe, glass pie plate. Cover with plastic wrap vented at one side. Microwave on *Low* (30% power) for 15 minutes; turn the plate 90 degrees. Microwave on *Low* (30% power) 10 minutes more. Microwave on *High* (100% power) for 6 minutes; turn the plate 90 degrees. Microwave on *High* for 12 minutes more or until juices run clear. Let stand 5 minutes. Serve as in Step 3.

# Turkey Teriyaki Kebabs

Per serving: Calories 201; Protein 22 g;
Carbohydrate 19 g; Fat 4 g; Sodium 189 mg;
Cholesterol 95 mg.

**For the marinade:**
- ⅓   cup white wine vinegar
- ¼   cup low-sodium soy sauce
- 2   tablespoons sugar
- 1   teaspoon minced fresh ginger
- 2   cloves garlic, minced
- ½   teaspoon hot chili oil or hot red pepper sauce, or to taste

**For the kebabs:**
- 1   pound fresh ground turkey
- 1   egg, beaten lightly
- ½   cup fine dry bread crumbs
- 1   large carrot, finely shredded
- 1   small onion, finely chopped
- ⅛   teaspoon each black pepper and Chinese 5-spice powder
- 12   small white onions
- 1   large sweet green pepper, cored, seeded, and cut into 12 pieces about 1 inch square
- 12   medium-size mushrooms
- 12   cherry tomatoes

1 To prepare the marinade: In a 10" x 6" x 2" casserole, combine the vinegar, soy sauce, sugar, ginger, garlic, and chili oil. Set aside.

2 To prepare the turkey kebabs: In a large bowl, mix the turkey, egg, bread crumbs, carrot, onion, pepper, and 5-spice powder. Shape the mixture into 36 (1¼-inch) balls.

3 Add the turkey balls to the marinade, gently turning them until well coated. Cover with plastic wrap and refrigerate for at least 2 hours but no more than 12, turning occasionally.

4 Preheat the broiler or grill. With a slotted spoon, remove the turkey balls from the marinade and thread onto six 8-inch skewers. While skewering the kebabs, soak the onions, green pepper, mushrooms, and cherry tomatoes in the marinade. Then thread six more skewers with 2 pieces of each vegetable. Reserve the marinade.

5 Lay the kebabs and vegetables on a lightly oiled broiler pan and broil 6 inches from the heat for 5 minutes. Brush with marinade, turn, and broil 5 minutes more. To grill, cook about 6 inches above medium hot coals for 10 minutes, brushing with the marinade and turning occasionally. Transfer to dinner plates and serve with herbed rice and garlic bread. Serves 6.

*Herbed Turkey Roll, the traditional holiday fowl given a new slant and an exciting presentation*

# Marinated Rock Cornish Hens

Per serving: Calories 369; Protein 61 g; Carbohydrate 1 g; Fat 11 g; Sodium 305 mg; Cholesterol 204 mg.

- 2 Rock Cornish hens (about 1½ pounds each), split
- ⅓ cup soy sauce
- ¼ cup vegetable oil
- ¼ cup brandy or dry sherry
- 3 cloves garlic, sliced
- 2 tablespoons sesame seeds, lightly toasted
- 1 1-inch piece fresh ginger, peeled and thinly sliced
- 1 tablespoon brown sugar
- 1 tablespoon fresh lime juice

1 Lay the Cornish hens skin side down in a glass dish just large enough to hold them in a single layer. Prick each hen several times with a fork.

2 In an electric blender or food processor, blend the soy sauce, oil, brandy, garlic, sesame seeds, ginger, sugar, and lime juice until smooth — about 1 minute. Pour the marinade over the hens, cover loosely with aluminum foil, and refrigerate for at least 6 hours and up to 24 hours, turning occasionally.

3 Preheat the oven to 400° F. With a slotted spoon, transfer the hens to a 13" x 9" x 2" baking dish, arranging them in a single layer, skin side up. Reserve the marinade. Roast, uncovered, basting with the marinade every 15 minutes, until the juices run clear and the meat is no longer pink on the inside — 35 to 40 minutes. Serve hot, accompanied by a casserole of white rice, wild rice, and mushrooms, chutney, and green beans with dill. Or serve at room temperature, accompanied by Pasta Rings in Piquant Cucumber Sauce (page 158) and baked tomatoes. Serves 4.

*Marinated Rock Cornish Hens — a succulent repast in an elegant setting — what better way to celebrate a special occasion?*

# Meats

The most suitable meat recipes for cooking ahead of time are those that contain a sauce. Should a meal be delayed, such dishes can be put on "hold," and they won't dry out. In fact, sauced pot roasts and stews are usually improved by reheating because the flavors become better blended and often more concentrated.

Marinated meats, of course, *must* be started a day or two before they are to be served. Since marinades give you more flavor and a tenderer product for your money, they are worth the extra effort it may require to plan ahead.

One of the most versatile of make-ahead meat recipes is the meat loaf. It can be served hot or cold as an entrée or a sandwich filling. It can also be frozen in the raw state, so you can prepare two or three at a time and have one available at a moment's notice. See page 110 for three delectable meatloaf recipes.

Broiled or roasted meats generally should not be reheated: their texture toughens and their flavor becomes less palatable. The best thing to do with leftovers in this category is to slice them and serve at room temperature, with a nippy sauce, a salad, and some warm bread.

# Pot-Roasted Brisket

Per serving: Calories 407; Protein 56 g; Carbohydrate 25 g; Fat 27 g; Sodium 142 mg; Cholesterol 170 mg.

- 1 boneless beef brisket (2½ to 3 pounds)
- 1 clove garlic, bruised
- 2 tablespoons unsalted butter or margarine
- 2 teaspoons vegetable oil
- 1 medium-size yellow onion, finely chopped
- 1 medium-size carrot, peeled and chopped
- 1 small tomato, peeled, seeded, and chopped
- 1 teaspoon minced fresh thyme or ¼ teaspoon dried thyme, crumbled
- 2 teaspoons minced fresh basil or ½ teaspoon dried basil, crumbled
- 1 tablespoon minced parsley
- 1½ cups Beef Stock (page 48) or canned beef broth
- 4 small potatoes, peeled, halved, and cooked
- 2 medium-size carrots, peeled, quartered, and cooked
- 1 pound fresh pumpkin, peeled, cut into 1½-inch pieces, and cooked
  Minced parsley for garnish

1 Preheat the oven to 350° F. Pat the meat dry with paper toweling and rub it with the bruised garlic. Mince the garlic and reserve.

2 Heat the butter and oil in a large flameproof casserole over moderately high heat. Add the meat, brown it on all sides — about 4 minutes — and transfer it to a platter. Add the onion to the casserole and stir for 1 minute. Add the carrot, tomato, and reserved garlic. Reduce the heat to moderate and stir for 3 minutes. Add the thyme, basil, parsley, and stock. Bring the mixture to a simmer and add the browned meat.

3 Cover the casserole, transfer to the oven, and bake for 2½ to 3 hours or until the meat is tender. While cooking, periodically skim the fat from the surface of the stock.

▽ At this point the brisket can be cooled to room temperature and stored. *Refrigerate* in the covered casserole for up to 3 days. For freezing, cut it in half. *Freeze* in a 2½-quart microwave-safe casserole or labeled, 1-gallon freezer bag for up to 1 month at 0° F.

4 Add the cooked vegetables to the casserole; simmer 5 to 10 minutes longer or until the vegetables are heated through. Garnish with the parsley before serving. Hot rolls and a green salad go well with this dish. Serves 6.

## Serving Later

**From refrigerator:** Bring to a simmer, covered, over moderate heat — about 15 minutes. Reduce the heat to moderately low and cook 15 to 20 minutes more or until heated through. Proceed as in Step 4. **From freezer:** Thaw in the refrigerator overnight. Transfer to a covered flameproof casserole and proceed as above. **To microwave:** Heat in a covered microwave-safe casserole on *Low* (30% power) for 15 minutes. Rearrange the meat, cover again, and then heat on *Low* (30% power) another 10 to 15 minutes, until defrosted. Microwave, covered, on *High* (100% power) for 10 to 15 minutes. Rearrange the meat again, add the vegetables, cover, and microwave on *High* (100% power) 2 to 5 minutes longer or until the vegetables are hot.

*Tip: To give a faint garlic flavor to meat or to a salad bowl, rub it with a bruised garlic clove or one cut in half to release its essence. Bruise garlic by slamming it against the cutting board with the side of a heavy knife, then remove the skin.*

# Pot Roast Venetian-Style

Per serving: Calories 323; Protein 32 g; Carbohydrate 2 g; Fat 19 g; Sodium 113 mg; Cholesterol 123 mg.

- 2 stalks celery, coarsely chopped
- 2 cloves garlic, minced
- 6 whole peppercorns
- 1 teaspoon salt
- 2 whole cloves
- 1 sprig fresh rosemary or 2 teaspoons dried rosemary, crumbled
- ⅛ teaspoon ground cinnamon
- 1½ cups red wine vinegar
- 3½ pounds beef eye round, bottom round, or rump roast
- 6 tablespoons (¾ stick) unsalted butter or margarine
- 1 small yellow onion, finely chopped
- ½ teaspoon black pepper
- ¼ cup Marsala wine
- ¼ cup dry white wine

1 In a large, glass or ceramic bowl, mix the celery, garlic, peppercorns, salt, cloves, rosemary, cinnamon, and vinegar. Add the beef roast, cover tightly, and refrigerate for 12 hours, turning occasionally.

2 Transfer the beef from the marinade to a platter lined with paper toweling; blot as dry as possible. Strain the marinade through a large sieve or a cheesecloth-lined colander. Reserve the vegetables; discard the marinade.

3 Melt the butter in a large flameproof casserole over moderate heat. Add the onion and reserved vegetables. Cook, uncovered, stirring frequently, for 5 minutes or until soft. Sprinkle the meat with pepper and add it to the casserole. Stir in the Marsala and white wine. Cover the casserole with buttered aluminum foil or wax paper and then with the lid. Reduce the heat to low and cook for about 2½ hours or until the meat is fork tender.

4 Transfer the meat to a heated platter and slice about ½ inch thick. Purée the liquid in an electric blender or food processor for 30 seconds or until smooth. Return the sauce to the casserole and heat through, covered, over low heat. Pour the sauce over the pot roast and serve right away with glazed carrots and boiled new potatoes. Makes 8 servings.

*Pot Roast Venetian-Style and Polenta Pie (page 158) take you on a culinary excursion.*

*Steak Cubes Southwestern-Style served with Mexican Cheese-Rice Casserole (page 152) — delectable snap and sassiness*

# Marinated London Broil

Per serving: Calories 228; Protein 27 g;
Carbohydrate 1 g; Fat 12 g; Sodium 157 mg;
Cholesterol 83 mg.

*Equally good served hot or cold, this meat is excellent for a buffet dinner.*

- 2 tablespoons vegetable oil
- 1 medium-size yellow onion, chopped
- 2 cloves garlic, minced
- ¼ cup minced parsley
- 1 tablespoon brown sugar
- 1 teaspoon each ground ginger and allspice
- 1 cup low-sodium beef broth or Beef Stock (page 48)
- ⅓ cup soy sauce
- 3 tablespoons red wine vinegar
- 2 pounds boneless beef, chuck or round, in one piece (about 1½ inches thick)

1 Heat the oil in a medium-size saucepan over moderate heat. Add the onion, and sauté until soft — about 5 minutes. Add all the remaining ingredients except the beef and bring to a simmer. Remove the marinade from the heat and cool.

▽ At this point the marinade can be stored. *Refrigerate* in a tightly covered, glass or ceramic container for up to 1 week. *Freeze* in a labeled, freezable container or 1-quart freezer bag for up to 1 month at 0° F.

2 Place the beef in a glass or ceramic dish just large enough to hold it. Pour the marinade over the meat, cover with plastic wrap, and refrigerate for 12 to 24 hours, turning the meat occasionally. Transfer the beef to a platter and bring to room temperature; discard the marinade.

3 Preheat a broiler pan or barbecue grill. Broil or grill the beef 3 to 4 inches from the heat for 8 to 10 minutes on each side. Let the beef cool for 5 minutes, then slice it at an angle, ¼ inch thick. Serve with Potatoes Roasted with Garlic and Rosemary (page 180), and slices of tomatoes and Bermuda onions. Serves 6.

## Serving Later

**From freezer:** Thaw the marinade in the refrigerator overnight. Proceed as in Steps 2 and 3.

# Steak Cubes Southwestern-Style

Per serving: Calories 529; Protein 43 g;
Carbohydrate 16 g; Fat 29 g; Sodium 620 mg;
Cholesterol 124 mg.

- 1 cup dry white wine
- 3 tablespoons red wine or red wine vinegar
- 2 canned green chilies, drained and finely chopped, or to taste
- 1 tablespoon brown sugar
- ½ teaspoon salt
- 1 clove garlic, minced
- 2 pounds lean beef round, cut into 1½-inch cubes and pierced with a fork
- 1 tablespoon vegetable oil
- ½ cup low-sodium beef broth or Beef Stock (page 48)
- ¼ cup chili sauce or ketchup
- 1 medium-size yellow onion, thinly sliced
- ½ cup pitted black olives

*Garnishes:*
- 2 medium-size tomatoes, quartered
  Avocado wedges, sprinkled with lime juice
  Parsley sprigs

1 In a medium-size, glass or ceramic bowl, mix the white wine, red wine, chilies, sugar, salt, garlic, and meat. Refrigerate overnight or for up to 2 days, stirring occasionally.

2 Preheat the oven to 325° F. Drain the meat, reserving 1 cup of the marinade, and pat dry. Heat the oil in a large flameproof casserole over moderately high heat for 1 minute. Add the meat in batches; brown on all sides — about 4 minutes per batch. Add the marinade, the broth, chili sauce, and onion; bring to a simmer. Cover, transfer to the oven, and cook for 1¼ to 1½ hours or until the meat is tender.

▽ At this point the meat can be cooled to room temperature and stored. *Refrigerate* in the casserole for up to 3 days. *Freeze* in a lined, 2-quart, microwave-safe casserole (see Tip, page 138) or in a labeled, 1-gallon freezer bag for up to 1 month at 0° F.

3 Return the casserole to high heat and stir in about half of the olives. Cook, uncovered, until the liquid is reduced and lightly thickened. With a slotted spoon transfer the meat and olives to a heated platter, and spoon some of the sauce over them. Garnish with the remaining olives, the tomatoes, avocado, and parsley. Serve the remaining sauce separately. A good accompaniment is Mexican Cheese-Rice Casserole (page 152). Serves 4.

## Serving Later

**From refrigerator:** Reheat in the covered casserole over moderately low heat, stirring occasionally, until simmering — 15 to 20 minutes. Proceed as in Step 3. **From freezer:** Thaw in the refrigerator overnight. Transfer to a flameproof casserole and proceed as above. **To microwave:** Heat in the covered microwave-safe casserole on *Low* (30% power) for 10 minutes; stir and break apart the meat. Microwave, covered, on *Low* (30% power) 10 to 13 minutes more, until defrosted. Microwave on *High* (100% power) for 15 minutes or until bubbling, stirring after 8 minutes. Let stand for 3 minutes. Garnish and serve as in Step 3.

# Italian Beef Rolls

Per serving: Calories 361; Protein 32 g;
Carbohydrate 13 g; Fat 21 g; Sodium 752 mg;
Cholesterol 84 mg.

1¼  pounds lean top round, cut
     into four slices, each about
     ¼ inch thick
1    clove garlic, bruised
⅓   cup freshly grated Parmesan
     cheese
⅓   cup minced parsley
1    cup soft bread crumbs
½   teaspoon salt
¼   teaspoon black pepper
¼   cup pine nuts (optional)
2    tablespoons olive oil
1    can (14½ ounces) tomatoes,
     puréed with their liquid
2    tablespoons tomato paste
½   teaspoon each dried thyme
     and basil, crumbled

1 Between 2 sheets of wax paper,
pound each slice of meat as thin as
possible, using a meat mallet, a small
heavy skillet, or a rolling pin. Rub the
meat with the garlic.

2 In a medium-size bowl, mix the
cheese, parsley, bread crumbs, salt,
pepper, and pine nuts, if desired.
Spread the mixture on the meat slices,
dividing it evenly. Roll up each piece
and secure with toothpicks or string.

3 Heat the olive oil in a medium-size
flameproof casserole over moderately high heat. Add the meat rolls and
brown on all sides for 6 to 8 minutes.

Add the tomatoes, tomato paste,
thyme, and basil and bring to a boil.
Reduce the heat to low, cover, and
simmer for 1¼ to 1½ hours or until the
meat rolls are fork tender. Or transfer to
an au gratin dish, cover with aluminum
foil, and bake for 1¼ to 1½ hours in a
preheated 350° F oven.

▽ At this point the meat rolls can be
cooled to room temperature and
stored. *Refrigerate* in the casserole or
au gratin dish for up to 2 days. *Freeze* in
a labeled, tightly covered container for
up to 1 month at 0° F.

4 Transfer the meat rolls to heated
plates. Accompany with steamed
broccoli or Savory Spinach Balls (page
184) and orzo (a pasta that resembles
rice). Serves 4.

*Italian Beef Rolls enfolding a savory blend of cheese, pine nuts, and a subtle mixture of herbs*

**From freezer:** Defrost the beef rolls in the refrigerator overnight. Preheat the oven to 400° F. Bake in a covered casserole for 35 to 40 minutes or until heated through. Serve as in Step 4.

# Vegetable-Stuffed Flank Steak

Per serving: Calories 439; Protein 44 g; Carbohydrate 10 g; Fat 24 g; Sodium 1252 mg; Cholesterol 196 mg.

*In this colorful steak roll, East meets West: It is a delicious example of Spanish influence on Filipino cuisine.*

1½ pounds flank steak, butterflied
2 tablespoons soy sauce
1 tablespoon fresh lime juice
1 clove garlic, minced
2 slices bacon
2 carrots, julienned
4 ounces pepperoni, julienned
2 hard-cooked eggs
2 dill pickles (each about 4 inches long), julienned
2 tablespoons olive oil
2 medium-size yellow onions, coarsely chopped
2 medium-size tomatoes, coarsely chopped
2 bay leaves
2 cups Beef Stock (page 48) or canned beef broth
¼ teaspoon black pepper

1 Place the flank steak between 2 sheets of wax paper or plastic wrap, and with a meat mallet, a small heavy skillet, or a rolling pin, pound it to a ⅜-inch thickness. In a small bowl, combine the soy sauce, lime juice, and garlic; using a pastry brush, coat both sides of the steak with this mixture.

2 Lay the bacon slices on the steak across the grain, about 2 inches from one end. Arrange the carrots, pepperoni, eggs, and pickles in roughly a 3-inch-wide mound on top of the bacon, leaving a 1½-inch border at each side. Fold the steak's short flap completely over the filling; fold the long flap over the short one to form a roll, and pull it snug. Fasten with toothpicks or tie with string at 2-inch intervals. Secure the sides, too, to keep the filling in.

3 Heat the oil in a large flameproof casserole over high heat for 1 minute. Add the rolled steak and cook for about 12 minutes, browning on all sides. Add the onions and tomatoes, reduce the heat to low, and simmer, uncovered, for 10 minutes. Add the bay leaves, beef stock, and pepper, and cover. Barely simmer, turning the rolled steak once or twice, for about 1½ hours or until the meat can be pierced easily with a fork. Transfer to a heated platter, cover with aluminum foil, and keep warm. Raise the heat to high and cook the sauce, uncovered, for about 12 minutes or until it is reduced by one-quarter. Cool the sauce slightly, transfer to an electric blender or food processor, and purée.

▽ At this point the stuffed steak and the sauce can be cooled to room temperature and stored separately. Wrap the steak in heavy-duty aluminum foil. Transfer the sauce to a tightly sealed container or to a labeled, 1-quart freezer bag. *Refrigerate* both for up to 2 days. *Freeze* the steak and the sauce for up to 3 months at 0° F.

4 Return the sauce to the casserole, set over low heat, and bring to a simmer. Untie the stuffed steak, slice it 2 inches thick, and arrange it to display the colorful mosaic of meat, eggs, and vegetables. Pass the sauce separately. Potatoes with Parsley Butter (page 223) go well with this dish. Serves 6.

**From refrigerator:** Preheat the oven to 400° F. Set the stuffed steak in a baking dish and heat for 1 hour and 10 minutes. Reheat the sauce in a small covered saucepan over moderately low heat, stirring occasionally, until simmering — about 10 minutes. Serve as in Step 4. **From freezer:** Thaw in the refrigerator overnight. Proceed as directed above. **To microwave:** Unwrap the frozen steak roll and place it in a 10-inch, microwave-safe pie plate. Cover loosely with plastic wrap and microwave on *Low* (30% power) for 40 minutes, rotating the pie plate 90 degrees twice. Microwave on *High* (100% power) for 20 minutes, rotating 90 degrees once. (If using a microwave meat thermometer, it should read 170° F.) Loosen the sauce from the freezer bag by running warm water over the bag; put the frozen block of sauce in a small saucepan. Cover and warm over moderately low heat until defrosted — about 10 minutes. Continue heating, stirring occasionally, another 10 minutes or until simmering. Serve as in Step 4.

*Tip: To julienne (cut in long thin strips) such foods as carrots, pickles, and pepperoni, first cut them in half lengthwise. Place the flat surface of one half against the cutting board and cut it into slices of desired thickness, usually ⅛ to ¼ inch; repeat with the second half. Stack the slices and cut again to make uniform strips.*

# Beef with Chestnuts

Per serving: Calories 671; Protein 40 g;
Carbohydrate 37 g; Fat 37 g; Sodium 378 mg;
Cholesterol 174 mg.

*Hearty fare for robust appetites, this is
an ideal dish to serve after a day of
winter sports.*

| | |
|---|---|
| 3 | tablespoons vegetable oil |
| 2½ | pounds lean boneless beef chuck, cut into 1½-inch cubes |
| 1 | medium-size yellow onion, sliced |
| 1 | clove garlic, minced |
| 2 | tablespoons all-purpose flour |
| 1¼ | cups hard cider or beer |
| 1½ | cups low-sodium beef broth or Beef Stock (page 48) |
| 2 | teaspoons ketchup |
| ½ | teaspoon each dried thyme and marjoram, crumbled |
| ½ | teaspoon salt |
| ¼ | teaspoon black pepper |
| 1 | can (16 ounces) whole chestnuts, drained |
| 2 | tablespoons minced parsley |

**1** Preheat the oven to 325° F. Heat the oil in a large flameproof casserole over moderate heat for 1 minute. Meanwhile, pat the beef dry with paper toweling. Add the beef in batches to the casserole, stirring occasionally to brown it on all sides — about 4 minutes per batch. Using a slotted spoon, transfer the browned beef to a platter lined with paper toweling.

**2** Add the onion and garlic to the casserole, and cook, uncovered, stirring well, until the onion is soft — about 5 minutes. Gradually stir in the flour to make a smooth paste; cook, stirring frequently, for 2 minutes. While stirring well, add the cider, broth, ketchup, thyme, marjoram, salt, and pepper. Return the beef to the casserole, cover, and bring to a simmer. Place the covered casserole in the oven and bake for 1½ hours or until the beef is fork tender.

▽ At this point the beef can be cooled to room temperature and stored. *Refrigerate* in the covered casserole for up to 2 days.

**3** Stir in the chestnuts and cook, uncovered, 10 minutes longer. Sprinkle with the parsley before serving. Noodles and steamed Brussels sprouts are good accompaniments. Serves 6.

## Serving Later

Remove the beef from the refrigerator and allow it to come to room temperature before stirring in the chestnuts and transferring it to a preheated 325° F oven. Cook and serve as in Step 3.

# Jugged Beef

Per serving: Calories 676; Protein 44 g;
Carbohydrate 33 g; Fat 37 g; Sodium 491 mg;
Cholesterol 180 mg.

*This stew, which freezes well, has a rich, gamy flavor. The recipe calls for jugging the meat — stewing it in an earthenware casserole — but a glass or enameled casserole will do as well.*

| | |
|---|---|
| 2½ | pounds lean boneless beef chuck, cut into 1½-inch cubes |
| ½ | teaspoon each salt and black pepper |
| ¼ | cup all-purpose flour |
| ¼ | pound slab bacon, cut into small cubes |
| 1 | tablespoon vegetable oil |
| 3 | large yellow onions, coarsely chopped |
| 1 | pound mushrooms, trimmed and thinly sliced |
| 1 | pound carrots, peeled and cut into 2-inch chunks |
| ½ | teaspoon each dried rosemary and marjoram, crumbled |
| ¼ | teaspoon dried thyme, crumbled |
| ⅛ | teaspoon ground nutmeg |
| 1 | cinnamon stick |
| 1 | cup dry red wine |
| ¼ | cup port, Madeira, or dry sherry |
| ½ | cup whole or jellied cranberry sauce or tart currant jelly |
| 2 | tablespoons minced parsley |

**1** Season the beef with the salt and pepper, dredge it in the flour, and set aside. Cook the bacon, uncovered, in a 12-inch skillet over moderately high heat until brown — about 10 minutes. Using a slotted spoon, transfer the bacon to paper toweling; set aside.

**2** Working in batches, brown the beef in the bacon drippings over moderately high heat — about 4 minutes per batch. Transfer to a platter or bowl. Discard the drippings and wipe out the skillet with paper toweling.

**3** Preheat the oven to 300° F. Heat the oil in the skillet over moderate heat for 1 minute. Add the onions and mushrooms, and cook, uncovered, until the onions are limp and lightly browned — about 10 minutes. Stir in the carrots, rosemary, marjoram, thyme, nutmeg, and cinnamon stick; cook, stirring, 2 minutes longer. Transfer to a large earthenware or other ovenproof casserole.

**4** Return the beef to the skillet. Add the wine, port, and cranberry sauce and bring to a boil. Transfer all these ingredients to the casserole. Cover and bake in the oven for 2 to 2½ hours or until the meat is fork tender. Stir in the reserved bacon bits.

▽ At this point the jugged beef can be cooled to room temperature and stored. *Refrigerate* in the casserole

*Jugged Beef, a full-bodied dish to satisfy the appetites of the most impassioned snow-fort architects and bobsledders*

for up to 3 days. *Freeze* in a labeled freezable container or 1-gallon freezer bag for up to 3 months at 0° F.

5 Remove the casserole from the oven. Stir in the parsley. Serve with boiled new potatoes or egg noodles and whole grain bread. Serves 6.

### Serving Later

**From refrigerator:** Reheat in a pre-heated 350° F oven for 50 minutes or until warmed through. Proceed as in Step 5. **From freezer:** Thaw overnight in the refrigerator. Transfer to a casserole, cover, and reheat as directed above. **To microwave:** Transfer to a microwave-safe casserole, cover, and heat on *Low* (30% power) for 25 minutes. Break the frozen pieces apart with a wooden spoon. Microwave, covered, on *Low* (30% power) until defrosted — about 12 minutes longer. Stir well, re-cover, and microwave on *High* (100% power) until bubbling — about 12 minutes. Let stand for 3 minutes; proceed as in Step 5.

# Beef and Mushroom Ragout

Per serving: Calories 568; Protein 37 g;
Carbohydrate 11 g; Fat 40 g; Sodium 444 mg;
Cholesterol 169 mg.

    2  tablespoons olive oil
 1 ½  pounds lean boneless beef
       chuck, cut into 1-inch cubes
    2  medium-size yellow onions,
       coarsely chopped
    1  clove garlic, minced
   10  ounces mushrooms, sliced
    4  teaspoons paprika
  ⅛   teaspoon dried thyme,
       crumbled
  ½   cup dry white wine
    1  cup Beef Stock (page 48) or
       canned beef broth
  ½   teaspoon salt
  ¼   teaspoon black pepper
  ½   cup sour cream

1 Heat the oil in a medium-size
flameproof casserole over moderate
heat for 1 minute. Add half the beef
and brown it on all sides — about 4
minutes. With a slotted spoon, transfer
to a platter lined with paper toweling.
Repeat with the remaining beef. Add
the onions, garlic, and mushrooms to
the skillet; sauté for 6 to 8 minutes or
until the onions are soft and the mushrooms have released their liquid.

2 Add the paprika, thyme, wine,
stock, salt, pepper, and the
browned beef. Cover and simmer for
1 ¼ hours. Uncover and simmer, stirring occasionally, 30 minutes more or
until the sauce has thickened.

▽ At this point the ragout can be
cooled to room temperature and
stored. *Refrigerate* in the casserole for
up to 3 days. *Freeze* in a labeled
freezable container or in a 1-gallon
freezer bag for up to 3 months at 0° F.

3 Stir in the sour cream over low heat,
and cook, uncovered, for 3 minutes
or just until heated through. Do not
allow to boil or the sauce will curdle.

Serve over steamed rice or egg noodles,
accompanied by green peas. Serves 4.

## Serving Later

**From refrigerator:** Reheat in the covered casserole over low heat for 15 to
20 minutes, stirring occasionally. Proceed as in Step 3. **From freezer:** Follow directions above but allow 40
minutes for reheating. **To microwave:**
Transfer the contents of the freezer bag
to a medium-size microwave-safe casserole. Microwave, covered, on *Low*
(30% power) for 20 minutes, stirring
once. Microwave, covered, on *High*
(100% power) for 7 minutes or until
heated through. Stir in the sour cream
and serve immediately.

# Orange-Cumin Beef Stew

Per serving: Calories 497; Protein 36 g;
Carbohydrate 16 g; Fat 32 g; Sodium 535 mg;
Cholesterol 157 mg.

*This is a delicious, full-bodied stew,
enhanced by an appealing mixture of
exotic flavors.*

    3  tablespoons vegetable oil
    3  pounds lean boneless chuck
       for stew, cut into 1-inch
       cubes
       Grated rind of 1 orange
       (about 1 tablespoon)
    1  cup orange juice
    1  cup low-sodium beef broth
       or Beef Stock (page 48)
    1  can (6 ounces) tomato paste
  ¼   cup red wine vinegar
    2  tablespoons brown sugar
    3  cloves garlic, minced
 4 ½  teaspoons ground cumin
    2  teaspoons dried oregano,
       crumbled
    1  teaspoon ground allspice
    1  bay leaf
    1  teaspoon salt
  ¼   teaspoon black pepper
    8  ounces small white onions

    1  pound small mushrooms,
       trimmed, or larger
       mushrooms, trimmed and
       halved

1 Heat the oil in a heavy 12-inch
skillet over moderately high heat for
1 minute. Working in batches, brown
the beef on all sides — about 4 minutes
per batch. Transfer the browned beef to
a large flameproof casserole.

2 Stir in the orange rind, orange juice,
broth, tomato paste, vinegar, sugar,
garlic, cumin, oregano, allspice, bay
leaf, salt, and pepper. Bring to a boil,
then reduce the heat to moderately
low. Simmer, covered, for 2 hours or
until fork tender. Add the onions during the last 30 minutes and the mushrooms during the last 15 minutes.

▽ At this point the stew can be
cooled to room temperature and
stored. *Refrigerate* in a tightly covered
container for up to 3 days. *Freeze* in a
labeled, 1-gallon freezer bag for up to 4
months at 0° F.

3 Serve with sautéed red peppers or
Creamy Broccoli Purée (page 188),
and noodles or rice. Serves 8.

## Serving Later

**From refrigerator:** Reheat in a covered
flameproof casserole over low heat for
20 to 30 minutes or in a preheated
350° F oven for the same length of
time. Proceed as in Step 3. **From freezer:** Thaw in the refrigerator overnight
and proceed as above. **To microwave:**
Transfer to a large, covered, microwave-safe casserole and microwave on
*Low* (30% power) for 30 minutes.
Break the frozen pieces apart with a
wooden spoon and stir well. Microwave, covered, on *Low* (30% power)
until defrosted — about 15 minutes
more. Stir, cover, and microwave on
*High* (100% power) until bubbling —
about 8 minutes. Let stand for 3 minutes and proceed as in Step 3.

# Skewered Beef with Peanut Sauce

Per serving: Calories 401; Protein 41 g; Carbohydrate 6 g; Fat 24 g; Sodium 456 mg; Cholesterol 101 mg.

*This modified Indonesian specialty can be served for a snack as well as a meal. Make the sauce ahead, if you like, and refrigerate it overnight.*

- 3 tablespoons peanut oil
- 1 large yellow onion, finely chopped
- 1 2-inch piece fresh ginger, peeled and finely chopped
- 2 cloves garlic, minced
- ½ cup creamy-style peanut butter
- ½ cup water
- 2 tablespoons soy sauce
- 1 teaspoon sesame oil
- 1 teaspoon cayenne pepper
- 2 tablespoons brown sugar
- 1 tablespoon grated lemon rind
- 2¼ pounds boneless sirloin or sirloin tip steak, cut into 1½-inch cubes

*For the peanut sauce:*
- ½ cup chunky peanut butter
- ½ cup water
- ½ teaspoon cayenne pepper
- 1 tablespoon grated fresh ginger or 1 teaspoon ground ginger
- 4 teaspoons soy sauce
- 6 green onions, trimmed and julienned
  Chopped peanuts for garnish
- 1 can (8 ounces) whole, peeled water chestnuts

1 Heat the peanut oil in a 10-inch skillet over moderate heat for 1 minute. Add the onion, chopped ginger, and garlic. Cook, stirring, for 5 minutes or until the onion is soft. Stir in the peanut butter, water, soy sauce, sesame oil, cayenne pepper, and brown sugar. Simmer, stirring, for 3 minutes. Stir in the lemon rind, then transfer to a medium-size bowl. Cool to room temperature. Toss the meat in the marinade until well coated. Cover tightly with plastic wrap and refrigerate overnight. Will keep for up to 2 days.

2 Meanwhile, prepare the sauce: In a small bowl, stir together the peanut butter, water, cayenne pepper, ginger, soy sauce and green onions. Sprinkle with the chopped peanuts.

3 Preheat the broiler. Stir the water chestnuts into the marinade, then thread them alternately with the meat on metal skewers. Arrange on a broiler pan. Broil 4 to 6 inches from the heat, turning once, for 6 to 8 minutes or until the meat is springy to the touch. Transfer the skewers to dinner plates and pass the sauce separately. Serve with Indonesian Rice (page 152) and a green salad. Serves 6.

*Skewered Beef with Peanut Sauce, here for two, with Indonesian Rice (page 152) — a Spice Islands' breeze*

# Fiesta Burgers

Per serving: Calories 326; Protein 45 g; Carbohydrate 1 g; Fat 15 g; Sodium 383 mg; Cholesterol 137 mg.

*Make up a double batch of these and keep them in the freezer for quick last-minute meals.*

- 1 tablespoon bacon drippings, lightly salted butter, or margarine
- 2 tablespoons minced green onion
- 1 clove garlic, minced
- 2 tablespoons each minced sweet green pepper and minced sweet red pepper
- ½ teaspoon dried oregano, crumbled
- 1¼ pounds lean ground beef round
- ½ teaspoon salt
- ¼ teaspoon black pepper
- 1 tablespoon vegetable oil

1 Heat the bacon drippings in a heavy 10-inch skillet over moderately low heat for 1 minute. Add the green onion, garlic, green and red pepper, and oregano. Reduce the heat to its lowest point, cover the skillet, and cook for 5 minutes. Remove from the heat and cool to room temperature. Thoroughly combine the skillet mixture with the beef, salt, and pepper and shape into 4 round patties.

▽ At this point the burgers can be stored. *Refrigerate*, individually wrapped in aluminum foil or plastic wrap, for up to 12 hours. *Freeze*, individually wrapped and labeled in heavy-duty aluminum foil or plastic wrap, for up to 1 month at 0° F.

2 Heat the vegetable oil in a 10-inch skillet over moderate heat. Add the burgers, and cook, uncovered, turning them once, for 10 to 15 minutes, depending on desired doneness.

3 Serve as is or with a dollop of Mexican Tomato Sauce (page 217) and accompany with French-fried potatoes. Or pop the burgers into warmed, poppy seed buns and top with lettuce and your favorite condiments. Coleslaw rounds out the meal. Serves 4.

### Serving Later

**From freezer:** Heat 1 tablespoon of vegetable oil in a 10-inch skillet over high heat. Cook the frozen burgers, uncovered, for 5 minutes on each side or until brown. Reduce the heat to moderately low, cover, and cook for 15 to 20 minutes, depending on desired doneness, turning them once. Serve as in Step 4. **To microwave:** Place the unwrapped frozen burgers on a microwave-safe plate, cover with plastic wrap vented at one side, and microwave on *Low* (30% power) until defrosted — about 10 minutes. Microwave on *High* (100% power) for 6 to 8 minutes, depending on desired doneness; turn the burgers once and rotate the plate 90 degrees twice during this stage. Serve as in Step 4. Microwaved burgers do not have the crisp, browned finish that grilled burgers do. If you prefer your burgers crisp, use the skillet method above.

# Avocado-Stuffed Burgers

Per serving: Calories 527; Protein 55 g; Carbohydrate 18 g; Fat 27 g; Sodium 877 mg; Cholesterol 198 mg.

*These are plenty spicy and perfect for a teenager's party or for a patio supper.*

- 1¼ pounds lean ground beef round
- ⅓ cup fine dry bread crumbs
- 1¼ cups tomato juice
- 1 egg, beaten lightly
- 1 small yellow onion, finely grated
- 2 teaspoons chili powder
- ½ teaspoon dried oregano, crumbled
- ½ teaspoon salt
- 4 teaspoons Worcestershire sauce
- 1 small ripe avocado, peeled, pitted, and thinly sliced
- ¾ cup shredded Monterey Jack cheese
- 1 can (4 ounces) green chilies, drained and chopped

1 Preheat the oven to 400° F. In a medium-size bowl, combine the meat, bread crumbs, ½ cup of the tomato juice, the egg, onion, 1½ teaspoons of the chili powder, the oregano, salt, and Worcestershire sauce.

2 Divide the meat mixture into 8 equal portions and form each into a patty about ⅜ inch thick and 4 inches in diameter.

3 Place 4 patties in a lightly greased, 9″ x 9″ x 2″ baking pan. In the center of each, place ¼ of the avocado slices, ¼ of the shredded cheese, and 1 tablespoon of the green chilies. Top each patty with a second one and firmly seal the edges.

▽ At this point the stuffed hamburgers can be stored. Cover the baking pan tightly with plastic wrap. *Refrigerate* for up to 8 hours.

4 Bake the hamburgers, uncovered, for 15 to 20 minutes or until they remain only slightly pink on the inside. Meanwhile, in a small saucepan bring the remaining tomato juice, chili powder, and chilies to a boil over moderate heat. Lower the heat and simmer, uncovered, for 15 minutes.

5 Transfer the hamburgers to a heated platter and spoon the sauce over them. Serve on hamburger buns, if desired. Good accompaniments are refried beans and a green salad. Serves 4.

*Molten Monterey Jack cheese cascades from the steaming center of a freshly baked Avocado-Stuffed Burger.*

# Blue Cheese–Stuffed Burgers

Per serving: Calories 396; Protein 52 g;
Carbohydrate 2 g; Fat 19 g; Sodium 772 mg;
Cholesterol 219 mg.

1¼  pounds lean ground beef
     round
1    egg, beaten lightly
1    small yellow onion, finely
     chopped
1    teaspoon Worcestershire
     sauce (optional)
½    teaspoon each salt and black
     pepper
4    ounces blue cheese

1 In a large bowl, combine the beef, egg, onion, Worcestershire sauce, if desired, salt, and pepper. Divide the meat into 8 equal portions and form each portion into a patty ⅜ inch thick and 4 inches in diameter.

2 Divide the cheese into 4 equal portions and form each into a flat, round cake about the size of a silver dollar. Place a cheese patty in the center of each of 4 meat patties. Top with a second meat patty and seal the edges.

▽ At this point the stuffed burgers can be stored. Arrange them in a single layer on a wax-paper-lined tray; cover with plastic wrap or aluminum foil. *Refrigerate* overnight. *Freeze*, indi-vidually wrapped and labeled in heavy-duty aluminum foil or plastic wrap, for up to 1 month at 0° F.

3 Broil the burgers 3 inches from the heat, allowing 5 minutes on each side for rare, 6 minutes for medium, and 7 for well done. Serve with Zucchini Slaw (page 196). Serves 4.

### Serving Later

**From freezer:** To cook the frozen burgers, follow the directions for Fiesta Burgers (page 106) and serve as in Step 3. **To microwave:** Follow the microwave directions for Fiesta Burgers (page 106) and serve as in Step 3.

# European Meatballs in Cream Sauce with Dill

Per serving: Calories 493; Protein 30 g; Carbohydrate 13 g; Fat 35 g; Sodium 692 mg; Cholesterol 147 mg.

*To vary this dish, omit the heavy cream and stir in ½ cup sour cream or yogurt during the last minute of cooking; do not let the sauce boil or it will curdle. European meatballs can also be made in a 1-inch size and served in a chafing dish as an appetizer.*

    8   ounces each lean ground
        beef round and lean ground
        pork or veal shoulder
    1   small yellow onion, finely
        chopped
    ½   teaspoon each salt and black
        pepper
    ¼   teaspoon each dried thyme
        and marjoram or oregano,
        crumbled
    ¼   teaspoon ground nutmeg
    1½  cups fresh bread crumbs
    ½   cup water

*For the sauce:*
    2   tablespoons butter
    2   tablespoons all-purpose flour
    1½  cups Beef Stock (page 48),
        canned beef broth, or beef
        consommé
    2   tablespoons snipped dill or 2
        teaspoons dried dill weed
    ½   cup heavy or light cream

*Garnishes:*
        Paprika
        Snipped dill or minced
        parsley

1 Preheat the broiler. In a bowl, mix the beef, pork, onion, salt, pepper, thyme, marjoram, nutmeg, bread crumbs, and water with your hands.

2 Shape the mixture into 2-inch balls and arrange about ½ inch apart on a lightly oiled broiler pan. Broil 4 inches from the heat for 4 minutes on each side or until lightly browned.

3 To prepare the sauce, melt the butter in a heavy 10-inch skillet over moderate heat. Blend in the flour to make a smooth paste, and cook, stirring, for 2 to 3 minutes. Gradually add the stock, stirring until thickened — 3 to 4 minutes. Transfer the meatballs to the sauce.

▽ At this point the meatballs and sauce can be cooled to room temperature and stored. *Refrigerate* in a tightly covered container for up to 24 hours. *Freeze* in a labeled, 1-gallon freezer bag or in a 2-quart microwave-safe casserole, tightly covered, for up to 3 months at 0° F.

4 Stir in the dill and reduce the heat to its lowest point; simmer, covered, for 15 minutes, basting the meatballs several times. Add the cream and stir until the sauce is smooth — about 1 minute. Transfer the meatballs and sauce to a heated serving dish. Add a blush of paprika and the dill. Serve with peas and potatoes with Garlic Butter (page 223) or buttered egg noodles tossed with poppy seeds. Serves 4.

## Serving Later

**From refrigerator:** Heat in a covered 10-inch skillet over moderate heat for 10 minutes or until simmering; stir occasionally. Proceed as in Step 4.
**From freezer:** Heat in a covered 10-inch skillet over low heat until simmering — about 20 minutes. Stir occasionally and, if necessary, add a few tablespoons of water to prevent sticking. Proceed as in Step 4. **To microwave:** In a covered microwave-safe casserole, heat on *High* (100% power) for 10 minutes. Stir in the dill and turn the meatballs. Microwave on *High* (100% power) 6 minutes more. Add the cream; stir until the sauce is smooth. Microwave on *High* (100% power) 1 minute longer. Serve as in Step 4.

*Tip: You can grind uncooked meats in a food processor if you first cube the meat, then freeze it slightly. Process for 8 to 10 seconds until finely chopped.*

# Fresh Sausage Patties

Per patty: Calories 287; Protein 15 g; Carbohydrate tr; Fat 25 g; Sodium 220 mg; Cholesterol 69 mg.

*For those desiring sausage without preservatives, these can be prepared ahead and frozen until needed.*

- 2 pounds lean, boneless pork shoulder or 1 pound each lean, boneless pork shoulder and veal shoulder, cut into 1-inch cubes
- 8 ounces pork fat, cut into 1-inch cubes
- 1½ teaspoons dried sage, crumbled,
- 1 teaspoon salt, or to taste
- ½ teaspoon dried thyme, crumbled
- ½ teaspoon cayenne pepper, or to taste
- ¼ teaspoon black pepper
  Sautéed pears or apples for garnish (optional)

1 Put the meat and pork fat through a meat grinder set for fine, or grind in a food processor (see Tip, opposite page) until finely chopped — about 30 seconds. Add the sage, salt, thyme, cayenne pepper, and black pepper, and mix until just combined. (Pulse 5 or 6 times in the food processor.) Divide this mixture into fourths, then divide each fourth into thirds. Shape each portion into a ½-inch-thick patty about 3 inches in diameter.

▽ At this point the patties can be individually wrapped in plastic wrap and **refrigerated** overnight. *Freeze*, individually wrapped and labeled in heavy-duty aluminum foil, for up to 1 month at 0° F.

2 Brown the patties on both sides in a 12-inch skillet over moderate heat — about 15 minutes or until well done. Transfer to a heated serving platter and garnish, if desired, with pear or apple slices sautéed for 5 minutes in a little butter and sprinkled with ground cinnamon and brown sugar. Serve with waffles, pancakes, or eggs cooked any style. Makes 12 patties.

## Serving Later

**From freezer:** Heat 1 tablespoon vegetable oil in a 10-inch skillet over high heat. Cook the frozen patties, uncovered, for 5 minutes on each side or until brown. Reduce the heat to moderately low, cover, and cook for 15 to 20 minutes or until well done, turning them once. Serve as in Step 2. **To microwave:** Place 2 frozen patties in an 8-inch, microwave-safe pie plate. Cover with plastic wrap vented at one side. Microwave on *Low* (30% power) until defrosted — about 3 minutes. Microwave on *High* (100% power) for 1½ minutes; rotate the plate 90 degrees. Microwave on *High* (100% power) another 1½ minutes or until the meat is well done. Serve as in Step 2.

*European Meatballs in Cream Sauce with Dill — incomparable!*

# German Meatloaf

Per serving: Calories 375; Protein 37 g; Carbohydrate 8 g; Fat 21 g; Sodium 497 mg; Cholesterol 194 mg.

- 1 cup soft rye bread crumbs
- ¼ cup milk
- 1 tablespoon vegetable oil
- 1 large yellow onion, finely chopped
- 2 cloves garlic, minced
- 1 pound lean ground beef round
- 8 ounces lean ground pork shoulder
- ½ cup each grated Parmesan cheese and minced fresh parsley
- 2 eggs
- 1 teaspoon fennel seeds
- ½ teaspoon salt
- 1 teaspoon black pepper

1 Preheat the oven to 375° F. In a small bowl, soak the bread crumbs in the milk and set aside. Heat the oil in a small skillet over moderate heat for 1 minute. Add the onion and garlic, and sauté, stirring often, until soft — about 5 minutes. Cool until warm to the touch. In a large bowl, mix the beef, pork, Parmesan cheese, parsley, eggs, fennel seeds, salt, pepper, bread crumb mixture, and onion-garlic mixture with your hands. Pack the mixture into a greased 9" x 5" x 3" loaf pan.

▽ At this point the meatloaf can be covered tightly with aluminum foil and stored. *Refrigerate* for up to 4 hours. *Freeze* for up to 3 months at 0° F. (Place the covered loaf in the freezer; when frozen, remove it from the pan, wrap it in heavy-duty aluminum foil, and label it.) If you intend to microwave the frozen loaf, shape the meat into an 8-inch round, set it in a 9-inch, microwave-safe pie plate, and cut it in half. Cover tightly with heavy-duty aluminum foil and label it.

2 Bake the meatloaf, uncovered, for 50 to 55 minutes or until it pulls away from the sides of the pan and has a dark brown crust. Slice to desired thickness and serve with mashed potatoes, dilled carrots, and tiny green peas. Serves 6.

## Serving Later

**From freezer:** Unwrap the meatloaf, return it to the loaf pan, and cover with aluminum foil. Bake in a preheated 325° F oven for 35 minutes. Remove the foil and bake 40 to 50 minutes longer or until the loaf pulls away from the sides of the pan; serve as in Step 2.
**To microwave:** Replace the aluminum foil with plastic wrap vented at one side. Microwave on *Low* (30% power) for 20 minutes. Rotate the plate 90 degrees and microwave on *Low* (30% power) another 20 minutes or until the meatloaf is defrosted in the center. Microwave on *High* (100% power) for 10 minutes. Rotate the plate 90 degrees and microwave on *High* (100% power) until the juices run clear when the loaf is pierced in the center, or a microwave meat thermometer registers 180° F — about 10 minutes longer. Serve as in Step 2.

# Lamb, Oat, and Apple Loaf

Per serving: Calories 408; Protein 52 g; Carbohydrate 18 g; Fat 13 g; Sodium 403 mg; Cholesterol 232 mg.

- 2 pounds lean ground lamb shoulder or lean ground beef round or a mixture of the two
- 1 cup rolled oats
- 1 medium-size yellow onion, finely chopped
- 1 small tart apple, peeled, cored, and finely chopped
- 2 medium-size carrots, peeled and finely grated
- ½ cup milk or apple cider
- 2 eggs, lightly beaten
- ¾ teaspoon salt

- ¼ teaspoon black pepper
- ¼ teaspoon each dried rosemary, thyme, and sage, crumbled

1 Preheat the oven to 375° F. In a large bowl, mix all the ingredients with your hands until well combined. Pack the mixture into a greased 9" x 5" x 3" loaf pan.

▽ At this point the meatloaf mixture can be stored. Follow directions in German Meatloaf (above) for storing and serving later. *Refrigerate* for up to 4 hours. *Freeze* for up to 3 months at 0° F.

2 Bake the meatloaf, uncovered, for 50 to 55 minutes or until it pulls away from the sides of the pan and has a dark brown crust. Remove the meatloaf from the oven and carefully pour the accumulated drippings into a bowl; cover them with plastic wrap and reserve for use in a soup, if desired. Let the meatloaf sit for 10 minutes before serving. Slice to desired thickness and serve with Baked Potatoes Stuffed with Brie (page 178) and Sautéed Cucumbers (page 176). Cold slices are good for sandwiches. Serves 6.

# Cajun Meatloaf

Per serving: Calories 372; Protein 34 g; Carbohydrate 12 g; Fat 20 g; Sodium 549 mg; Cholesterol 198 mg.

*Here is a meatloaf that bites back. Spices can be adjusted to make it hotter or cooler, depending on personal taste.*

- 1 medium-size yellow onion, chopped
- 1 stalk celery, chopped
- ½ medium-size sweet green pepper, cored, seeded, and chopped
- 2 green onions, minced
- 1 clove garlic, minced
- 2 bay leaves
- ¾ teaspoon salt

*Cajun Meatloaf, for those who like it hot even when it's served cold, and Zucchini, Pepper, and Tomato Gratin (page 186)*

½ teaspoon each cayenne pepper and black pepper

¼ teaspoon each ground cumin and nutmeg

1 tablespoon Worcestershire sauce

¼ teaspoon hot red pepper sauce

2 tablespoons unsalted butter or margarine

¼ cup milk

¼ cup ketchup

½ cup fine dry bread crumbs

1 pound lean ground beef round

8 ounces lean ground pork shoulder

2 eggs

1 Preheat the oven to 375° F. Mix the onion, celery, green pepper, green onions, garlic, bay leaves, salt, cayenne pepper, black pepper, cumin, nutmeg, Worcestershire sauce, and hot red pepper sauce in a medium-size bowl.

2 Melt the butter in a heavy 10-inch skillet over moderate heat. Add the vegetable-spice mixture, and cook, uncovered, for 6 minutes, stirring constantly, until the onions and peppers are soft. Remove from the heat and cool slightly. Discard the bay leaves. Stir in the milk, ketchup, and bread crumbs.

3 In a large bowl, combine the beef, pork, eggs, and the bread crumb mixture. Pack the meat mixture into a greased, 9" x 5" x 3" loaf pan.

▽ At this point the meatloaf can be stored. Follow the directions in German Meatloaf (page 110) for storing and serving later. *Refrigerate* for up to 8 hours. *Freeze* for up to 3 months at 0° F.

4 Bake the meatloaf, uncovered, for 50 to 55 minutes or until it is dark brown and pulls away from the sides of the pan. Slice to desired thickness and serve with boiled red-skin potatoes and Zucchini, Pepper, and Tomato Gratin (page 186). Serves 6.

# Tuscan Roast Pork

Per serving: Calories 540; Protein 29 g; Carbohydrate 1 g; Fat 46 g; Sodium 592 mg; Cholesterol 119 mg.

*Although this succulent dish tastes very good when hot, it is at its best served at room temperature.*

- 6 cloves garlic, crushed
- 2 tablespoons fennel seeds
- 2 teaspoons salt
- ¼ teaspoon black pepper
- 3 pounds boneless pork rib roast or loin roast
- 2 tablespoons olive oil
  Cherry tomatoes for garnish

1 Using a mortar and pestle or a small bowl and a fork, mash the garlic, fennel seeds, salt, and pepper into a coarse paste.

2 Untie and unroll the roast. Spread all but 1 tablespoon of the paste on the exposed inside. Reroll and tie the roast, with the pale tenderloin more or less in the center, surrounded by the darker meat of the loin. With a sharp knife, make several ½-inch-deep cuts in the roast and insert some of the paste into these incisions. Rub the remaining paste, then the olive oil, over the roast. Place in a roasting pan, cover, and refrigerate for up to 8 hours.

3 Preheat the oven to 350° F. Roast the meat, uncovered, basting occasionally for 2 hours or until a meat thermometer registers 170° F. Cool for 10 minutes, then slice ½ inch thick. Arrange the slices on a serving platter and garnish with cherry tomatoes. Serve with potatoes sautéed with sage, and steamed broccoli drizzled with lemon. If the roast is served at room temperature, both accompaniments can also be prepared ahead and served that way. Serves 8.

*Zucchini and Pork Mexicana, a delicious concoction embraced by a golden taco shell*

# Roast Loin of Pork in Ginger Marinade

Per serving: Calories 376; Protein 29 g; Carbohydrate 1 g; Fat 28 g; Sodium 141 mg; Cholesterol 102 mg.

- ½ cup Beef Stock or Chicken Stock (page 48) or canned beef or chicken broth
- 1 3-inch by 1½-inch piece fresh ginger, peeled and minced or grated
- ¼ cup firmly packed brown sugar
- 2 tablespoons soy sauce
- 2 tablespoons tomato purée
- 1 tablespoon wine vinegar
- 1 clove garlic, minced
- 2¼ pounds boneless pork loin, trimmed of fat and sinew

*Optional garnishes:*
  Baked apple slices
  Watercress

1 In a large glass or ceramic bowl, mix the beef or chicken stock, ginger, brown sugar, soy sauce, tomato purée, vinegar, and garlic. Add the pork loin, coating all sides with the marinade. Tightly cover the bowl with plastic wrap and refrigerate overnight.

2 Preheat the oven to 350° F. Transfer the pork loin and marinade to a shallow roasting pan. Roast, basting frequently, for about 1 hour and 40 minutes or until a meat thermometer registers 165° F. Pour off the remaining marinade and discard.

▽ At this point the roast can be cooled to room temperature, wrapped in heavy-duty aluminum foil, and *refrigerated* for up to 2 days.

3 Let the roast rest for 10 minutes, then slice it thin. Arrange on a heated platter with baked apple slices and watercress for garnish, if desired. Accompany with Indonesian Rice (page 152) and a salad of radicchio and romaine lettuce. Serves 6.

## Serving Later

One hour before serving, set the roast out to come to room temperature. Slice it thin and arrange on a platter with watercress sprigs for garnish, if desired. Accompany with Curried Rice Salad (page 209). Serves 6.

# Zucchini and Pork Mexicana

Per serving: Calories 560; Protein 33 g; Carbohydrate 38 g; Fat 33 g; Sodium 316 mg; Cholesterol 97 mg.

*Easily doubled or tripled, this handy make-ahead is ideal for a buffet party or for a special family dinner.*

- 4 small zucchini, cut into ¾-inch cubes (about 1 pound)
- 1 teaspoon salt
- 3 tablespoons vegetable oil
- 1 pound lean, boneless pork shoulder, trimmed of fat and cut into ⅜-inch cubes
- 1 small yellow onion, thinly sliced
- 2 cloves garlic, minced
- 1 medium-size tomato, peeled and diced
- 1 large fresh chile poblano, roasted, peeled, seeded, and diced, or 2 pickled jalapeño peppers, rinsed, seeded, and diced
- 1 cup fresh corn kernels (1 large ear) or 1 cup frozen corn kernels, thawed
- ½ teaspoon dried oregano, crumbled
- ¼ teaspoon each dried thyme and marjoram, crumbled
- 2 bay leaves
- 1½ cups water
- 3 ounces Mexican *queso fresco* or mild fresh goat or farmer's cheese, cut into ½-inch cubes
- 12 warm taco shells or tortillas

1 Place the zucchini in a colander and sprinkle with the salt. Toss several times and let drain for 30 minutes.

2 Heat 2 tablespoons of the oil in a heavy 12-inch skillet over moderately high heat. Add the pork in a single layer and brown well on all sides — about 7 minutes. With a slotted spoon, transfer to a small bowl.

3 Add the remaining tablespoon of oil to the skillet, if needed, and reduce the heat to moderate. Add the onion, and sauté, stirring frequently, until lightly browned — about 7 minutes. Stir in the garlic and tomato. Continue cooking, stirring occasionally, for 5 minutes.

4 Rinse the zucchini and dry on paper toweling. Add them to the tomato mixture, along with the pork, chili, corn, herbs, and water. Reduce the heat to moderately low and simmer, uncovered, for 30 to 40 minutes or until the meat is tender and the juices have been absorbed into the sauce.

▽ At this point the zucchini and pork can be cooled to room temperature and *refrigerated* in a tightly covered container for up to 2 days.

5 Spoon into the taco shells and top with the cheese. Accompany with a salad of mixed greens. Serves 4.

## Serving Later

In a covered medium-size saucepan or 10-inch skillet, bring mixture to a simmer over moderately low heat — about 15 minutes. Proceed as in Step 5.

# Pork Chops with Plum Sauce

Per serving: Calories 471; Protein 23 g; Carbohydrate 11 g; Fat 34 g; Sodium 330 mg; Cholesterol 119 mg.

*The delicious sauce for this dish is made with baby food — plums with tapioca or rice.*

- 4 pork loin chops (about 6 ounces each)
- 1 tablespoon flour
- ½ teaspoon salt
- ¼ teaspoon each black pepper and dried sage, crumbled
- 1 jar (4½ ounces) strained plums with tapioca or rice
- ½ cup Port or Beef Stock (page 48) or canned beef broth
- 1 teaspoon grated lemon rind
- ½ teaspoon ground cinnamon
- ¼ teaspoon ground cloves

1 Trim the excess fat from the pork chops; cut the fat into cubes and reserve. Combine the flour, salt, pepper, and sage on wax paper. Coat both sides of the pork chops with the mixture, shaking off any excess.

2 Heat the reserved pork fat in a 12-inch skillet over moderate heat until slightly rendered — 3 to 5 minutes. Discard the browned pieces of fat. Brown the chops until golden, turning them over once — about 10 minutes.

3 Preheat the oven to 325° F. Meanwhile, in a shallow, 2-quart baking dish, combine the plums, Port, lemon rind, cinnamon, and cloves. Put the chops in the dish and coat both sides with the sauce.

▽ At this point the chops can be stored. Cover with plastic wrap and *refrigerate* for up to 12 hours.

4 Bake, uncovered, for 50 to 65 minutes or until fork tender. If the sauce starts to dry out, add a little water.

Serve with buttered boiled potatoes or dumplings, green peas with pearl onions, and a radicchio and curly endive salad. Serves 4.

# Pork and Sauerkraut Stew

Per serving: Calories 586; Protein 28 g; Carbohydrate 15 g; Fat 46 g; Sodium 975 mg; Cholesterol 108 mg.

*This mouth-watering Hungarian dish is superb cold-weather fare. Americans tend to like sauerkraut crisp, while Europeans prefer it soft. If you want the traditional texture, add the sauerkraut to the skillet when you add the meat and spices, so that it can cook longer.*

- 2 tablespoons vegetable oil
- 2 large yellow onions, coarsely chopped
- 2 cloves garlic, minced
- 2 pounds boneless pork butt, cut into 1-inch cubes
- 1 cup water
- 2 tablespoons paprika
- 1 teaspoon caraway seeds
- ½ teaspoon salt
- 3 cups sauerkraut, rinsed and drained
- 2 tablespoons all-purpose flour, blended with 1 tablespoon cold water
- 1 cup plain low-fat yogurt or sour cream

1 Heat the oil in a heavy 12-inch skillet or a flameproof casserole over moderate heat. Add the onions and garlic, and cook, stirring occasionally, until translucent — about 3 minutes.

2 Add the pork, water, paprika, caraway seeds, and salt and bring to a boil over high heat. Reduce the heat to low, cover, and simmer for 1 hour or until the meat is almost tender. Add the sauerkraut and continue simmering for 15 to 20 minutes. Stir the flour paste into the stew and continue cooking and stirring 5 minutes longer.

▽ At this point the stew can be cooled to room temperature and stored. *Refrigerate*, tightly covered, in the flameproof casserole or in a glass or ceramic container for up to 4 days.

3 Stir in the yogurt, and heat through; do not let it boil or it will curdle. Serve with hot noodles and Sautéed Cucumbers (page 176). Serves 6 to 8.

## Serving Later

Reheat the stew in the covered casserole over moderately low heat until the pork is heated through and the sauce simmering — about 20 minutes. Proceed as in Step 3.

# Spicy Pork and Bean Curd

Per serving: Calories 386; Protein 19 g; Carbohydrate 7 g; Fat 32 g; Sodium 557 mg; Cholesterol 39 mg.

- 3 tablespoons vegetable oil
- 3 cloves garlic, minced
- 7 green onions (including some green), sliced
- 1 tablespoon minced fresh ginger
- 8 ounces lean ground pork
- 1 pound firm bean curd (tofu), cut into ¾-inch cubes
- 1 cup water
- ½ teaspoon hot red pepper sauce, or to taste
- 3 tablespoons soy sauce
- 1 tablespoon sherry
- 4 teaspoons cornstarch mixed with 2 tablespoons cold water
- 2 cups hot cooked rice or 8 ounces hot boiled noodles

1 Heat the oil in a wok or a heavy 12-inch skillet over high heat for 1 minute. Add the garlic, green onions, and ginger and stir-fry for 1 minute. Stir in the pork, breaking it up with a

wooden spoon; cook until no longer pink — 3 to 5 minutes. Add the bean curd, water, hot red pepper sauce, soy sauce, and sherry. As the sauce begins to boil, reduce the heat to low, cover, and cook for 3 minutes. Blend in the cornstarch mixture; stir until the sauce has thickened — about 3 minutes.

▽ At this point the sauce can be cooled to room temperature and stored. *Refrigerate* in a tightly covered container for up to 2 days.

2 Serve immediately over the hot rice or noodles. A salad of mixed greens and water chestnuts makes a good accompaniment. Serves 4.

### Serving Later

Reheat in a covered 12-inch skillet over moderately low heat, stirring occasionally, until warmed through — about 10 minutes. Add more soy sauce and hot red pepper sauce, if desired.

*A simple preparation elegantly presented — Pork Chops with Plum Sauce*

# Marinated Spareribs

Per serving: Calories 533; Protein 25 g; Carbohydrate 1 g; Fat 47 g; Sodium 86 mg; Cholesterol 109 mg.

*These tasty ribs are perfect for a picnic. Take them, along with the marinade, in a plastic bag. After the meal, put the bones in the bag and toss it into a refuse bin. Go home empty-handed.*

- 4 pounds pork spareribs, cut into ribs
- 6 tablespoons lime juice
- 6 tablespoons orange juice
- ¼ cup orange marmalade
- ¼ cup peanut or corn oil
- 2 tablespoons plus 1 teaspoon soy sauce
- 3 cloves garlic, crushed
- 1 teaspoon ground ginger
- ½ teaspoon hot red pepper sauce

1 Place the ribs in a large saucepan or flameproof casserole and add water to cover. Bring to a boil over high heat; then reduce the heat to moderate and simmer for 10 minutes. Drain the ribs and set aside.

2 Whisk the lime juice, orange juice, marmalade, oil, soy sauce, garlic, ginger, and hot red pepper sauce in a medium-size bowl.

3 When the ribs have cooled to room temperature, transfer them to a 1-gallon freezer bag or a large, glass or ceramic bowl. Coat the ribs with the marinade and seal the bag or tightly cover the bowl. Refrigerate for at least 12 and up to 24 hours, turning the ribs occasionally.

4 Remove the ribs from the container, reserving the marinade. To barbecue, arrange the ribs on an oiled grill 3 to 4 inches from hot coals. Grill until crisp and cooked through — about 10 minutes on each side — brushing them periodically with the marinade.

5 To bake the ribs, preheat the oven to 400° F. Arrange the ribs, one layer deep, in a large, greased baking or roasting pan. Bake, brushing occasionally with the reserved marinade, for 20 minutes. Turn them over and bake another 20 minutes. Baked sweet potatoes and a cucumber salad with Yogurt Dressing (page 214) make good accompaniments. Serves 6.

# Ham Steaks with Sherried Pear Sauce

Per serving: Calories 305; Protein 30 g; Carbohydrate 25 g; Fat 8 g; Sodium 1712 mg; Cholesterol 75 mg.

*For those watching their fat or sodium intake, low-fat and reduced sodium hams are available.*

- 2 tablespoons dry sherry or Port
- 1 tablespoon lemon juice
- 1 tablespoon Worcestershire sauce
- 2 teaspoons tomato paste
- 1 bay leaf
- 1 clove garlic, crushed
- 4 drops hot red pepper sauce
- 1/8 teaspoon black pepper
- 2 ham steaks (10 ounces each)

*For the sauce:*
- 2 large pears, peeled, cored, and cut in 1/2-inch cubes
- 3 tablespoons dry sherry or Port
- 2 tablespoons honey
- 1 tablespoon lemon juice
- 1/4 teaspoon grated lemon rind

1 In a shallow 2-quart casserole, stir together the sherry, lemon juice, Worcestershire sauce, tomato paste, bay leaf, garlic, hot red pepper sauce, and pepper. Add the ham steaks, and coat with the marinade. Cover and refrigerate for at least 8 hours or overnight. Will keep for up to 2 days.

2 Preheat the oven to 375° F. Cover and bake the steaks in the marinade for 45 to 55 minutes or until tender.

3 Meanwhile, in a small saucepan, bring the pears, sherry, honey, lemon juice, and lemon rind to a boil over moderate heat. Reduce the heat to moderately low and simmer, covered, for 15 minutes or until the pears are fork tender. Cool slightly, then purée in an electric blender or food processor for 30 seconds. Return to the saucepan and bring to a simmer.

4 Cut the ham steaks in half before serving. Pass the sauce separately. Creamy Broccoli Purée (page 188), sliced pears, and sweet potatoes are good accompaniments. Serves 4.

# Ham Balls with Orange Sauce

Per serving: Calories 337; Protein 19 g; Carbohydrate 16 g; Fat 22 g; Sodium 489 mg; Cholesterol 148 mg.

- 2 eggs
- 7 ounces ground boiled or baked ham (about 1 1/2 cups)
- 12 ounces ground pork
- 1 medium-size yellow onion, finely chopped
- 1/2 cup soft bread crumbs (1 slice)
- 1 teaspoon grated orange rind
- 2 tablespoons vegetable oil

- 1 cup orange juice
- 1/3 cup red wine vinegar
- 2 tablespoons apple jelly or orange marmalade
- 4 teaspoons cornstarch
- 2 teaspoons Worcestershire sauce
- 1 teaspoon dry mustard
  Orange slices for garnish (optional)

1 Beat the eggs in a large mixing bowl. Add the ham, pork, onion, bread crumbs, and orange rind; mix with your hands until well combined. Shape the mixture into 1-inch balls.

▽ At this point the ham balls can be arranged on a 15" x 10" x 1" baking sheet, covered tightly with plastic wrap or aluminum foil, and *refrigerated* for up to 12 hours.

2 Heat the oil in a heavy 12-inch skillet over moderately high heat. Cook the meatballs in several batches, turning occasionally, until all sides are well browned — 5 to 8 minutes per batch. Transfer the meatballs to a platter lined with paper toweling.

3 Meanwhile, in a small bowl, mix the orange juice, vinegar, apple jelly, cornstarch, Worcestershire sauce, and mustard. Stir until the cornstarch has completely dissolved.

4 Return all of the meatballs to the skillet and pour the sauce over them. Bring to a boil over moderate heat; reduce the heat to low and simmer, covered, for 5 to 10 minutes. Transfer the meatballs and the sauce to a heated serving dish, and garnish with the orange slices, if desired. Serve with steamed carrots and coleslaw with pineapple. Serves 6.

*A surprising and pleasing blend of flavors and textures, Ham Steaks with Sherried Pear Sauce*

# Veal Breast Stuffed with Spinach, Pine Nuts, and Raisins

Per serving: Calories 626; Protein 42 g; Carbohydrate 15 g; Fat 42 g; Sodium 503 mg; Cholesterol 141 mg.

*This spectacular dish is perfect for a special occasion, and it's easy on the budget, too.*

For the stuffing:
- 4 tablespoons (½ stick) unsalted butter or margarine
- 1 medium-size yellow onion, finely chopped
- 1 clove garlic, minced
- 8 ounces mushrooms, coarsely chopped
- ¼ cup coarsely chopped pine nuts
- ¼ teaspoon each dried rosemary, sage, and thyme, crumbled
- 1 package (10 ounces) frozen chopped spinach, thawed
- 1 cup soft whole-wheat bread crumbs (2 slices)
- ⅓ cup golden raisins
- 2 tablespoons dry sherry, Port, or Madeira
- ½ teaspoon salt
- ¼ teaspoon black pepper

For the veal:
- 3½ to 4 pounds boneless veal breast, trimmed
- ½ teaspoon each salt and black pepper
- ½ teaspoon each dried rosemary and sage, crumbled

For the poaching liquid:
- 2 cups Chicken Stock (page 48) or canned chicken broth
- 6 cups water
- 1 cup dry white wine
- 1 medium-size carrot, peeled and thinly sliced
- 4 green onions, thinly sliced
- ¼ teaspoon each dried rosemary and thyme, crumbled
- 3 sprigs parsley

1 Melt the butter in a heavy 12-inch skillet over moderate heat. Add the onion, and sauté until golden — about 10 minutes. Stir in the garlic, mushrooms, pine nuts, rosemary, sage, thyme, and spinach. Reduce the heat to low and cook, uncovered, stirring occasionally, until all the juices have evaporated — 10 to 12 minutes. Add the bread crumbs, raisins, sherry, salt, and pepper; cook, stirring, until the flavors are blended — 2 to 3 minutes more. Set aside.

▽ At this point the stuffing can be cooled to room temperature and stored. *Refrigerate* in a covered container for up to 24 hours.

2 Pound the veal on both sides with a meat mallet, a small heavy skillet, or a rolling pin to produce a uniform thickness. Sprinkle with the salt, pepper, rosemary, and sage. Fill the center of the veal with the stuffing, leaving a 1½-inch margin all around.

3 Wrap the long sides of the veal over the stuffing, overlapping them to make a sausage-shaped roll, and sew it shut with a needle and heavy-duty thread or thin twine. (Do not sew too close to the edge of the meat, or the seam will burst during cooking.) Tuck the ends under the side seam and sew them shut to encase the stuffing.

4 Place the stuffed veal in a large flameproof casserole. Add all the ingredients for the poaching liquid and bring to a simmer over moderate heat. Reduce the heat to low, cover, and cook until the veal is tender when pierced with a fork — 2 to 2½ hours. Transfer the veal to a shallow baking dish or ovenproof platter, cover with aluminum foil, and keep warm.

5 Skim any fat from the broth. Boil the broth, uncovered, over moderately high heat until reduced by half — 15 to 20 minutes. Cool slightly. Transfer the broth and vegetables to an electric blender or food processor and

purée, in 2 batches if necesssary, for about 30 seconds. Return the purée to the casserole and boil over moderate heat, uncovered, until slightly thickened — 15 to 20 minutes.

▽ At this point the veal and sauce can be cooled to room temperature and stored. Return the meat to the casserole and *refrigerate*, tightly covered, for up to 24 hours.

6 Remove the thread from the veal and cut the roll into slices ½ inch thick. Arrange the slices on a heated serving platter, and spoon some of the sauce over them. Pass the remaining sauce separately. Accompany with Baked Carrot Ring (page 173) and hot buttered noodles tossed with poppy seeds. Serves 8.

## Serving Later

Reheat the veal in the covered casserole over moderately low heat until the meat is warmed through and the sauce is simmering — about 30 minutes. Proceed as in Step 6.

# Veal Shanks Italian-Style

Per serving: Calories 420; Protein 31 g; Carbohydrate 14 g; Fat 23 g; Sodium 436 mg; Cholesterol 136 mg.

*Slow cooking makes the meat tender and succulent. If veal shanks are not available, try substituting 2 pounds of boneless, cubed veal shoulder for a different but equally delicious stew.*

- 6 veal shanks (2 to 2½ inches thick)
- ½ cup all-purpose flour
- ¼ cup olive oil
- 1 teaspoon salt
- ⅛ teaspoon black pepper
- 2 medium-size yellow onions, finely chopped

2 cloves garlic, minced
2 tablespoons each finely chopped basil and parsley or 2 teaspoons each dried basil and parsley, crumbled
2 teaspoons minced marjoram or ½ teaspoon dried marjoram, crumbled
1 teaspoon minced rosemary or ¼ teaspoon dried rosemary, crumbled
1 large ripe tomato, peeled and coarsely chopped
1¼ cups dry white wine
1 clove garlic, minced
2 teaspoons grated lemon rind
2 tablespoons minced parsley

1 Dredge the veal shanks in the flour until well coated, shaking off any excess. Heat the oil in a large, heavy, flameproof casserole over moderately high heat for 1 minute. Brown the shanks, 3 at a time — about 5 minutes per batch. Transfer to a platter lined with paper toweling. Sprinkle with the salt and pepper.

2 Add the onions, garlic, basil, parsley, marjoram, and rosemary to the casserole, and cook, uncovered, over very low heat, stirring occasionally, until the onions are soft but not brown — about 15 minutes. Add the tomato, wine, and shanks and bring to a boil over moderate heat. Reduce the heat to low, cover, and simmer until the meat is very tender but not falling off the bone — 2 to 2½ hours.

▽ At this point the veal shanks can be cooled to room temperature and stored. *Refrigerate* in the covered casserole for up to 2 days.

3 Just before serving, stir the garlic, lemon rind, and parsley into the sauce. Serve each veal shank on a bed of hot rice with some of the juices spooned over it. Spinach sautéed with garlic in olive oil, and a salad of sliced tomatoes and artichoke hearts make good accompaniments. Serves 6.

### Serving Later

Reheat, covered, over very low heat until the shanks are warmed through and the juices simmering — about 20 minutes. Proceed as in Step 3.

*Waiting to be served — a mouthwatering Veal Shank Italian-Style on a bed of buttered rice*

*Veal Marengo, a delectable reminder that a classic recipe can be given an interesting new life*

# Veal in Cider

Per serving: Calories 367; Protein 31 g; Carbohydrate 11 g; Fat 21 g; Sodium 436 mg; Cholesterol 141 mg.

2 tablespoons vegetable oil
1 tablespoon unsalted butter or margarine
2 pounds boneless veal shoulder, cut into 1½-inch cubes
12 shallots, peeled and separated into cloves, or 20 green onions

12 small white onions, peeled
1 cup plus 2 tablespoons hard cider or 1 cup fresh cider mixed with 2 tablespoons dry vermouth or sherry
1 bay leaf
½ teaspoon dried thyme, crumbled
2 sprigs parsley
3 medium-size cucumbers, peeled, quartered lengthwise, seeded, and sliced ¾ inch thick
6 ounces snow peas, trimmed
1 teaspoon salt
¼ teaspoon black pepper

1 Heat the oil and butter in a large, heavy, flameproof casserole over moderately high heat until very hot — about 1 minute. Add the veal and brown on all sides — 7 to 10 minutes. Transfer to a platter lined with paper toweling. Add the shallots and onions to the casserole, and sauté, stirring, for 2 minutes.

2 Pour off any remaining fat from the casserole. Add 1 cup of the cider, and cook over moderate heat, scraping

120

up any brown bits, until the pan is deglazed — about 1 minute. Add the veal, bay leaf, thyme, and parsley sprigs and bring to a boil. Reduce the heat to moderately low. Lay a buttered round of brown or wax paper over the casserole, cover, and simmer gently until the meat is tender — 1 1/4 to 1 1/2 hours. Remove the buttered paper.

▽ At this point the veal can be cooled to room temperature and stored. *Refrigerate*, tightly covered, in the flameproof casserole for up to 2 days. *Freeze*, labeled, in a 1-gallon freezer bag or a lined, 2 1/2-quart, covered, microwave-safe casserole (see Tip, page 138) for 3 months at 0° F.

3 Lay the cucumbers and snow peas on top of the veal, cover, and cook over moderate heat for 4 minutes or until the vegetables are just cooked but still slightly crunchy.

4 With a slotted spoon, transfer the meat and vegetables to a heated platter and keep warm. Skim any fat from the sauce and discard the parsley sprigs and bay leaf. Add the remaining cider, and boil, uncovered, over moderately high heat until reduced to about 3/4 cup. Stir in the salt and pepper, then strain the sauce over the meat and vegetables. Accompany with garlic bread and braised endive. Serves 6.

## Serving Later

**From refrigerator:** Remove any solidified fat. Cover and warm the meat over moderately low heat, stirring occasionally, until heated through — 15 to 20 minutes. Proceed as in Steps 3 and 4.
**From freezer:** Let the veal and sauce defrost overnight in the refrigerator. Transfer to a large, heavy, flameproof casserole and proceed as directed above. **To microwave:** Heat in the covered casserole on *Low* (30% power) for 8 minutes. Stir to break up frozen chunks. Microwave on *Low*

(30% power) 7 minutes more; stir again. Arrange the snow peas around the outside edge of the casserole and the cucumbers in the center. Cover and microwave on *Low* (30% power) until the vegetables are cooked but still crisp — 5 to 7 minutes more. Let stand for 2 minutes. Serve as in Step 4.

*Tip: Placing a buttered round of brown or wax paper just under the lid of a saucepan or casserole helps retain the liquid and concentrates the flavors. The technique is especially useful when making stews.*

# Veal Marengo

Per serving: Calories 651; Protein 48 g; Carbohydrate 22 g; Fat 35 g; Sodium 537 mg; Cholesterol 204 mg.

*This veal version of the classic chicken dish, which was originally created for Napoleon at the Battle of Marengo, makes a wonderful party dish.*

- 1/2 cup all-purpose flour
- 1/2 teaspoon salt
- 1/4 teaspoon black pepper
- 2 pounds boned veal shoulder, trimmed and cut into 1 1/2-inch cubes
- 4 tablespoons olive oil
- 1 large yellow onion, coarsely chopped
- 1 clove garlic, minced
- 1 1/2 cups dry white wine
- 1/2 cup water
- 1/4 cup tomato paste
- 1/2 teaspoon each dried thyme and tarragon, crumbled
- 1 teaspoon finely grated orange rind
- 6 ounces button mushrooms, trimmed
- 2 tablespoons minced parsley for garnish (optional)

1 Preheat the oven to 325° F. In a shallow bowl, blend the flour, salt, and pepper. Dredge the veal, shaking off any excess.

2 Heat 3 tablespoons of the oil in a heavy 12-inch skillet over moderately high heat for 1 minute. Add the veal; brown on all sides — 5 to 7 minutes. Transfer to a 2-quart casserole.

3 Add the remaining oil, the onion, and garlic to the skillet; sauté, stirring, over moderate heat until the onion is soft — about 5 minutes. Add the wine, water, tomato paste, thyme, tarragon, and orange rind and bring to a boil over moderately high heat. Pour the mixture over the veal, cover, and bake for 2 hours.

▽ At this point the Veal Marengo can be cooled to room temperature and stored. *Refrigerate* in the covered casserole for up to 2 days. *Freeze* in a labeled, 1-gallon freezer bag for up to 1 month at 0° F.

4 Add the mushrooms to the casserole, re-cover, and bake 30 minutes more. Garnish with the parsley, if desired. Accompany with hot buttered noodles, tiny green peas, and Caramelized Onions (page 177). Serves 4.

## Serving Later

**From refrigerator:** One hour before baking, set the stew out to come to room temperature. Preheat the oven to 325° F. Stir in the mushrooms; bake, covered, for 35 to 45 minutes or until the mushrooms are cooked. Serve as in Step 4.
**From freezer:** Defrost overnight in the refrigerator. Proceed as above.

# Veal with Tuna Sauce

Per serving: Calories 612; Protein 44 g; Carbohydrate 1 g; Fat 47 g; Sodium 279 mg; Cholesterol 265 mg.

*This delightful veal dish is a natural for summer dining. The chicken variation is equally appealing; turkey breast can also be used.*

*For the veal:*
- 2¼ pounds boneless leg or shoulder of veal, trimmed, rolled, and tied
- 2 anchovy fillets, chopped

*For the poaching liquid:*
- 1 medium-size yellow onion stuck with 2 whole cloves
- 1 bay leaf
- 1 stalk celery
- 1 medium-size carrot, peeled and quartered
- 3 parsley sprigs
- 1 teaspoon salt

*For the tuna sauce:*
- 2 egg yolks
- ¾ cup olive oil
- 1 can (6½ ounces) oil-packed tuna, drained
- 3 anchovy fillets
- 2 tablespoons plus 1 teaspoon lemon juice
- 3 tablespoons capers
- ⅛ teaspoon white pepper

*Optional garnishes:*
    Parsley sprigs
    Lemon wedges

1 Using a sharp paring knife, make small incisions in the veal at regular intervals and fill them with pieces of the anchovies.

2 Place the veal in a large heavy saucepan and pour in enough hot boiling water to cover. Add the poaching ingredients and bring to a boil over high heat. Reduce the heat to low, cover, and simmer until the veal is tender — 1¼ to 1¾ hours. Transfer the veal to a cutting board and let cool. Reserve ¼ cup of the poaching liquid for the sauce. (You can use the rest in a soup, if you like.)

3 Meanwhile, prepare the tuna sauce. Beat the egg yolks in an electric blender or food processor for 5 seconds; then with the motor running, add the oil 1 tablespoon at a time. As the sauce begins to thicken, add the oil in a thin stream.

4 Add the tuna and anchovies and continue blending until smooth. Blend in the reserved poaching liquid and the lemon juice. Transfer the sauce to a medium-size mixing bowl and gently stir in the capers and pepper.

5 Carve the veal into thin slices. Spoon some sauce over the bottom of a serving platter and arrange the veal slices, overlapping, in a layer on top. Drizzle with more sauce; serve any remaining sauce separately. Cover tightly with plastic wrap and refrigerate for at least 8 and up to 24 hours.

6 Serve at room temperature, garnished with parsley sprigs and lemon wedges, if desired. Accompany with Potatoes Roasted with Garlic and Rosemary (page 180) and asparagus with lemon and dill. Serves 6.

## Chicken Variation

Per serving: Calories 519; Protein 50 g; Carbohydrate 1 g; Fat 31 g; Sodium 175 mg; Cholesterol 189 mg.

Substitute **3 whole boneless, skinless chicken breasts (12 ounces each), halved,** for the veal and omit the anchovies and poaching ingredients. Bring **2 cups Chicken Stock (page 48) or canned chicken broth** to a boil in a heavy 12-inch skillet. Reduce the heat to low, add the chicken breasts, and simmer until no longer pink on the inside — 10 to 15 minutes. Transfer to a cutting board and cool. Reserve ¼ cup of the poaching liquid for the tuna sauce. (Use the rest in a soup, if you like.) Slice the chicken breasts to make 12 thin slices. Proceed as in Steps 3 through 6. Serves 6.

## Artichoke Sauce Variation

Per serving for veal: Calories 553; Protein 35 g; Carbohydrate 2 g; Fat 45 g; Sodium 172 mg; Cholesterol 244 mg.

Cook the veal as in Veal with Tuna Sauce or the chicken as in the Chicken Variation, reserving ⅓ cup of the cooking liquid. For the Artichoke Sauce, combine **2 egg yolks** with **2 teaspoons lemon juice** in an electric blender or food processor. Add **¾ cup olive oil** as in Step 3, then add **3 anchovy fillets, 1 cup canned artichoke hearts, drained, or frozen artichoke hearts, cooked according to package directions,** and the reserved poaching liquid. Blend until smooth — about 20 seconds. Transfer to a medium-size bowl, fold in 3 tablespoons capers and ⅛ teaspoon white pepper. Proceed as in Steps 5 and 6.

# Lamb Stew with White Beans

Per serving: Calories 666; Protein 34 g; Carbohydrate 35 g; Fat 39 g; Sodium 390 mg; Cholesterol 102 mg.

- 1 cup dried Great Northern or navy beans, washed and picked over, or 1 can (19 ounces) cannellini beans, drained
- 2 cups water
- 2 slices bacon, diced
- 1 tablespoon olive oil
- 1 large yellow onion, chopped
- 1 medium-size carrot, peeled and sliced ½ inch thick
- 1¼ pounds boneless lamb shoulder, trimmed and cut into 1-inch cubes
- 1 cup dry white wine
- 1 clove garlic, minced
- 1 teaspoon dried rosemary, crumbled

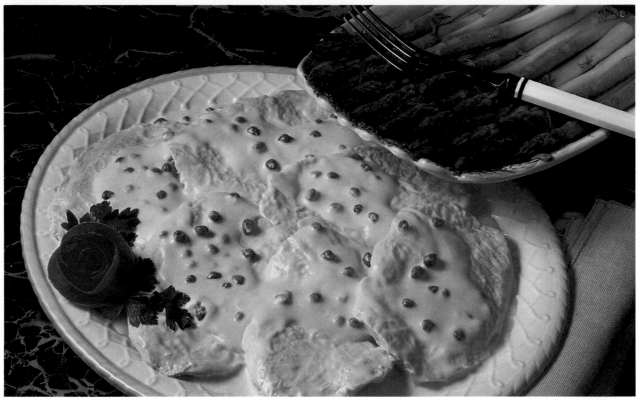

*Succulent Veal with Tuna Sauce punctuated by pungent capers*

¼ teaspoon dried thyme,
crumbled
½ teaspoon salt
1 bay leaf
1 2-inch strip orange zest
(colored part of the rind)

1 In a medium-size saucepan, cover the beans with water and bring to a boil over moderately high heat. Remove from the heat, cover, and let sit for 1 hour. Drain the beans. Add the 2 cups of water, cover, and bring to a boil over moderately high heat. Reduce the heat to low and simmer, covered, adding more water if necessary, just until the beans are tender — about 1 hour. Drain and set aside.

2 Meanwhile, in a heavy, medium-size flameproof casserole, cook the bacon over moderately low heat until barely crisp — about 4 minutes. Transfer to a plate lined with paper toweling. Drain off the fat. Add the olive oil,

onion, and carrot to the casserole, and cook, uncovered, until the onion is soft — about 5 minutes.

3 Add the lamb, wine, garlic, rosemary, thyme, salt, bay leaf, orange zest, and bacon. Bring to a boil over moderately high heat; then reduce the heat to low, cover, and simmer until the lamb is fork tender and the sauce has thickened — about 1¾ hours. Stir in the beans.

▽ At this point the lamb and beans can be cooled to room temperature and stored. *Refrigerate*, tightly covered, in the flameproof casserole for up to 3 days. *Freeze*, labeled, in a 1-gallon freezer bag or lined, 2-quart, covered, microwave-safe casserole (see Tip, page 138) for 3 months at 0° F.

4 Simmer the lamb and beans, covered, until the beans are heated through — about 10 minutes. Accom-

pany with Zucchini, Pepper, and Tomato Gratin (page 186) and French bread. Serves 4.

### Serving Later

**From refrigerator:** Reheat in the covered casserole over moderate heat until the lamb is warmed through and the sauce simmering — about 20 minutes. Serve as in Step 4. **From freezer:** Thaw overnight in the refrigerator. Transfer to a heavy, medium-size flameproof casserole and proceed as above. **To microwave:** Heat the frozen stew in the covered casserole on *Low* (30% power) for 20 minutes; stir, re-cover, and rotate the dish 90 degrees. Heat on *Low* (30% power) 15 minutes more. Increase the setting to *High* (100% power) and microwave for 5 minutes; stir, re-cover, and microwave 5 minutes more on *High* (100% power).

# Lamb with Almonds and Raisins

Per serving: Calories 491; Protein 25 g; Carbohydrate 13 g; Fat 38 g; Sodium 326 mg; Cholesterol 99 mg.

1¼ pounds boneless lamb shoulder, trimmed and cut into 1-inch cubes
1 medium-size yellow onion, coarsely chopped
1 clove garlic, minced
1 medium-size tomato, peeled and coarsely chopped
½ teaspoon each salt, black pepper, and ground turmeric
¼ teaspoon ground ginger
⅛ teaspoon cayenne (ground red) pepper
½ cup water
1 tablespoon minced parsley or cilantro (coriander leaves)
¼ cup golden raisins
¼ cup whole, toasted, blanched almonds

1 In a large, heavy, flameproof casserole, bring the lamb, onion, garlic, tomato, salt, black pepper, turmeric, ginger, cayenne pepper, and water to a boil over moderately high heat. Cover, reduce the heat to low, and cook for 1 hour, stirring occasionally.

2 Add the parsley and raisins, and cook, covered, 30 minutes more. Stir more frequently during the last 10 minutes of cooking, when the sauce should be quite thick.

▽ At this point the lamb can be cooled to room temperature and stored. *Refrigerate*, tightly covered, in the casserole for up to 3 days. *Freeze*, labeled, in a 1-gallon freezer bag or a lined, 1½-quart, covered, microwave-safe casserole (see Tip, page 138) for up to 3 months at 0° F.

3 Serve over hot saffron rice or couscous, accompanied by zucchini sautéed in Mint Butter (page 223). Makes 4 servings.

## Serving Later

**From refrigerator:** Reheat the lamb in the covered casserole over moderately low heat until the meat is warmed through and the sauce simmering — about 20 minutes. Serve as in Step 3.
**From freezer:** Defrost in the refrigerator overnight. Transfer to a large, heavy, flameproof casserole and proceed as above. **To microwave:** Heat the frozen stew in the covered casserole on *Low* (30% power) for 7 minutes. Stir, re-cover, and microwave on *Low* (30% power) 3 minutes more. Microwave on *High* (100% power) for 3 minutes. Stir, re-cover, and microwave on *High* (100% power) 2 minutes more or until heated through. Serve as in Step 3.

# Braised Lamb with Black Olives

Per serving: Calories 566; Protein 24 g; Carbohydrate 10 g; Fat 46 g; Sodium 656 mg; Cholesterol 99 mg.

¼ cup all-purpose flour
1¼ pounds boneless lamb shoulder, trimmed and cut into 1-inch cubes
2 tablespoons olive oil
1 large yellow onion, minced
1 clove garlic, minced
¾ cup Beef Stock (page 48) or canned beef broth
½ cup dry red wine
¾ cup sliced pitted black olives
2 tablespoons lemon juice
¾ teaspoon salt
¼ teaspoon black pepper
1 teaspoon each dried rosemary and sage, crumbled

1 Place the flour in a shallow bowl or on a sheet of wax paper. Coat the lamb well, shaking off any excess. Heat the oil in a heavy 10-inch skillet over moderately high heat for 1 minute. Add the lamb and brown on all sides — 7 to 10 minutes.

2 Add the onion and garlic, and sauté, stirring occasionally, over moderately low heat until the onion is soft — about 5 minutes. Add the beef stock, wine, olives, lemon juice, salt, pepper, rosemary, and sage and bring to a boil over moderately high heat. Reduce the heat to low, cover, and simmer, stirring occasionally, until the lamb is fork tender — about 1¾ hours.

▽ At this point the braised lamb can be cooled and stored. *Refrigerate*, tightly covered, in a medium-size flameproof casserole for up to 3 days. *Freeze*, labeled, in a 1-gallon freezer bag or lined, 1½-quart, covered, microwave-safe casserole (see Tip, page 138) for up to 3 months at 0° F.

3 Serve the lamb and sauce over hot rice accompanied by Baked Tomatoes Stuffed with Orzo (page 184) and a crusty garlic bread. Serves 4.

## Serving Later

**From refrigerator:** Reheat in the covered casserole over moderate heat until the lamb is warmed through and the sauce simmering — about 20 minutes. Serve as in Step 3. **From freezer:** Let the stew defrost in the refrigerator overnight. Transfer to a medium-size flameproof casserole and proceed as directed above. **To microwave:** Defrost the frozen stew in the covered casserole on *Low* (30% power) for 15 minutes; stir to break up any frozen pieces. Re-cover and microwave 5 minutes more on *Low* (30% power). Microwave on *High* (100% power) 5 minutes longer. Serve as in Step 3.

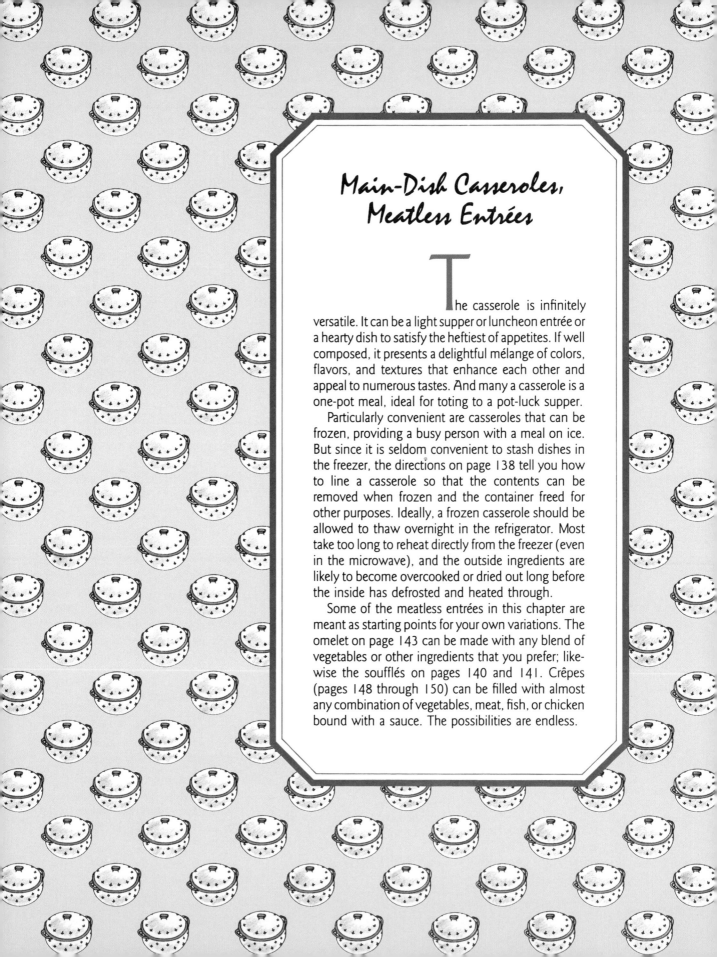

# Main-Dish Casseroles, Meatless Entrées

The casserole is infinitely versatile. It can be a light supper or luncheon entrée or a hearty dish to satisfy the heftiest of appetites. If well composed, it presents a delightful mélange of colors, flavors, and textures that enhance each other and appeal to numerous tastes. And many a casserole is a one-pot meal, ideal for toting to a pot-luck supper.

Particularly convenient are casseroles that can be frozen, providing a busy person with a meal on ice. But since it is seldom convenient to stash dishes in the freezer, the directions on page 138 tell you how to line a casserole so that the contents can be removed when frozen and the container freed for other purposes. Ideally, a frozen casserole should be allowed to thaw overnight in the refrigerator. Most take too long to reheat directly from the freezer (even in the microwave), and the outside ingredients are likely to become overcooked or dried out long before the inside has defrosted and heated through.

Some of the meatless entrées in this chapter are meant as starting points for your own variations. The omelet on page 143 can be made with any blend of vegetables or other ingredients that you prefer; likewise the soufflés on pages 140 and 141. Crêpes (pages 148 through 150) can be filled with almost any combination of vegetables, meat, fish, or chicken bound with a sauce. The possibilities are endless.

# Spicy Shrimp and Rice Casserole

Per serving (hot version): Calories 452; Protein 28 g; Carbohydrate 53 g; Fat 14 g; Sodium 330 mg; Cholesterol 157 mg.

*This zesty dish can can be served either hot or at room temperature.*

- 3 tablespoons olive oil
- 2 medium-size yellow onions, finely chopped
- 3 cloves garlic, crushed
- 1 medium-size sweet green or sweet red pepper, cored, seeded, and coarsely chopped
- 1 bottle (8 ounces) clam broth
- 2 strips orange zest (colored part of rind), ½ inch by 2 inches each
- ¾ cup fresh orange juice
- 1 cup crushed tomatoes
- 10 pitted black olives, halved
- 1 bay leaf
- 2 teaspoons hot red pepper sauce
- 3 cups cooked rice
- 1 pound shrimp, shelled and deveined

*For the cold version:*

- ⅓ cup olive oil
- 2½ tablespoons fresh lemon juice

1 Preheat the oven to 350° F. Heat the olive oil in a medium-size flameproof casserole over moderate heat for 1 minute. Add the onions and garlic, and sauté until golden — about 10 minutes. Add the green pepper, and cook, uncovered, 5 minutes more.

2 Stir in the clam broth, orange zest, and orange juice, raise the heat to high, and cook, uncovered, for 2 minutes. Add the tomatoes, olives, bay leaf, and hot red pepper sauce and bring to a boil. Stir in the cooked rice.

▽ At this point the casserole can be cooled to room temperature and stored. *Refrigerate* in the tightly covered casserole for up to 3 days.

3 Add the shrimp to the casserole, cover, and bake for 15 minutes or until the shrimp are cooked through. Serve with hot crusty bread and steamed artichokes with lemon butter. For the cold version, add the olive oil and lemon juice while still hot. Serve at room temperature, accompanied by pumpernickel rolls and asparagus with dill. Serves 4.

## Serving Later

One hour before baking the casserole, set it out to come to room temperature. Preheat the oven to 350° F. Proceed as in Step 3, baking 25 to 30 minutes.

# Captain's Seafood Casserole

Per serving: Calories 486; Protein 30 g; Carbohydrate 45 g; Fat 21 g; Sodium 870 mg; Cholesterol 154 mg.

*The flavorful sauce in this dish dresses up any seafood combination. We've used shrimp, crab, and white fish, but you could use a combination of any two, or substitute lobster, so long as there are 18 ounces of seafood in all.*

- 3 tablespoons unsalted butter or margarine
- 1 medium-size sweet green pepper, cored, seeded, and finely chopped
- 1 medium-size yellow onion, finely chopped
- 1 cup thinly sliced mushrooms (about 3 ounces)
- 1 cup White Sauce (page 221)
- ½ cup mayonnaise
- 1 tablespoon Dijon or spicy brown mustard
- 6 ounces crabmeat, flaked, shell and cartilage removed
- 6 ounces cooked white fish such as halibut, hake, or flounder, flaked
- 6 ounces cooked shrimp, shelled and deveined
- 2 cups cooked rice
- ½ cup soft bread crumbs

1 Preheat the oven to 350° F. Melt the butter in a heavy 12-inch skillet over moderately low heat. Add the green pepper, onion, and mushrooms. Cook, stirring frequently, until the mushroom liquid has evaporated — about 10 minutes.

2 Remove from the heat and stir in the White Sauce, mayonnaise, and mustard. Fold in the crabmeat, white fish, shrimp, and rice; then spoon the mixture into a 2-quart casserole.

▽ At this point the seafood casserole can be cooled to room temperature and stored. *Refrigerate*, covered tightly, for up to 8 hours.

3 Sprinkle the bread crumbs over the top and bake, uncovered, for 30 minutes or until the casserole is heated through and the top a golden brown. Accompany with sautéed zucchini and carrot sticks. Serves 4.

## Serving Later

Preheat the oven to 350° F. Bake the casserole, tightly covered with aluminum foil, for 20 minutes. Uncover, sprinkle with the bread crumbs, and bake 30 minutes more or until heated through and golden. Serve as in Step 3.

### Tuna Variation

Per serving: Calories 503; Protein 36 g; Carbohydrate 45 g; Fat 21 g; Sodium 914 mg; Cholesterol 91 mg.

Proceed as above, increasing the cooked white fish to 12 ounces and substituting 1 can (6½ ounces) water-packed tuna for the shrimp and crabmeat. Serves 4.

# Turkey and Ham Casserole with Water Chestnuts

Per serving: Calories 240; Protein 21 g; Carbohydrate 16 g; Fat 11 g; Sodium 540 mg; Cholesterol 56 mg.

- 2 tablespoons unsalted butter or margarine
- 2 medium-size yellow onions, chopped
- 12 ounces mushrooms, sliced
- 3 tablespoons all-purpose flour
- ½ teaspoon salt
- ¼ teaspoon black pepper
- 1¼ cups milk
- 12 ounces cooked turkey, cut into ½-inch cubes (about 2 cups)
- 6 ounces cooked ham, cut into ½-inch cubes (about 1 cup)
- 1 can (8 ounces) sliced water chestnuts, drained
- 1 small hot red pepper, seeded and chopped, or ¼ cup chopped canned green chilies, drained
- 2 tablespoons dry sherry
- ½ cup freshly grated Parmesan cheese
- 1 cup soft whole-wheat bread crumbs (2 slices)
- 4 teaspoons unsalted butter or margarine, melted

1 Melt the 2 tablespoons of butter in a heavy 12-inch skillet over moderately low heat. Add the onions, and sauté, stirring occasionally, until soft — about 5 minutes. Add the mushrooms, and cook, uncovered, stirring occasionally, 3 minutes longer.

2 Preheat the oven to 400° F. Blend the flour, salt, and pepper into the vegetable mixture, and cook, stirring, for 2 to 3 minutes. Increase the heat to moderate, gradually stir in the milk, and bring to a boil; cook, stirring constantly, 3 to 4 minutes longer or until the sauce has thickened.

3 Add the turkey, ham, water chestnuts, hot red pepper, and sherry. Stir until well mixed and transfer to a shallow, 2-quart baking dish.

▽ At this point the dish can be cooled to room temperature and stored. *Refrigerate*, covered, for up to 24 hours.

4 Sprinkle the Parmesan cheese over the turkey-ham mixture. In a small bowl, mix the bread crumbs and melted butter; sprinkle on top of the cheese. Bake, uncovered, for 15 minutes. Reduce the heat to 350° F and continue baking until hot and bubbling — about 40 minutes. Buttered egg noodles and steamed Brussels sprouts are good accompaniments. Serves 8.

### Serving Later

Preheat the oven to 400° F. Uncover and proceed as in Step 4, baking the casserole for 20 minutes at 400° F, 50 to 55 minutes at 350° F.

*Spicy Shrimp and Rice Casserole — subtle undercurrents in a peppery medium*

*A sunken treasure of bright colors and savory flavors beneath a sea of golden corn kernels, Chicken-Corn Pie*

# Chicken-Corn Pie

Per serving: Calories 497; Protein 41 g;
Carbohydrate 28 g; Fat 26 g; Sodium 708 mg;
Cholesterol 257 mg.

- 4 tablespoons (½ stick)
  unsalted butter or margarine
- 4 eggs
- 1 package (16 ounces) frozen
  corn kernels, thawed
- 3 cups shredded Monterey Jack
  cheese (about 12 ounces)
- ½ cup diced sweet red pepper
- 2 green onions (including the
  green part), thinly sliced
- 2 teaspoons Dijon or spicy
  brown mustard
- ¾ teaspoon salt
- ¼ teaspoon cayenne pepper
- ¼ teaspoon mace
- 1 medium-size yellow onion,
  finely chopped
- 1 cup cooked diced carrots
- 1 cup uncooked green peas
- 1 cup uncooked, 2-inch
  lengths of green beans
- ½ cup sliced pitted black olives
- ½ cup diced sweet green
  pepper
- ½ teaspoon dried thyme
- ¼ teaspoon black pepper
- 1 clove garlic, minced
- 1 cup Chicken Stock (page 48)
  or canned chicken broth
- 1 tablespoon cornstarch
- 3 cups diced cooked chicken
  (about 18 ounces)
- 2 tablespoons dark raisins

**1** Grease a shallow, 2-quart baking dish with 1 tablespoon of the butter. In a medium-size bowl, beat the eggs slightly; stir in the corn, cheese, sweet red pepper, green onions, mustard, ½ teaspoon of the salt, the cayenne pepper, and mace. Pour half of this mixture into the baking dish.

**2** Melt 1 tablespoon of the remaining butter in a heavy 12-inch skillet over moderate heat. Add the onion, and sauté until soft — about 5 minutes. Add the carrots, peas, green beans, olives, sweet green pepper, remaining salt, thyme, and black pepper. Sauté, stirring occasionally, for 3 minutes; stir in the garlic, and cook 1 minute more.

**3** Preheat the oven to 350° F. In a small bowl or measuring cup, stir the stock and the cornstarch together until smooth. Add the liquid to the skillet and bring to a simmer over moderate heat. Stir in the chicken, then pour the skillet mixture over the corn mixture. Top with the remaining corn.

▽ At this point the pie can be cooled to room temperature and stored. *Refrigerate*, covered tightly with plastic wrap, for up to 8 hours.

**4** Dot the pie with the remaining 2 tablespoons of butter. Bake, uncovered, for 1 hour or until hot and bubbling. Serve with cranberry-orange relish and French rolls. Serves 6 to 8.

## Serving Later

Preheat the oven to 350° F. Uncover the pie and proceed as in Step 4, baking the pie for about 1 hour and 15 minutes or until hot and bubbling.

128

# Tortilla Casserole

Per serving: Calories 516; Protein 39 g;
Carbohydrate 37 g; Fat 25 g;
Sodium 1221 mg; Cholesterol 47 mg.

- 1 pound lean ground beef round
- 1/4 teaspoon each salt and black pepper
- 3 cups Mexican Tomato Sauce (page 217)
- 12 corn tortillas
- 2 cups shredded Cheddar cheese (about 8 ounces)
- 3 green onions (both white and green parts), finely chopped
- 1/2 cup sliced pitted black olives

1 In a heavy 12-inch skillet set over moderately low heat, sauté the ground beef, stirring frequently, until browned — about 5 minutes. Drain off any fat. Season with the salt and pepper and stir in 1 cup of the tomato sauce; set aside.

2 Preheat the oven to 350° F. Spread a thin layer of the tomato sauce across the bottom of a 13" x 9" x 2" baking dish. Cut each tortilla in half. Dip 8 of the tortilla halves in the remaining sauce and arrange them, overlapping, in a layer in the baking dish. Top with half of the beef mixture, then a third of the cheese, smoothing to make the layers even. Sprinkle with half of the green onions and half of the olives. Repeat the layers; top with the remaining tortillas, sauce, and cheese.

▽ At this point the tortilla casserole can be stored. Cover tightly and *refrigerate* for up to 12 hours.

3 Bake, uncovered, for 30 to 40 minutes or until heated through and bubbling. Serve with endive and Bibb lettuce with Herbed Vinaigrette Dressing (page 214). Makes 6 servings.

**Serving Later**

One hour before baking the casserole, set it out to come to room temperature. Preheat the oven to 350° F. Proceed as in Step 3.

# Tamale Pie

Per serving: Calories 503; Protein 44 g;
Carbohydrate 44 g; Fat 17 g; Sodium 798 mg;
Cholesterol 154 mg.

*This is a wonderful buffet dish. The recipe can easily be doubled or tripled for a large crowd.*

- 1 tablespoon vegetable oil
- 1 large yellow onion, chopped
- 1 large sweet green pepper, cored, seeded, and diced
- 2 pounds lean ground beef round
- 1 package (10 ounces) frozen corn kernels, thawed
- 1 cup tomato purée
- 1/2 cup sliced, pimiento-stuffed green olives
- 2 tablespoons yellow cornmeal
- 1 tablespoon cocoa powder (not a mix)
- 1 tablespoon chili powder, or to taste
- 2 teaspoons ground cumin
- 2 teaspoons Worcestershire sauce
- 1 teaspoon salt
- 3/4 teaspoon ground allspice
- 1/2 teaspoon hot red pepper sauce, or to taste
- 1/4 teaspoon black pepper

*For the topping:*
- 1 cup all-purpose flour
- 1 cup yellow cornmeal
- 2 tablespoons sugar
- 2 teaspoons baking powder
- 1 egg
- 1/2 cup milk
- 2 tablespoons unsalted butter or margarine, melted
- 1/2 cup shredded Cheddar cheese (about 2 ounces)
- 2 tablespoons chopped green chilies

1 Heat the vegetable oil in a heavy 12-inch skillet over moderate heat for 1 minute. Add the onion and green pepper, and sauté, stirring occasionally, until soft — about 5 minutes. Add the ground beef, and sauté, stirring and breaking up the clumps, until it loses its pink color — about 4 minutes.

2 Add the corn, tomato purée, olives, the 2 tablespoons cornmeal, the cocoa, chili powder, cumin, Worcestershire sauce, salt, allspice, hot red pepper sauce, and black pepper. Bring to a boil. Reduce the heat to low, cover, and simmer, stirring occasionally, for 10 minutes. Pour the mixture into a shallow, 2 1/2- to 3-quart baking dish.

▽ At this point the mixture can be cooled to room temperature and stored. Cover with plastic wrap. *Refrigerate* for up to 3 days.

3 Preheat the oven to 400° F. In a large bowl, mix the flour, cornmeal, sugar, and baking powder. In a medium-size bowl, beat the egg slightly, then blend in the milk and melted butter. Stir the egg mixture into the dry ingredients until well combined; stir in the cheese and chilies. Drop large spoonfuls of this topping around the edges of the baking dish.

4 Bake, uncovered, for 10 minutes. Reduce the oven temperature to 350° F and bake, uncovered, 30 to 40 minutes longer or until bubbling and hot. A watercress salad or North African Carrot Salad (page 195) makes a good accompaniment. Serves 8 to 10.

**Serving Later**

One hour before baking the pie, set it out to come to room temperature. Proceed as in Steps 3 and 4.

# Casserole of Stuffed Braised Lamb Steaks

Per serving: Calories 631; Protein 32 g;
Carbohydrate 36 g; Fat 40 g; Sodium 479 mg;
Cholesterol 110 mg.

4 lamb shoulder steaks (about
6 ounces each)
3 ounces cooked ham,
chopped
3 tablespoons chopped yellow
onion
2 tablespoons minced parsley
1 tablespoon lemon juice
1½ teaspoons dried rosemary,
crumbled
4 teaspoons vegetable oil
4 all-purpose potatoes, peeled
and sliced ¼ inch thick
3 stalks celery, sliced ½ inch
thick diagonally

3 carrots, peeled and sliced ¾
inch thick diagonally
*For the sauce:*
1½ cups Chicken Stock (page
48) or canned chicken broth
1 tablespoon minced parsley
2 tablespoons chopped yellow
onion
½ teaspoon dried rosemary,
crumbled
¼ teaspoon black pepper
1 bay leaf

1 Cut a pocket horizontally in the
side of each steak. Mix the ham,
onion, parsley, lemon juice, and rosemary. Stuff the pockets with this mixture and secure with toothpicks.

▽ At this point the lamb steaks can
be stored. *Refrigerate*, individually wrapped in plastic wrap, for up to 6

hours. *Freeze*, labeled and individually
wrapped in heavy-duty aluminum foil,
for up to 1 month at 0° F.

2 Heat the oil in a 12-inch skillet over
high heat for about 1 minute. Add
the steaks, and cook, partially covered
to prevent spattering, until golden
brown on each side — about 12 minutes. Meanwhile, in a 2-quart casserole, layer the vegetables in the order
listed. Top them with the steaks.

3 Preheat the oven to 350° F. Discard
the fat from the skillet, add the
stock, parsley, onion, rosemary, pepper, and bay leaf, and bring to a boil,
scraping any bits from the skillet. Pour
over the casserole, cover, and bake
until the vegetables are tender — about
1 hour and 10 minutes. Serve with
crusty whole-wheat bread. Serves 4.

*Curried Lamb Casserole — the blatant heat of curry subtly subdued by creamy yogurt, golden raisins, and pistachios*

**From freezer:** Heat the oil in a 12-inch skillet over moderate heat for about 1 minute. Add the frozen steaks and cook, partially covered, until golden brown on each side — about 20 minutes. Continue as in Steps 2 and 3. **To microwave:** Layer the vegetables in a 2-quart microwave-safe casserole. Add the parsley, onion, rosemary, pepper, and bay leaf to the stock and pour over the vegetables. Cover with plastic wrap vented at one side and microwave on *High* (100% power) for 10 minutes. Rotate the casserole 90 degrees and stir the vegetables. Re-cover and microwave on *High* (100% power) another 10 minutes or until the vegetables are tender. Stir once more. Meanwhile, brown the frozen steaks as directed in the *From freezer* instructions above.

Add them to the casserole along with the pan juices (add ¼ cup water to deglaze the skillet, if necessary). Cover with plastic wrap vented at one side; microwave on *High* (100% power) for 2 minutes. Serve as in Step 3.

# Curried Lamb Casserole

Per serving: Calories 757; Protein 35 g; Carbohydrate 59 g; Fat 43 g; Sodium 282 mg; Cholesterol 102 mg.

- 3 tablespoons olive oil
- 1 cup white rice
- ¼ teaspoon ground turmeric
- 2 cups water
- 1¼ pounds boneless lamb (from the leg), cubed
- 3 tablespoons all-purpose flour
- 1 medium-size yellow onion, sliced
- 2 cloves garlic, minced
- 1 tablespoon chopped fresh ginger
- ½ cup Chicken Stock (page 48) or canned chicken broth
- ⅓ cup golden raisins
- 1 tablespoon curry powder
- ¼ teaspoon ground cinnamon
- 2 teaspoons tomato paste
- ¼ teaspoon salt
- ¼ cup plain low-fat yogurt
- 1 tablespoon half-and-half
- ½ cup chopped roasted pistachios or almonds

1 Heat 1 tablespoon of oil in a medium-size saucepan over moderate heat. Add the rice and turmeric, and cook, stirring, for 1 minute. Add the water, cover, and bring to a boil. Reduce the heat to low; cook until the rice is done — about 20 minutes. Set aside.

2 Coat the lamb with the flour. Heat the remaining 2 tablespoons of oil in a heavy 12-inch skillet over moderately high heat. Sauté the lamb in batches until brown — about 5 minutes per batch. Transfer to a platter lined with paper toweling.

3 Add the onion, garlic, and ginger to the skillet; sauté for 4 minutes. Add the browned lamb along with the stock, raisins, curry, cinnamon, tomato paste, and salt. Cook, covered, for 15 minutes over low heat, stirring occasionally. Remove from the heat and stir in the yogurt and half-and-half.

4 Preheat the oven to 375° F. Fluff the rice with a fork and put half in a 2-quart ovenproof casserole. (If you plan to freeze the casserole, see Tip, page 138, on lining the dish.) Spoon half of the lamb mixture on top, then sprinkle it with half of the nuts. Repeat with the remaining ingredients, leaving a 1-inch border of exposed rice.

▽ At this point the dish can be cooled to room temperature and stored. *Refrigerate* in the covered casserole for up to 2 days. *Freeze* in the covered casserole or in a shallow, 2½-quart, covered, microwave-safe casserole for up to 2 months at 0° F.

5 Bake, covered, for 45 to 55 minutes or until heated through. Sautéed zucchini and steamed carrots make good accompaniments. Serves 4.

**From refrigerator:** Preheat the oven to 375° F. Proceed as in Step 5, baking the casserole for 1 to 1¼ hours. **From freezer:** Thaw the casserole in the refrigerator overnight and proceed as above. **To microwave:** Heat, covered, in the microwave-safe casserole on *Low* (30% power) for 15 minutes. Rotate the casserole 90 degrees; then heat, covered, on *Low* (30% power) 10 minutes more. Stir, rotate it 90 degrees again, and microwave, covered, on *Low* (30% power) 10 minutes longer. Microwave, covered, on *High* (100% power) for 10 minutes; rotate 90 degrees and stir. Microwave, covered, on *High* (100% power) 10 minutes longer. Serve as in Step 5.

# Zucchini Moussaka

Per serving: Calories 496; Protein 31 g; Carbohydrate 17 g; Fat 35 g; Sodium 905 mg; Cholesterol 127 mg.

*This delicious variation on a classic Greek dish, usually made with eggplant, is a wonderful way to use up a plentiful harvest of zucchini.*

| | |
|---|---|
| 6 | medium-size zucchini, sliced lengthwise ¼ inch thick (about 2 pounds) |
| 2 | teaspoons salt |
| ¼ | cup olive oil |
| 6 | tablespoons (¾ stick) unsalted butter or margarine |
| 1 | large yellow onion, finely chopped |
| 1 | clove garlic, minced |
| 1½ | pounds lean ground lamb shoulder |
| 1½ | teaspoons dried oregano, crumbled |
| ¾ | teaspoon ground cinnamon |
| ¼ | teaspoon each ground nutmeg and black pepper |
| 4 | tablespoons all-purpose flour |
| 1½ | cups milk |
| 1 | egg, lightly beaten |
| 8 | ounces feta cheese, crumbled |

**1** Sprinkle the zucchini with 1 teaspoon of the salt, place them in a colander set in the sink, and weight with a heavy plate. Let stand for 1 hour. Press the slices to squeeze out as much water as possible, then rinse off the salt and pat dry with paper toweling.

**2** In a heavy 12-inch skillet, heat 2 tablespoons of the oil over moderate heat for 1 minute. Sauté the zucchini in 3 batches until lightly browned — 5 to 6 minutes per batch. Add the remaining oil as needed. With a slotted spatula, transfer to a platter lined with paper toweling.

**3** In the same skillet, melt 2 tablespoons of the butter over moderate heat. Add the onion and garlic, and sauté, stirring, for 1 minute. Add the lamb, oregano, the remaining teaspoon of salt, the cinnamon, nutmeg, and pepper. Cook, uncovered, stirring occasionally, until the lamb is brown — about 7 minutes. Drain off the fat.

**4** Preheat the oven to 350° F. In a small heavy saucepan, melt the remaining 4 tablespoons of butter over moderately low heat. Whisk in the flour, and cook, stirring constantly, for 2 minutes. Gradually add the milk, stirring constantly. Add the egg, and cook, still stirring, until the sauce has thickened — 3 to 4 minutes.

**5** In a greased 13″ x 9″ x 2″ baking dish, arrange half of the zucchini in an even layer. Top with the lamb mixture and half of the feta cheese. Cover with the remaining zucchini and feta. Pour the sauce over all.

▽ At this point the moussaka can be cooled to room temperature and stored. *Refrigerate*, tightly covered with plastic wrap, for up to 24 hours.

**6** Bake, uncovered, until golden and bubbling — 50 minutes to 1 hour. Accompany with a rice pilaf or pita bread, and a salad of tomatoes, onions, and black olives. Serves 6 to 8.

## Serving Later

Preheat the oven to 350° F. Bake, uncovered, for 1 to 1¼ hours. Serve as in Step 6.

## Eggplant Variation

Per serving: Calories 520; Protein 31 g; Carbohydrate 23 g; Fat 35 g; Sodium 904 mg; Cholesterol 127 mg.

For the zucchini, substitute **2 medium-size eggplants, trimmed, halved lengthwise, and cut into ¾-inch slices.** Prepare as in Step 1 to remove excess water. Sauté the eggplant as in Step 2, adding more olive oil, if necessary. Continue as in Steps 3, 4, 5, and 6.

# Quick Cassoulet

Per serving: Calories 728; Protein 45 g; Carbohydrate 37 g; Fat 44 g; Sodium 986 mg; Cholesterol 134 mg.

*A faster and less calorie-laden version of the classic French dish, which calls for a whole duck, this hearty one-pot meal is perfect for a cold winter's night.*

| | |
|---|---|
| 1 | pound dried Great Northern beans, washed and picked over |
| ½ | pound slab or thick-sliced bacon, diced |
| 1 | pound boneless pork shoulder or butt, trimmed and cut into ¾-inch cubes |
| 1 | pound boneless lamb shoulder, trimmed and cut into ¾-inch cubes |
| 2 | boneless chicken thighs or drumsticks, cut into ¾-inch cubes |
| 1 | pound garlic sausage or kielbasa, cut into ½-inch slices |
| 3 | medium-size yellow onions, coarsely chopped |
| 6 | cloves garlic, coarsely chopped |
| ½ | cup dry white wine |
| 1 | can (28 ounces) crushed tomatoes |
| 1 | teaspoon each dried thyme and basil, crumbled |
| ½ | cup chopped parsley |
| 3 | bay leaves |
| ¼ | teaspoon black pepper |
| ½ | cup soft bread crumbs |
| 3 | tablespoons unsalted butter or margarine, melted |

**1** In a large saucepan, cover the beans with water and bring to a boil over moderately high heat. Remove from the heat, cover, and let stand 1 hour.

**2** Meanwhile, in a very large, heavy, flameproof casserole, cook the bacon over moderate heat, stirring occasionally, until all the fat is rendered — about 10 minutes. With a slotted spoon, transfer to a platter lined with paper toweling. Remove all but 3 tablespoons of the fat from the casserole and reserve it.

3 Add the pork and lamb to the casserole and brown over moderate heat — 8 to 10 minutes. Add the chicken and sausage, and sauté, stirring occasionally, 5 minutes more. With a slotted spoon, transfer the meats to a platter lined with paper toweling.

4 Add enough reserved fat to the casserole to make 3 tablespoons. Add the onions and garlic, and sauté over moderate heat until soft — about 5 minutes. Stir in the wine, raise the heat to moderately high, and cook, uncovered, for 5 minutes, stirring and scraping up any brown bits.

5 Add the tomatoes, thyme, basil, parsley, bay leaves, and pepper to the casserole. Cover and simmer over moderately low heat for 30 minutes or until thickened.

6 Preheat the oven to 350° F. Drain the beans, reserving the liquid. Return the meats to the casserole, add the beans, and mix well.

▽ At this point the cassoulet can be cooled to room temperature and stored. *Refrigerate* in the covered casserole for up to 2 days.

7 Sprinkle the mixture with the bread crumbs, then drizzle with the melted butter. Bake, uncovered, for 2 hours or until the beans are tender and the top is crusty brown. Check during the baking; if the casserole seems too dry, add a little of the reserved bean liquid. Accompany with hot garlic bread and an arugula salad. Serves 10 to 12.

### Serving Later

One hour before baking the casserole, set it out to come to room temperature. Preheat the oven to 350° F. Proceed as in Step 7, adding a little chicken broth, if necessary, during the baking.

*A generous portion of Zucchini Moussaka — new variation on an old theme*

# Sausage-Stuffed Zucchini

Per serving: Calories 302; Protein 19 g; Carbohydrate 15 g; Fat 19 g; Sodium 832 mg; Cholesterol 118 mg.

- 4 medium-size zucchini, cut in half lengthwise (about 1½ pounds)
- 8 ounces Italian sausage, hot or sweet
- 1 medium-size yellow onion, chopped
- 3 tablespoons minced parsley
- 2 tablespoons minced basil or 2 teaspoons dried basil, crumbled
- ¼ teaspoon dried marjoram or thyme, crumbled
- ¼ cup fine dry bread crumbs
- ¼ cup grated Parmesan cheese
- ¼ teaspoon each salt and black pepper
- 1 egg

1 Place the zucchini halves in a large saucepan, weigh them down with a small plate so they will cook evenly, and cover with boiling water. Over moderately low heat, simmer for 6 to 8 minutes or until the zucchini are almost tender. Drain and refresh under cold running water.

2 With a spoon, scoop the pulp from the zucchini, leaving a ¼-inch border all around. Chop the pulp coarsely, transfer to a sieve, and press it with the back of a large spoon to extract any excess liquid; set pulp aside. Invert the zucchini on paper toweling to drain.

3 Remove and discard the sausage casings, break up the meat, and sauté in a 10-inch skillet over moderate heat for 5 minutes. Add the onion, parsley, basil, and marjoram; cook 5 minutes more or until the onion is soft. Remove from the heat, add the bread crumbs, 2 tablespoons of the Parmesan cheese, and the salt and pepper.

▽ At this point the stuffing can be cooled to room temperature and stored; store the zucchini separately. *Refrigerate* each in a tightly sealed container for up to 24 hours.

4 Preheat the oven to 350° F. Mix the egg with the stuffing mixture and fill the zucchini boats with equal amounts of the stuffing. Place the zucchini boats in a 13" x 9" x 2" baking dish and sprinkle with the remaining 2 tablespoons of Parmesan cheese. Bake, uncovered, for 35 to 45 minutes or until the zucchini are heated through and the filling has a lightly browned crust. Serve with Potato, Tomato, and Onion Gratin (page 178). Serves 4.

# Baked Rice with Sausage, Peppers, and Mushrooms

Per serving: Calories 605; Protein 30 g; Carbohydrate 46 g; Fat 33 g; Sodium 1199 mg; Cholesterol 76 mg.

- 2 tablespoons olive oil
- 12 ounces Italian sausage, hot or sweet, cut into ½-inch slices
- 1 medium-size yellow onion, finely chopped
- 1 medium-size sweet red pepper, cored, seeded, and cut into ½-inch squares
- 1 cup thinly sliced mushrooms (about 4 ounces)
- 1 small zucchini, halved lengthwise and thinly sliced
- 3 cups white rice
- 2¾ cups Chicken Stock (page 48) or canned chicken broth
- ½ cup grated Parmesan cheese
- 1 tablespoon minced basil or 1 teaspoon dried basil, crumbled
- ¼ teaspoon black pepper

1 Heat the oil in a heavy 12-inch skillet over moderately high heat. Add the sausage, and sauté for 5 minutes or until browned. Transfer

with a slotted spoon to a bowl. Pour off all but 1 tablespoon of the fat from the skillet and discard.

2 Preheat the oven to 350° F. Add the onion to the skillet, and sauté, stirring, for 5 minutes. Add the red pepper, mushrooms, and zucchini, and sauté, stirring occasionally, 5 minutes longer. Stir in the rice, tossing to coat. Add the stock, bring to a boil, and stir in the Parmesan cheese, basil, pepper, and sausage. Transfer the mixture to a lightly oiled, 2-quart casserole.

▽ At this point the casserole can be cooled to room temperature and stored. *Refrigerate*, tightly covered, for up to 24 hours.

3 Bake, covered, for 25 minutes. Uncover and bake 10 minutes longer or until almost all the liquid has been absorbed, the rice is tender, and the top is slightly crusty. Serve hot or at room temperature, accompanied by marinated vegetables. Serves 4.

### Serving Later

Preheat the oven to 350° F. Bake the casserole, covered, for 40 to 45 minutes. Uncover and proceed as in Step 3.

# Sausage and Lentil Casserole

Per serving: Calories 495; Protein 25 g; Carbohydrate 33 g; Fat 30 g; Sodium 1079 mg; Cholesterol 64 mg.

- 1 pound dried lentils, washed and picked over
- 1 teaspoon salt
- 2 pounds kielbasa (Polish sausage)
- 2 tablespoons vegetable oil
- 2 medium-size yellow onions, coarsely chopped
- 3 cloves garlic, crushed

*Sausage-Stuffed Zucchini boats, piping hot and ready to serve*

1   can (16 ounces) tomatoes, broken up, with their juice
1   bay leaf
1   teaspoon sugar
½   teaspoon black pepper

1 Place the lentils and salt in a large saucepan, add water to cover, and bring to a boil over high heat. Reduce the heat to low, cover, and simmer for 35 to 45 minutes or until the lentils are tender but still hold their shape. Add a little more water while they are cooking, if needed.

2 Meanwhile, slit the casing on the kielbasa lengthwise and remove it. Slice the meat ½ inch thick; set aside.

3 Preheat the oven to 350° F. Heat the oil in a large flameproof casserole over moderately high heat. Add the onions and garlic, and sauté, stirring occasionally, for 5 minutes or until the onions are soft. Stir in the lentils, kielbasa, tomatoes, bay leaf, sugar, and pepper until well mixed.

▽ At this point the dish can be cooled to room temperature and stored. Cover and *refrigerate* in the casserole for up to 2 days.

4 Bake, covered, for 30 minutes or until hot and bubbling. Serve with sauerkraut, dilled cucumbers, and hard rolls. Serves 8 to 10.

### Serving Later

One hour before baking the casserole, set it out to come to room temperature. Preheat the oven to 350° F. Proceed as in Step 4.

# Sure-Fire Black Bean Chili

Per serving: Calories 334; Protein 17 g; Carbohydrate 51 g; Fat 8 g; Sodium 192 mg; Cholesterol 0 mg.

*This meatless chili is low on fat and high on taste. If there's time, it's worth the effort to make your own ground chili (see Tip, page 137) and also to cook the spices as directed in Step 3. For a change of pace, use pinto beans to make a red chili.*

- 2 cups (12 ounces) dried black turtle beans, washed and picked over
- 1 bay leaf
- 4 teaspoons cumin seeds or 4 teaspoons ground cumin
- 4 teaspoons dried oregano, crumbled
- 4 teaspoons paprika
- ½ teaspoon cayenne (ground red) pepper
- 3 tablespoons corn oil
- 3 medium-size yellow onions, coarsely chopped
- 4 cloves garlic, coarsely chopped
- ½ teaspoon salt
- 2 tablespoons chili powder
- 5 medium-size tomatoes, peeled, seeded, and chopped, or 2½ cups crushed tomatoes
- 1 teaspoon chopped chilpotle chili or crushed red pepper flakes, or to taste
- 1 tablespoon rice wine vinegar or cider vinegar
- ¼ cup chopped cilantro (coriander leaves) or parsley

*Optional garnishes:*

- ½ cup shredded Muenster or Monterey Jack cheese
- ½ cup sour cream
- 2 poblano or Anaheim chilis, roasted, peeled, and diced, or 2 ounces canned green chilies, rinsed and diced
- 6 sprigs cilantro (coriander leaves) or parsley

1. In a large, heavy, flameproof casserole, cover the beans with water and bring to a boil over moderately high heat. Remove from the heat, cover, and let stand for 1 hour.

2. Drain the beans and cover with fresh water. Add the bay leaf and bring to a boil over moderate heat. Reduce the heat to low, cover, and simmer for 1½ hours.

3. Meanwhile, heat a heavy 10-inch skillet over moderate heat for 1 minute. Add the cumin seeds, and cook until they begin to color — about 30 seconds. Add the oregano, and cook, shaking the pan frequently so

136

that the herbs don't scorch, until the fragrance is strong and robust — about 20 seconds. Remove from the heat, stir in the paprika and cayenne pepper, and transfer to a mortar or spice mill. Grind to a coarse powder and set aside. Or, if you are using ground cumin, combine the spices in a small bowl and set aside.

4 In the same skillet, heat the oil over moderately low heat for 1 minute. Add the onions, and sauté until soft — about 5 minutes. Add the garlic, salt, ground herbs, and chili powder, and sauté 5 minutes more. Add the tomatoes and the chilpotle chili and simmer, uncovered, for 15 minutes.

5 Stir the skillet mixture into the simmering beans, adding more water, if necessary, so that the beans are covered by 1 inch of liquid. Continue cooking until the beans are tender — 15 to 20 minutes. Then add the vinegar, cilantro, and if desired, more chilpotle pepper and salt.

▽ At this point the chili can be cooled to room temperature and stored. *Refrigerate* in the covered casserole for up to 3 days.

6 Ladle the chili into soup plates and garnish with the cheese, sour cream, green chilies, and a sprig of cilantro, if you like. Accompany with rice or corn bread and an avocado salad. Serves 6.

## Serving Later

Heat the chili, covered, over moderately low heat, stirring occasionally, until warmed through — about 20 minutes. Serve as in Step 6.

*Sure-Fire Black Bean Chili, a wholesome, all-vegetable chili spiked with a bold mixture of herbs and spices*

*Tip: As a substitute for commercial chili powder, try making your own ground chili. Dry chili negros or ancho chilis in a 375° F oven for 3 to 5 minutes. When cool enough to handle, remove the stems, seeds, and veins. (Use gloves when handling chilis and be careful not to touch your eyes.) Tear the pods into small pieces and grind them into a powder in a spice mill or blender. One chili yields 1 tablespoon of ground chili.*

# Chuckwagon Chili

Per serving: Calories 356; Protein 38 g; Carbohydrate 24 g; Fat 12 g; Sodium 600 mg; Cholesterol 70 mg.

|   |   |
|---|---|
| ⅔ | cup dried pinto beans, washed and picked over |
| 1½ | cups water |
| 1 | pound ground beef chuck |
| 8 | ounces ground pork shoulder |
| 2 | medium-size yellow onions, chopped |
| 1 | medium-size sweet green pepper, cored, seeded, and chopped |
| ¼ | cup chopped parsley |
| 2 | cloves garlic, minced |
| 1 | can (16 ounces) whole tomatoes in purée |
| 1 | tablespoon tomato paste |
| 3 | tablespoons chili powder |
| 1 | teaspoon ground cumin |
| 1 | teaspoon each salt and black pepper |

Optional garnishes:
　Sour cream
　Chopped onion
　Shredded Cheddar cheese
　Chopped green chilies

1 In a medium-size saucepan, bring the beans and water to a boil over high heat. Remove from the heat, cover, and let stand for 1 hour.

2 Meanwhile, brown the beef and pork in a medium-size flameproof casserole over moderately high heat — 5 to 7 minutes. Drain and discard all but 1 tablespoon of the fat. Add the onions, green pepper, parsley, and garlic; cook, uncovered, for 5 minutes, stirring occasionally. Add the tomatoes, tomato paste, chili, cumin, salt, and pepper. Bring to a boil; reduce the heat to moderately low and simmer, uncovered, for 15 minutes.

3 Add the beans and their liquid and return to a boil over moderately high heat. Reduce the heat to moderately low, cover, and simmer, stirring occasionally, for 1 hour and 15 minutes or until the beans are tender.

▽ At this point the chili can be cooled to room temperature and stored. *Refrigerate* in the covered casserole for up to 3 days. *Freeze* in labeled, 1-quart freezer bags (2 servings per bag) for 2 months at 0° F.

4 Ladle the chili into soup bowls and serve the sour cream, onion, Cheddar cheese, and chilies on the side. Good accompaniments are rice and a green salad. Serves 6.

## Serving Later

**From refrigerator:** Add 2 tablespoons water. Cover and reheat, stirring occasionally, over moderately low heat for 35 minutes or until warmed through. Serve as in Step 4. **From freezer:** Thaw in the refrigerator overnight. Transfer to a medium-size flameproof casserole and reheat as above. **To microwave:** In a 2-quart, covered, microwave-safe casserole, heat on *Low* (30% power) for 15 minutes. Rotate the casserole 90 degrees and microwave on *Low* (30% power) 15 minutes longer. Break up any clumps with a wooden spoon, re-cover, and microwave on *High* (100% power) for 7 minutes or until heated through. Serve as in Step 4.

# White Bean and Eggplant Casserole

Per main-dish serving: Calories 270;
Protein 12 g; Carbohydrate 39 g; Fat 9 g;
Sodium 568 mg; Cholesterol 2 mg.

- 1 cup dried Great Northern beans, washed and picked over
- 5½ cups water
- 3 cloves garlic, 1 clove bruised, 2 minced
- 2 bay leaves
- 1 tablespoon minced sage or 1 teaspoon dried sage, crumbled
- 2 tablespoons olive oil
- 2 large yellow onions, sliced
- 1 medium-size eggplant, cut into ¾-inch cubes
- 1 can (28 ounces) whole tomatoes with their juice
- ¾ teaspoon salt
- ¼ teaspoon dried thyme, crumbled

*For the topping:*
- ½ cup fine dry bread crumbs
- 2 tablespoons grated Parmesan cheese
- 1 tablespoon olive oil
- ⅛ teaspoon black pepper

1 Place the beans and 2½ cups of the water in a heavy, medium-size, flameproof casserole and bring to a boil over high heat. Remove from the heat, cover, and let stand for 1 hour. Drain off the liquid. Add the remaining 3 cups water, the bruised garlic, bay leaves, and 1½ teaspoons of the sage and bring to a boil over high heat. Reduce the heat to low, cover, and simmer for 1 hour or until tender. Drain and set aside.

2 Meanwhile, heat the oil in a heavy 12-inch skillet over moderately low heat for 1 minute. Add the onions, and sauté, stirring occasionally, until soft — about 5 minutes. Add the eggplant, and cook, covered, 10 minutes more, stirring occasionally.

3 Add the tomatoes, minced garlic, salt, thyme, and remaining 1½ teaspoons of sage, breaking up the tomatoes with a spoon. Return to a boil over moderate heat. Then simmer, uncovered, for 20 minutes over moderately low heat.

4 Preheat the oven to 350° F. Stir the eggplant-tomato mixture into the the beans and bring to a boil over moderate heat. Reduce the heat to moderately low, cover, and simmer for 10 minutes.

▽ At this point the mixture can be cooled to room temperature and stored. *Refrigerate* in the tightly covered casserole for up to 24 hours.

5 Cover and bake the casserole for 20 minutes. Meanwhile, combine the topping ingredients in a small bowl.

6 Sprinkle the topping over the vegetables. Bake, uncovered, for 40 minutes more or until the topping is brown and the vegetables heated through. Serve as a meatless entrée, accompanied by hot rice and a salad of watercress and mushrooms, or use as a side dish with roasted meats or poultry. Serves 6 as a main dish, 8 as a side dish.

## Serving Later

One hour before baking the casserole, set it out to come to room temperature. Preheat the oven to 350° F. Proceed as in Steps 5 and 6.

# Black Beans with Ham in Sour Cream

Per main-dish serving: Calories 482;
Protein 27 g; Carbohydrate 52 g; Fat 19 g;
Sodium 677 mg; Cholesterol 56 mg.

*For a special treat, top this hearty dish with crumbled bacon — about ½ pound, cooked until crisp.*

- 1 pound dried black beans, washed and picked over, or 2 cans (16 ounces each) black beans
- 8 ounces cooked ham, diced (about 1⅓ cups)
- 2 cups sour cream
- ⅓ cup orange juice
- 1 teaspoon dried mint, crumbled
- ½ teaspoon salt
- ¼ teaspoon black pepper

1 In a 2-quart flameproof casserole, cover the dried beans with water and bring to a boil over high heat. Remove from the heat, cover, and let stand for 1 hour. Bring to a boil again over high heat. Reduce the heat to low, cover, and simmer until tender — about 1 hour. Add more water, if necessary, to prevent scorching. Drain

*Tip: To freeze a casserole without losing the use of the dish for several weeks, line the dish with overlapping sheets of plastic wrap that are long enough to encase the food when folded over. Add the food, fold and seal the plastic wrap, and cover the dish with heavy-duty aluminum foil.*

*When frozen solid — 12 to 24 hours — take the frozen food block out of the dish, wrap it tightly in heavy-duty aluminum foil, and label it.*

*When ready to reheat the casserole, remove the foil and plastic wrapper. Then slip the food block into the dish in which it was frozen, oiling the dish first. Proceed according to recipe.*

*Through a crown of cheese, a scoop of mouth-watering White Bean and Eggplant Casserole*

and return to the casserole. If using canned beans, drain, rinse, and place them in the casserole.

**2** Preheat the oven to 350° F. Stir the ham, sour cream, orange juice, mint, salt, and pepper into the beans.

▽ At this point the beans can be stored. *Refrigerate* in the covered casserole for up to 2 days.

**3** Bake the beans, covered, until heated through — 30 to 40 minutes. Serve as an entrée, accompanied by hot rice and a spinach salad with mushrooms and sliced red onions. Or use as a side dish to accompany roasted meat or game. Serves 6 as a main dish, 8 as a side dish.

### Serving Later

One hour before baking the casserole, set it out to come to room temperature. Preheat the oven to 350° F. Proceed as in Step 3.

# Cottage Cheese Soufflé

Per serving: Calories 309; Protein 16 g; Carbohydrate 13 g; Fat 22 g; Sodium 550 mg; Cholesterol 320 mg.

- 4 tablespoons (½ stick) unsalted butter or margarine
- ¼ cup all-purpose flour
- ¾ cup milk
- 1 cup cottage cheese
- 1 jar (7 ounces) pimientos, drained and chopped (about ⅔ cup)
- 4 eggs, separated
- 1 tablespoon finely chopped yellow onion
- ½ teaspoon salt
- ⅛ teaspoon black pepper
- 1 tablespoon fine dry bread crumbs

1 Melt the butter in a heavy medium-size saucepan over moderate heat. Add the flour, and cook, stirring constantly, until smooth — about 2 minutes. Gradually add the milk and bring to a boil, stirring constantly. Reduce the heat to low; cook and stir until thickened and smooth — 3 to 4 minutes.

2 Remove from the heat and add the cottage cheese, pimientos, egg yolks, onion, salt, and pepper, stirring until well blended. Transfer the mixture to a large bowl.

▽ At this point the egg whites and the cottage cheese mixture, after it has cooled to room temperature, can be stored separately. *Refrigerate*, tightly covered, for up to 24 hours.

3 Preheat the oven to 350° F. Lightly butter a straight-sided, 6-cup soufflé dish; dust it with the bread crumbs. In a medium-size bowl, beat the egg whites until stiff but not dry. Gradually fold them into the cottage cheese mixture until well blended. Turn into the soufflé dish and bake, uncovered, until puffed and golden — 50 to 55 minutes.

Serve immediately, accompanied by asparagus with Lemon Butter (page 223). Serves 4.

## Serving Later

Proceed as in Step 3, baking the soufflé for 60 to 70 minutes.

## Garlic-Ricotta Variation

Per serving: Calories 349; Protein 16 g; Carbohydrate 11 g; Fat 27 g; Sodium 635 mg; Cholesterol 344 mg.

Proceed as in Step 1 but, before adding the flour, sauté **2 tablespoons minced garlic** in the melted butter until soft — about 2 minutes. In Step 2, substitute **1 cup ricotta cheese** for the cottage cheese, omit the pimiento and onion, and add ¾ **teaspoon dried basil, crumbled**, and an additional ½ **teaspoon salt**. Proceed as in Step 3. Serve with a green salad or marinated vegetables.

# Eggplant and Cheese Soufflé

Per serving: Calories 387; Protein 18 g; Carbohydrate 12 g; Fat 30 g; Sodium 404 mg; Cholesterol 346 mg.

- 1 medium-size eggplant, peeled and cubed (about 1 pound)
- 1 teaspoon salt
- 4 tablespoons (½ stick) unsalted butter or margarine
- 2 tablespoons all-purpose flour
- ⅔ cup milk
- 1 cup shredded Cheddar cheese (about 4 ounces)
- 4 eggs, separated
- ⅛ teaspoon black pepper
- 3 tablespoons grated Parmesan cheese

1 Place the eggplant cubes in a colander or a sieve set over a large bowl. Sprinkle with the salt, toss together, and set aside for 30 minutes. Rinse under cold running water and pat dry with paper toweling.

2 Melt 2 tablespoons of the butter in a heavy 10-inch skillet over moderately low heat. Add the eggplant; cook, stirring occasionally, until golden and tender — 8 to 10 minutes. Purée in an electric blender or food processor — about 30 seconds — and set aside.

3 Melt the remaining 2 tablespoons of butter in a medium-size saucepan over moderate heat. Gradually stir in the flour, and cook, stirring constantly, for 2 to 3 minutes or until smooth. Stir in the milk and bring to a boil, stirring constantly. Reduce the heat to low and cook, stirring constantly, until thickened and smooth — 3 to 4 minutes. Remove from the heat, add the Cheddar cheese, and stir until melted. Stir in the eggplant purée, egg yolks, and pepper until well blended.

▽ At this point the egg whites and the eggplant mixture, after it has cooled to room temperature, can be stored separately. *Refrigerate* in tightly covered bowls for up to 24 hours.

4 Preheat the oven to 350° F. Lightly butter a 6-cup soufflé dish and dust it with 1 tablespoon of the Parmesan cheese. Beat the egg whites until stiff but not dry. Fold them into the eggplant mixture until evenly mixed, spoon into the prepared dish, and sprinkle with the remaining 2 tablespoons of Parmesan cheese.

5 Bake, uncovered, until puffy and golden — 50 to 55 minutes. Serve immediately with a brioche and a salad of mandarin oranges, red onions, and spinach. Serves 4.

## Serving Later

Proceed as in Steps 4 and 5, baking the soufflé for 60 to 70 minutes.

### Onion, Herb, and Cheese Variation

Per serving: Calories 417; Protein 20 g; Carbohydrate 12 g; Fat 33 g; Sodium 276 mg; Cholesterol 355 mg.

Substitute for the eggplant **2 large yellow onions, chopped**, and skip Step 1. Cook as in Step 2, using **3 tablespoons unsalted butter or margarine**; do *not* purée. Proceed as in Step 3, substituting **1 cup shredded Gruyère cheese** for the Cheddar and adding **½ teaspoon each dried marjoram and thyme, crumbled**. Proceed as in Steps 4 and 5, baking from 35 to 45 minutes.

## Zucchini-Cheese Puff

Per serving: Calories 320; Protein 19 g; Carbohydrate 18 g; Fat 20 g; Sodium 568 mg; Cholesterol 312 mg.

  4  medium-size zucchini, shredded (about 1½ pounds)
1½  teaspoons salt
  2  teaspoons vegetable oil
  1  small yellow onion, chopped
  4  eggs, lightly beaten
  ½  cup ricotta cheese
  ¾  cup shredded Cheddar or mozzarella cheese (about 3 ounces)
  ½  cup fine dry bread crumbs
  2  tablespoons chopped parsley
  1  tablespoon minced basil or 1 teaspoon dried basil, crumbled
  ¼  teaspoon black pepper

**1** In a large colander, mix the zucchini with the salt and let stand for 20 minutes. Press the zucchini with a wooden spoon to extract the liquid.

**2** Heat the oil in a heavy 10-inch skillet over moderate heat. Sauté the onion until soft — about 5 minutes.

**3** Preheat the oven to 350° F. In a large bowl, mix the eggs and ricotta. Stir in the zucchini, onion, Cheddar cheese, bread crumbs, parsley, basil, and pepper. Pour into a lightly oiled, 1½-quart soufflé dish or casserole.

▽ At this point the mixture can be stored. *Refrigerate* in the tightly covered casserole for up to 12 hours.

**4** Bake, uncovered, until the center is set — 45 to 55 minutes. The mixture will rise slightly. Serve immediately with buttered mixed vegetables and Yeast Corn Rolls (page 240). Serves 4.

### Serving Later

Preheat the oven to 350° F. Proceed as in Step 4, baking the zucchini puff for 60 to 70 minutes.

*Direct from the oven and table ready, Cottage Cheese Soufflé*

*Broccoli Omelette Supreme, pebbled with ham and tender florets*

# Eggs in Casserole

Per serving: Calories 411; Protein 20 g;
Carbohydrate 24 g; Fat 26 g; Sodium 615 mg;
Cholesterol 247 mg.

- 3 tablespoons unsalted butter
  or margarine, melted
- 6 ounces mushrooms, thinly
  sliced
- 4 green onions, thinly sliced
- 6 slices French bread, about 1
  inch thick, crusts removed,
  and cubed (about 2 cups)
- 1 cup each shredded Cheddar
  cheese and Colby cheese, or
  2 cups shredded Cheddar
  (about 8 ounces total)
- 4 eggs
- 2 cups milk
- 2 teaspoons Dijon or spicy
  brown mustard
- ¼ teaspoon salt
- ¼ teaspoon each black pepper,
  cayenne (ground red)
  pepper, and paprika

1 Melt the butter in a heavy 10-inch
skillet over moderate heat. Pour all
but 1 tablespoon into a small bowl and
reserve. Add the mushrooms to the
skillet; sauté until the juices have been
released and have evaporated — 4 to 5
minutes. Add the green onions, and
cook, stirring, for 1 minute.

2 Arrange the bread cubes in the
bottom of a buttered, 8" x 8" x 2"
baking pan. Drizzle the reserved butter
over the bread. Scatter the mushroom
mixture over the bread and top with all
but ½ cup of the cheeses.

3 Preheat the oven to 325° F. In a
large bowl, whisk the eggs, milk,
mustard, salt, black pepper, cayenne
pepper, and paprika until well mixed.
Pour the egg mixture into the pan and
sprinkle with the remaining cheese.

▽ At this point the casserole can be
stored. Cover the baking pan
tightly with plastic wrap and *refrigerate*
for up to 24 hours.

4 Bake, uncovered, until the eggs are
puffed and golden brown — about
1 hour. Fresh Sausage Patties (page
109) and a green salad make good
accompaniments. Serves 6.

### Serving Later

Preheat the oven to 325° F. Proceed as
in Step 4, baking about 1¼ hours.

# Broccoli Omelet Supreme

Per main-dish serving: Calories 420;
Protein 20 g; Carbohydrate 8 g; Fat 35 g;
Sodium 808 mg; Cholesterol 471 mg.

*This Italian omelet, called* frittata, *may
be served hot or at room temperature. It
is a good choice for brunch and does
well as an appetizer, too.*

- 1 tablespoon olive oil
- 5 tablespoons unsalted butter
  or margarine
- 1 medium-size yellow onion,
  finely chopped
- 1 clove garlic, minced
- ½ cup chopped cooked ham or
  Canadian bacon (about 3
  ounces)
- 2 cups broccoli florets, coarsely
  chopped (about 8 ounces)
- ½ ounce cooked spaghetti,
  coarsely chopped (about 20
  strands)
- 6 eggs
- ½ cup freshly grated Parmesan
  cheese (about 2 ounces)
- ¼ teaspoon salt
- ½ teaspoon crushed red pepper
  flakes

1 Heat the oil and 3 tablespoons of
the butter in a heavy 10-inch skillet
over moderate heat until the butter
melts. Add the onion, and sauté, stirring, until golden — about 7 minutes.

Add the garlic and ham, and cook,
stirring, for 3 minutes. Stir in the broccoli and spaghetti, toss until well coated, and then remove from the heat.

2 In a large bowl, whisk the eggs until
frothy. Add the broccoli mixture, all
but 2 tablespoons of the Parmesan
cheese, and the salt.

3 Melt 1 tablespoon of the remaining
butter in the skillet over moderate
heat. Add the egg mixture, reduce the
heat to low, and cook, uncovered, for 8
to 10 minutes or until the eggs are firm
and brown on the underside.

4 Carefully run a spatula under the
edges of the omelet, then under the
bottom to loosen it from the pan. Place
a shallow plate over the skillet and
quickly invert the omelet onto it. (If you
prefer not to flip the omelet, run it
under the broiler for 3 to 4 minutes to
brown the top.)

5 Melt the remaining 1 tablespoon of
butter in the skillet over moderate
heat. Carefully slide the omelet back
into the pan. Sprinkle it with the
crushed pepper and the remaining 2
tablespoons of Parmesan cheese. Cook
3 to 4 minutes longer.

▽ At this point the omelet can be
cooled to room temperature and
stored. Transfer to a plate, cover tightly,
and *refrigerate* for up to 2 days.

6 Serve in wedges, directly from the
pan, along with crusty bread and a
tomato salad. Serves 4 as an entrée, 6
as a first course, or 8 as an appetizer.

### Serving Later

Allow the omelet to come to room
temperature and cut it into wedges.

# Spinach and Cheese Pie

Per main-dish serving: Calories 438; Protein 31 g; Carbohydrate 11 g; Fat 31 g; Sodium 757 mg; Cholesterol 362 mg.

- 1 tablespoon unsalted butter or margarine
- 8 medium-size green onions (including some of the green), chopped (about 1 cup)
- 2 pounds spinach, cooked, chopped, and squeezed dry
- 5 eggs
- ½ cup milk
- 2 cups shredded Monterey Jack cheese (about 8 ounces)
- ¼ cup shredded Cheddar cheese (about 1 ounce)
- ¼ teaspoon each salt and black pepper

1 Melt the butter in a heavy 10-inch skillet over moderate heat. Sauté the onions until soft — about 5 minutes. Add the spinach and stir until any excess liquid has evaporated — 3 to 5 minutes. Let cool.

2 Preheat the oven to 350° F. In a large bowl, whisk the eggs and milk, then add the spinach mixture, cheeses, salt, and pepper.

▽ At this point the mixture can be tightly covered and stored. *Refrigerate* for up to 24 hours.

3 Lightly butter a 9-inch pie pan, pour in the spinach mixture, and bake, uncovered, until the top is golden and a knife inserted near the center comes out clean — 35 to 45 minutes.

4 Serve hot, at room temperature, or chilled. Accompany with a pasta salad and crisp vegetable sticks. Serves 4 as an entrée, 8 as a first course, or 16 as an appetizer.

## Serving Later

Preheat the oven to 350° F. Proceed as in Steps 3 and 4, baking the pie for 45 to 55 minutes.

# Spinach, Broccoli, and Zucchini Casserole

Per main-dish serving: Calories 209; Protein 17 g; Carbohydrate 10 g; Fat 12 g; Sodium 599 mg; Cholesterol 378 mg.

- 10 ounces spinach, rinsed, and coarse stems removed
- 12 ounces broccoli, stems trimmed (about ½ large bunch)
- 2 small zucchini (about 4 ounces each), trimmed, quartered lengthwise, and sliced ½ inch thick
- 1 medium-size sweet red pepper, cored, seeded, and cut into ½-inch squares
- 8 eggs
- 1 cup milk
- 2 tablespoons Dijon or spicy brown mustard
- ½ teaspoon salt
- 2 teaspoons dried basil, crumbled
- ½ teaspoon black pepper
- ½ cup grated Parmesan cheese

1 Bring 1 inch of water to a boil in the bottom of a large steamer or saucepan over moderate heat. Put the spinach in the steamer basket, tearing up any large leaves. Steam for 2 minutes; transfer to a large bowl. Trim the florets from the broccoli and cut up the larger florets. Peel the stems, quarter lengthwise, and cut into ½-inch pieces. Steam the stems for 2 minutes. Add the florets and steam 6 minutes longer. Transfer to the bowl. Steam the zucchini and red pepper for 6 minutes. Add to the vegetables in the bowl.

▽ At this point the vegetable mixture can be cooled to room temperature and stored. *Refrigerate*, tightly covered, for up to 2 days.

2 Preheat the oven to 350° F. In a medium-size mixing bowl, whisk together the eggs, milk, mustard, salt, basil, and pepper.

3 Lightly grease a shallow 2-quart casserole. Mix the vegetables and spread them evenly in the prepared dish. Pour the egg mixture over the vegetables, sprinkle with the Parmesan cheese, and bake, uncovered, until the top is golden brown around the edges and a knife inserted near the center comes out clean — about 45 minutes.

4 Wait at least 15 minutes before cutting the pie. Cut it into wedges and serve hot or at room temperature. Serve as a light entrée, accompanied by whole wheat rolls or as a side dish with roasted meat or fish. Serves 6 as a main course, 10 as a side dish.

## Serving Later

Proceed as in Steps 3 and 4, baking the casserole for 50 minutes to 1 hour.

# Layered Broccoli–Wild Rice Casserole

Per serving: Calories 421; Protein 15 g; Carbohydrate 44 g; Fat 21 g; Sodium 447 mg; Cholesterol 57 mg.

*This dish is ideal for a luncheon entrée or a light supper. Use 1⅓ cups wild rice to yield about 4 cups cooked.*

- 3 tablespoons unsalted butter or margarine
- ¼ cup finely chopped yellow onion
- 2 tablespoons all-purpose flour
- 1½ cups milk

*Spinach, Broccoli, and Zucchini Casserole — a combination that pleases, whatever the presentation, plain or fancy*

½ cup sour cream
4 cups hot cooked wild rice, white rice, or a mixture of the two
½ teaspoon salt, or to taste
¼ teaspoon black pepper
1 pound broccoli, trimmed and halved lengthwise (about 1 small bunch)
1 cup shredded Cheddar cheese (about 4 ounces)
6 slices bacon, cooked, drained, and crumbled

1 Melt the butter in a heavy 10-inch skillet over moderate heat. Add the onion, and sauté, stirring occasionally, until soft — about 5 minutes. Blend in the flour, and cook, stirring, for 2 minutes. Gradually stir in the milk and bring to a boil, then reduce the heat to low. Simmer, stirring, for 3 to 4 minutes or until thickened and smooth. Remove from the heat, blend in the sour cream, and stir the mixture into the rice. Stir in the salt and pepper.

2 Preheat the oven to 350° F. Steam the broccoli until just tender — about 4 minutes. Refresh under cold water and pat dry. Layer half the rice mixture in a buttered, 11″ x 7″ x 2″ baking dish. Arrange the broccoli halves, cut sides down, along the sides of the casserole and add the remaining rice mixture within this border. Sprinkle the cheese and bacon over the rice. Cover tightly with aluminum foil.

▽ At this point the casserole can be cooled to room temperature and *refrigerated* for up to 24 hours.

3 Bake, covered, for 30 minutes; then uncover and bake until the cheese is bubbling — 10 minutes longer. Serve with Gazpacho Aspic With Avocado Dressing (page 212). Serves 6.

### Serving Later

Preheat the oven to 350° F. Proceed as in Step 3, baking, covered, for 45 to 50 minutes; uncovered, for 10 minutes.

# Onion, Rice, and Dill Casserole

Per serving: Calories 332; Protein 17 g; Carbohydrate 37 g; Fat 14 g; Sodium 691 mg; Cholesterol 99 mg.

- 2 tablespoons unsalted butter or margarine
- 2 medium-size yellow onions, chopped
- 2 medium-size sweet red peppers, cored, seeded, and chopped
- ¼ cup Chicken Stock (page 48) or canned chicken broth
- 1 cup thinly sliced mushrooms (about 2 ounces)
- 1 clove garlic, minced
- 2 cups cooked brown rice
- 1 cup cottage cheese
- 1 egg, lightly beaten
- ⅓ cup plus 1 tablespoon grated Parmesan cheese
- ⅓ cup minced dill or 2 teaspoons dried dill weed
- ⅓ cup minced parsley
- ½ teaspoon salt
- ¼ teaspoon black pepper
- ⅓ cup soft whole-wheat bread crumbs

1 Melt the butter in a heavy 12-inch skillet over moderately low heat; remove and reserve 1 tablespoon. Add the onions, red peppers, and stock, and cook, covered, until the vegetables are soft — about 10 minutes. Add the mushrooms and garlic, raise the heat to moderate, and cook, uncovered, until the mushrooms are soft and the liquid has evaporated — about 10 minutes longer. Add the rice, mixing well. Transfer to a large bowl.

▽ At this point the mixture can be cooled to room temperature, covered tightly with plastic wrap, and *refrigerated* for up to 2 days.

2 Preheat the oven to 375° F. In a medium-size bowl, combine the cottage cheese, egg, ⅓ cup of the Parmesan cheese, the dill, parsley, salt, and pepper. Fold into the rice-vegetable mixture, and spoon into a lightly buttered, 9″ x 9″ x 2″ baking pan.

3 Mix the bread crumbs, the remaining Parmesan cheese, and the reserved butter in a small bowl until well combined. Sprinkle over the casserole. Bake, uncovered, until it is set and has a golden brown crust — about 30 minutes. A salad of dandelion leaves or endive and bacon bits with a vinaigrette dressing makes a good accompaniment. Serves 4.

Proceed as in Steps 2 and 3, baking the casserole for 45 to 50 minutes or until it is set and has a brown crust.

# Rice, Zucchini, and Walnut Loaf with Cheddar Sauce

Per serving: Calories 351; Protein 15 g; Carbohydrate 20 g; Fat 25 g; Sodium 540 mg; Cholesterol 175 mg.

1½ cups water
1½ teaspoons salt
1 cup brown rice
1 pound zucchini, coarsely grated
3 eggs
3 green onions, thinly sliced
¾ cup walnuts, coarsely chopped
½ teaspoon each dried sage and marjoram, crumbled

¼ teaspoon dried rosemary, crumbled
¼ teaspoon black pepper

*For the sauce:*
2 tablespoons unsalted butter or margarine
3 tablespoons all-purpose flour
1¼ cups milk
1 cup shredded Cheddar cheese (about 4 ounces)
2 teaspoons Dijon or spicy brown mustard
½ cup plain low-fat yogurt
Walnut halves for garnish (optional)

1 In a heavy medium-size saucepan, bring the water and ½ teaspoon of the salt to a boil over moderately high heat. Add the rice, reduce the heat to low, and cook, covered, for 35 minutes. Remove from the heat and let stand for at least 20 minutes. Meanwhile, put the zucchini in a colander or a large sieve set over a bowl. Toss with ½ teaspoon of the remaining salt and let drain for 30 minutes.

2 In a large bowl, whisk the eggs slightly. Stir in the zucchini, separating the strands. Add the rice, green onions, walnuts, the remaining ½ teaspoon of salt, the sage, marjoram, rosemary, and pepper, mixing until well

blended. Lightly butter a 9" x 5" x 3" loaf pan and pour the mixture into it. Cover tightly with aluminum foil.

3 Preheat the oven to 350° F. Melt the butter in a small saucepan over moderately low heat. Blend in the flour, stirring constantly for 2 to 3 minutes or until bubbly. Gradually stir in the milk and bring to a boil. Cook, stirring constantly, until thickened and smooth — 3 to 4 minutes. Add the cheese and mustard, stirring until the cheese has melted.

▽ At this point the rice loaf and the cheese sauce, after it has cooled to room temperature, can be stored separately. *Refrigerate*, tightly covered, for up to 24 hours.

4 Bake the covered loaf for 50 minutes. Remove the foil and bake until the surface is dry and firm — 10 to 15 minutes longer. Let rest for 5 to 10 minutes before removing from the pan.

5 Meanwhile, over low heat, add the yogurt gradually to the sauce and stir until smooth and heated through.

6 Loosen the loaf by running a thin metal spatula around the edges. Invert onto a heated platter and garnish with walnut halves, if desired. Cut into ½-inch slices; pass the sauce separately. Accompany with sautéed red, green, and yellow peppers. Serves 6.

Preheat the oven to 350° F. Bake the covered loaf for 1 hour; uncover and continue as in Step 4. Meanwhile, heat the sauce over low heat, stirring occasionally. Proceed as in Steps 5 and 6.

*Rice, Zucchini, and Walnut Loaf with Cheddar Sauce, each slice a symphony of tastes, textures, and hues*

# Crêpes Florentine

Per serving: Calories 606; Protein 32 g; Carbohydrate 28 g; Fat 42 g; Sodium 780 mg; Cholesterol 305 mg.

*An impressive company dish, crêpes are actually quite easy to prepare, especially if made in stages. Some can even be frozen and just popped in the oven. However, if you plan to freeze crêpes, use only fresh ingredients to start with. Bacteria can develop when frozen foods are thawed and refrozen.*

1½ cups ricotta cheese
1½ cups chopped cooked spinach, squeezed dry (about 1 pound fresh)
 2 tablespoons finely grated yellow onion, squeezed dry
 1 egg, lightly beaten
 ½ teaspoon salt, or to taste
 ¼ teaspoon black pepper
 ⅛ teaspoon freshly grated nutmeg, or to taste
 4 tablespoons (½ stick) unsalted butter or margarine
 ¼ cup all-purpose flour
2½ cups milk
 2 cups shredded Cheddar cheese (about 8 ounces)
 ¼ teaspoon white pepper
 ⅛ teaspoon ground mace, or to taste
12 seven-inch Basic French Crêpes (page 236)
 3 tablespoons grated Parmesan cheese (for topping)

*Cheesy Chicken and Mushroom Crêpes, bundles that pamper the palate*

1 To prepare the filling: In a large bowl, combine the ricotta cheese, spinach, onion, egg, salt, black pepper, and nutmeg.

2 To prepare the sauce: Melt the butter in a heavy medium-size saucepan over moderate heat. Add the flour, and cook, stirring constantly, until bubbly — 2 to 3 minutes. Slowly blend in the milk and bring to a boil,

stirring constantly. Reduce the heat to low and simmer, still stirring, for 3 to 4 minutes or until thickened and smooth. Remove from the heat and stir in the cheese, white pepper, and mace.

3 One at a time, place each crêpe with the most attractive side face-down, so that it will be on the outside when rolled. Spoon 3 to 4 tablespoons of filling down the center, then fold the sides over. The crêpe should be snugly filled, but not so stuffed that the filling spills out at the ends.

4 Preheat the oven to 350° F. Lay the crêpes seam-side down, just touching one another, in a lightly greased, 13″ x 9″ x 2″ baking dish. (If you plan to freeze the crêpes, see Tip, page 138, on lining the dish.) Pour the sauce over all; top with the Parmesan cheese.

▽ At this point, the crêpes can be stored. *Refrigerate* in the baking dish, tightly covered, for up to 24 hours. *Freeze* in the labeled, tightly covered dish for up to 1 month at 0° F.

**5** Bake the crêpes, uncovered, for 30 to 40 minutes or until the sauce is bubbling. Run them under the broiler until browned — 2 to 3 minutes. Accompany with a salad of sliced tomatoes and red onions with a creamy vinaigrette. Serves 6.

**From refrigerator:** Preheat the oven to 350° F. Bake, covered, for 15 to 20 minutes. Uncover and proceed as in Step 5. **From freezer:** Preheat the oven to 400° F. Do not thaw the crêpes. Bake, uncovered, for 1 to 1¼ hours or until the crêpes are heated through and the sauce is simmering. Brown and serve as in Step 5. **To microwave:** Cover with plastic wrap vented at one side and heat on *Low* (30% power) for 15 minutes. Turn the dish 90 degrees and microwave on *Low* (30% power) 15 minutes more. Microwave on *High* (100% power) for 9 minutes. Turn the dish 90 degrees and microwave on *High* (100% power) 8 to 9 minutes more. Let stand for 3 minutes, then brown and serve as in Step 5.

## Cheesy Chicken and Mushroom Crêpes

Per serving: Calories 631; Protein 37 g; Carbohydrate 26 g; Fat 42 g; Sodium 827 mg; Cholesterol 276 mg.

- 8 tablespoons (1 stick) unsalted butter or margarine
- 1 small yellow onion, finely chopped
- 4 ounces mushrooms, minced
- ½ cup chopped cooked spinach, squeezed dry (about 6 ounces fresh or half a 10-ounce package frozen)
- 1½ cups diced cooked chicken (about 9 ounces)
- 1 tablespoon minced tarragon, chives, or parsley
- 6 tablespoons all-purpose flour
- ¾ cup milk
- 2 tablespoons sour cream
- 2 tablespoons grated Parmesan cheese
- 1 tablespoon dry sherry or Madeira
- ¼ teaspoon each salt and black pepper
- 1½ cups Chicken Stock (page 48) or canned chicken broth
- ¾ cup each shredded Swiss Cheese and grated Parmesan cheese or 1½ cups shredded Cheddar cheese
- ½ cup half-and-half or milk
- 2 tablespoons dry sherry or Madeira (optional)
- ⅛ teaspoon cayenne (ground red) pepper
- 12 seven-inch Basic French Crêpes (page 236)
- 2 tablespoons grated Parmesan cheese (for topping)

**1** To prepare the filling: Melt 2 tablespoons of the butter in a heavy 10-inch skillet over moderately low heat. Add the onion, and sauté, stirring frequently, until soft — about 5 minutes. Add the mushrooms, and sauté, stirring frequently, until the mushrooms begin to give off their liquid — 2 to 3 minutes. Add the spinach, and sauté, stirring frequently, until the mixture is dry — about 2 minutes more. Transfer to a large mixing bowl and stir in the chicken and tarragon; set aside.

**2** Melt 2 tablespoons of the remaining butter in a small heavy saucepan over moderate heat. Add 2 tablespoons of the flour, and cook, stirring constantly, for 2 to 3 minutes or until bubbly. Slowly blend in the milk and bring to a boil, stirring constantly. Reduce the heat to low and simmer, still stirring, until thickened and smooth — 3 to 4 minutes. Stir the sauce into the chicken mixture, then blend in the sour cream, 2 tablespoons of the cheese, the sherry, salt, and black pepper.

**3** To prepare the cheese sauce: Melt the remaining 4 tablespoons of butter in a heavy medium-size saucepan over moderate heat. Add the remaining 4 tablespoons of flour, and cook, stirring constantly, until bubbly — 2 to 3 minutes. Slowly blend in the chicken stock, bring to a boil, and cook, stirring constantly, until thickened and smooth — 3 to 4 minutes. Remove from the heat and stir in the Swiss and Parmesan cheeses. Then stir in the cream, sherry, if desired, and cayenne.

**4** Preheat the oven to 350° F. Fill and roll the crêpes as in Step 3 of Crêpes Florentine (opposite page). Pour the sauce over all and sprinkle the Parmesan cheese on top.

▽ At this point the crêpes can be stored. *Refrigerate* them, tightly covered, for up to 24 hours.

**5** Bake the crêpes, uncovered, for 30 to 40 minutes or until the sauce is bubbling. Run under the broiler to brown lightly — 2 to 3 minutes. Accompany with a salad of watercress and cherry tomatoes. Serves 6.

Preheat the oven to 350° F. Bake, covered, for 15 minutes. Uncover, bake, brown, and serve as in Step 5.

# Herbed Crêpes California-Style

Per serving: Calories 439; Protein 13 g; Carbohydrate 16 g; Fat 36 g; Sodium 472 mg; Cholesterol 253 mg.

*This imaginative combination makes a delightful luncheon dish.*

- 1 large ripe avocado, peeled and diced
- 4 ounces cream cheese, at room temperature
- 4 teaspoons lemon juice
- ¼ teaspoon salt
- ¼ teaspoon white pepper
- ⅛ teaspoon hot red pepper sauce, or to taste
- 2 tablespoons minced chives or green onion tops
- 1 tablespoon minced tarragon or 1 teaspoon dried tarragon
- 8 ounces cooked shrimp, shelled, deveined, and minced (5 or 6 large)
- ½ cup (1 stick) lightly salted butter or margarine, melted
- 1 clove garlic, crushed
- 12 Basic French Crêpes (page 236) to which have been added 2 tablespoons minced parsley or chives

1 To prepare the filling: In a medium-size bowl, combine the avocado, cream cheese, 2 teaspoons of the lemon juice, the salt, ⅛ teaspoon of the pepper, the red pepper sauce, chives, and tarragon. Fold in the shrimp.

2 To prepare the sauce: Melt the butter in a small saucepan over low heat. Stir in the garlic, the remaining 2 teaspoons of lemon juice, and remaining ⅛ teaspoon of pepper.

3 Preheat the oven to 325° F. Fill and roll the crêpes as in Step 3 of Crêpes Florentine (page 148). Pour the sauce over all.

▽ At this point the crêpes can be stored. *Refrigerate*, tightly covered, for up to 4 hours.

4 Bake the crêpes, uncovered, for 20 minutes (30 to 35 minutes if they have been refrigerated) or until just heated through. Do not overcook or the filling will become bitter. Accompany with Spicy Salsa (page 218), French-fried zucchini, and a hearts of palm salad. Serves 6.

# Asparagus-Cheese-Filled Crêpes

Per serving: Calories 573; Protein 24 g; Carbohydrate 30 g; Fat 41 g; Sodium 753 mg; Cholesterol 244 mg.

- 6 tablespoons (¾ stick) unsalted butter or margarine
- 1 medium-size yellow onion, finely chopped
- 1 clove garlic, minced
- 4 ounces prosciutto or smoked ham, diced
- 1½ pounds asparagus, trimmed and cut into 1½-inch lengths
- ⅓ cup dry white wine
- ¼ teaspoon black pepper
- ¼ cup all-purpose flour
- 2½ cups milk
- ½ cup shredded Swiss cheese (about 2 ounces)
- ½ cup grated Parmesan cheese (about 2 ounces)
- 12 Whole Wheat Crêpes (page 237)
- 3 cups Classic Tomato Sauce (page 216)
- 2 tablespoons grated Parmesan cheese (for topping)

1 To prepare the filling: Melt 2 tablespoons of the butter in a heavy 12-inch skillet over moderately low heat. Add the onion, garlic, and prosciutto, and cook, stirring occasionally, until the onion is soft — about 5 minutes. Add the asparagus, wine, and ⅛ teaspoon of the pepper. Increase the heat to moderately high, cover, and bring to a boil. Steam for 3 to 4 minutes or until the asparagus is just tender. Transfer to a bowl; let cool.

2 To prepare the sauce: In a heavy medium-size saucepan, melt the remaining 4 tablespoons of butter over moderate heat. Blend in the flour, and cook, stirring constantly, until bubbly — 2 to 3 minutes. Gradually blend in the milk and bring to a boil, stirring constantly. Reduce the heat to low and simmer, stirring constantly, until thickened and smooth — 3 to 4 minutes. Remove from the heat, then blend in the cheeses and the remaining ⅛ teaspoon of pepper.

3 Add ½ cup of the sauce to the asparagus and mix gently; set the rest of the sauce aside.

4 Preheat the oven to 350° F. Fill and roll the crêpes as in Step 3 of Crêpes Florentine (page 148). (If you plan to freeze the crêpes, see Tip, page 138, on lining the dish.) Spoon the remaining cheese sauce over the crêpes and pour the tomato sauce over all. Sprinkle with the 2 tablespoons of Parmesan cheese.

▽ At this point the crêpes can be tightly covered and stored. *Refrigerate* in the baking dish for up to 24 hours. *Freeze* in the labeled baking dish for up to 1 month at 0° F.

5 Bake the crêpes, uncovered, for 30 to 40 minutes or until the sauce is bubbling. Run under the broiler until browned — 2 to 3 minutes. Accompany with rice and a green salad. Serves 6.

## Serving Later

**From refrigerator:** Preheat the oven to 350° F. Bake, covered, for 20 minutes. Brown and serve as in Step 5. **From freezer:** Preheat the oven to 400° F. Bake, uncovered, for 1 to 1¼ hours. Brown and serve as in Step 5.

# Rice, Grains, Pasta, and Pizza

Fortunately for the busy cook, rice and grains are sturdy and generally amenable to reheating. They are particularly agreeable when mixed with cheese or a sauce and then baked. Although unadorned rice is easy to prepare at the last minute, you can, if you like, cook it ahead; instructions for one method are given in the Tip, page 299.

Baked pasta, too, is a wonderful make-ahead (see pages 154 and 160-165); but even freshly cooked pastas require little last-minute fuss. Just prepare the sauce ahead of time (see pages 216 to 218 for several that are freezable). Put the pasta water on to heat as soon as the guests arrive (keep it simmering if it boils too soon); then ten minutes before sitting down to eat, put the pasta in to cook (see Tip, page 161, for cooking it perfectly every time).

Pizza is not a typical do-ahead dish, but a few recipes have been included in this chapter to demonstrate that it can be done in stages. The key is to prepare the dough in advance, refrigerating or freezing it until needed. If you want to take the process a step further, substitute a tomato sauce (pages 216 to 218) for the fresh tomatoes; then freeze the freshly baked and cooled pizza for a future treat.

# Confetti Rice Squares

Per serving: Calories 126; Protein 6 g; Carbohydrate 6 g; Fat 8 g; Sodium 397 mg; Cholesterol 142 mg.

*Brown rice lends a nutlike taste (as well as more nutritive value) to these appealing squares. White rice, however, can be substituted.*

| | |
|---|---|
| 2 | tablespoons vegetable oil |
| ¾ | cup brown rice or 1 cup white rice |
| 1¾ | cups water (2 cups for white rice) |
| 1 | teaspoon salt |
| 1 | large yellow onion, finely chopped |
| ½ | medium-size sweet red pepper, seeded, cored, and coarsely chopped |
| ½ | cup grated Parmesan cheese |
| ¼ | cup minced parsley |
| 2 | tablespoons minced basil or 2 teaspoons dried basil, crumbled |
| ¼ | teaspoon black pepper |
| 4 | eggs |

1 Heat 1 tablespoon of the oil in a medium-size saucepan over moderate heat for 1 minute. Add the rice, and cook for 1 minute, stirring to coat. Add the water and ½ teaspoon of the salt and bring to a boil. Reduce the heat to low, cover, and cook for 45 minutes (20 minutes for white rice) or until all the liquid has been absorbed. Cool to room temperature.

2 Heat the remaining tablespoon of oil in a heavy 10-inch skillet over moderately low heat for 1 minute. Sauté the onion and sweet red pepper, stirring occasionally, until soft — about 7 minutes. Remove from the heat and stir in the cooked rice, 6 tablespoons of the Parmesan cheese, the parsley, basil, the remaining ½ teaspoon of salt, and the black pepper.

▽ At this point the rice mixture can be cooled to room temperature and stored. *Refrigerate* in a tightly covered container for up to 2 days.

3 Preheat the oven to 350° F. In a large bowl, beat the eggs. Stir in the rice mixture and blend well. Pour into a lightly oiled, 11" x 7" x 2" baking dish and sprinkle with the remaining 2 tablespoons of Parmesan cheese. Bake, uncovered, for 25 to 30 minutes or until the center is set.

4 Cut into 8 portions and serve hot with Cheese-Stuffed Chicken Rolls (page 89) or Halibut in Wine Sauce (page 68). Or serve at room temperature with cold roasted meats or poultry. Serves 8 as a side dish.

## Serving Later

Allow the rice to come to room temperature; proceed as in Steps 3 and 4.

# Indonesian Rice

Per serving: Calories 129; Protein 5 g; Carbohydrate 10 g; Fat 8 g; Sodium 281 mg; Cholesterol 0 mg.

| | |
|---|---|
| 2 | tablespoons vegetable oil |
| 3 | cloves garlic, minced |
| 2 | tablespoons minced fresh ginger or 2 teaspoons ground ginger |
| 1 | teaspoon cumin seeds |
| ⅛ | teaspoon crushed red pepper flakes |
| 2¾ | cup Chicken Stock (page 48) or canned chicken broth or water |
| 1 | cup brown rice |
| ½ | teaspoon each ground cinnamon, coriander, and nutmeg |
| ½ | teaspoon salt |
| ⅓ | cup blanched slivered almonds or coarsely chopped roasted peanuts (about 5 ounces) |
| 2 | green onions, thinly sliced |

1 Heat the oil in a heavy medium-size saucepan over moderate heat for 1 minute. Add the garlic, ginger, cumin seeds, and red pepper flakes, and sauté, stirring occasionally, for 1 to 2 minutes or until the garlic and ginger are soft.

2 Add the chicken stock and bring to a boil. Stir in the rice, cinnamon, coriander, nutmeg, and salt. Reduce the heat to low, cover, and simmer about 50 minutes or until all of the liquid has been absorbed.

▽ At this point the rice can be cooled to room temperature and stored. *Refrigerate* in a tightly covered container for up to 48 hours.

3 Transfer to a heated serving dish and sprinkle with the slivered almonds and green onions. Serve with meat, fish or poultry. This dish goes especially well with spicy or curried foods, such as Creamy Shrimp Curry (page 74). Serves 6.

## Serving Later

Transfer the rice mixture to the top of a double boiler. Cover, set it over gently boiling water, and heat, stirring occasionally, until warmed through — about 30 minutes. Serve as in Step 3.

# Mexican Cheese-Rice Casserole

Per side-dish serving: Calories 340; Protein 12 g; Carbohydrate 42 g; Fat 15 g; Sodium 840 mg; Cholesterol 11 mg.

| | |
|---|---|
| 3 | cups cooked rice |
| 1½ | cups shredded Monterey Jack or Cheddar cheese (about 6 ounces) |
| 1 | can (1 pound, 1 ounce) cream-style corn |
| ⅔ | cup sour cream |

1 bunch green onions, thinly sliced (about ½ cup)
1 can (4 ounces) green chilies, drained and coarsely chopped
2 tablespoons minced cilantro (coriander leaves) or parsley (optional)
½ teaspoon salt, or to taste
⅛ teaspoon cayenne (ground red) pepper

1 Preheat the oven to 400° F. In a large bowl, combine the rice, cheese, corn, sour cream, green onions, chilies, cilantro, if desired, salt, and cayenne. Transfer the mixture to a lightly oiled, 1½-quart casserole.

▽ At this point the casserole can be stored. *Refrigerate*, tightly covered, for up to 24 hours.

2 Bake the casserole, uncovered, for 35 to 40 minutes or until golden. Serve as a side dish with Steak Cubes Southwestern-Style (page 99). Or present it as a meatless main dish, accompanied by steamed artichoke hearts topped with buttered bread crumbs, and a mixed green salad. Serves 6 as a side dish, 4 as a main dish.

### Serving Later

Preheat the oven to 400° F. Bake the casserole, covered, for 20 minutes. Uncover and bake another 35 to 40 minutes or until golden. Serve as in Step 2.

*Uncommonly festive as well as delicious, Confetti Rice Squares*

# Creamy Baked Hungarian Noodles

Per main-dish serving: Calories 522; Protein 27 g; Carbohydrate 55 g; Fat 22 g; Sodium 849 mg; Cholesterol 85 mg.

- 8 ounces fine egg noodles
- 1 tablespoon unsalted butter or margarine
- 1 small yellow onion, coarsely chopped
- 1 clove garlic, minced
- 1 pound low-fat cottage cheese
- 1 cup sour cream
- 1 cup plain low-fat yogurt
- 2 tablespoons Worcestershire sauce
- 2 tablespoons poppy seeds
- ½ teaspoon salt
- ¼ teaspoon black pepper
- 2 dashes hot red pepper sauce

*Optional garnishes:*
Paprika
Grated Parmesan cheese

1 Cook the noodles according to package directions until *al dente* (see Tip, page 161). Drain in a colander, then rinse under cold running water to stop the cooking.

2 Meanwhile, melt the butter in a 6-inch skillet over moderately low heat. Add the onion and garlic, and sauté, stirring occasionally, until softened — about 5 minutes. Set aside.

3 Preheat the oven to 350° F. In a large bowl, combine the cottage cheese, sour cream, yogurt, Worcestershire sauce, poppy seeds, salt, black pepper, hot red pepper sauce, and onion mixture. Stir in the noodles. Spoon the mixture into a lightly oiled, shallow, 2-quart casserole. Cover with aluminum foil.

▽ At this point the mixture can be *refrigerated* for up to 24 hours.

4 Bake the foil-wrapped casserole for 30 minutes. Uncover and bake 10 to 15 minutes longer or until heated through and bubbling. Sprinkle with the paprika and Parmesan, if desired.

5 Serve as a main dish, accompanied by bread sticks and a mélange of marinated vegetables, such as steamed green beans, steamed carrots, and chick peas; or as a side dish with meatloaf, roasted meat or poultry, or Turkey Teriyaki Kebabs (page 93). Serves 4 as a main dish, 8 as a side dish.

### Serving Later

Preheat the oven to 350° F. Bake the casserole, covered, for 45 minutes. Uncover and continue as in Steps 4 and 5.

# Noodle Pie with Spicy Cajun Ham

Per serving: Calories 323; Protein 15 g; Carbohydrate 29 g; Fat 16 g; Sodium 516 mg; Cholesterol 247 mg.

- 8 ounces egg noodles, broken into 1-inch pieces
- 3 tablespoons unsalted butter or margarine
- 2 cloves garlic, minced
- 4 eggs
- 1 cup finely diced Cajun Smoked Ham (page 294) or other spicy smoked ham (about 6 ounces)
- ½ cup shredded Cheddar cheese (about 2 ounces)
- 2 tablespoons minced parsley
- 2 teaspoons paprika
- ½ teaspoon salt
- ¾ teaspoon each dried oregano and thyme, crumbled
- ¼ teaspoon hot red pepper sauce, or to taste
- ¼ teaspoon each cayenne (ground red) pepper and black pepper

*Optional garnishes:*
Pimiento strips
Parsley sprigs

1 Preheat the oven to 350° F. Cook the noodles according to package directions until *al dente* (see Tip, page 161). Drain in a colander, then rinse under cold water to stop the cooking. Set aside.

2 Melt the butter in a heavy 6-inch skillet over moderately low heat. Add the garlic, and cook until just golden — about 1 minute. Set aside.

3 In a large bowl, beat the eggs. Add the garlic and butter mixture, ham, cheese, parsley, paprika, salt, oregano, thyme, hot red pepper sauce, cayenne pepper, and black pepper and mix well. Stir in the noodles. Spoon into a lightly oiled, 10-inch quiche dish or pie pan. Bake, uncovered, for 30 to 35 minutes or until firm and lightly browned. Cool to room temperature and refrigerate, tightly covered, for at least 2 hours and up to 24 hours.

4 Cut into wedges and serve cold, garnished with the pimiento strips and parsley, if desired. Accompany with poppy seed rolls and Zucchini Slaw (page 196). Serves 6.

# Sesame Noodles Oriental-Style

Per side-dish serving: Calories 492; Protein 16 g; Carbohydrate 54 g; Fat 25 g; Sodium 881 mg; Cholesterol 0 mg.

*Make extra sauce when preparing this dish. The spicy peanut taste is delicious with grilled chicken, meats, or fish.*

- 8 ounces Chinese noodles or spaghetti
- 3 tablespoons dark sesame oil
- ⅓ cup creamy peanut butter
- ¼ cup Chicken Stock (page 48) or canned chicken broth
- 4 teaspoons rice or red wine vinegar
- 3 tablespoons soy sauce
- 2 cloves garlic, minced

1 tablespoon minced fresh ginger
1 tablespoon dry sherry
2 teaspoons sugar
1 teaspoon chili oil or 1/8 teaspoon cayenne (ground red) pepper, or to taste
1/4 teaspoon black pepper
2 green onions, including tops, minced
2 tablespoons toasted sesame seeds

1 Cook the noodles according to package directions until *al dente* (see Tip, page 161). Drain in a colan- der, then rinse under cold water to stop the cooking. In a large bowl, toss the cooked noodles with 1 tablespoon of the sesame oil.

2 In an electric blender or food pro- cessor, combine the peanut butter, chicken stock, vinegar, soy sauce, gar- lic, ginger, sherry, sugar, chili oil, and black pepper and process until well combined — about 1 minute.

▽ At this point the noodles and the sauce can be stored separately. *Refrigerate*, tightly covered, for up to 24 hours.

3 Add the sauce and green onions to the noodles and toss to coat. Trans- fer to a serving dish and sprinkle with the sesame seeds. Serve at room tem- perature with grilled meats, fish, poul- try, or any spicy Oriental dish, such as Himalayan Chicken (page 85) or Ori- ental Spiced Fish (page 68). Serves 4 as a side dish, 6 as an appetizer.

*The piquancy of Noodle Pie with Spicy Cajun Ham tempered by the coolness of Zucchini Slaw (page 196)*

*Good-luck fare at New Year's — a good dish anytime, Hoppin' John*

# Hoppin' John

Per main-dish serving: Calories 504;
Protein 23 g; Carbohydrate 69 g; Fat 15 g;
Sodium 837 mg; Cholesterol 24 mg.

*This traditional Southern dish can be
served hot as an accompaniment to
pork or poultry, or tossed with a
vinaigrette dressing and served at room
temperature as a main-dish salad.*

- 1 cup dried cowpeas or black-eyed peas, washed and picked over
- 4 ounces lean slab bacon, cut into ½-inch cubes
- 2½ cups water
- ¾ teaspoon salt, or to taste
- ⅛ teaspoon each cayenne (ground red) pepper and black pepper, or to taste
- 3 cups hot cooked rice

1 In a medium-size saucepan, bring the peas, bacon, and water to a boil over moderately high heat. Reduce the heat to low, cover, and simmer until the peas are just tender — about 25 minutes for cowpeas, 40 to 45 minutes for black-eyed peas.

2 Drain the peas, reserving the liquid for a soup, if you like, and transfer to a large bowl. Add the salt, cayenne pepper, and black pepper and mix well. Stir in the rice and add more salt and pepper, if desired.

▽ At this point the Hoppin' John can be cooled to room temperature and stored. *Refrigerate*, tightly covered, for up to 2 days.

3 Transfer to a heated serving dish and serve with baked ham, pork sausages, or Roast Loin of Pork in Ginger Marinade (page 113). Or cool to room temperature, stir in ¾ to 1 cup

vinaigrette dressing, and serve as a main-dish salad, garnished with lettuce, sliced tomatoes, and black olives. Serves 4 as an entrée, 6 as a side dish.

### Serving Later

To serve hot, preheat the oven to 350° F. Transfer to a buttered 2-quart casserole. Cover and bake until heated through — about 30 minutes. Serve as in Step 3. To serve as a salad, allow it to come to room temperature; then proceed as in Step 3.

# Barley-Mushroom Casserole

Per serving: Calories 200; Protein 6 g; Carbohydrate 32 g; Fat 6 g; Sodium 86 mg; Cholesterol 15 mg.

*Barley, with its slightly chewy texture, makes an interesting change of pace from the usual rice or potatoes. For a meatless main dish, try topping this casserole with shredded Cheddar or Monterey Jack cheese.*

- 2 tablespoons unsalted butter or margarine
- 2 shallots or 4 green onions, coarsely chopped
- 4 ounces mushrooms, trimmed and sliced
- ¾ cup barley
- 1¾ cups Chicken Stock (page 48) or canned chicken broth
- ¼ teaspoon dried thyme, crumbled
- ¼ teaspoon black pepper
- 2 green onions (including tops), thinly sliced

1 Melt the butter in a 2-quart flame-proof casserole over low heat. Add the shallots, and sauté, stirring occa-

sionally, until golden brown — 5 to 7 minutes. Add the barley, chicken stock, thyme, and pepper and bring to a boil over high heat. Reduce the heat to low, cover, and simmer for 45 minutes, stirring occasionally.

▽ At this point the barley can be cooled to room temperature and stored. *Refrigerate* in a covered 1-quart casserole for up to 3 days. *Freeze* in a labeled, 1-quart freezable container or freezer bag for up to 1 month at 0° F.

2 Stir in the sliced green onions and transfer to a heated serving dish. This casserole would go well with Veal Breast Stuffed with Spinach, Pine Nuts, and Raisins (page 118) or Italian Beef Rolls (page 100). Serves 4.

### Serving Later

**From refrigerator:** Preheat the oven to 325° F. Stir in the sliced green onions and bake, covered, for 30 to 35 minutes or until heated through. Serve as in Step 2. **From freezer:** Thaw in the refrigerator overnight. Preheat the oven to 325° F. Transfer to a 1-quart casserole, breaking up the barley with a wooden spoon. Stir in ¼ cup water and the sliced green onions. Bake, covered, for 30 to 35 minutes or until heated through. Serve as in Step 2.

# Cheesy Sage Grits

Per serving: Calories 258; Protein 14 g; Carbohydrate 11 g; Fat 18 g; Sodium 331 mg; Cholesterol 182 mg.

- 2 tablespoons unsalted butter or margarine
- 1 small yellow onion, coarsely chopped
- 2 cups Chicken Stock (page 48) or canned chicken broth
- 1 cup grits (not the quick-cooking type)

- 2 eggs
- 1 cup shredded Cheddar cheese (about 4 ounces)
- 2 tablespoons finely chopped sage or 2 teaspoons dried sage, crumbled

1 Preheat the oven to 375° F. Melt the butter in a heavy medium-size saucepan over moderately low heat. Add the onion, and sauté until soft — about 5 minutes.

2 Increase the heat to moderate, add the chicken stock, and bring to a boil. Reduce the heat to low and gradually whisk in the grits. Cook, stirring constantly, for 1 to 2 minutes or until the grits begin to thicken. Remove from the heat.

3 In a small bowl, beat the eggs slightly. Gradually beat several spoonfuls of the hot grits into the eggs, then stir the egg mixture into the saucepan with the grits. Blend in the cheese and sage. Pour into an oiled 1-quart casserole.

▽ At this point the grits can be cooled to room temperature and stored. *Refrigerate*, tightly covered, for up to 24 hours.

4 Bake, uncovered, for 45 minutes or until golden. Serve in place of rice or potatoes. This dish goes particularly well with German Meatloaf (page 110) or Marinated Spareribs (page 116). Serves 4 to 6.

### Serving Later

Preheat the oven to 375° F. Bake, covered, for 30 minutes. Uncover and bake another 25 to 30 minutes or until golden. Serve as in Step 4.

# Polenta Pie

Per main-dish serving: Calories 524; Protein 18 g; Carbohydrate 46 g; Fat 30 g; Sodium 594 mg; Cholesterol 90 mg.

- 4 cups water
- 1 cup yellow cornmeal
- ¾ teaspoon salt
- 6 tablespoons (¾ stick) unsalted butter or margarine
- 12 ounces mushrooms, trimmed and sliced
- 4 tablespoons all-purpose flour
- 3 cups milk
- ⅛ teaspoon white pepper Pinch freshly grated nutmeg
- ½ cup shredded Swiss cheese (about 2 ounces)
- ¼ cup grated Parmesan cheese

1 In a heavy medium-size saucepan, combine the water, cornmeal, and 1 teaspoon of the salt. Whisk while bringing it to a boil over moderate heat. Reduce the heat to low and simmer, uncovered, whisking occasionally, for 15 minutes or until thick. Pour into a lightly oiled, 8" x 4" x 3" loaf pan and let cool to room temperature. Refrigerate, covered with plastic wrap, for at least 2 hours or overnight.

2 Melt 2 tablespoons of the butter in a heavy 10-inch skillet over moderately low heat. Add the mushrooms, and cook, stirring frequently, until lightly browned — about 10 minutes. Set aside.

3 Melt the remaining 4 tablespoons of butter in a heavy medium-size saucepan over moderate heat. Stir in the flour, forming a smooth paste. Cook, stirring constantly, until bubbly — 2 to 3 minutes. Gradually blend in the milk and bring to a boil, stirring constantly. Reduce the heat to moderately low and simmer, still stirring, until thickened and smooth — 3 to 4 minutes. Stir in the pepper, nutmeg, Swiss cheese, and mushrooms. Set aside.

4 Preheat the oven to 400° F. Invert the polenta onto a cutting board and cut into ½-inch slices. To assemble: In a lightly oiled, 2½-quart casserole, alternate layers of polenta slices with layers of the sauce, ending with the sauce. Top with the Parmesan.

▽ At this point the pie can be cooled to room temperature and stored. *Refrigerate*, tightly covered, for up to 24 hours.

5 Bake, uncovered, for 35 to 40 minutes or until the pie is heated through and the top golden. Serve as a meatless main dish, accompanied by dilled carrots and Winter Salad (page 192), or as a side dish with Pot Roast Venetian Style (page 96) or Tuscan Roast Pork (page 112). Serves 4 as a main dish, 8 as a side dish.

### Serving Later

Preheat the oven to 400° F. Proceed as in Step 5, baking the pie, uncovered, for 45 to 50 minutes.

# Pasta Rings in Piquant Cucumber Sauce

Per serving: Calories 262; Protein 11 g; Carbohydrate 50 g; Fat 2 g; Sodium 321 mg; Cholesterol 4 mg.

*Cool, refreshing, and wonderfully spicy, this pairing of pasta with raita (an Indian sauce usually served with curries) makes an excellent side dish for roast meats and poultry.*

- 2 medium-size cucumbers, peeled, seeded, and coarsely grated
- 2 tablespoons grated yellow onion
- 1¼ teaspoons salt
- 2 cups plain yogurt
- 1 small tomato, finely chopped
- 2 green onions, minced
- 2 tablespoons fresh lemon or lime juice
- 2 tablespoons minced mint or parsley or 2 teaspoons dried mint, crumbled
- 1 clove garlic, minced
- 2 teaspoons ground cumin
- ⅛ teaspoon each cayenne (ground red) pepper and black pepper
- 1 pound small rings or wagon wheels pasta Mint leaves or parsley sprigs for garnish (optional)

1 In a medium-size bowl, combine the cucumber, onion, and ¼ teaspoon of the salt; let stand for 10 minutes at room temperature. Drain in a colander, rinse under cold water, and squeeze dry; set aside.

2 Wipe the bowl dry and in it combine the yogurt, tomato, green onions, lemon juice, mint, garlic, cumin, cayenne pepper, black pepper, and the remaining teaspoon of salt. Add the cucumber mixture and stir well.

▽ At this point the sauce can be stored. *Refrigerate*, tightly covered, for up to 2 days.

3 Cook the pasta according to package directions until *al dente* (see Tip, page 161). Drain and return to the pot. While the pasta is still warm, add the cucumber sauce and mix well. Transfer to a serving dish and garnish with the mint leaves, if desired. Serve with roasted meats, broiled fish, or Marinated Rock Cornish Hens (page 94). Serves 8 as a side dish.

### Serving Later

Allow the sauce to come to room temperature, then proceed as in Step 3.

# Pasta Twists with Fresh Tomatoes, Basil, and Garlic

Per main-dish serving: Calories 692; Protein 16 g; Carbohydrate 93 g; Fat 29 g; Sodium 384 mg; Cholesterol 0 mg.

*This is a dish to make when fresh tomatoes and basil are at their peak. Leftovers will keep for two days and can be eaten as pasta salad.*

- 4 medium-size ripe tomatoes, diced
- ½ cup minced basil
- 2 cloves garlic, minced
- 2 tablespoons lemon juice
- ½ cup olive oil
- ¾ teaspoon salt, or to taste
- ¼ teaspoon black pepper
- 1 pound pasta twists or linguine

1 In a medium-size bowl, mix all of the ingredients except the pasta. Cover and let sit at room temperature for at least 2 and up to 6 hours.

2 Cook the pasta according to package directions until *al dente* (see Tip, page 161). Drain, toss with the sauce, and serve immediately. Serve as a first course, followed by Veal with Tuna Sauce (page 122) and cold asparagus. Or present it as the main course, followed by cheese and a green salad. Serves 4 as an entrée, 6 as a first course.

# Green and White Fettuccine with Chicken and Ham

Per main-dish serving: Calories 623; Protein 41 g; Carbohydrate 67 g; Fat 21 g; Sodium 601 mg; Cholesterol 120 mg.

- 1 quart water
- 2 whole boneless, skinless chicken breasts (about 12 ounces each)
- 8 ounces each fettuccine and spinach fettuccine
- 3 tablespoons unsalted butter or margarine
- 1 large yellow onion, slivered
- 8 ounces mushrooms, sliced thin (about 2½ cups)
- 2 cloves garlic, minced
- 1 cup Classic Tomato Sauce (page 216) or 1 can (8 ounces) tomato sauce
- 8 ounces ham, julienned (optional)
- 1 teaspoon salt
- ¾ teaspoon black pepper
- 2 cups half-and-half Grated Parmesan cheese for topping

1 Bring the water to a boil in a heavy 12-inch skillet. Add the chicken breasts, reduce the heat to moderately low, cover, and simmer until the chicken is no longer pink at the center — 15 to 20 minutes. Pour off the liquid, reserving it for use in a soup, if desired. Let the chicken cool, then cut it into julienne slices.

2 Cook the fettuccine according to package directions until *al dente* (see Tip, page 161). Drain in a colander, then rinse under cold water to stop the cooking. Rinse the pot as well and return the fettuccine to it.

*Sauce-drenched ribbons of Green and White Fettuccine with Chicken and Ham, an edible celebration*

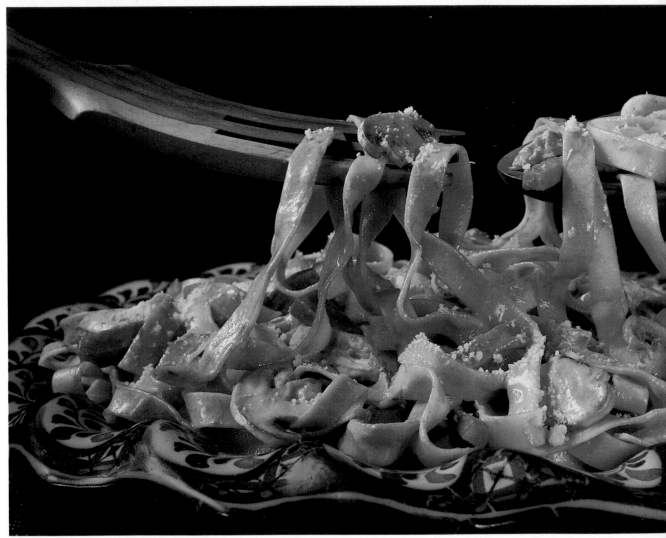

3 Melt the butter in the skillet over moderately low heat. Add the onion, and sauté until soft—about 5 minutes. Add the mushrooms, and cook 7 minutes longer or until golden. Add the garlic, and cook 1 minute more. Remove the skillet from the heat and stir in the tomato sauce. Add the vegetable mixture to the fettuccine, then stir in the ham, if desired, the chicken, salt, and pepper. Toss well.

▽ At this point the pasta mixture can be *refrigerated* in a tightly covered container for up to 24 hours.

4 Preheat the oven to 350° F. Add the half-and-half to the pasta and toss to coat. Pour into a 13" x 9" x 2" baking dish and cover with heavy-duty aluminum foil. Bake for 40 minutes, tossing twice during this period. Transfer to a heated serving dish, top with the grated Parmesan cheese, and accompany with a Caesar salad and whole-wheat Italian bread. Serves 6 as an entrée, 8 as a first course.

### Serving Later

One hour before baking, set the casserole out to come to room temperature. Proceed as in Step 4.

## Macaroni & Cheese, Italian-Style

Per serving: Calories 633; Protein 24 g; Carbohydrate 74 g; Fat 27 g; Sodium 952 mg; Cholesterol 75 mg.

- 1 pound thick macaroni, such as ziti or penne
- 4 tablespoons (½ stick) unsalted butter or margarine
- ¼ cup all-purpose flour
- 3 cups milk
- ¼ teaspoon black pepper
- 2 cups grated Parmesan cheese (about 4 ounces)
- 3 cups Classic Tomato Sauce (page 216), Marinara Sauce (page 216), or canned spaghetti sauce

1 Cook the pasta according to package directions until *al dente* (see Tip, below). Drain in a colander, then rinse under cold water to stop the cooking. Return to the pot.

2 While the pasta cooks, melt the butter in a heavy medium-size saucepan over moderate heat. Stir in the flour, forming a smooth paste, and cook for 2 minutes, stirring constantly. Gradually stir in the milk and bring to a

boil. Reduce the heat to moderately low, add the pepper, and cook, still stirring, until thickened and smooth—3 to 4 minutes. Blend in the cheese and remove from the heat.

3 Preheat the oven to 375° F. Add the cheese sauce to the ziti and mix well. In a 3-quart casserole or a 13" x 9" x 2" baking dish, alternate layers of the ziti and cheese sauce with layers of tomato sauce, ending with the ziti.

▽ At this point the casserole can be stored. *Refrigerate*, tightly covered, for up to 24 hours.

4 Bake, uncovered, for 20 minutes or until the top is browned and the sauce bubbling. Accompany with hot garlic bread and Avocado with Sweet Red Pepper Sauce (page 197).

### Serving Later

Preheat the oven to 375° F. Bake, covered, for 15 to 20 minutes. Uncover and bake another 20 minutes. Serve as in Step 4.

*Tip: Perfect pasta, as any Italian will tell you, is cooked al dente, which, loosely translated, means firm to the bite. It should never be mushy. Keep testing the pasta, and the moment it becomes flexible and tender — with no hard, uncooked center — remove it from the heat. Drain, and toss with sauce immediately. Or if making pasta salad, rinse under cold water to stop the cooking. Try different brands of pasta until you find a good one. Some are too soft even when properly cooked.*

# Giant Shells Stuffed with Spinach and Ricotta

Per serving: Calories 725; Protein 39 g;
Carbohydrate 64 g; Fat 37 g;
Sodium 1324 mg; Cholesterol 174 mg.

1½  pounds fresh spinach,
    trimmed, or 2 packages (10
    ounces each) frozen
    chopped spinach, thawed
2   green onions, finely chopped
1   cup grated Parmesan cheese
1   cup shredded mozzarella
    cheese (about 4 ounces)
1   cup ricotta cheese
1   egg, lightly beaten
¼   teaspoon black pepper
⅛   teaspoon ground nutmeg
8   ounces (about 36) jumbo
    shells, or cannelloni or
    manicotti shells (about 14)
3   cups Marinara Sauce (page
    216) or canned spaghetti
    sauce

1 Put the fresh spinach in a large heavy saucepan with just the water that clings to its leaves. Cover and cook over moderate heat until wilted — 4 to 5 minutes. Drain, let cool, squeeze dry, and chop fine. If using frozen spinach, squeeze it dry.

2 In a large bowl, combine the green onions, ½ cup of the Parmesan cheese, both the mozzarella and ricotta cheeses, the egg, pepper, nutmeg, and chopped spinach.

3 Cook the pasta according to package directions until *al dente* (see Tip, page 161). Drain off half of the water and refill the pot with cold water. Remove the shells, a few at a time, and drain well on a cloth kitchen towel.

4 Preheat the oven to 375° F. Spread 1 cup of the sauce over the bottom of a shallow 2-quart casserole. Stuff the pasta shells with the spinach mixture and arrange them on top of the sauce.

*A generous topping of rich tomato sauce completes the dress of Giant Shells Stuffed with Spinach and Ricotta*

Ladle the remaining 2 cups of sauce over all and sprinkle with the remaining ½ cup of Parmesan.

▽ At this point the shells can be *refrigerated* in the casserole, tightly covered, for up to 24 hours.

5 Bake, uncovered, for 20 minutes or until heated through and bubbling. Accompany with sesame bread sticks and Winter Salad (page 192). Serves 4.

### Serving Later

Preheat the oven to 350° F. Bake, covered with aluminum foil, for 20 minutes. Remove the foil and bake until the shells are heated through and the sauce bubbling — 10 to 20 minutes more. Serve as in Step 5.

## Mushroom Variation

Per serving: Calories 796; Protein 39 g; Carbohydrate 68 g; Fat 43 g; Sodium 1227 mg; Cholesterol 193 mg.

Prepare 12 ounces fresh spinach or 1 package (10 ounces) frozen spinach as in Step 1 of Stuffed Shells. In a heavy 10-inch skillet set over moderate heat, melt 2 tablespoons unsalted butter or margarine. Add ⅓ cup finely chopped celery, ⅓ cup finely chopped shallots or green onions, and 8 ounces trimmed and finely chopped mushrooms. Sauté, stirring frequently, until the vegetables are tender and the mushroom liquid has evaporated — about 10 minutes. Transfer to a large bowl, add the spinach, ½ cup Parmesan cheese, 2 cups ricotta cheese, 1 egg, ¼ teaspoon black pepper, and ⅛ teaspoon nutmeg and mix well. Proceed as in Steps 3 through 5 of Stuffed Shells.

## Sausage Variation

Per serving: Calories 795; Protein 41 g; Carbohydrate 63 g; Fat 43 g; Sodium 1579 mg; Cholesterol 191 mg.

Prepare 12 ounces fresh spinach or 1 package (10 ounces) frozen spinach as in Step 1 of Stuffed Shells. In a heavy 10-inch skillet set over moderate heat, cook 8 ounces sweet Italian sausage, casings removed, until browned — about 5 minutes. With a slotted spoon, transfer to a plate lined with paper toweling. Let cool, then chop fine. In the skillet with the drippings, sauté 1 small yellow onion, finely chopped, and 1 clove garlic, minced, over moderate heat, stirring frequently, until soft — about 5 minutes. In a large bowl, combine the onion mixture, sausage, spinach, ¼ cup Parmesan cheese, 1 cup ricotta cheese, 1 egg, 1 tablespoon minced parsley, ½ teaspoon dried oregano, crumbled, and ½ teaspoon black pepper. Proceed as in Steps 3 through 5 of Stuffed Shells.

# Classic Lasagne

Per square: Calories 378; Protein 30 g; Carbohydrate 27 g; Fat 17 g; Sodium 549 mg; Cholesterol 96 mg.

*Food fads come and go, but lasagne — an ideal party dish — remains a favorite with just about everyone.*

| | |
|---|---|
| 12 | lasagne noodles (about 12 ounces) |
| 1 | pound ricotta cheese |
| ¼ | cup minced parsley |
| 1 | egg |
| ½ | cup grated Parmesan cheese |
| ¼ | teaspoon black pepper |
| 5 | cups Tomato-Meat Sauce (page 218) or canned spaghetti sauce with meat |
| 3 | cups shredded part-skim mozzarella cheese (about 12 ounces) |

1 Cook the lasagne noodles according to package directions until *al dente* (see Tip, page 161). Drain in a colander, then rinse under cold water to stop the cooking.

2 In a medium-size bowl, combine the ricotta, parsley, egg, ¼ cup of the Parmesan cheese, and the pepper.

3 Preheat the oven to 375° F. To assemble the lasagne: Spread ½ cup of the meat sauce on the bottom of a lightly oiled, 13" x 9" x 2" baking pan. (If you plan to freeze it, see Tip, page 138, on lining the dish.) Then layer on 4 lasagne noodles, followed by half the ricotta mixture, ¾ cup of the mozzarella, and 1½ cups sauce. Repeat, beginning with the noodles. Top with the remaining 4 noodles, 1½ cups sauce, and 1½ cups mozzarella. Sprinkle the remaining ¼ cup of Parmesan over all.

▽ At this point the lasagne can be stored. *Refrigerate*, tightly covered, for up to 2 days. *Freeze* in the lined, labeled, and tightly covered casserole for up to 3 months at 0° F.

4 Place the lasagne on a baking sheet and bake, covered, for 15 minutes. Uncover and bake another 20 to 25 minutes or until heated through and bubbling. Remove from the oven and let stand for 15 minutes. Cut into 12 squares and serve with garlic bread and a salad of lettuce with red onion and shredded carrot. Serves 8 to 12.

### Serving Later

**From refrigerator:** Preheat the oven to 375° F. Proceed as in Step 4, baking the lasagne, covered, for 30 minutes; then, uncovered, for 25 to 30 minutes. **From freezer:** Thaw the lasagne in the refrigerator overnight. Proceed as above.

# Chicken Lasagne

Per square: Calories 437; Protein 27 g; Carbohydrate 31 g; Fat 23 g; Sodium 719 mg; Cholesterol 84 mg.

- 12 lasagne noodles (about 12 ounces)
- 6 cups Classic Tomato Sauce (page 216) or canned spaghetti sauce
- ½ cup coarsely chopped chicken livers (optional)
- ½ cup diced cooked ham (about 3 ounces)
- 1 pound ricotta cheese
- ½ cup grated Parmesan cheese
- 1 egg
- ¼ teaspoon black pepper
- 2 cups diced cooked chicken (about 12 ounces)
- 3 cups shredded part-skim mozzarella cheese (about 12 ounces)

1 Cook the lasagne noodles according to package directions until *al dente* (see Tip, page 161). Drain in a colander, then rinse under cold water to stop the cooking.

2 Meanwhile, in a heavy medium-size saucepan, mix the tomato sauce, livers, and ham, and cook, uncovered, over moderate heat for 10 minutes or until the sauce is thickened and the livers cooked through.

3 In a medium-size bowl, combine the ricotta, ¼ cup of the Parmesan cheese, the egg, and pepper.

4 Preheat the oven to 375° F. To assemble the lasagne: Spread ½ cup of the sauce on the bottom of a lightly oiled, 13" x 9" x 2" baking pan. (If you plan to freeze it, see Tip, page 138, on lining the dish.) Place 4 lasagne noodles in a layer over the sauce. Then layer on half of the ricotta mixture, followed by half of the chicken, ¾ cup of the mozzarella, and 1½ cups of the sauce. Repeat, beginning with the noodles. Top with the remaining 4 noodles, 2½ cups of sauce, and 1½ cups of mozzarella. Sprinkle the remaining ¼ cup of Parmesan over all.

▽ At this point the lasagne can be stored. *Refrigerate*, tightly covered, for up to 2 days. *Freeze* in the lined, labeled, and tightly covered casserole for up to 3 months at 0° F.

5 Place the lasagne on a baking sheet and bake, covered, for 15 minutes. Uncover and bake another 20 to 25 minutes or until heated through and bubbling. Remove from the oven and let stand for 15 minutes. Cut into 12 squares and accompany with sesame bread sticks and spinach sautéed in olive oil and garlic. Serves 8 to 12.

## Serving Later

**From refrigerator:** Preheat the oven to 375° F. Proceed as in Step 5, baking the lasagne, covered, for 30 minutes; then uncovered, for 25 to 30 minutes. **From freezer:** Thaw the lasagne in the refrigerator overnight. Proceed as above.

# Vegetarian Lasagne

Per square: Calories 417; Protein 20 g; Carbohydrate 36 g; Fat 23 g; Sodium 708 mg; Cholesterol 83 mg.

- 12 lasagne noodles (about 12 ounces)
- 6 cups Classic Tomato Sauce (page 216) or canned spaghetti sauce
- 1 medium-size carrot, peeled and finely chopped
- ¼ teaspoon fennel seeds
- 2 tablespoons olive oil
- 1 large yellow onion, coarsely chopped
- 12 ounces mushrooms, trimmed and thinly sliced
- 3 medium-size zucchini, trimmed and sliced ½ inch thick (about 1 pound)
- ½ teaspoon salt
- ¾ teaspoon black pepper
- 1 tablespoon each minced oregano and rosemary or 1 teaspoon each dried oregano and rosemary, crumbled
- 3 cloves garlic, minced
- 1 pound ricotta cheese
- ½ cup grated Parmesan cheese
- 1 egg
- 3 cups shredded part-skim mozzarella cheese (about 12 ounces)

1 Cook the noodles according to package directions until *al dente* (see Tip, page 161). Drain in a colander, then rinse under cold water to stop the cooking. Set aside.

2 While the noodles cook, mix the tomato sauce, carrot, and fennel seeds in a heavy medium-size saucepan. Bring to a boil over moderate heat. Reduce the heat to low, cover, and simmer for 10 minutes. Set aside.

3 Heat the oil in a large flameproof casserole over moderate heat for 1 minute. Add the onion, and sauté, stirring occasionally, until soft — about 5 minutes. Add the mushrooms, zucchini, salt, and ½ teaspoon of the pepper. Increase the heat to moderately high, and sauté, stirring occasionally, until the zucchini is crisp-tender and the liquid has evaporated — about 10 minutes. Add the oregano, rosemary, and garlic, and cook 1 minute more.

4 In a medium-size bowl, combine the ricotta, ¼ cup of the Parmesan, the egg, and the remaining ¼ teaspoon of pepper.

5 Preheat the oven to 375° F. To assemble the lasagne: Spread ½ cup of sauce over the bottom of a lightly oiled, 13" x 9" x 2" baking dish.

*Vegetarian Lasagne — zucchini, mushrooms, and onion sandwiched by layers of pasta and cheese*

(If you are planning to freeze it, see Tip, page 138, on lining the dish.) Place 4 lasagne noodles in a layer over the sauce. Then layer on half of the ricotta mixture, followed by ¾ cup of the mozzarella, half of the vegetable mixture, and 1½ cups of sauce. Repeat, beginning with the noodles. Top with the remaining 4 lasagne noodles, 2½ cups of sauce, and 1½ cups of mozzarella. Sprinkle the remaining ¼ cup of Parmesan over all.

▽ At this point the lasagne can be stored. *Refrigerate*, tightly covered, for up to 24 hours. *Freeze* in the lined, labeled, and tightly covered casserole for up to 3 months at 0° F.

6 Place the lasagne on a baking sheet and bake, covered, for 15 minutes. Uncover and bake 20 to 25 minutes more or until heated through and bubbling. Remove from the oven and let stand for 15 minutes, then cut into 12 squares. Accompany with whole-wheat Italian bread and a salad of arugula and endive with walnuts. Serves 8 to 12.

### Serving Later

**From refrigerator:** Preheat the oven to 375° F. Proceed as in Step 6, baking the lasagne, covered, for 30 minutes; then uncovered, for 25 to 30 minutes. **From freezer:** Thaw the lasagne overnight in the refrigerator. Proceed as above.

*Pizza Napoli,
a matchless classic*

# Pizza Napoli

Per main-dish serving: Calories 703;
Protein 39 g; Carbohydrate 54 g; Fat 36 g;
Sodium 965 mg; Cholesterol 133 mg.

*Though a baked pizza can be stored for
a day in the refrigerator, then reheated,
pizza tastes best when freshly baked.
Make the dough ahead and assemble a
pie when the mood strikes. If you like
Pesto (page 222), spread ½ cup of it
on the dough before adding the
mozzarella; omit the anchovies.*

*For the crust:*
½ cup lukewarm water (105° to
    115° F)
1 envelope active dry yeast
1 tablespoon light brown sugar
¾ teaspoon salt
2 cups sifted all-purpose flour
1 egg, lightly beaten
2 tablespoons olive oil

*For the filling:*

- 2 tablespoons olive oil
- 1 pound part-skim mozzarella cheese, thinly sliced
- 2 medium-size tomatoes, peeled and thinly sliced
- 2 teaspoons dried oregano, crumbled, or ground fennel
- 1 can (2 ounces) anchovy fillets, drained
- 8 black Italian olives (such as Gaeta) or other flavorful black olives, halved and pitted

1 To prepare the crust: In a small bowl, combine the water, yeast, and sugar. Let sit until bubbly — about 5 minutes. In a large bowl, mix together the salt and flour. Stir in the yeast mixture, egg, and olive oil.

2 On a lightly floured surface or in an electric mixer with a dough hook, knead the dough until smooth and elastic — about 10 minutes by hand, 3 to 4 minutes in a mixer. Transfer the dough to a clean, lightly oiled bowl, cover with plastic wrap, and let rise in a warm, draft-free place until doubled in size — about 1 hour. Punch the dough down and form into a ball.

▽ At this point the dough can be covered tightly with plastic wrap and stored. *Refrigerate* for up to 2 days. *Freeze*, labeled, for up to 3 months at 0° F.

3 Preheat the oven to 375° F. On a lightly floured surface, roll out the dough into a circle ⅛ inch thick and 12 inches in diameter. Press into a lightly oiled, 12-inch, round pizza pan and brush with the olive oil.

4 Spread the mozzarella cheese evenly over the dough and arrange the tomatoes on top. Sprinkle with the oregano. Arrange the anchovy fillets

like wheel spokes and place the pitted olive halves between them. Bake on the lower oven rack until the bottom crust is crisp — about 30 minutes.

5 Cut into wedges and accompany with a tossed green salad. Serves 4 as a main dish, 8 as an appetizer.

## Serving Later

**From refrigerator:** Let the dough come to room temperature — about 30 minutes. Proceed as in Steps 3 through 5. **From freezer:** Let the dough come to room temperature — about 2 hours — and proceed as above.

# Tomato, Bacon, and Onion Pizza

Per main-dish serving: Calories 763; Protein 33 g; Carbohydrate 43 g; Fat 50 g; Sodium 1009 mg; Cholesterol 137 mg.

- 1 Recipe Pizza Crust (see Pizza Napoli, opposite page), ready to roll out
- 6 ounces thinly sliced bacon
- 4 medium-size yellow onions, diced
- ⅛ teaspoon black pepper
- ¼ cup olive oil
- 12 ounces mozzarella, Fontina, or Bel Paese cheese, thinly sliced
- 3 medium-size tomatoes, cut into 15 slices
- 2 tablespoons snipped chives or thinly sliced green onion tops

1 To prepare the filling: In a heavy 12-inch skillet, cook the bacon over moderate heat until almost crisp — about 5 minutes. With a slotted spoon, transfer to a plate lined with paper toweling. Cut into ½-inch-long pieces. Set aside.

2 Add the onions and pepper to the skillet with the bacon drippings, and sauté, stirring occasionally, until golden — about 10 minutes.

3 Preheat the oven to 375° F. Lightly oil a 15½" x 10½" x 1" jelly roll pan. Roll out the dough to a ⅛-inch thickness and shape to fit the pan. Press the dough into the pan and sprinkle 2 tablespoons of the olive oil evenly over the top.

4 Scatter the onions evenly on top of the dough, then the cheese. Sprinkle the bacon over all and then lay the tomatoes in rows on top. Sprinkle with the remaining 2 tablespoons of olive oil. Bake on the lower rack of the oven until the bottom crust is crisp and the top is bubbly — about 30 minutes.

▽ At this point the pizza can be cooled to room temperature and stored. *Refrigerate* in the pan, tightly covered, for up to 24 hours.

5 Sprinkle the pizza with the chives and cut into squares. Accompany with a tossed green salad. Serves 5 as a main course, 10 as an appetizer.

## Serving Later

Preheat the oven to 400° F. Drizzle the pizza with a little olive oil. Then heat, uncovered, until warmed through — about 10 minutes. Serve as in Step 5.

# Onion-Olive Pie

Per main-dish serving: Calories 595;
Protein 11 g; Carbohydrate 61 g; Fat 35 g;
Sodium 570 mg; Cholesterol 69 mg.

- 7 tablespoons olive oil
- 4 large yellow onions, thinly sliced
- 1 clove garlic, crushed
- 1½ teaspoons dried thyme, crumbled
- ¼ teaspoon salt
- ⅛ teaspoon black pepper
- 1 recipe Pizza Crust (see Pizza Napoli, page 166), ready to roll out
- 1 pimiento, cut into 8 strips
- 16 black Italian olives, halved and pitted
- 8 cherry tomatoes, halved
- 1 can (2 ounces) anchovy fillets, drained (optional)

1 Heat 4 tablespoons of the olive oil in a heavy 10-inch skillet over moderate heat for 1 minute. Reduce the heat to moderately low, add the onion and garlic, and sauté until golden — 15 to 20 minutes. Season with the thyme, salt, and pepper.

2 Preheat the oven to 375° F. On a lightly floured surface, roll out the dough into a circle ⅛ inch thick and 12 inches in diameter. Press into a lightly oiled, 12-inch, round pizza pan. Spread the onions over the dough and arrange the pimiento, olives, tomatoes, and the anchovy fillets, if desired, decoratively on top. Sprinkle with the remaining 3 tablespoons of olive oil. Bake until the bottom is crisp — 30 to 40 minutes.

*Onion-Olive Pie — one slice per guest may not be enough.*

▽ At this point the pizza can be cooled to room temperature and stored. *Refrigerate* in the pan, tightly covered, for up to 24 hours.

3 Cut into wedges and accompany with a tossed green salad. Serves 4 as a main course, 8 as an appetizer.

## Serving Later

Preheat the oven to 400 °F. Drizzle with a little olive oil and heat until warmed through — about 10 minutes. Serve as in Step 3.

# Pizza Mexicali

Per main-dish serving: Calories 714;
Protein 28 g; Carbohydrate 57 g; Fat 43 g;
Sodium 898 mg; Cholesterol 69 mg.

- 1 recipe Pizza Crust (see Pizza Napoli, page 166), ready to roll out
- ¾ cup Spicy Salsa (page 218)
- 1 small red onion, thinly sliced
- 10 ounces Monterey Jack cheese, thinly sliced
- 1 pimiento, cut into thin strips
- 1 small ripe avocado, peeled, pitted, and diced
- 2 tablespoons chopped cilantro (coriander leaves), optional

1 Preheat the oven to 375° F. On a lightly floured surface, roll out the dough into a circle ⅛ inch thick and 12 inches in diameter. Press into a lightly oiled, 12-inch, round pizza pan. Spread the sauce over the dough and lay the onion slices on top. Arrange the cheese and pimiento strips on top of the onion. Bake, uncovered, on the lower rack of the oven until the bottom crust is crisp — about 30 minutes.

▽ At this point the pizza can be cooled to room temperature and stored. *Refrigerate* in the pan, tightly covered, for up to 24 hours.

2 Arrange the avocado on top of the pizza and sprinkle with the cilantro. Cut into wedges and accompany with a salad of romaine, endive, orange slices, and walnuts topped with a vinaigrette dressing. Serves 4 as a main course, 8 as an appetizer.

## Serving Later

Preheat the oven to 400° F. Heat the pizza, uncovered, until warmed through — about 10 minutes. Proceed as in Step 2.

# Vegetables

Baking and braising are two of the most convenient ways to prepare vegetables ahead. But even a busy hostess, who wants everything done before the guests arrive, can serve fresh vegetables very simply cooked to a perfect degree of crisp tenderness. The secret is to parboil them. In a large saucepan, bring to a boil sufficient water to cover the vegetables, drop them in, and cook until barely tender and still quite crisp. Drain in a colander and refresh immediately in ice cold water to stop the cooking. Cover and store at room temperature for up to 4 hours; in the refrigerator for up to 24 hours. When ready to serve, reheat them in a covered saucepan containing about $1/2$ inch of boiling water, or sauté them in a little butter or oil flavored with herbs. If you want to preserve the minerals lost to the parboiling water, use it to cook rice or add some of it to a soup or a sauce.

Puréeing is another way to have your vegetables and eat them too. When seasonal types, such as summer squash, eggplants, or peas are abundant, buy extra quantities, purée them, and freeze to enjoy when the season is long past.

## Artichokes with Wine, Anchovies, and Capers

Per serving: Calories 205; Protein 4 g; Carbohydrate 14 g; Fat 14 g; Sodium 113 mg; Cholesterol 0 mg.

*This flavorful recipe will perhaps inspire you to include artichokes in your diet more often. Rich in calcium, vitamin A, potassium, and phosphorus, they are low in calories.*

2 quarts water
4 medium-size artichokes or 12 miniature artichokes
¼ cup olive oil
½ cup dry white wine
4 anchovy fillets, chopped
2 tablespoons minced parsley
2 cloves garlic, minced
1 tablespoon drained capers
½ teaspoon black pepper

1 In a large saucepan, bring the water to a boil over moderately high heat. Reduce the heat to moderate, add the artichokes, and cook, covered, for 15 minutes. Drain the artichokes in a colander, then pat dry on paper toweling. Remove a layer or two of the tough outer leaves, cut off the tips of all remaining leaves, and trim the stems. Quarter the artichokes lengthwise and scrape out the chokes with a sharp paring knife. If using miniature artichokes, which have no chokes, simply halve lengthwise.

▽ At this point, the artichokes can be cooled to room temperature and stored. *Refrigerate*, in a tightly covered bowl, for up to 2 days.

2 Heat the oil in a heavy 12-inch skillet over moderately low heat for 1 minute. Add the artichokes and sauté gently for 1 minute, then add the wine. Cook, covered, until the artichokes are tender when pierced with a knife — 15 to 20 minutes. (If necessary, add a little water to prevent sticking.)

3 Transfer the artichokes to a serving platter. Stir the anchovies, parsley, garlic, and capers into the skillet, then spoon the skillet mixture over the artichokes. Sprinkle with the pepper. Serve hot or at room temperature as an appetizer or as a side dish with Turkey Mushroom Loaf (page 92) or Tuscan Roast Pork (page 112). Serves 4.

## Baked Beet Casserole

Per serving: Calories 136; Protein 2 g; Carbohydrate 20 g; Fat 6 g; Sodium 554 mg; Cholesterol 15 mg.

*This ultra-simple recipe brings out the best in beets.*

3 tablespoons unsalted butter or margarine
¼ cup fine dry bread crumbs
2 tablespoons all-purpose flour
⅔ cup cold water or beet liquid
2 tablespoons brown sugar
1½ tablespoons prepared horseradish
¼ teaspoon salt
2 cans (1 pound each) small beets, drained and halved

1 Preheat the oven to 375° F. Melt the butter in a medium-size saucepan over moderate heat. Remove 1 tablespoon and toss with the bread crumbs in a small bowl; set aside. Add the flour to the skillet, and cook for 1 minute, stirring constantly. Blend in the water, sugar, horseradish, and salt. Cook, stirring, 1 minute more, remove from the heat, and stir in the beets. Pour into a 1½-quart casserole.

▽ At this point the casserole and bread crumbs can be covered and stored separately. When the casserole has cooled to room temperature, *refrigerate* it for up to 24 hours.

2 Sprinkle the buttered crumbs evenly over the casserole. Bake, uncovered, for 45 minutes or until the beets are heated through and the topping is golden brown. Serve with roasted meat or broiled fish. This dish goes particularly well with German Meatloaf (page 110). Serves 6.

### Serving Later

One hour before baking the casserole, set it out to come to room temperature. Preheat the oven to 375° F. Proceed as in Step 2.

## Beets with Dill and Sour Cream

Per serving: Calories 98; Protein 2 g; Carbohydrate 13 g; Fat 4 g; Sodium 338 mg; Cholesterol 9 mg.

*These Swedish-style beets are sweeter and more succulent than boiled beets. For richer color, cook the beets as directed below.*

8 small beets, trimmed of all but ½ inch of the tops and scrubbed (about 1½ pounds)
1 tablespoon minced yellow onion
2 tablespoons fresh lemon juice, or to taste
½ teaspoon sugar
½ teaspoon salt
Pinch black pepper, or to taste
⅓ cup sour cream
3 tablespoons snipped fresh dill or 2 teaspoons dried dill weed

*Artichokes with Wine, Anchovies, and Capers — a glorious way to feature this ancient vegetable*

1 Preheat the oven to 400° F. If the beets are of uniform size, place 4 in a line on a sheet of aluminum foil and wrap securely. Repeat with the remaining beets. If they are not the same size, wrap separately. Place the beets on a baking sheet and bake for about 45 minutes or until they can be easily pierced with a knife.

▽ At this point the wrapped beets can be cooled to room temperature and stored in their foil wrappers. *Refrigerate* for up to 4 days.

2 When cool enough to handle, unwrap the beets and, using paper toweling, slip off their skins. Cut the beets into ⅜-inch slices and place in a medium-size bowl.

3 Add the onion, lemon juice, sugar, salt, and pepper; toss to coat. Add the sour cream and dill; toss until the dill is well distributed. Let stand at room temperature for 1 hour before serving. Or refrigerate for up to 24 hours, then remove from the refrigerator 30 minutes before serving. Serve with roast chicken and potato salad, or with a salad made of potatoes, apples, and chunks of chicken. Serves 4.

## Braised Cabbage with Apples

Per serving: Calories 149; Protein 4 g; Carbohydrate 28 g; Fat 3 g; Sodium 224 mg; Cholesterol 0 mg.

1 tablespoon olive or vegetable oil
1 large yellow onion, coarsely chopped
1 tablespoon sugar
2 medium-size apples, peeled, cored, and coarsely chopped
1 medium-size red cabbage, trimmed, cored, quartered, and thinly sliced (about 2 pounds)

1/4 cup red wine vinegar
1 cup Chicken or Beef Stock (page 48) or canned chicken or beef broth
1/2 teaspoon salt
2 bay leaves
1/2 cup dry red wine
2 tablespoons all-purpose flour
2 tablespoons currant or grape jelly

1 Heat the oil in a large flameproof casserole over moderate heat for 1 minute. Add the onion, sugar, and apples, and cook, uncovered, stirring occasionally, for 5 minutes or until the onions are soft. Add the cabbage, and cook, stirring occasionally, until wilted — about 5 minutes.

2 Add the vinegar, 1/2 cup of the stock, the salt, and bay leaves. Bring to a boil, stirring all the while. Reduce the heat to low, cover, and simmer for 8 to 10 minutes or until the cabbage is crisp-tender.

▽ At this point the casserole can be cooled to room temperature and stored. *Refrigerate*, tightly covered, for up to 24 hours.

3 Add the wine and remaining 1/2 cup of stock and bring to a simmer. Sprinkle with the flour and stir well. Add the jelly and simmer, stirring often, for 5 minutes or until slightly thickened; remove the bay leaves. Serve with Tuscan Roast Pork (page 112). Serves 6 to 8.

### Serving Later

Bring the casserole to a simmer over moderate heat, stirring occasionally — 10 to 15 minutes. Proceed as in Step 3.

# Baked Carrot Ring

Per serving: Calories 206; Protein 4 g; Carbohydrate 17 g; Fat 14 g; Sodium 320 mg; Cholesterol 136 mg.

*This delicious but somewhat delicate ring should be handled gently. The compliments it draws, however, make the extra care worth the trouble. Filling the center with tiny green peas makes a more dramatic presentation.*

16 medium-size carrots, peeled, cut into 1-inch pieces, and boiled until tender (about 2 pounds)
3 eggs
2 tablespoons brown sugar
1 tablespoon all-purpose flour
1 teaspoon salt
1/4 teaspoon ground cinnamon
1/8 teaspoon white pepper
1/2 cup milk
1/2 cup (1 stick) unsalted butter or margarine, melted
Cooked carrot slices for garnish (optional)

1 Preheat the oven to 350° F. In an electric blender or food processor, purée the carrots until smooth — about 30 seconds. Blend in the eggs, one at a time, then add the sugar, flour, salt, cinnamon, pepper, milk, and butter.

▽ At this point the mixture can be stored. Pour into a large bowl, cover tightly with plastic wrap, and *refrigerate* for up to 4 hours.

2 Butter a 10-cup, ovenproof ring mold or casserole. Pour the carrot mixture into the mold (stir it first, if it's been refrigerated) and bake, uncovered, for 50 minutes to 1 hour or until a knife inserted in the center comes out clean. Let it stand for 10 minutes before unmolding. Run a small knife around the inner edge of the mold. Carefully invert onto a serving dish and garnish with the carrot slices, if you like. Serve with Lime Chicken Stuffed with Goat Cheese (page 80), Veal Breast Stuffed with Spinach, Pine Nuts, and Raisins

(page 118), or Herbed Turkey Roll (page 92). It is also good with baked ham. Serves 8.

# Carrot Burgers

Per serving: Calories 173; Protein 4 g; Carbohydrate 16 g; Fat 11 g; Sodium 307 mg; Cholesterol 85 mg.

5 medium-size carrots, shredded (about 2 cups)
1 small yellow onion, finely chopped
3 tablespoons all-purpose flour
2 tablespoons cornmeal
1 egg, lightly beaten
2 tablespoons milk, half-and-half, or sour cream
1 tablespoon snipped dill or 1 teaspoon dried dill weed (optional)
1/2 teaspoon sugar
1/2 teaspoon salt
1/4 teaspoon baking powder
1/8 teaspoon black pepper
2 tablespoons unsalted butter or margarine
1 tablespoon vegetable oil

1 In a medium-size bowl, mix the carrots, onion, flour, cornmeal, egg, milk, dill, if desired, sugar, salt, baking powder, and pepper. Shape the mixture into 8 patties about 1 1/2 inches thick. Transfer to a platter, cover with plastic wrap, and refrigerate for at least 1 hour. Will keep for up to 12 hours.

2 Heat the butter and the oil in a heavy 10-inch skillet over moderate heat until sizzling — about 1 minute. Brown the patties for about 3 minutes on each side. Drain on a platter lined with paper toweling, then serve immediately. Serve as a side dish with Marinated Spareribs (page 116), or as a light luncheon dish accompanied by a salad of mixed greens and whole grain bread. Laced with a little maple syrup, Carrot Burgers also make an interesting breakfast alternative. Serves 4.

# Cauliflower and Ham Gratin

Per main-dish serving: Calories 345; Protein 26 g; Carbohydrate 14 g; Fat 21 g; Sodium 992 mg; Cholesterol 84 mg.

- 2 quarts water
- 1 large cauliflower, trimmed and cored (about 1 ½ pounds)
- 3 tablespoons unsalted butter or margarine
- 2 shallots or 4 green onions, minced
- 8 ounces cooked ham, finely chopped
- 1 tablespoon Madeira or sherry
- 2 tablespoons all-purpose flour
- 1 cup Chicken Stock (page 48) or canned chicken broth
- ¼ teaspoon each salt and black pepper, or to taste
- ⅛ teaspoon each ground ginger and ground nutmeg
  Pinch cayenne (ground red) pepper
- 1 cup grated Gruyère cheese (about 4 ounces)

1 Preheat the oven to 350° F. In a medium-size saucepan, bring the water to a boil over moderately high heat. Add the cauliflower, and cook, covered, until just tender — about 8 minutes. Transfer to a colander and rinse under cold running water. Separate the florets and set aside.

2 While the cauliflower is cooking, melt 1 tablespoon of the butter in a heavy 10-inch skillet over moderate heat. Add the shallots, and sauté for about 1 minute. Add the ham; sauté until lightly browned — 3 to 4 minutes. Stir in the Madeira. Cook for 1 minute, remove from the heat, and set aside.

3 Melt the remaining 2 tablespoons of butter in a medium-size saucepan over moderate heat. Blend in the flour gradually and stir constantly for 2 minutes. Gradually whisk in the chicken stock, bring to a boil, then cook and stir until thickened and smooth — 3 to 4 minutes. Stir in the salt, black pepper, ginger, nutmeg, and cayenne pepper.

4 Arrange half of the cauliflower in a buttered 2-quart casserole, spoon the ham mixture over it, and then spoon half the sauce over the ham mixture. Sprinkle with half of the cheese. Top with the remaining cauliflower, sauce, and cheese. Cover tightly with aluminum foil.

▽ At this point the dish can be cooled to room temperature and stored. *Refrigerate* for up to 24 hours.

5 Bake, covered, until bubbling — 15 to 20 minutes. Serve as a light supper dish accompanied by a spinach salad. Or serve as a side dish with roast chicken or beef. Serves 4 as an entrée, 6 as a side dish.

## Serving Later

Transfer from the refrigerator to a preheated 350° F oven and bake, covered, until bubbling — about 40 minutes. Serve as in Step 5.

# Baked Celery and Onions with Herbs

Per serving: Calories 113; Protein 3 g; Carbohydrate 8 g; Fat 8 g; Sodium 239 mg; Cholesterol 22 mg.

*If you like the taste of caraway, substitute 1 teaspoon of the seeds for the marjoram and thyme.*

- 4 tablespoons (½ stick) unsalted butter or margarine
- 1 large bunch celery, base and leafy sections removed, and cut into 1-inch pieces
- 1½ tablespoons cornstarch
- 2 cups Chicken Stock (page 48) or canned chicken broth
- ½ teaspoon dried marjoram, crumbled
- ¼ teaspoon dried thyme, crumbled
- ¼ teaspoon each salt and black pepper
- 2 tablespoons minced fresh parsley
- 2 medium-size yellow onions, thinly sliced

1 Melt the butter in a heavy 12-inch skillet over moderate heat. Add the celery, and sauté, stirring occasionally, for 3 minutes or until crisp-tender.

2 In a small bowl, whisk together the cornstarch and chicken stock until smooth and add to the skillet. Bring to a boil, stirring; reduce the heat to moderately low. Simmer, stirring occasionally, for 5 minutes. Add the marjoram, thyme, salt, pepper, and parsley.

3 Preheat the oven to 350° F. Scatter the onion rings over the bottom of a buttered, 12" x 8" x 2" baking dish; spoon the celery mixture over them. Cover tightly with aluminum foil.

▽ At this point the casserole can be cooled to room temperature and *refrigerated* for up to 24 hours.

4 Bake, covered, for 50 to 55 minutes or until the celery is tender. Serve with roast poultry, or meat. Serves 6.

## Serving Later

One hour before baking the casserole, set it out to come to room temperature. Preheat the oven to 350° F. Proceed as in Step 4.

# Pueblo Baked Corn and Harvest Vegetables

Per serving: Calories 140; Protein 7 g; Carbohydrate 16 g; Fat 6 g; Sodium 379 mg; Cholesterol 17 mg.

*In this recipe, based on typical fare of Indians in the Southwest, the vegetables are cooked for a long time. If you prefer crisper vegetables, reduce the overall cooking time by 15 minutes.*

3 slices bacon, cut crosswise in julienne strips
2 large yellow onions, coarsely chopped
2 cups fresh corn kernels (2 large ears) or 2 cups frozen corn kernels, thawed
2 teaspoons chili powder, or to taste
1 teaspoon dried oregano, crumbled
1 teaspoon salt
¼ teaspoon each ground cumin and black pepper
3 medium-size yellow squash, cut into ½-inch slices (about 1 pound)
2 large ripe tomatoes, peeled and cut in slim wedges (about 1 pound)
1 large sweet green pepper, cored, seeded, and cut into 1-inch squares
1 cup shredded Cheddar cheese (about 4 ounces)

*Pueblo Baked Corn and Harvest Vegetables, the bounty of late summer in one dish*

1 Preheat the oven to 350° F. Cook the bacon in a heavy 10-inch skillet over moderately high heat until crisp — about 5 minutes. Transfer to a platter lined with paper toweling and reserve.

2 Reduce the heat to moderate. Add the onions to the skillet, and cook, stirring, for 5 to 8 minutes or until lightly browned. Add the corn, chili powder, oregano, salt, cumin, and black pepper, and cook, uncovered, for about 5 minutes or until the corn is crisp-tender.

3 Meanwhile, in a 13" x 9" x 2" baking dish, combine the squash, tomatoes, and green pepper. Add the corn mixture and toss well. Cover with aluminum foil.

▽ At this point the dish can be *refrigerated* for up to 8 hours.

4 Bake, covered, for 30 minutes. Stir, then bake, uncovered, 30 minutes longer or until the squash is tender. Sprinkle the cheese evenly over the top and bake, uncovered, 10 to 15 minutes

longer or until the cheese is melted. Serve with beef or chicken tostadas or with roast chicken or pork. Serves 8.

### Serving Later

Preheat the oven to 350° F. Bake, covered, for 40 minutes. Uncover, stir, and bake 35 minutes longer or until the squash is tender. Continue as in Step 4.

# Sautéed Cucumbers

Per serving: Calories 79; Protein 1 g; Carbohydrate 7 g; Fat 6 g; Sodium 69 mg; Cholesterol 15 mg.

- 3 medium-size cucumbers, trimmed and peeled (about 2 pounds)
- 1 tablespoon salt
- 2 tablespoons unsalted butter or margarine
- 2 tablespoons each minced chives and snipped dill or minced tarragon
- ¼ teaspoon black pepper

1 Halve the cucumbers lengthwise, then scrape out the seeds with a teaspoon and discard. Cut the cucumbers crosswise into 1½-inch pieces. Place them in a colander, sprinkle with the salt, and toss well; allow to drain for at least 30 minutes. Rinse the cucumbers in cold water, drain well, and pat dry with paper toweling.

▽ At this point the cucumbers can be stored. Cover tightly and *refrigerate* for up to 12 hours.

2 Melt the butter in a heavy 12-inch skillet over moderate heat. Add the cucumbers, and sauté, tossing frequently, for 3 to 5 minutes or until crisp-tender. Sprinkle with the chives, dill, and pepper. Serve immediately. This dish goes well with Himalayan Chicken (page 85) and with Pork and Sauerkraut Stew (page 114). Serves 4.

*Certain to please —
Onions Stuffed with Pecans,
Mushrooms, and Rice*

# Caramelized Onions

Per serving: Calories 203; Protein 4 g;
Carbohydrate 22 g; Fat 13 g; Sodium 374 mg;
Cholesterol 33 mg.

- 4 tablespoons (½ stick) unsalted butter or margarine
- 3 large Bermuda onions, halved and thinly sliced (about 2½ pounds)
- 3 tablespoons red wine vinegar
- ¾ teaspoon salt
- ¼ teaspoon black pepper

1 Melt the butter in a heavy 14-inch skillet (or two smaller heavy skillets) over moderately low heat. Add the onions, and cook, covered, until very tender — about 30 minutes.

2 Increase the heat to moderate and cook, uncovered, stirring occasionally, until the onions are a light caramel color — about 45 minutes. (If the onions darken too rapidly, reduce the heat to low and cover for a few minutes. Uncover and continue cooking.)

3 Stir in the vinegar, salt, and pepper, and cook over over high heat, stirring constantly, until the vinegar has evaporated — about 5 minutes.

▽ At this point the onions can be cooled to room temperature and stored. Transfer to a buttered casserole and *refrigerate*, covered tightly with plastic wrap, for up to 3 days.

4 Serve with braised liver, sausage and peppers, roast turkey, or Veal Marengo (page 121). Serves 4 to 6.

### Serving Later

One hour before reheating, set the onions out to come to room temperature. Preheat the oven to 350° F; bake, covered, until heated through — about 15 minutes. Serve as in Step 4. Or transfer directly from the refrigerator to a skillet containing 1 tablespoon of melted butter; reheat, covered, over moderately low heat until warmed through — about 15 minutes. Serve as in Steps 4 to 6.

## Onion Sauce Variation

Per serving: Calories 303; Protein 9 g;
Carbohydrate 39 g; Fat 13 g; Sodium 465 mg;
Cholesterol 34 mg.

Add ½ cup Chicken Stock (page 48) or canned chicken broth to the caramelized onions; cook, stirring, over moderately high heat. When bubbling, remove from the heat; pour over 8 ounces cooked spaghetti and top with grated Parmesan cheese. Serves 4.

# Onions Stuffed with Pecans, Mushrooms, and Rice

Per serving: Calories 360; Protein 6 g;
Carbohydrate 24 g; Fat 28 g; Sodium 342 mg;
Cholesterol 51 mg.

- 1½ teaspoons salt
- 6 large Spanish onions, 1 inch cut from tops and peeled (about 5 pounds)
- 1 tablespoon unsalted butter or margarine
- 2 ounces mushrooms, finely chopped (about ½ cup)
- 1 cup cooked rice
- 8 ounces pecans, finely chopped (about ⅔ cup)
- 1 egg, slightly beaten
- ¼ teaspoon dried thyme, crumbled
- ⅛ teaspoon black pepper Pinch ground nutmeg or mace

1 Pour 1½ inches of water into a large saucepan, add ½ teaspoon of the salt, and bring to a boil over high heat. Add the onions, return to a boil, and reduce the heat to moderate. Cook, covered, for 10 to 15 minutes or until the onions are almost tender but retain their shape.

2 Meanwhile, melt the butter in a heavy 10-inch skillet over moderately low heat. Add the mushrooms, and sauté for 3 to 5 minutes or until tender. Set aside.

3 Drain the onions on a platter lined with paper toweling. When cool enough to handle, gently scoop out the insides with a serving spoon, leaving shells ⅜ to ½ inch thick. Make sure that the bottom of each shell remains intact. Chop up the pulp.

4 Preheat the oven to 350° F. In a medium-size bowl, mix 1 cup of chopped pulp (use the remainder for soup, stew, or meatloaf), the mushrooms, rice, pecans, egg, the remaining teaspoon of salt, the thyme, pepper, and nutmeg until well blended.

5 Stuff the onions with equal amounts of pulp mixture (about ½ cup per onion) and place in a lightly greased, 13" x 9" x 2" baking dish.

▽ At this point the dish can be stored. *Refrigerate*, tightly covered, for up to 24 hours.

6 Bake, covered, for 45 minutes; uncover and bake 10 minutes longer. Serve with Marinated Rock Cornish Hens (page 94) or Tuscan Roast Pork (page 112). Makes 6 large servings.

### Serving Later

Preheat the oven to 350° F. Bake the onions, covered, for 55 minutes, then uncover and bake 10 minutes longer. Serve as in Step 6.

# Tender Baked Parsnips

Per serving: Calories 143; Protein 2 g; Carbohydrate 23 g; Fat 6 g; Sodium 258 mg; Cholesterol 15 mg.

- 4 parsnips, peeled, trimmed, halved, and boiled until tender (about 1 pound)
- 1 tablespoon lemon juice
- 1 teaspoon grated lemon rind
- ½ teaspoon salt
- ¼ teaspoon each black pepper and ground nutmeg
- 2 tablespoons unsalted butter or margarine
- 2 tablespoons minced parsley

1 Preheat the oven to 350° F. In the saucepan in which you cooked the parsnips, toss them with the lemon juice, lemon rind, salt, pepper, and nutmeg. Transfer all to an oiled, 8" x 8" x 2" baking dish.

▽ At this point the parsnips can be covered with plastic wrap and left at room temperature for up to 4 hours.

2 Dot the parsnips with the butter and bake, uncovered, until the butter has melted and the parsnips are heated through — about 20 minutes. Transfer to a serving dish and sprinkle with the parsley. Serve with pot roast, pork chops, or ham. This dish is particularly good with Beef with Chestnuts (page 102) and Orange-Cumin Beef Stew (page 104). Serves 4.

### Serving Later

Preheat the oven to 350° F and proceed as in Step 2.

# Baked Potatoes Stuffed with Brie

Per main-dish serving: Calories 158; Protein 4 g; Carbohydrate 17 g; Fat 9 g; Sodium 173 mg; Cholesterol 57 mg.

*An easy way to dress up potatoes, this dish is equally delicious made with Camembert, Monterey Jack, Fontina, or a creamy blue cheese.*

- 4 medium-size, hot, baked potatoes (Idahoes or russets)
- 2 ounces Brie cheese, cut into 1-inch cubes
- 4 tablespoons (½ stick) unsalted butter or margarine, at room temperature
- 1 egg yolk
- 1 tablespoon minced chives or green onion tops, or to taste
- ½ teaspoon salt
- ¼ teaspoon black pepper Ground nutmeg to taste (optional)

1 Preheat the oven to 375° F. Slice ½ inch lengthwise off each potato. Taking care not to pierce the skin, scoop out the flesh, leaving a ¼-inch-thick shell.

2 In a medium-size bowl, mash the potato flesh until smooth. Add the Brie, butter, egg yolk, chives, salt, pepper, and nutmeg, if desired; mix well.

3 Stuff each potato shell with the mixture, mounding it in the center; transfer to a shallow baking dish.

▽ At this point the potatoes can be stored. *Refrigerate*, tightly covered, for up to 24 hours.

4 Bake the potatoes, uncovered, until the cheese has melted and the stuffing is heated through — 12 to 15 minutes. Run under the broiler, five inches from the flame, until lightly browned — 3 to 5 minutes. Serve as a side dish with steak, roasts, poultry, or broiled fish, such as Herbed Bluefish

Fillets (page 70), or as a light luncheon dish, accompanied by a spinach salad with tomatoes and mushrooms. Serves 4 as an entrée, 8 as a side dish.

### Serving Later

Preheat the oven to 375° F. Bake the potatoes, uncovered, until the cheese has melted and the stuffing is heated through — 20 to 25 minutes. Brown and serve as in Step 4.

# Potato, Tomato, and Onion Gratin

Per serving: Calories 250; Protein 4 g; Carbohydrate 35 g; Fat 12 g; Sodium 418 mg; Cholesterol 0 mg.

*This appealing Provençal dish is even better when prepared with home-grown tomatoes and fresh thyme, preferably lemon thyme. If serving at room temperature, add the capers for a more piquant flavor.*

- 3 quarts water
- 3½ teaspoons salt
- 3 large baking potatoes, peeled and sliced ¼ inch thick (about 1½ pounds)
- 4 large ripe tomatoes, peeled, halved, and seeded (about 2 pounds)
- ¼ cup olive oil
- 2 medium-size red onions, sliced ¼ inch thick
- 4 teaspoons thyme leaves or 1¼ teaspoons dried thyme, crumbled
- 3 cloves garlic, thinly sliced
- ½ teaspoon fennel seeds
- ¼ teaspoon black pepper, or to taste
- ½ cup pitted green or black olives, coarsely chopped
- 1 tablespoon drained capers (optional)

1 In a large saucepan, bring the water and 3 teaspoons of the salt to a boil. Add the potatoes, and parboil, uncovered, for 3 minutes or until slightly tender; drain and set aside. Meanwhile, coarsely chop one of the tomato halves, and slice the rest 1/4 inch thick. Set aside.

2 Preheat the oven to 400° F. Heat 2 tablespoons of the oil in a heavy 10-inch skillet over moderate heat for 1 minute. Add the onions, 2 teaspoons of the thyme, half of the garlic, the fennel seeds, 1/4 teaspoon of the salt, and 1/8 teaspoon of the pepper. Sauté, stirring occasionally, for 3 minutes or until barely tender. Set aside.

3 In a lightly oiled, 13" x 9" x 2" baking dish, layer half of the onion mixture and top with the chopped tomato and the olives. Sprinkle with 1 teaspoon of the remaining thyme. Layer the potatoes on top, then the sliced tomatoes. Tuck in the remaining garlic. Sprinkle the remaining 1/4 teaspoon salt and 1/8 teaspoon pepper over all. If serving at room temperature, add the capers, if desired. Top with the remaining onions and drizzle with the remaining 2 tablespoons of olive oil. Cover the baking dish with aluminum foil.

▽ At this point the gratin can be *refrigerated* for up to 8 hours.

4 Bake the casserole for about 20 minutes. Uncover and bake 20 minutes longer or until the potatoes are done. Sprinkle with the remaining teaspoon of thyme. Can be served hot or at room temperature. Serve with grilled chicken or Italian sausages, French bread, and a green salad. Serves 4 to 6.

### Serving Later

Preheat the oven to 400° F. Bake the foil-covered casserole for 30 minutes. Uncover and bake 20 to 25 minutes more or until the potatoes are done. Serve as in Step 4.

*A scrumptious Baked Potato Stuffed with Brie, almost a meal by itself*

## Potatoes Roasted with Garlic and Rosemary

Per serving: Calories 255; Protein 3 g; Carbohydrate 32 g; Fat 14 g; Sodium 131 mg; Cholesterol 0 mg.

*These crispy potatoes are equally tasty straight from the oven or at room temperature. The roasted garlic has a mellow flavor. If you like, you can squeeze the garlic cloves out of their skins and eat them with the potatoes.*

- 4 medium-size baking potatoes, peeled (1¼ to 1½ pounds)
- ¼ cup olive oil
- 4 cloves garlic, unpeeled
- 1 teaspoon dried rosemary, crumbled
- ¼ teaspoon salt or ½ teaspoon coarse (Kosher) salt

1 Preheat the oven to 375° F. Cut the potatoes in half lengthwise, then crosswise into 1-inch-thick pieces.

2 In a 13″ x 9″ x 2″ baking dish, stir together the oil, garlic, and rosemary and bake, uncovered, for 5 minutes. Add the potatoes and bake, uncovered, turning occasionally, until tender and crispy brown — 30 to 40 minutes. Sprinkle with the salt.

▽ At this point the potatoes can be stored, uncovered, at room temperature for up to 6 hours.

3 Serve hot or at room temperature with roasted meats or poultry. This dish goes especially well with Chicken Escabeche (page 90), Veal with Tuna Sauce (page 122), or Zucchini Stuffed with Sausage (page 132). Serves 4.

## Potato Salad Variation

Per serving: Calories 267; Protein 3 g; Carbohydrate 33 g, Fat 14 g; Sodium 158 mg; Cholesterol 0 mg.

Proceed as in Steps 1 and 2 of Potatoes Roasted with Garlic and Rosemary; transfer the potatoes to a medium-size mixing bowl. Add **3 tablespoons white wine or white wine vinegar, 2 tablespoons minced onion or shallot,** and **1½ teaspoons Dijon or spicy brown mustard;** toss well. Serve hot or at room temperature. Serves 4.

## Potato Pie

Per side-dish serving: Calories 249; Protein 14 g; Carbohydrate 28 g; Fat 9 g; Sodium 481 mg; Cholesterol 114 mg.

- 2 tablespoons soft bread crumbs
- ¾ cup grated Parmesan cheese (about 1½ ounces)
- 1 tablespoon minced parsley
- 3 large, hot, baked potatoes (about 1½ pounds)
- 1 cup part skim-milk ricotta or low-fat cottage cheese, pressed through a sieve
- 2 eggs, beaten lightly
- ¼ cup half-and-half or milk (optional)
- 2 tablespoons minced chives
- ½ teaspoon salt
- ¼ teaspoon black pepper

1 Preheat the oven to 350° F. In a small bowl, mix the bread crumbs, ¼ cup of the Parmesan cheese, and the parsley. Sprinkle the mixture over the bottom and sides of a well-buttered, 9-inch pie pan; shake out any excess. Chill, uncovered, until ready to use.

2 Cut the potatoes in half lengthwise and scoop the flesh into a large bowl. (Reserve the skins for Potato-Skin Nachos, below.) While the potato flesh is still hot, stir in the ricotta and, using an electric mixer, a whisk, or a wooden spoon, beat until smooth.

Gradually beat in the eggs. If a creamier consistency is desired, stir in the half-and-half. Blend in the chives, salt, pepper, and ¼ cup of the remaining Parmesan cheese.

3 Spoon the mixture into the prepared pie plate and sprinkle with the last ¼ cup of Parmesan cheese.

▽ At this point the pie can be *refrigerated*, tightly covered, for up to 24 hours.

4 Bake the pie, uncovered, until puffed and lightly browned — 35 to 45 minutes. Can be eaten hot or at room temperature. Serve as a meatless main dish, accompanied by steamed asparagus with Dill Butter (page 222), or as a side dish with German Meatloaf (page 110). Serves 4 as an entrée, 6 as a side dish.

### Serving Later

Preheat the oven to 350° F. Bake the pie, uncovered, until puffed and lightly browned — 45 to 55 minutes. Serve as in Step 4.

## Potato-Skin Nachos

Per side-dish serving: Calories 263; Protein 12 g; Carbohydrate 28 g; Fat 12 g; Sodium 217 mg; Cholesterol 10 mg.

*When you plan mashed potatoes, cook the potatoes in the oven and save the skins for this zesty dish, which also makes a delicious appetizer.*

- 6 large baked potatoes (about 3 pounds)
- 2 cups shredded Monterey Jack or sharp Cheddar cheese (about 8 ounces)
- 1 can (4 ounces) green chilies, drained and coarsely chopped

1 Preheat the oven to 400° F. Slice each potato in half lengthwise and scoop out the flesh, reserving it for a purée or Potato Pie (above). Cut each skin in half again, crosswise.

▽ At this point the potato skins can be refrigerated, tightly covered with plastic wrap, for up to 2 days.

2 Place the skins on a large baking sheet and bake, uncovered, until crisp — 10 to 15 minutes.

3 Preheat the broiler. Sprinkle each skin with cheese, then top with the green chilies. Broil 6 inches from the heat until the cheese melts — 1 to 2 minutes. Serve with grilled meats or poultry. This dish is particularly good with Steak Cubes Southwestern-Style (page 98) or Cottage Cheese Soufflé (page 136). Serves 6 as a side dish, 8 to 12 as an appetizer.

### Spiced Potato Strips

Per serving: Calories 137; Protein 2 g; Carbohydrate 20 g; Fat 5 g; Sodium 192 mg; Cholesterol 16 mg.

Preheat the oven to 500° F. Proceed as in Steps 1 and 2 of Potato-Skin Nachos, cutting the skins lengthwise into 1-inch strips rather than quarters. Brush the strips on both sides with **4 tablespoons melted unsalted butter or margarine** and sprinkle with ½ **teaspoon salt**. In place of the cheese and chilies, sprinkle with ¾ **teaspoon chili or curry powder**, or 1½ **teaspoons poppy or caraway seeds**, or **2 tablespoons** grated Parmesan cheese blended with ¾ teaspoon paprika and a dash of cayenne (ground red) pepper. Bake, uncovered, for 8 to 10 minutes or until crisp. Serves 8 to 12 as an appetizer.

### Bacon-Pimiento Variation

Per side-dish serving: Calories 287; Protein 13 g; Carbohydrate 28 g; Fat 13 g; Sodium 285 mg; Cholesterol 14 mg.

Proceed as in Steps 1 and 2 of Potato-Skin Nachos. In Step 3, after sprinkling the skins with cheese, substitute **4 slices bacon, cooked crisp and crumbled**, and **1 jar (4 ounces) pimientos, drained and chopped**, for the green chilies. Broil and serve as in Step 3.

*Irresistible munchies — Spiced Potato Strips*

# Potatoes and Apples with Bacon

Per serving: Calories 201; Protein 4 g; Carbohydrate 41 g; Fat 3 g; Sodium 340 mg; Cholesterol 5 mg.

*The combination of flavors in this unusual dish is simply heavenly — a wonderful accompaniment to roasts, grilled meats, or sausages.*

- 1   cup water
- 1   teaspoon salt
- 6   medium-size all-purpose potatoes, peeled and sliced ¼ inch thick (about 2 pounds)
- 6   medium-size MacIntosh, Cortland, or winesap apples, peeled, cored, and thinly sliced (about 2 pounds)
- 7   slices bacon (about 6 ounces)
- 1   medium-size yellow onion, diced

1  In a large saucepan, bring the water and salt to a boil over high heat. Add the potatoes, reduce the heat to moderate, cover, and cook until almost tender — 12 to 15 minutes.

2  Add the apples, reduce the heat to low, and re-cover. Cook, stirring occasionally, until the apples are crisp-tender — 4 to 5 minutes more.

3  Meanwhile, in a heavy 10-inch skillet, cook the bacon over moderate heat until crisp — about 5 minutes. With a slotted spatula, transfer to a platter lined with paper toweling; when it has cooled, crumble the bacon.

4  In the skillet with the bacon drippings, sauté the onion over moderate heat, stirring occasionally, until golden — about 7 minutes. Set aside.

5  Remove the saucepan from the heat and mash the potatoes and apples with the remaining liquid until almost smooth, but leaving some texture. Stir in the bacon and the onion.

*Baked Acorn Squash with Cranberries, two holiday favorites happily combined*

▽ At this point the mixture can be cooled to room temperature and *refrigerated* in a lightly oiled, covered, 2-quart casserole for up to 24 hours.

6 Transfer to a heated serving dish and serve with Turkey Mushroom Loaf (page 93) or Roast Loin of Pork with Ginger Marinade (page 114). Serves 8.

### Serving Later

Preheat the oven to 350° F. Dot the top of the casserole with butter, cover with foil, and bake until heated through — about 20 minutes. Serve as in Step 6. (If there are any leftovers, add a little milk and reheat in a saucepan over low heat, stirring often.)

# Orange-Praline Sweet Potatoes

Per serving: Calories 370; Protein 5 g; Carbohydrate 57 g; Fat 14 g; Sodium 362 mg; Cholesterol 72 mg.

*The crunchy praline on top of the creamy sweet potatoes is just about irresistible. If you double the recipe, use 2 casseroles to keep the correct proportion of topping to potatoes.*

- 6 medium-size sweet potatoes, peeled, quartered, and boiled until tender (about 2½ pounds)
- ⅓ cup orange juice
- 1 teaspoon grated orange rind
- 1 tablespoon brandy
- 1 teaspoon salt
- ½ teaspoon ground ginger
- ¼ teaspoon black pepper

- 5 tablespoons unsalted butter or margarine
- 1 egg
- ¼ cup brown sugar
- ¼ teaspoon ground cinnamon
- ¼ cup coarsely chopped pecans or walnuts

1 Preheat the oven to 375° F. In a large bowl, mash the sweet potatoes. Add the orange juice, orange rind, brandy, salt, ginger, pepper, 2 tablespoons of the butter, and the egg. Beat with an electric mixer, a whisk, or a wooden spoon until smooth and fluffy. Spoon the potatoes into a buttered, shallow, 1½-quart casserole or 10-inch quiche pan, smoothing the top.

2 In a small saucepan, combine the remaining 3 tablespoons of butter, the sugar, and cinnamon. Over low heat, cook, uncovered, stirring frequently, until blended — about 3 minutes. Spread the mixture on top of the potatoes and sprinkle with the pecans.

▽ At this point the potatoes can be *refrigerated*, tightly covered, for up to 24 hours.

3 Bake, covered, for 15 minutes. Uncover and bake another 15 minutes or until heated through. Serve with poultry, pork chops, or ham. This dish goes especially well with Herbed Turkey Roll (page 92) or Marinated Rock Cornish Hens (page 94). Serves 6.

### Serving Later

Preheat the oven to 375° F. Bake, covered, for 25 minutes. Uncover and bake another 15 to 20 minutes or until heated through. Serve as in Step 3.

# Baked Acorn Squash with Cranberries

Per serving: Calories 182; Protein 2 g; Carbohydrate 41; Fat 3 g; Sodium 38 mg; Cholesterol 8 mg.

- 2 small acorn squash, halved lengthwise and seeded
- 2 tablespoons orange juice or water
- 3 tablespoons sugar
- 1 teaspoon grated orange rind
- 1 tablespoon lightly salted butter
- ¾ cup cranberries, washed, stemmed, and picked over

1 Preheat the oven to 350° F. Set the squash, cut side up, in a 13" x 9" x 2" baking pan. Cover with aluminum foil and bake until tender but not mushy — 30 to 35 minutes.

2 Meanwhile, in a small saucepan, heat the orange juice, sugar, orange rind, and butter over moderate heat, stirring, until the sugar is dissolved and the butter melted — about 3 minutes. Add the cranberries; stir until coated.

▽ At this point the squash and cranberries can be cooled, covered tightly, and stored separately. *Refrigerate* for up to 24 hours.

3 Spoon some of the cranberry mixture into each squash cavity. Bake, uncovered, for 15 to 20 minutes or until the cranberries are soft. Serve with roast chicken, turkey, or baked ham. Makes 4 generous servings.

### Serving Later

Preheat the oven to 350° F. Reheat the squash, covered, in a 13" x 9" x 2" baking pan until warmed — 10 to 15 minutes. Proceed as in Step 3.

# Savory Spinach Balls

Per serving: Calories 193; Protein 12 g; Carbohydrate 16 g; Fat 10 g; Sodium 645 mg; Cholesterol 90 mg.

*These tender spinach morsels can be served plain with an entrée that has a sauce, such as Italian Beef Rolls (page 100). Topped with their own sauce, they're a lively accompaniment for grilled meats, fish, or poultry.*

- 2 tablespoons unsalted butter or margarine
- 1 medium-size yellow onion, finely chopped
- 2 cloves garlic, minced
- 1½ pounds spinach, cooked, chopped, and squeezed dry, or 2 packages (10 ounces each) frozen chopped spinach, thawed and squeezed dry (about 2 cups)
- ½ teaspoon salt
- ⅛ teaspoon black pepper
- ¼ cup fine dry bread crumbs
- ⅓ cup grated Parmesan cheese
- 1 egg
- 3 cups Classic Tomato Sauce (page 216) or Marinara Sauce (page 216) (optional)

1 Melt the butter in a heavy 12-inch skillet over moderately low heat. Add the onion and garlic, and sauté, stirring occasionally, until golden but not brown — 10 to 15 minutes. Add the spinach, salt, and pepper. Cover, turn the heat to its lowest point, and steam for 15 minutes.

2 Remove the skillet from the heat and stir in the bread crumbs, Parmesan cheese, and egg. Transfer to a bowl, cover tightly, and refrigerate for at least 2 hours or until firm enough to shape. Will keep for up to 24 hours.

3 Preheat the oven to 350° F. Roll the spinach mixture into 1-inch balls, then arrange them in a single layer in an oiled, 9" x 9" x 2" baking dish. Bake,

uncovered, for 30 minutes. Transfer to a heated serving dish, and top with some of the sauce, if desired; pass the rest. Serves 4 to 6.

# Baked Tomatoes Stuffed with Orzo

Per serving: Calories 305; Protein 13 g; Carbohydrate 37 g; Fat 8 g; Sodium 307 mg; Cholesterol 32 mg.

*An Italian favorite, orzo is pasta shaped like grains of rice. It is delicious in soups or tossed with butter and served as a side-dish.*

- 6 large firm-ripe tomatoes (about 3 pounds)
- ½ teaspoon salt
- 4 tablespoons (½ stick) unsalted butter or margarine
- 1 medium-size yellow onion, finely chopped
- 8 ounces orzo pasta
- 3½ to 4 cups Chicken Stock (page 48) or canned chicken broth
- ¼ cup grated Parmesan cheese
- ¼ teaspoon sugar
- ½ teaspoon dried oregano, crumbled
- ¼ teaspoon black pepper
- ½ cup cubed mozzarella cheese (about 2 ounces)

1 Slice ¼ inch off the top of each tomato and discard. Using a spoon, scoop out the pulp and seeds and discard them. Sprinkle the insides with salt, place the tomato shells upside down on a platter lined with paper toweling, and let drain for 15 minutes.

2 Meanwhile, in a large saucepan, melt the butter over moderate heat. Add the onion, and sauté, stirring occasionally, until soft — about 5 minutes. Stir in the orzo, coating it well with the butter, then pour in 2 cups of the chicken stock. Simmer, stirring, until

the stock is absorbed — about 5 minutes. Gradually add more of the stock (1 to 1½ cups) until the orzo is almost cooked but still very firm — 8 to 10 minutes more. Stir in the Parmesan cheese and remove from the heat.

3 Preheat the oven to 375° F. Pat the tomatoes dry and sprinkle with the sugar, oregano, and pepper. Divide the mozzarella equally among the tomatoes, then top with the orzo mixture. Arrange the stuffed tomatoes in a 13" x 9" x 2" baking dish, adding ½ cup more of the stock to the dish. Cover the dish tightly with aluminum foil.

▽ At this point the tomatoes can be stored. When the stuffing has cooled to room temperature, *refrigerate* for up to 8 hours.

4 Bake the tomatoes for 30 minutes. Uncover and bake 10 minutes more or until heated through. Serve as a meatless main dish with a green vegetable and garlic bread or as a side dish with broiled meats or poultry. This dish

goes particularly well with Flounder Soufflé (page 71) and Braised Lamb with Black Olives (page 124). Serves 6.

(page 71) ... (page 124)

### Serving Later

One hour before baking, set the tomatoes out to come to room temperature. Preheat the oven to 375° F. Proceed as in Step 4.

# Baked Tomatoes Sicilian-Style

Per serving: Calories 156; Protein 4 g; Carbohydrate 14 g; Fat 10 g; Sodium 204 mg; Cholesterol 0 mg.

- 6 medium-size firm-ripe tomatoes
- 1 teaspoon salt
- 8 anchovy fillets, drained and finely chopped
- 4 teaspoons drained capers
- 2 tablespoons minced parsley
- 1 large yellow onion, finely chopped
- 1/8 teaspoon each black pepper and ground nutmeg
- 1/2 cup fine dry bread crumbs
- 4 tablespoons olive oil

1 Preheat the oven to 375° F. Slice 1/4 inch off the top of each tomato and discard. Using a spoon, scoop out the seeds and some of the pulp and discard them. Sprinkle the insides with the salt, place the tomato shells upside down on a platter lined with paper toweling, and let drain for 10 minutes.

2 Meanwhile, in a small bowl, mix the anchovies, capers, parsley, onion, pepper, nutmeg, 3 tablespoons of the bread crumbs, and 2 tablespoons of the olive oil. Stuff the tomatoes with the mixture and place them in a lightly oiled, 9-inch pie pan.

3 In the same small bowl, toss the remaining bread crumbs with the remaining 2 tablespoons of olive oil and sprinkle over the tomatoes. Bake, uncovered, for 30 minutes or until the tomatoes are soft but not mushy.

▽ At this point the tomatoes can be cooled to room temperature and *refrigerated*, covered with plastic wrap, for up to 2 days.

4 Serve hot from the oven or at room temperature, but do not reheat. This dish is good with steaks, lamb chops, as part of an antipasto, or as a light luncheon dish, accompanied by cheese, cold cuts, and Italian bread. It goes especially well with Zucchini Cheese Puff (page 141). Serves 6.

### Serving Later

Before serving, let the tomatoes come to room temperature.

*Stuffed fit to burst — Baked Tomatoes Sicilian-Style*

*Spring Vegetable Casserole, sure signs of that favored season*

# Zucchini, Pepper, and Tomato Gratin

Per serving: Calories 193; Protein 4 g; Carbohydrate 16 g; Fat 14 g; Sodium 269 mg; Cholesterol 0 mg.

*This colorful vegetable mélange tastes as good as it looks, and can be served either hot or at room temperature.*

- 4 tablespoons olive oil
- 2 medium-size yellow onions, thinly sliced
- 2 cloves garlic, minced
- 2 medium-size zucchini, sliced ¼ inch thick
- 1 large sweet red pepper, cored, seeded, and diced
- 3 medium-size tomatoes, halved, seeded, and sliced ¼ inch thick
- 1½ teaspoons each thyme and rosemary leaves or ½ teaspoon each dried thyme and rosemary, crumbled
- 1 teaspoon dried oregano, crumbled
- ½ teaspoon salt
- ¼ teaspoon black pepper
- 3 tablespoons fresh bread crumbs

1 Preheat the oven to 375° F. Heat 2 tablespoons of the olive oil in a heavy 12-inch skillet over moderate heat. Add the onions and garlic; sauté until golden — about 10 minutes.

2 In a 12″ x 8″ x 2″ baking dish, arrange a row of zucchini slices, overlapping slightly, then a row of the onion mixture, followed by the diced pepper and the sliced tomatoes. Repeat until all of the vegetables have been attractively arranged.

3 Sprinkle the vegetables with the herbs, salt, pepper, and the bread crumbs. Drizzle with the remaining 2 tablespoons of olive oil.

▽ At this point the vegetables can be *refrigerated*, tightly covered, for up to 4 hours.

4 Bake, uncovered, until the vegetables are tender — 50 to 60 minutes. Serve hot or at room temperature with fish, poultry, or grilled meats. This dish goes especially well with Cajun Meatloaf (page 111) and Lamb Stew with White Beans (page 122). Serves 4 to 6.

### Serving Later

One hour before baking the gratin, set it out to come to room temperature. Preheat the oven to 375° F. Proceed as in Step 4.

# Spring Vegetable Casserole

Per serving: Calories 356; Protein 4 g; Carbohydrate 25 g; Fat 28 g; Sodium 273 mg; Cholesterol 0 mg.

- 1 cup olive oil
- ½ cup Chicken Stock (page 48) or canned chicken broth
- ½ cup dry white wine
- 3 tablespoons lemon juice
- 1 tablespoon honey
- 1 teaspoon salt
- ½ teaspoon black pepper
- 3 medium-size zucchini, thinly sliced (about 1 pound)
- 1 large yellow onion, thinly sliced and separated into rings
- 12 ounces green beans, trimmed and cut into 2- to 3-inch sections
- 1 pound cherry tomatoes, halved, or 2 cups sliced canned tomatoes
- 3 medium-size red-skin potatoes, washed and thinly sliced (about 1 pound)
- ¼ cup minced parsley
- 1 tablespoon minced oregano or 1½ teaspoons dried oregano, crumbled

1 In a medium-size bowl, whisk together the olive oil, chicken stock, wine, lemon juice, honey, salt, and pepper until well mixed. Set aside.

2 Preheat the oven to 350° F. Line the bottom of a 3-quart casserole with the zucchini, slightly overlapping the slices. Next, layer on the onion rings, green beans, tomatoes, and potatoes. Sprinkle the parsley and oregano evenly over all.

3 Pour the olive oil mixture over the vegetables. Cover loosely with aluminum foil and bake for 1½ to 2 hours or until the potatoes are fork tender.

4 After the casserole has cooled to room temperature — about 30 minutes — suction some of the juice from the bottom with a baster and drizzle it over the vegetables.

▽ At this point the casserole can be stored. *Refrigerate*, tightly covered, for up to 24 hours.

5 Serve at room temperature with cold roast chicken or Marinated London Broil (page 99). Serves 8.

# Pepper, Onion, and Tomato Sauté

Per serving: Calories 126; Protein 2 g; Carbohydrate 10 g; Fat 10 g; Sodium 336 mg; Cholesterol 0 mg.

- ¼ cup olive oil
- 2 medium-size yellow onions, thinly sliced
- 4 large sweet red or sweet green peppers or a combination of both, cored, seeded, and cut into ½-inch strips
- 4 medium-size tomatoes, peeled, seeded, and chopped, or 1 can (28 ounces) Italian tomatoes, drained and chopped
- 3 cloves garlic, minced
- 1 teaspoon salt
- ¼ teaspoon black pepper
- 1 tablespoon minced basil or 1 teaspoon dried basil, crumbled

1 In a heavy 12-inch skillet, heat the oil over moderate heat. Add the onions, and sauté, stirring occasionally, until golden — about 10 minutes.

2 Add the sweet peppers, and sauté, stirring frequently, until softened — about 5 minutes more. Add the tomatoes, garlic, salt, and pepper. Cover and cook until the peppers are tender — 10 to 15 minutes. Uncover and cook 5 minutes more or until most of the liquid has evaporated. Stir in the basil.

▽ At this point the vegetables can be cooled to room temperature and *refrigerated* in a tightly covered container for up to 3 days.

3 Transfer to a serving dish. Serve hot or at room temperature with omelets or grilled meats. This dish is especially good with Blue Cheese–Stuffed Burgers (page 107) and Sausage-Stuffed Zucchini (page 134). Serves 4 to 6.

### Serving Later

Reheat, covered, in a heavy 12-inch skillet over low heat until warmed through — 10 to 15 minutes. Or 1 hour before serving, set the vegetables out to come to room temperature. Serve as in Step 3.

# Creamy Broccoli Purée

Per serving: Calories 88; Protein 4 g;
Carbohydrate 7 g; Fat 6 g; Sodium 162 mg;
Cholesterol 15 mg.

- 1 bunch broccoli (1¼ to 1½ pounds)
- ¼ teaspoon salt
- ⅛ teaspoon each black pepper and ground nutmeg
- 2 tablespoons unsalted butter or margarine
- ¼ cup heavy cream (optional)

1 Peel the broccoli stems and cut them into 1-inch pieces; divide the tops into florets. Place the stems in a large saucepan of boiling water and cook until tender — about 10 minutes. Add the florets, and cook until tender — 2 to 3 minutes more. Drain and refresh under cold water.

2 In an electric blender or food processor, purée the broccoli, salt, pepper, and nutmeg for about 1 minute.

▽ At this point the purée can be stored. *Refrigerate* in a tightly covered container for up to 24 hours. *Freeze* in a labeled, 1-quart freezer bag or covered, 1½ quart, microwave-safe casserole for up to 1 month at 0° F.

3 Transfer the purée to a heavy medium-size saucepan and warm over moderate heat, stirring constantly, until hot — 3 to 4 minutes. Beat in the butter and the cream, if desired. Continue heating until the butter is melted and the cream is warmed through — about 2 minutes more. Serve with roasted or broiled meat or poultry. This dish goes particularly well with Chicken Provençal (page 88) and Marinated London Broil (page 99). Serves 4.

## Serving Later

**From refrigerator:** Proceed as in Step 3, extending the rewarming time to 5 to 8 minutes. **From freezer:** Reheat, covered, in a heavy medium-size saucepan over moderately low heat until thawed and heated through — 20 to 25 minutes. Proceed as in Step 3. **To microwave:** In the covered, microwave-safe casserole, heat on *High* (100% power) for 6 minutes. Turn the casserole 90 degrees and heat on *High* (100% power) 5 more minutes. Stir and break up any remaining frozen clumps. Heat on *High* (100% power) 2 minutes longer. Beat in the butter and cream, if desired. Re-cover and heat on *High* (100% power) for 1 minute. Serve as in Step 3.

# Zucchini Boats with Carrot Purée

Per serving: Calories 138; Protein 3 g;
Carbohydrate 25 g; Fat 4 g; Sodium 118 mg;
Cholesterol 10 mg.

*For this colorful, easy dish, choose plump rather than skinny squash.*

- 3 medium-size zucchini (about 1 pound)
- 8 medium-size carrots, peeled, sliced, and boiled until tender (about 1 pound)
- 3 medium-size parsnips, peeled, cubed, and boiled until tender (about 1 pound)
- 2 tablespoons unsalted butter or margarine
- ¼ teaspoon salt
- ⅛ teaspoon black pepper

1 Preheat the oven to 350° F. Drop the zucchini into a large saucepan of boiling water, and cook, uncovered, over moderately high heat until slightly tender — 2 to 3 minutes. Drain and refresh under cold water. Halve the zucchini lengthwise and cut each half crosswise into 2 pieces. Scoop out and discard the flesh and seeds, leaving a ¼-inch shell all around. Pat dry with paper toweling.

2 Place the carrots and parsnips in an electric blender or food processor and, working in batches if necessary, purée — about 1 minute. Add the butter, salt, and pepper and blend — 20 seconds more. (The purée should be thick. If too runny, return to the pan, and cook, stirring, over moderately low heat until thickened.)

3 Fill the zucchini boats with the purée and arrange them in an oiled, shallow, 2-quart casserole.

▽ At this point the zucchini boats can be cooled to room temperature and *refrigerated*, tightly covered, for up to 24 hours.

4 Bake, uncovered, until heated through — about 20 minutes. Serve with fish, meat, or poultry. These go especially well with Captain's Seafood Casserole (page 126) and Andalusian Chicken (page 82). Serves 6.

## Serving Later

Preheat the oven to 350° F. Bake, uncovered, until heated through — 30 to 35 minutes. Serve as in Step 4.

# Watercress and Green Pea Purée

Per serving: Calories 148; Protein 6 g;
Carbohydrate 14 g; Fat 8 g; Sodium 338 mg;
Cholesterol 22 mg.

- 4 pounds green peas, shelled (about 4 cups), or 2 packages (10 ounces each) frozen green peas
- 2 bunches watercress, with 2 inches of stem removed, or 2 medium-size heads Bibb lettuce, cored

4 tablespoons (½ stick)
  unsalted butter or margarine
¾ teaspoon salt
½ teaspoon black pepper

1 Preheat the oven to 350° F. Bring a large saucepan of water to a boil over moderately high heat. Add the peas and cover. When the water returns to a boil, stir in the watercress and re-cover. Remove from the heat and let stand for 5 minutes.

2 Drain the vegetables, then purée in an electric blender or food processor — working in batches if necessary — about 1 minute. Add the butter, salt, and pepper and process until well combined — about 20 seconds more.

▽ At this point the purée can be cooled to room temperature and stored in a tightly covered container. *Refrigerate* for up to 24 hours. *Freeze* for up to 1 month at 0° F.

3 Transfer the purée to an oiled, shallow, 1-quart baking dish. Bake, covered, until heated through — 25 to 30 minutes. Serve with roasts and chops. This dish goes particularly well with Lamb, Oat, and Apple Loaf (page 110) and Lime Chicken Stuffed with Goat Cheese (page 80). Serves 6.

### Serving Later

**From refrigerator:** Preheat the oven to 350° F. Proceed as in Step 3, baking the purée for 35 to 40 minutes. **From freezer:** Thaw overnight in the refrigerator and proceed as above. Or transfer to a heavy medium-size saucepan, cover, and heat over moderately low heat until thawed and warmed through — 20 to 25 minutes.

*Flowers of Creamy Broccoli Purée ringing succulent slices of Marinated London Broil (page 99)*

# White Turnip and Potato Purée

Per serving: Calories 185; Protein 6 g; Carbohydrate 24 g; Fat 8 g; Sodium 398 mg; Cholesterol 22 mg.

*Two workmanlike vegetables make a sophisticated duo — the perfect way to dress up a roast.*

- 6 medium-size white turnips, peeled, cubed, and boiled until tender (about 2 pounds)
- 2 large Idaho or russet potatoes, peeled, cubed, and boiled until tender (about 1 pound)
- 3 tablespoons unsalted butter or margarine
- 1/2 teaspoon salt
- 1/4 teaspoon black pepper
- 1/2 cup grated Parmesan cheese or a combination of Parmesan and shredded Swiss cheese

1 Preheat the oven to 400° F. In an electric blender or food processor, purée the turnips — about 30 seconds — and transfer to a large saucepan. Mash the potatoes or press them through a ricer or food mill and add to the turnips. Cook over moderately low heat, stirring constantly, until dry — about 3 minutes. Beat in 2 tablespoons of the butter, the salt, pepper, and 1/4 cup of the Parmesan cheese.

2 Transfer the purée to a gratin dish or a shallow, 1 1/2-quart baking dish. Smooth the top and sprinkle with the remaining 1/4 cup of cheese. Dot with the remaining tablespoon of butter.

▽ At this point the purée can be cooled to room temperature and stored. *Refrigerate*, tightly covered, for up to 24 hours.

3 Bake, uncovered, until the purée is heated through — 10 to 15 minutes. Serve with German Meatloaf (page 110) or Vegetable-Stuffed Flank Steak (page 101). Serves 6.

### Serving Later

Preheat the oven to 400° F. Bake, uncovered, until warmed through — 20 to 30 minutes. Serve as in Step 3.

# Purée of Red Beans, Bacon, and Onions

Per serving: Calories 268; Protein 14 g; Carbohydrate 39 g; Fat 5 g; Sodium 307 mg; Cholesterol 10 mg.

- 6 cups water
- 1 pound dried kidney beans, washed and picked over
- 4 slices bacon, cut crosswise in julienne strips
- 2 medium-size yellow onions, coarsely chopped
- 1 clove garlic, minced
- 1 medium-size carrot, coarsely chopped
- 1/2 teaspoon each dried marjoram and thyme, crumbled
- 1/4 teaspoon dried rosemary, crumbled
- 1 1/2 cups dry red wine
- 1 bay leaf
- 2 tablespoons unsalted butter or margarine
- 1 teaspoon salt
- 1/8 teaspoon black pepper

1 In a large heavy saucepan, bring 5 cups of the water and the kidney beans to a boil over moderately high heat. Remove from the heat, cover, and let sit for 1 hour.

2 Add the remaining cup of water to the beans and bring to a boil over moderately high heat. Reduce the heat

to low. Cook, covered, for 1 1/2 hours or until the beans are tender.

3 Meanwhile, in a heavy 10-inch skillet over moderate heat, cook the bacon until crisp. Transfer to a small platter lined with paper toweling.

4 Discard all but 1 tablespoon of the drippings. Add the onions, garlic, and carrot; sauté, stirring occasionally, for 10 to 15 minutes or until golden. Stir in the marjoram, thyme, rosemary, wine, and bay leaf. Reduce the heat to low and cook, uncovered, for 30 to 45 minutes or until just a thin layer of liquid remains. Discard the bay leaf.

5 Drain the liquid from the cooked beans, reserving 1/2 cup. In an electric blender or food processor, working in batches, purée the beans, onion mixture, bacon, butter, salt and pepper, adding some of the reserved liquid if necessary — about 30 seconds. The purée should have the consistency of whipped potatoes.

▽ At this point the purée can be cooled to room temperature and stored in a tightly covered container. *Refrigerate* for up to 5 days. *Freeze* for up to 1 month at 0° F.

6 Transfer to a heated serving dish. Serve with roast pork or poultry, or present as a luncheon dish, accompanied by a green vegetable, salad, and Herbed Garlic Bread (page 243). Serves 8 to 10.

### Serving Later

**From refrigerator:** Transfer to the top section of a double boiler. Heat over gently boiling water for 25 minutes or until heated through; stir occasionally. Serve as in Step 6. **From freezer:** Reheat as above until thawed and heated through — 40 to 50 minutes.

# Salads and Salad Dressings

The versatile salad is suitable for a first course, an entrée, a side dish, or even a snack. Conveniently, all or most of the ingredients can be prepared ahead of time and, if necessary, combined at the last minute.

If the salad includes greens, these should be fresh, crisp, and dry, so that their texture is crunchy and the dressing clings well and is not diluted. Wash and spin-dry them; wrap in a dish towel or paper toweling; place in a salad bowl or enclose in a plastic bag; then store in the refrigerator for at least 2 hours or until ready to use. (If properly dried, many greens will keep well for up to 5 days in a plastic bag in the refrigerator.) If other ingredients are to be included in the salad, they should be cut up, wrapped, and stored separately. Combine them with the greens and dressing just before serving.

Salads made with root vegetables (potatoes and beets, for example), legumes (all types of beans), and rice usually benefit from at least several hours of marinating. These are natural selections for making ahead. To be ready for quick last-minute salads, create some planned leftovers of meat, fish, chicken, and/or vegetables and toss them with cooked pasta and a creamy dressing just before serving.

# Radish and Swiss Cheese Salad

Per serving: Calories 191; Protein 5 g; Carbohydrate 4 g; Fat 18 g; Sodium 154 mg; Cholesterol 13 mg.

- 4 large bunches radishes, sliced (about 5 cups)
- 1 cup diced Swiss cheese (about 3 ounces)
- 2 tablespoons tarragon vinegar
- 6 tablespoons olive oil
- 1 teaspoon anchovy paste or mashed anchovies
- 1 teaspoon Dijon or spicy brown mustard
- 1 clove garlic, minced
- 4 green onions (including some of the green), minced
- ¼ teaspoon each salt and black pepper, or to taste

Optional garnishes:
  Parsley sprigs
- 1 cup pitted black olives
- 12 rolled anchovy fillets

1 In a large bowl, toss together the radishes and Swiss cheese. Put the vinegar, olive oil, anchovy paste, mustard, garlic, green onions, salt, and pepper in a jar, cover tightly, and shake until the dressing is well mixed and creamy. Add to the salad and toss.

▽ At this point the salad can be stored. *Refrigerate*, tightly covered, for up to 6 hours.

2 Transfer to a salad platter or individual salad plates and garnish with the parsley, black olives, and anchovies, if desired. Serve as a first course with crusty French bread. Serves 6 to 8.

# Winter Salad

Per serving: Calories 205; Protein 3 g; Carbohydrate 10 g; Fat 18 g; Sodium 300 mg; Cholesterol 0 mg.

*Jícama, a turniplike tuber from the tropics, lends a special crunch to this nippy salad. So that the vegetables will retain their crispness, combine them with the dressing just before serving.*

- 1 tablespoon cider vinegar
- 1 tablespoon lemon juice
- 1 teaspoon Dijon or spicy brown mustard
- ½ teaspoon salt
- ⅛ teaspoon black pepper
- ⅓ cup olive oil or a combination of olive and salad oil
- 3 tablespoons minced parsley
- 8 ounces mushrooms, trimmed, rinsed, and thinly sliced
- 2 bunches radishes (about 12), trimmed, washed, and thinly sliced
- ¼ jícama or 1 medium-size white turnip, peeled and thinly sliced
- 6 green onions (including 1 inch of the green), thinly sliced
- 1 clove garlic, minced
  Lettuce leaves for garnish

1 In a small bowl whisk together the vinegar, lemon juice, mustard, salt, pepper, and oil. Stir in the parsley.

▽ At this point the dressing and prepared vegetables can be stored separately in tightly covered containers. *Refrigerate* for up to 12 hours.

2 Put the mushrooms, radishes, jícama, green onions, and garlic in a medium-size bowl. Add the dressing, toss well, and transfer to salad plates lined with the lettuce leaves. Serve as a first course to precede Beef, Barley, and Yogurt Soup (page 66) or as a side dish with Polenta Pie (page 158) or Giant Shells Stuffed with Spinach and Ricotta (page 162). Serves 4.

# Ratatouille Vinaigrette

Per serving: Calories 157; Protein 3 g; Carbohydrate 14 g; Fat 11 g; Sodium 363 mg; Cholesterol 0 mg.

- 1 large eggplant, sliced crosswise into ½-inch-thick rounds (about 1½ pounds)
- 3 teaspoons salt
- 3 medium-size zucchini, trimmed and sliced crosswise into ¼-inch-thick rounds (about 1 pound)
- 4 tablespoons olive oil
- 2 medium-size sweet green peppers, cored, seeded, and cut crosswise into ¼-inch slices
- 2 large yellow onions, thinly sliced
- 2 cloves garlic, minced
- 3 medium-size tomatoes, peeled, seeded, and coarsely chopped (about 1 pound), or 1 can (1 pound) crushed tomatoes
- ¾ cup sliced pitted Kalamata or other Greek-style olives
- 3 tablespoons minced basil or 2 teaspoons dried basil, crumbled
- 2 tablespoons drained capers
- ¼ teaspoon black pepper
- 2 tablespoons minced chives for garnish (optional)

For the vinaigrette:
- 1 tablespoon olive oil
- 3 tablespoons fresh lemon juice
- 1 tablespoon white wine vinegar

1 In a large colander, sprinkle the eggplant evenly with 2 teaspoons of the salt, cover with a heavy plate, and leave to drain for 30 minutes. Do the same with the zucchini, using the remaining salt. Rinse the vegetables under cold running water, then pat dry with paper toweling.

*Often just a bit player, the radish is a star in Radish and Swiss Cheese Salad.*

**2** Preheat the oven to 400° F. Lightly brush a 15½" x 10½" x 1" baking sheet with 1 tablespoon of the oil. Arrange the eggplant slices on the sheet, overlapping them slightly in a single layer. Bake for 10 to 15 minutes on each side or until tender. Quarter the slices and transfer to a large bowl. Brush the baking sheet with 1 tablespoon of the remaining oil and bake the zucchini for 5 to 7 minutes on each side; transfer to the bowl.

**3** Heat the remaining 2 tablespoons of olive oil in a heavy 12-inch skillet over moderately low heat and sauté the peppers for 10 minutes. Add the onions and garlic, and cook, uncovered, stirring occasionally, until tender but not brown — about 10 minutes. Add the tomatoes, and cook, stirring occasionally, 4 to 5 minutes more or until most of the juices have evaporated. Mix the sautéed vegetables with the eggplant and zucchini. Stir in the olives, basil, capers, and pepper.

**4** Meanwhile, in a small bowl, whisk together the olive oil, lemon juice, and vinegar. Pour the dressing over the vegetables and toss well.

▽ At this point the salad can be stored. *Refrigerate*, tightly covered, for up to 3 days.

**5** Garnish with the chives, if desired, just before serving. Serve chilled or at room temperature as an accompaniment to cold Marinated London Broil (page 99) or Tuscan Roast Pork (page 112). Serves 8.

## Tender Beet Salad

Per serving: Calories 83; Protein 2 g;
Carbohydrate 19 g; Fat tr; Sodium 884 mg;
Cholesterol 0 mg.

2   pounds small fresh beets or 2
    cans (1 pound each) sliced
    beets, drained
1   small red onion, thinly sliced
1   tablespoon prepared
    horseradish
2   teaspoons sugar
½   teaspoon caraway seeds
1   tablespoon red wine vinegar
½   teaspoon salt
¼   teaspoon black pepper

1 In a large saucepan, bring 2 inches
of water to a boil over high heat.
Add the beets and cover. When the
water reboils, reduce the heat to moderate and simmer until the beets are
tender when pierced with a knife — 30
to 40 minutes. Drain and let cool.

2 Remove and discard the skins and
slice the beets ¼ inch thick. Put
them in a medium-size bowl along
with the onion. In a small bowl, combine the horseradish, sugar, caraway
seeds, vinegar, salt (omit if using
canned beets), and pepper. Pour over
the vegetables and toss well. Refrigerate, covered, for at least 2 hours. Will
keep for up to 3 days.

3 Serve chilled as a first course or a
side dish. This salad makes a good
accompaniment for hard-cooked eggs,
sardines, cold meats, and smoked fish.
Serves 4 to 6.

## Layered Vegetable Salad

Per serving: Calories 115; Protein 8 g;
Carbohydrate 9 g; Fat 5 g; Sodium 387 mg;
Cholesterol 10 mg.

For the topping:
1   pint cottage cheese
2   tablespoons mayonnaise
1   tablespoon grated yellow
    onion
½   teaspoon salt
¼   teaspoon white pepper

For the salad:
1   head Boston lettuce, torn
    into bite-size pieces
2   large tomatoes, thinly sliced
1   small Spanish onion, thinly
    sliced
1   medium-size cucumber,
    thinly sliced
1   pound beets, cooked, peeled,
    and sliced (about 2 cups), or
    2 cans (8 ounces each)
    sliced beets, drained
3   tablespoons chopped chives

*Common ingredients in
an uncommon presentation —
Layered Vegetable Salad*

1 In a small bowl, combine the cottage cheese, mayonnaise, onion, salt, and pepper; set aside.

2 Line the bottom of a 3-quart, straight-sided glass bowl with a bed of the lettuce. Dot with 1 cup of the cottage cheese topping. Next make 1 layer each of the tomatoes, onion, cucumber, and beets, with each layer touching the sides of the bowl for display. Spread the remaining topping over the beets.

▽ At this point the salad can be stored. *Refrigerate*, covered with plastic wrap, for up to 24 hours.

3 Sprinkle with the chives just before serving. Serve as a light luncheon dish, a first course, or as an accompaniment for cold roasted chicken or Fiesta Burgers (page 106). Serves 8.

# North African Carrot Salad

---

Per serving: Calories 84; Protein 1 g; Carbohydrate 13 g; Fat 3 g; Sodium 163 mg; Cholesterol 0 mg.

*The barely steamed carrots in this salad take on an exotic character when flavored with cumin and cinnamon.*

- 2 cloves garlic, unpeeled
- 8 medium-size carrots, peeled, halved lengthwise, and cut in 1/2-inch pieces (about 1 pound)
- 1 green onion (including some of the green), minced
- 2 tablespoons minced parsley
- 2 tablespoons snipped dill or 1 teaspoon dried dill weed, crumbled
- 2 tablespoons lemon juice
- 1 tablespoon olive oil, or to taste
- 1/2 teaspoon cumin seeds, crushed
- 1/4 teaspoon paprika
- 1/8 teaspoon ground cinnamon
- 1/4 teaspoon salt, or to taste
  Cayenne (ground red) pepper to taste

1 In the bottom of a steamer or in a medium-size saucepan, bring 1 inch of water to a boil and add the garlic. Insert the steamer basket with the carrots, cover, and steam over moderately high heat for 5 minutes or until crisp-tender. Transfer to a medium-size bowl and toss with the green onion, parsley, and dill.

2 Remove the garlic from the saucepan and peel it. In a small bowl, using a fork and the back of a spoon, mash the garlic into a paste. Add the lemon juice, oil, cumin seeds, paprika, salt, cinnamon, and cayenne pepper. Pour over the carrots and toss well.

▽ At this point the salad can be stored. *Refrigerate*, tightly covered, for up to 3 days.

3 Serve cold or at room temperature as a side dish to Chicken Marrakesh with Almonds and Chick Peas (page 83) or to roasted or broiled meats or poultry. Serves 4.

# Sauerkraut and Cabbage Salad

---

Per serving: Calories 106; Protein 1 g; Carbohydrate 18 g; Fat 5 g; Sodium 571 mg; Cholesterol 6 mg.

*Taste the sauerkraut before you start this recipe. If it's too salty, rinse it in a colander, with cold water, then squeeze it dry in a towel. If you prefer, 1 1/2 cups vinaigrette dressing can be substituted for the mayonnaise type.*

- 1 1/2 cups low-calorie mayonnaise-type salad dressing
- 1/4 cup sugar
- 1 tablespoon celery seeds or caraway seeds
- 1/4 teaspoon each salt and black pepper
- 1 tablespoon Dijon or spicy brown mustard
- 2 cups sauerkraut (1-pound package), drained
- 1/2 small head green cabbage, thinly sliced (about 2 1/2 cups)
- 1/2 small head red cabbage, thinly sliced (about 2 1/2 cups)

1 In a medium-size saucepan, combine the salad dressing, sugar, celery seeds, salt, pepper, and mustard; stir in the sauerkraut. Cook, uncovered, over moderately low heat, stirring frequently, for 10 minutes. Do not boil.

2 Place the red and green cabbage in a large bowl. Pour the sauerkraut mixture over the cabbage and toss well.

▽ At this point the salad can be stored. *Refrigerate*, tightly covered, for up to 12 hours.

3 Serve hot or at room temperature with a sausage such as kielbasa or knockwurst, or as an accompaniment to Marinated Spareribs (page 116). Makes 8 servings.

### Serving Later

One hour before serving, set the salad out to come to room temperature.

# Summer Corn Salad

Per serving: Calories 107; Protein 2 g; Carbohydrate 21 g; Fat 2 g; Sodium 286 mg; Cholesterol 5 mg.

*Here is summer's bounty in a refreshing and colorful combination.*

- 6 large ears of corn or 1 package (1 pound) frozen corn kernels, cooked according to package directions
- 1 large sweet green pepper, cored, seeded, and chopped
- 1 large tomato, seeded and cut into 1/2-inch cubes
- 4 green onions, bulbs and green parts chopped separately
- 1 small red onion, chopped
- 2 shallots, thinly sliced
- 3 tablespoons low-calorie mayonnaise
- 3 tablespoons sour cream
- 2 tablespoons plain low-fat yogurt
- 2 tablespoons Beef Stock (page 48) or canned beef broth
- 1 tablespoon red wine vinegar
- 3/4 teaspoon salt
- 1/8 teaspoon black pepper
  Pimiento strips for garnish (optional)

1 Half fill a very large saucepan or a stockpot with water and bring to a boil over high heat. Add the corn, cover, and when the water returns to a boil, cook for 3 minutes. Drain the ears in a colander and rinse under cold running water until cool enough to handle. Cut the kernels from the cobs into a large bowl.

2 Add the green pepper, tomato, chopped green-onion bulbs, red onion, and shallots. Toss together until well mixed; set aside.

3 In a small bowl, stir together the mayonnaise, sour cream, yogurt, beef stock, vinegar, salt, and pepper until smooth. Stir into the vegetable mixture until well combined. Cover and refrigerate for at least 2 hours. Will keep for up to 24 hours.

4 Before serving, garnish with the chopped green-onion tops and the pimiento strips, if desired. Serve with cold meat or chicken or Curried Tuna Mousse (page 72). Serves 6.

# Zucchini Slaw

Per serving: Calories 33; Protein 1 g; Carbohydrate 5 g; Fat 2 g; Sodium 237 mg; Cholesterol 2 mg.

- 1/2 cup low-calorie mayonnaise
- 1/4 cup plain low-fat yogurt
- 1/4 cup snipped dill or 2 teaspoons dried dill weed, crumbled
- 1 teaspoon salt
- 1/4 teaspoon white pepper
- 6 medium-size zucchini, coarsely shredded (about 2 pounds)

*Optional garnishes:*
Lettuce leaves
Grated orange rind
Tomato wedges

1 In a large bowl, combine the mayonnaise, yogurt, dill, salt, and pepper. Add the zucchini and toss well.

▽ At this point the salad can be stored. *Refrigerate*, tightly covered, for up to 3 hours.

2 Line salad plates with the lettuce leaves, if you like, and spoon the zucchini slaw onto them. Garnish with the grated orange rind and surround with the tomatoes, if desired. Serve with Herbed Bluefish Fillets (page 70), Steak Cubes Southwestern-Style (page 99), or Noodle Pie with Spicy Cajun Ham (page 154). Serves 10 to 12.

# Hearts of Palm Salad with Avocado Dressing

Per serving: Calories 319; Protein 7 g; Carbohydrate 20 g; Fat 24 g; Sodium 367 mg; Cholesterol 19 mg.

*For the dressing:*
- 1 cup sour cream
- 1 cup plain low-fat yogurt
- 1 large ripe avocado, peeled, pitted, and cubed (about 1 pound)
- 3 tablespoons lemon juice, or to taste
- 2 cloves garlic, minced
- 1/2 teaspoon salt, or to taste
  Hot red pepper sauce to taste

*For the salad:*
- 1 small head iceberg lettuce, torn into bite-size pieces
- 1 can (14 ounces) hearts of palm, drained and sliced 1/4 inch thick
- 1 small red onion, finely chopped
- 1 small sweet green pepper, cored, seeded, and finely chopped
- 2 large ripe tomatoes, cut into wedges
- 1 can (3 1/2 ounces) pitted black olives, drained

1 Blend the sour cream, yogurt, avocado, lemon juice, garlic, salt, and hot red pepper sauce in an electric blender or food processor until smooth — about 30 seconds.

▽ At this point the dressing can be *refrigerated* in a tightly covered container for up to 24 hours.

2 On a large salad platter or individual plates, arrange the lettuce, hearts of palm, onion, green pepper, tomatoes, and black olives. Cover and refrigerate until ready to serve — up to 6 hours. Pass the dressing separately. Serve with Halibut in Wine Sauce (page 68). Serves 6.

# Avocado with Sweet Red Pepper Sauce

Per serving: Calories 232; Protein 2 g; Carbohydrate 9 g; Fat 22 g; Sodium 78 mg; Cholesterol 0 mg.

- 1 medium-size sweet red pepper
- 1 clove garlic, minced
- 1 tablespoon olive oil
- 1 tablespoon sherry or red wine vinegar
- 1/8 teaspoon each salt and black pepper
- 2 medium-size avocados

1 Roast the red pepper over a burner or under a broiler until blackened on all sides — about 10 minutes. Place in a paper bag, seal tightly, and set aside for 10 minutes to steam the skin loose. Peel under cold running water. Discard the skin, seeds, and core.

2 In an electric blender or food processor, blend the red pepper, garlic, olive oil, vinegar, salt, and black pepper until smooth — about 1 minute.

▽ At this point the sauce can be stored. *Refrigerate*, tightly covered, for up to 2 days.

3 Peel and halve the avocados and remove the pits. Slice each piece lengthwise into 5 wedges. Place an avocado half on each plate, spoon 2 tablespoons of sauce over it, and serve immediately. Serve as a first course for Poisson Mariné (page 70) or Piquant Chicken with Sausage and Raisins (page 80), or as an accompaniment to Macaroni and Cheese Italian-Style (page 161). Serves 4.

*Avocado with Sweet Red Pepper Sauce, a winning way to preface the main course*

# Green Beans with Walnut Vinaigrette

Per serving: Calories 372; Protein 4 g; Carbohydrate 12 g; Fat 36 g; Sodium 170 mg; Cholesterol 0 mg.

|  |  |
|---|---|
| 3 | quarts water |
| 1 1/2 | pounds green or wax beans or a combination of both, trimmed |
| 3/4 | cup coarsely chopped walnuts (about 3 ounces) |
| 8 | green onions (including some of the green), minced |
| 1/4 | cup each minced parsley and snipped dill |
| 3/4 | cup olive oil |
| 1/4 | cup cider vinegar |
| 1/2 | teaspoon salt, or to taste |
| 1/4 | teaspoon black pepper |

*Optional garnishes:*

|  |  |
|---|---|
| 1/2 | cup thinly sliced radishes or a few radish roses |
| 2 | tablespoons minced parsley or snipped dill |

1 In a large saucepan, bring the water to a boil over high heat. Add the beans, reduce the heat to moderate, cover, and cook until crisp-tender — about 5 minutes. Drain the beans in a colander and rinse under cold water. Drain well and place in a serving bowl.

2 Blend the walnuts, green onions, parsley, dill, olive oil, vinegar, salt, and pepper in an electric blender or food processor until smooth — about 1 minute. Spoon over the beans and toss well. Refrigerate, tightly covered, for 1 hour. Will keep for up to 24 hours.

3 Just before serving, garnish with the radishes and parsley, if desired. Serve as a side dish with cold chicken or Layered Salmon and Cucumber Mousse (page 72). Or serve as a light luncheon dish, accompanied by cheese and a crusty bread. Serves 6.

*At the peak of perfection — Green Beans with Walnut Vinaigrette*

# Vegetable Mélange with Walnut-Basil Dressing

Per serving: Calories 72; Protein 3 g; Carbohydrate 10 g; Fat 3 g; Sodium 285 mg; Cholesterol 0 mg.

- 3 medium-size carrots, peeled and sliced ¼ inch thick
- 1 medium-size yellow squash, halved and sliced ¼ inch thick
- ½ cup frozen peas
- ½ medium-size sweet red pepper, cored, seeded, and cut into ½-inch squares
- 2 tablespoons minced red onion

*For the dressing:*
- 1 clove garlic, minced
- ¼ cup walnut halves
- 1 cup minced basil or 1 cup minced parsley mixed with 2 teaspoons dried basil, crumbled
- ¼ cup Chicken Stock (page 48) or canned chicken broth
- 2 tablespoons red wine vinegar
- ¾ teaspoon salt
- ¼ teaspoon black pepper

1 In the bottom section of a steamer or in a medium-size saucepan, bring 1 inch of water to a boil. Insert the steamer basket with the carrots, cover, and steam over moderately high heat for 5 minutes. Add the squash and steam 4 more minutes; add the peas and steam 2 minutes longer. Transfer to a large bowl and add the red pepper and the onion.

2 Meanwhile, blend all dressing ingredients in an electric blender or food processor until smooth — about 1 minute. Pour over the vegetables and mix well.

▽ At this point the salad can be stored. *Refrigerate*, tightly covered, for up to 24 hours.

3 Serve the salad cold or at room temperature with grilled chicken or fish and crusty rolls. Or serve as a luncheon dish with assorted cheeses and pumpernickel bread. Serves 6.

## Mixed Bean Variation

Per serving: Calories 167; Protein 9 g; Carbohydrate 25 g; Fat 4 g; Sodium 747 mg; Cholesterol 0 mg.

Prepare the dressing as in Step 2 of Vegetable Mélange. In a large bowl, mix 1 can (19 ounces) red kidney beans, drained and rinsed, 1 can (10 ounces) chick peas, drained and rinsed, 1 stalk celery, diced, and 2 tablespoons minced red onion. Stir in the dressing and mix well. Store as above and serve as in Step 3 above. Serves 6.

# Lentil Salad with Hot Italian Sausage

Per serving: Calories 648; Protein 38 g; Carbohydrate 43 g; Fat 41 g; Sodium 1202 mg; Cholesterol 88 mg.

- 1 pound dried lentils, washed and picked over
- 3 cups water
- 1 teaspoon salt
- ⅓ cup plus 1 tablespoon olive oil
- 2 pounds hot Italian sausages
- 2 tablespoons plus 2 teaspoons lemon juice
- 2 teaspoons ground cumin
- ¾ teaspoon dried oregano, crumbled
- ½ teaspoon black pepper
- 2 large sweet green peppers, cored, seeded, and diced
- 2 large sweet red peppers, cored, seeded, and diced
- 2 large cucumbers, peeled, seeded, and diced
- 3 stalks celery, diced
- 1 large red onion, finely chopped
- 2 cloves garlic, minced
  Romaine leaves for garnish (optional)

1 In a large saucepan, bring the lentils, water, and salt to a boil over high heat. Reduce the heat to low, cover, and simmer, stirring occasionally, until the lentils are almost tender — 35 to 40 minutes. Drain and set aside.

2 Meanwhile, in a 12-inch skillet, heat 1 tablespoon of the olive oil over moderately high heat. Add the sausages, and sauté, turning occasionally, until cooked through — about 15 minutes. Transfer to a platter lined with paper toweling, cool slightly, then slice into bite-size pieces.

3 In a large bowl, whisk together the remaining ⅓ cup of olive oil, the lemon juice, cumin, oregano, and black pepper until well blended. Add the lentils, sausages, green and red peppers, cucumbers, celery, onion, and garlic and mix well. Cover and marinate in the refrigerator for at least 8 hours. Will keep for up to 3 days.

4 Before serving, set the salad out to come to room temperature — about 1 hour. Transfer to a serving dish and garnish with the Romaine leaves, if desired. Serve as a luncheon or light supper dish with dilled baby carrots and garlic bread. Serves 6 to 8.

## Black Bean and Sweet Pepper Salad

Per side-dish serving: Calories 260; Protein 10 g; Carbohydrate 30 g; Fat 12 g; Sodium 263 mg; Cholesterol 0 mg.

*A vinaigrette dressing with cumin and cilantro gives this colorful dish lots of zip. For an even spicier salad, add some chopped green chilies.*

1¼ cups dried black beans, washed and picked over
1 small yellow onion, peeled
2 bay leaves
1 large sweet red pepper, cored, seeded, and diced
½ large sweet yellow pepper, cored, seeded, and diced
½ large sweet green pepper, cored, seeded, and diced
1 small red onion, diced
1 stalk celery, diced

*For the vinaigrette:*
5 tablespoons olive oil
2 tablespoons lemon juice
2 tablespoons red wine vinegar
1 clove garlic, minced
¾ teaspoon salt
¼ teaspoon ground cumin
2 dashes hot red pepper sauce, or to taste
2 tablespoons minced cilantro (coriander leaves) or parsley
1 tablespoon minced mint for garnish (optional)

1 In a large saucepan, cover the beans with water and bring to a boil over high heat. Remove from the heat, cover, and let sit for 1 hour. Drain the beans, return them to the saucepan, and cover with water. Add the yellow onion and bay leaves; cook, covered, over low heat until tender — about 1 hour and 10 minutes. Add more water, if necessary, to prevent scorching.

2 Meanwhile, in a large bowl, combine the vinaigrette ingredients. Stir in the red, yellow, and green peppers, the red onion, and celery; mix well. Drain the beans and, while still warm, stir them into the pepper mixture.

▽ At this point the salad can be stored. *Refrigerate*, tightly covered, for up to 3 days.

3 Transfer the salad to a serving dish and garnish with the mint, if desired. Serve hot or at room temperature as a side dish with meat, poultry, or fish. Or add 1 cup diced Monterey Jack or Swiss cheese and serve as a main dish, accompanied by Sage-Corn Bread (page 236) and a green vegetable. Serves 4 as an entrée, 6 as a side dish.

### Serving Later

One hour before serving, set the salad out to come to room temperature, then proceed as in Step 3.

## Tangy Potato Salad with Bacon

Per side-dish serving: Calories 229; Protein 8 g; Carbohydrate 33 g; Fat 7 g; Sodium 674 mg; Cholesterol 65 mg.

½ cup sour cream
¼ cup low-calorie mayonnaise
2 green onions (including some of the green), sliced
3 tablespoons coarsely chopped dill pickle
2 tablespoons dill pickle juice
2 tablespoons diced sweet red pepper
1 teaspoon salt
½ teaspoon dry mustard
8 small new potatoes, scrubbed, boiled until tender, and quartered (about 2 pounds)
4 slices Canadian bacon, cooked until crisp and diced
1 hard-cooked egg, chopped

1 In a large bowl, mix the sour cream, mayonnaise, green onions, pickles, pickle juice, red pepper, salt, and mustard. Add the potatoes, bacon, and egg and mix well. Refrigerate, tightly covered, for at least 1 hour. Will keep for up to 2 days.

2 Serve chilled with barbecued chicken or hamburgers. Or serve as a light luncheon dish, accompanied by sliced tomatoes and a cooked and chilled green vegetable. Serves 4 as an entrée, 6 as a side dish.

## Some-Like-It-Hot Potato Salad

Per serving: Calories 222; Protein 3 g; Carbohydrate 34 g; Fat 9 g; Sodium 334 mg; Cholesterol 0 mg.

*The name says it all. To make your own chili powder, see Tip, page 137.*

¼ cup olive or vegetable oil
1 small sweet red pepper, cored, seeded, and diced
1 small sweet green pepper, cored, seeded, and diced
1 small red onion, diced
1 tablespoon chili powder
½ teaspoon ground cumin
1 clove garlic, minced
8 small new potatoes, scrubbed, boiled until tender, and quartered (about 2 pounds)
⅓ cup cider vinegar
1 teaspoon salt
¼ teaspoon black pepper
2 dashes hot red pepper sauce, or to taste (optional)
2 tablespoons chopped cilantro (coriander leaves) or parsley
Parsley leaves for garnish (optional)

*Black Bean and Sweet Pepper Salad, a true adventure in taste*

1 In a 10-inch skillet, heat the olive oil over moderately high heat. Add the red and green peppers and the onion, and sauté, stirring occasionally, until slightly softened — about 4 minutes. Add the chili powder, cumin, and garlic, and sauté 1 minute more.

2 In a large bowl, combine the potatoes, vinegar, salt, pepper, hot red pepper sauce, if desired, and cilantro. Stir in the skillet mixture. Refrigerate, tightly covered, for at least 6 hours. Will keep for up to 2 days.

3 Transfer to a serving bowl and garnish with the parsley, if desired. Serve with barbecued chicken, baby back ribs, or hamburgers. Serves 6.

# Shrimp with Vegetables and Lime Dressing

Per main-dish serving: Calories 173;
Protein 16 g; Carbohydrate 3 g; Fat 10 g;
Sodium 252 mg; Cholesterol 118 mg.

- 1 quart water
  Grated rind and juice of 1 lime
- 3 bay leaves
- ½ teaspoon black pepper
- ¼ teaspoon ground allspice
- 12 ounces medium-size shrimp

- 2 medium-size tomatoes, chopped (about 1 cup)
- 2 tablespoons chopped red onion
- 5 medium-size radishes, chopped (about ½ cup)
- 3 tablespoons minced cilantro (coriander leaves)

*For the dressing:*
- 4 teaspoons lime juice
- 4 teaspoons each olive and vegetable oil
- ¼ teaspoon salt

*Optional garnishes:*
  Romaine or leaf lettuce
  Cilantro sprigs
  Radish roses

1 In a medium-size covered saucepan, bring the water, lime rind and juice, bay leaves, pepper, and allspice to a boil over high heat. Reduce the heat to low; simmer for 10 minutes.

2 Increase the heat to high, add the shrimp, cover, and bring to a full boil. Remove from the heat and drain the liquid. Re-cover and set aside for 15 minutes. Rinse under cold water. Peel and devein the shrimp; set aside.

3 In a medium-size bowl, combine the shrimp, tomato, red onion, radishes, and cilantro. In a small jar with a

*Nesting on a bed of crisp lettuce — Scallop Salad with Snow Peas*

tight-fitting lid, shake the dressing ingredients until well blended. Add to the shrimp and vegetables and toss to coat.

▽ At this point the salad can be stored. *Refrigerate*, tightly covered, for up to 24 hours.

4 Serve on a platter lined with romaine leaves and garnished with cilantro sprigs and radish roses, if desired. Accompany with a green salad and bread, or fill warm taco shells with the mixture and accompany with crisp vegetables. Serves 4 as a light supper dish, 6 as a first course or appetizer.

# Salmon Salad with Sweet Pickles

Per serving: Calories 253; Protein 22 g; Carbohydrate 9 g; Fat 13 g; Sodium 850 mg; Cholesterol 44 mg.

- 1 can (15½ ounces) salmon, drained and flaked
- 1 stalk celery, thinly sliced
- 1 medium-size carrot, shredded (about ½ cup)
- ⅓ cup finely chopped sweet pickle
- 1 small yellow onion, finely chopped
- 2 tablespoons vegetable oil
- 1 tablespoon wine vinegar
- 1½ teaspoons prepared horseradish
- ½ teaspoon sugar
- ¼ teaspoon salt
- ¼ teaspoon dry mustard
  Cayenne (ground red) pepper to taste
  Romaine leaves for garnish

*Optional garnishes:*
- 2 hard-cooked eggs, shelled and sliced
- 4 radishes, thinly sliced
- 1 tablespoon chopped parsley

1 In a large bowl, gently mix together the salmon, celery, carrot, pickle, and onion. Set aside.

2 In a small bowl, whisk together the oil, vinegar, horseradish, sugar, salt, mustard, and cayenne pepper. Pour over the salmon mixture and toss until well mixed. Refrigerate, tightly covered, for at least 12 and up to 24 hours.

3 Line a salad platter with the romaine leaves. Spoon the salmon salad over them and garnish with the eggs, radishes, and parsley, if desired. Serve with boiled new potatoes and cold marinated green beans. Serves 4.

# Scallop Salad with Snow Peas

Per serving: Calories 261; Protein 29 g; Carbohydrate 20 g; Fat 7 g; Sodium 736 mg; Cholesterol 327 mg.

*Even those who claim they don't especially care for fish are bound to be won over by this agreeable and subtly spiced summer entrée.*

- 1½ pounds sea scallops, cut into ¾-inch pieces, or 1½ pounds bay scallops
- ¼ cup dry white wine
- 1 medium-size shallot, minced
- ¼ teaspoon salt
- ⅛ teaspoon black pepper
- 4 ounces snow peas, trimmed
- 4 green onions (including the green), thinly sliced
- 1 medium-size sweet red pepper, cored, seeded, and cut into 1½- by ⅛-inch strips
- 2 tablespoons minced cilantro (coriander leaves) or dill
  Lettuce leaves

*For the dressing:*
- ¾ cup low-calorie mayonnaise
- ¼ cup plain low-fat yogurt
- 1 tablespoon lemon juice
- 2 teaspoons Dijon or spicy brown mustard
- 1 teaspoon curry powder, or to taste
- 1 clove garlic, minced
- ¼ teaspoon black pepper

*Optional garnishes:*
  Tomato slices
  Pitted black olives

1 In a 10-inch skillet, combine the scallops, wine, shallot, salt, and pepper with enough cold water to just cover the scallops. Bring to a boil over moderately high heat, then immediately reduce the heat to low, and simmer gently for 1 minute or until tender. (When done, sea scallops spring back to your touch; bay scallops lose their pinkish color.) Remove from the heat, drain in a colander, and cool.

▽ At this point the scallops can be stored. *Refrigerate*, tightly covered, for up to 24 hours.

2 In a large saucepan, bring 2 quarts of water to a boil over high heat, add the snow peas, and cook until they turn bright green — about 1 minute. Drain and refresh under cold running water; pat dry. Wrap the snow peas, green onions, and red pepper separately in dampened paper towels and store in plastic bags. Refrigerate until ready to serve. Will keep for up to 24 hours.

3 To make the dressing: In a small bowl, whisk together the mayonnaise, yogurt, lemon juice, mustard, curry powder, garlic, and pepper until well combined. Refrigerate until ready to use. Will keep for up to 4 days.

4 In a large bowl, toss together the scallops, vegetables, and dressing. Transfer to plates lined with lettuce leaves; garnish with the tomato slices and olives, if desired. Serve as an entrée for lunch or a light supper. Crusty French bread or Brown-and-Serve Dinner Rolls (page 238) would make a good accompaniment. Serves 4.

# Curried Chicken Salad with Grapes and Pineapple

Per serving: Calories 369; Protein 24 g; Carbohydrate 22 g; Fat 21 g; Sodium 436 mg; Cholesterol 66 mg.

*For a showier presentation, serve this colorful salad mounded in avocado, papaya, or pineapple halves.*

- ²/₃ cup mayonnaise
- ²/₃ cup plain low-fat yogurt
- 2 tablespoons lemon juice
- 2 tablespoons soy sauce
- 1 tablespoon curry powder
- 1 tablespoon minced yellow onion
- 1 tablespoon minced chutney (optional)
- 3 cups diced cooked chicken or turkey breast (about 18 ounces)
- 2 stalks celery, chopped
- 1 can (8 ounces) water chestnuts, drained and sliced
- 2 cups seedless green grapes, halved lengthwise
- 1 can (20 ounces) pineapple chunks, drained (about 2¹/₂ cups)
- 1 jar (4 ounces) pimiento, drained and julienned (about ¹/₃ cup)
  Lettuce leaves
- ¹/₂ cup toasted slivered almonds (about 2¹/₂ ounces)

1 In a medium-size bowl, combine the mayonnaise, yogurt, lemon juice, soy sauce, curry powder, onion, and chutney, if desired. Set aside.

2 In a large bowl, mix the chicken, celery, water chestnuts, grapes, and pineapple. Stir in the dressing. Cover and chill for at least 12 hours. Will keep, refrigerated, for up to 2 days.

3 Just before serving, stir in the pimiento. Mound the salad on lettuce leaves and scatter the almonds lightly over each portion. Serve accompanied by Poppy Seed Bowknots (page 241). Serves 8.

# Mexican Chicken Salad

Per serving: Calories 322; Protein 41 g; Carbohydrate 7 g; Fat 14 g; Sodium 363 mg; Cholesterol 99 mg.

- 3 whole boneless, skinless chicken breasts (about 12 ounces each), cooked and diced
- 1 can (4 ounces) green chilies, seeded and minced
- 1 large pickled jalapeño pepper, seeded and minced
- 1 small yellow onion, finely chopped
- 4 plum tomatoes, diced
- ¹/₂ cup minced cilantro (coriander leaves) or ¹/₂ cup minced parsley plus 1 teaspoon dried cilantro

*For the dressing:*
- 3 tablespoons white wine vinegar
- 2 cloves garlic, minced
- ³/₄ teaspoon salt
- ¹/₂ teaspoon black pepper
- ¹/₃ cup olive oil

1 In a large bowl, gently mix the chicken, chilies, jalapeño pepper, onion, tomatoes, and cilantro.

2 In a small bowl, whisk together the vinegar, garlic, salt, and pepper. Still whisking, add the oil in a stream until the dressing is well combined. Add the dressing to the salad and toss well.

▽ At this point the salad can be stored. *Refrigerate*, tightly covered, for up to 12 hours.

3 Serve as an entrée accompanied by crusty French bread or present in tortilla shells, as with Taco Salad (page 206). Serves 6.

# Cashew-Orange Chicken Salad

Per serving: Calories 483; Protein 44 g; Carbohydrate 17 g; Fat 26 g; Sodium 292 mg; Cholesterol 99 mg.

- 1 cup orange juice
- ¹/₄ cup chopped cilantro (coriander leaves) or ¹/₄ cup chopped parsley plus 1 teaspoon dried cilantro
- ¹/₄ cup peanut or olive oil
- 1 tablespoon red wine vinegar
- 2 teaspoons Dijon or spicy brown mustard
- ¹/₂ teaspoon grated orange rind
- ¹/₂ teaspoon sugar
- ¹/₄ teaspoon each salt and black pepper
- 2 whole boneless, skinless chicken breasts (about 12 ounces each), poached and cut into ³/₄-inch cubes
- 2 stalks celery, cut into matchsticks (about 1 cup)
- 2 green onions, sliced
- 1 large sweet red pepper, cored, seeded, and cut into ³/₄-inch squares
- ²/₃ cup roasted cashews
- 2 cups shredded romaine (about ¹/₄ head)

1 In a small saucepan, boil the orange juice over moderate heat until reduced to ¹/₂ cup. Set aside to cool.

2 In a medium-size bowl, mix the juice, cilantro, oil, vinegar, mustard, orange rind, sugar, salt, and pepper.

3 In a large bowl, mix the chicken, celery, green onions, sweet red pepper, and cashews. Pour the dressing over and toss gently until well mixed.

▽ At this point the salad and greens can be covered and *refrigerated* separately for up to 24 hours.

4 Toss the romaine with the chicken mixture. Serve as a main course, accompanied by hot croissants or Herb Biscuits (page 231). Serves 4.

*Cashew-Orange Chicken Salad, its many flavors deliciously underscored by a nutty crunch*

# Tarragon Turkey Salad with Hazelnuts

Per serving: Calories 356; Protein 48 g; Carbohydrate 5 g; Fat 15 g; Sodium 251 mg; Cholesterol 133 mg.

2 pounds cooked turkey or chicken breasts, diced
1 small red onion, minced
4 stalks celery, finely chopped
¼ cup plus 2 tablespoons minced tarragon or 2 tablespoons dried tarragon, crumbled
¼ cup minced parsley
Dash hazelnut, vegetable, or walnut oil
½ cup plain low-fat yogurt
¼ cup mayonnaise
¼ teaspoon each salt and black pepper, or to taste
½ cup hazelnuts, roasted, skinned, and coarsely chopped, or walnuts, coarsely chopped

1 In a large bowl, toss the turkey, red onion, celery, tarragon, parsley, and oil until well mixed.

▽ At this point the salad can be stored. *Refrigerate*, tightly covered, for up to 12 hours.

2 In a small bowl, whisk the yogurt, mayonnaise, salt, and pepper. Add to the salad and toss gently. Sprinkle with the nuts. Serve with French bread and sliced tomatoes. Serves 6.

*Tip: To skin hazelnuts, roast them on a baking sheet in a 375° F oven for about 10 minutes. Transfer to a paper bag, seal, and then shake them to loosen the skins. Leave the nuts in the bag 10 minutes longer to steam, then rub off the skins, using a kitchen towel or heavy-duty paper toweling.*

# Taco Salad

Per serving: Calories 751; Protein 38 g;
Carbohydrate 48 g; Fat 47 g; Sodium 645 mg;
Cholesterol 89 mg.

*If you don't have time to make the cup-shaped shells, serve the salad on tortilla chips.*

   1   pound lean ground beef round
   1   large yellow onion, minced
2 ½   teaspoons chili powder
   2   teaspoons ground cumin
   2   cloves garlic, minced
 ½    teaspoon dried oregano, crumbled
   1   can (8 ounces) whole-kernel corn, drained
   1   can (8 ounces) tomato sauce
         Vegetable oil for deep frying
   6   corn or flour tortillas
 ¼    cup red or white wine vinegar
   1   clove garlic, minced
   2   teaspoons Dijon or spicy brown mustard
 ¼    teaspoon salt
 ⅓    cup each olive oil and vegetable oil
   1   tablespoon minced cilantro (coriander leaves) or minced parsley
 ½    large head iceberg lettuce, shredded
   1   can (10 ounces) chick peas, drained
   2   green onions (including the tops), minced
   2   large tomatoes, sliced in thin wedges
   1   large avocado, peeled, pitted, and sliced
   1   cup shredded Cheddar cheese (about 4 ounces)

*Optional garnishes:*
         Sour cream
         Minced cilantro (coriander leaves)

1 In a 10-inch skillet, sauté the ground beef and onion over moderate heat until the meat is browned and the onion soft — about 5 minutes. Add 2 teaspoons of the chili powder, 1½ teaspoons of the cumin, the garlic, oregano, corn, and tomato sauce; simmer, uncovered, stirring occasionally, until most of the liquid has evaporated — 3 to 5 minutes.

▽ At this point the meat mixture can be cooled to room temperature and *refrigerated* in a tightly covered container for up to 24 hours.

2 In a deep-fat fryer or large heavy saucepan, heat the vegetable oil to 375° F or until a 1-inch bread cube takes 1 minute to brown. To form tortilla cups, hold one tortilla at a time between 2 ladles, or in a basket ladle used to make potato nests, and fry until crisp — about 1 minute. Transfer to a platter lined with paper toweling. Or holding an empty 3-inch can with tongs, gently push a tortilla to the bottom of the hot oil, where it will fold up around the can, and hold it there until crisp. The cups can sit at room temperature for up to 4 hours.

3 In a small bowl, whisk together the vinegar, garlic, mustard, the remaining ½ teaspoon each of cumin and chili, the salt, oils, and cilantro.

4 In a large bowl, toss the lettuce, chick peas, green onions, tomatoes, and avocado with the dressing.

5 Place a tortilla cup on each of 6 plates, fill it with the meat, and top with the Cheddar cheese. Arrange the lettuce mixture around the cups and garnish with sour cream and cilantro, if desired. Serves 6.

### Serving Later

Let the meat mixture come to room temperature — about 30 minutes. Preheat the oven to 400° F. Bake the tortilla cups on a baking sheet until warm and crisp — 5 to 7 minutes. Proceed as in Steps 3, 4, and 5.

# Pork, Potato, and Apple Salad

Per serving: Calories 388; Protein 26 g;
Carbohydrate 22 g; Fat 22 g; Sodium 132 mg;
Cholesterol 78 mg.

   1   small red onion, thinly sliced
   3   small new potatoes, peeled, diced, and boiled until tender (about 8 ounces)
 12   ounces cooked roast pork or ham cut into 3" x ¼" x ¼" julienne (about 2 cups)
   1   Granny Smith or other tart apple, peeled, cored, and thinly sliced
   1   recipe Sweet-Bite Dressing (page 214)
   4   cups torn assorted greens

1 Put the red onion slices in a small bowl, cover with cold water, and soak for about 20 minutes to remove some of the sharpness. Drain and pat dry on paper toweling.

**2** In a large bowl, combine the onion, potatoes, pork strips, and apple slices with the Sweet-Bite Dressing.

▽ At this point the salad and the greens can be covered tightly with plastic wrap and *refrigerated* in separate containers for up to 24 hours.

**3** Add the greens to the salad and toss together until well combined. Serve accompanied by crisp carrot and cucumber sticks or Green Beans with Walnut Vinaigrette (page 199) and a crusty rye bread. Serves 4.

### Serving Later

Proceed as in Step 3.

# Piquant Beef and Vegetable Salad

Per serving: Calories 278; Protein 22 g; Carbohydrate 7 g; Fat 18 g; Sodium 139 mg; Cholesterol 54 mg.

- 1 quart water
- 2 cups broccoli florets (about ¹/₂ bunch)
- 1 cup cauliflower florets (about ¹/₄ head)
- 1 medium-size carrot, peeled and thinly sliced
- 10 ounces cooked roast beef or Marinated London Broil (page 99), cut into 3" x ¹/₄" x ¹/₄" julienne (about 1²/₃ cups)
- 1 recipe Sweet-Bite Dressing (page 214)

**1** In a large saucepan, bring the water to a boil over high heat. Add the broccoli, and cook until crisp-tender —

about 4 minutes. Remove with a slotted spoon, transfer to a colander, and rinse under cold water. Drain and transfer to a medium-size bowl.

**2** In the same boiling water, cook the cauliflower until crisp-tender — about 4 minutes — and then the carrots — 3 to 4 minutes. Rinse and drain as in Step 1, then add to the broccoli.

▽ At this point the vegetables and beef can be covered and *refrigerated* separately for up to 24 hours.

**3** Add the beef strips to the vegetables, pour the dressing over all, and toss to coat. Transfer to a serving dish and serve with Whole-Wheat Refrigerator Rolls (page 240). Serves 4.

### Serving Later

Let the vegetables and beef come to room temperature — about 30 minutes — then proceed as in Step 3.

*Tex-Mex outdoes itself in this eye-appealing Taco Salad.*

*Rice Salad with Ham and Cheese, a crowd-pleasing dish, impressively presented*

# Rice Salad with Ham and Cheese

Per main-dish: Calories 502; Protein 19 g; Carbohydrate 47 g; Fat 26 g; Sodium 655 mg; Cholesterol 42 mg.

*This versatile dish can be varied by substituting sausage or chicken for the ham, black olives for the green, or tomatoes, green beans, or cucumber for any of the vegetables.*

- 4 cups Chicken Stock (page 48) or 1 can (13½ ounces) chicken broth plus enough water to equal 4 cups liquid
- ¼ teaspoon ground saffron or turmeric
- 1½ cups white rice
- ⅔ cup diced cooked ham (about 4 ounces)
- 10 green onions (including some of the green), coarsely chopped
- 2 medium-size carrots, shredded
- 1 cup chopped parsley
- ½ cup shelled fresh peas or ½ cup frozen peas, cooked
- 1 small sweet red pepper, cored, seeded, and diced
- 1 small sweet green pepper, cored, seeded, and diced
- ½ cup chopped basil or 1 tablespoon dried basil, crumbled
- ½ cup sliced green olives
- ¼ cup toasted pine nuts
- ¼ teaspoon black pepper
- 1 cup diced fontina, Swiss, or Cheddar cheese (about 6 ounces)
- 6 tablespoons olive oil
- 3 tablespoons wine vinegar
  Lettuce leaves
  Cherry tomatoes for garnish (optional)

1 In a large saucepan, bring the stock and saffron to a boil over high heat. Stir in the rice, cover, reduce the heat to low, and cook until the rice is tender — 15 to 20 minutes. Transfer to a large bowl and cool to room temperature; then stir in all of the remaining ingredients except the oil, vinegar, and lettuce.

▽ At this point the salad can be *refrigerated*, tightly covered, for up to 24 hours.

2 Four hours before serving, add the oil and vinegar and toss well. Serve at room temperature on lettuce leaves, and garnish with cherry tomatoes, if

desired. Serve as a luncheon or light supper dish, accompanied by cold asparagus dressed with lemon, and pumpernickel rolls. This also makes an excellent buffet or picnic dish. Serves 6 as an entrée, 8 as a side dish.

> *Tip: To mold rice salad for an attractive presentation, lightly oil the mold, then fill it with the salad, packing the rice firmly without mashing it. Chill for 30 minutes. To unmold, dip in hot water for 30 seconds; invert onto a serving platter.*

# Herbed Rice Salad

Per serving: Calories 337; Protein 6 g; Carbohydrate 42 g; Fat 16 g; Sodium 120 mg; Cholesterol 0 mg.

*Hot rice is recommended for this and other rice salads because it absorbs the dressing better.*

- ¼ cup olive oil
- 2 tablespoons tarragon or white wine vinegar
- 1 teaspoon Dijon or spicy brown mustard
- 1 teaspoon soy sauce
- 3 cups hot cooked brown or white rice
- 1 small carrot, minced
- 1 small stalk celery, minced
- 1 small sweet green pepper, cored, seeded, and minced
- 2 tablespoons minced parsley
- 1 shallot or 2 green onions, minced
- 2 tablespoons sunflower seeds or pine nuts
- 2 tablespoons snipped chives
- 1 tablespoon snipped dill or 1 teaspoon dried dill weed
- 1 teaspoon minced tarragon or ¼ teaspoon dried tarragon, crumbled
- ¾ teaspoon minced rosemary or ¼ teaspoon dried rosemary, crumbled

1 In a large bowl, whisk together the olive oil, vinegar, mustard, and soy sauce. Add the remaining ingredients and toss well. Refrigerate, tightly covered, for at least 2 and up to 24 hours.

2 Before serving, let the salad come to room temperature — about 30 minutes. This dish goes especially well with Seviche (page 76), cold steamed shrimp or lobster, or barbecued meats or poultry. Serves 4 to 6.

# Curried Rice Salad

Per serving: Calories 332; Protein 5 g; Carbohydrate 49 g; Fat 13 g; Sodium 254 mg; Cholesterol 0 mg.

*With the addition of 2 cups diced cooked chicken, this salad of Basmati rice from India can be turned into a light supper dish.*

*For the dressing:*
- ⅓ cup peanut or corn oil
- ¼ cup lemon juice
- 1 tablespoon curry powder
- 1 teaspoon ground cumin
- 1 teaspoon salt
- ½ teaspoon each ground coriander and black pepper Pinch cayenne (ground red) pepper

*For the salad:*
- 6 cups hot cooked Basmati or other rice
- 4 green onions, thinly sliced
- 1 medium-size carrot, finely shredded
- ½ cup dried black currants or raisins, soaked in hot water for 10 minutes, then drained
- ½ cup shelled pistachio nuts, coarsely chopped

1 In a large bowl, whisk together the dressing ingredients. Add the hot rice and mix well. Stir in the green onions, carrot, currants, and pistachio nuts. Cover tightly and refrigerate for at least 2 and up to 48 hours.

2 Transfer the salad to a serving dish and serve with grilled chicken, pork chops, or shrimp. This dish goes especially well with Roasted Loin of Pork in Ginger Marinade (page 113). Serves 8.

# Rice, Egg, Tuna, and Tomato Salad

Per serving: Calories 296; Protein 21 g; Carbohydrate 33 g; Fat 10 g; Sodium 491 mg; Cholesterol 117 mg.

- ¾ cup low-calorie mayonnaise
- ¼ cup milk
- 3 tablespoons lemon juice
- ¼ teaspoon each salt and black pepper
- 3 cups hot cooked white rice
- 1 can (12½ ounces) water-packed tuna, drained and flaked
- 2 hard-cooked eggs, minced
- 1 large firm-ripe tomato, seeded and chopped
- 1 medium-size yellow onion, minced
- ½ cup chopped pitted Kalamata or other flavorful black olives
- ¼ cup minced parsley Lettuce leaves Tomato wedges for garnish (optional)

1 In a large bowl, combine the mayonnaise, milk, lemon juice, salt, and pepper. Add the rice, tuna, eggs, tomato, onion, olives, and parsley and stir well. Refrigerate, tightly covered, for at least 1 and up to 8 hours.

2 Before serving, let the salad come to room temperature — about 30 minutes. Transfer to a serving dish or individual plates lined with the lettuce leaves; garnish with tomato wedges, if desired. Accompany with Herbed Garlic Bread (page 243). Serves 6 to 8.

# Creamy Pasta Salad with Chicken

Per main-dish serving: Calories 644;
Protein 42 g; Carbohydrate 49 g; Fat 30 g;
Sodium 366 mg; Cholesterol 107 mg.

- ⅔ cup sour cream
- ⅓ cup olive oil
- 2 tablespoons lemon juice
- 2 tablespoons minced basil or
  2 teaspoons dried basil,
  crumbled
- 2 tablespoons minced parsley
- 1 teaspoon minced oregano or
  ½ teaspoon dried oregano,
  crumbled
- ½ teaspoon salt
- ⅛ teaspoon black pepper
- 8 ounces rotelli, fusilli, or other
  corkscrew pasta
- 2½ cups cubed cooked chicken
  breasts (about 15 ounces)
- 1 small zucchini, cubed
- 1 small tomato, seeded and
  diced
- 2 stalks celery, chopped
  Chopped walnuts for garnish
  (optional)

1 In a large bowl, whisk the sour cream, olive oil, lemon juice, basil, parsley, oregano, salt, and pepper.

2 In a large saucepan, cook the rotelli according to package directions until al dente (see Tip, page 161). Drain but do not rinse.

3 Add the pasta, chicken, zucchini, tomato, and celery to the dressing and toss to coat. Refrigerate, tightly covered, for at least 4 hours. Will keep for up to 24 hours.

4 Serve cold or at room temperature, sprinkled with walnuts, if desired, and accompanied by Italian bread, olives, and cucumber sticks. Serves 4 as an entrée, 6 to 8 as a side dish.

# Pasta Salad with Shrimp, Snow Peas, and Oranges

Per main-dish serving: Calories 480;
Protein 23 g; Carbohydrate 52 g; Fat 20 g;
Sodium 601 mg; Cholesterol 104 mg.

- 12 ounces tricolor pasta
- 2 quarts water
- 4 ounces snow peas, strings
  removed
- 2 bay leaves
- 2 tablespoons chopped yellow
  onion
- 1½ teaspoons salt
- 1 pound medium-size shrimp
- ½ cup olive oil
- ⅓ cup white wine vinegar
- 1 teaspoon grated orange rind
- ½ teaspoon black pepper
- 2 seedless oranges, peeled and
  sectioned, or 1 can (11
  ounces) mandarin oranges,
  drained
- 6 green onions (green part
  only), sliced (about ¾ cup)
  Watercress for garnish
  (optional)

1 Cook the pasta according to package directions until al dente (see Tip, page 161). Drain and rinse under cold water.

2 In a large saucepan, bring the water to a boil over high heat. Add the snow peas, and cook until they turn bright green — about 1 minute. Remove the snow peas with a slotted spoon and plunge into a bowl of cold water to stop the cooking.

3 Add the bay leaves, onion, and ½ teaspoon of the salt to the saucepan and return to a boil. Add the shrimp; cook, uncovered, until they are opaque in the center — about 3 minutes. Drain, discarding the onion and bay leaf. Peel and devein the shrimp.

4 In a large bowl, whisk together the olive oil, vinegar, grated orange rind, the remaining teaspoon of salt, and the pepper. Add the shrimp, snow peas, pasta, orange sections, and green onions and toss to coat.

5 Refrigerate, tightly covered, for at least 3 and up to 24 hours. Serve cold or at room temperature, garnished with the watercress, if desired, and accompanied by sourdough bread. Serves 6 as an entrée, 10 as a side dish.

# Pasta Salad with Tuna, Pine Nuts, and Red Peppers

Per serving: Calories 501; Protein 20 g;
Carbohydrate 60 g; Fat 20 g; Sodium 513 mg;
Cholesterol 11 mg.

*This salad also tastes good the day after it's prepared. Just give it an hour to come to room temperature.*

- 6 tablespoons olive oil
- ½ cup pine nuts
- 2 cloves garlic, minced
- 1 large tomato, peeled, seeded,
  and coarsely chopped
- 1 can (6½ ounces) water-
  packed tuna, drained
- 1 jar (5 ounces) roasted red
  peppers or pimientos, cut
  into strips (about ½ cup)
- ½ cup pitted black olives,
  coarsely chopped
- 2 tablespoons red wine vinegar
- 1 teaspoon salt
- ¼ teaspoon black pepper
- 1 pound regular or spinach
  fettuccine or linguine
- 2 tablespoons minced parsley

1 Heat the oil in a heavy 6-inch skillet over moderate heat for 1 minute. Add the pine nuts and cook until lightly browned — about 2 minutes. Stir in the garlic, and cook until golden — 1 minute more. Stir in the tomato.

*More than just a meal — Pasta Salad with Tuna, Pine Nuts, and Red Peppers*

pound each cooked green beans and wax beans, cut into 2-inch pieces, and add 1 small red onion, thinly sliced. Garnish with the minced parsley and 2 hard-cooked eggs, quartered. Serve with Italian or French bread. Serves 6.

# BLT Macaroni Salad

Per serving: Calories 225; Protein 7 g; Carbohydrate 34 g; Fat 7 g; Sodium 273 mg; Cholesterol 10 mg.

| | |
|---|---|
| 8 | ounces elbow macaroni or other small pasta |
| ²⁄₃ | cup low-calorie mayonnaise |
| ¹⁄₃ | cup plain low-fat yogurt |
| 1 | tablespoon white wine vinegar |
| ¹⁄₄ | teaspoon each salt and black pepper |
| 6 | slices bacon, cooked until crisp and crumbled (about 4 ounces) |
| 4 | green onions, finely chopped |
| 1 | large tomato, seeded and chopped |
| 2 | tablespoons chopped parsley Lettuce leaves for garnish (optional) |

**1** Cook the pasta according to package directions until *al dente* (see Tip, page 161). Drain and rinse under cold water.

**2** Meanwhile, in a large bowl, combine the mayonnaise, yogurt, vinegar, salt, and pepper. Add the pasta, bacon, green onions, tomato, and parsley; mix well. Refrigerate, tightly covered, for at least 1 and up to 24 hours.

**3** Transfer the salad to a serving dish lined, if desired, with lettuce leaves. Serve cold or at room temperature with hamburgers, hot dogs, or barbecued chicken. This dish goes especially well with Turkey Mushroom Loaf (page 92). Serves 6 as a side dish.

**2** Transfer the mixture to a large bowl. Stir in the tuna, red peppers, olives, vinegar, salt, and pepper.

▽ At this point the sauce can be covered and allowed to stand at room temperature for up to 2 hours.

**3** Cook the pasta according to package directions until *al dente* (see Tip, page 161). Drain in a colander, then add the pasta to the tuna sauce

and mix well. Sprinkle with the parsley. Serve at room temperature, accompanied by sesame bread sticks and steamed asparagus. Serves 6.

## Green Bean Variation

Per serving: Calories 292; Protein 15 g; Carbohydrate 13 g; Fat 21 g; Sodium 539 g; Cholesterol 11 g.

Proceed as in Steps 1 and 2 above. In step 3, substitute for the pasta ¾

# Gazpacho Aspic with Avocado Dressing

Per serving: Calories 111; Protein 3 g; Carbohydrate 7 g; Fat 9 g; Sodium 139 mg; Cholesterol 7 mg.

*This refreshing combination is especially appealing on a hot summer evening. If you have a food processor, you can save time by chopping all the vegetables in it.*

- 2 envelopes unflavored gelatin
- 3 cups tomato or mixed vegetable juice
- 1/3 cup red wine vinegar
- 3 dashes hot red pepper sauce, or to taste
- 1 clove garlic, minced
- 2 small tomatoes, coarsely chopped
- 1 medium-size cucumber, peeled, seeded, and coarsely chopped
- 1/2 small sweet green pepper, cored, seeded, and coarsely chopped
- 1 stalk celery, coarsely chopped
- 1/2 small yellow onion, coarsely chopped
  Lettuce leaves for garnish (optional)

*For the dressing:*
- 1 medium-size avocado, peeled, pitted, and cubed
- 1 green onion, minced
- 1/2 cup sour cream
- 1/4 cup mayonnaise
- 2 tablespoons lemon juice
- 1/4 teaspoon salt

1 In a small saucepan, sprinkle the gelatin over 1/2 cup of the tomato juice. Stir over low heat until the gelatin has dissolved — 4 to 5 minutes. Set aside.

2 In a medium-size bowl, mix the remaining tomato juice, the vinegar, hot red pepper sauce, and gelatin. Stand the mixture in a large bowl of ice water, stirring occasionally, until al-

*Where hot flavors and cool textures exist in delicious tandem — Gazpacho Aspic*

most set (the consistency of raw egg whites) — about 15 minutes. Or chill in the refrigerator for about 30 minutes.

3 Add the garlic, tomatoes, cucumber, green pepper, celery, and onion to the juice mixture and stir well. Pour into a lightly oiled, 6-cup mold and chill until set — about 3 hours. Will keep for up to 2 days.

4 Blend the dressing ingredients in an electric blender or food processor until smooth — about 1 minute. Or in a small bowl, mash the avocado with a fork and whisk in the other ingredients.

▽ At this point the dressing can be stored. *Refrigerate*, covered with plastic wrap, for up to 24 hours.

5 To unmold the salad, loosen the sides with a thin-bladed knife or spatula, then dip in a pan of hot water for 30 seconds. Invert onto a serving platter and garnish with lettuce leaves, if desired. Pass the dressing separately. This dish goes well with fish or barbecued chicken. Serves 6.

# Guacamole Aspic

Per salad serving: Calories 168; Protein 5 g; Carbohydrate 7 g; Fat 14 g; Sodium 139 mg; Cholesterol 0 mg.

- 2 packages unflavored gelatin
- 1/2 cup cold water
- 3 medium-size avocados (8 ounces each)
- 2 tablespoons lemon juice
- 1 medium-size tomato, diced
- 2 green onions (including some of the green), sliced
- 2 tablespoons chopped cilantro (coriander leaves) or 2 tablespoons chopped parsley plus 1/2 teaspoon dried cilantro
- 1 clove garlic, minced
- 2 dashes hot red pepper sauce, or to taste
- 1/4 teaspoon salt
- 2 cups Chicken Stock (page 48) or canned chicken broth

*Optional garnishes:*
  Sour cream
  Sprigs of cilantro (coriander leaves)

*with Avocado Dressing and Guacamole Aspic*

1 In a large saucepan, sprinkle the gelatin over the water. Set over low heat and stir until the gelatin has dissolved — 4 to 5 minutes. Set aside.

2 Halve the avocados, remove their pits, and scoop the pulp into a medium-size bowl. Immediately spoon the lemon juice over the pulp, coarsely mash it with a fork, and set aside.

3 Add the tomato, green onions, cilantro, garlic, hot red pepper sauce, salt, and stock to the saucepan with the gelatin; mix well. Stand the mixture in a bowl of ice water, stirring occasionally, until almost set (the consistency of raw egg whites) — about 15 minutes. Or refrigerate for about 30 minutes.

4 Add the avocado to the gelatin mixture and stir well. Pour into a lightly oiled, nonmetallic, 6-cup mold and cover with plastic wrap, pressing it onto the surface of the aspic. Refrigerate until set — about 3 hours. Will keep for up to 2 days.

5 To unmold the aspic, first loosen the sides with a thin-bladed knife or spatula, then dip in a pan of hot water for 30 seconds. Invert onto a serving platter. Garnish with dollops of sour cream and sprigs of cilantro, if desired. Slice in wedges and serve with taco chips as a first course. Or serve as an appetizer with crackers. Serves 8 as a first course, 16 as an appetizer.

# Molded Cranberry-Chicken Salad

Per main-dish serving: Calories 308; Protein 20 g; Carbohydrate 40 g; Fat 8 g; Sodium 225 mg; Cholesterol 52 mg.

*For the cranberry layer:*
- 1 tablespoon unflavored gelatin
- 3 tablespoons orange juice
- 1 can (1 pound) whole-berry cranberry sauce
- 1 can (8 ounces) crushed pineapple in juice
- 1 small stalk celery, finely diced
- ¼ cup coarsely chopped walnuts

*For the chicken layer:*
- ¼ cup cold water
- 1 tablespoon unflavored gelatin
- 2 cups diced cooked chicken (about 12 ounces)
- ½ cup low-calorie mayonnaise
- ½ cup plain low-fat yogurt
- 3 tablespoons chopped parsley
- ¼ teaspoon salt
- ⅛ teaspoon pepper
  Lettuce leaves for garnish

1 To make the cranberry layer: In a small bowl, sprinkle the gelatin on top of the orange juice. Set aside to soften — about 4 minutes.

2 In a medium-size saucepan, bring the cranberry sauce to a boil over moderate heat. Remove from the heat, add the gelatin, and stir until completely dissolved — 2 to 3 minutes. Stir in the pineapple, celery, and walnuts; pour into a 9″ x 9″ x 2″ pan. Refrigerate until nearly set — about 30 minutes.

3 Meanwhile, make the chicken layer: Pour the water into a small saucepan and sprinkle the gelatin on top. Over low heat, stir until the gelatin has dissolved — 4 to 5 minutes. Set aside.

4 In a medium-size bowl, combine the chicken, mayonnaise, yogurt, parsley, salt, and pepper; stir in the dissolved gelatin. Pour the mixture on top of the cranberry layer. Refrigerate until firmly set — about 1 hour. Will keep for up to 24 hours.

5 To unmold the salad, first loosen the sides with a thin-bladed knife or spatula, then dip the mold in a pan of hot water for 30 seconds. Invert onto a serving platter and garnish with the lettuce leaves. Serves 6 as a main dish, 16 as an appetizer.

# Cottage-Cheese and Chives Dressing

Per serving: Calories 33; Protein 3 g; Carbohydrate 4 g; Fat tr; Sodium 271 mg; Cholesterol 2 mg.

- ⅔ cup low-fat cottage cheese
- ½ cup plain low-fat yogurt
- 1 tablespoon honey
- 1 teaspoon lemon juice
- 2 tablespoons minced chives
- 1 green onion (both white and green parts), thinly sliced
- ½ clove garlic, crushed
- 1 teaspoon paprika
- ¾ teaspoon salt
- ⅛ teaspoon black pepper

1 In an electric blender or food processor, blend all ingredients until smooth — about 1 minute. Serve as a dressing for a green or potato salad, as a topping for baked potatoes, or as a pasta sauce. Will keep, tightly covered and refrigerated, for up to 4 days. Makes about 1⅓ cups or enough to dress 2 salads of 4 servings each.

# Basil Cottage-Cheese Dressing

Per serving: Calories 75; Protein 2 g; Carbohydrate 1 g; Fat 7 g; Sodium 124 mg; Cholesterol 1 mg.

*This versatile dressing is delicious also as a topping for baked potatoes or as a dip for vegetables.*

- ½ cup low-fat cottage cheese
- ¼ cup plain low-fat yogurt or low-fat milk
- 4 teaspoons basil, white wine, or cider vinegar

- 1 tablespoon minced basil or 1 teaspoon dried basil, crumbled
- 1 teaspoon minced oregano or ½ teaspoon dried oregano, crumbled
- 1 clove garlic, crushed
- ¼ teaspoon salt
- ¼ cup olive oil

1 In an electric blender or food processor, blend the cottage cheese, yogurt, and vinegar until smooth — about 30 seconds. Add the basil, oregano, garlic, and salt and blend until smooth — about 30 seconds more. With the motor running, slowly pour in the oil and process until blended — about 1 minute.

2 The dressing will be thick. If a thinner dressing is preferred, blend in 1 to 3 more tablespoons of yogurt or milk and adjust the seasonings. Will keep, refrigerated and covered, for up to 3 days. Makes 1 cup or enough to dress 2 salads of 4 servings each.

# Yogurt Dressing

Per serving: Calories 39; Protein 2 g; Carbohydrate 2 g; Fat 2 g; Sodium 143 mg; Cholesterol 2 mg.

- ½ cup plain yogurt
- 2 teaspoons olive oil
- ½ teaspoon ground cumin
- ¼ teaspoon salt
- ⅛ teaspoon cayenne (ground red) pepper
- 1 tablespoon chopped mint, parsley, or dill or 1 teaspoon dried mint or dill weed, crumbled
- 1 green onion, thinly sliced

1 In a small bowl, combine all ingredients. Serve over sliced tomatoes or a mixed green salad. This dressing is especially good on thinly sliced cucumbers as an accompaniment to curried dishes, such as Himalayan Chicken

(page 85). Will keep, tightly covered and refrigerated, for up to 3 days. Makes about ½ cup or enough to dress 2 cucumbers or a salad of 4 servings.

# Sweet-Bite Dressing

Per serving: Calories 98; Protein tr; Carbohydrate 2 g; Fat 10 g; Sodium 55 mg; Cholesterol 0 mg.

- 2 tablespoons Sweet-Bite Salad Dressing Mix (page 17)
- 4 teaspoons vinegar
- 3 tablespoons olive or vegetable oil

1 In a small bowl, combine the dressing mix and vinegar. Whisk in the olive oil. Will keep, tightly covered, for up to 2 weeks. Makes enough to dress a salad of 4 servings.

# Herb Vinaigrette Dressing

Per serving: Calories 120; Protein 0 g; Carbohydrate 1 g; Fat 13 g; Sodium 245 mg; Cholesterol 2 mg.

- ¼ cup olive or vegetable oil
- 2 tablespoons vinegar
- 1 teaspoon Herb Salad Dressing Mix (page 17)

1 In a small jar with a tight-fitting lid, combine all ingredients and shake well. Let stand for 5 minutes before using. Will keep, tightly covered and refrigerated, for up to 1 month. Makes about ⅓ cup or enough to dress a salad of 4 servings.

# Sauces and Condiments

**M**any sauces are freezable, so you can save time and take advantage of seasonal specials by making a double batch of sauce and freezing the extra. For convenience in reheating, freeze sauces in small portions, 1 to 1½ cups in a small freezable container or 1-pint freezer bag, leaving ½ to 1 inch of headspace. For quick thawing and warming, transfer the contents to a small saucepan, or pop the bag into a microwave oven. (Note that emulsions made with raw egg — for example, Garlic Mayonnaise or Piquant Sauce for Fish and Poultry, page 220 — and any sauce that is thickened with flour or cornstarch should not be frozen because they separate upon thawing. If used, though, to bind other ingredients, as in a filled crêpe or pot pie, separation in the latter type will not be noticeable.)

A sampling of condiments has been included in this chapter to give you an idea of how relatively easy they are to prepare, and to inspire you perhaps to try your own versions when your favorite fruits or vegetables are plentiful. A few months later — when you liven up a simple, last-minute meal with a dollop of homemade Zucchini Relish (page 228) or present a friend with a jar of Gingered Pear Marmalade (page 224) — you will be delighted with your foresight.

# Classic Tomato Sauce

Per ½ cup: Calories 104; Protein 2 g; Carbohydrate 7 g; Fat 8 g; Sodium 425 mg; Cholesterol 22 mg.

*Store this or any sauce in quantities that are convenient for you and your family. A 1-pint freezer bag comfortably holds up to 1½ cups.*

- ¼ cup unsalted butter or margarine
- 1 medium-size yellow onion, finely chopped
- 1 can (28 ounces) plum tomatoes with their liquid, puréed, or 1 can (28 ounces) tomato purée
- 2 tablespoons minced basil or 2 teaspoons dried basil, crumbled
- ½ teaspoon salt
- ¼ teaspoon black pepper

| Melt the butter in a medium-size saucepan over moderate heat. Add the onion, and sauté, stirring frequently, for 5 minutes or until soft. Stir in the tomato purée, basil, salt, and pepper. Bring to a simmer, reduce the heat to low, and cook, uncovered, for 25 minutes or until thick. Makes about 3 cups or enough sauce for 1 pound of pasta.

▽ At this point the sauce can be cooled to room temperature and stored. *Refrigerate* in a tightly covered, glass or ceramic container for up to 3 days. *Freeze* in labeled, 1-pint freezer bags for up to 3 months at 0° F.

## Serving Later

**From refrigerator:** Warm in a covered medium-size saucepan over moderate heat, stirring occasionally, until heated through — about 20 minutes. **From freezer:** In a covered medium-size saucepan, warm over moderately low heat until thawed — 15 to 20 minutes. Continue heating as above. **To microwave:** Open a freezer bag 1 inch and stand it in a deep, 1½-quart, microwave-safe casserole. Microwave on *High* (100% power) for 2 minutes. Transfer the sauce to the casserole, cover, and microwave on *High* (100% power) for 3 minutes. Stir and break up the frozen block, cover, and microwave 2 minutes or until heated through.

# Marinara Sauce

Per ½ cup: Calories 114; Protein 2 g; Carbohydrate 8 g; Fat 9 g; Sodium 424 mg; Cholesterol 0 mg.

- ¼ cup olive oil
- 1 medium-size yellow onion, finely chopped
- 2 cloves garlic, minced
- 2 pounds ripe plum tomatoes, peeled and chopped, or 1 can (28 ounces) crushed tomatoes
- 1 teaspoon dried oregano, crumbled
- ½ teaspoon salt
- ¼ teaspoon black pepper

| Heat the olive oil in a medium-size saucepan over moderate heat. Add the onion, and sauté, stirring occasionally, until soft — about 5 minutes.

2 Stir in the garlic, tomatoes, oregano, salt, and pepper. Bring to a simmer, then reduce the heat to low. Cook, uncovered, for 25 minutes or until thick. Makes about 3 cups, or enough for 1 pound of pasta. For storing and serving later, see Classic Tomato Sauce (page 216).

# Spicy Tomato Sauce

Per ½ cup: Calories 92; Protein 1 g; Carbohydrate 7 g; Fat 7 g; Sodium 319 mg; Cholesterol 0 mg.

- ¼ cup olive oil
- 2 cloves garlic
- 8 green onions, minced (about ½ cup)
- 1 small sweet green pepper, cored, seeded, and finely chopped
- 6 medium-size, fully ripe tomatoes, peeled, seeded, and chopped (about 3 cups), or 1 can (28 ounces) crushed tomatoes
- ½ cup Chicken Stock (page 48) or canned chicken broth
- 1½ teaspoons black pepper, or to taste
- 1 teaspoon salt
- ½ teaspoon dried oregano, crumbled
- ½ teaspoon crushed red pepper flakes
  Dash of hot red pepper sauce
- ½ cup minced parsley

| Heat the oil in a large saucepan over moderate heat. Add the garlic, green onions, and green pepper, and sauté, stirring occasionally, until the onions are soft — about 5 minutes. Add the tomatoes, chicken stock, black pepper, salt, oregano, red pepper flakes, and hot red pepper sauce. Bring to a boil and simmer, partly covered, over moderately low heat for 1 hour, stirring occasionally.

2 In an electric blender or food processor, purée the sauce in batches until smooth — about 30 seconds per batch. If a thicker sauce is desired, return it to the saucepan, and cook, uncovered, over moderate heat until reduced to desired thickness.

3 Just before serving, stir in the minced parsley. Use this sauce with pasta or South-of-the-Border Chicken Rolls (page 88). Makes about 4 cups. For storing and serving later, see Classic Tomato Sauce (left).

# Mexican Tomato Sauce

Per ½ cup: Calories 105; Protein 2 g; Carbohydrate 7 g; Fat 7 g; Sodium 558 mg; Cholesterol 0 mg.

- 1 can (28 ounces) plum tomatoes with their liquid
- 1 small yellow onion, coarsely chopped
- 1 jalapeño pepper, seeded and coarsely chopped (optional)
- 1 clove garlic, peeled
- 1 tablespoon chili powder
- ½ teaspoon each ground cumin and dried oregano, crumbled
- ½ teaspoon salt
- 3 tablespoons corn oil

1 In an electric blender or food processor, purée all of the ingredients, except the corn oil, until smooth — about 1 minute.

2 In a medium-size saucepan, combine the oil and the tomato mixture. Bring to a simmer over moderate heat. Reduce the heat to low and cook, uncovered, stirring frequently, until the sauce is thick — about 25 minutes. Use in Tortilla Casserole (page 129) or serve with Fiesta Burgers (page 106). Makes about 3 cups. For storing and serving later, see Classic Tomato Sauce (page 216).

*Marinara Sauce, what better way to blanket the pasta of your choice?*

217

# Tomato-Meat Sauce

Per ½ cup: Calories 130; Protein 15 g;
Carbohydrate 5 g; Fat 6 g; Sodium 359 mg;
Cholesterol 41 mg.

*Double or triple the recipe so that you always have plenty of this all-time favorite on hand.*

- 2 tablespoons olive oil
- 1 medium-size yellow onion, finely chopped
- 1 pound lean ground beef round
- 2 cloves garlic, minced
- 1 can (28 ounces) plum tomatoes with their liquid, puréed, or 1 can (28 ounces) tomato purée
- 2 tablespoons minced basil or 2 teaspoons dried basil, crumbled
- ½ teaspoon salt
- ¼ teaspoon black pepper

1 Heat the olive oil in a medium-size flameproof casserole over moderate heat. Add the onion, and sauté, stirring occasionally, until soft — 5 minutes.

2 Stir in the ground beef, and sauté, stirring to break up the lumps, until browned — about 5 minutes. Stir in the garlic, tomatoes, basil, salt, and pepper. Bring the sauce to a simmer and reduce the heat to low. Cook, uncovered, stirring occasionally, for 1 hour or until the sauce is thick. Serve with pasta or use when making Classic Lasagne (page 163). Makes about 5 cups. For storing and serving later, see Classic Tomato Sauce (page 216), but allow an additional 10 to 15 minutes for reheating in a saucepan.

# Hot Cajun Sauce

Per ¼ cup: Calories 54 g; Protein 1 g;
Carbohydrate 3 g; Fat 4 g; Sodium 104 mg;
Cholesterol 0 mg.

*This is, indeed, a spicy sauce, but you can tone it down by omitting the jalapeño peppers. For a hotter sauce, increase the cayenne to ¾ teaspoon.*

- ¼ cup vegetable or corn oil
- ¼ cup plus 1 tablespoon all-purpose flour
- 1 medium-size yellow onion, chopped
- 1 small sweet green pepper, cored, seeded, and chopped
- 1 stalk celery, chopped
- ¼ teaspoon cayenne (ground red) pepper, or to taste
- ½ teaspoon each white and black pepper
- 2 bay leaves
- 3 jalapeño peppers or 1 can (4 ounces) jalapeños, drained, seeded, and minced (about ¼ cup)
- 2 cloves garlic, minced
- 3 cups Beef Stock (page 48) or canned beef broth

1 Heat the oil in a heavy medium-size saucepan over moderately low heat. Gradually whisk in the flour, forming a smooth paste. Cook, stirring constantly, until the mixture turns a light brown — about 3 minutes.

2 Remove from the heat and stir in the onion, green pepper, celery, and cayenne, white, and black pepper. Return to the stove, turn the heat to high, and cook, stirring constantly, for 3 minutes. Stir in the bay leaves, jalapeño peppers, and garlic, and cook, stirring constantly, 2 minutes longer.

3 In a separate medium-size saucepan, bring the beef stock to a rolling boil over moderately high heat. Add the flour and vegetable mixture by the spoonful, stirring until each addition is

dissolved. Return to a boil, reduce the heat to low, and simmer, uncovered, until the sauce is reduced to 3½ cups — about 15 minutes.

▽ At this point the sauce can be cooled to room temperature and stored. *Refrigerate* in a tightly covered container for up to 4 days. *Freeze* in a labeled, tightly covered, freezable container or 1-pint freezer bags for up to 3 months at 0° F.

4 Transfer to a sauceboat and serve on meatloaf, roast beef, or hamburgers. Makes about 3½ cups.

### Serving Later

See Serving Later instructions for Classic Tomato Sauce (page 216).

# Spicy Salsa

Per ¼ cup: Calories 9; Protein tr;
Carbohydrate 2 g; Fat tr; Sodium 125 mg;
Cholesterol 0 mg.

*If using canned jalapeño chilies, omit the vinegar from this recipe.*

- 4 large tomatoes, peeled, seeded, and finely chopped
- 2 jalapeño chilies or 2 canned jalapeño chilies, drained, seeded, and minced (about 1 tablespoon)
- 2 tablespoons minced cilantro (coriander leaves) or 2 tablespoons minced parsley plus ½ teaspoon dried cilantro
- 1 small red onion, minced
- 1 clove garlic, minced
- 1 teaspoon red wine vinegar or lemon juice
- 1 teaspoon salt

1 In a medium-size bowl, mix the tomatoes, chilies, cilantro, onion, garlic, vinegar, and salt. Refrigerate, tightly covered, for at least 2 hours. Will keep for up to 3 days.

2 One hour before serving, set the sauce out to come to room temperature. Serve as a condiment with Tex-Mex dishes, broiled meats, poultry, and seafood. Makes about 4 cups.

## Firecracker Barbecue Sauce

Per ¼ cup: Calories 275; Protein 1 g; Carbohydrate 29 g; Fat 18 g; Sodium 794 mg; Cholesterol 50 mg.

- ½  cup cider vinegar
- 1  cup water
- ¼  cup sugar
- 2  tablespoons prepared mild yellow mustard
- ¼  teaspoon salt
- 1  teaspoon black pepper
- ½  teaspoon paprika
- 1  medium-size yellow onion, thinly sliced
- 2  thick slices lemon
- ½  cup (1 stick) unsalted butter or margarine
- 1  cup ketchup
- ¼  cup Worcestershire sauce

1 In a small heavy saucepan, combine the vinegar, water, sugar, mustard, salt, pepper, paprika, onion, lemon, and butter and bring to a boil over moderately high heat. Reduce the heat to low and simmer, uncovered, stirring occasionally, for 20 minutes. Remove from the heat and stir in the ketchup and Worcestershire sauce.

▽ At this point the sauce can be cooled to room temperature and stored. *Refrigerate* in a tightly covered

*Fourth-of-July flavor anytime — Firecracker Barbecue Sauce*

container for up to 4 days. *Freeze* in a labeled, tightly covered, freezable container or a 1-pint freezer bag for up to 3 months at 0° F.

2 Use for basting grilled, broiled, or roasted meats or poultry. Makes about 1¼ cups.

### Serving Later

**From freezer:** Transfer to a small saucepan, cover, and warm over moderately low heat until thawed — 10 to 15 minutes. **To microwave:** See Classic Tomato Sauce (page 216).

219

*Piquant Sauce for Fish and Poultry, a dressy accompaniment for a simple meal*

# Garlic Mayonnaise

Per tablespoon: Calories 105; Protein tr;
Carbohydrate tr; Fat 11 g; Sodium 9 mg;
Cholesterol 11 mg.

*In France the garlic for* aïoli, *as this potent sauce is called, is pounded in a mortar, then blended by hand with the other ingredients. This modified version is done in an electric blender or food processor.*

    4   cloves garlic, minced
    1   large egg or 2 yolks (for
        thicker mayonnaise)
    1   tablespoon lemon juice
    2   teaspoons Dijon or spicy
        brown mustard
    ¼   teaspoon white pepper
    1¼  cups vegetable or olive oil

1 In an electric blender or food processor, blend the garlic, egg, lemon juice, mustard, and pepper for about 30 seconds. With the motor running, drizzle ¼ cup of the oil very slowly into

the mixture. Continue adding the remaining oil in a thin, steady stream. The mayonnaise will thicken as the oil is added.

▽ At this point the mayonnaise can be stored. *Refrigerate*, tightly covered, for up to 4 days.

2 This makes a wonderful dip for raw vegetables and a fine accompaniment for cold meats, fish, or hard-cooked eggs. Makes about 1½ cups.

*Tip: Should your mayonnaise curdle or separate, transfer it to a bowl or measuring cup. Put an egg yolk, 1 tablespoon of vinegar or lemon juice, and a teaspoon of mustard in the blender. With the motor running, drizzle the mayonnaise into the egg mixture and continue blending until the sauce is smooth.*

# Piquant Sauce for Fish and Poultry

Per ¼ cup: Calories 227; Protein 2 g;
Carbohydrate 1 g; Fat 24 g; Sodium 34 mg;
Cholesterol 109 mg.

    2   egg yolks
    1   teaspoon Dijon or spicy
        brown mustard
    2   anchovy fillets
    2   teaspoons lemon juice
    1   teaspoon white wine vinegar
        or lemon juice
    ½   cup olive oil
    ⅓   cup buttermilk
    2   teaspoons minced tarragon
        or ¼ teaspoon dried
        tarragon, crumbled
        Pinch white pepper

1 In an electric blender or food processor, blend the egg yolks, mustard, anchovies, lemon juice, and vinegar until smooth — about 30 seconds. With the motor running, add the oil drop by drop until the mixture begins

to thicken, then continue to add it in a very thin stream. Blend in the buttermilk, tarragon, and pepper.

▽ At this point the sauce can be stored. *Refrigerate*, tightly covered, for up to 5 days.

2 Transfer to a sauceboat and serve with grilled poultry or fish. This sauce is also good in tuna salad or on meat sandwiches. Makes 1¼ cups.

# Basic White Sauce

Per ¼ cup: Calories 102; Protein 3 g; Carbohydrate 6 g; Fat 8 g; Sodium 153 mg; Cholesterol 24 mg.

*The possibilities for varying this sauce are almost endless. A few suggestions: Add ½ teaspoon curry powder, 1 teaspoon dried herbs, 2 teaspoons Dijon or spicy brown mustard, or ¼ cup grated Parmesan, shredded Swiss, or crumbled Blue Cheese to 1 cup of thickened sauce. You can also substitute chicken broth or clam juice for the milk.*

    2  slices (½ inch thick) White
       Sauce Mix (page 17)
    1  cup milk

1 In a small saucepan, thaw the sauce-mix slices over moderately low heat and cook, stirring, until smooth and bubbly — about 2 minutes. Gradually blend in the milk and bring to a boil, stirring constantly. Cook until thickened and smooth — 2 to 3 minutes longer. For a thinner sauce, add more liquid. Makes 1 cup sauce.

## Mushroom Sauce

Per ¼ cup: Calories 87; Protein 2 g; Carbohydrate 4 g; Fat 7 g; Sodium 102 mg; Cholesterol 21 mg.

Proceed as for Basic White Sauce, adding to the thickened sauce 1 cup thinly sliced mushrooms, sautéed in 1 tablespoon unsalted butter or margarine until lightly browned — about 10 minutes. Makes about 1½ cups.

## Onion Sauce

Per ¼ cup: Calories 104; Protein 3 g; Carbohydrate 6 g; Fat 8 g; Sodium 181 mg; Cholesterol 24 mg.

Proceed as for Basic White Sauce, stirring into the thawed White Sauce Mix 2 tablespoons minced onion. Makes about 1 cup.

# Basic Brown Sauce

Per ¼ cup: Calories 51; Protein 2 g; Carbohydrate 3 g; Fat 3 g; Sodium 110 mg; Cholesterol 8 mg.

*The addition of 2 more tablespoons of Madeira, 2 teaspoons Dijon or spicy brown mustard, or 1 tablespoon minced fresh herbs, such as marjoram or parsley, per cup of thickened sauce are just three of the ways in which this classic can be varied.*

    3  tablespoons unsalted butter
       or margarine
    3  large shallots, minced (about
       ⅓ cup)
    4  ounces mushrooms,
       chopped
    3  tablespoons flour
    5  cups Beef Stock (page 48) or
       canned beef broth
   ⅓  cup dry Madeira or sherry
    1  tablespoon tomato paste
   ½  teaspoon dried thyme,
       crumbled
    8  whole peppercorns
   12  sprigs parsley
    1  bay leaf

1 Melt the butter in a large saucepan over moderate heat. Add the shallots and mushrooms, and sauté, stirring occasionally, until the shallots are soft — about 5 minutes. Blend in the flour, and cook, stirring, for 3 minutes or until thickened and smooth. Stir in the beef stock, Madeira, tomato paste, thyme, peppercorns, parsley, and bay leaf and bring to a boil, stirring constantly. Simmer, uncovered, over moderate heat for 25 to 30 minutes or until the sauce is reduced to 3 cups and lightly thickened. Strain.

▽ At this point the sauce can be cooled to room temperature and stored. *Refrigerate* in a tightly covered container for up to 1 week. *Freeze* in labeled, 1-pint freezer bags for up to 2 months at 0° F.

2 Serve with roasted, broiled, or grilled meats. This sauce, with additional Madeira, is especially good with Turkey Mushroom Loaf (page 92). Makes about 3 cups.

### Serving Later

**From refrigerator:** Heat in a small saucepan over low heat, stirring occasionally, until simmering — 5 to 7 minutes. **From freezer:** Heat in a small saucepan over moderately low heat, stirring occasionally, until simmering — 15 to 20 minutes.

## Piquant Sauce for Meat

Per ¼ cup: Calories 56; Protein 2 g; Carbohydrate 4 g; Fat 3 g; Sodium 125 mg; Cholesterol 7 mg.

In a heavy medium-size saucepan, bring ⅓ cup each white wine and white wine vinegar and 2 large minced shallots to a boil over moderate heat. Cook, uncovered, until reduced to 2 tablespoons — 7 to 10 minutes. Add 3 cups Basic Brown Sauce, bring to a boil, and simmer, uncovered, for 5 minutes. Before serving, stir in 3 tablespoons chopped gherkin pickle and 1 tablespoon each minced parsley and chives. Serve with pork, beef, or veal. Makes about 3¼ cups.

# Pesto

Per ¼ cup: Calories 191; Protein 3 g; Carbohydrate 1 g; Fat 20 g; Sodium 369 mg; Cholesterol 5 mg.

*The Italians blend this sauce with hot pasta, but it can be used in myriad other ways: for example, to flavor soups, stews, baked potatoes, and salad dressings.*

    2   cups firmly packed basil
        leaves
    2   tablespoons chopped parsley
    2   cloves garlic
    ½   teaspoon salt
    ¼   teaspoon black pepper
    ⅓   cup olive oil
    ¼   cup grated Parmesan cheese

1 In an electric blender or food processor, chop the basil, parsley, and garlic — 10 to 15 seconds. Add the salt, pepper, and olive oil; blend until smooth — about 20 seconds.

▽ At this point the mixture can be stored. *Refrigerate* in a tightly covered jar for up to 5 days. *Freeze* in a labeled, 1-pint freezer bag or jar for up to 3 months at 0° F.

2 Stir in the Parmesan cheese. Makes about 1 cup, or enough sauce for 1 pound of pasta.

## Serving Later

**From refrigerator:** One hour before serving the pesto, set it out to come to room temperature. Proceed as in Step 2. **From freezer:** Let thaw overnight in the refrigerator. Proceed as in Step 2. Or transfer to a small covered saucepan and warm over low heat, stirring occasionally, until completely defrosted — 10 to 15 minutes. Stir in the cheese.

## Parsley Pesto

Per ¼ cup: Calories 199; Protein 3 g; Carbohydrate 3 g; Fat 20 g; Sodium 375 mg; Cholesterol 5 mg.

Proceed as for Pesto, substituting **2 cups parsley** for the basil. Use to garnish White Bean and Fresh Tomato Soup with Parsley Pesto (page 62) or serve over pasta, poached chicken, or grilled fish. Makes about 1 cup.

## Broccoli Pesto

Per ¼ cup: Calories 123; Protein 1 g; Carbohydrate 3 g; Fat 12 g; Sodium 333 mg; Cholesterol 0 mg.

Proceed as for Pesto, adding **2 cups cooked broccoli florets** and using only **½ cup basil** or **1 teaspoon dried basil**. Use **1 teaspoon salt** and omit the Parmesan. This bulky variation makes 1½ to 1¾ cups or enough sauce for 1 pound of pasta.

# Red Pepper Butter

Per teaspoon: Calories 21; Protein tr; Carbohydrate tr; Fat 2 g; Sodium 34 mg; Cholesterol 6 mg.

*Flavored butters are wonderful to have on hand — to add zest to simply prepared foods. The recipes below suggest a few possibilities. You can create your own combinations with your favorite herbs.*

    2   tablespoons lightly salted
        butter or margarine
    2   tablespoons finely chopped
        sweet red pepper
    2   tablespoons finely chopped
        yellow onion
    1   clove garlic, minced
    ¼   teaspoon dried rosemary,
        crumbled
    ¼   teaspoon black pepper
    ½   cup (1 stick) lightly salted
        butter or margarine, at room
        temperature

1 Melt the 2 tablespoons of butter in a small saucepan over moderate heat. Add the sweet red pepper, onion, and garlic; sauté until the vegetables are soft — about 5 minutes. Add the rosemary and black pepper. Remove from the heat and allow to cool to room temperature.

2 In a medium-size bowl, blend the red pepper mixture with the ½ cup butter using a wooden spoon. Transfer to a sheet of heavy-duty aluminum foil; roll the foil around the mixture, forming a log 8 inches long by ¾ inch in diameter. Tuck in the ends of the foil, label, and freeze. Will keep for up to 2 months at 0° F. Use to flavor rice and vegetables or to spread on bread. A ¼-inch slice equals 1 teaspoon; a ¾-inch slice equals 1 tablespoon.

# Dill Butter

Per teaspoon: Calories 26; Protein 0 g; Carbohydrate 0 g; Fat 3 g; Sodium 29 mg; Cholesterol 8 mg.

    ½   cup (1 stick) lightly salted
        butter or margarine, at room
        temperature
    ¼   cup minced dill or 1
        tablespoon dried dill weed
    1½  teaspoons lemon juice

1 In a medium-size bowl, cream the butter with a wooden spoon until light and fluffy. Add the dill and lemon juice and blend well.

2 Transfer to a sheet of heavy-duty aluminum foil; roll the foil around the butter mixture, forming a log 8 inches long by ¾ inch in diameter. Tuck in the ends of the foil, label, and freeze. Will keep for up to 3 months at 0° F. Use to flavor potatoes and other cooked vegetables, rice, or fish. A ¼-inch slice equals 1 teaspoon; a ¾-inch slice equals 1 tablespoon.

### Parsley Butter

Per teaspoon: Calories 26; Protein 0 g; Carbohydrate 0 g; Fat 3 g; Sodium 29 mg; Cholesterol 8 mg.

Proceed as for Dill Butter, substituting ¼ cup minced parsley for the dill. Use to flavor potatoes and other vegetables, rice, fish, soups, and sauces.

### Mint Butter

Per teaspoon: Calories 26; Protein 0 g; Carbohydrate 0 g; Fat 3 g; Sodium 29 mg; Cholesterol 8 mg.

Proceed as for Dill Butter, substituting ¼ cup chopped mint for the dill and omitting the lemon juice. Use to flavor cooked vegetables and rice.

### Garlic Butter

Per teaspoon: Calories 26; Protein 0 g; Carbohydrate 0 g; Fat 3 g; Sodium 29 mg; Cholesterol 8 mg.

Proceed as for Dill Butter, substituting **2 cloves crushed garlic** for the dill and omitting the lemon juice. Use to flavor potatoes and other cooked vegetables, rice, pasta, and pasta sauces.

### Lemon Butter

Per teaspoon: Calories 26; Protein 0 g; Carbohydrate 0 g; Fat 3 g; Sodium 29 mg; Cholesterol 8 mg.

Proceed as for Dill Butter, omitting the dill, using **2 tablespoons lemon juice**, and adding **2 teaspoons grated lemon rind**. Serve with broiled fish or warm asparagus or artichokes, or spread on Simple Muffins (page 230).

*Red Pepper Butter and other flavored butters can be served in any number of attractive ways.*

# Gingered Pear Marmalade

Per tablespoon: Calories 40; Protein 0 g; Carbohydrate 10 g; Fat 0 g; Sodium 0 mg; Cholesterol 0 mg.

*Ginger gives this marmalade its zip. You could use up to 8 ounces.*

- 4 ounces preserved ginger in syrup, or to taste
- 4 pounds hard unripe pears, such as Kieffer or Seckel, peeled, cored, and diced
- 5½ cups sugar
- ½ cup lemon juice

1 Remove the ginger from the syrup and cut into small even cubes. Return to the syrup and set aside. In a large, heavy, enamel or stainless steel pan, combine the pears, sugar, and lemon juice. Bring to a boil over moderate heat and cook, stirring, until the sugar dissolves — about 5 minutes.

2 Add the ginger and syrup to the pears and return to a boil. Reduce the heat to low and simmer, uncovered, stirring occasionally, for 2 to 2½ hours — until a candy thermometer reads 220° F. Or test by scooping a small amount onto a metal spoon, then letting it slide back into the pan. When droplets merge and fall as one drop, the syrup has reached 220° F.

3 About 15 minutes before the pears are done, wash and sterilize 4 pint jars, their dome lids, and screw bands by boiling them in a kettle of water for at least 10 minutes. As soon as the marmalade is ready, remove one jar at a time from the water, using jar grippers, and fill it, leaving ¼ inch of head space. Wipe the rims clean with a damp clean cloth and seal.

*Sublime — Gingered Pear Marmalade, Heavenly Lemon Marmalade, and Fabulous Spiced Grapes*

4 When all jars are filled, process them in a boiling water bath (212° F), with the water at least 1 inch above the jar tops, for 10 minutes. (Add 1 minute for each 1,000 feet above sea level.) Using a jar gripper, lift the jars straight up out of the bath. Tipping the contents can ruin the seal.

5 After 24 hours, check the seals by tapping the dome lids lightly. If properly sealed, they will give off a clear metallic ping. Unsealed jars will thud. The lids should also be slightly depressed and completely rigid. If in doubt, remove the screw bands, roll the contents around the neck of the jar, and check for leakage. Reprocess any jars with imperfect seals. Label and store in a cool dry place. The marmalade will keep for up to 1 year. Refrigerate after opening.

6 Or cool to room temperature and freeze in labeled, tightly covered, freezable containers, leaving 1 inch of head space. Will keep for up to 6 months at 0° F. Or cool to room temperature, spoon into jars, cover tightly, and refrigerate for up to 1 month. Serve as an accompaniment to lamb or pork, on crackers with cream cheese, or on toast. Makes 2 quarts.

# Heavenly Lemon Marmalade

Per tablespoon: Calories 19; Protein 0 g; Carbohydrate 5 g; Fat 0 g; Sodium 0 mg; Cholesterol 0 mg.

*This sweet yet tart preserve pleases almost every palate and makes a wonderful Christmas gift.*

- 4 medium-size lemons
- 2 cups sugar

1 Peel the zest (colored part of the rind) from the lemons and cut into slivers. In a heavy, medium-size, enamel or stainless steel saucepan, cover the zest with water and bring to a boil over high heat. Reduce the heat to low; simmer, uncovered, for 10 minutes. Drain and set aside.

2 Meanwhile, scrape the pith (white part of the rind) from the lemons and discard it. Chop the pulp coarsely, transfer to a pint measuring cup, and add enough water to make 2 cups. Add the pulp to the drained zest and bring to a boil over high heat. Reduce the heat to low, cover, and simmer for 15 minutes, stirring occasionally.

3 Add the sugar, stirring constantly until it dissolves. Raise the heat to moderately low and return the mixture to a slow boil. Cook, uncovered, stirring occasionally, for 30 to 40 minutes — until the temperature on a candy thermometer reaches 220° F. Or test by scooping a small amount onto a metal spoon, then letting it slide back into the pan. When two or more droplets merge and fall as one drop, the syrup has reached 220° F. Remove from the heat and skim off any foam.

4 Ladle into 5 hot, sterilized, ½-pint preserving jars (see Step 3, Gingered Pear Marmalade, opposite page), leaving ½ inch of head space. Wipe the jar rims clean, seal, and process in a boiling water bath for 10 minutes (see Steps 4 and 5, Gingered Pear Marmalade). Label and store in a cool dry place. Will keep for up to 1 year. Refrigerate after opening.

5 Or cool to room temperature and freeze in labeled, tightly covered, ½-pint freezable containers, leaving 1 inch of head space. Will keep at 0° F for 6 months. Or cool to room temperature and refrigerate, tightly covered, for up to 1 month. Serve on buttered English muffins or toast or with banana fritters. Makes 2½ pints.

# Fabulous Spiced Grapes

Per tablespoon: Calories 36; Protein 0 g; Carbohydrate 10 g; Fat 0 g; Sodium 0 mg; Cholesterol 0 mg.

*This spicy-sweet condiment makes a wonderful holiday treat with roasted meats or poultry.*

- 5 pounds small, underripe, thin-skinned seedless grapes, stemmed and halved
- 6 cups sugar
- 1 cup cider vinegar
- ½ cup water
- 2 thin slices lemon, seeded
- 1 cinnamon stick (about 2½ inches)
- 1 tablespoon whole cloves

1 In a large, heavy, enamel or stainless steel pan, bring the grapes, sugar, vinegar, water, lemon slices, and spices to a boil over moderately high heat. Reduce the heat to low, cover, and simmer until the grapes have turned a deep amber — about 1½ hours. (To test doneness, place a spoonful on a plate and let cool; the syrup should be thick.)

2 Ladle the grapes and syrup into hot, sterilized, pint preserving jars (see Step 3, Gingered Pear Marmalade, page 224), leaving ¼ inch of head space. Wipe the jar rims clean, seal, and process in a boiling water bath for 10 minutes (see Steps 4 and 5, Gingered Pear Marmalade). Label and store in a cool dry place. Will keep for up to 1 year. Refrigerate after opening.

3 Or cool to room temperature and freeze in labeled, tightly covered, 1-pint freezable containers, leaving 1 inch of head space. Will keep for up to 1 year at 0° F. Or cool to room temperature and refrigerate in tightly covered jars for up to 6 weeks. Serve as an accompaniment to chicken, game birds, or ham. Makes about 5 pints.

## Four-Fruit Chutney

Per tablespoon: Calories 17; Protein 0 g; Carbohydrate 5 g; Fat 0 g; Sodium 47 mg; Cholesterol 0 mg.

*For this sweet but slightly hot condiment, you can adjust the texture to your taste by cutting the fruit in larger or smaller pieces.*

- 4 cups cider vinegar
- 1½ cups water
- 1 large yellow onion, coarsely chopped
- 2 medium-size sweet red peppers, cored, seeded, and coarsely chopped
- 3 cloves garlic, minced
- 2 tablespoons salt
- 2 tablespoons finely grated orange zest (the colored part of the rind)
- 2 tablespoons each mustard seeds and ground ginger
- 1 teaspoon each cayenne (ground red) pepper and ground cinnamon
- 2 cups firmly packed light brown sugar
- 1 cup granulated sugar
- 2 pounds firm-ripe pears, cored, peeled, and quartered, sliced, or chopped
- 2 pounds firm-ripe freestone plums or prune plums, pitted and quartered or chopped
- 2 cups blueberries, picked over
- 1 cup golden raisins

1 In a large, heavy, enamel or stainless steel saucepan, bring the vinegar, water, onion, sweet red peppers, garlic, salt, orange zest, mustard seeds, ginger, cayenne, and cinnamon to a boil over high heat. Reduce the heat to low; simmer, uncovered, for 15 minutes or until the onion is translucent.

2 Stir in the sugars, pears, and plums, increase the heat to high, and return to a boil. Then reduce the heat to low and simmer, uncovered, stirring occasionally, for 50 to 60 minutes or until slightly thickened.

3 Add the blueberries and raisins to the chutney and simmer, uncovered, stirring occasionally, for 15 minutes more or until it has reached the desired thickness. Ladle the chutney into 4 hot, sterilized, pint preserving jars (see Step 3, Gingered Pear Marmalade, page 224), leaving ¼ inch of head space. Wipe the jar rims clean, seal, and process in a boiling water bath for 10 minutes (see Steps 4 and 5, Gingered Pear Marmalade). Label and store in a cool dry place. Let the chutney mellow for at least 3 weeks before serving. Will keep for up to 1 year. Refrigerate after opening.

4 The chutney can also be cooled to room temperature and stored in the refrigerator, tightly covered, for up to 6 weeks. Serve as an accompaniment to meats, poultry, game, or curried dishes. Makes 4 pints.

## Tangy Apple Chutney

Per tablespoon: Calories 35; Protein 0 g; Carbohydrate 10 g; Fat 0 g; Sodium 47 mg; Cholesterol 0 mg.

- 5 medium-size greening, Granny Smith, or other tart apples, cored and coarsely chopped (about 2 pounds or 2 quarts chopped)
- 2 medium-size sweet green or red peppers, cored, seeded, and coarsely chopped
- 3 medium-size yellow onions, coarsely chopped
- 1¼ cups dried currants or dark raisins
- 1½ cups cider vinegar
- 1 cup honey
- ¾ cup orange juice
  Juice of 2 medium-size lemons
  Grated rind of 1 lemon
- 1½ teaspoons salt
- 1 teaspoon ground ginger
- ¼ teaspoon cayenne (ground red) pepper

- 1 clove garlic, cut in half
- 1 cinnamon stick, broken into several pieces
- 1 teaspoon whole cloves

1 In a large, heavy, enamel or stainless steel saucepan, mix the apples, sweet peppers, onions, currants, vinegar, honey, orange juice, lemon juice, lemon rind, salt, ginger, and cayenne pepper. Tie the garlic, cinnamon, and cloves in a cheesecloth bag and add to the other ingredients. Bring to a boil over high heat. Reduce the heat to low and simmer, uncovered, stirring occasionally, until the volume is reduced by half and the mixture is thick and glossy — about 2½ hours. Remove and discard the cheesecloth bag.

2 Ladle the chutney into 2 hot, sterilized, pint preserving jars (see Step 3, Gingered Pear Marmalade, page 224), leaving ¼ inch of head space. Wipe the jar rims clean, seal, and process in a boiling water bath for 10 minutes (see Steps 4 and 5, Gingered Pear Marmalade). Label and store in a cool dry place for several weeks before using. Will keep for up to 1 year. Refrigerate after opening.

3 The chutney can also be cooled to room temperature and refrigerated, tightly covered, for up to 6 weeks. Serve with roast pork, poultry, or curried dishes. Makes 1 quart.

## Sweet and Crunchy Watermelon Pickles

Per pickle: Calories 6; Protein 0 g; Carbohydrate 2 g; Fat 0 g; Sodium 4 mg; Cholesterol 0 mg.

- 8 pounds thick-rinded watermelon
- 6 tablespoons kosher salt or 3 tablespoons pickling or non-iodized table salt

*Tickling to the taste buds — Four-Fruit Chutney, Tangy Apple Chutney, and Sweet and Crunchy Watermelon Pickles*

6   quarts plus ½ cup water
4   cups sugar
2   cups white vinegar
24  whole cloves
2   cinnamon sticks
1   lemon, sliced

1 Scoop out the watermelon flesh, leaving a ⅜-inch strip of fruit attached to the rind. Slice the rind into 1-inch-wide strips, then peel off and discard the skin. Cut into 1-inch cubes.

2 In a large bowl, combine the salt, 2 quarts of the water, and the rind; soak for 24 hours. Drain and rinse.

3 In an enamel or stainless steel kettle or stockpot, bring 4 quarts of the remaining water to a boil over moderately high heat. Add the rind, return to a boil, and cook, uncovered, until the pieces are tender when pierced with a fork — 10 to 12 minutes. Drain well and return to the pot.

4 Meanwhile, in a large enamel or stainless steel saucepan, bring the sugar, vinegar, the remaining ½ cup of water, the cloves, cinnamon, and lemon to a boil over moderately high heat. Cook, uncovered, for 5 minutes; remove from the heat and let stand for 15 minutes. Using a slotted spoon, remove the spices and lemon and discard. Add the syrup to the rind, bring to a boil over moderate heat, and boil, uncovered, until the rind is translucent — 25 to 30 minutes.

5 Pack into 4 hot, sterilized, half-pint preserving jars (see Step 3, Gingered Pear Marmalade, page 224), leaving ½ inch of head space. Wipe the jar rims clean, seal, and process in a boiling water bath for 5 minutes (see Steps 4 and 5, Gingered Pear Marmalade). Label and store in a cool dry place. Will keep for up to 1 year. Refrigerate after opening. Serve with sandwiches or macaroni, potato, tuna, or chicken salad. Makes 2 pints.

# Old-Fashioned Hamburger Relish

Per tablespoon: Calories 5; Protein 0 g; Carbohydrate 2 g; Fat 0 g; Sodium 62 mg; Cholesterol 0 mg.

- 2 medium-size cucumbers, peeled, seeded, and chopped (about 2 cups)
- 1 medium-size yellow onion, chopped
- 1 medium-size sweet green pepper, cored, seeded, and chopped
- 1 medium-size sweet red or yellow pepper, cored, seeded, and chopped
- 1 stalk celery, chopped
- 2 tablespoons kosher salt or 1 tablespoon pickling or non-iodized table salt
- 1/2 teaspoon turmeric
- 3 cups cold water
- 1 cinnamon stick
- 12 whole cloves
- 1/4 teaspoon ground allspice (optional)
- 2 cups cider vinegar
- 4 medium-size ripe tomatoes, peeled, seeded, and chopped (about 2 cups)
- 1 cup sugar
- 2 teaspoons mustard seeds

1 In a large enamel or stainless steel bowl, mix the cucumbers, onion, peppers, celery, salt, turmeric, and water. Let stand for 12 hours or overnight, then drain in a strainer, lightly pressing out any excess liquid. Set aside.

2 Tie up the cinnamon, cloves, and allspice in a piece of cheesecloth. In a large, heavy, enamel or stainless steel saucepan, bring the spices and vinegar to a boil over moderate heat. Reduce the heat to low and simmer, uncovered, for 15 minutes.

3 Add the tomatoes, increase the heat to moderate, and bring the mixture to a boil. Reduce the heat to low and simmer, partially covered, until the tomatoes resemble a purée — about 30 minutes. Add the sugar and mustard seeds, cover, and let stand overnight at room temperature.

4 Add the drained vegetables to the tomato mixture and bring to a boil over moderately high heat. Then reduce the heat to low and simmer, uncovered, until most of the liquid has evaporated — 25 to 30 minutes. Remove the spice bag.

5 Ladle into 4 hot, sterilized, 1/2-pint preserving jars (see Step 3, Gingered Pear Marmalade, page 224), leaving 1/2 inch of head space. Wipe the jar rims clean, seal, and process in a boiling water bath for 10 minutes (see Steps 4 and 5, Gingered Pear Marmalade). Label, then let the relish mellow in a cool dry place for at least 3 weeks before using. Will keep for up to 1 year. Refrigerate after opening.

6 Or cool to room temperature and refrigerate, tightly covered, for up to 1 month. Serve with hamburgers and hot dogs. Makes 2 pints.

# Zucchini Relish

Per 1/4 cup: Calories 12; Protein 0 g; Carbohydrate 3 g; Fat 0 g; Sodium 7 mg; Cholesterol 0 mg.

- 4 large zucchini, cut into 3/8-inch cubes (about 2 pounds)
- 1 large yellow onion, quartered and sliced
- 1 tablespoon kosher salt or 1 1/2 teaspoons pickling or non-iodized table salt
- 1 small sweet red pepper, cored, seeded, and diced
- 1 cup cider vinegar
- 1 cup sugar
- 1/2 teaspoon each celery seeds and mustard seeds

1 In a large bowl, mix the zucchini and onion with the salt. Let stand for 1 hour, then drain.

2 In a large, heavy, enamel or stainless steel saucepan, mix the sweet red pepper, vinegar, sugar, celery seeds, and mustard seeds. Bring to a boil, uncovered, over moderately high heat. Stir in the zucchini and onions; return to a boil and cook for 1 minute. Remove from the heat.

3 Pack into 5 hot, sterilized, 1/2-pint preserving jars (see Step 3, Gingered Pear Marmalade, page 224), leaving 1/2 inch of head space. Wipe the jar rims clean, seal, and process in a boiling water bath for 10 minutes (see Steps 4 and 5, Gingered Pear Marmalade). Label; store in a cool dry place for up to 1 year. Refrigerate after opening.

4 Or cool to room temperature and refrigerate in tightly covered containers for up to 1 month. Serve with hamburgers or with potato or macaroni salad. Makes 2 1/2 pints.

*Welcome at any time of year — Zucchini Relish and Old-Fashioned Hamburger Relish*

# Breads

Homemade bread conveys a sense of caring. But for anyone with a busy schedule, this special touch to a meal may seem difficult if not impossible to achieve. Prepared in stages, however, many breads are relatively easy. The recipes on the following pages provide a variety of possibilities to suit any time frame.

First, there are biscuits, muffins, and other quick breads that can be put together in a thrice using Griddle Quick-Mix or Shortcut Biscuit Mix (page 16). With Angel Biscuits (page 238), Whole-Wheat Refrigerator Rolls, and Yeast Corn Rolls (page 240), you can prepare the dough when you have a few spare moments, store it in the refrigerator, and roll and cut out a batch a few days later.

Or make up Refrigerator White Bread (page 242) a day before guests are expected. Pop it in the oven shortly before they arrive so that the aroma greets them at the door. Brown-and-Serve Rolls (page 238) are another possibility. Partially baked, then frozen, they can be transferred from freezer to oven whenever you please — for freshly baked rolls in just minutes.

Fully baked breads are freezable, too (see Tip, page 233). Bake the loaves when the mood strikes and enjoy them when the moment is right.

# Feather-Light Pancakes

Per pancake: Calories 83; Protein 3 g; Carbohydrate 11 g; Fat 3 g; Sodium 126 mg; Cholesterol 52 mg.

*Separating the eggs is optional but does result in a lighter pancake.*

- 2 eggs, separated
- 2 tablespoons unsalted butter or margarine, melted
- ¾ cup water
- 1½ cups Griddle Quick Mix (page 16)

1 In a 1-quart measuring cup or small bowl, whisk the egg yolks, butter, and water. In a medium-size bowl, beat the egg whites until stiff but not dry.

2 Put the Griddle Quick Mix in a 2-quart measuring cup or large bowl and stir in the liquid ingredients until just blended; do not overmix. Gently fold in the egg whites.

3 Heat a well-oiled griddle or 12-inch skillet over moderate heat. When hot but not smoking, pour a scant ¼ cup of batter per pancake onto the griddle and cook until bubbles have formed across the top — about 2 minutes. Turn the pancakes and cook 2 minutes longer. Makes about 12 five-inch pancakes, or enough to serve 4.

# Golden Waffles

Per waffle: Calories 298; Protein 9 g; Carbohydrate 32 g; Fat 15 g; Sodium 380 mg; Cholesterol 172 mg.

- 3 eggs, separated
- 6 tablespoons (¾ stick) unsalted butter or margarine, melted
- 1¾ cups water or milk
- 2¼ cups Griddle Quick Mix (page 16)

1 Preheat the waffle iron. In a 1-quart measuring cup or small bowl, whisk the egg yolks with the butter and water. In a medium-size bowl, beat the egg whites until stiff but not dry.

2 Put the Griddle Quick Mix in a 2-quart measuring cup or large bowl and stir in the egg-yolk mixture until just blended; do not overmix. Gently fold in the egg whites.

3 Pour enough batter into the center of each waffle iron section to cover about ⅔ of the surface. (It will spread out to the edges as it cooks.) Close and bake until the waffles stop steaming — about 5 minutes.

4 Serve immediately with maple syrup or Heavenly Lemon Marmalade (page 225) or top with strawberries and whipped cream for a dessert. Makes 6 to 8 waffles.

# Simple Muffins

Per muffin: Calories 183; Protein 6 g; Carbohydrate 22 g; Fat 8 g; Sodium 254 mg; Cholesterol 88 mg.

*To vary these muffins, mix in 1 tablespoon dried herbs, such as parsley, chives, or dill; or ½ cup shredded Cheddar cheese; or ¼ cup chopped walnuts. If using walnuts, sprinkle 2 tablespoons sugar mixed with 1 teaspoon cinnamon over the muffins just before baking.*

- 2 eggs, lightly beaten
- ¼ cup (½ stick) unsalted butter or margarine, melted
- ¾ cup water
- 2 cups plus 1 tablespoon Griddle Quick Mix (page 16)

1 Preheat the oven to 400° F. In a 1-quart measuring cup or small bowl, whisk together the eggs, butter, and water. Put the Griddle Quick Mix in a large bowl and stir in the liquids until just blended; do not overmix.

2 Spoon into 8 greased, 2¼-inch muffin cups and bake until golden and a toothpick inserted in the center comes out clean — 10 to 12 minutes. Remove from the pan and cool on a wire rack. Makes 8 muffins.

# Onion-Sage Bread

Per ¾-inch slice: Calories 194; Protein 4 g; Carbohydrate 18 g; Fat 12 g; Sodium 178 mg; Cholesterol 25 mg.

*This bread is slightly sweet with a delicate crumb.*

- 2 tablespoons plus ½ cup olive oil
- 2 medium-size yellow onions, finely chopped
- 1 egg
- ⅔ cup water
- 2¼ cups Griddle Quick Mix (page 16)
- 1½ teaspoons dried sage, crumbled, or 1 teaspoon ground sage

1 Preheat the oven to 350° F. Heat the 2 tablespoons of olive oil in a 10-inch skillet over moderately low heat. Add the onions, and sauté until soft — about 5 minutes. Remove from the heat and cool to room temperature.

2 In a small bowl, whisk the remaining ½ cup olive oil with the egg and water. In a large bowl, stir together the Griddle Quick Mix and sage and make a well in the center. Add the onion and liquid ingredients and stir until just combined; do not overmix.

3 Pour the batter into a greased 9″ x 5″ x 3″ loaf pan. Bake, uncovered, for 30 minutes, then cover with foil and bake 20 minutes longer or until a toothpick inserted in the center comes out clean. Cool in the pan on a wire rack to room temperature. Turn out, slice, and serve. Makes 1 loaf.

# Shortcut Biscuits

Per biscuit: Calories 64; Protein 1 g;
Carbohydrate 8 g; Fat 3 g; Sodium 102 mg;
Cholesterol 3 mg.

- 1¾ cups Shortcut Biscuit Mix
  (page 16)
- ½ to ⅔ cup water
- 2 tablespoons milk

1 Preheat the oven to 450° F. Put the Shortcut Biscuit Mix in a large bowl, make a well in the center, and add ½ cup water. Mix gently, just enough for the dough to come together. If it seems too dry, add a little more water.

2 Transfer the dough to a lightly floured surface, roll out ½ inch thick, and cut into 2-inch rounds. Brush the biscuits with the milk and bake on an ungreased baking sheet until golden — 10 to 12 minutes. Serve immediately. Makes 8 biscuits.

## Herb Biscuit Variation

Per biscuit: Calories 64; Protein 1 g;
Carbohydrate 8 g; Fat 3 g; Sodium 102 mg;
Cholesterol 3 mg.

Proceed as in Shortcut Biscuits, adding to the biscuit mix 3 tablespoons

chopped basil, dill, parsley, or chives or 1 tablespoon dried basil or dill weed, crumbled, or any combination of herbs that you prefer.

## Ham-and-Cheese Biscuit Variation

Per biscuit: Calories 82; Protein 3 g;
Carbohydrate 8 g; Fat 4 g; Sodium 149 mg;
Cholesterol 7 mg.

Proceed as in Shortcut Biscuits, adding to the biscuit mix ½ cup shredded Cheddar or Swiss cheese, ¼ cup finely chopped ham, and ⅛ teaspoon cayenne (ground red) pepper.

## Shortcake Variation

Per shortcake: Calories 207; Protein 4 g;
Carbohydrate 29 g; Fat 8 g; Sodium 307 mg;
Cholesterol 9 mg.

Proceed as in Shortcut Biscuits, adding to the biscuit mix 2 tablespoons sugar, and substituting ½ cup milk or heavy cream for the water. Roll out ¾ inch thick and cut into 3-inch rounds, preferably with a fluted cutter. Brush with the 2 tablespoons milk, then sprinkle with 1 tablespoon sugar. Serve with sliced peaches or strawberries and whipped cream. Makes 6 shortcakes.

*For starters —
Feather-Light Pancakes
and Shortcut Biscuits*

# Sweet-Potato Muffins

Per muffin: Calories 245; Protein 5 g; Carbohydrate 31 g; Fat 11 g; Sodium 196 mg; Cholesterol 77 mg.

*These taste best when eaten fresh from the oven. Otherwise, rewarm them in a 350° F oven for about 5 minutes.*

- ¼ cup (½ stick) unsalted butter or margarine
- 3 tablespoons light brown sugar
- 1½ cups all-purpose flour
- 1 tablespoon baking powder
- ¼ teaspoon salt, or to taste
- 1 medium-size sweet potato or yam, boiled, peeled, and mashed (about 1 cup)
- 2 eggs, separated
- ¼ to ½ cup milk
- ½ cup coarsely chopped pecans
- 1 tablespoon granulated sugar mixed with ¼ teaspoon ground cinnamon

**1** Preheat the oven to 375° F. In a large bowl or 2-quart measuring cup, cream the butter and brown sugar until light and fluffy. Sift the flour, baking powder, and salt onto a sheet of wax paper.

**2** In a medium-size bowl, mix the sweet potato with the egg yolks and ¼ cup of the milk until smooth; stir in the pecans. In a small bowl, beat the egg whites until stiff but not dry.

**3** Alternately stir the flour and potato mixtures into the creamed butter until well combined. Add more milk if the mixture is very stiff and dry; fold in the egg whites.

**4** Fill nine 2¼-inch muffin cups three-quarters full with batter, then sprinkle with the cinnamon and sugar. Bake for 35 minutes or until a toothpick inserted in the center of a muffin comes out clean. Serve warm with butter or cream cheese. Makes 9 muffins.

# Pumpkin Muffins

Per muffin: Calories 156; Protein 4 g; Carbohydrate 22 g; Fat 6 g; Sodium 77 mg; Cholesterol 34 mg.

- 1¼ cups whole wheat flour
- ¼ cup each bran and wheat germ or ½ cup wheat germ
- ¼ cup coarsely chopped pecans
- 1 teaspoon baking soda
- ½ teaspoon ground cinnamon
- ¼ teaspoon ground nutmeg
- 1 cup puréed cooked pumpkin
- ¼ cup (½ stick) unsalted butter or margarine, melted
- ¼ cup honey
- ¼ cup orange juice
- 2 tablespoons molasses
- 1 egg

**1** Preheat the oven to 375° F. In a large bowl or 2-quart measuring cup, stir together the flour, bran, wheat germ, pecans, baking soda, cinnamon, and nutmeg until well mixed. Set aside.

**2** In a medium-size bowl, beat together the pumpkin, butter, honey, orange juice, molasses, and egg until well blended. Add all at once to the dry ingredients, stirring until just blended; do not overmix.

**3** Fill 12 lightly greased, 2¼-inch muffin cups three-quarters full with batter. Bake for about 20 minutes or until a toothpick inserted in the center of a muffin comes out clean.

**4** Cool the muffin tins on a wire rack for 5 minutes, then remove the muffins. Serve hot with butter, cream cheese, or preserves. See Tip (opposite page) for storing and serving later. Makes 1 dozen muffins.

# Carrot Wheat-Germ Muffins

Per muffin: Calories 192; Protein 4 g; Carbohydrate 23 g; Fat 9 g; Sodium 202 mg; Cholesterol 47 mg.

*Make a double batch of these nutritious gems and freeze the extras for future breakfasts or snack treats.*

- 1½ cups sifted all-purpose flour
- ¼ cup wheat germ
- 2 teaspoons baking powder
- ½ teaspoon salt
- ½ teaspoon ground ginger
- ½ cup coarsely chopped walnuts
- 2 eggs
- ¼ cup vegetable oil
- ½ cup light brown sugar
- ½ cup milk
- 1 cup finely grated carrot (about 4 medium-size carrots)

**1** Preheat the oven to 400° F. In a large bowl or 2-quart measuring cup, stir together the flour, wheat germ, baking powder, salt, ginger, and walnuts. Set aside.

**2** In a medium-size bowl, whisk together the eggs, oil, and sugar. Still whisking, add the milk and carrots. Add the liquid mixture to the dry ingredients and stir until just combined. Do not overmix.

**3** Fill 12 lightly greased, 2¼-inch muffin cups three-quarters full with batter. Bake until golden brown — about 20 minutes — or until a toothpick inserted in the middle of a muffin comes out clean. Serve hot with butter or honey. See Tip (opposite page) for storing and serving later. Makes 1 dozen muffins.

*Rivulets of butter explore the lively texture of Carrot Wheat-Germ Muffins.*

# Fig Bread

Per ½-inch slice: Calories 143; Protein 2 g;
Carbohydrate 26 g; Fat 4 g; Sodium 62 mg;
Cholesterol 40 mg.

- 1 cup apple juice
- ¼ cup (½ stick) unsalted butter
  or margarine
- ¼ teaspoon salt
- 1½ cups dried figs, stems
  removed
- 1¾ cups all-purpose flour
- ½ teaspoon baking powder
- ¼ teaspoon baking soda
- 2 eggs
- ⅓ cup sugar
- ½ teaspoon vanilla
- 1 teaspoon grated lemon or
  orange rind

1 In a small saucepan, heat the apple juice over moderately high heat just until boiling — about 3 minutes. Remove from the heat, add the butter, and stir until melted; then stir in the salt and figs. Cool to room temperature.

2 Preheat the oven to 350° F. In a large bowl, sift together the flour, baking powder, and baking soda. In a medium-size bowl, beat the eggs, sugar, and vanilla until well mixed; stir in the fig mixture and lemon rind. Add all to the dry ingredients and stir until just moistened. Do not overmix.

3 Spoon the batter into a greased, 8½" x 4" x 2½" loaf pan. Bake for about 1 hour or until a toothpick inserted in the center comes out clean. Let cool upright in the pan on a wire rack for at least 10 minutes. Remove and let cool completely. Makes 1 loaf.

*Tip: To store bread for more than a day after baking, wrap it snugly in aluminum foil or seal it in 2 plastic bags. If the weather is cool and dry, yeast bread will keep at room temperature for 4 to 5 days, quick bread (made with baking powder) for 2 to 3 days. Refrigerating bread is preferable in hot and humid weather (which encourages mildew), though the texture will be coarsened slightly. Most yeast breads will keep in the refrigerator for up to 2 weeks, quick breads for up to 1 week. When frozen, both yeast and quick breads retain their original texture and freshness for up to 3 months at 0° F. For convenience, slice yeast bread before freezing; you can then remove a slice or two at a time. To defrost frozen bread, leave it at room temperature for a couple of hours. Or defrost in a microwave oven according to the manufacturer's directions — usually for 1 to 4 minutes. Or wrap in aluminum foil and warm in a preheated 400° F oven for 15 to 25 minutes. Whatever the storage method, rewarm bread to restore freshness.*

# Apricot-Almond Bread

Per ¾-inch slice: Calories 280; Protein 5 g;
Carbohydrate 40 g; Fat 12 g; Sodium 227 mg;
Cholesterol 43 mg.

1½ cups sifted all-purpose flour
1 cup unsifted whole-wheat flour
1 tablespoon baking powder
¾ teaspoon salt
½ cup coarsely chopped toasted almonds (about 2 ounces)
1½ cups dried apricots, thinly sliced
½ cup orange juice
½ cup firmly packed light brown sugar
⅓ cup (⅔ stick) unsalted butter or margarine
1 egg, beaten
¾ cup sour cream or buttermilk

1 Preheat the oven to 350° F. In a large bowl, mix the flours, baking powder, salt, and almonds. Set aside.

2 In a medium-size saucepan, bring the apricots and orange juice to a boil over high heat — 3 to 5 minutes. Reduce the heat to low and cook, uncovered, for about 6 minutes. The apricot slices will partially disintegrate. Remove from the heat and stir in the sugar and butter. Allow to cool to room temperature, then add the egg and sour cream, beating until smooth.

3 Add the liquids to the dry ingredients all at once and stir lightly with a fork just until the liquid is absorbed. Do not overmix. Spoon into a greased and floured, 9" x 5" x 3" loaf pan.

4 Bake for 40 minutes or until a toothpick inserted in the center of the bread comes out clean. Let cool upright in the pan on a wire rack for 10 minutes, then turn out onto the rack and cool completely. Wrap tightly in aluminum foil and store at room temperature overnight. Serve plain or with cream cheese. See Tip (page 233) for storing and serving later.

*Oven-fresh and delectable: (clockwise from bottom left) Apricot-Almond Bread, Light Zucchini Bread (page 236), Boston Bran Bread (page 236), Sage Corn Bread (page 236), and Cheddar-Walnut-Cranberry Bread*

# Apple-Walnut Sour-Cream Bread

Per ¾-inch slice: Calories 263; Protein 4 g;
Carbohydrate 21 g; Fat 18 g; Sodium 205 mg;
Cholesterol 75 mg.

- 1 cup all-purpose flour
- 1 teaspoon each baking powder and baking soda
- 1 teaspoon ground cardamom
- ½ teaspoon salt
- ½ cup (1 stick) unsalted butter or margarine, softened
- ½ cup firmly packed light brown sugar
- 2 eggs
- 1 teaspoon vanilla
- 1 cup sour cream
- 1 medium-size apple, cored and coarsely chopped (about 1½ cups)
- 1 cup coarsely chopped walnuts (about 4 ounces shelled)

1 Preheat the oven to 350° F. In a small bowl, sift together the flour, baking powder, baking soda, cardamom, and salt. Set aside.

2 In a large bowl, cream the butter and sugar until fluffy. Add the eggs and vanilla, beating until smooth.

3 Alternately fold the dry ingredients and sour cream into the creamed mixture until just combined. Do not overmix; the batter should be somewhat thick and lumpy. Fold in the apple and walnuts. Spread in a greased and floured, 9" x 5" x 3" loaf pan and smooth the top.

4 Bake for 1 hour or until a toothpick inserted in the center of the bread comes out clean. Let cool upright in the pan for 10 minutes; turn out on a wire rack and cool completely. Wrap tightly in aluminum foil and store at room temperature overnight. Serve either plain or with cream cheese. See Tip (page 233) for storing and serving later. Makes 1 loaf.

# Orange-Oat Bread

Per ¾-inch slice: Calories 216; Protein 4 g;
Carbohydrate 47 g; Fat 2 g; Sodium 183 mg;
Cholesterol 26 mg.

- Grated rind of 2 oranges (about ¼ cup)
- 1 cup orange juice
- 1¼ cups sugar
- 1 cup milk
- 1 egg, beaten lightly
- 2 cups all-purpose flour
- 1 cup rolled oats
- 1 tablespoon baking powder
- ½ teaspoon salt

1 Preheat the oven to 350° F. In a medium-size saucepan, bring the rind and juice to a boil over moderately high heat. Reduce the heat to moderately low and simmer, uncovered, for about 5 minutes. Add the sugar, stirring until dissolved. Increase the heat to moderately high, bring the mixture to a boil, and cook, stirring occasionally, until syrup threads form on the tip of the spoon when lifted — 5 to 7 minutes. Remove from the heat and let cool to room temperature.

2 Whisk the milk and egg into the syrup until well blended. Combine the flour, rolled oats, baking powder, and salt in a large bowl. Add the liquid and stir until the batter is just combined. Do not overmix.

3 Pour the batter into a buttered and floured, 9" x 5" x 3" loaf pan; bake for 55 to 60 minutes or until a toothpick inserted in the center comes out clean. Let cool upright in the pan for 10 minutes; turn out onto a wire rack to cool completely. This bread is especially good with cream cheese. See Tip (page 233) for storing and serving later. Makes 1 loaf.

# Cheddar-Walnut-Cranberry Bread

Per ¾-inch slice: Calories 379; Protein 9 g;
Carbohydrate 48 g; Fat 18 g; Sodium 267 mg;
Cholesterol 61 mg.

- 3 cups sifted all-purpose flour
- 1⅓ cups sugar
- 2¼ teaspoons baking powder
- 1½ teaspoons baking soda
- Grated rind of 1 orange (about 2 tablespoons)
- Grated rind of 1 lemon (about 2 teaspoons)
- ⅓ cup cold vegetable shortening
- Juice of 1 orange and 1 lemon plus enough water to make 1⅛ cups
- 1½ cups shredded sharp Cheddar cheese (about 6 ounces)
- 2 eggs, lightly beaten
- 1½ cups fresh or frozen raw cranberries, coarsely chopped
- 1 cup coarsely chopped walnuts (about 4 ounces shelled)

1 Preheat the oven to 350° F. In a large bowl, sift together the flour, sugar, baking powder, and baking soda. Stir in the orange and lemon rinds. Cut the shortening in with a pastry blender or two knives until the mixture resembles a coarse meal.

2 In a medium-size bowl, stir together the mixed juices, cheese, and eggs. Add to the flour mixture, stirring until just combined; do not overmix. Fold in the cranberries and walnuts.

3 Pour the batter into a buttered and floured, 9¼" x 5¼" x 3" loaf pan; bake for 1¼ hours or until a toothpick inserted in the center comes out clean. Let cool upright in the pan for 10 minutes; turn out onto a wire rack to cool completely. Serve warm with butter or cream cheese. See Tip (page 233) for storing and serving later.

# Light Zucchini Bread

Per ¾-inch slice: Calories 316; Protein 6 g;
Carbohydrate 44 g; Fat 13 g; Sodium 266 mg;
Cholesterol 69 mg.

- 3 cups sifted all-purpose flour
- 2 teaspoons baking powder
- 1 teaspoon baking soda
- ¾ teaspoon salt
- ½ teaspoon ground cinnamon
- ¼ teaspoon ground ginger
- ½ cup finely chopped walnuts
- 3 eggs
- ½ cup vegetable oil
- 1¼ cups sugar
- 3 medium-size zucchini, shredded (about 2 cups)
- 1 teaspoon grated lemon rind
- 1 tablespoon lemon juice
- 1 teaspoon vanilla

1 Preheat the oven to 350° F. Mix together the dry ingredients in a large bowl and set aside.

2 In a medium-size bowl, beat the eggs until frothy. Add the oil in a thin stream, beating until well blended — about 2 minutes. Add the sugar and beat 2 minutes longer or until the mixture is light in color. Add the zucchini, lemon rind, lemon juice, and vanilla. Stir until well combined.

3 Add the zucchini mixture to the dry ingredients, stirring until just moistened; do not overmix. Spoon into a lightly greased and floured, 9″ x 5″ x 3″ loaf pan. Bake for 1¼ hours or until a toothpick inserted in the center of the bread comes out clean. Cool upright in the pan for 10 minutes; turn out onto a wire rack and cool completely. See Tip (page 233) for storing and serving later. Makes 1 loaf.

# Sage Corn Bread

Per square: Calories 198; Protein 5 g;
Carbohydrate 29 g; Fat 6 g; Sodium 331 mg;
Cholesterol 81 mg.

- 1 cup all-purpose flour
- 1 cup cornmeal
- 1½ teaspoons baking powder
- ½ teaspoon baking soda
- ½ teaspoon salt
- 2 tablespoons minced sage or 1½ teaspoons dried sage, crumbled, or 1 teaspoon ground sage
- 2 tablespoons brown sugar
- 2 eggs
- 1 cup buttermilk
- 3 tablespoons butter, melted

1 Preheat the oven to 425° F. Sift the flour, cornmeal, baking powder, baking soda, and salt into a large bowl. Stir in the sage and brown sugar.

2 In a small bowl, beat the eggs, buttermilk, and butter together. Stir the liquids into the dry ingredients until just moistened. Do not overmix.

3 Pour the batter into a lightly buttered, 8″ x 8″ x 2″ pan and bake for 25 to 30 minutes or until the top is golden and a toothpick inserted into the center of the bread comes out clean. Cut into 9 squares. Serve warm.

# Boston Bran Bread

Per ½-inch slice: Calories 146; Protein 4 g;
Carbohydrate 32 g; Fat 1 g; Sodium 206 mg;
Cholesterol 1 mg.

- 2 cups whole wheat flour
- 1 cup all-purpose flour
- ½ cup wheat germ
- 1 teaspoon salt
- ½ cup raisins
- 1½ teaspoons baking soda
- 1¾ cups buttermilk
- ½ cup molasses
- ½ cup firmly packed light brown sugar

1 Preheat the oven to 350° F. Mix the flours, wheat germ, salt, and raisins in a large bowl and set aside.

2 In a medium-size bowl, stir together the baking soda and ¼ cup of the buttermilk. Stir in the remaining buttermilk, the molasses, and brown sugar. Add the liquids to the dry ingredients, stirring until just combined; do not overmix. Spoon into a lightly greased, 9″ x 5″ x 3″ loaf pan.

3 Bake for 1¼ hours or until a toothpick inserted in the center of the bread comes out clean. Loosen the loaf and turn out onto a wire rack; let cool completely. Cut in thin slices and serve with butter or cream cheese. This bread is tasty with baked beans. See Tip (page 233) for storing and serving later. Makes 1 loaf.

# Basic French Crêpes

Per crêpe: Calories 72; Protein 3 g;
Carbohydrate 6 g; Fat 4 g; Sodium 66 mg;
Cholesterol 76 mg.

- 3 eggs
- ¾ cup milk
- 2 tablespoons cold water
- 2 tablespoons unsalted butter or margarine, melted
- ¼ teaspoon salt
- ¾ cup all-purpose flour

1 In a small bowl, beat the eggs, milk, water, butter, and salt until well combined — about 20 seconds. Sift the flour into a medium-size bowl or a 2-quart measuring cup, then add the liquid mixture, beating until well combined — about 1 minute. Or blend the first 5 ingredients in an electric blender or food processor for 15 seconds; sprinkle in the flour and blend until smooth — about 30 seconds. Cover loosely with plastic wrap; let stand for at least 1 hour refrigerated or at room temperature. (The flour will swell to make a softer batter.) Will keep, refrigerated, for up to 4 hours.

*As versatile as they are appealing — Basic French Crêpes*

2 Brush butter on the bottom of a crêpe pan or heavy 7-inch skillet. Set over moderate heat for about 30 seconds or until a drop of batter sizzles. Stir the batter well, pour 2 tablespoonfuls into the skillet, and quickly tip it back and forth so that the batter evenly coats the bottom. Cook until the crêpe edges are golden brown — about 1 minute. Slide a spatula under the crêpe, flip it over, and cook for about 30 seconds. Transfer to a warm plate. Repeat with the remaining batter, re-buttering the skillet when necessary.

▽ At this point the crêpes can be cooled to room temperature, separated by sheets of wax paper, and stored. *Refrigerate*, wrapped tightly with plastic wrap, for up to 24 hours. *Freeze*, wrapped with aluminum foil and labeled, for up to 1 month at 0° F.

3 Serve with your own favorite crêpe filling or use for Crêpes Florentine (page 148) or Cheesy Chicken and Mushroom Crêpes (page 149). Makes 1 dozen 7-inch crêpes.

## Whole Wheat Crêpes

Per crêpe: Calories 56; Protein 2 g; Carbohydrate 3 g; Fat 4 g; Sodium 24 mg; Cholesterol 75 mg.

Proceed as in Basic French Crêpes, using ⅔ **cup milk**, omitting the cold water and salt, and substituting ⅓ **cup whole wheat flour** for the all-purpose flour. Use for Asparagus-Cheese-Filled Crêpes (page 150).

## Dessert Crêpes

Per crêpe: Calories 79; Protein 3 g; Carbohydrate 8 g; Fat 4 g; Sodium 66 mg; Cholesterol 76 mg.

Proceed as for Basic French Crêpes, adding **2 tablespoons sugar** to the batter. Use for Cinnamon Crêpes with Caramel Sauce and Pecans (page 250) or Walnut Crêpes with Mocha Sauce (page 250).

237

# Angel Biscuits

Per biscuit: Calories 149; Protein 3 g; Carbohydrate 20 g; Fat 6 g; Sodium 115 mg; Cholesterol 16 mg.

*You can enjoy homemade biscuits every night of the week with a batch of this handy dough in the refrigerator.*

- 1 envelope active dry yeast
- 3 tablespoons lukewarm water (see Tip, at right)
- 6½ to 7 cups all-purpose flour
- ¼ cup sugar
- 1 teaspoon each baking powder and baking soda
- 1 teaspoon salt
- 1 cup unsalted butter or margarine (2 sticks) or vegetable shortening
- 2 cups buttermilk

1 In a large bowl, an electric mixer fitted with a dough hook, or a food processor, sprinkle the yeast over the water, stir, and let stand for 5 minutes. Stir until dissolved.

2 In a large bowl, sift together 6 cups of the flour, the sugar, baking powder, baking soda, and salt. With a pastry blender or 2 knives, cut in the butter until the mixture resembles a coarse meal.

3 Stir the buttermilk into the yeast, then add the flour mixture and mix well. On a lightly floured board or in the mixer or food processor, knead the dough until it is smooth and elastic — about 5 minutes by hand, 2½ minutes in the mixer, or no more than 45 seconds (see Tip, page 243) in the processor. Add more flour as needed to keep the dough from sticking (see Tip, page 245). Transfer to a large, lightly greased bowl, cover, and refrigerate for at least 8 hours and up to 1 week.

4 Preheat the oven to 425° F. Divide the dough in half and roll out each half to a ¾-inch thickness. Using a floured, 2½-inch, round cutter, cut out the biscuits. Place on a lightly greased baking sheet and bake until lightly browned — 10 to 15 minutes. For storing and serving later, see Tip (page 233). Makes 32 biscuits.

*Tip: Active dry yeast needs lukewarm liquid (between 105° and 115° F) in which to dissolve. You can test it with a candy thermometer or by placing a drop on the inside of your wrist. Like baby formula, it should feel slightly warm but not hot.*

# Brown-and-Serve Dinner Rolls

Per roll: Calories 122; Protein 3 g; Carbohydrate 16 g; Fat 5 g; Sodium 93 mg; Cholesterol 35 mg.

*These light rolls can be shaped in a variety of ways. The dough can also be frozen, or the rolls can be partially baked, frozen, and browned later.*

- 1 envelope active dry yeast
- 2 tablespoons lukewarm water (see Tip, above)
- 2 tablespoons light brown sugar
- ½ cup (1 stick) unsalted butter or margarine, at room temperature
- 1 cup milk, scalded and cooled to lukewarm
- 2 eggs, beaten
- 4 cups sifted all-purpose flour
- 1 teaspoon salt
- ¼ cup (½ stick) lightly salted butter or margarine, melted (optional)

1 In a small bowl, stir together the yeast, water, and 1 tablespoon of the sugar and let stand until bubbly — about 5 minutes. Stir until dissolved.

2 In an electric mixer fitted with a dough hook or in a food processor, cream the ½ cup butter and the remaining tablespoon of sugar until light and fluffy — about 3 minutes in the mixer, or 30 seconds in the food processor. Add the milk, yeast, and eggs and continue beating until very light — about 1 minute in the mixer, or 15 seconds in the processor. Sift in the flour and salt; mix until smooth — 2 minutes in the mixer, 30 seconds (see Tip, page 245) in the processor.

3 This dough is too soft to knead. Transfer to a large, lightly greased bowl, turn to coat with the grease, and cover with plastic wrap. Let rise in a warm, draft-free place until doubled in bulk — about 1¼ hours.

4 Punch the dough down, place it on a lightly floured board, and roll out ⅓ inch thick. For dinner rolls, cut into 3-inch rounds. Brush each round with the melted butter, if desired; top with a second round. For pocketbook rolls, cut into small ovals, brush with some of the melted butter, and fold over. Place 2 inches apart on ungreased baking sheets. For a cloverleaf roll, place 3 balls, each the size of a walnut, in a lightly greased, 2¼-inch muffin cup. For crescent rolls, cut the dough into 4-inch squares, then cut each square into a triangle (see photograph, right). Brush with the melted butter or sprinkle with cinnamon and sugar; roll up from the wide end to the point and shape into a crescent. Place 2 inches apart on ungreased baking sheets.

▽ At this point the rolls can be stored. *Freeze* on the baking sheets, tightly covered with aluminum foil, for up to 1 month at 0° F.

*Crescent-shaped Brown-and-Serve Dinner Rolls in the making*

**5** Preheat the oven to 400° F. Brush the top of each roll with the remaining melted butter, if desired, cover with plastic wrap, and let rise in a warm, draft-free place until doubled in bulk — about 25 minutes. For brown-and-serve rolls, bake until they just begin to brown — about 5 minutes.

▽ At this point the rolls can be cooled to room temperature and stored. Wrap in aluminum foil, label, and *freeze* for up to 3 months at 0° F.

**6** If serving immediately, continue baking until golden brown — about 13 minutes more. Makes 2 dozen rolls.

### Serving Later

**For frozen dough:** Remove the foil. Thaw the rolls at room temperature and let rise until doubled in bulk — 2 to 3 hours in all. Preheat the oven to 400° F. Brush the rolls with butter, if desired; bake until golden brown — about 18 minutes. **For frozen, partially baked rolls:** Preheat the oven to 400° F. Remove the foil and place the rolls on an ungreased baking sheet. Bake until golden brown — 13 to 15 minutes.

# Whole-Wheat Refrigerator Rolls

Per roll: Calories 143; Protein 4 g; Carbohydrate 23 g; Fat 4 g; Sodium 93 mg; Cholesterol 10 mg.

*These rolls have a full hearty flavor, and the dough will keep for up to 5 days in the refrigerator.*

- 1 envelope active dry yeast
- ¼ cup lukewarm water (see Tip, page 238)
- 3 tablespoons plus 1 teaspoon sugar
- ¼ cup (½ stick) unsalted butter or margarine, melted
- 1½ cups warm milk
- ¾ teaspoon salt
- ¼ cup wheat germ
- 2½ cups all-purpose flour
- 1½ cups whole wheat flour
- 2 tablespoons lightly salted butter or margarine, melted, for glaze (optional)

1 In a large bowl, an electric mixer fitted with a dough hook, or a food processor, combine the yeast, water, and 1 teaspoon of the sugar; let stand until bubbly — about 5 minutes. Stir in the ¼ cup of butter, the milk, the remaining 3 tablespoons of sugar, and the salt. Add the wheat germ, all-purpose flour, and enough whole-wheat flour (start with about 1 cup) to make a soft dough.

2 On a lightly floured board or in the mixer or food processer, knead the dough until smooth and elastic — 3 minutes by hand, 2 minutes in a mixer, or no more than 45 seconds (see Tip, page 245) in the food processor. Add more whole-wheat flour as needed to keep the dough from sticking (see Tip, page 243).

▽ At this point the dough can be stored. Place in a 1-gallon food-storage bag, push out all of the air, and secure with a twist-tie, leaving room at the end for expansion. *Refrigerate* for up to 5 days.

3 Transfer to a large, lightly greased bowl, turn to coat with the grease, and cover with a clean dry towel. Let rise in a warm place until doubled in bulk — 45 minutes to 1 hour.

4 On a lightly floured surface, roll the dough out ½ inch thick and cut into 3-inch rounds, rerolling scraps as necessary. Or make cloverleafs, as in Step 4 of Brown-and-Serve Dinner Rolls (page 238). Place the rounds 2 inches apart on lightly greased baking sheets and cover with a dry towel. Let rise in a warm place until doubled in bulk — 45 minutes to 1 hour.

5 Preheat the oven to 400° F. Brush the rolls lightly with the 2 tablespoons melted butter, if desired. Bake until golden brown — 18 to 20 minutes. Makes 18 rolls.

### Serving Later

Let the dough sit at room temperature for 2 to 2½ hours. Knead a few turns on a lightly floured surface, then proceed as in Steps 4 and 5.

# Yeast Corn Rolls

Per roll: Calories 138; Protein 3 g; Carbohydrate 23 g; Fat 4 g; Sodium 153 mg; Cholesterol 23 mg.

- 1 envelope active dry yeast
- ¼ cup lukewarm water (see Tip, page 238)
- ¼ cup plus 1 teaspoon sugar
- ¼ cup (½ stick) butter or margarine, melted and cooled
- 1 cup buttermilk or milk
- 1 egg
- 1 teaspoon salt
- ¾ cup plus 2 tablespoons cornmeal
- 3 cups all-purpose flour

1 In a large bowl, an electric mixer fitted with a dough hook, or a food processor, combine the yeast, water, and 1 teaspoon of the sugar and let stand until bubbly — about 5 minutes. Stir in the remaining ¼ cup of sugar, the butter, buttermilk, egg, salt, and ¾ cup of the cornmeal; blend well. Stir in enough flour (start with about 2 cups) to make a soft dough.

2 On a lightly floured board or in the mixer or food processor, knead the dough until smooth and elastic — 7 to 10 minutes by hand, 5 minutes in a mixer, or 40 seconds (see Tip, page 245) in the food processor. Add more flour as needed to keep the dough from sticking. (See Tip, page 243).

▽ At this point the dough can be stored. Place in a 1-gallon food-storage bag, push out all of the air, and secure with a twist-tie, leaving room at the end for expansion. *Refrigerate* for up to 3 days.

3 Transfer to a large, lightly greased bowl, turn to coat with the grease, and cover with a clean dry towel. Let rise in a warm, draft-free place until doubled in bulk — about 1 hour.

4 Punch the dough down and roll it out ½ inch thick on a lightly floured surface. Cut into eighteen 3-inch rounds and set 2 inches apart on lightly greased baking sheets. Cover with dry towels and let rise until almost doubled in bulk — 35 to 45 minutes. Meanwhile, preheat the oven to 375° F.

5 Sprinkle the rolls lightly with the remaining 2 tablespoons of cornmeal and bake until golden brown — 17 to 20 minutes. Makes 18 rolls.

### Serving Later

Let the dough sit at room temperature for 2 to 2½ hours. Knead a few turns on a lightly floured board, then proceed as in Steps 4 and 5.

*Home-baked Whole-Wheat Refrigerator Rolls, Brown-and-Serve Dinner Rolls (page 238), and Poppy Seed Bowknots*

# Poppy Seed Bowknots

Per roll: Calories 101; Protein 3 g; Carbohydrate 16 g; Fat 3 g; Sodium 182 mg; Cholesterol 6 mg.

- 1   envelope active dry yeast
- ¼   cup lukewarm water (see Tip, page 238)
- 4   to 4½ cups all-purpose flour
- 1   tablespoon sugar
- 2   teaspoons salt
- ¼   cup (½ stick) unsalted butter, melted and cooled
- 1½  cups buttermilk, at room temperature
- 1   egg white, lightly beaten, for glaze
- 2   tablespoons poppy seeds, or to taste

1 In a large bowl, an electric mixer fitted with a dough hook, or a food processor, sprinkle the yeast over the water, stir, and let stand for 5 minutes. Stir until dissolved.

2 Add 4 cups of the flour, the sugar, salt, butter, and buttermilk to the yeast mixture and mix thoroughly. On a lightly floured board or in the mixer or food processor, knead the dough until smooth and elastic — about 4 minutes by hand, 2 minutes in the mixer, or 30 seconds (see Tip, page 245) in the processor. Add more flour as needed to keep the dough from sticking (see Tip, page 243). This is more malleable and softer than a bread dough.

3 Transfer the dough to a large, lightly greased bowl, turn to coat with the grease, and cover with a clean dry towel. Let rise in a warm, draft-free spot until doubled in bulk — about 1 hour.

4 Punch the dough down and knead it on a lightly floured surface for 2 minutes. Roll the dough out to a 24″ x 6″ x ½″ rectangle, then cut into 6″ x 1″ x ½″ strips. Gently tie each strip into a bowknot by slipping one end over, under, then back over the other.

5 Lay the rolls 2 inches apart on a lightly oiled baking sheet; cover with a clean dry towel. Place in a warm, draft-free spot until the rolls have doubled in bulk — about 25 minutes.

6 Preheat the oven to 375° F. Brush the tops with the egg white and sprinkle with poppy seeds. Bake on the middle shelf of the oven until golden brown and a toothpick inserted in a knot comes out clean — 20 to 25 minutes. Cool on the baking sheet, then serve. For storing and serving later, see Tip (page 233). Makes 24 rolls.

*Diamonds of crusty Herbed Garlic Bread drenched with a butter-rich blend of pungent flavors*

# Refrigerator White Bread

Per ½-inch slice: Calories 95; Protein 2 g; Carbohydrate 16 g; Fat 2 g; Sodium 121 mg; Cholesterol 1 mg.

*You will remember how good white bread can be.*

- 2 envelopes active dry yeast
- ½ cup lukewarm water (see Tip, page 238)
- 5½ to 6 cups all-purpose flour
- ¼ cup sugar
- 2 teaspoons salt
- 1½ cups warm milk
- ¼ cup vegetable oil

1 In a large bowl, an electric mixer fitted with a dough hook, or a food processor, sprinkle the yeast over the water, stir, and let stand for 5 minutes. Stir until dissolved.

2 Add 3 cups of the flour, the sugar, salt, milk, and oil to the yeast mixture and blend well. Gradually work in the remaining flour until the dough is firm enough to handle.

3 On a lightly floured board or in the mixer or food processor, knead the dough until smooth and elastic — 8 to 10 minutes by hand, 4 to 5 minutes in

the mixer, no more than 45 seconds (see Tip, page 245) in the processor. Add flour as needed to keep dough from sticking (see Tip, opposite page).

4 Transfer to a large, lightly greased bowl, turn to coat with the grease, and cover with a dry towel. Let rise in a warm, draft-free place until doubled in bulk — about 1 hour.

5 Punch the dough down and divide it in half. On a lightly floured board, roll out one half to a 12- by 8-inch rectangle. Tightly roll up the dough from the 8-inch side, pinch the ends and side seam to seal, and place in a lightly greased, 8½" x 4½" x 2½" pan.

242

Repeat with the second half. Cover the pans with plastic wrap and refrigerate for at least 8 and up to 24 hours.

6 Preheat the oven to 400° F. Remove the plastic wrap and let the loaves stand at room temperature for 15 minutes. Bake until they are a deep golden brown and sound hollow when tapped on the bottom — 40 to 45 minutes. Remove from the pans and let cool on wire racks. For storing and serving later, see Tip (page 233). Makes 2 loaves.

# Rye Bread with Beer

Per serving: Calories 118; Protein 3 g; Carbohydrate 20 g; Fat 2 g; Sodium 86 mg; Cholesterol 17 mg.

- 2 envelopes active dry yeast
- ¼ cup lukewarm water (see Tip, page 238)
- 1 can (12 ounces) beer
- ¼ cup (½ stick) unsalted butter or margarine
- ¼ cup molasses
- 1 tablespoon anise or fennel seeds
- 1 tablespoon grated orange rind (optional)
- 1 teaspoon salt
- 3½ cups rye flour
- 2 to 3 cups all-purpose flour
- 1 egg, beaten with 1 tablespoon water, for glaze

1 In a large bowl or an electric mixer fitted with a dough hook, sprinkle the yeast over the water, stir, and let stand for about 5 minutes. Then stir until dissolved.

2 In a small saucepan, heat the beer and butter over low heat until the butter melts. Let cool to lukewarm. To the yeast mixture, add the molasses, anise seeds, orange rind, if desired, salt, and beer mixture. Stir together, then add the rye flour and beat until smooth. Gradually stir in enough of the all-purpose flour (start with 2 cups) to make a soft dough.

3 On a lightly floured board or in the electric mixer, knead the dough until smooth and elastic — 8 to 10 minutes by hand, 4 to 5 minutes in the mixer. Add more flour as needed to keep the dough from sticking (see Tip, below).

4 Transfer to a large, lightly greased bowl, turn to coat with the grease, and cover with a clean dry towel. Let rise in a warm, draft-free place until doubled in bulk — about 1½ hours. Punch the dough down and knead lightly a few times; cover with the towel and let rest 10 minutes more.

5 Divide the dough in half, shape each half into a round, and place on a lightly greased baking sheet. Cover with a towel and let rise in a warm, draft-free place until doubled in bulk — 30 to 40 minutes.

6 Preheat the oven to 350° F. With a sharp knife, cut an X, ¼ inch deep, on the top of each loaf, then brush with the glaze. Bake until the loaves are brown and sound hollow when tapped on the bottom — 40 to 45 minutes. See Tip (page 233) for storing and serving later. This bread goes well with corned beef and cabbage, roast pork, or sauerbraten, or use it to make pastrami or ham sandwiches. Makes two 10-inch loaves of 12 servings each.

*Tip: The secret of a light bread is a dough that is soft and pliable yet firm enough to hold its shape. A stiff or claylike dough will yield a leaden loaf. If bread dough is still very sticky or slack after a couple of minutes of kneading, work in another 3 or 4 tablespoons of flour. Continue to work in flour only if needed to keep the dough from sticking to the board. The dough will become less tacky and more manageable as you knead it.*

# Herbed Garlic Bread

Per ½ ounce: Calories 73; Protein 1 g; Carbohydrate 7 g; Fat 4 g; Sodium 140 mg; Cholesterol 10 mg.

- 1 long loaf (8 ounces) French, sourdough, or Italian bread
- 5 tablespoons unsalted butter or margarine, at room temperature
- 2 tablespoons minced parsley
- 2 green onions (including some of the green), trimmed and finely chopped
- 1 clove garlic, crushed
- ½ teaspoon dried basil, crumbled
- ½ teaspoon salt

1 Preheat the oven to 400° F. Cut the bread diagonally into 1-inch slices, leaving the bottom intact. Cut 1-inch diagonal slices in the opposite direction, forming diamond shapes.

2 In a small bowl, thoroughly blend the butter, parsley, green onions, garlic, basil, and salt with a fork. Butter both sides of the bread slices, then the top crust.

▽ At this point, the bread can be wrapped tightly with heavy-duty aluminum foil and stored. *Refrigerate* for up to 3 days. *Freeze*, labeled, for up to 1 month at 0° F.

3 Wrap the loaf loosely with aluminum foil and place it on a baking sheet. Bake for about 15 minutes. Serve with soup or salad, or as an appetizer.

### Serving Later

**From refrigerator:** Loosen the aluminum foil and bake in a preheated 400° F oven for about 20 minutes or until golden brown. Serve as in Step 3.
**From freezer:** Follow the directions above but bake for 30 to 35 minutes.

# Fennel Bread

Per serving: Calories 77; Protein 2 g;
Carbohydrate 13 g; Fat 2 g; Sodium 42 mg;
Cholesterol 5 mg.

| | |
|---|---|
| 1 | envelope active dry yeast |
| 1 ½ | cups lukewarm water (see Tip, page 238) |
| 3 | tablespoons molasses |
| 4 | tablespoons ( ½ stick) unsalted butter or margarine, melted |
| 1 ½ | teaspoons fennel seeds, lightly crushed |
| ½ | teaspoon salt |
| 2 | cups rye flour |
| 1 ½ | to 2 cups all-purpose flour |

1 In a large bowl, an electric mixer fitted with a dough hook, or a food processor, sprinkle the yeast over the water, stir, and let stand for 5 minutes. Stir until dissolved, then add the molasses, 2 tablespoons of the butter, the fennel seeds, and salt. Add the rye flour gradually, beating until the mixture is smooth. Gradually add enough of the all-purpose flour (start with 1 ½ cups) to make a workable dough.

2 On a lightly floured surface or in the mixer or food processor, knead the dough until smooth and elastic — about 10 minutes by hand, 5 minutes in the mixer, or no more than 45 seconds (see Tip, opposite page) in the food processor. Add more flour as needed to keep the dough from sticking (see Tip, page 243). Shape the dough into 2 balls and let rest for 15 minutes on a lightly floured board, covered by a towel.

*Fennel Bread — a taste
experience that lingers favorably
long after the last bite*

**3** With your hands, flatten each ball, to form a 9-inch circle. Using a 2-inch, round biscuit cutter, cut a hole in the center of each. Place the loaves on lightly oiled baking sheets, prick the tops with a fork, and cover loosely with a towel. Let rise for 1 hour.

**4** Preheat the oven to 425° F. Bake the loaves, one at a time, for 15 to 20 minutes or until golden. Transfer to wire racks and brush with the remaining 2 tablespoons of melted butter. Let cool before cutting into wedges. See Tip (page 233) for storing and serving later. Makes two 10-inch loaves of 12 servings each.

# Divine Bread

Per slice: Calories 177; Protein 5 g; Carbohydrate 30 g; Fat 4 g; Sodium 176 mg; Cholesterol 64 mg.

*This slightly sweet Southern favorite is very adaptable — how about splitting it and adding an apple-raisin or cheese-salami filling? For a sinfully delicious treat, try French toast with slices of the prune-walnut variation.*

- 2 envelopes active dry yeast
- 1½ cups lukewarm water (see Tip, page 238)
- ½ cup sugar
- 2 teaspoons salt
- ¼ cup (½ stick) unsalted butter or margarine, melted and cooled
- 4 eggs
- 7 cups sifted all-purpose flour
- 1 egg yolk, beaten with 2 tablespoons heavy cream, for glaze
  Poppy seeds for garnish (optional)

**1** In a large bowl or an electric mixer fitted with a dough hook, sprinkle the yeast over the water. Stir, let stand 5 minutes, then stir until dissolved.

**2** Add the sugar, salt, butter, and eggs to the yeast mixture and blend well. Gradually add about 6½ cups of the flour, 1 cup at a time, mixing well after each addition.

**3** On a lightly floured board or in the mixer, knead the dough until smooth and elastic — about 3 minutes by hand, or 1½ minutes in the mixer. Add flour as needed to keep dough from sticking (see Tip, page 243).

**4** Transfer to a large, lightly greased bowl and turn to coat with the grease; cover with a clean dry towel. Let rise in a warm, draft-free place until doubled in bulk — about 1 hour.

**5** Punch the dough down. On a lightly floured surface, roll it out ½ inch thick, then shape into 2 oblong loaves or 2 round loaves, as desired.

▽ At this point the dough can be stored. Place the loaves on a baking sheet, cover with foil, and freeze. When frozen solid — about 8 hours — remove from the pan and rewrap tightly in aluminum foil. Label and *freeze* for up to 1 month at 0° F.

**6** Place the loaves on lightly greased baking sheets, cover with a clean dry towel, and let rise in a warm, draft-free place until doubled in bulk — about 45 minutes.

**7** Preheat the oven to 350° F. Brush the loaves with the glaze and sprinkle with the poppy seeds, if desired. Bake, one loaf at a time, on the middle shelf of the oven until the loaf is golden brown and sounds hollow when tapped on the bottom — about 45 minutes. Cut into 12 slices. See Tip (page 233) for storing and serving later. Makes two 13- by 5-inch loaves.

## Serving Later

**To bake frozen dough:** Remove the foil and place a loaf on a lightly greased baking sheet. Cover with a clean dry towel and let rise until doubled in bulk — about 6 hours in a warm, draft-free place or overnight in the refrigerator. Bake and serve as in Step 7.

### Prune-Walnut Variation

Per slice: Calories 241; Protein 6 g; Carbohydrate 39 g; Fat 7 g; Sodium 177 mg; Cholesterol 64 mg.

Mix **2 cups coarsely chopped pitted prunes** with **1 cup chopped walnuts.** Proceed as in Steps 1 through 4 of Divine Bread. In Step 5, roll out each half to a 9- by 11-inch rectangle. Spread each rectangle with half of the filling, gently pressing it into the dough; roll up jelly-roll—style. Tuck the ends under; proceed as in Steps 6 and 7. Makes 2 loaves of 12 slices each.

*Tip: Food processors make the job of kneading dough easier, but you should knead for no more than 45 seconds because the dough may overheat, which would kill the yeast. Some doughs become sufficiently elastic in as few as 30 seconds. You will know when the dough is fully kneaded: it will roll into a ball and ride up the spindle, leaving the sides of the processor relatively clean. Never use a food processor to knead a very sticky dough, such as brioche, because you risk stalling and burning out the motor.*

# Orange-Almond Sweet Bread

Per ¾-inch slice: Calories 306; Protein 6 g;
Carbohydrate 44 g; Fat 12 g; Sodium 103 mg;
Cholesterol 68 mg.

- 2 envelopes active dry yeast
- ½ cup lukewarm water (see Tip, page 238)
- 1 cup warm milk
- ½ cup sugar
- ½ cup (1 stick) unsalted butter or margarine, melted
- 1 teaspoon salt
- 3 eggs, lightly beaten
- 6 to 7 cups all-purpose flour

*For the filling:*
- ½ cup (1 stick) unsalted butter, at room temperature
  Grated rind of 2 oranges (about ¼ cup)
- ¾ cup honey
- 1 cup blanched almonds, finely chopped (about 4 ounces)
- 1¼ cups golden raisins, plumped in hot water and patted dry
- ½ cup chopped candied orange peel
- 1 egg, beaten with 1 tablespoon water, for glaze
  Slivered almonds for garnish

1 In a large bowl or an electric mixer fitted with a dough hook, sprinkle the yeast over the water, stir, and let stand for 5 minutes. Stir until dissolved. Add the milk, sugar, butter, salt, and eggs and mix well.

2 Add 3 cups of the flour and beat until smooth. Add enough of the remaining flour (start with 1½ cups) to form a soft but not sticky dough.

3 On a lightly floured board or in the mixer, knead the dough until satiny and smooth — 8 to 10 minutes by hand, 4 to 5 minutes in the mixer. Add more flour as needed to keep dough from sticking (see Tip, page 243).

4 Transfer to a large, lightly greased bowl, turn to coat with the grease, and cover with a clean dry towel. Let rise in a warm, draft-free place until doubled in bulk — 1¼ to 1½ hours. Punch down.

▽ At this point the dough can be covered with plastic wrap and *refrigerated* for up to 8 hours.

5 Let rise again until doubled in bulk — 1 to 1¼ hours. Meanwhile, make the filling: In a medium-size bowl, an electric mixer, or a food processor, beat the butter, orange rind, and honey until smooth and light — 2 to 3 minutes by hand, 1 to 2 minutes in the mixer, or about 30 seconds in the food processor.

6 On a lightly floured board, roll out the dough to a 16- by 16-inch square. Using a spatula, spread the filling evenly over the dough to within ½ inch of the edges. Sprinkle the almonds, raisins, and candied orange peel on top. Roll the dough up jelly-roll–style and seal the seam.

7 Flatten the roll slightly with your hands. Then, using a rolling pin, flatten it to about 1 inch. With a sharp knife, divide the roll lengthwise into 3 strips; cut each strip in half crosswise, making 6 pieces in all. Braid or twist 3 of the strips together and place in a lightly greased, 9″ x 5″ x 3″ loaf pan. Repeat. Cover the loaves with a clean dry towel and let them rise in a warm dry place until puffed up over the tops of the pans — about 45 minutes.

8 Preheat the oven to 350° F. Brush the loaves with the egg wash and decorate with slivered almonds. Bake until a toothpick inserted in the center of a loaf comes out clean and the loaves are brown — about 45 minutes.

9 Let cool in the pan for 10 minutes, then loosen with a spatula and turn out onto wire racks. Do not slice the bread until thoroughly cooled. For stor-ing and serving later, see Tip (page 233). Serve at room temperature or toasted. Makes 2 loaves.

### Serving Later

Remove the plastic wrap and let the dough come to room temperature — 20 to 30 minutes. Proceed as in Steps 5 through 9.

# Sweet Buns with Cinnamon-Raisin Swirls

Per bun: Calories 123; Protein 2 g;
Carbohydrate 21 g; Fat 4 g; Sodium 71 mg;
Cholesterol 26 mg.

*You can make these luscious buns the night before and just pop them in the oven the next morning. For an even richer swirl, add ½ cup chopped walnuts or pecans with the raisins.*

- 1 envelope active dry yeast
- ¼ cup lukewarm water (see Tip, page 238)
- 1 cup milk
- ¼ cup sugar
- 8 tablespoons (1 stick) unsalted butter or margarine
- 2 eggs
- 1 teaspoon salt
- 4 to 4½ cups all-purpose flour
- ½ cup granulated sugar mixed with 1½ teaspoons ground cinnamon
- 1 cup raisins
- ⅓ cup confectioners' sugar
- 1½ teaspoons milk
- 2 drops vanilla

1 In a large bowl, an electric mixer fitted with a dough hook, or a food processor, sprinkle the yeast over the water, stir, and let stand for 5 minutes. Stir until dissolved.

*Tea with Orange-Almond Sweet Bread, an unbeatable combination*

2 In a small saucepan, scald the milk, then stir in the sugar and 4 tablespoons of the butter. Let cool to lukewarm. Stir into the yeast mixture, add the eggs, and beat until well blended. Stir in the salt and enough flour (start with 3½ cups) to make a soft dough.

3 On a lightly floured board or in the mixer or food processor, knead the dough until smooth and elastic — about 5 minutes by hand, 2½ minutes in the mixer, or no more than 45 seconds (see Tip, page 245) in the food processor. Add more flour as needed to keep the dough from sticking (see Tip, page 243).

4 Transfer to a large, lightly greased bowl, turn to coat with the grease, and cover with a clean dry towel. Let rise in a warm, draft-free place until doubled in bulk — about 1 hour.

5 Meanwhile, in the small saucepan, melt the remaining 4 tablespoons of butter. Punch the dough down and divide in quarters. Roll out one quarter to a 12- by 9-inch rectangle. (Keep the remaining dough in the refrigerator, covered with plastic wrap.) Brush the rectangle with 1 tablespoon of the butter, then sprinkle with 2 tablespoons of the sugar mixture and ¼ cup of the raisins. Starting from the 12-inch side, tightly roll up the dough, then cut it into eight 1½-inch-thick slices. Place the slices, cut side up, in a lightly greased, 8″ x 8″ x 2″ pan. Repeat with the remaining dough, filling 4 pans. Cover with plastic wrap and refrigerate for at least 8 and up to 24 hours.

6 Preheat the oven to 375° F. Remove the plastic wrap and let the rolls stand at room temperature for 15 minutes. Bake until golden brown — about 25 minutes. Let cool slightly in the pan on wire racks. Meanwhile, in a small bowl, combine the confectioners' sugar, milk, and vanilla. Drizzle over the buns and serve. It's best to serve these the day they are baked. Makes 32 buns.

# Caramel Bubble Loaf

Per serving: Calories 257; Protein 4 g; Carbohydrate 39 g; Fat 9 g; Sodium 118 mg; Cholesterol 31 mg.

*This rich raisin- and nut-filled loaf is a special favorite with children, who love to break off the "bubbles."*

> 1   envelope active dry yeast
> ¼   cup lukewarm water (see Tip, page 238)
> 1   cup plus 1 teaspoon sugar
> ¾   cup (1½ sticks) unsalted butter or margarine
> 1   cup milk
> ½   teaspoon salt
> 1   egg
> 1   teaspoon vanilla
> 4 to 5 cups all-purpose flour
> 1   teaspoon cinnamon
> ½   cup finely chopped pecans or walnuts
> ½   cup raisins

1 In a large bowl, an electric mixer fitted with a dough hook, or a food processor, combine the yeast, water, and 1 teaspoon of the sugar and let stand until bubbly — about 5 minutes.

2 Meanwhile, in a small saucepan, combine ½ cup of the sugar, ¼ cup of the butter, the milk, and salt and stir over low heat until the butter melts. Let cool, then stir into the yeast mixture. Beat in the egg and vanilla.

3 Add 2 cups of the flour and beat until smooth. Gradually stir in enough of the remaining flour (start with 1½ cups) to make a soft dough. On a lightly floured board or in the mixer or food processor, knead the dough until smooth and elastic — 8 to 10 minutes by hand, 4 to 5 minutes in the mixer, or no more than 45 seconds (see Tip, page 245) in the processor.

4 Place in a large, lightly greased bowl, turn to coat with the grease, and cover with a clean dry towel. Let rise in a warm, draft-free spot until doubled in bulk — 1 to 1½ hours. Punch the dough down and knead lightly in the bowl. Re-cover with the towel and let rise again until doubled in bulk — 30 to 40 minutes more. Knead the dough briefly — about 1 minute more by hand. Re-cover and let rest for 10 minutes.

5 Meanwhile, in a small saucepan, combine the remaining ½ cup sugar, the remaining ½ cup butter, and the cinnamon and stir over low heat just until the butter is melted. Set aside.

6 Pinch off about 2 tablespoons of the dough, roll into a ball, dip the top of the ball into the glaze, and place in a well-buttered, 10-inch tube pan. Repeat until the bottom of the pan is covered with balls, then sprinkle with half of the nuts and raisins. Continue to fill the pan with glazed balls until all of the dough is used. Sprinkle with the remaining nuts and raisins; pour the remaining glaze over all.

7 Cover with a sheet of greased wax paper and a clean dry towel; let rise in a warm, draft-free place until doubled in bulk — 30 to 40 minutes.

8 Preheat the oven to 350° F. Bake for 40 to 45 minutes or until the loaf is golden brown and sounds hollow when tapped on the bottom. Turn out onto a serving platter or wire rack with foil beneath to catch excess syrup. Serve warm or at room temperature. For storing and serving later, see Tip (page 233). Makes 1 loaf that serves 16.

# Desserts

Serve a delightful dessert, and you end a meal on a memorable note. Fortunately, most desserts can be made ahead of time; notable exceptions are hot soufflés and fried fruits. Even whipped cream, once a last-minute must, can be prepared up to 24 hours in advance, following directions in the Tip on page 272.

Most of the recipes in this chapter were selected not only for their good keeping qualities, but also for their appeal to many tastes — from tart to ultra sweet. A number of them can be frozen, allowing you to make dessert when you have the time, and put it aside for a future event or unexpected company.

Fruit pies, which lend themselves especially well to freezing, are a good way to take advantage of seasonal specials on fruits (see recipes, page 274). You can freeze the filling by itself, then drop it into a freshly made shell for baking. Or prepare a whole pie for freezing coating the inside of the crust with egg white to prevent sogginess. Meringue-topped or cream pies, unfortunately, cannot be frozen; meringue toughens and shrinks in the freezer and custard separates on thawing

All cakes freeze well (see Tip, page 265), and cookies too, though their bulk can monopolize freezer space. Try, instead, the Basic Cookie Mix (page 16) or Ginger Icebox Cookies (page 268) and produce freshly baked cookies in a jiffy.

# Meringue Shells

Per shell: Calories 98; Protein 1 g; Carbohydrate 24 g; Fat 0 g; Sodium 25 mg; Cholesterol 0 mg.

*Make these when the weather is dry. Humidity prevents them from drying properly. For a fancy presentation, pipe scalloped edges with a pastry bag and large star tip.*

- 4 egg whites, at room temperature
- 1 cup sugar
- 1 teaspoon vanilla

**1** Preheat the oven to 250° F. In a large bowl, beat the egg whites until frothy — about 30 seconds. Still beating, gradually add the sugar. Add the vanilla and beat 5 minutes longer or until the mixture is glossy and stands in stiff peaks.

**2** Drop the meringue in mounds onto 2 baking sheets, lightly buttered and floured or lined with aluminum foil. Make eight 4-inch or two 8-inch mounds, swirling each into a shell with the back of a spoon, then depressing each center to form a raised border about 1-inch high. Bake for about 1 hour or until firm. Turn off the oven but leave the meringues in it to dry out — about 2 hours.

**3** Carefully remove the shells from the pans or, if you used aluminum foil, peel it from the shells. Will keep in an airtight container for about 2 weeks. Fill with sherbet, ice cream, fresh fruit, or a combination of these. Makes eight 4-inch or two 8-inch shells.

# Walnut Crêpes with Mocha Sauce

Per serving: Calories 734; Protein 13 g; Carbohydrate 70 g; Fat 47 g; Sodium 154 mg; Cholesterol 170 mg.

- 1½ cups ground walnuts (about 6 ounces shelled)
- ¾ cup sugar
- ¾ cup milk
- ¼ cup raisins
- ½ teaspoon ground cinnamon
- ½ teaspoon grated lemon rind
- 6 ounces semisweet chocolate, cut into small pieces
- ⅔ cup strong coffee
- 2 tablespoons rum
- 3 tablespoons unsalted butter or margarine
- 12 Dessert Crêpes (page 237)
- 1 cup heavy cream (optional)

**1** In a small saucepan, bring the walnuts, ½ cup of the sugar, the milk, raisins, cinnamon, and lemon rind to a simmer over moderately low heat. Cook, uncovered, for 5 minutes, stirring occasionally. Let cool completely.

**2** Meanwhile, prepare the sauce: In the top of a double boiler, warm the chocolate, the remaining ¼ cup of sugar, and the coffee over simmering water, stirring, until the chocolate melts and the mixture is smooth. Remove from the heat and stir in the rum and butter. Set aside.

**3** Preheat the oven to 350° F. Place a crêpe with the more attractive side down and spread with 1 tablespoon of the walnut mixture. Roll up tightly and place, seam side down, in a buttered, 13" x 9" x 2" baking dish. Repeat until all crêpes are filled. Cover with foil.

▽ At this point the dessert can be stored. Let the sauce cool to room temperature; transfer to a tightly covered container. *Refrigerate* the crêpes and sauce for up to 5 days or label and *freeze* for up to 1 month at 0° F.

**4** Preheat the oven to 350° F. Bake the foil-covered crêpes for 10 minutes. Uncover and bake until heated through — about 5 minutes more. At the same time, reheat the sauce in the double boiler over moderate heat until warmed through — about 5 minutes.

**5** Meanwhile, in a medium-size bowl, whip the cream, if desired, until soft peaks form. Drizzle the hot crêpes with some of the mocha sauce and pass the remaining sauce and the whipped cream. Serves 6.

### Serving Later

**From refrigerator:** Proceed as in Steps 4 and 5, extending the reheating time for the covered crêpes to 15 to 20 minutes and for the sauce to 10 minutes. **From freezer:** Thaw in refrigerator overnight, then proceed as above.

# Cinnamon Crêpes with Caramel Sauce and Pecans

Per serving: Calories 619; Protein 12 g; Carbohydrate 68 g; Fat 35 g; Sodium 232 mg; Cholesterol 200 mg.

*This unusual Mexican dessert is very rich and utterly delicious.*

- 1 quart milk
- 2 teaspoons cornstarch
- ⅛ teaspoon baking soda
- 1¼ cups sugar
- 1 cinnamon stick (about 2½ inches)
- 5 tablespoons unsalted butter or margarine
- 1 cup pecans, coarsely chopped (about 3½ ounces)
- 12 Dessert Crêpes (page 237), with ½ teaspoon ground cinnamon and ⅛ teaspoon ground cloves added to the batter

*Meringue Shells — elegant and edible — lend a crunchy accent to their contents; here, an assortment of fruits in season.*

1 In a small bowl, combine 1 table-spoon of the milk, the cornstarch, and baking soda. Set aside.

2 In a large heavy saucepan, bring the remaining milk to a boil over mod-erate heat. Remove the pan from the heat and stir in the cornstarch mixture. (The milk will bubble up.) Return to the heat, reduce the heat to low, and stir in the sugar and cinnamon. Simmer, un-covered, for 30 minutes, stirring occa-sionally. Remove the cinnamon stick and continue to simmer, stirring fre-quently, until the sauce is very thick — about 30 minutes more. Set aside.

3 Meanwhile, melt the butter in a 7-inch skillet over moderate heat. Add the pecans, and sauté, stirring

frequently, until the nuts are toasted and the butter is browned — about 10 minutes. Remove from the heat. With a slotted spoon, remove the nuts and set aside. Reserve the butter.

4 Preheat the oven to 325° F. Place a crêpe with the more attractive side down, brush with the browned butter, and put 1 tablespoon of caramel in the center. Fold the crêpe in half, pressing gently to spread out the filling; then fold it in half again to form a wedge. Brush the edges with butter and place the crêpe in a buttered, 13" x 9" x 2" baking dish. Repeat, overlapping the crêpes slightly in the pan.

▽ At this point the dessert can be stored. Cover the crêpes with foil and place the nuts in a tightly covered

container. Cool the sauce to room temperature, then cover tightly. *Refrig-erate* all for up to 24 hours.

5 Bake the crêpes, uncovered, until heated through — 8 to 10 minutes. Meanwhile, heat the remaining sauce over low heat, stirring frequently, until warmed through — about 5 minutes. Drizzle the caramel over the crêpes, then sprinkle with the pecans. Serves 6.

### Serving Later

Preheat the oven to 325° F. Uncover the crêpes and bake until warmed through — 12 to 14 minutes. Mean-while, gently reheat the sauce — 7 to 10 minutes. Continue as in Step 5.

# Cold Raspberry Soufflé with Framboise Sauce

Per serving: Calories 397; Protein 7 g;
Carbohydrate 61 g; Fat 14 g; Sodium 84 mg;
Cholesterol 54 mg.

*What more elegant way to end a meal
than with a cooling soufflé sweet with
the flavor of summer fruit? Whipped
cream could be substituted for the
sauce, if desired.*

- 1 envelope unflavored gelatin
- 2 tablespoons cold water
- 2 packages (10½ ounces each)
  frozen raspberries in syrup,
  thawed, puréed, and strained
- 1 cup sugar
- 2 tablespoons framboise,
  kirsch, or cassis
- 8 egg whites, at room
  temperature (about 1 cup)
- 1 cup heavy cream

*Optional garnishes:*
  Fresh raspberries
  Mint leaves dusted with a
  little confectioners' sugar

1 Tear off a piece of wax paper long
enough to fit around a 1-quart
soufflé dish. Fold the paper in half
lengthwise and brush one side lightly
with vegetable oil. Tie the paper around
the soufflé dish with the oiled side
inward and the folded edge extending
2 inches above the rim.

2 In a medium-size saucepan, heat
the gelatin, the water, half of the
raspberries, and ½ cup of the sugar
over moderate heat. Stir constantly
until the sugar and gelatin have dissolved—about 5 minutes. Transfer to
a large bowl and refrigerate, covered,
until syrupy—15 to 20 minutes.

3 Meanwhile, prepare the sauce. In a
medium-size bowl combine the remaining raspberries, ¼ cup of the
remaining sugar, and the framboise.
Cover and refrigerate until ready to use.
Will keep for up to 3 days.

4 Beat the egg whites until soft peaks
form. Add the remaining ¼ cup of
sugar a little at a time and continue
beating until the whites are stiff but not

*Cold Raspberry Soufflé with Framboise Sauce — an irresistible treat*

dry. Fold them gently but thoroughly into the gelatin mixture. Whip the cream until soft peaks form, and fold it into the gelatin mixture also. Pour into the prepared soufflé dish and cover loosely with plastic wrap.

5 Refrigerate for at least 2 and up to 24 hours. When ready to serve, remove the collar and garnish the soufflé with the fresh raspberries and mint leaves, if desired. Pass the sauce separately. Serves 6 to 8.

# Frozen Cointreau Soufflé

Per serving: Calories 355; Protein 4 g; Carbohydrate 26 g; Fat 27 g; Sodium 36 mg; Cholesterol 286 mg.

- ⅔ cup sugar
- 3 tablespoons water
  Grated rind of 1 orange
- 6 egg yolks
- ⅓ cup Cointreau or fresh orange juice
- 2 cups heavy cream
- 12 ladyfingers, halved lengthwise

Optional garnishes:
  Thin orange slices or grated orange rind
  Shaved chocolate

1 Fit a 1½-quart soufflé dish with a wax-paper collar (see Step 1, Cold Raspberry Soufflé, opposite page). In a small saucepan, bring the sugar, water, and orange rind to a boil over moderate heat, stirring, until the sugar dissolves — 3 to 4 minutes.

2 In a large bowl, using an electric beater on high speed, beat the egg yolks while adding the hot syrup in a steady stream. Continue to beat until the mixture is thick and falls in a heavy ribbonlike stream when poured from a spoon — about 8 minutes. Add the Cointreau and mix well.

3 In a medium-size bowl, whip the cream until stiff peaks form. Stir ¼ of the whipped cream into the egg yolk mixture, then gently but thoroughly fold in the remaining cream.

4 Arrange a layer of ladyfingers like spokes of a wheel on the bottom of the prepared dish, then top with ⅓ of the soufflé mixture. Repeat, adding two more layers of each, cover with plastic wrap, and freeze for at least 8 hours.

▽ At this point the soufflé can be stored. Rewrap tightly with plastic wrap and aluminum foil and *freeze* for up to 1 month at 0° F.

5 When ready to serve, remove the collar. Garnish with the orange slices or grated rind or shaved chocolate, if desired. Serves 8 to 12.

# Cold Chocolate Soufflé

Per serving: Calories 446; Protein 8 g; Carbohydrate 32 g; Fat 33 g; Sodium 59 mg; Cholesterol 197 mg.

*This dessert and Summery Lemon Soufflé (page 254) are equally delicious served chilled or frozen.*

- 4 egg yolks
- 1 cup sugar
- ¼ cup water
- 8 ounces unsweetened chocolate, melted
- 2 tablespoons coffee-flavored liqueur, dark rum, or strong coffee
- 6 egg whites, at room temperature
- 1½ cups heavy cream

Optional garnishes:
  Warm chocolate sauce
  Whipped cream

1 Fit a 1-quart soufflé dish with a wax-paper collar (see Step 1, Cold Raspberry Soufflé, opposite page). In a small bowl, beat the egg yolks until thick and creamy.

2 In a small heavy saucepan, bring ¾ cup of the sugar and the water to a boil over moderate heat, stirring until the sugar has dissolved. Boil, uncovered, until a candy thermometer registers 238° F or until a soft ball forms when a small amount of the syrup is dropped into a saucer of cold water — 5 to 7 minutes.

3 Beating constantly with an electric mixer at high speed, add the syrup to the yolks in a steady stream. Continue to beat until the mixture is room temperature — 8 to 10 minutes. Blend in the chocolate and liqueur.

4 In a medium-size bowl, beat the egg whites until they form soft peaks. Add the remaining ¼ cup of sugar a little at a time and continue to beat until stiff. Stir ¼ of the whites into the chocolate mixture, then gently but thoroughly fold in remaining whites.

5 In the bowl in which the egg whites were beaten, whip the cream until soft peaks form. Gently but thoroughly fold the whipped cream into the chocolate mixture, then spoon into the prepared mold. Cover loosely with plastic wrap.

▽ At this point the soufflé can be stored. *Freeze* until solid, about 8 hours, then rewrap tightly with plastic wrap and aluminum foil. Will keep for up to 5 days at 0° F.

6 Chill for at least 2 and up to 24 hours. When ready to serve, remove the collar; serve the soufflé with a warm chocolate sauce and whipped cream, if desired. Serves 8.

### Serving Later

Serve as in Step 6. Do not thaw.

# Summery Lemon Soufflé

Per serving: Calories 410; Protein 7 g; Carbohydrate 36 g; Fat 28 g; Sodium 66 mg; Cholesterol 354 mg.

- 1 envelope unflavored gelatin
- ¼ cup cold water
- 6 egg yolks
- 1 cup sugar
- ⅔ cup fresh lemon juice (about 4 medium-size lemons)
- 1 tablespoon grated lemon rind
- 4 egg whites, at room temperature
- 1½ cups heavy cream

*Optional garnishes:*
  Thin lemon slices
  Whipped cream

1 Fit a 1-quart soufflé dish with a wax-paper collar (see Step 1, Cold Raspberry Soufflé, page 252). In a small bowl, soften the gelatin in the water for 5 minutes.

2 In a medium-size nonaluminum saucepan, beat the yolks with ½ cup of the sugar until light and thick. Stir in the lemon juice, and cook, stirring constantly, over low heat until lightly thickened — 7 to 10 minutes. Do not boil. Add the gelatin; cook, stirring constantly, until dissolved — 1 minute more. Transfer the mixture to a large bowl, stir in the lemon rind, and chill, loosely covered, until syrupy — 15 to 20 minutes.

3 In a medium-size bowl, beat the egg whites until they form soft peaks. Add the remaining sugar, a little at a time, and continue beating the whites until stiff but not dry. Stir ¼ of the whites into the yolk mixture, then gently but thoroughly fold in the remaining whites.

4 In the bowl in which the egg whites were beaten, whip the cream until soft peaks form. Gently but thoroughly fold the cream into the lemon mixture, then spoon into the prepared dish. Cover loosely with plastic wrap.

▽ At this point the soufflé can be stored. *Freeze* until solid — about 8 hours. Rewrap tightly with plastic wrap and aluminum foil and *freeze* for up to 5 days at 0° F.

5 Refrigerate the soufflé for at least 2 and up to 24 hours. When ready to serve, remove the collar and garnish with the lemon slices and whipped cream, if desired. Fresh blueberries, strawberries, or raspberries make a nice accompaniment. Serves 6 to 8.

### Serving Later

Serve as in Step 5. Do not thaw.

# Strawberry Mousse in Praline Baskets

Per serving without basket: Calories 188; Protein 3 g; Carbohydrate 12 g; Fat 15 g; Sodium 33 mg; Cholesterol 54 mg.

*This impressive dessert offers a wonderful combination of flavors and textures. You could also serve the mousse in Meringue Shells (page 250) or heaped in parfait glasses.*

- 2 envelopes unflavored gelatin
- ¼ cup cold water
- 3 cups strawberries, hulled and quartered (about 1½ pints)
- 4 egg whites
- ⅛ teaspoon cream of tartar
- ½ cup sugar
- 2 cups heavy cream
- 1 recipe Lacy Chocolate Praline Baskets (page 270)

*Optional garnishes:*
  Sliced strawberries
  Mint sprigs

1 In a small saucepan, heat the gelatin and the water over low heat, stirring, until the gelatin dissolves — about 5 minutes.

2 Meanwhile, purée the strawberries in an electric blender or food processor, then pour them into a large bowl. Add the gelatin mixture and stir well. Refrigerate until the consistency of raw egg whites — 15 to 20 minutes.

3 In a medium-size bowl, beat the egg whites with the cream of tartar until soft peaks form. Gradually beat in the sugar and continue beating until glossy — about 3 minutes. Gently but thoroughly fold the egg-white mixture into the strawberries.

4 In the bowl in which the egg whites were beaten, whip the cream until stiff peaks form. Gently but thoroughly fold the whipped cream into the strawberry mixture. Refrigerate, lightly covered with plastic wrap, for at least 4 and up to 24 hours.

5 Just before serving, spoon ½ cup of the mousse into each praline basket and garnish with sliced strawberries and sprigs of mint, if desired. If the mousse is presented in parfait glasses, it serves 12; in the praline baskets, it makes 22 servings.

# Light-as-Clouds Orange Mousse

Per serving: Calories 315; Protein 15 g; Carbohydrate 37 g; Fat 12 g; Sodium 166 mg; Cholesterol 428 mg.

*Serve this refreshing dessert in your prettiest stemmed glasses.*

- 2 envelopes unflavored gelatin
- ⅔ cup fresh orange juice (2 medium-size oranges)
- 1 quart milk

*Strawberry Mousse in Praline Baskets — for those who take their desserts seriously*

Grated rind of 1 orange
(about 2 tablespoons)
1 cup granulated sugar
12 eggs, separated
⅓ cup confectioners' sugar

1 In a small bowl, stir the gelatin into the orange juice and set aside. In a medium-size saucepan, scald the milk over low heat. Remove from the heat, add the gelatin mixture, orange rind, and sugar and stir until dissolved.

2 In a medium-size bowl, beat the egg yolks lightly. Slowly add 1 cup of the milk in a steady stream, beating until well combined. Pour the mixture into the pan with the milk and beat until well blended.

3 Cook over low heat, stirring constantly, until lightly thickened — about 15 minutes. Do not allow to boil or the custard will curdle. Pour into a large bowl, cover loosely, and chill until syrupy — about 1 hour.

4 In a medium-size bowl, beat the egg whites to soft peaks, gradually adding the confectioners' sugar. Gently but thoroughly fold the whites into the orange mixture. Transfer to a glass serving bowl or individual goblets and chill, covered, for at least 12 and up to 48 hours. Serves 8.

# Spiced Pears in Red Wine

Per serving: Calories 206; Protein 1 g; Carbohydrate 34 g; Fat 1 g; Sodium 12 mg; Cholesterol 0 mg.

- 2 cups dry red wine
- 1 cup cold water
- 2 tablespoons sugar
- 1 tablespoon lemon juice
- 1 cinnamon stick, broken
- 6 whole cloves
- 6 medium-size firm-ripe pears, such as Bartlett, cored, peeled, and with the stems left on
- 1 cup Vanilla Sauce (page 262) (optional)

1 In a large stainless steel or enamel saucepan, bring the wine, water, sugar, lemon juice, cinnamon stick, and cloves to a boil over moderate heat.

2 Place the pears, stem side up, in the saucepan, adjusting the heat so that the wine mixture barely simmers. Cook the pears, uncovered, basting frequently, until barely tender — about 15 minutes. Remove from the heat and let cool to room temperature, continuing to baste frequently.

3 Discard the cinnamon stick and cloves. Cover the pears and chill for at least 2 and up to 24 hours, basting occasionally. To serve, spoon into each dish about ⅓ cup Vanilla Sauce, if desired, and stand a pear in it. Or spoon about ¼ cup of the poaching liquid over each pear. Serves 6.

*Spiced Pears in Red Wine — served here with Vanilla Sauce — a simply beautiful dessert that deserves applause*

# Baked Apples in Apricot-Wine Sauce

Per serving: Calories 258; Protein 1 g; Carbohydrate 49 g; Fat 4 g; Sodium 7 mg; Cholesterol 10 mg.

- 6 large baking apples, such as Rome, Macintosh, Cortland, or Granny Smith
- ¾ cup raisins soaked in 2 tablespoons light rum for 30 minutes
- ½ teaspoon grated lemon rind
- ¼ cup sugar
- 2 tablespoons unsalted butter or margarine
- 1 cup white wine
- ½ cup boiling water
- 2 tablespoons apricot preserves
  Whipped cream for topping (optional)

1 Preheat the oven to 375° F. Remove all but the bottom ½ inch of the core of each apple, then peel a ½-inch-wide strip around the top of the cavity. Stand the apples in a shallow baking dish large enough to accommodate all of them in a single layer.

2 Stuff each apple with the raisins, then sprinkle with the lemon rind and sugar and dot with the butter. Spoon the wine over all. Add the boiling water to the pan, cover with aluminum foil, and bake for 25 minutes. Remove the foil and continue baking, basting frequently, until the apples are tender — 15 to 20 minutes more. Transfer to a serving platter.

3 Pour the pan juices into a small saucepan, stir in the apricot preserves, and cook over moderate heat until the preserves are melted and the sauce is hot — 3 to 4 minutes.

▽ At this point the apples and sauce can be cooled to room temperature and stored. Cover the ap-ples with aluminum foil and pour the sauce into a container and cover tightly. *Refrigerate* for up to 3 days.

4 Pour the sauce over the apples and pass the whipped cream on the side, if desired. Serves 6.

## Serving Later

Serve at room temperature or preheat the oven to 350° F and bake the foil-covered apples for 15 minutes or until warmed through. Add a little water to the pan if the apples seem dry. Reheat the sauce in a small saucepan over moderately low heat — about 5 minutes.

# Pear Custard

Per 6-ounce serving: Calories 456; Protein 10 g; Carbohydrate 42 g; Fat 29 g; Sodium 218 mg; Cholesterol 255 mg.

*This subtly flavored dessert tastes best when made with maple syrup.*

- 2 large firm-ripe pears, such as Bosc or Anjou (about 1 pound)
- 2 tablespoons water
- 1 tablespoon unsalted butter or margarine
- 1 teaspoon maple syrup or honey
- ¼ teaspoon each ground cinnamon and ground nutmeg

*For the custard:*
- 3 eggs
- 2 cups milk
- 2 tablespoons maple syrup or honey
- 2 teaspoons vanilla
- ⅛ teaspoon salt

*For the topping:*
- ½ cup chopped pecans
- 2 tablespoons unsalted butter or margarine, melted
- 2 tablespoons maple syrup or honey
- 2 tablespoons heavy cream or milk

1 Preheat the oven to 350° F. Peel, quarter, and core the pears. Cut them into ½-inch slices and mix with the water, butter, maple syrup, cinnamon, and nutmeg in a heavy 12-inch skillet. Cook, covered, over moderate heat, until the pears are tender but not mushy — about 5 minutes. Uncover and cook until all of the liquid has evaporated and the pears have started to caramelize — 4 minutes longer. Remove from the heat and set aside.

2 To prepare the custard: In a medium-size bowl or 2-quart measuring cup, whisk the eggs, milk, maple syrup, vanilla, and salt. Distribute the pears among four 6-ounce or six 4-ounce flameproof custard cups. Pour the custard over the pears.

3 Set the cups in a baking pan and pour hot water into the pan until it comes halfway up the sides of the cups. Bake, uncovered, for about 35 minutes or until a knife inserted midway between the rim and the center comes out clean. Transfer the cups to a wire rack and cool to room temperature — 30 to 40 minutes. Cover with plastic wrap and refrigerate for at least 2 hours. Will keep for up to 3 days.

4 Preheat the broiler. Sprinkle the cold custards with the pecans. Whisk together the butter, maple syrup, and cream; spoon the mixture over the custards. Broil 6 inches from the heat for about 3 minutes or until the topping bubbles. Serve immediately. Serves 4 to 6.

# Cranberry Fool

Per serving: Calories 306; Protein 1 g; Carbohydrate 28 g; Fat 22 g; Sodium 226 mg; Cholesterol 82 mg.

- 2 cups cranberries, picked over, stemmed, and rinsed
- 1 cup sugar
- 2 cups heavy cream

*Optional garnishes:*
- Fresh mint leaves
- Whole cranberries

1 In a heavy medium-size saucepan, cook the cranberries and sugar, uncovered, over moderately low heat for 15 to 20 minutes or until a thick syrup has formed. Stir occasionally, lightly crushing the berries against the side of the pan with the back of the spoon.

2 Remove from the heat and transfer to a medium-size bowl. Cool to room temperature. Cover with plastic wrap and refrigerate for about 2 hours.

3 In a large bowl, whip the cream until stiff peaks form. Fold the cranberry mixture into the whipped cream. Cover tightly with plastic wrap and refrigerate for at least 2 hours and up to 24 hours. Garnish with the mint leaves and cranberries, if desired. Serves 8.

*A smart, sweet pairing — Cranberry Fool and Steamed Ginger Pudding*

# Noodle Pudding with Vanilla Sauce

Per square without sauce: Calories 295; Protein 10 g; Carbohydrate 41 g; Fat 11 g; Sodium 118 mg; Cholesterol 111 mg.

- 8 ounces medium-width egg noodles
- 4 eggs
- 1 cup cottage cheese
- 1 cup apple sauce
- 1 cup coarsely chopped walnuts
- ¾ cup sugar
- ¾ cup golden raisins
- 2 cups milk or half-and-half
- 2 teaspoons ground cinnamon
- 2 teaspoons vanilla
- ½ teaspoon ground cloves
  Confectioners' sugar (optional)
- 2¼ cups Vanilla Sauce (page 262)

1 Cook the pasta according to package directions until *al dente* (see Tip, page 161). Drain and rinse under cold running water.

2 Preheat the oven to 350° F. In a large bowl, whisk the eggs until light and frothy. Whisk in the cottage cheese, apple sauce, walnuts, sugar, raisins, milk, cinnamon, vanilla, and cloves. Stir in the noodles. Pour into a buttered, 13" x 9" x 2" baking dish, spreading the mixture evenly.

3 Bake, covered loosely with aluminum foil, for about 1 hour or until a skewer inserted midway between the center and the rim comes out clean. Let cool to room temperature on a rack.

▽ At this point the pudding can be covered tightly with plastic wrap and *refrigerated* for up to 4 days.

4 Divide the pudding into 12 squares. Dust with confectioners' sugar, if desired. Spoon 3 tablespoons of Vanilla Sauce into each dessert dish and top with a square of pudding. Serves 12.

### Serving Later

About ½ hour before serving, set the pudding out to come to room temperature. Serve as in Step 4.

# Steamed Ginger Pudding

Per serving: Calories 618; Protein 9 g; Carbohydrate 70 g; Fat 34 g; Sodium 303 mg; Cholesterol 180 mg.

*For Christmas, this is a light and pleasing alternative to the traditional plum pudding.*

- 5 cups all-purpose flour
- 2 tablespoons baking powder
- 1 tablespoon ground ginger
- ½ teaspoon ground cloves
- ½ teaspoon salt
- 2 cups (4 sticks) unsalted butter or margarine, at room temperature
- 1 cup sugar
- 4 eggs
- 4 ounces candied ginger, finely chopped
- 2 cups milk
- ¾ cup golden raisins (optional)
- ¾ cup red currant jelly

1 Sift together the flour, baking powder, ginger, cloves, and salt onto a sheet of wax paper.

2 In a large bowl, cream the butter and sugar until fluffy. Beat in the eggs, one at a time, until well combined. Stir in the candied ginger. Using a wooden spoon, alternately stir in the dry ingredients and milk by fourths. Stir in the raisins, if desired.

3 Spoon the mixture into 2 lightly greased, 1½-quart pudding molds or other molds, or a 3-quart Bundt pan. Cover tightly with heavy-duty aluminum foil and secure with string. Set wire racks in the bottom of 2 steamers or large saucepans, pour in boiling water until it touches the racks, and set a mold on each rack.

4 Cover and simmer over moderately low heat for 2½ to 3 hours or until a skewer poked through the aluminum foil into the center of each pudding comes out clean. Keep the steamer water at rack level, adding boiling water when needed. Let the molds cool on wire racks for about 45 minutes.

▽ At this point the puddings can be cooled completely and stored. *Refrigerate*, tightly covered with aluminum foil, for up to 2 days.

5 To prepare the glaze: Heat the jelly in a small heavy saucepan over moderately low heat, stirring occasionally, until syrupy — about 5 minutes. Carefully unmold the warm pudding onto a serving plate. Brush with the currant glaze and serve in thin slices with Cranberry Fool (page 258) or hard sauce. Serves 12 to 16.

### Serving Later

Transfer the puddings to 2 large saucepans; cover and steam, as in Steps 3 and 4, for about 45 minutes. Serve as in Step 5.

# Apple-Ginger Sorbet

Per ½-cup serving: Calories 163; Protein tr;
Carbohydrate 42 g; Fat tr; Sodium 1 mg;
Cholesterol 0 mg.

- 1½ cups sugar
- ¾ cup water
- ¾ cup apple cider or juice
- 1 teaspoon ground ginger
- ¼ teaspoon ground cinnamon
- 6 large tart apples, such as
  Granny Smith, peeled, cored,
  and coarsely chopped (about
  2¾ pounds)
- ¼ cup lemon juice
- ½ cup Calvados or apple juice

Optional garnishes:
   Calvados
   Chopped candied ginger
   Mint leaves

1 In a medium-size saucepan, whisk
together the sugar, water, and apple
juice. Heat over moderate heat, stirring
occasionally, just until the sugar dissolves and bubbles begin to form in the
bottom of the pan — 8 to 10 minutes.
Transfer to a large mixing bowl. Add
the spices, stirring constantly until they
dissolve. Refrigerate for 20 minutes.

2 Meanwhile, in an electric blender or
food processor, purée the apples
along with the lemon juice and Calvados. Add to the chilled syrup.

3 Pour into a 13" x 9" x 2" pan, cover
tightly with heavy-duty aluminum
foil, and freeze until ice crystals begin
to form — about 45 minutes.

4 Scrape into a large bowl and beat
until the crystals have dissolved
and the mixture is relatively smooth
(apple-sauce consistency). Re-cover
and refreeze. Repeat this process until
the sorbet has a smooth, firm, and
finely grained consistency. Refreeze,
covered tightly, for at least 2 hours and
up to 1 week. Or freeze in an ice-cream
freezer according to the manufacturer's
instructions and store in the freezer
until ready to serve.

5 About 30 minutes before serving,
transfer the sorbet from the freezer
to the refrigerator to allow it to soften
slightly. Top each serving with 1 tablespoon Calvados, fresh mint leaves, and
chopped candied ginger, if desired.
Makes about 3 pints.

# Chocolate-Orange Sorbet

Per ½-cup serving: Calories 247; Protein 2 g;
Carbohydrate 63 g; Fat 2 g; Sodium 2 mg;
Cholesterol 0 mg.

- 1⅔ cups sugar
- 1½ cups water
- 4 strips orange zest (colored
  part of the rind), each ½ inch
  by 2 inches
- 1 cup orange juice
- ¾ cup unsweetened cocoa

1 In a medium-size saucepan, bring
the sugar, water, and orange zest to
a boil over moderate heat, stirring until
the sugar dissolves — 4 to 5 minutes.
Remove from the heat, cover, and cool
to room temperature. Discard the zest.

2 In a large bowl, gradually stir the
orange juice into the cocoa until no
lumps remain. Blend in the sugar syrup.

3 For freezing and storing, see Steps 3
and 4 of Apple-Ginger Sorbet (left).
About 30 minutes before serving,
transfer the sorbet to the refrigerator to
allow it to soften slightly. Serve on
Meringue Shells (page 250) or with
cookies. Makes about 1 quart.

# Lime-Pineapple-Buttermilk Sherbet

Per ½-cup serving: Calories 166; Protein 4 g;
Carbohydrate 35 g; Fat 2 g; Sodium 97 mg;
Cholesterol 71 mg.

*In this refreshing low-calorie dessert,
you can substitute lemon or orange
juice for the lime, and plain yogurt for
the buttermilk, if you like.*

- 2 eggs
- ½ cup sugar
- ½ cup light corn syrup
- 2 cups buttermilk
- ¼ cup fresh lime juice
- 1 can (8 ounces) crushed
  pineapple, drained

1    teaspoon grated lime or
     lemon rind for garnish
     (optional)

1  In a large bowl, beat the eggs until
   thick and creamy. Still beating,
gradually add the sugar. Stir in the corn
syrup, buttermilk, lime juice, and pineapple until well mixed.

2  For freezing and storing, see Steps 3
   and 4 of Apple-Ginger Sorbet (opposite page). About 30 minutes before
serving, transfer the sherbet from the
freezer to the refrigerator to allow it to
soften slightly. Serve with gingersnaps.
Or add 1 scoop to a glass of ginger ale
for a tasty float. Makes about 1 quart.

# Honeydew Ice

Per ½-cup serving: Calories 133; Protein 2 g;
Carbohydrate 33 g; Fat tr; Sodium 20 mg;
Cholesterol 0 mg.

1    envelope unflavored gelatin
3    tablespoons cold water
1    small honeydew melon (5
     inches in diameter), peeled,
     seeded, and coarsely
     chopped
¼    cup honey
1½   tablespoons lime juice, or to
     taste

1  In a small saucepan, soften the
   gelatin in the cold water for about 5
minutes. Set over low heat and stir until
dissolved — about 3 minutes.

2  In an electric blender or food processor, purée the melon in batches,
then transfer to a medium-size bowl.
Stir in the gelatin, honey, and lime juice
until well mixed. Pour the mixture into
a nonaluminum, 9-inch baking dish,
cover tightly with plastic wrap, and
freeze until firm — 2 to 4 hours.

3  In an electric blender or food processor, purée the ice in batches
until smooth but not liquefied; refreeze. Will keep for up to 3 days at
0° F. Makes about 1 pint.

## Watermelon Ice

Per ½-cup serving: Calories 127; Protein 2 g;
Carbohydrate 30 g; Fat tr; Sodium 24 mg;
Cholesterol 0 mg.

Follow directions for Honeydew Ice, substituting the flesh of **3 pounds of watermelon, seeded and coarsely chopped,**
for the honeydew melon, **½ cup light
corn syrup, or to taste,** for the honey,
and **2 tablespoons lemon juice** for the
lime juice. Makes about 1½ pints.

## Cantaloupe Ice

Per ½-cup serving: Calories 136; Protein 3 g;
Carbohydrate 32 g; Fat tr; Sodium 17 mg;
Cholesterol 0 mg.

Follow directions for Honeydew Ice,
substituting **¼ cup orange juice** and
the flesh of **2½ pounds of cantaloupe,
seeded and coarsely chopped,** for the
honeydew melon, and **1 tablespoon
lemon juice** for the lime juice. Add **2
teaspoons finely grated orange rind.**
Makes about 1 pint.

*To be shared, to be savored — Cantaloupe Ice and Watermelon Ice*

# Peach Melba Torte

Per serving: Calories 393; Protein 4 g;
Carbohydrate 70 g; Fat 11 g; Sodium 133 mg;
Cholesterol 44 mg.

- 1 cup graham cracker, vanilla
  wafer, or gingersnap crumbs
- 2 tablespoons unsalted butter
  or margarine, at room
  temperature
- ½ gallon vanilla ice cream,
  softened

*For the peach sauce:*
- 3 medium-size peaches,
  peeled and sliced (2½ cups)
- ¾ cup sugar
- ¼ cup light corn syrup
- 2 tablespoons cornstarch
  blended with 2 tablespoons
  water

*For the raspberry sauce:*
- 3 cups fresh or frozen
  raspberries
- ⅔ cup sugar
- ⅓ cup light corn syrup
- ¼ cup cornstarch blended with
  ⅓ cup water

*Optional garnishes:*
  Fresh whole raspberries
  Mint leaves

1 In an ungreased, 9-inch springform pan, toss together the crumbs and butter until blended. Set aside 1 tablespoon, then press the remainder evenly over the bottom of the pan. Set in the freezer while preparing the sauces.

2 To prepare the peach sauce: In an electric blender or food processor, purée the peaches — about 30 seconds. In a medium-size saucepan, combine the purée, sugar, corn syrup, and cornstarch paste. Bring to a boil over moderate heat, and cook, stirring constantly, until the mixture thickens slightly and mounds when dropped from a spoon — 2 to 3 minutes. Transfer to a medium-size bowl; press a piece of plastic wrap directly on the surface. Refrigerate until thoroughly chilled and thick enough to spread — 20 to 30 minutes.

3 Meanwhile, in another medium-size saucepan, prepare the raspberry sauce: Bring all of the ingredients to a boil over moderate heat, and cook, stirring constantly, until the mixture thickens slightly — 2 to 3 minutes. Press through a fine sieve into another medium-size bowl. Press a piece of plastic wrap directly on the surface and refrigerate until chilled and thick enough to spread — 20 to 30 minutes.

4 Spread ⅓ of the ice cream evenly over the graham cracker crust and top with about ¼ of the peach sauce and ½ of the raspberry sauce. Repeat; then top with the remaining ice cream and sprinkle with the reserved graham cracker crumbs. Refrigerate the remaining peach sauce until ready to serve. Cover the torte tightly with aluminum foil and freeze for at least 6 hours or until firm. Will keep for up to 3 days.

5 To serve, loosen the sides of the springform pan; let the torte sit at room temperature for about 10 minutes before cutting it into wedges. Pass the remaining peach sauce. Serves 12.

# Frozen Banana Pops

Per pop: Calories 258; Protein 2 g;
Carbohydrate 28 g; Fat 15 g; Sodium 1 mg;
Cholesterol 0 mg.

- 6 firm-ripe bananas
- 12 popsickle or lollipop sticks
- 1 package (12 ounces)
  semisweet chocolate chips
- 6 tablespoons vegetable oil
  Sprinkles, coconut, or
  chopped nuts for garnish
  (optional)

1 Peel the bananas and cut in half crosswise. Insert a popsickle stick halfway into the cut end of each banana half and lay on a baking sheet. Freeze for at least 1 hour or overnight.

2 Melt the chocolate in the top of a double boiler over simmering water. Stir in the oil. Dip each frozen banana into the chocolate mixture, turning to coat all over. While the coating is still soft, roll in the sprinkles, coconut, or nuts, if you wish. Let the coating set — about 5 minutes — then store in the freezer. When thoroughly frozen, wrap each pop in aluminum foil. Will keep for up to 2 weeks at 0° F. Makes 12 pops.

# Vanilla Sauce

Per ¼ cup serving: Calories 114; Protein 3 g;
Carbohydrate 15 g; Fat 5 g; Sodium 66 mg;
Cholesterol 144 mg.

- 2 cups milk
- 4 egg yolks, lightly beaten
- ½ cup sugar
- ⅛ teaspoon salt
- 1 teaspoon vanilla

1 In the top of a double boiler, scald the milk over moderate heat. Whisk a little of the hot milk into the egg yolks, stir the mixture back into the pan, and set over simmering water. Add the sugar and salt. Stir constantly until the mixture begins to thicken — about 3 minutes. Do not allow to boil or the sauce may curdle. Remove from the heat and stir in the vanilla.

▽ At this point the sauce can be cooled to room temperature and stored. Transfer to a medium-size bowl, lay a piece of plastic wrap on the surface to prevent skin from forming, and *refrigerate* for up to 3 days.

2 Serve warm, at room temperature, or chilled over fresh or cooked fruit, warm unfrosted cake, a cobbler, or a fruit crumble. This sauce goes especially well with Noodle Pudding (page 259) or Spiced Pears in Red Wine (page 256). Makes about 1 pint.

## Serving Later

Let the sauce come to room temperature — about 20 minutes. Or heat in a double boiler, stirring constantly, until just warmed through — 5 to 8 minutes.

# Orange-Ginger Sauce

Per 1/4-cup serving: Calories 162; Protein 1 g; Carbohydrate 34 g; Fat 3 g; Sodium 2 mg; Cholesterol 42 mg.

*If you prefer a more tart sauce, reduce the sugar to 3/4 cup.*

- 1 cup sugar
- 2 tablespoons cornstarch
- 1 1/2 cups water
  Juice of 1 orange
  Juice of 1 lemon
- 1 egg yolk
- 2 teaspoons grated orange rind
- 2 tablespoons unsalted butter or margarine
- 1/3 cup chopped candied or preserved ginger

1 In a medium-size saucepan, combine the sugar and cornstarch. Stir in the water, orange and lemon juices, and bring to a boil over moderate heat. Cook, stirring constantly, until thickened and clear — about 5 minutes.

2 In a small bowl, beat the egg yolk with the orange rind. Still beating, pour a little of the hot mixture into the yolk; pour the yolk mixture into the saucepan. Cook over low heat, stirring constantly, for about 2 minutes or until no taste of raw egg remains.

3 Remove from the heat and add the butter, stirring until it melts and the mixture is smooth. Stir in the ginger.

▽ At this point the sauce can be cooled to room temperature, tightly covered with plastic wrap, and *refrigerated* for up to 3 days.

4 Let stand for about 5 minutes before serving. Spoon the warm sauce over gingerbread or vanilla ice cream. Makes 1 pint.

## Serving Later

Remove the plastic wrap and reheat over moderately low heat, stirring, for about 8 minutes or until the sauce is warm. Do not boil. Serve as in Step 4.

# Lemon Curd

Per 1/4-cup serving: Calories 232; Protein 3 g; Carbohydrate 22 g; Fat 15 g; Sodium 55 mg; Cholesterol 202 mg.

*This easy-to-make sweet is sublime as a filling for Meringue Shells (page 250) or simply spread it on bread.*

- 3 eggs plus 2 egg yolks
- 8 tablespoons (1 stick) unsalted butter or margarine, cut up
- 3/4 cup granulated sugar
- 2 tablespoons light brown sugar
- 1/2 cup fresh lemon juice (about 3 medium-size lemons)
  Pinch of salt

1 Combine all ingredients in the top of a double boiler or in a large heatproof bowl set over, not in, boiling water. Cook over moderately high heat, beating constantly with a whisk or an electric mixer on low speed, until the mixture is the consistency of thick honey — 15 to 20 minutes.

2 Pour into 2 sterilized, 1/2-pint preserving jars; cover tightly. (See Step 3, Gingered Pear Marmalade, page 224 for sterilizing; you do not have to seal the jars or use a water bath.) Or let cool to room temperature and transfer to a tightly covered container. Refrigerate for up to 2 weeks in the sterilized jars, up to 5 days in the covered container. Makes about 1 pint.

# Plum Sauce

Per 1/4 cup serving: Calories 202; Protein tr; Carbohydrate 32 g; Fat 9 g; Sodium 1 mg; Cholesterol 26 mg.

*If you like your desserts less sweet, use only 1/2 cup sugar.*

- 3/4 cup sugar
- 1 1/2 tablespoons cornstarch
- 1/2 teaspoon ground nutmeg
- 4 large ripe purple plums, peeled, pitted, and puréed (about 3/4 pound)
- 6 tablespoons (3/4 stick) unsalted butter or margarine
- 1 teaspoon lemon juice, or to taste

1 In a medium-size saucepan, combine the sugar, cornstarch, and nutmeg. Add the puréed plums and bring to a boil over moderate heat, stirring constantly. Cook, stirring, until thickened and clear — about 3 minutes.

2 Reduce the heat to low. Add the butter, stirring occasionally until it is melted and blended in. Stir in the lemon juice, then remove the sauce from the heat.

▽ At this point the sauce can be cooled to room temperature and stored. *Refrigerate* in a tightly covered container for up to 5 days.

3 Cool the sauce slightly, then transfer to a serving dish. Spoon over vanilla ice cream, gingerbread, or sponge cake. Makes about 1 3/4 cups.

## Serving Later

In a small saucepan, reheat the sauce, stirring constantly, over moderately low heat until warmed through — 3 to 4 minutes.

*Ease into a Maine state of mind with irresistible Down East Blueberry Buckle.*

# Orange Brownie Cake

Per serving: Calories 437; Protein 7 g;
Carbohydrate 35 g; Fat 30 g; Sodium 53 mg;
Cholesterol 135 mg.

*This chocoholic's delight is easy to
prepare in the food processor. But be
careful not to overprocess the nuts or
they will turn to paste.*

   4   ounces semisweet chocolate
   1   cup blanched shelled
       almonds or walnuts, finely
       ground
   ¼   cup plain dry bread crumbs
   1   tablespoon grated orange
       rind
   ⅔   cup sugar
   ½   cup (1 stick) unsalted butter
       or margarine, at room
       temperature

   3   eggs
   1   tablespoon orange-flavored
       liqueur (optional)

*For the glaze:*
   2   ounces semisweet chocolate
   1   ounce unsweeteened
       chocolate
   3   tablespoons unsalted butter
       or margarine
   1   tablespoon honey
       Sliced almonds for garnish

1 Preheat the oven to 375° F. Melt
the 4 ounces of semisweet chocolate in the top of a double boiler set
over simmering water. Meanwhile, in a
large bowl, mix the nuts, bread crumbs,
orange rind, and 3 tablespoons of the
sugar. Transfer to a sheet of wax paper
and set aside.

2 In the same bowl, cream the butter
and the remaining sugar until light
and fluffy. Add the eggs 1 at a time,
beating until well incorporated. Add
the melted chocolate, the nut mixture,
and the liqueur, if desired, and blend
just until combined.

3 Pour the batter evenly into an 8-
inch, round cake pan, the bottom
lined with greased wax paper lightly
dusted with flour. Smooth the batter
and bake until the top of the cake is
firm and slightly cracking — about 25
minutes. Do not test with a toothpick.

4 Cool upright in the pan on a rack for
10 minutes, then turn out onto a
plate and cool completely. (The cake
will fall slightly.)

▽ At this point the cake can be
wrapped in aluminum foil and
*refrigerated* for up to 3 days or *frozen*
for up to 1 month at 0° F.

**5** For the glaze: In the top of a double boiler set over simmering water, melt the chocolates and the butter over low heat. Stir in the honey. Meanwhile, brush any crumbs off the cake and lay 3 strips of wax paper on a serving plate. Place the cake in the center of the plate, arranging the paper strips to keep the glaze from running onto the plate.

**6** Spoon the glaze over the cake; using a thin spatula, spread it over the top and sides. Carefully slide out the paper strips and garnish the cake with the almonds. Refrigerate until the glaze is firm — at least 1 hour. Will keep for up to 3 days. Serves 8.

# Lemon Tea Cake

Per serving: Calories 321; Protein 4 g; Carbohydrate 33 g; Fat 20 g; Sodium 231 mg; Cholesterol 120 mg.

*If you prefer, substitute for the confectioners' sugar 1 cup of puréed raspberries or a glaze made with 1/2 cup confectioners' sugar and 1 tablespoon lemon juice.*

1 1/2   cups all-purpose flour
1   teaspoon baking powder
1   cup (2 sticks) unsalted butter or margarine, at room temperature
4   ounces cream cheese, at room temperature
1 1/3   cups sugar
3   eggs
1   tablespoon grated lemon rind
  Confectioners' sugar

**1** Preheat the oven to 350° F. On a large piece of wax paper, sift together the flour and baking powder.

**2** In a large mixing bowl, beat together the butter and cream cheese until well blended. Beat in the sugar, eggs, and lemon rind until the mixture is light and fluffy. Add the flour mixture, stirring just until smooth.

**3** Spoon the batter into a 10-inch tube pan, the bottom lined with greased wax paper lightly dusted with flour. Smooth the top and bake until the cake is a light golden brown and springs back when pressed lightly — 55 to 60 minutes.

**4** Cool in the upright pan on a wire rack for 15 minutes; turn out onto the rack and let cool completely. See Tip, right, for storing and serving later. Just before serving, sprinkle with the confectioners' sugar. Serves 12 to 16.

# Down East Blueberry Buckle

Per serving: Calories 427; Protein 5 g; Carbohydrate 57 g; Fat 20 g; Sodium 437 mg; Cholesterol 87 mg.

*This luscious dessert can also be made with apricots, peaches, pears, or apples. It's good for breakfast, too.*

For the topping:
1/2   cup sugar
1/2   cup flour
3/4   teaspoon ground cinnamon
5   tablespoons unsalted butter or margarine, chilled

For the buckle:
2   cups all-purpose flour
2 1/2   teaspoons baking powder
1/2   teaspoon salt
1/2   cup (1 stick) unsalted butter or margarine, softened
1/2   cup sugar
1   egg
1/2   cup milk
1   pint fresh blueberries, stemmed and washed, or frozen dry-pack blueberries (not defrosted)

**1** Preheat the oven to 375° F. To prepare the topping: In a medium-size bowl, mix together the sugar, flour, and cinnamon. Cut the butter in with a pastry blender or 2 knives until the mixture resembles coarse meal. Transfer to a sheet of wax paper.

**2** To prepare the buckle: On a sheet of wax paper, sift together the flour, baking powder, and salt. Set aside. Wipe out the topping bowl and in it cream together the butter and sugar until light. Add the egg and beat for 1 minute or until fluffy. Blend in 1/2 of the flour mixture, then the milk, then the remaining flour.

**3** Spoon the batter into a greased, 8" x 8" x 2" baking pan. Spread on the blueberries in an even layer, then sprinkle with the topping. Bake until puffed and nicely browned — about 1 1/4 hours. Cool in the upright pan on a rack for 15 minutes. Cut into squares and serve hot or warm. Vanilla ice cream or whipped cream makes a nice topping. For storing and serving later, see Tip, below. Serves 8 to 10.

*Tip: Most cakes will keep well for a day or two at room temperature if protected by a cake cover or by a wrapping of aluminum foil or plastic. If you plan to freeze a cake, it is best to freeze it unfrosted (frosting a frozen cake is easier, too). Wrap each layer in heavy-duty aluminum foil, label, and freeze at 0° F for up to 8 months. If you choose to freeze a frosted cake, use a frosting made with butter and confectioners' sugar; it should not contain egg whites, brown sugar, or artificial flavorings. Partially freeze the cake first, then protect the icing with a layer of wax paper before wrapping it in aluminum foil. Allow 1 to 2 hours for a cake to defrost at room temperature.*

# Penuche and Raisin Layer Cake

Per serving: Calories 534; Protein 5 g; Carbohydrate 73 g; Fat 25 g; Sodium 207 mg; Cholesterol 148 mg.

*As rich and sugary as penuche candy, this cake is for real sweets-lovers.*

  2   cups sifted all-purpose flour
  1   teaspoon baking powder
  ¼   teaspoon salt
  5   tablespoons unsalted butter or margarine, at room temperature
  1   cup granulated sugar
  3   eggs
  1   teaspoon vanilla
  ⅔   cup milk

*For the frosting:*
  ½   cup golden raisins
  3   tablespoons bourbon or rum
  4   tablespoons unsalted butter or margarine
  2   cups firmly packed dark brown sugar
  2   cups heavy cream

**1** Preheat the oven to 400° F. On a piece of wax paper, sift together the flour, baking powder, and salt. Set aside. In a large bowl, cream the butter and sugar until light and fluffy. Add the eggs one at a time, beating after each addition. Stir in the vanilla.

**2** Add ⅓ of the milk, then ⅓ of the flour mixture to the egg mixture, stirring until just combined. Repeat twice more. Divide the batter between two 9-inch, round baking pans, the bottoms lined with greased wax paper lightly dusted with flour. Smooth the tops and bake until a toothpick inserted in the center comes out clean — about 25 minutes.

**3** Cool the cakes in the pans on racks for 5 minutes, then turn out onto the racks and let cool completely.

▽ At this point the the cakes can be stored. Wrap tightly in aluminum foil and *refrigerate* for up to 24 hours; *freeze* for up to 1 month at 0° F.

**4** To prepare the frosting: In a small bowl, marinate the raisins in the bourbon for at least 30 minutes. Meanwhile, in a heavy medium-size saucepan, bring the sugar and 1 cup of the cream to a boil over moderate heat. Reduce the heat to low; cook, uncovered, until the mixture reaches 238° F on a candy thermometer or a small quantity dropped in a cup of cold water forms a soft ball — about 15 minutes.

**5** Remove from the heat and stir in the butter. Set the pan in a large bowl filled with ice and water and let cool, stirring occasionally, until the temperature reaches 160° F. Stir in the raisins and bourbon; cool to room temperature. Chill for 15 minutes.

**6** In a large bowl, whip the remaining cup of cream until stiff peaks form. Gently fold in the raisin mixture and refrigerate until well chilled — about 30 minutes. Meanwhile, using a long thin knife, slice each cake in half horizontally, making 4 layers.

**7** Place one layer on a serving plate and spread about 1/6th of the frosting over the top. Repeat with the remaining layers, then frost the sides of the cake. This cake can be refrigerated, loosely covered with an aluminum foil tent or a large bowl, for up to 3 days. Serves 12 to 16.

## Serving Later

Set the cake out to come to room temperature, then proceed as in Steps 4 through 7.

# Chocolate Trifle

Per serving: Calories 608; Protein 11 g; Carbohydrate 62 g; Fat 36 g; Sodium 188 mg; Cholesterol 406 mg.

*Here is a wonderful chocolate version of a favorite English dessert. Tradition calls for it to be presented in a pretty glass bowl to show off the layers.*

*For the chocolate sponge cake:*
  6   eggs
  1   cup sugar
  1 ½   teaspoons vanilla
  ⅔   cup all-purpose flour
  ⅓   cup unsweetened cocoa powder
  ½   teaspoon salt
  6   tablespoons (¾ stick) unsalted butter or margarine, melted

*For the custard cream:*
  6   egg yolks
  ½   cup sugar
  3   tablespoons flour
  3   cups half-and-half, scalded
  1   teaspoon vanilla

*For the assembly:*
  ¾   cup strained raspberry preserves
  ¾   cup toasted slivered almonds
  ⅓   cup raspberry liqueur or crème de cassis (optional)
  ½   cup dry sherry
  1   cup heavy cream
      Chocolate curls for garnish

**1** Preheat the oven to 350° F. To prepare the chocolate sponge cake: In a medium-size bowl, whisk together the eggs and sugar until well combined. Set the bowl over simmering water and whisk until the sugar has dissolved — 3 to 4 minutes.

**2** Remove from the water and, using an electric mixer, beat until the mixture forms a thick ribbonlike stream when dropped from a spoon — about 10 minutes. Then beat in the vanilla.

3 Sift together the flour, cocoa, and salt onto a piece of wax paper, then gradually fold these dry ingredients into the egg mixture until just combined. Fold in the butter.

4 Divide the batter between two 8" x 8" x 2" pans, the bottoms lined with buttered wax paper lightly dusted with flour. Smooth the top and bake until a toothpick inserted in the center comes out clean — 30 to 35 minutes. Cool the pans upright on racks for 5 minutes, then turn the cakes out onto the racks and let cool completely.

5 Meanwhile, prepare the custard cream: In a medium-size bowl, beat the egg yolks lightly. Add the sugar and beat until thick and pale. Beat in the flour, then add the half-and-half in a slow stream, stirring constantly. Transfer to a medium-size saucepan, and cook over moderately low heat, stirring, until thickened — about 5 minutes. Do not boil. Strain the custard into a bowl and stir in the vanilla. Press a sheet of plastic wrap directly on the surface and chill until cold — about 1 hour.

▽ At this point the cake and custard can be stored. Wrap the cake in plastic wrap and *store* in a cool dry place for up to 24 hours. *Refrigerate* the custard for up to 24 hours.

6 To assemble: Spread the top of each cake layer with the raspberry preserves and sprinkle with ½ cup of the almonds. Sandwich the coated sides together, then cut into 1- by 3-inch fingers. Arrange the fingers on the bottom and partially up the sides of a deep 10- to 12-inch glass serving bowl. Pour the liqueur, if desired, and the sherry evenly over the cake and let them soak in for 10 minutes. Spoon the custard cream on top, cover, and chill for at least 2 and up to 24 hours.

7 In a medium-size bowl, whip the cream until stiff peaks form (see Tip, page 272, on preparing it ahead), then spoon on top of the custard. Garnish the trifle with the chocolate curls. Serves 10 to 12.

*Superlative's the word —
Chocolate Trifle*

# Sugar Cookies

Per cookie: Calories 51; Protein 1 g;
Carbohydrate 6 g; Fat 3 g; Sodium 37 mg;
Cholesterol 15 mg.

- 2 cups Basic Cookie Mix (page 16)
- ½ cup (1 stick) unsalted butter or margarine, melted
- 1 egg, lightly beaten
- 1 teaspoon vanilla

1 Preheat the oven to 350° F. In a large bowl, combine all ingredients. With lightly floured hands, shape the dough into 1-inch balls; arrange them about 2 inches apart on 2 lightly greased, 13" x 9" x 1" baking sheets.

2 Bake for 12 to 15 minutes or until golden. Let cool for 1 to 2 minutes on the baking sheets; using a spatula, transfer to wire racks to cool completely. The cookies can be stored in a tightly covered container at room temperature for up to 1 week. Makes about 3 dozen 2½-inch cookies.

# Ginger Icebox Cookies

Per cookie: Calories 60; Protein 1 g;
Carbohydrate 8 g; Fat 3 g; Sodium 14 mg;
Cholesterol 7 mg.

- 3½ cups sifted all-purpose flour
- ½ teaspoon baking soda
- ¼ teaspoon salt
- 1 tablespoon ground ginger
- ½ teaspoon ground cinnamon
- ¼ teaspoon ground allspice
- 1 cup (2 sticks) unsalted butter or margarine, at room temperature
- 1 cup firmly packed light brown sugar
- ½ cup molasses

1 Onto a sheet of wax paper, sift together the flour, baking soda, salt, and spices. In a large bowl, cream the butter and sugar until light and fluffy.

2 Alternately mix the dry ingredients and the molasses into the butter mixture until the dough is smooth. Divide the dough in half and form each into a roll about 2 inches in diameter. Wrap in aluminum foil or plastic wrap; chill until firm — about 3 hours.

▽ At this point the dough can be stored. *Refrigerate* for up to 10 days. *Freeze*, wrapped in heavy-duty aluminum foil and labeled, for up to 2 months at 0° F.

3 Preheat the oven to 350° F. Slice each roll ⅛ inch thick, space the slices 1½ inches apart on ungreased baking sheets, and bake for about 10 minutes or until firm. Let cool for 1 minute on the pans, then transfer to wire racks to cool completely. Makes about 6 dozen 2-inch cookies.

### Serving Later

**From the freezer:** Proceed as in Step 3, baking for 10 to 12 minutes or until firm.

## Peanut Butter Cookies

Per cookie: Calories 64; Protein 2 g; Carbohydrate 7 g; Fat 3 g; Sodium 54 mg; Cholesterol 11 mg.

*If you use all-natural peanut butter, add an extra tablespoon of butter or margarine to the dough.*

- 2 cups Basic Cookie Mix (page 16)
- 1 egg, lightly beaten
- 5 tablespoons unsalted butter or margarine, melted
- ½ cup chunky or creamy peanut butter
- 1 teaspoon vanilla

1 Preheat the oven to 350° F. In a large bowl, stir together all of the ingredients until well combined. With lightly floured hands, roll the dough into 1-inch balls and arrange them 2 inches apart on 2 lightly greased, 13" x 9" x 1" baking sheets. Flatten each cookie slightly with a fork.

2 Bake for 12 to 15 minutes or until golden. Let cool for 1 to 2 minutes on the baking sheets; using a spatula, transfer to wire racks to cool completely. The cookies can be stored in a tightly covered container at room temperature for up to 1 week. Makes about 3 dozen 2½-inch cookies.

*Sugar, Peanut Butter, and Chocolate Chip Cookies — there'll never be enough on hand.*

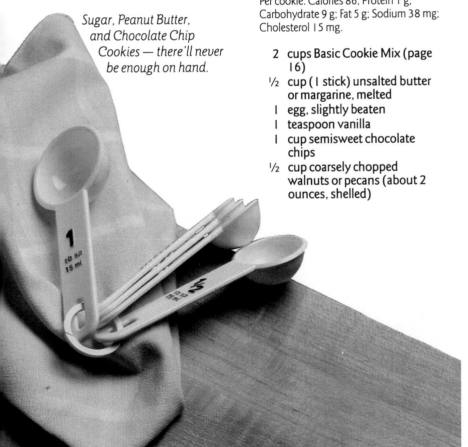

## Chocolate Chip Cookies

Per cookie: Calories 86; Protein 1 g; Carbohydrate 9 g; Fat 5 g; Sodium 38 mg; Cholesterol 15 mg.

- 2 cups Basic Cookie Mix (page 16)
- ½ cup (1 stick) unsalted butter or margarine, melted
- 1 egg, slightly beaten
- 1 teaspoon vanilla
- 1 cup semisweet chocolate chips
- ½ cup coarsely chopped walnuts or pecans (about 2 ounces, shelled)

1 Preheat the oven to 350° F. In a large bowl, combine the Basic Cookie Mix, butter, egg, and vanilla. Stir in the chocolate chips and walnuts, distributing them well. With lightly floured hands, roll the dough into 1-inch balls; arrange them 2 inches apart on 2 lightly greased, 13" x 9" x 1" baking sheets.

2 Bake for 12 to 15 minutes or until golden. Let cool for 1 to 2 minutes on the baking sheets; using a spatula, transfer to wire racks to cool completely. The cookies can be stored in a tightly covered container at room temperature for up to 1 week. Makes about 3 dozen 2½-inch cookies.

## Brownies

Per brownie: Calories 138; Protein 2 g; Carbohydrate 15 g; Fat 8 g; Sodium 85 mg; Cholesterol 28 mg.

- 2 cups Basic Cookie Mix (page 16)
- 1 egg, lightly beaten
- ⅓ cup cold water
- ⅓ cup (⅔ stick) unsalted butter or margarine, melted
- ¼ cup sifted unsweetened cocoa or 2 envelopes no-melt unsweetened chocolate
- ¾ cup chopped pecans or walnuts (about 3 ounces, shelled)

1 Preheat the oven to 375° F. In a large bowl, stir together all ingredients, except the pecans, until smooth. Add the nuts, stirring until well distributed in the mixture. Pour into a lightly greased, 9" x 9" x 2" baking pan.

2 Bake for about 20 minutes or until the center springs back when lightly touched. Let cool completely in the upright pan on a wire rack — about 1 hour. Cut into 2¼-inch squares. Can be stored in a tightly covered container for up to 3 days. Makes 16 brownies.

# Lacy Chocolate Praline Cookies and Baskets

Per cookie: Calories 121; Protein 1 g; Carbohydrate 16 g; Fat 6 g; Sodium 50 mg; Cholesterol 11 mg.

*Making praline baskets may take a little practice, but the results are worth the effort.*

- ½ cup (1 stick) lightly salted butter or margarine
- ⅔ cup firmly packed light brown sugar
- ½ cup light corn syrup
- 2 tablespoons unsweetened cocoa
- ½ teaspoon vanilla
- 1 cup all-purpose flour
- ½ cup finely chopped pecans or walnuts (about 2½ ounces, shelled)

1 Preheat the oven to 375° F. Melt the butter in a large saucepan over moderate heat. Add the brown sugar, corn syrup, cocoa, and vanilla. Cook the mixture, stirring occasionally, for 3 minutes or until heated through. Remove from the heat and add the flour and nuts; stir until well mixed.

2 Drop level tablespoonfuls of batter, 3 inches apart, in the center of 2 greased baking sheets: 3 cookies per sheet. Bake for 8 minutes or until the cookies just darken around the edges.

3 Cool the baking sheets on wire racks for 1 minute, then remove the cookies. When the pans are completely cool, repeat with the remaining batter but do not regrease the pans.

4 To make baskets: Bake the cookies as in Steps 2 and 3; cool the baking sheets on racks for 30 seconds only. Quickly transfer each cookie to a 2¼-inch muffin cup and mold it to that

shape; or shape it over the bottom of a 2¼-inch-wide tumbler (see page 11). Repeat with the remaining batter.

5 Fill the praline baskets with ice cream, Strawberry Mousse (page 254), or fresh berries and whipped cream. The cookies can be stored in a tightly covered container at room temperature for up to 1 week. Makes 22 four-inch cookies or 22 baskets.

# Hazelnut Meringues

Per meringue: Calories 41; Protein 1 g; Carbohydrate 4 g; Fat 3 g; Sodium 4 mg; Cholesterol 0 mg.

*Crisp and nutty, this variation on Meringue Shells (page 350) melts in your mouth. Avoid making them in humid or rainy weather, however.*

- 4 egg whites, at room temperature
- 1 teaspoon lemon juice
- 1 cup sugar
- 2 cups ground unblanched hazelnuts (about 8 ounces, shelled)
  Grated rind of 1 lemon (about 2 teaspoons)

1 Preheat the oven to 250° F. In a large bowl, beat the egg whites until frothy. Still beating, add the lemon juice, then gradually add the sugar. Continue beating until the mixture is glossy and stands in stiff peaks. Fold in the hazelnuts and the lemon rind.

2 Drop the mixture by teaspoonfuls onto two 15½" x 10½" x 1" baking sheets lined with aluminum foil (dull side up). Bake for about 40 minutes or until the meringues are firm.

3 Transfer to wire racks, let cool, then peel off any aluminum foil that still sticks. Will keep in an airtight container for up to 2 weeks. Serve with vanilla ice cream or Light-as-Clouds Orange Mousse (page 254). Makes about 4½ dozen 2-inch cookies.

# Chocolate Hazelnut Truffles

Per truffle: Calories 68; Protein 1 g; Carbohydrate 5 g; Fat 5 g; Sodium 1 mg; Cholesterol 41 mg.

- 1½ pounds semisweet chocolate
- ½ cup heavy cream
- 3 tablespoons Grand Marnier or Frangelico liqueur
- ½ cup unsweetened cocoa
- 2 tablespoons ground cinnamon
  About 66 toasted hazelnuts

1 In the top of a double boiler set over simmering water, heat the chocolate, stirring occasionally, until it melts.

*A delightful gift, for a friend or yourself — Chocolate Hazelnut Truffles*

Add the cream and Grand Marnier and stir until smooth. Let the mixture cool to room temperature — about 30 minutes. Beat until fluffy. Refrigerate until firm but pliable — about 30 minutes.

2 In a small bowl, combine the cocoa and cinnamon. Form the chilled chocolate mixture into balls approximately 1 inch in diameter, molding each ball around a hazelnut. Roll the balls in the cocoa-cinnamon mixture, place on a baking sheet lined with wax paper, and refrigerate, uncovered, until firm — about 2 hours. Transfer to tightly covered containers; refrigerate for up to 3 weeks. Makes about 5½ dozen truffles.

# Date-Nut Tart

Per serving: Calories 366; Protein 7 g; Carbohydrate 56 g; Fat 15 g; Sodium 37 mg; Cholesterol 137 mg.

- 3 eggs, separated
- ½ cup sugar
- 2 tablespoons flour
- 1 package (10 ounces) pitted dates, coarsely chopped
- 1 cup walnuts or pecans, coarsely chopped (about 4 ounces, shelled)
- ⅛ teaspoon cream of tartar

1 Preheat the oven to 325° F. In a large bowl, beat the egg yolks and sugar until light in color and thick — about 3 minutes. In a medium-size bowl, mix the flour with the dates and nuts, then stir into the egg mixture.

2 In a clean medium-size bowl, beat the egg whites with the cream of tartar until soft peaks form. Stir about ⅓ of the egg whites into the date mixture until blended, then fold in the remaining whites until just combined.

3 Spoon the mixture into a lightly greased, 11-inch tart pan or 10-inch pie pan, smoothing the top. Bake until the tart is brown and springs back when lightly touched — about 45 minutes. Cool in the pan on a wire rack.

▽ At this point the tart can be stored. Cover with aluminum foil and *refrigerate* for up to 4 days.

4 Serve warm or at room temperature. Whipped cream makes a good topping. Serves 6 to 8.

# Pear-Almond Tart

Per slice: Calories 689; Protein 9 g;
Carbohydrate 83 g; Fat 34 g; Sodium 70 mg;
Cholesterol 165 mg.

*This is as good a tart as you'd find in
the best French restaurant, and it's easy
to make when prepared in stages.*

*For the pastry:*
1 ½   cups all-purpose flour
  2   tablespoons sugar
 ⅛   teaspoon salt
 ½   cup (1 stick) cold unsalted
      butter or margarine, cut into
      pieces
  1   egg, lightly beaten
  1   to 2 tablespoons ice water
  1   teaspoon vanilla (optional)

*For the pear filling:*
  2   cups dry white wine or water
      (or 1 cup wine, 1 cup water)
  2   tablespoons lemon juice
 ½   cup sugar
  1   cinnamon stick
  3   large ripe pears, peeled,
      cored, and halved

*For the almond custard:*
 ½   cup (1 stick) unsalted butter
      or margarine, at room
      temperature
 ½   cup sugar
  2   eggs
  1   cup ground almonds (about
      6 ounces whole blanched
      almonds)
  2   tablespoons flour
  1   to 2 tablespoons pear eau de
      vie or kirsch (optional)

*For the glaze:*
 ½   cup apricot preserves,
      strained
  1   tablespoon sugar
  1   to 2 tablespoons toasted
      slivered almonds (optional)

1 To prepare the pastry: In a large
bowl or food processor, combine
the flour, sugar, and salt. Add the
butter, cutting it in with a pastry blender or 2 knives or processing until the
mixture resembles coarse meal.

2 In a small bowl, combine the egg, 1
tablespoon of the water, and the
vanilla, if desired. Sprinkle the egg mixture over the flour and mix with your
hands or process just until the dough
comes together in large pieces. Add
more water if the mixture is crumbly.

3 Transfer the dough to a work surface and, with the heel of your
hand, push 3 to 4 tablespoons of
dough at a time away from you, completely blending the flour and butter.
Form the dough into a ball and cover
with aluminum foil. Chill for at least 1
hour or overnight.

4 On a lightly floured surface, roll out
the dough to a circle ⅛ inch thick
and 12 inches across. Fit into a 10-inch
tart pan with removable bottom and
crimp the edges decoratively. Prick the
bottom of the dough with a fork; chill
for at least 30 minutes or overnight.

5 Preheat the oven to 425° F. Line the
pastry shell with wax paper, weight
it with dried beans or rice, and bake on
a baking sheet in the lower third of the
oven for 15 minutes. Remove the paper
and beans and bake 15 minutes more.
Transfer the shell to a rack and let cool.

▽ At this point the shell can be
wrapped in aluminum foil and
*frozen* for up to 1 month at 0° F.

6 Meanwhile, prepare the filling: In a
large saucepan, bring the wine,
lemon juice, sugar, and cinnamon to a
boil over moderate heat. Reduce the
heat to low and simmer, uncovered,
until the the syrup is clear — 5 to 7
minutes. Add the pears and simmer,
covered, until tender — 10 to 15 minutes. Let cool to room temperature.

7 To prepare the custard: In a medium-size bowl, cream the butter and
sugar. Add the eggs, 1 at a time,
beating well after each addition. Stir in
the almonds, flour, and pear eau de vie,
if desired.

▽ At this point the pears and custard can be stored. Transfer the
pears to a small bowl and cover with
plastic wrap. Cover the custard and
*refrigerate* both for up to 24 hours.

8 Preheat the oven to 425° F. Spoon
the custard into the shell. Slice the
pears ¼ inch thick but retain the pear
form; arrange them on top like the
spokes of a wheel, rounded sides up
and fanned (see photograph, opposite
page). Bake until the custard is puffed
and golden — about 30 minutes.

9 In a small saucepan, combine the
preserves and sugar; simmer over
moderate heat, stirring, until the sugar
has dissolved. Spoon the glaze over the
tart and sprinkle with the slivered almonds, if desired. Serves 8.

## Serving Later

**From refrigerator:** About ½ hour before baking, set the pears and custard
out to come to room temperature.
Proceed as in Steps 8 and 9. **From
freezer:** Defrost the tart shell in a
preheated 350° F oven for 15 minutes.
Proceed as in Steps 6 through 9.

*Tip: Whipped cream can be
prepared ahead of time by
adding gelatin to it. For each cup
of whipping cream, put 1
tablespoon cold water in a
heatproof cup, stir in ½
teaspoon of unflavored gelatin,
and set the cup in a pan of
simmering water. Stir until the
gelatin dissolves; allow to cool.
Whip the cream until soft peaks
form; add the dissolved
gelatin and 1 tablespoon sugar,
if desired. Continue whipping
until the cream is stiff. Cover and
refrigerate for up to 24 hours.
When ready to serve, whisk the
cream lightly.*

*Pear-Almond Tart — a masterpiece in design and flavor*

# Walnut Pie

Per serving: Calories 529; Protein 6 g;
Carbohydrate 60 g; Fat 30 g; Sodium 216 mg;
Cholesterol 119 mg.

1¾ cups Flaky Pie Crust Mix
    (page 16)
  4 to 5 tablespoons ice water
  3 eggs, lightly beaten
  ½ cup firmly packed light
    brown sugar
  1 cup light corn syrup
  ¼ cup (½ stick) unsalted butter
    or margarine, melted
  1 teaspoon ground cinnamon
  ⅛ teaspoon salt
  1 teaspoon vanilla
  1 cup walnut halves (about
    3½ ounces)

1 Preheat the oven to 375° F. In a medium-size bowl, toss the Flaky Pie Crust Mix and 4 tablespoons of the ice water lightly with a fork. Form the mixture into a ball, adding more of the ice water if the mixture is crumbly. Wrap in plastic wrap and chill for at least 1 hour or overnight.

2 On a lightly floured surface, roll out the dough to a circle ⅛ inch thick and 12 inches across and fit into a 9-inch pie pan. Trim the dough, leaving a ½-inch overhang; crimp the edges and lightly prick the bottom and sides. Chill for at least 1 hour or overnight.

3 In a medium-size bowl, combine the eggs, brown sugar, corn syrup, butter, cinnamon, salt, and vanilla. Stir in the nuts and pour the filling into the pastry shell. Bake on a baking sheet in the lower third of the oven until the filling jiggles slightly when the pan is gently shaken — about 50 minutes.

4 Transfer the pie to a rack and let cool for at least 2 hours before cutting. This pie is at its best when prepared 24 hours ahead but kept unrefrigerated. Serve with whipped cream or ice cream. Serves 8.

# Blueberry Pie

Per serving: Calories 508; Protein 5 g;
Carbohydrate 55 g; Fat 30 g; Sodium 293 mg;
Cholesterol 12 mg.

*Make several batches of pie filling when the fruit is in season. Freeze them and have fresh pies all year round.*

-   1 quart blueberries, raspberries, strawberries, or blackberries, rinsed, stemmed, and picked over
-   1/2 to 2/3 cup sugar, depending on sweetness of the fruit
-   1/2 cup flour or 1/4 cup cornstarch
-   1 teaspoon lemon juice, or to taste
-   1 teaspoon grated lemon or orange rind, or to taste
-   1/2 teaspoon ground cinnamon, or to taste
-   3 tablespoons lightly salted butter or margarine, melted
-   3 1/2 cups Flaky Pie Crust Mix (page 16)
-   6 to 8 tablespoons ice water
-   1 egg yolk mixed with a little water or 1 tablespoon milk for glaze (optional)

1 In a large bowl, gently toss the blueberries with the sugar, flour, lemon juice, lemon rind, cinnamon, and butter. Set aside.

▽ At this point the filling can be stored. Line a 9-inch pie pan with plastic wrap, add the filling, mounding it, and freeze for 3 to 4 hours or until solid. Remove the filling and lining from the pan; wrap in additional plastic wrap and heavy-duty aluminum foil; label. *Freeze* for up to 4 months at 0° F.

2 In a medium-size bowl, combine the Flaky Pie Crust Mix and 6 tablespoons of the water with a fork, adding more water if the mixture is crumbly. Cover with plastic wrap and chill for at least 1 hour or overnight.

3 Preheat the oven to 425° F. On a lightly floured surface, roll out a little more than half of the dough to a circle 1/8 inch thick and 12 inches across. Fit into a 9-inch pie pan; trim the excess. Spoon the filling into the shell. Roll out the remaining dough to form a circle about 1 inch larger than the pan. Fit over the top of the pie, crimp and trim the edges decoratively, and prick all over to allow steam to escape. Brush with the glaze, if desired.

4 Set on a baking sheet and bake for 10 minutes; reduce the heat to 350° F and bake another 35 to 40 minutes or until the crust is golden. Cool the pie to lukewarm before cutting. Serve with ice cream or whipped cream, if desired. Serves 8.

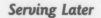
## Serving Later

Preheat the oven to 450° F. Unwrap the frozen filling and carefully set it in the pie shell prepared as in Steps 2 and 3; top as in Step 3. Bake on a baking sheet in the lower third of the oven for 20 minutes. Reduce the heat to 375° F, transfer the pie to the center of the oven, and bake for 1 to 1 1/4 hours more or until the crust is golden and the filling bubbly.

## Peach Pie Variation

Per serving: Calories 522; Protein 5 g;
Carbohydrate 57 g; Fat 31 g; Sodium 304 mg;
Cholesterol 15 mg.

Proceed as for Blueberry Pie, substituting 1 quart peeled, pitted, and sliced firm-ripe peaches, apricots, nectarines, or pitted whole sour cherries (2 to 2 1/2 pounds) for the blueberries. Use 2/3 to 1 cup sugar, 1/3 cup flour or 3 tablespoons cornstarch, 2 teaspoons lemon juice, or to taste, 1/2 teaspon grated lemon rind, 1/2 teaspoon ground cinnamon, nutmeg, or ginger, and 4 tablespoons lightly salted butter or margarine, melted. Proceed as in Steps 2, 3, and 4.

## Apple Pie Variation

Per serving: Calories 536; Protein 4 g;
Carbohydrate 63 g; Fat 30 g; Sodium 290 mg;
Cholesterol 12 mg.

Proceed as for Blueberry Pie, substituting 6 large tart apples, peeled, cored, and sliced (2 to 2 1/2 pounds) for the blueberries. Use 2/3 to 1 cup sugar, 1/4 cup flour or 2 tablespoons cornstarch, 2 teaspoons lemon juice, or to taste, 1/2 teaspoon grated lemon rind, 1/4 teaspoon each ground cinnamon and nutmeg, 1/8 teaspoon ground cloves, and 3 tablespoons lightly salted margarine or butter, melted. Proceed as in Steps 2, 3, and 4.

*A summer favorite — Peach Pie*

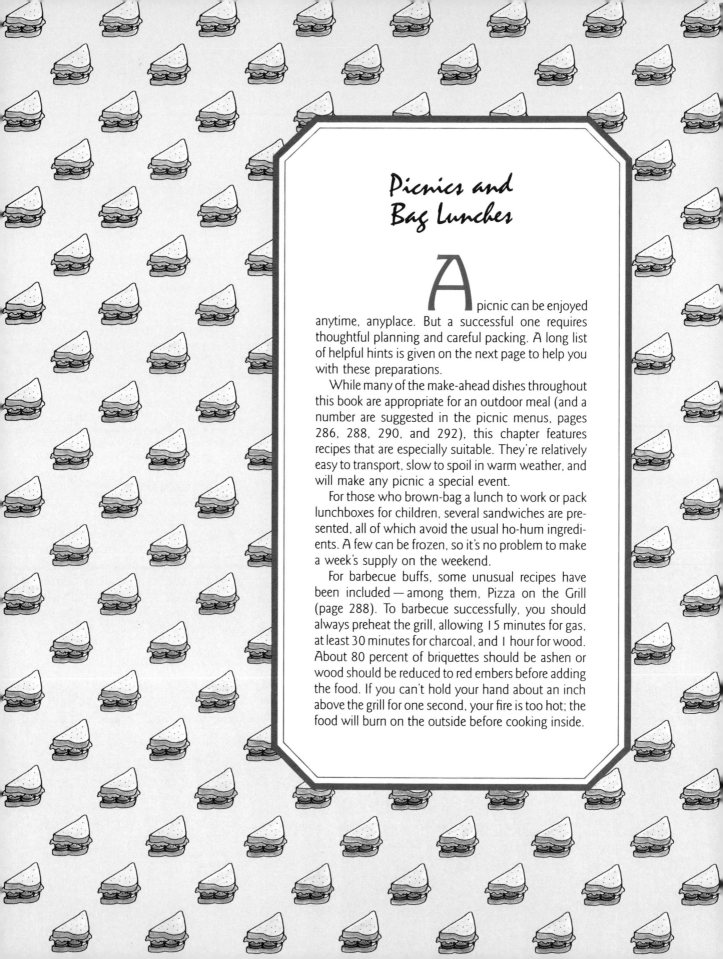

# Picnics and Bag Lunches

A picnic can be enjoyed anytime, anyplace. But a successful one requires thoughtful planning and careful packing. A long list of helpful hints is given on the next page to help you with these preparations.

While many of the make-ahead dishes throughout this book are appropriate for an outdoor meal (and a number are suggested in the picnic menus, pages 286, 288, 290, and 292), this chapter features recipes that are especially suitable. They're relatively easy to transport, slow to spoil in warm weather, and will make any picnic a special event.

For those who brown-bag a lunch to work or pack lunchboxes for children, several sandwiches are presented, all of which avoid the usual ho-hum ingredients. A few can be frozen, so it's no problem to make a week's supply on the weekend.

For barbecue buffs, some unusual recipes have been included — among them, Pizza on the Grill (page 288). To barbecue successfully, you should always preheat the grill, allowing 15 minutes for gas, at least 30 minutes for charcoal, and 1 hour for wood. About 80 percent of briquettes should be ashen or wood should be reduced to red embers before adding the food. If you can't hold your hand about an inch above the grill for one second, your fire is too hot; the food will burn on the outside before cooking inside.

## Planning a Picnic Menu

With careful organization and packing, almost any sort of dish, even a very elaborate one, can be toted to a picnic. But if your idea of the perfect alfresco feast is one that allows you to relax, select foods that pack easily, won't spoil readily, and require a minimum of dishes and utensils. Good candidates are finger foods, including most sandwiches, cooked but unsauced poultry and meats, olives, crisp vegetables, fruits, and cookies. Casseroles or main dish salads that are best served at room temperature are also good choices. In hot weather avoid foods that might spoil easily — those with homemade mayonnaise, for example. Whatever you choose for a winter picnic should require a minimum of preparation at the picnic site.

## Packing Tips

■ Put any food that contains liquid in a leakproof container *and*, as an extra precaution, seal the container in a plastic bag.

■ Pack bruisables or squishables — tomatoes, peaches, pears, bananas, and deviled eggs, for example — in hard-sided containers. Plastic boxes with tight-fitting lids are ideal.

■ Tote cakes in the pans in which they were baked. Disposable aluminum pans are ideal for this purpose.

■ Wrap breakable items in the picnic cloth, napkins, or dish towels (always handy to have on a picnic).

■ For a cookout, cushion or wrap picnic items with extra layers of brown bags or newspapers, which can be used in starting the fire. Don't forget the matches.

■ Put perishables in a cooler or insulated bag. To keep foods cold for several hours, add frozen gel packs. You can freeze juices and water in their containers, but be sure to leave at least 2 inches of space at the top for expansion.

■ If traveling some distance to a cookout without a cooler, freeze meat patties and kebabs to prevent spoilage.

■ Pack salad greens and salad dressing separately; leave tomatoes and cucumbers whole. Slice vegetables and toss with salad greens and dressing just before serving.

■ For foods that are to be assembled or cut up at the picnic site, a cutting/serving board is indispensable, as are a knife and serving/mixing utensils. Also pack a bottle opener and corkscrew, if these are needed.

## Secrets of Successful Sandwiches

The best sandwiches are those that are freshly made, with no sog in the bread, no wilt in the vegetables. For sandwiches that won't be eaten until several hours after preparation, use the following techniques:

■ Pack the bread, fillings, and spread separately, if possible, and assemble everything when ready to eat. Keep perishables well chilled in transit.

■ Spread the bread with a thin layer of butter, margarine, cream cheese, or peanut butter, whichever is appropriate. Their fat content prevents soft fillings from soaking in.

■ For a zippier taste, use one of the flavored butters (see pages 222 and 223 for recipes).

■ Assemble the sandwich, but add a layer of plastic wrap between the filling and bread. Remove the plastic wrap at the last minute.

■ Make sandwiches that can be frozen (see pages 280 and 281 for recipes). These take a couple of hours to thaw and reach room temperature, at which time they will taste freshly made.

■ Use the drugstore wrap (page 9) to keep sandwiches their freshest.

■ If the bread is a little dry, wrap the sandwich in a dampened paper or dish towel for a couple of hours to restore freshness.

# Bread Stuffed with Mushrooms

Per serving: Calories 398; Protein 14 g; Carbohydrate 51 g; Fat 15 g; Sodium 740 mg; Cholesterol 84 mg.

*Slice this picnic treat carefully, using a good bread knife.*

- 4 tablespoons (½ stick) unsalted butter or margarine
- 1 large yellow onion, finely chopped
- 1 clove garlic, minced
- 2 pounds medium-size mushrooms, thinly sliced
- 1½ teaspoons minced thyme or ½ teaspoon dried thyme, crumbled
- 1 teaspoon salt
- ¼ teaspoon black pepper
- 1 cup dry white wine
- 1 round loaf (9 inches) French or Italian bread or 2 small loaves (about 6 inches each) or 8 hard-crusted rolls
- 2 eggs
- ½ cup chopped parsley
- 2 tablespoons olive oil

**1** Melt the butter in a 12-inch skillet over moderate heat. Sauté the onion and garlic for about 5 minutes or until soft. Add the mushrooms, thyme, salt, and pepper, and sauté about 5 minutes more, stirring occasionally. Add the wine and cook, uncovered, for 25 to 30 minutes or until most of the liquid has evaporated.

**2** Preheat the oven to 375° F. Slice off the top quarter of the round loaf (or a thin slice from the top of each small loaf or roll) and set aside. With a fork, scrape out most of the soft insides of the bottom section, leaving a ½-inch shell; set it aside. (Reserve the insides for bread crumbs.)

**3** In a large bowl, beat the eggs slightly, then gradually stir in the mushroom mixture and the parsley.

Spoon into the cavity of the loaf, replace the top, and lightly coat the entire loaf with the olive oil. Place on a greased 15½" x 10" x 1" baking sheet.

4 Bake for 15 to 20 minutes or until the eggs are cooked. Cut into wedges. If desired, this sandwich can be wrapped in aluminum foil and frozen for up to 1 month at 0°F. Allow at least 3 hours to thaw and come to room temperature. Serves 8 to 10.

# Bread Stuffed with Meat and Eggs

Per serving: Calories 403; Protein 25 g; Carbohydrate 49 g; Fat 11 g; Sodium 718 mg; Cholesterol 114 mg.

- 2 cups ground cooked chicken, ham, roast beef, pork, veal, or a combination of these (about 1 pound)
- 2 hard-cooked eggs, peeled and chopped
- ¼ cup finely chopped parsley
- ¼ cup mayonnaise
- 3 tablespoons finely chopped yellow onion
- 2 tablespoons finely chopped sour pickles
- 1 tablespoon Worcestershire sauce
- ½ teaspoon salt
- ¼ teaspoon black pepper
  Hot red pepper sauce to taste
- 2 loaves Italian bread (each about 12 by 3½ inches), 4 small loaves ( each 6 inches round), or 8 large firm-crusted rolls
- 4 teaspoons unsalted butter or margarine, at room temperature

1 In a large bowl, combine all of the ingredients except the bread and butter. Set aside.

2 Slice off the top quarter of each loaf (or a thin slice from the top of each small loaf or roll). Using a fork, remove most of the insides of the bottom section, leaving a ½- to ¾-inch shell. (Reserve the insides for bread crumbs.) Spread the butter in the cavities.

3 Pack an equal portion of the mixture into each cavity. Press the tops on; wrap securely in aluminum foil. Refrigerate for several hours before slicing. See opposite page for storing and serving later directions. Serves 8 to 10.

# Pocket Beanwiches

Per serving: Calories 432; Protein 15 g; Carbohydrate 46 g; Fat 21 g; Sodium 848 mg; Cholesterol 15 mg.

- 1 can (19 ounces) chick peas
- 2 green onions, minced
- 2 teaspoons chili powder
- ⅛ teaspoon black pepper
- ¼ cup olive oil
- 1 tablespoon lemon juice
- ½ cup diced Cheddar or Monterey Jack cheese (about 2 ounces)
- 4 pita breads
- 4 large lettuce leaves

1 Rinse the beans in a colander and drain well. In a large bowl, mash the beans with a wooden spoon. Stir in the green onions, chili powder, pepper, olive oil, and lemon juice. Add the cheese, distributing it well.

▽ At this point the filling can be covered tightly and *refrigerated* for up to 3 days.

2 Partially split the pita breads to form pockets. Line with the lettuce and fill with the bean mixture. If desired, the sandwiches can be wrapped with aluminum foil or plastic wrap and stored at room temperature or refrigerated for up to 6 hours. Makes 4 sandwiches.

*Bread Stuffed with Meat and Eggs*

# Spunkies

Per serving: Calories 589; Protein 29 g; Carbohydrate 52 g; Fat 29 g; Sodium 1008 mg; Cholesterol 39 mg.

*When low on spunk, try this robust combination to get going again.*

**For the basil vinaigrette:**
- 1 cup loosely packed basil leaves
- 1 clove garlic, chopped
- 6 tablespoons olive oil
- 2 tablespoons freshly grated Parmesan or Romano cheese
- 1 tablespoon red wine vinegar
- ⅛ teaspoon black pepper or to taste

**For the filling:**
- 1 can (6½ ounces) water-packed tuna, drained and flaked
- 2 medium-size ripe tomatoes, seeded and chopped
- 1 medium-size cucumber, peeled, seeded, and chopped
- ½ cup canned chick peas, drained
- 1 large sweet red pepper, roasted, peeled, seeded, and chopped (see Roasted Sweet Red Pepper Paste, page 35, for roasting method) or 3 canned pimientos
- 6 marinated artichoke hearts, quartered and chopped
- 10 pitted black olives, chopped
- 3 tablespoons pine nuts

**For the assembly:**
- 6 round hard rolls (about 2 ounces each)
- 8 ounces provolone cheese, thinly sliced

1 To prepare the vinaigrette: In an electric blender or food processor, purée the basil and garlic with the olive oil. Transfer to a small bowl; stir in the cheese, vinegar, and pepper.

2 In a large bowl, combine all the filling ingredients, add the vinaigrette, and toss well. Slice off the top third of each roll. Scrape out the insides, leaving a ½-inch shell. (Reserve the insides for bread crumbs.) Spoon about ¼ cup of the tuna filling into each roll, add a slice of cheese, and repeat. Add a final layer of the tuna.

3 Wrap each sandwich in aluminum foil and refrigerate for at least 3 and up to 24 hours. Serves 6.

*A diversity of tastes and textures — Chicken and Hummus Sandwich*

## Provençale Sandwiches

Per serving: Calories 372; Protein 13 g; Carbohydrate 38 g; Fat 19 g; Sodium 531 mg; Cholesterol 25 mg.

- 1 small eggplant, cut crosswise into ½-inch slices (about 12 ounces)
- 1 teaspoon salt
- ¼ cup olive oil
- ¼ teaspoon dried thyme, crumbled
- ⅛ teaspoon black pepper
- 1 loaf French bread (about 8 ounces) or 4 large firm-crusted rolls
- 1 clove garlic, peeled and halved
- 2 medium-size tomatoes, thinly sliced
- 1 small red onion, thinly sliced
- 12 basil leaves
- 1 can (3½ ounces) Norwegian sardines, drained

1 Sprinkle the eggplant with the salt, layer in a colander set in the sink or over a bowl, and weight with a heavy plate. Let stand for 1 hour. Press the slices to squeeze out as much liquid as possible, rinse off the salt, and pat dry with paper toweling.

2 Preheat the oven to 400° F. Brush a large baking sheet with a little of the olive oil. Arrange the eggplant slices in a single layer on the sheet. Brush with the remaining olive oil and sprinkle with the thyme and pepper. Bake, uncovered, for 10 minutes. Turn over and bake 10 minutes more or until tender. Let cool to room temperature.

3 Cut the bread in half lengthwise (or slice the tops off the rolls). Remove the soft insides, leaving shells ½ inch thick. (Reserve the insides for bread crumbs.) Rub the interiors with the cut side of the garlic. Layer the bottom half with the eggplant, tomatoes, onion, basil, and sardines. Cover with the loaf top; slice to make 4 sandwiches. If desired, these can be wrapped and refrigerated for up to 24 hours.

## Salami, Cheese, and Olive Sandwich

Per serving: Calories 604; Protein 25 g; Carbohydrate 35 g; Fat 40 g; Sodium 1603 mg; Cholesterol 58 mg.

- ½ cup pitted green olives, chopped
- ½ cup pitted black oil-cured or Kalamata olives, chopped
- ¼ cup olive oil, or to taste
- ¼ cup chopped pimiento
- ¼ cup minced parsley
- ¼ cup minced basil or 2 teaspoons dried basil, crumbled, or 2 tablespoons minced oregano or ½ teaspoon dried oregano, crumbled
- 2 tablespoons drained capers
- 1 clove garlic, crushed
- ¼ teaspoon black pepper
- 1 loaf (about 8 inches long) semolina or Italian bread
- ¼ pound sliced sopressata or other Italian salami
- ½ pound sliced provolone, smoked mozzarella, or similar cheese

1 In a medium-size bowl, stir the olives, olive oil, pimiento, parsley, basil, capers, garlic, and black pepper until well mixed. Refrigerate, tightly covered with plastic wrap, for at least 2 and up to 24 hours.

2 Halve the bread lengthwise and scoop out the soft insides (reserve for crumbs), leaving ½-inch shells. Gently press half of the olive salad into each shell. Arrange the salami and cheese in alternating layers on top of the salad in the bottom shell. Press the halves together and wrap tightly with plastic wrap and aluminum foil. Refrigerate for at least 2 and up to 24 hours. Cut into 4 equal pieces while still cold, rewrap, and let come to room temperature before serving. Serves 4.

## Chicken and Hummus Sandwich

Per serving: Calories 692; Protein 46 g; Carbohydrate 80 g; Fat 21 g; Sodium 1216 mg; Cholesterol 72 mg.

- 2 cloves garlic
- 1 can (19 ounces) chick peas, drained
- 2 tablespoons lemon juice
- 2 tablespoons tahini (sesame seed paste)
- 1 sheet lavash bread (14 to 16 inches long) or 2 large flour tortillas (about 8 inches each) or 2 large pita breads (about 8 inches each), split in half
- 1 small cucumber, thinly sliced
- 12 pitted black (preferably oil-cured) olives, sliced
- 6 ounces cooked chicken, thinly sliced
- 1 tablespoon toasted sesame seeds (optional)

1 In an electric blender or food processor, mince the garlic. Add the chick peas, lemon juice, and tahini and blend together until smooth — about 30 seconds.

2 Lay out the lavash bread on a clean dry surface, trim any ragged edges, and spread the hummus on top. Arrange the cucumber slices, olives, chicken, and sesame seeds, if desired, in rows on the bread. Roll up fairly tight and cut in half or quarters. If desired, wrap each portion in aluminum foil or plastic wrap and refrigerate for up to 24 hours. Serves 2 or 3.

*A Ham and Chutney Sandwich takes the blah out of a brown-bag lunch.*

## Salad Sandwiches

Per serving: Calories 397; Protein 12 g; Carbohydrate 41 g; Fat 21 g; Sodium 762 mg; Cholesterol 21 mg.

2 medium-size tomatoes, thinly sliced
1 small cucumber, peeled and thinly sliced
1 small red onion, thinly sliced
3 tablespoons olive oil
2 teaspoons red or white wine vinegar
½ teaspoon dried oregano, crumbled
¼ teaspoon black pepper

4 large firm-crusted rolls or 1 loaf (8 ounces) French bread, cut into 4 sections
4 ounces goat cheese or blue cheese, thinly sliced

1 In a large bowl, toss all the vegetables with the olive oil, vinegar, oregano, and pepper.

2 Slice the tops off the rolls and remove some of the crumb from the bottom halves. Fill the bottoms with the vegetable mixture, cover with the cheese, and replace the tops. Wrap in aluminum foil and weight with a cutting board or 1-pound cans for at least 1 and up to 6 hours before serving. Makes 4 sandwiches.

## Tuna and White Bean Sandwiches

Per sandwich: Calories 411; Protein 26 g; Carbohydrate 50 g; Fat 12 g; Sodium 486 mg; Cholesterol 40 mg.

*White beans take the place of mayonnaise and make for a creamy, nutritious dressing.*

3 cloves garlic, peeled
1 can (16 ounces) cannellini beans, drained and rinsed
4 teaspoons lemon juice
½ teaspoon hot red pepper sauce
1 can (6½ ounces) oil-packed chunk light tuna, with its liquid

 ¼ cup coarsely chopped, pitted
   black olives
 2 tablespoons finely chopped
   red onion
 4 teaspoons unsalted butter or
   margarine, at room
   temperature
 8 slices sandwich bread

1 Blanch the garlic in a small pan of
  boiling water for 2 minutes. Drain
well. In an electric blender or food
processor, blend the garlic, beans, lemon juice, and hot red pepper sauce until
smooth — about 30 seconds.

2 Transfer to a medium-size bowl;
  stir in the tuna, olives, and onion
until well mixed. Butter one side of
each slice of bread with ½ teaspoon of
butter. Spread ¼ of the filling on each
of 4 slices, then top with second slices.

3 If desired, the sandwiches can be
  frozen for 1 month at 0°F. See page
276 for directions on wrapping and
thawing. Makes 4 sandwiches.

# Ham and Chutney Sandwiches

Per sandwich: Calories 405; Protein 18 g;
Carbohydrate 35 g; Fat 21 g;
Sodium 1283 mg; Cholesterol 61 mg.

*Here is an interesting combination that
is also good made with chicken.*

 ¼ cup ( ½ stick) unsalted butter
   or margarine, at room
   temperature
 1 tablespoon apple cider or
   orange juice
 ½ cup chutney, finely chopped
 1 tablespoon Dijon or spicy
   brown mustard
 1 ½ cups finely chopped ham
   (about 9 ounces)
 4 teaspoons unsalted butter or
   margarine, at room
   temperature
 8 slices sandwich bread

1 In a small bowl, beat the ¼ cup of
  butter and the apple cider until light
and fluffy. Beat in the chutney and
mustard, then stir in the ham.

2 Butter one side of each bread slice
  with ½ teaspoon of butter. Spread
¼ of the filling on each of 4 slices, then
top with second slices. If desired, these
can be frozen for 1 month at 0°F. See
page 276 for directions on wrapping
and thawing. Makes 4 sandwiches.

# Cream Cheese and Pesto Sandwiches

Per sandwich: Calories 464; Protein 10 g;
Carbohydrate 28 g; Fat 35 g; Sodium 599 mg;
Cholesterol 73 mg.

 1 ½ cups basil leaves
 2 cloves garlic
 4 teaspoons pine nuts
 2 tablespoons plus 1 teaspoon
   olive oil
 ¼ teaspoon salt
 1 package (8 ounces) cream
   cheese, at room temperature
 4 teaspoons unsalted butter or
   margarine, at room
   temperature
 8 slices sandwich bread

1 In an electric blender or food processor, blend the basil, garlic, pine
nuts, olive oil, and salt until smooth. In
a medium-size bowl, beat the cream
cheese with an electric mixer until
smooth — about 2 minutes. Add the
basil mixture; stir until well combined.

▽ At this point the mixture can be
   stored. *Refrigerate*, tightly covered, for up to 5 days.

2 Butter one side of each bread slice
  with ½ teaspoon of butter. Spread
¼ of the filling on each of 4 slices, then
top with second slices. If desired, these
can be frozen. See page 276 for directions on wrapping and thawing. Makes
4 sandwiches.

# Oriental Chicken-Salad Sandwich

Per serving: Calories 537; Protein 30 g;
Carbohydrate 35 g; Fat 31 g; Sodium 707 mg;
Cholesterol 48 mg.

 ½ cup peanut butter
 3 tablespoons peanut or
   vegetable oil
 1 teaspoon dark (Oriental)
   sesame oil
 2 tablespoons rice wine
   vinegar
 1 tablespoon honey
 1 tablespoon soy sauce
 ⅛ teaspoon cayenne (ground
   red) pepper
 ¼ cup water
 2 cups shredded cooked
   chicken (about 8 ounces)
 1 tablespoon minced green
   onion
 4 teaspoons unsalted butter or
   margarine, at room
   temperature
 8 slices sandwich bread

1 Using a small bowl and a fork or an
  electric blender, blend the peanut
butter with the peanut and sesame oils
until smooth. Add the vinegar, honey,
soy sauce, cayenne pepper, and water.
Blend until smooth. Transfer to a medium-size bowl.

2 Fold in the chicken and green onions. Butter one side of each bread
slice with ½ teaspoon of butter. Spread
¼ of the filling on each of 4 slices, then
top with second slices. If desired, these
can be frozen. See page 276 for directions on wrapping and thawing. Makes
4 sandwiches.

# Strawberry Soup

Per 1-cup serving: Calories 58; Protein 2 g; Carbohydrate 9 g; Fat tr; Sodium 86 mg; Cholesterol 0 mg.

*You can tote this soup to a picnic in a thermos jug or serve it at home for an elegant start to a meal on the patio.*

- 1 quart very ripe strawberries, hulled, or 1 quart frozen dry-pack strawberries, thawed
- 1 large ripe peach, peeled, pitted, and sliced, or 1 cup frozen dry-pack peach slices, thawed
- ½ cup unsweetened pineapple juice
- 2 cups Chicken Stock (page 48) or canned chicken broth

*Optional garnishes:*
- ½ cup sour cream or plain yogurt
- 2 tablespoons toasted sliced almonds

1 In an electric blender or food processor, purée the strawberries, peach, and pineapple juice. Transfer to a large bowl and stir in the chicken stock. Cover tightly with plastic wrap and chill thoroughly for at least 1 hour. Will keep for up to 3 days.

2 To serve, ladle into clear glass bowls or cups, garnish each serving with a dollop of the sour cream, and sprinkle with the toasted almonds, if desired. Makes 6 one-cup servings.

# Herbed Cheese in Pepper Crust

Per serving: Calories 46; Protein 1 g; Carbohydrate tr; Fat 5 g; Sodium 45 mg; Cholesterol 15 mg.

- 1 package (8 ounces) cream cheese, at room temperature
- 2 tablespoons dry white wine
- 1 tablespoon minced rosemary or 1 teaspoon dried rosemary, crumbled
- 1 clove garlic, minced
- ¼ teaspoon salt
- ½ cup heavy cream
- 1 tablespoon black peppercorns or 1 tablespoon cracked Java peppercorns

1 In a medium-size bowl, beat the cream cheese, wine, rosemary, garlic, and salt with an electric mixer until smooth.

2 In a small bowl, whip the heavy cream to stiff peaks; fold into the cream cheese mixture just until combined. Spoon the mixture into a small (2-cup) bowl lined with plastic wrap and smooth the top. Cover with plastic wrap and refrigerate for at least 6 hours and up to 3 days.

3 Meanwhile, place the peppercorns in a plastic bag and lay it on a cutting board. Using a meat mallet or heavy skillet, crush the peppercorns.

4 When ready to serve, invert the cheese onto a piece of wax paper, remove the plastic, and coat evenly with the pepper. Transfer to a serving platter. If taking to a picnic, wrap in several layers of plastic wrap and keep chilled. Serve with crackers or thinly sliced baguettes and fresh fruit.

# Summer Chicken Tarragon

Per serving: Calories 419; Protein 43 g; Carbohydrate 5 g; Fat 25 g; Sodium 419 mg; Cholesterol 109 mg.

- 2 whole boneless, skinless chicken breasts (about 12 ounces each)
- ¼ teaspoon salt
- ⅛ teaspoon black pepper
- 1 tablespoon olive oil
- 1 tablespoon unsalted butter or margarine
- 2 medium-size shallots, peeled and minced
- ½ cup dry white wine
- 1 cup Chicken Stock (page 48) or canned chicken broth
- 1½ teaspoons dried tarragon, crumbled
- 2 strips lemon zest

*For the dressing:*
- 1 tablespoon Dijon or spicy brown mustard
- 2 tablespoons lemon juice
- 1 clove garlic, minced
- ⅛ teaspoon each salt and black pepper
- ¼ cup olive oil
- 2 tablespoons sour cream
- 2 tablespoons minced tarragon, chives, or parsley

1 Season the chicken with the salt and pepper. Heat the olive oil and butter in a 10-inch skillet over moderately high heat for about 1 minute. Add the chicken, and sauté for 2 minutes on each side. Transfer to a plate.

2 Add the shallots to the skillet, and sauté for 1 minute over moderate heat. Add the wine and boil, uncovered, 1 minute more. Stir in the stock, tarragon, and zest, add the chicken, and return to a boil. Reduce the heat to moderately low; simmer, covered, for 6 to 8 minutes or just until the chicken is no longer pink at the center. Remove from the heat and let cool. Cut the chicken into bite-size pieces and transfer to a medium-size bowl. Save the poaching liquid for soup, if desired.

3 For the dressing: In a small bowl, whisk together the mustard, lemon juice, garlic, salt, and pepper. Add the oil in a steady thin stream, whisking until well combined. Add the sour cream and tarragon and mix well.

4 Toss the dressing with the chicken and serve immediately, accompanied by sliced tomatoes and roasted sweet peppers. Or refrigerate for up to 24 hours; about 45 minutes before serving, set the chicken out to come to room temperature. Serves 4.

# Garlic-Crumbed Chicken Drumsticks

Per serving: Calories 492; Protein 54 g;
Carbohydrate 15 g; Fat 24 g;
Sodium 650 mg; Cholesterol 201 mg.

- 1 ½ cups plain yogurt
- ⅓ cup lemon juice
- 6 cloves garlic, minced
- 1 ½ teaspoons salt
- ¾ teaspoon hot red pepper sauce
- ¾ teaspoon cayenne (ground red) pepper
- 30 chicken drumsticks, skinned (5 to 6 pounds)
- 3 cups finely crushed saltine crackers (about 6 dozen)
- 2 tablespoons dried oregano, crumbled
- 1 tablespoon each dry mustard and paprika
- 6 tablespoons (¾ stick) unsalted butter or margarine, melted

1 In a medium-size bowl, combine the yogurt, lemon juice, garlic, 1 teaspoon of the salt, the hot red pepper sauce, and ½ teaspoon of the cayenne. Divide among 2 shallow, 2-quart baking dishes or pour into a large enamel or stainless steel baking pan. Add the drumsticks, coat well with the mixture, cover, and refrigerate for at least 3 and up to 24 hours.

2 Preheat the oven to 375° F. Meanwhile, in a large brown paper bag, combine the cracker crumbs, oregano, mustard, paprika, and the remaining ½ teaspoon of salt and ¼ teaspoon of cayenne. Shake the drumsticks in the bag to coat with crumbs. Arrange in two 15 ½" x 10" x 1" baking pans lined with aluminum foil and drizzle with the melted butter.

3 Bake, uncovered, for 45 minutes or until fork tender and golden brown. Serve hot or at room temperature. If desired, the chicken can be cooled to room temperature, wrapped in aluminum foil, and refrigerated for up to 3 days. Serves 12 to 15.

# Sardines in Dill Sauce

Per serving: Calories 257; Protein 14 g;
Carbohydrate 4 g; Fat 20 g; Sodium 645 mg;
Cholesterol 57 mg.

- 2 cans (4 ounces each) oil-packed sardines, drained
- ¼ cup lemon juice
- 3 tablespoons Dijon or spicy brown mustard, or to taste
- 1 tablespoon red wine vinegar
- 1 ½ teaspoons sugar
- ¼ teaspoon salt
- ⅛ teaspoon black pepper, or to taste
- ¼ cup olive oil
- 3 tablespoons snipped dill or 1 tablespoon dried dill weed
- 1 tablespoon minced parsley
  Lettuce leaves
- ¼ cup chopped radishes for garnish (optional)

1 Arrange the sardines in a shallow dish. Sprinkle with 3 tablespoons of the lemon juice, cover, and marinate in the refrigerator for 2 hours.

2 Discard the lemon juice, drain the sardines on paper toweling, and return them to the dish. In a small bowl, combine the remaining tablespoon of lemon juice, the mustard, vinegar, sugar, salt, and pepper. Beat in the oil until the dressing is creamy, then stir in the dill and parsley.

3 Spoon the dressing over the sardines, cover, and refrigerate for at least 2 and up to 24 hours. Arrange the sardines on a bed of lettuce leaves and garnish with the radishes, if desired. Serves 4 as an appetizer.

# Dilled Tuna Salad with Capers

Per serving: Calories 183; Protein 34 g;
Carbohydrate 4 g; Fat 4 g; Sodium 507 mg;
Cholesterol 44 mg.

*This versatile salad can also be puréed and used as a dip for crisp vegetables.*

- 1 medium-size yellow onion, sliced into slim wedges
- ¼ cup loosely packed dill sprigs or 2 teaspoons dried dill weed
- 1 teaspoon minced marjoram or ½ teaspoon dried marjoram, crumbled
- ¼ teaspoon black pepper
- 2 cans (12 ½ ounces each) water-packed solid white tuna, drained and broken into chunks
- ¼ cup low-calorie mayonnaise
- ¼ cup plain low-fat yogurt
- 1 tablespoon lime or lemon juice
- 3 tablespoons low-fat milk
- 2 tablespoons capers, drained

1 In an electric blender or food processor, chop the onion with the dill, marjoram, and pepper. Add the tuna, mayonnaise, yogurt, lime juice, and milk and process until the mixture is the texture you desire. If too dry, add up to 2 more tablespoons of milk. Transfer to a medium-size bowl and stir in the capers until well mixed.

▽ At this point the salad can be stored. *Refrigerate*, tightly covered, for up to 2 days.

2 Serve on lettuce leaves as a light luncheon entrée or use as a spread or sandwich filling. It goes especially well with rice wafers. Serves 6.

# Spicy Beef Turnovers

Per turnover: Calories 229; Protein 9 g; Carbohydrate 16 g; Fat 14 g; Sodium 247 mg; Cholesterol 34 mg.

*Prepare a double batch and stash the extras in the freezer for snacks or a last-minute supper. To make turnovers for an appetizer, cut the dough in 3-inch squares and bake for 15 to 20 minutes.*

**For the crust:**
- 1½ cups all-purpose flour
- ½ teaspoon salt
- 6 tablespoons (¾ stick) cold margarine, cut into pieces
- ¼ cup (½ stick) cold unsalted butter, cut into pieces
- 5 to 6 tablespoons ice water

**For the filling:**
- 2 teaspoons olive oil
- 1 small yellow onion, finely chopped
- 1 clove garlic, finely chopped
- 8 ounces ground beef
- ½ teaspoon each ground coriander and ground cumin
- ⅛ teaspoon each ground cinnamon and cayenne (ground red) pepper
- ¼ teaspoon salt
- 2 tablespoons finely chopped dried apricots (6 halves)
- 1 large tomato, chopped (about ¾ cup)

**1** To prepare the crust: In a large bowl, combine the flour and salt. Cut in the margarine and butter, using a pastry blender or 2 knives, until the mixture resembles coarse meal. Add 5 tablespoons of the water and stir lightly with a fork until the mixture forms a dough. (Add the remaining tablespoon of water if the dough crumbles.) Wrap the dough in plastic wrap and refrigerate for at least 1 hour.

▽ At this point the dough can be stored. *Refrigerate* for up to 3 days or wrap in aluminum foil, label, and *freeze* for up to 3 months at 0° F.

**2** For the filling: Heat the oil in a 12-inch skillet over moderate heat. Add the onion, and sauté until soft — about 5 minutes. Add the garlic and beef, and sauté until the beef is browned — about 5 minutes. Stir in the coriander, cumin, cinnamon, cayenne, and salt, and sauté 30 seconds more.

**3** Add the apricots and tomato and simmer, uncovered, until the mixture has thickened and is a rich mahogany color — about 25 minutes. Let cool to room temperature.

▽ At this point the mixture can be stored. Transfer to a covered container and *refrigerate* for up to 2 days.

**4** Meanwhile, preheat the oven to 350° F. Roll out the dough to a ⅛-inch thickness. Cut it into ten 5-inch squares and place 2 tablespoons of the filling in the center of each. Dampen 2 adjacent sides of each square with water, then fold over to form a triangle. Crimp the edges with a fork.

**5** Bake on greased baking sheets until golden brown — 20 to 25 minutes. Cool on wire racks. Serve hot or at room temperature. Makes 10 turnovers. When cool, the turnovers can be stored. Wrap in aluminum foil and freeze for up to 2 months at 0° F. To reheat, bake the foil-covered turnovers in a preheated 375° F oven until heated through — 25 to 30 minutes.

## Chicken, Walnut, and Red Pepper Variation

Per turnover: Calories 227; Protein 8 g; Carbohydrate 14 g; Fat 15 g; Sodium 294 mg; Cholesterol 30 mg.

Prepare the crust as in Step 1 of Spicy Beef Turnovers. In a 10-inch skillet, melt 1 **tablespoon unsalted butter or** margarine with 1 tablespoon vegetable oil over moderately low heat. Add 2 tablespoons finely chopped yellow onion and 3 tablespoons finely chopped sweet red pepper; sauté, stirring occasionally, until soft — about 5 minutes. Add 8 ounces ground chicken or turkey breast and 2 tablespoons coarsely chopped walnuts, and sauté until the chicken is no longer pink — about 5 minutes. Remove from the heat; stir in 3 tablespoons plain yogurt, ½ teaspoon salt, and ⅛ teaspoon ground black pepper. Let cool to room temperature, then proceed as in Steps 4 and 5. Makes 10 turnovers.

## Black Olive Variation

Per turnover: Calories 265; Protein 2 g; Carbohydrate 16 g; Fat 22 g; Sodium 425 mg; Cholesterol 13 mg.

Prepare the crust as in Step 1 of Spicy Beef Turnovers. Heat 2 tablespoons of olive oil in a 10-inch skillet over moderately low heat. Add ½ cup finely chopped yellow onion and 3 cloves garlic, minced. Sauté, stirring occasionally, until the onion is soft — about 5 minutes. Add 1 small tomato, peeled, seeded, and chopped, and sauté until all the liquid has evaporated — 4 to 5 minutes. In a medium-size bowl, combine the onion mixture, 3 tablespoons olive oil, ½ cup pitted black Greek olives, coarsely chopped, ½ cup pitted black Italian olives, coarsely chopped, 1¼ teaspoons drained capers, and 3 tablespoons lemon juice. Let cool to room temperature, then proceed as in Steps 4 and 5. Makes 10 turnovers.

*Spicy Beef Turnovers — grand casings for ground meat*

# Sliced Beef in Orange Juice

Per serving: Calories 326; Protein 30 g; Carbohydrate 13 g; Fat 17 g; Sodium 482 mg; Cholesterol 85 mg.

*This unusual and quite wonderful dish tastes a bit like sauerbraten.*

- 3 cloves garlic, crushed
- ½ teaspoon each ground cumin and ground cloves
- ½ teaspoon salt
- ¼ teaspoon white pepper
- 1½ cups orange juice
- 2 pounds boneless beef sirloin, round, or chuck roast, about 2 inches thick
- 2 tablespoons olive oil
- 1 cup beef stock (page 48) or canned beef broth
- 1 medium-size yellow onion, peeled
- 1 bay leaf

*Garnishes:*
- Watercress or shredded lettuce
- 2 ounces cooked ham, diced (about ⅓ cup)
- 1 medium-size red onion, sliced
- 1 orange, sliced

1 In a small bowl, combine the garlic, cumin, cloves, salt, pepper, and 1 tablespoon of the orange juice and blend to a paste. With a small sharp knife, make several ½-inch-deep slits in the beef. Using your fingers, stuff the slits with the paste.

2 In a large flameproof casserole, heat the oil over moderate heat. Add the meat and brown on both sides — about 15 minutes. Drain off the oil and add the beef stock, onion, and bay leaf. Cover and cook over low heat for 1½ to 2 hours or until the meat is tender. Let cool to room temperature.

3 Carve the beef into thin slices, cutting across the grain and removing any fat. Place the slices in a container just large enough to hold them in two layers. Add the remaining orange juice, cover, and refrigerate for at least 24 hours or up to 3 days.

4 To serve, remove the beef from the marinade and arrange on a platter lined with the watercress. Sprinkle with the ham and garnish with the red onion and orange slices. Serves 6 to 8.

# Creole Stuffed Eggs

Per serving: Calories 115; Protein 6 g;
Carbohydrate 2 g; Fat 9 g; Sodium 177 mg;
Cholesterol 277 mg.

- 12  hard-cooked eggs, peeled
- ¼  cup mayonnaise
- 1  tablespoon sherry vinegar or white wine vinegar
- 2  teaspoons lemon juice
- 2  teaspoons paprika
- ½  teaspoon cayenne (ground red) pepper
- ½  cup finely chopped celery
- ⅓  cup finely chopped sour pickles
- ¼  cup finely chopped red onion
- 2  cloves garlic, minced
     Parsley sprigs for garnish (optional)

1 Halve the eggs lengthwise and transfer the yolks to a small bowl. Mash the yolks, then combine them with the mayonnaise, vinegar, lemon juice, paprika, and cayenne pepper. Stir in the celery, pickles, onion, and garlic.

2 Stuff the whites with the filling, then arrange the eggs on a platter. Garnish with the parsley, if you like. If desired, the eggs can be refrigerated in a tightly covered container for up to 3 days. For a picnic, wrap each egg individually, halves together, in aluminum foil, or pack close together in a plastic box and keep cool. Serves 12.

# Parmesan Chicken

Per serving: Calories 649; Protein 43 g;
Carbohydrate 6 g; Fat 69 g; Sodium 603 mg;
Cholesterol 286 mg.

- 3  cups fresh bread crumbs (about 6 slices)
- 1  cup grated Parmesan cheese
- ¾  cup chopped parsley
- 3  cloves garlic, minced
- ¾  teaspoon each salt, black pepper, and paprika
- 3  whole broiler/fryer chickens, each cut into 8 pieces (7 ½ to 9 pounds)
- ¾  cup (1 ½ sticks) unsalted butter or margarine, melted

1 Preheat the oven to 375° F. Combine the bread crumbs, cheese, parsley, garlic, salt, pepper, and paprika in a 1-gallon food-storage bag.

2 Dip the chicken in the butter. Shake 2 pieces at a time in the bag to coat with crumbs. Arrange in two 15½" x 10" x 1" baking pans lined with aluminum foil and sprinkle any remaining coating mixture over the chicken.

▽ At this point the chicken can be covered tightly with plastic wrap and *refrigerated* for up to 6 hours.

3 Bake, uncovered, for 45 minutes or until the juices run clear when the chicken is pierced with a knife. (If browning too quickly, cover the chicken loosely with aluminum foil.) Serve hot or at room temperature. Will keep, tightly wrapped and refrigerated, for up to 3 days. Serves 12.

*To celebrate with pizzazz:
Creole Stuffed Eggs, Parmesan Chicken, Summer Corn Salad (page 196), and Chocolate Nut Torte*

# Chocolate Nut Torte

Per serving: Calories 612; Protein 8 g;
Carbohydrate 74 g; Fat 32 g; Sodium 178 mg;
Cholesterol 100 mg.

*If taking this torte to a picnic, leave it right in the baking pan.*

For the crust:
- 3 cups all-purpose flour
- 1 cup firmly packed light brown sugar
- 3 teaspoons grated orange rind
- ½ teaspoon salt
- 1 cup (2 sticks) unsalted butter or margarine

For the filling:
- 1 package (12 ounces) semisweet chocolate chips
- 4 eggs
- 2 cups firmly packed light brown sugar
- ½ cup all-purpose flour
- 1 teaspoon baking powder
- ½ teaspoon salt
- 2 teaspoons vanilla
- 3 cups coarsely chopped walnuts (about 12 ounces)

1 Preheat the oven to 375° F. In a large bowl, combine the flour, brown sugar, orange rind, and salt. Cut in the butter, using a pastry blender or 2 knives, until the mixture is crumbly. Press half of the mixture evenly over the bottom of an ungreased, 8-inch spring-form pan. Repeat with another spring-form pan. Bake for 10 minutes or until firm. Remove the pans from the oven but leave the heat on.

2 Sprinkle half of the chocolate chips over each baked crust and let stand for 2 minutes. Using a spatula, spread the chocolate evenly over the crusts.

3 In a large bowl, beat the eggs until frothy. Stir in the brown sugar, flour, baking powder, salt, and vanilla until smooth. Fold in the walnuts. Spread half of the the mixture on top of each chocolate-covered crust. Bake until the tops are firm and golden — about 20 minutes. Cool completely, then remove from the pans. Store in a cool place for up to 24 hours. Do not refrigerate. Each cake serves 8.

## Backyard Barbecue

### MENU FOR SIX

MUSHROOM PÂTÉ
*page 38*

OR

HOT & SPICY EGGPLANT
*page 40*

ASSORTED CRACKERS

•

SOUTHERN-STYLE
PICKLED SHRIMP

OR

SHRIMP WITH VEGETABLES
AND LIME DRESSING
*page 202*

OR

HEARTS OF PALM SALAD
WITH AVOCADO DRESSING
*page 196*

•

PIZZA ON THE GRILL

OR

BARBECUED PEPPERS

AND

HERBED GARLIC BREAD
*page 243*

GRILLED MUSHROOMS

•

MINTED PEACHES AND MELON
*page 309*

•

COLD CHOCOLATE SOUFFLÉ
*page 253*

OR

CHOCOLATE-ORANGE SORBET
*page 260*

OR

PEACH MELBA TORTE
*page 262*

SUGAR COOKIES
*page 268*

*A dynamic trio — Barbecued Peppers, Grilled Mushrooms
and Zucchini, and Pizza on the Grill*

# Southern-Style Pickled Shrimp

Per serving: Calories 119; Protein 21 g; Carbohydrate 3 g; Fat 2 g; Sodium 199 mg; Cholesterol 157 mg.

- 2 cups white vinegar
- 2 quarts plus ½ cup water
- 3 tablespoons coriander seeds
- 2 teaspoons mustard seeds
- 1 piece (1 inch long) fresh ginger, peeled and sliced (optional)
- ¼ teaspoon dry mustard
- ¼ teaspoon salt
  Pinch ground nutmeg
- 1½ pounds medium-size shrimp, shelled and deveined
- 1 medium-size yellow onion, thinly sliced
- 1 lemon, thinly sliced
- 2 bay leaves, crumbled
- ¼ teaspoon crushed red pepper flakes

1 In a small saucepan, bring the vinegar, the ½ cup of water, the coriander seeds, mustard seeds, ginger, mustard, salt, and nutmeg to a boil over high heat. Reduce the heat to low and simmer, uncovered, for 10 minutes. Let cool to room temperature.

2 Meanwhile, in a large saucepan, bring the remaining 2 quarts of water to a boil over moderate heat. Add the shrimp; cook for 2 minutes or until they turn pink; drain well.

3 Pack a 1-quart glass jar, alternating each layer of shrimp with a layer of onion, lemon, bay leaf, and red pepper flakes. Pour in the marinade and pack the shrimp down until they are completely covered, adding more vinegar, if necessary. Cover and refrigerate for at least 36 hours, turning the jar upside down occasionally to distribute the spices. Will keep, refrigerated, for up to 3 days. Serve cold as an appetizer, or arrange on a bed of lettuce and present as a salad. Serves 6.

# Pizza on the Grill

Per serving: Calories 469; Protein 26 g; Carbohydrate 36 g; Fat 24 g; Sodium 643 mg; Cholesterol 89 mg.

*You can vary this pizza by adding 1 cup cooked chopped spinach, broccoli, artichoke hearts, or sliced mushrooms.*

- 1 recipe Pizza Napoli (page 166), substituting 6 plum tomatoes for 2 medium-size tomatoes

1 Prepare the dough as in Steps 1 and 2 of Pizza Napoli. Divide it into 6 pieces and roll out each piece to a 6½-inch round. Brush one side of each round with olive oil. Set on the grill, about 6 inches from glowing coals, and cook until grill marks appear and the dough puffs slightly — 3 to 4 minutes.

2 Using a spatula, remove the pizzas from the grill. Arrange the topping ingredients on the cooked side, then return the pizzas to the grill, uncooked side down. Cook until the cheese melts — 3 to 4 minutes. Serves 6.

# Barbecued Peppers

Per serving: Calories 483; Protein 20 g; Carbohydrate 18 g; Fat 37 g; Sodium 692 mg; Cholesterol 67 mg.

- 6 large sweet red, yellow, or green peppers (about 8 ounces each)
- 18 ounces mozzarella cheese, cut into ½-inch cubes (about 3 cups)
- 6 plum tomatoes, peeled, cored, seeded, and chopped (about 2 cups)
- 9 anchovy fillets, chopped
- ¾ cup pitted black Italian olives, chopped
- ⅓ cup olive oil
- ½ cup chopped fresh basil or parsley
- ¾ teaspoon salt, or to taste
- ½ teaspoon black pepper
- 2 tablespoons lemon juice (optional)

1 Cut a large wedge from one side of each pepper and remove the seeds and core. Leave the stem intact.

2 In a medium-size bowl, stir together the mozzarella, tomatoes, anchovies, olives, olive oil, basil, salt, pepper, and lemon juice, if desired. Fill each pepper with the stuffing.

▽ At this point the stuffed peppers can be stored. *Refrigerate*, tightly covered, for up to 24 hours.

3 Set the peppers, open side up, on the grill about 6 inches from glowing coals; cover the grill or tent with aluminum foil. Cook for 12 minutes or until just tender. Serves 6.

# Grilled Mushrooms

Per serving: Calories 83; Protein 2 g; Carbohydrate 4 g; Fat 7 g; Sodium 66 mg; Cholesterol 0 mg.

*If you like, combine the mushrooms with other fresh vegetables.*

- 1 clove garlic, halved
- ¾ teaspoon dried thyme, crumbled
- ¼ teaspoon each salt and black pepper
- ⅓ cup olive oil
- 18 ounces large mushrooms, stems removed

1 In a small bowl, combine the garlic, thyme, salt, pepper, and olive oil. Thread the mushrooms onto skewers and lay on a baking sheet. Brush with the oil mixture, let stand for at least 1 and up to 6 hours at room temperature.

2 Lay the mushrooms on the grill, 5 to 6 inches from glowing coals. Cook, turning occasionally, until soft — 3 to 5 minutes. Serve hot or at room temperature. Serves 6.

# Shellfish Brochettes

Per serving: Calories 186; Protein 25 g; Carbohydrate 8 g; Fat 6 g; Sodium 529 mg; Cholesterol 275 mg.

- ½ cup honey or firmly packed light brown sugar
- ½ cup Dijon or spicy brown mustard
- ½ cup low-sodium soy sauce
- ⅓ cup bourbon, rye, or scotch
- 3 cloves garlic, pressed
- 1 tablespoon minced fresh ginger or 1 teaspoon ground ginger
- ½ teaspoon crushed red pepper flakes
- 2 pounds sea scallops or large shrimp, shelled and deveined, or 1 pound of each
- 9 thin slices bacon

1 In a large bowl, combine the honey, mustard, soy sauce, bourbon, garlic, ginger, and red pepper flakes; add the scallops and toss to coat. Refrigerate for at least 1 and up to 2 hours.

2 Drain the scallops. Thread onto 6 skewers, interweaving the bacon between them. Grill 6 inches from glowing coals, turning and basting with the marinade, until cooked through — 10 to 12 minutes. Serves 6.

## Pork Variation

Per serving: Calories 234; Protein 28; Carbohydrate 4 g; Fat 11 g; Sodium 124 mg; Cholesterol 95 mg.

Prepare the marinade as in Step 1 of Shellfish Brochettes, and substitute for the scallops **2 pounds boneless pork shoulder, cut into 1½-inch cubes.** Marinate for 2 hours or overnight, then proceed as in Step 2, omitting the bacon. Grill until cooked through — 20 to 25 minutes. Serves 6.

*Herbed Cheese in Pepper Crust (page 282), a flavorful beginning*

## Chicken or Turkey Variation

Per serving: Calories 172; Protein 33; Carbohydrate 5 g; Fat 2 g; Sodium 108 mg; Cholesterol 82 mg.

Prepare the marinade as in Step 1 of Shellfish Brochettes, substituting for the scallops **2 pounds boneless chicken or turkey, cut into 1½-inch cubes.** Marinate for 2 hours or overnight, then proceed as in Step 2, including the bacon, if desired. Grill until cooked through — 10 to 12 minutes. Serves 6.

# Corn on the Grill

Per serving: Calories 156; Protein 3 g; Carbohydrate 18 g; Fat 8 g; Sodium 74 mg; Cholesterol 33 mg.

- 6 medium-size ears of corn
- ¼ cup (½ stick) unsalted butter or margarine, at room temperature
- 2 tablespoons minced chives, chervil, tarragon, parsley, or a combination of these herbs
- ¼ teaspoon each salt and black pepper

*For a memorable day at the beach, Shellfish Brochettes, Corn on the Grill, and Marinated Vegetables*

1 Peel back the husks from the corn without detaching them from the stem and remove the silk. In a small bowl, combine the butter, herbs, salt, and pepper and spread on the kernels. Rewrap the husks around each ear, then wrap in aluminum foil.

▽ At this point the corn can be stored in a cool place or *refrigerated* for up to 8 hours.

2 Grill the corn 6 inches from glowing coals, turning occasionally, until tender — about 30 minutes. Or broil the corn 5 inches from the heat, turning occasionally — 20 to 25 minutes. Remove the foil and husks and serve immediately. Serves 6.

## Marinated Vegetables

Per serving: Calories 60; Protein 1 g; Carbohydrate 15 g; Fat tr; Sodium 100 mg; Cholesterol 0 mg.

12 medium-size carrots, trimmed, peeled, and cut into 1-inch pieces
1 small sweet red, 1 small sweet yellow, and 1 small sweet green pepper, cored, seeded, and cut into 1-inch squares
1 medium-size red onion, halved from root to stem and thinly sliced
1½ cups cider vinegar
½ cup sugar
⅛ teaspoon cayenne (ground red) pepper
1 teaspoon red pepper flakes
1 piece (1 inch) fresh ginger, peeled and chopped
2 teaspoons paprika
2 teaspoons salt

1 In a large saucepan of boiling water, blanch the carrots for 4 to 5 minutes or until crisp-tender. Add the peppers and bring the water back to a boil. Drain in a colander and rinse under cold water. Transfer the carrots and peppers to a large bowl and toss with the onion.

2 In a small saucepan, bring the vinegar, sugar, cayenne, red pepper flakes, ginger, paprika, and salt to a boil over moderately high heat. Reduce the heat to moderately low and simmer, uncovered, until the liquid is reduced by one-third — 8 to 10 minutes. Cool slightly, then strain over the vegetables, discarding the solids. Cover tightly and refrigerate, stirring occasionally, for at least 24 hours. Will keep for up to 1 week. Serves 6.

## Country Pâté

Per ½-inch slice: Calories 167; Protein 13 g;
Carbohydrate 3 g; Fat 12 g; Sodium 299 mg;
Cholesterol 74 mg.

 1 pound ground turkey or veal
 1 pound ground pork
 1 cup diced boiled ham (about
   6 ounces)
 1 medium-size yellow onion,
   chopped
 2 cloves garlic, minced
 ½ cup chopped parsley
 ¼ cup dried bread crumbs
 ¼ cup shelled pistachio nuts
 ¼ cup heavy cream
 2 eggs
 1 teaspoon each salt and black
   pepper
 ½ teaspoon each ground
   allspice and cinnamon
 ¼ teaspoon dried thyme,
   crumbled
 8 slices bacon
12 pitted prunes (optional)

1 Preheat the oven to 400° F. In a large bowl, mix the turkey, pork, ham, onion, garlic, parsley, bread crumbs, pistachios, cream, eggs, salt, pepper, allspice, cinnamon, and thyme.

2 Line the bottom and sides of a 9" x 5" x 3" loaf pan crosswise with the bacon strips, and spoon half of the meat mixture on top. Make a groove down the center of the meat and fill it with a line of prunes, if desired. Add the remaining meat, packing it in lightly and smoothing the top.

3 Cover the loaf pan with a double thickness of aluminum foil and set in a larger baking pan. Transfer to the oven and add enough boiling water to the baking pan to come halfway up the sides of the loaf pan.

4 Bake until the pâté is cooked to an internal temperature of 180° F or the meat is no longer pink — about 2 hours. Remove from the oven and weight the top with a foil-covered brick or with a second loaf pan filled with two 1-pound cans.

▽ At this point the pâté can be cooled to room temperature and stored. Remove from the pan, wrap in heavy-duty aluminum foil, and *refrigerate* for up to 5 days. Or *freeze* for up to 1 month at 0° F.

5 When cool, turn out onto a cutting board. Slice ½ inch thick and arrange attractively on the board or a serving platter. Makes 18 slices.

### Serving Later

**From refrigerator:** About 1 hour before serving, set the pâté out to come to room temperature, then proceed as in Step 5. Or serve cold. **From freezer:** Allow to thaw overnight in the refrigerator, then proceed as above.

## Marinated Mushrooms

Per serving: Calories 66; Protein 2 g;
Carbohydrate 7 g; Fat tr; Sodium 190 mg;
Cholesterol 0 mg.

1¾ cups dry white wine
 1 cup water
 ¼ cup white wine vinegar
 1 medium-size yellow onion,
   thinly sliced
12 black peppercorns
 1 teaspoon coriander seeds
 1 teaspoon dried marjoram,
   crumbled
 ¾ teaspoon salt
1½ pounds small mushrooms,
   trimmed and halved
   Minced parsley for garnish

1 In a large enamel or stainless steel saucepan, bring the wine, water, and vinegar to a boil over high heat. Reduce the heat to moderately low, add the onion, peppercorns, coriander seeds, marjoram, and salt, and simmer, uncovered, for 10 minutes.

2 Stir in the mushrooms, cover, and simmer until the mushrooms are tender — about 10 minutes more. Let cool to room temperature, then transfer to a 1-quart jar and cover tightly. Refrigerate for at least 24 hours and up to 10 days. When ready to serve, drain, reserving the liquid to add to a salad dressing or sauce, if desired. Transfer to a serving dish, and garnish with the parsley. Makes about 3½ cups, enough to serve 8 as an appetizer.

*A portable feast — Country Pâté, Marinated Mushrooms, Tomato Tart with Two Cheeses (page 294), and Curried Winter Squash Soup (page 65)*

# Cajun Smoked Ham

Per serving: Calories 252; Protein 38 g;
Carbohydrate 7 g; Fat 8 g; Sodium 2008 mg;
Cholesterol 84 mg.

- 1 1/4 teaspoons each black pepper, onion powder, garlic powder, and ground cumin
- 3/4 teaspoon each white pepper, cayenne (ground red) pepper, paprika, and dry mustard
- 3 tablespoons brown sugar
- 2 pounds boneless smoked ham or smoked pork butt

1 Preheat the oven to 300° F. In a large bowl, combine all the ingredients except the ham.

2 Remove and discard the ham's casing. Prick the ham all over with a fork, then press firmly into the spice mixture to coat.

3 Bake, uncovered, for 1 1/2 hours. Increase the oven temperature to 400° F and bake 15 minutes more or until the ham is golden brown.

▽ At this point, the ham can be stored. Wrap in heavy-duty aluminum foil and *refrigerate* for up to 5 days. Label and *freeze* for up to 3 months at 0° F.

4 Serve hot or at room temperature, accompanied by potato or pasta salad and marinated vegetables. Or use for Noodle Pie with Spicy Cajun ham (page 154). Serves 6 to 8.

### Serving Later

**From refrigerator:** Bake, uncovered, in a preheated 400° F oven until warmed through — 20 to 25 minutes — or serve at room temperature.
**From freezer:** Thaw overnight in the refrigerator. Follow directions above.

# Tomato Tart with Two Cheeses

Per serving: Calories 402; Protein 13 g;
Carbohydrate 29 g; Fat 26 g; Sodium 233 mg;
Cholesterol 52 mg.

*This summery pie is at its best with vine-ripened tomatoes. For a variation, omit the anchovies and crumble 3 slices of cooked bacon over the tart during the last few minutes of baking.*

For the crust:
- 1 1/3 cups all-purpose flour
- 3/4 cup shredded extra-sharp Cheddar cheese (about 3 ounces)
- 1/4 cup (1/2 stick) cold unsalted butter or margarine, cut into pieces
- 1 tablespoon vegetable shortening
- 3 to 4 tablespoons cold dry white wine or water

For the filling:
- 1/3 cup fine plain cracker crumbs
- 1/2 cup shredded Jarlsberg cheese (2 ounces)
- 1/4 cup shredded extra-sharp Cheddar cheese (1 ounce)
- 4 medium-size ripe tomatoes, each cut into 8 wedges
- 2 tablespoons olive oil
- 1 can (2 ounces) anchovy fillets, rinsed and dried (optional)
- 12 pitted black olives, preferably Kalamata
- 1/4 cup minced chives
- 2 tablespoons chopped basil or 2 tablespoons chopped parsley combined with 1 teaspoon dried basil, crumbled
- 1/4 teaspoon black pepper, or to taste

1 To prepare the crust: In a medium-size bowl, combine the flour and cheese. Cut in the butter and shortening, using a pastry blender or 2 knives, until the mixture resembles coarse meal. Add 3 tablespoons of the wine and stir lightly with a fork until the mixture forms a dough. (Add the remaining tablespoon of wine if the dough crumbles.) Shape the dough into a ball and cover with plastic wrap. Refrigerate for at least 2 hours.

▽ At this point the dough can be stored. *Refrigerate* overnight or *freeze*, wrapped in aluminum foil, for up to 3 months at 0° F.

2 Preheat the oven to 375° F. On a lightly floured surface, roll the dough out to an 11- by 1/8-inch round and fit into a 9-inch tart pan with a removable bottom. Lightly butter a sheet of aluminum foil and place it, buttered side down, in the prepared shell. Fill with uncooked rice, beans, or pie weights. Bake for 15 minutes, remove the foil and rice, and bake 5 minutes longer. Set on a wire rack.

3 Meanwhile, in a small bowl, combine the cracker crumbs and cheeses. Sprinkle over the bottom of the shell, then bake 8 minutes more. Lay the tomato wedges, overlapping slightly, in two concentric circles over the cheese mixture and brush with the olive oil. Lay the anchovies on top like the spokes of a wheel, if desired, and space the olives in between. Scatter the chives, basil, and pepper on top.

4 Bake, uncovered, until the tomatoes are soft but not shriveled — 15 to 20 minutes. Cool in the pan on a wire rack. If desired, wrap the cooled tart with aluminum foil and refrigerate overnight. One hour before serving, set it out to come to room temperature. Serve at room temperature. Serves 6.

# Holidays and Entertaining

Some of life's most wonderful memories emanate from holiday feasts or incomparable parties. To be the creator of such an event brings special rewards — and sometimes headaches from the exertion of putting it all together. While the menus and recipes on the following pages do require effort, almost everything can be prepared far enough in advance that you will be free to relax with the guests, instead of hovering in the kitchen. Also, many of the dishes are easily transported, in case any relatives or friends volunteer to help.

In arranging a menu for entertaining, select dishes with an eye for appearance as well as taste. There should be both harmony and contrast in colors, shapes, sizes, flavors, and textures. Naturally, presentation is important, too; for ideas and techniques in creating beautiful garnishes, see pages 12-14.

Because holidays often bring houseguests as well as party-goers, recipes included in the brunch menu were chosen with breakfast making in mind. Baked French Toast (page 308) and Overnight Coffeecake (page 309) are ideal for those times when you have extra people to feed in the morning.

## Roast Turkey with Herbed Stuffing

Per serving: Calories 502; Protein 59 g;
Carbohydrate 18 g; Fat 21 g; Sodium 594 mg;
Cholesterol 180 mg.

*You can make stuffing in a jiffy with Herbed Stuffing Mix, but don't stuff the turkey until you are ready to roast it. If the turkey darkens too quickly while roasting, tent it with aluminum foil.*

- 1 recipe (8 cups) Herbed Stuffing Mix (page 16)
- 1 cup Chicken Stock (page 48) or canned chicken broth
- 1 turkey (12 to 14 pounds), neck and giblets removed, rinsed and patted dry
- 1 teaspoon salt (optional)
- 1/4 cup (1/2 stick) unsalted butter or margarine, melted

1 Preheat the oven to 325° F. In a large bowl, combine the Herbed Stuffing Mix and stock. Loosely stuff the turkey's breast and neck cavities three-quarters full. Put any remaining stuffing in a lightly greased baking pan and cover with aluminum foil.

2 Skewer or sew the openings of the turkey and then truss it (see page 11). Rub the outside of the turkey with the salt, if desired.

3 Place the turkey, breast side up, on a rack in a roasting pan. Roast, uncovered, basting every 30 minutes with the butter and pan drippings, for 4 to 4 1/2 hours or until the juices run clear when the thigh is pierced with a knife, and the leg feels loose at the joint when pulled up and down. During the final half hour of roasting, bake the reserved stuffing. Serves 12.

## Sausage Stuffing

Per 3/4-cup serving: Calories 269; Protein 11 g;
Carbohydrate 15 g; Fat 18 g; Sodium 678 mg;
Cholesterol 29 mg.

- 1 pound sweet or hot Italian sausage, removed from casings and crumbled
- 1 large sweet red or sweet green pepper, cored, seeded, and diced
- 1/4 cup dry red wine
- 6 1/2 cups Herbed Stuffing Mix (page 16)

1 Brown the sausage in a 12-inch skillet over moderate heat, breaking up any clumps — about 6 minutes. Drain; reserve the sausage and drippings separately.

2 Return 2 tablespoons of the drippings to the skillet. Add the sweet pepper, and sauté over moderate heat until the pepper is soft — about 6 minutes. Add the drained sausage and the wine, then raise the heat to high. Sauté until almost all the liquid has evaporated — about 5 minutes. Transfer to a large bowl, and toss with the Herbed Stuffing Mix and 3 more tablespoons of the drippings until well mixed. Makes enough to stuff a 12- to 14-pound turkey or two 6-pound chickens.

## Fruit and Rice Stuffing

Per 3/4-cup serving: Calories 209; Protein 4 g;
Carbohydrate 40 g; Fat 4 g; Sodium 314 mg;
Cholesterol 11 mg.

- 1/4 cup (1/2 stick) unsalted butter or margarine
- 1 large yellow onion, finely chopped
- 1 large stalk celery, finely chopped
- 2 cups white rice
- 3 cups Chicken Stock (page 48), turkey broth, or canned chicken broth

*Roast turkey with a few of the elegant trimmings — Cornbread-Pecan Stuffing, Cranberry-Walnut Relish (page 298), Orange-Praline Sweet Potatoes (page 183), and steamed green beans with Dill Butter (page 222)*

| | |
|---|---|
| 3 | cups water |
| 1½ | cups finely chopped, mixed dried fruits such as apricots, prunes, raisins, and dates |
| 1½ | teaspoons salt |
| 1 | teaspoon dried thyme, crumbled |
| ¼ | teaspoon black pepper |

1 In a large saucepan, melt the butter over moderate heat. Add the onion and celery, and sauté, stirring occasionally, until the onion is soft — about 5 minutes. Stir in the rice, stock, water, dried fruit, salt, thyme, and pepper and bring to a simmer.

2 Cover and reduce the heat to low. Cook for 15 to 20 minutes or until the liquid is absorbed. Cool to room temperature. Will keep, covered and refrigerated, for up to 3 days. Makes enough to fill a 12- to 14-pound turkey or two 6-pound chickens.

# Cornbread-Pecan Stuffing

Per ¾-cup serving: Calories 367; Protein 12 g; Carbohydrate 23 g; Fat 25 g; Sodium 824 mg; Cholesterol 93 mg.

- 1 pound sweet Italian sausage, removed from casings and crumbled
- ¾ cup unsalted butter or margarine
- 2 large yellow onions, finely chopped
- 1 cup diced celery (about 3 stalks)
- 3 cloves garlic, minced
- 1 recipe Sage Corn Bread (page 236), minus the sage, crumbled (about 8 cups)
- 1½ cups chopped pecans (about 6 ounces, shelled)
- ½ cup minced parsley
- ½ cup Chicken Stock (page 48) or canned chicken broth
- 1 tablespoon rubbed sage, crumbled, or to taste
- 1 teaspoon each dried thyme and marjoram, crumbled
- 1 teaspoon salt
- ½ teaspoon black pepper

1 In a 12-inch skillet over moderate heat, brown the sausage, breaking up any clumps—about 6 minutes. Transfer to a large bowl. Drain the skillet, wipe it clean with paper toweling, and return it to the heat.

2 Melt the butter. Add the onions and celery, and sauté, stirring, for about 7 minutes or until golden. Add the garlic and stir for 1 minute. Transfer to the bowl and add the remaining ingredients. Stir until well combined, add more seasoning, if desired, and let cool completely. Will keep, covered and refrigerated, for up to 24 hours. See Roast Turkey with Herbed Stuffing (page 296) for directions on filling a turkey and baking extra stuffing. Makes about 10 cups or enough to fill a 12- to 14-pound turkey.

# Cranberry-Walnut Relish

Per serving: Calories 188; Protein tr; Carbohydrate 36 g; Fat 5 g; Sodium 5 mg; Cholesterol 0 mg.

- 12 ounces fresh cranberries, stemmed, washed, and drained, or frozen cranberries, thawed
- ¾ cup sugar
- ¾ cup coarsely chopped walnuts
- ¾ cup orange marmalade
- 1 tablespoon lemon juice

1 Preheat the oven to 350° F. Put the cranberries in a shallow, 1½-quart baking dish; sprinkle with the sugar. Cover with aluminum foil and bake for 35 minutes. Sprinkle with the walnuts, re-cover, and bake 10 minutes longer.

2 Remove from the oven and stir in the marmalade and lemon juice until well mixed. Ladle into glass jars or storage containers. Let cool to room temperature, cover tightly, and refrigerate for at least 3 hours. Will keep, refrigerated, for up to 3 weeks. Can be frozen for up to 3 months at 0° F. Serve with poultry or pork. Makes 2½ cups.

# Mince-Pumpkin Pie

Per serving: Calories 306; Protein 4 g; Carbohydrate 35 g; Fat 16 g; Sodium 243 mg; Cholesterol 42 mg.

- 1¾ cups Flaky Pie Crust Mix (page 16)
- 4 to 5 tablespoons ice water
- 1 cup pumpkin purée
- ⅔ cup half-and-half or light cream
- ⅓ cup firmly packed light brown sugar
- 1 egg
- ½ teaspoon ground cinnamon
- ¼ teaspoon ground ginger
- ⅛ teaspoon ground allspice or cloves
- 1½ cups prepared mincemeat
- 1 cup heavy cream, whipped, for garnish (optional)

1 In a medium-size bowl, toss the Flaky Pie Crust Mix and 4 tablespoons of the ice water lightly with a fork. Form the mixture into a ball, adding more of the ice water if the mixture is crumbly. Wrap in plastic wrap and refrigerate for at least 1 hour or overnight.

2 On a lightly floured surface, roll out the dough to a circle ⅛ inch thick and 12 inches in diameter. Fit it into a 9-inch pie pan. Trim the dough, leaving a ½-inch overhang; crimp the edges decoratively and lightly prick the bottom and sides. Refrigerate for at least 1 hour and up to 24 hours.

3 Preheat the oven to 425° F. In a medium-size bowl, beat the pumpkin, half-and-half, sugar, egg, cinnamon, ginger, and allspice until smooth.

4 Spoon the mincemeat into the pie crust and level it with the back of a spoon. Pour the pumpkin mixture evenly on top.

5 Place in the center of the oven and bake for 15 minutes. Reduce the heat to 375° F. Bake 45 to 50 minutes longer or until the pumpkin filling is puffy and golden and a knife inserted in the center comes out clean.

6 Cool completely on a rack. Will keep, covered with plastic wrap and refrigerated, for up to 2 days. Remove from the refrigerator 1 hour before serving and top with whipped cream, if desired. Makes 8 servings.

## Christmas Buffet

MENU FOR TWELVE

CRUDITÉS WITH
ANCHOVY-PARSLEY DIP
*page 34*
AND

ROASTED SWEET
RED PEPPER PASTE
*page 35*

ARTICHOKE SQUARES
*page 45*

•

CRAB IN
MUSTARD-MADEIRA SAUCE
OR

EUROPEAN MEATBALLS
IN CREAM SAUCE WITH DILL*
*page 108*

•

STEAMED RICE
WITH PARSLEY BUTTER
*page 223*

SPINACH-MUSHROOM RING
*page 300*

ZUCCHINI SLAW
*page 196*

•

SOURDOUGH ROLLS

•

RED BERRY
PUDDING WITH VANILLA CREAM
*page 301*
AND

CHRISTMAS COOKIES
OR

STEAMED GINGER PUDDING
*page 259*
AND

CRANBERRY FOOL
*page 258*

*\*Recipe must be tripled.*

# Crab in Mustard-Madeira Sauce

Per serving: Calories 345; Protein 23 g;
Carbohydrate 7 g; Fat 24 g; Sodium 455 mg;
Cholesterol 183 mg.

| | |
|---|---|
| 8 | tablespoons (1 stick) unsalted butter or margarine |
| 1/3 | cup minced shallots or green onions |
| 10 | ounces mushrooms, trimmed and sliced |
| 1/2 | teaspoon salt |
| 1/4 | teaspoon black pepper |
| 2/3 | cup dry Madeira or sherry |
| 1/3 | cup all-purpose flour |
| 3 | cups Chicken Stock (page 48), fish broth, or canned chicken broth |
| 2 | tablespoons tomato paste |
| 1 | bay leaf |
| 1 | cup heavy cream |
| 1 | cup light cream or half-and-half |
| 3 | tablespoons cognac or dry Madeira |
| 2 | tablespoons Dijon or spicy brown mustard, or to taste |
| 3 | pounds crabmeat, picked over, or 3 pounds skinned and boned chicken breasts, cooked and cut into slivers Paprika for garnish |

1 In a 12-inch skillet, melt 2 tablespoons of the butter over moderately high heat. Add the shallots and stir for about 2 minutes or until softened. Add the mushrooms, salt, and pepper, and cook, stirring, for 4 to 5 minutes or until almost all the juices have evaporated. Add the Madeira and boil for 1 minute. Set aside.

2 In a large saucepan, melt the remaining 6 tablespoons of butter over moderate heat. Add the flour and stir for 3 minutes or until a smooth paste has formed. Add the stock, tomato paste, bay leaf, and mushroom mixture and bring to a boil, stirring constantly. Reduce the heat to moder-

ately low and cook, stirring, until thickened and smooth — 2 to 3 minutes. Simmer, uncovered, stirring occasionally, for 15 minutes.

3 Add the heavy and light creams, bring to a boil, and cook, uncovered, for 5 minutes or until the sauce is thick enough to coat a spoon. Stir in the cognac and mustard; add more salt and pepper, if desired. Remove and discard the bay leaf.

▽ At this point the sauce can be cooled to room temperature and stored. *Refrigerate*, tightly covered, for up to 24 hours.

4 Gently fold the crabmeat into the sauce, and cook over moderately low heat until warmed through — about 5 minutes. Transfer to a chafing dish and sprinkle with the paprika. Serve with rice or noodles. Serves 12.

### Serving Later

In a large saucepan, warm the sauce over moderate heat stirring constantly, until it comes to a simmer — 10 to 12 minutes. Proceed as in Step 4.

*Tip: To prepare rice ahead, boil it for about 3/4 of the normal cooking time: 15 minutes for white rice, 30 minutes for brown. Drain it in a colander and cover to prevent drying. To reheat, set the covered colander in a large saucepan or kettle containing about 1 inch of boiling water. Steam the rice to the perfect degree of doneness — 5 to 7 minutes for white rice, 10 to 12 minutes for brown rice — fluffing occasionally with a fork to allow the steam to penetrate.*

# Spinach-Mushroom Ring

Per serving: Calories 309; Protein 13 g; Carbohydrate 20 g; Fat 20 g; Sodium 493 mg; Cholesterol 137 mg.

*Serve this delectable dish either hot or at room temperature. For a showier presentation, fill the center of the hot version with steamed julienned carrots, the cool one with cherry tomatoes.*

2 cups chopped walnuts (about 8 ounces)
1½ pounds mushrooms
5 tablespoons olive oil
2 large yellow onions, chopped
4 pounds spinach, cooked, chopped, and squeezed dry, or 4 packages (10 ounces each) frozen chopped spinach, drained and squeezed dry
3 cups soft whole-wheat bread crumbs (about 6 slices)
6 eggs, lightly beaten
2 teaspoons lemon juice
1½ teaspoons salt
½ teaspoon ground nutmeg
¼ teaspoon black pepper

1 Preheat the oven to 375° F. Spread the walnuts on a baking sheet and bake until lightly toasted — 7 to 10 minutes. (Check frequently to ensure that they do not burn.)

2 Remove the stems from 8 ounces of the mushrooms. Thinly slice the caps and brush lightly with 1 tablespoon of the olive oil. Arrange the slices around the bottoms of 2 lightly oiled, 1½-quart ring molds or one 3-quart mold. Chop the stems and the remaining mushrooms and set aside.

*Crab in Mustard-Madeira Sauce (page 299); Spinach-Mushroom Ring; crudités with Anchovy-Parsley Dip (page 34) and Roasted Sweet Red Pepper Paste (page 35); opposite page: Red Berry Pudding with Vanilla Cream and Christmas Cookies*

5½ to 6 cups cranberry or red
     grape juice
  1 cup plus 2 tablespoons sugar
     Grated rind of 2 lemons
     (about 4 teaspoons)
¼ cup lemon juice
  1 cup cornstarch
1½ cups dry red wine

*For the Vanilla Cream:*
1½ cups heavy cream
  1 teaspoon vanilla
  4 teaspoons confectioners'
     sugar

1 In a 2-quart measuring cup, combine the raspberry juice, strawberry purée, and if using canned cherries, the cherry juice. Add enough cranberry juice to yield 1½ quarts. Pour the mixture into a large enamel or stainless steel saucepan and add 3 cups more of the cranberry juice. Stir in the sugar, lemon rind, and lemon juice.

2 Bring to a boil over moderate heat, stirring occasionally. Meanwhile, in a medium-size bowl, whisk together the cornstarch and wine, making a smooth, thin paste. When the juice boils, slowly pour in the cornstarch mixture, whisking vigorously.

3 Reduce the heat to low; cook, stirring constantly, until the mixture bubbles and is thickened and clear — about 3 minutes. Stir in the raspberries and cherries; heat 1 minute more.

4 Transfer to a heatproof 5-quart serving bowl or individual serving dishes and lay plastic wrap directly on the surface. Let cool to room temperature, then refrigerate until completely chilled and thick — at least 8 hours and preferably overnight. Will keep for up to 3 days.

5 Just before serving, prepare the Vanilla Cream: In a large bowl, beat the cream, vanilla, and sugar until slightly thickened but thin enough to pour. Transfer to a serving dish and pass separately. Makes 12 servings.

---

3 Heat the remaining 4 tablespoons of oil in a large flameproof casserole over moderate heat. Add the onions, and sauté, stirring occasionally, until soft — about 5 minutes. Add the chopped mushrooms; sauté, stirring occasionally, until tender — about 3 minutes more.

4 Remove from the heat and stir in the spinach, bread crumbs, walnuts, eggs, lemon juice, salt, nutmeg, and pepper, blending well. Spoon into the prepared molds and set in 1 large roasting pan or 2 smaller baking pans. Add enough hot water to the pan to come halfway up the sides of the molds. Bake, uncovered, until the tops are set — 40 to 45 minutes.

▽ At this point the rings can be cooled to room temperature, covered with aluminum foil, and *refrigerated* for up to 24 hours.

5 Let cool in the molds on a wire rack for 10 to 15 minutes. Run a thin-bladed knife around each edge to loosen the spinach. Hold a plate over one mold and invert the ring onto the plate; repeat. Serves 12 to 16.

### Serving Later

To serve hot, preheat the oven to 375° F and heat the foil-covered molds until warmed through — 20 to 30 minutes. Proceed as in Step 5. To serve at room temperature, set them out one hour before serving; unmold and serve.

## Red Berry Pudding with Vanilla Cream

Per serving: Calories 489; Protein 2 g; Carbohydrate 95 g; Fat 11 g; Sodium 22 mg; Cholesterol 41 mg.

*For the pudding:*
  3 packages (10 ounces each) frozen raspberries, thawed and drained, juice reserved
  3 packages (10 ounces each) frozen strawberries, thawed and puréed
1½ pounds dark sweet red cherries, stemmed, pitted, and quartered, or 2 cans (1 pound each) pitted dark sweet cherries, drained, juice reserved

# Roast Fresh Ham

Per serving: Calories 3 | 6; Protein 43 g;
Carbohydrate tr; Fat 16 g; Sodium 269 mg;
Cholesterol 8 | mg.

- 2 tablespoons coarse salt
- 1 ¼ teaspoons rubbed sage
- 1 ¼ teaspoons ground ginger
- ½ teaspoon black pepper
- 4 bay leaves, crumbled
- 4 cloves garlic, minced
- 1 fresh half ham, shank or butt
  portion, including the bone
  (about 9 pounds)
  Grapes for garnish (optional)

1 In a small bowl, stir together the salt, sage, ginger, pepper, bay leaves, and garlic until well mixed.

2 Remove any rind from the ham but do not remove fat. Rub the salt mixture all over the ham. Wrap tightly in aluminum foil or plastic wrap and refrigerate overnight.

3 Preheat the oven to 425° F. Unwrap the ham and place it in a 13" x 9" x 2" roasting pan. Roast for 20 minutes. Reduce the heat to 325° F and baste with the pan drippings. Roast, uncovered, basting every 30 minutes, for about 4 hours or until a meat thermometer inserted near but not touching the bone registers 160° F. If the ham seems to be browning too fast, cover loosely with aluminum foil.

▽ At this point the ham can be cooled to room temperature, wrapped tightly in aluminum foil, and *refrigerated* for up to 3 days.

4 Transfer to a platter and let rest for 20 minutes before carving. Garnish with the grapes, if desired. Serves 12.

### Serving Later

Unwrap the ham; transfer to a roasting pan with 1 cup of water. Roast, uncovered, in a preheated 400° F oven for 30 minutes or until heated through.

# Brussels Sprout Salad

Per serving: Calories 235; Protein 3 g;
Carbohydrate 12 g; Fat 20 g; Sodium 278 mg;
Cholesterol 0 mg.

- 2 quarts water
- 4 pints fresh Brussels sprouts
  or four 10-ounce packages
  frozen Brussels sprouts
- 4 medium-size tomatoes, cut
  into wedges
- 2 small red onions, finely
  chopped
- 48 pitted small black olives
  (about 5 ounces)
- 1 cup olive oil
- ¼ cup white wine vinegar
- 2 tablespoons lemon juice
- 2 teaspoons Dijon or spicy
  brown mustard
- 1 teaspoon salt
- ½ teaspoon black pepper
- ¼ cup minced basil, dill, or
  parsley

*At the center of a gala event is Roast Fresh Ham, surrounded by Citrus Salad with Cumin Vinaigrette, Caraway Cheese Sticks (page 46), Brussels Sprout Salad, and Artichoke Mousse (page 304).*

1 In a large saucepan, bring the water to a boil over moderate heat. Add the fresh Brussels sprouts, cover, and cook for 10 to 15 minutes or until the sprouts are fork tender. (To cook frozen sprouts, follow package directions.) Drain and rinse under cold water.

2 In a large bowl, combine the Brussels sprouts, tomatoes, onions, and olives. Add the olive oil and toss to coat. Cover and refrigerate for at least 3 hours. Will keep for up to 24 hours.

3 In a small bowl, whisk together the vinegar, lemon juice, mustard, salt, and pepper. Add the dressing to the salad, toss, and sprinkle with the herbs. Serves 12 to 16.

## Citrus Salad with Cumin Vinaigrette

Per serving: Calories 152; Protein 1 g; Carbohydrate 11 g; Fat 12 g; Sodium 105 mg; Cholesterol 0 mg.

*The fruits and dressing can be prepared a day ahead; the salad arranged, covered, and refrigerated up to 6 hours in advance; and the dressing added at the last minute.*

**For the vinaigrette:**
- ²/₃ cup citrus juice, reserved from salad fruit
- ²/₃ cup olive oil
- ¹/₃ cup white wine vinegar
- 2 cloves garlic, minced
- 1 tablespoon Dijon or spicy brown mustard
- 1 teaspoon ground cumin
- ¹/₂ teaspoon salt
- ¹/₄ teaspoon black pepper

**For the salad:**
- 18 leaves red-leaf lettuce, cut in half crosswise
- 3 endives, sliced
- 3 large grapefruit, peeled, sectioned, and seeded, ¹/₃ cup juice reserved
- 2 oranges, peeled, sectioned, and seeded, ¹/₃ cup juice reserved
- 1 large red onion, chopped

1 Prepare the vinaigrette: In a small bowl, whisk together the citrus juice, olive oil, vinegar, garlic, mustard, cumin, salt, and pepper until blended.

2 Arrange the lettuce tips fanned out around the edge of a large platter; place the remaining leaves in the center. Arrange the endives and citrus fruits on top and garnish with the red onion. Pour the dressing over all and serve immediately. Serves 12.

# Artichoke Mousse

Per serving: Calories 189; Protein 10 g; Carbohydrate 13 g; Fat 11 g; Sodium 408 mg; Cholesterol 33 mg.

- 4 envelopes plain gelatin
- 1 cup cold water
- 3 tablespoons unsalted butter or margarine
- 8 green onions, finely chopped
- 12 ounces mushrooms, thinly sliced
- ¼ cup dry white wine (optional)
- 2 cans (16 ounces each) artichoke hearts, drained, or 3 packages (9 ounces each) frozen artichoke hearts, cooked according to package directions and drained
- 1 pound part-skim-milk ricotta cheese
- 1 cup sour cream
- ¼ cup packed parsley leaves
- 1 tablespoon snipped dill or 1 teaspoon dried dill weed
- 2 tablespoons lemon juice
- 1½ teaspoons salt
- ¼ teaspoon white pepper
- 2 cups milk

1 In a small saucepan, sprinkle the gelatin over the water. Warm over low heat, stirring constantly, until the gelatin is dissolved — about 5 minutes.

2 Melt the butter in a 12-inch skillet over moderate heat. Add the green onions and mushrooms, and sauté, stirring frequently, for 5 minutes.

Add the wine, if desired, and cook, uncovered, until all of the liquid has evaporated — about 5 minutes more.

3 In an electric blender or food processor, purée the artichoke hearts, ricotta, and sour cream. Add the parsley, dill, lemon juice, salt, and pepper; process until the parsley is minced.

4 Pour the mixture into a large bowl; stir in the milk, mushroom mixture, and gelatin. Divide the mousse between two 5- or 6-cup molds or pour it into one 12-cup mold. Cover and chill for at least 4 hours or overnight.

5 When ready to serve, run a thin-bladed knife or spatula around the edge of each mold, loosening the mousse. Dip in hot water for 30 seconds and invert onto a serving platter. Serves 12 to 14.

# Pecan Tassies

Per tart: Calories 130; Protein 1 g; Carbohydrate 11 g; Fat 9 g; Sodium 13 mg; Cholesterol 25 mg.

- 1½ cups (3 sticks) unsalted butter or margarine, at room temperature
- 6 ounces cream cheese, at room temperature
- 2 cups all-purpose flour
- 1 cup sugar
- 1 egg, lightly beaten
- 1½ cups chopped pecans (about 6 ounces, shelled)
- 1 cup chopped pitted dates
- 1 teaspoon vanilla
  Sifted confectioners' sugar

1 Preheat the oven to 350° F. In a large bowl or a food processor, thoroughly mix 1 cup of the butter, the cream cheese, and flour — about 2 minutes in the bowl, 20 to 30 seconds in the food processor.

2 Divide the dough into 4 equal parts and separate each part into 12 balls. Place each ball in a section of 4 un-greased miniature muffin tins. Using thumb and forefinger, press each ball into its cup, working the dough evenly up the sides to the rim.

3 In a medium-size bowl, beat the remaining ½ cup butter with the sugar until smooth. Stir in the egg, pecans, dates, and vanilla.

4 Divide the filling among the shells and bake in the oven for 30 to 35 minutes or until golden. Let cool completely on wire racks before removing. Sprinkle with the confectioners' sugar before serving. Will keep, tightly covered and refrigerated, for up to 3 days. Or wrap in heavy-duty aluminum foil, label, and freeze for up to 1 month at 0° F. Makes 48 tarts.

*Melt-in-the-mouth Pecan Tassies will disappear fast.*

# Brie and Leek Sandwiches

Per sandwich: Calories 224; Protein 8 g;
Carbohydrate 18 g; Fat 12 g; Sodium 380 mg;
Cholesterol 28 mg.

- 16 slices bread (each about 5 inches square)
- 4 tablespoons olive oil
- 2 cloves garlic, halved
- 6 leeks, cut into 4-inch lengths, then sliced into thirds lengthwise, and separated into strips
- 1 teaspoon sugar
- 1/2 teaspoon salt
- 1/4 teaspoon black pepper
- 1/3 cup cold water
- 1 1/2 pounds ripe brie cheese

1 Preheat the oven to 375° F. Trim the crusts from the bread slices and lay them on 2 baking sheets in a single layer. Drizzle with 3 tablespoons of the olive oil. Bake until crisp and golden — 5 to 7 minutes. Remove from the oven and rub one side of each slice with the cut side of the garlic.

2 Heat the remaining tablespoon of olive oil in a 12-inch skillet over moderate heat. Add the leeks, sugar, salt, and pepper, stir to coat, and sauté until lightly browned — about 5 minutes. Add the water, reduce the heat to low, cover, and simmer until soft — about 10 minutes more. Set aside.

3 Spread each slice of toast on the garlic-coated side with an equal amount of brie, discarding the rind. Cut each slice in half to form 2 rectangles. Lay the leeks on one half and top with the other half. (If desired, cut in half again to form squares.) Place on a baking sheet.

▽ At this point the sandwiches can be covered with plastic wrap and *refrigerated* for up to 8 hours.

4 Bake, uncovered, until the cheese is melted — 3 to 4 minutes from room temperature, 5 to 6 minutes from the refrigerator. Makes 16 sandwiches.

# Asparagus Tea Sandwiches

Per sandwich: Calories 83; Protein 3 g;
Carbohydrate 13 g; Fat 2 g; Sodium 136 mg;
Cholesterol 2 mg.

- 1 jar (7 ounces) roasted red peppers, 2 tablespoons finely chopped, the remainder cut into thin strips for garnish
- 2 tablespoons cream cheese
- 1/4 cup low-calorie or regular mayonnaise
- 1/4 teaspoon dried tarragon or oregano, crumbled
- 16 slices thin-cut sandwich bread, crusts removed
- 16 medium-thick asparagus tips (each 4 inches long) cooked until crisp-tender (about 1 pound)

1 In a medium-size bowl or a food processor, blend until smooth the 2 tablespoons chopped red pepper, the cream cheese, mayonnaise, and tarragon — about 2 minutes by hand, 20 seconds in the processor.

2 Flatten the bread slices with a rolling pin until half their original thickness. Do not allow to dry out.

3 For each sandwich: Spread a bread slice with about 1/2 tablespoon of the red pepper mixture. Center 1 asparagus spear diagonally on top, fold the two side points over it, and press together to seal. Garnish with 2 strips of red pepper. If desired, the sandwiches can be covered with plastic wrap and refrigerated for up to 4 hours. Makes 16 sandwiches.

# Ricotta Rounds with Baby Shrimp

Per sandwich: Calories 40; Protein 3 g; Carbohydrate 4 g; Fat 1 g; Sodium 67 mg; Cholesterol 9 mg.

- 1 large head garlic
- 1 pound part-skim-milk ricotta cheese
- 1 tablespoon chopped basil or 1 teaspoon dried basil, crumbled
- 1/4 teaspoon black pepper
- 36 party bread rounds (an 8-ounce package) or 2 1/2-inch rounds cut from any sliced firm-textured bread
- 1 bunch watercress
- 1 package (5 ounces) frozen baby shrimp, thawed and drained

1 Preheat the oven to 350° F. Place the garlic on a sheet of aluminum foil and roast until tender when pierced with a toothpick — 20 to 30 minutes. When cool enough to handle, separate the head into cloves (there should be 20 to 25) and peel them. In a medium-size bowl, mash the garlic with a fork. Add the ricotta, basil, and pepper and blend well.

▽ At this point the spread can be covered with aluminum foil and *refrigerated* overnight.

2 Fit a pastry bag with a star tip and fill with the ricotta mixture. Pipe about 1 teaspoon of the mixture onto each bread round. Top with several small sprigs of watercress, pressing down gently to secure the watercress and spread the filling. Pipe on an additional teaspoon of the mixture and top with 2 shrimp per round. (Save the remaining shrimp for another use.) Makes 36 rounds.

# Mushrooms Filled with Tarama Salad

Per filled mushroom: Calories 102; Protein 2 g; Carbohydrate 3 g; Fat 9 g; Sodium 23 mg; Cholesterol 13 mg.

*You can buy tarama, a Greek codfish roe, at specialty food stores and some supermarkets. Use leftovers for a dip or in a salad dressing.*

- 32 medium-size mushrooms, rinsed, patted dry, and stemmed (about 1 1/2 pounds)
- 1 cup olive oil, plus 1/4 cup if needed
- 1/4 cup lemon juice

*For the filling:*
- 6 slices firm-textured white bread, trimmed of crusts
- 2/3 cup cold water
- 1 small yellow onion, quartered
- 1/2 cup tarama or red caviar
- 1 tablespoon lemon juice
- 1 cup olive oil
  Parsley or coriander leaves for garnish, optional

1 In a medium-size bowl, toss the mushrooms with the olive oil and lemon juice. Cover with plastic wrap and refrigerate for at least 4 and up to 24 hours.

2 In a shallow bowl, soak the bread in the water for 10 minutes, then squeeze dry. In a food processor, mince the onion — 5 to 6 pulses. Add the bread, tarama, and lemon juice and process until creamy — about 5 seconds. With the motor running, drizzle in 1 cup of olive oil in a thin stream; after it is blended, let the processor run 10 seconds longer or until the mixture has the consistency of mayonnaise. Add more olive oil if needed.

▽ At this point the mixture can be stored. Transfer to a storage container, cover tightly, and *refrigerate* for up to 24 hours.

3 Remove the mushrooms from the marinade, reserving the marinade for salad dressing; pat them dry with paper toweling. Spoon or pipe the filling into each mushroom, and garnish with parsley or coriander leaves, if desired. Makes 32 stuffed mushrooms.

# Shaker Lemon Bread

Per 3/4-inch slice: Calories 203; Protein 3 g; Carbohydrate 33 g; Fat 7 g; Sodium 100 mg; Cholesterol 47 mg.

- 1/3 cup vegetable shortening or unsalted butter or margarine
- 1 cup sugar
- 2 eggs
- 1 1/2 cups sifted all-purpose flour
- 1 1/2 teaspoons baking powder
- 1/4 teaspoon salt
- 1/2 cup milk
  Grated rind of 1 lemon
- 1/2 cup chopped pecans or walnuts (optional)

*Glaze:*
- 1/3 cup sugar
  Juice of 1 lemon

1 Preheat the oven to 350° F. Cream the shortening and sugar until light and fluffy. Add the eggs, one at a time, beating well after each addition.

2 Sift the dry ingredients together; add 1/3 to the egg mixture, followed by 1/3 of the milk, and beat well. Repeat twice more. Fold in the lemon rind and, if desired, the nuts. Turn into a well-greased, 9" x 5" x 3" loaf pan and bake for 45 to 55 minutes or until the loaf springs back when lightly touched.

3 Meanwhile, combine the glaze ingredients, mixing well. As soon as the bread comes from the oven, spoon the glaze evenly over the loaf. Cool to room temperature before removing from the pan and slicing. Makes 1 loaf.

# Cranberry-Peach Cooler

Per serving: Calories 148; Protein 1 g; Carbohydrate 37 g; Fat tr; Sodium 14 mg; Cholesterol 0 mg.

- 2 quarts cranberry juice cocktail
- 2 quarts peach nectar
- 2 oranges, thinly sliced and seeded
  Ice in cubes or a block

1 In 2 large pitchers, combine the cranberry juice, peach nectar, and sliced oranges. Cover and refrigerate for at least 2 hours or overnight.

2 Place the ice cubes in tall glasses or an ice block in a punch bowl. Stir the cooler well, then pour over the ice. Makes sixteen 8-ounce or thirty-two 4-ounce servings.

*Tea on the terrace: Brie and Leek Sandwiches (page 305), Asparagus Tea Sandwiches (page 305), Mushrooms Filled with Tarama Salad, Shaker Lemon Bread, and Cranberry-Peach Cooler*

# Spicy Ham and Cheese Pudding

Per serving: Calories 470; Protein 27 g; Carbohydrate 28 g; Fat 28 g; Sodium 924 mg; Cholesterol 259 mg.

- 3 tablespoons bacon fat or lightly salted butter or margarine
- 2 medium-size Spanish onions, coarsely chopped
- 36 slices (each about 3 inches square) thin-cut whole-wheat, rye, or white sandwich bread, crusts removed (about 1¼ pounds)
- 1 pound cooked ham or tongue, coarsely chopped (about 2½ cups)
- 2 jalapeño chilies, roasted, seeded, and chopped, or 1 can (4 ounces) green chilies, chopped and drained
- 1 teaspoon each chili powder and dried oregano, crumbled
- 1 pound sharp Cheddar cheese, shredded (about 4 cups)
- 4 cups milk
- 8 eggs

1 Melt the bacon fat in a 12-inch skillet over moderate heat. Add the onions, and sauté, stirring frequently, until softened — about 5 minutes.

2 Cut each bread slice in half and arrange ⅓ of the slices in a single layer in a 14½" x 10½" x 2" roasting pan. Spoon on ½ of the cooked onion in an even layer, followed by ½ of the ham, ½ of the chilies, ½ teaspoon of the oregano, ½ teaspoon of the chili powder, and ⅓ of the shredded cheese. Repeat, then arrange the remaining bread on top.

3 In a large bowl, beat the eggs lightly, then slowly beat in the milk. Pour the mixture over the bread and sprinkle the remaining cheese on top. Cover and refrigerate for at least 2 hours or overnight.

4 Preheat the oven to 325° F. Bake, uncovered, until the center is puffed and golden brown — 50 to 60 minutes. Serves 12 to 14.

# Overnight Coffeecake

Per serving: Calories 485; Protein 6 g; Carbohydrate 68 g; Fat 21 g; Sodium 357 mg; Cholesterol 109 mg.

- 2 cups sifted all-purpose flour
- 1 teaspoon baking powder
- 1 teaspoon baking soda
- 1 teaspoon ground cardamom
- ¼ teaspoon salt
- ½ cup (1 stick) unsalted butter or margarine, at room temperature
- 1 cup sugar
- 2 eggs
- ¾ cup sour cream
- ½ cup firmly packed light brown sugar
- ½ cup chopped walnuts or pecans
- ¼ teaspoon each ground allspice and cinnamon

*Glaze:*
- ½ cup confectioners' sugar
- 2 teaspoons lemon juice
- ½ teaspoon vanilla or water

1 Sift together the flour, baking powder, baking soda, cardamom, and salt onto a sheet of wax paper.

2 In a large bowl, cream the butter and sugar until fluffy. Add the eggs and beat for 1 minute or until well blended. Add the sour cream and beat until just combined.

3 Add the sifted dry ingredients and beat until just combined. Spoon into a lightly greased and floured, 9" x 9" x 2" baking pan; spread evenly.

4 Stir together the brown sugar, nuts, allspice, and cinnamon. Sprinkle evenly over the batter. Cover the cake with plastic wrap and refrigerate for 8 hours or overnight.

5 Preheat the oven to 350° F. Bake, uncovered, for 50 minutes or until a toothpick inserted in the center comes out clean. (If it seems to be browning too quickly, cover loosely with aluminum foil.) Transfer to a wire rack and cool upright in the pan for 10 minutes.

6 Meanwhile, in a small bowl, combine the glaze ingredients. Drizzle over the cake. Serve warm or at room temperature. Will keep, tightly covered and refrigerated, for up to 3 days. Or label and freeze for up to 1 month at 0° F. Serves 8 to 12.

## Baked French Toast

Per slice: Calories 105; Protein 4 g; Carbohydrate 12 g; Fat 4 g; Sodium 118 mg; Cholesterol 67 mg.

- 6 eggs, beaten
- 3 cups milk
- 1/4 cup (1/2 stick) unsalted butter or margarine, melted
- 1/3 cup firmly packed brown sugar
- 1 teaspoon finely grated lemon rind
- 1/4 teaspoon each ground nutmeg and cinnamon
- 28 slices French bread, each about 3/4 inch thick (about 1 1/2 loaves)
- 2 tablespoons confectioners' sugar

1 In a large bowl, beat the eggs, milk, butter, sugar, lemon rind, nutmeg, and cinnamon. Pour half the mixture into 2 buttered, 17" x 11 1/2" x 3" roasting pans. Lay the bread slices on top in a single layer, pressing them as close together as possible. Pour the remaining milk mixture over all and cover with aluminum foil. Refrigerate for at least 2 hours or overnight.

2 Preheat the oven to 350° F. Bake, uncovered, until puffed and golden brown — 50 to 60 minutes. Sprinkle with the confectioners' sugar. Serve hot, accompanied by maple syrup, honey, or slices of fresh fruit and yogurt. Serves 10 to 12.

## Citrus-Honey Compote

Per serving: Calories 155; Protein 1 g; Carbohydrate 39 g; Fat tr; Sodium 1 mg; Cholesterol 0 mg.

- 2 cups water
- 1 cup honey
  Zest (colored part of the rind) and juice of 2 lemons
- 6 pink or white grapefruits, peeled, sliced, and seeded
- 6 oranges, peeled, sliced, and seeded

1 In a small saucepan, bring the water, honey, and lemon zest to a boil over moderate heat. Reduce the heat to low and simmer, uncovered, for 5 minutes. Let cool to room temperature.

2 In a large bowl, combine the grapefruit and orange slices, the lemon juice, and the honey mixture. Cover and refrigerate for at least 4 hours or overnight. Serves 12.

## Minted Peaches and Melon

Per serving: Calories 91; Protein 2 g; Carbohydrate 16 g; Fat 3 g; Sodium 8 mg; Cholesterol 0 mg.

- 2 small cantaloupes, peeled, seeded, and cut into 1/2-inch cubes (about 4 1/2 pounds)
- 6 medium-size peaches, peeled, pitted, and sliced (about 1 1/2 pounds)

- 1/2 cup slivered toasted almonds
- 1/2 cup orange juice
- 1/4 cup sugar
- 2 tablespoons lemon juice
- 1/4 cup chopped mint

1 In a large bowl, stir together the cantaloupe, peaches, almonds, orange juice, sugar, and lemon juice.

▽ At this point the fruit can be refrigerated, tightly covered, for up to 8 hours.

2 Just before serving, toss with the mint. Can be served cold or at room temperature. Serves 12.

## Spiced Coffee

Per serving without milk and sugar: Calories 83; Protein 1 g; Carbohydrate 11 g; Fat 4 g; Sodium 3 mg; Cholesterol 0 mg.

- 2 vanilla beans, split lengthwise
- 6 strips orange rind, each 2 inches by 1/2 inch
- 4 cinnamon sticks
- 10 slices candied ginger
- 10 cups hot, freshly brewed coffee
- 6 ounces semisweet chocolate, grated
  Light brown sugar
  Warm milk

1 Wrap the vanilla beans, orange rind, cinnamon sticks, and ginger in a piece of cheesecloth and tie it. Drop the bag into the coffee and leave to steep on a warmer for 20 minutes. (Or if you have a drip pot, add the spice bag to the pot before brewing.)

2 Just before serving, remove the spices and stir in the chocolate. Serve hot, accompanied by the sugar and milk. Serves 12.

# Acknowledgments

Grateful acknowledgment is made to the following sources for permission to use or adapt their recipes. Note: when our recipe title differs from the one under which the recipe originally appeared, the original title appears in parentheses.

**Harry N. Abrams, Inc.,** THE LOS ANGELES TIMES CALIFORNIA COOKBOOK, "Blue Cheese—Stuffed Eggs," "Carrot Vichyssoise," "Frozen Banana Pops" ("Frozen Chocolate Banana Pops"), "Halibut in Wine Sauce," "Roquefort Mousse Spread," "Taco Salad," "Turkey Teriyaki Kebabs," compiled and edited by Betsy Balsley, Food Editor, and the Food Staff of the Los Angeles Times. Published in 1981 by Harry N. Abrams, Inc. Reprinted by permission of the publisher.

**Atheneum Publishers,** COLD CUISINE by Helen Hecht, "Artichoke Mousse," "Honeydew Ice," "Piquant Sauce for Fish and Poultry" ("Piquant Sauce"), "Ratatouille Vinaigrette," "Tomato Tart with Two Cheeses" ("Tomato Tart"), "Veal with Tuna Sauce" ("Vitello Tonnato"), copyright © 1981 by Helen Hecht,. Reprinted by permission.

**Bantam Books,** SABLE & ROSENFELD ELEGANT ENTERTAINING COOKBOOK by Myra Sable, "Creamy Shrimp Curry" ("Sour Cream Jumbo Shrimp Curry"), "Eggs in Casserole," copyright © 1986 by Sable and Rosenfeld Foods, Ltd. THE GREENS COOK BOOK by Deborah Madison with Edward Espe Brown, "Creole Stuffed Eggs" ("Creole Egg Salad Sandwich"), "Spunkies" ("Pan Bagnat"), "Black Bean and Sweet Pepper Salad" ("Black Bean and Pepper Salad"), "Sure-Fire Black Bean Chili" ("Black Bean Chili"), "Potato, Tomato and Onion Gratin" ("Provençal Potato Gratin with Olives and Lemon Thyme"), "White Bean and Eggplant Casserole" ("White Bean and Eggplant Gratin"), "White Bean and Fresh Tomato Soup with Parsley Pesto" ("White Bean and Fresh Tomato Soup with Parsley Sauce"), "Yellow Split Pea Soup with Spiced Yogurt," copyright © 1987 by Edward Espe Brown and Deborah Madison. Reprinted by permission.

**Chronicle Books,** COLD PASTA by James McNair, "Lemon Soup" ("Avgolemono Soup with Pastina"), "Pasta Rings in Piquant Cucumber Sauce" ("Pasta Rings in Spicy Cucumber Raita"), "Noodle Pie with Spicy Cajun Ham," "Noodle Pudding with Vanilla Sauce" ("Noodle Pudding with Vanilla Bean Sauce"), published in 1985 by Chronicle Books. Reprinted by permission.

**Clarkson N. Potter, Inc.,** LEE BAILEY'S GOOD PARTIES by Lee Bailey, "Ham Steaks with Sherried Pear Sauce" ("Baked Marinated Ham Steaks"), "Chicken, Walnut, and Red Pepper Turnover" ("Chicken, Walnut, and Red Pepper Tarts"), "Black Olive Turnover" ("Black Olive Tarts"), "Date-Nut Tart" ("Date Tart"), copyright © 1986 by Lee Bailey. Reprinted by permission.

**Crown Publishers, Inc.,** THE GRAND CENTRAL OYSTER BAR AND RESTAURANT SEAFOOD COOKBOOK by Jerome Brody and Joan and Joseph Foley, "Salmon Salad with Sweet Pickles" ("Salmon Salad"), copyright © 1977 by Jerome Brody and Joseph Foley. READY WHEN YOU ARE by Elizabeth Schneider Colchie, "Barley-Mushroom Casserole" ("Barley, Mushroom, and Onion Casserole"), "Rice, Zucchini, and Walnut Loaf with Cheddar Sauce" ("Brown Rice, Zucchini, and Walnut Loaf with Cheddar Sauce"), "Spicy Ham and Cheese Pudding" ("Cheese, Ham, Chile, and Bread Pudding"), copyright © 1982 by Elizabeth Schneider Colchie. THE HOLIDAYS by John Hadamuscin, "Apple-Ginger Sorbet," "Cranberry Fool," "Chocolate-Hazelnut Truffles," "Lacy Chocolate Praline Cookies and Baskets" ("Chocolate Praline Lace Cookies"), "Fresh Sausage Patties," "Herbed Tomato Soup," "Lemon Tea Cake" ("Lemon Velvet Tea Cake"), "Prairie Caviar," "Quick Cassoulet," "Steamed Ginger Pudding," "Strawberry Mousse in Praline Baskets", copyright © 1986 by John Hadamuscin. Reprinted by permission of Harmony Books, Inc., a division of Crown Publishers, Inc. JANE BUTEL'S TEX-MEX COOKBOOK by Jane Butel, "Avocado Stuffed Burgers" ("Avocado-Stuffed Hamburgers"), "Chuckwagon Chili" ("Chasen's Chile"), "Chili Nuts" ("Chile Nuts"), "Gazpacho," "Tex-Mex Guacamole" ("Guacamole"), "Steak Cubes Southwestern-Style" ("Southwestern Swiss Steak"), copyright © 1980 by Jane Butel. Reprinted by permission of Jane Butel.

**Doubleday Publishing Co.,** THE DOUBLEDAY COOKBOOK by Jean Anderson and Elaine Hanna, "Sugar Cookies," "Ginger Icebox Cookies" ("Molasses Icebox Cookies"), "Basic French Crêpes" ("Basic Crepes"), "Watercress and Cream Cheese Wheels" ("Cream Cheese and Watercress Spread"), "Firecracker Barbecue Sauce" ("All-Purpose Barbecue Sauce"), "Confetti Corn," "Crêpes Florentine" ("Spinach and Ricotta Stuffed Ravioli"), "Vanilla Sauce," copyright © 1975 by Doubleday & Company, Inc. SAN FRANCISCO A LA CARTE, "Layered Vegetable Salad," copyright © 1979 by The Junior League of San Francisco, Inc. NEW YORK ENTERTAINS, "Chicken Liver and Sausage Terrine" ("Terrine de Chagny Lameloise"), "Peppery Ham Pâté" ("Ham Paste with Green Peppercorns"), "Cheesy Chicken and Mushroom Crêpes" ("Spinach and Chicken Crêpes"), "Giant Shells Stuffed with Spinach and Ricotta" ("Cannelloni with Spinach and Ricotta"), copyright © 1974 by The Junior League of The City of New York, Inc. SAN FRANCISCO ENCORE: A COOKBOOK, "Creamy Carrot-Basil Soup" ("Potage Crecy"), "Caraway Cheese Sticks," "Spicy Pork and Bean Curd" ("Drunken Aunt's Bean Curd"), "South-of-the-Border Chicken Rolls" ("Mexican Chicken Kiev"), "Sausage and Lentil Casserole" ("Polish Sausage and Lentil Casserole"), "Rice Salad with Ham and Cheese" ("Sausalito Rice Salad"), "Cashew-Orange Chicken Salad," "Peach Melba Torte" ("Sonoma Melba Torte"), copyright © 1986 by The Junior League of San Francisco. THE DINAH SHORE COOKBOOK by Dinah Shore, "Layered Broccoli Wild Rice Casserole," "Layered

Salmon and Cucumber Mousse" ("Salmon Mousse on Molded Cucumber Salad"), "Andalusian Chicken," copyright © 1983 by Sewanee Productions, Inc. TEXAS ON THE HALF SHELL by Phil Brittin and Joseph Daniel, "Guacamole Aspic with Avocado Dressing" ("Jellied Guacamole Phillips"), "Best Bean Dip Bar None" ("Best Bar-None Bean Dip"), text copyright © 1982 by Phil Brittin and Joseph Daniel. THE PARK AVENUE COOKBOOK by Sara Stamm, "Zucchini Slaw," copyright © 1981 by Sara Stamm. RECIPES FROM AMERICA'S RESTORED VILLAGES by Jean Anderson, "Plum Sauce," "Pueblo Baked Corn and Harvest Vegetables" ("Pueblo Baked Corn and Vegetables of the Vines"), copyright © 1975 by Jean Anderson. Reprinted by permission.

**Episcopal Churchwomen and Friends of Christ,** PASS THE PLATE, "Curried Chicken with Sweet Peppers and Almonds" ("Inglis Fletcher's Chicken Country Captain"), "Ham Balls with Orange Sauce," ("Ham Balls á L'Orange"), "Pasta Salad with Tuna, Pine Nuts, and Red Peppers" ("Fettuccine Fredde Alla Pronto"), "Sweet and Crunchy Watermelon Pickles" ("Watermelon Pickles"), copyright © 1984 by Pass the Plate, Inc. Reprinted by permission.

**Eubry Press,** COOKING AHEAD, "Eggplant and Cheese Soufflé," "Haddock and Shrimp Gratinée," "Beef with Chestnuts" ("Beef and Chestnut Casserole"), "Some-Like-It-Hot Potato Salad" ("Chili Potato Salad"), published in 1985 by Eubry Press, London, and Barron's Educational Series, Inc., Woodbury, New York. Copyright © 1985 The National Magazine Company. Reprinted by permission.

**Harper & Row Publishers,** MARLENE SOROSKY'S YEAR-ROUND HOLIDAY COOKBOOK, "Marinated London Broil" ("Marinated Chuck Roast"), "Orange-Praline Sweet Potatoes" ("Orange Praline Yams"), copyright © 1982 by Marlene Sorosky. THE VEGETARIAN FEAST, by Martha Rose Shulman, "Zucchini-Cheese Puff" ("Squash Soufflé"), copyright © 1979 by Martha Rose Shulman. THE MYSTIC SEAPORT COOKBOOK by Lillian Langseth-Christensen, "Cheese Crackers" ("Cheese Pigs"), copyright © 1970 by The Marine Historical Association, Inc. COUSCOUS AND OTHER GOOD FOOD FROM MOROCCO by Paula Wolfert, "Chicken Marrakesh with Almonds and Chick-Peas" ("Chicken Kdra with Almonds and Chick-Peas"), "Lamb with Almonds and Raisins" ("Tangine of Lamb with Raisins and Almonds, Tiznit Style"), copyright © 1973 by Paula Wolfert. HALF A CAN OF TOMATO PASTE AND OTHER CULINARY DILEMMAS by Jean Anderson and Ruth Buchan, "Orange-Ginger Sauce" ("Orange and Ginger Sauce"), "Lime-Pineapple Buttermilk Sorbet" ("Lime-Pineapple Buttermilk Sherbet"), "Tart and Tangy Apple Chutney" ("Honeyed Apple Chutney"), "Cottage Cheese and Chives Dressing" ("Low-Calorie Cottage Cheese Chive Salad Dressing"), "Sweet and Sour Chicken Chunks" ("Chunks of Chicken in Sweet-Sour Sauce"), "Curried Tuna Mousse," "Lamb, Oat, and Apple Loaf" ("Crofter's Oat, Apple, and Lamb Loaf"), "Chicken in Yogurt with Indian Spices" ("Chicken in Yogurt with Coriander, Cumin, and Cardamom"), "Braised Lamb with Black Olives" ("Braised Lamb with Black Olives in Wine Gravy"), "Onions Stuffed with Pecans, Mushrooms, and Rice" ("Spanish Onions Stuffed with Pecans, Mushrooms, and Rice"), "European Meatballs in Cream Sauce with Dill" ("Kotleti"), copyright © 1980 by Jean Anderson and Ruth Buchan. CUCINA FRESCA by Viana La Place and Evan Kleiman, "Tuscan Roast Pork" ("Arista"), "Herbed Turkey Roll" ("Turkey Breast with Herb Butter"), copyright © 1985 by Viana La Place and Evan Kleiman. FROM THE FARMER'S MARKET by Richard Sax with Sandra Gluck, "Pecan Cheese Crackers," "Zucchini, Pepper, and Tomato Gratin" ("Baked Zucchini, Pepper and Tomato Gratin"), copyright © 1986 by Richard Sax and Sandra Gluck. Reprinted by permission.

**Henry Holt & Co.,** THE SEASONAL KITCHEN, A RETURN TO FRESH FOODS by Perla Meyers, "Walnut Crêpes with Mocha Sauce" ("Crepes hongroises"), "Sea Scallops Creole" ("Sea Scallops a la Creole"), "Herbed Crêpes California-Style" ("Crepes aux fines herbes a la mexicaine"), "Green Bean Salad with Tuna, Pine Nuts, and Red Pepper" ("Palermo salad"), "Artichokes with Wine, Anchovies, and Capers" ("Artichokes valeuris"), "Radish and Swiss Cheese Salad" ("Radish salad lugano"), "Baked Apples in Apricot-Wine Sauce" ("Baked apples grandmere"), "Green Beans with Walnut Vinaigrette" ("Green beans tivoli"), copyright © 1973 by Perla Meyers. THE INTERNATIONAL DINNER PARTY COOKBOOK by Jan Bilton, "Tamale Pie," "Pistachio Dip," "Carrot Wheat-Germ Muffins" ("Carrot and Wheatgerm Muffins"), copyright © 1985 by Jan Bilton. Reprinted by permission.

**Houghton Mifflin Company,** PIRET'S: THE GEORGE AND PIRET MUNGER COOKBOOK by Piret Munger and George Munger, "Orange Brownie Cake," copyright © 1985 by Piret Munger and George Munger. THE NEW CARRY-OUT CUISINE by Phyllis Meras with Linda Glick, "Roast Loin of Pork in Ginger Marinade," "Orange-Cumin Beef Stew," "German Meatloaf," "Mushroom Pâté," "Tortilla Soup" ("Beth's Tortilla Soup"), "Zucchini Relish," "Curried Rice Salad," "Creamy Pasta Salad with Chicken" ("Chicken Pesto Salad"), "Tarragon Turkey Salad with Hazelnuts" ("Jerilyn's Turkey Salad with Tarragon Hazelnuts"), "Green and White Fettuccine with Chicken and Ham" ("Fettuccine Con Pollo"), "Artichoke Squares," copyright © 1986 by Phyllis Meras. Reprinted by permission.

**Junior League of Hampton Roads, Inc.,** VIRGINIA HOSPITALITY by the Junior League of Hampton Roads, Inc., "Molded Cranberry-Chicken Salad" ("Chicken Cranberry Layers"), "Minted Peaches and Melon" ("Peach and Melon Salad"), copyright © 1975 by the Junior League of Hampton Roads, Inc. Reprinted by permission.

310

# Index

Page numbers in *italic* type refer to illustrations.

Page numbers in *italic* type refer to illustrations.

Page numbers in *italic* type refer to illustrations.

Reader's Digest Fund for the Blind is
publisher of the Large Type Edition
of *Reader's Digest.* For subscription
information about this magazine,
please contact Reader's Digest Fund
for the Blind, Inc., Dept. 250, Pleasantville, N.Y. 10570

Page numbers in *italic* type refer to illustrations.